THE PHILOSOPHY OF THE CHRISTIAN RELIGION

Et inde admonitus redire ad memetipsum, intravi in intima mea, duce te ; et potui, quoniam factus es adjutor meus. Intravi, et vidi qualicumque oculo animæ meæ, supra eumdem oculum animæ meæ, supra mentem meam, lucem incommutabilem ; non hanc vulgarem et conspicuam omni carni : nec quasi ex eodem genere grandior erat, tanquam si ista multo multoque clarius claresceret, totumque occuparet magnitudine. Non hoc illa erat ; sed aliud, aliud valde ab istis omnibus. Nec ita erat supra mentem meam sicut oleum supra aquam, nec sicut cœlum super terram ; sed superior, quia ipsa fecit me, et ego inferior, quia factus sum ab ea. Qui novit veritatem, novit eam ; et qui novit eam, novit æternitatem. Charitas novit eam. O æterna veritas, et vera charitas, et chara æternitas ! tu es Deus meus ; tibi suspiro die ac nocte. Et cum te primum cognovi, tu assumpsisti me, ut viderem esse quod viderem, et nondum me esse qui viderem. Et reverberasti infirmitatem aspectus mei, radians in me vehementer, et contremui amore et horrore ; et inveni longe me esse a te in regione dissimilitudinis, tanquam audirem vocem tuam de excelso : Cibus sum grandium ; cresce, et manducabis me. Nec tu me in te mutabis, sicut cibum carnis tuæ ; sed tu mutaberis in me. Et cognovi quoniam pro iniquitate erudisti hominem, et tabescere fecisti sicut araneam animam meam ; et dixi : Numquid nihil est veritas, quoniam neque per finita, neque per infinita locorum spatia diffusa est. Et clamasti de longinquo : Imo vero, *Ego sum qui sum.* Et audivi sicut auditur in corde, et non erat prorsus unde dubitarem ; faciliusque dubitarem vivere me, quam non esse veritatem, quæ per ea quæ facta sunt, intellecta conspicitur.—AUGUSTINE.

There is not anything that I know, which hath done more mischief to *Religion*, than the disparaging of *Reason*, under pretence of respect and favour to it : For hereby the very Foundations of Christian Faith have been undermin'd, and the World prepared for Atheism. And if Reason must not be heard, the *Being* of a *God*, and the *Authority* of *Scripture*, can neither be proved nor defended ; and so our Faith drops to the Ground like a House that hath no Foundation.—GLANVILL.

THE PHILOSOPHY OF THE CHRISTIAN RELIGION

BY

A. M. FAIRBAIRN DD LLD

PRINCIPAL OF MANSFIELD COLLEGE, OXFORD

οὐ γάρ ἐστιν προσωπολημψία παρὰ τῷ Θεῷ

WIPF & STOCK · Eugene, Oregon

Wipf and Stock Publishers
199 W 8th Ave, Suite 3
Eugene, OR 97401

The Philosophy of the Christian Religion
By Fairbairn, A. M.
ISBN 13: 978-1-5326-1870-3
Publication date 3/9/2017
Previously published by Hodder and Stoughton, 1902

THIS BOOK
IS DEDICATED TO
ALEXANDER MACKENNAL
ALBERT SPICER
AND TO THE MEMORY OF
ROBERT WILLIAM DALE
IN GRATEFUL RECOGNITION OF
SERVICES
RENDERED FREELY AND WITHOUT STINT TO
MANSFIELD COLLEGE
AND OF
FRIENDSHIPS
WHICH HAVE ENHANCED THE WORTH AND THE JOY OF LIFE

χάρις τίκτει χάριν

PREFACE

THIS book may be described as an attempt to do two things: first, to explain religion through nature and man; and, secondly, to construe Christianity through religion. The author conceives religion to be a joint product of the mind within man and the nature around him, the mind being the source of the ideas which constitute its soul, the nature around determining the usages and customs which build up its body. He does not think, therefore, that any one of its special forms can be explained without the local nature which begot and shaped it, or that its general being can be resolved and construed without the reason or thought which is common to the race. He sees in religion the greatest of all man's unconscious creations, and the most potent of the means which the past, while it was still a living present, formed for the making of the man and the times that were yet to be.

The beliefs of the author are writ large on almost every page, and these he need neither explain nor justify here; but a word or two may be said as to the occasion which defined not so much the problem of the book as its scope and point of view. Some years ago he had the honour of being appointed by the University of Chicago lecturer on the Haskell foundation. The conditions of the endowment were that a certain number of lectures should be delivered in India, especially in the Presidency towns. In India the author suddenly found himself face to face with a religion he had studied in its literature and by the help of interpreters of many minds and tongues, and this contact with reality at once illuminated and perplexed him. It was not so much that his knowledge was incorrect or false, as that it was mistaken in its emphasis. No religion can be known in its Sacred Books alone, or simply through its speculative thinkers and religious reformers; and of all religions the one that these can least interpret is the encyclopædic aggregation of cults and customs we know as Hinduism. Hence he realized as he had never done before the force of custom and usage, of social convention and religious observance, the didactic and coercive power of a worship which can command obedience where its value is doubted, or even where it is denied and despised. He saw a religion which had an innumerable multitude of deities and an indescribable variety of worships, which had grown out of a simple and primitive naturalism that had no knowledge of these gods and rites, which had had hosts of reformers who had yet only added to the mythologies and cults they had set out to purge and reform, and which still amid so many changes was conceived and described as one religion, and as continuous with that of the ancient Aryan men. Hence he was confronted with certain philosophical problems which he had to attempt to solve before he could think of undertaking any large historical investigation:—What is religion in general? How and why has it arisen? What causes have made religions to differ? Is the multitude as good for man permanently as it has been necessary to his development? What are the ultimate constituents of religions,—ideas and beliefs, or customs and institutions? If by their usages and observances some religions are native to certain localities and peoples, and alien from certain other places and races,—can a religion whose institutions are at once local and essential be universal? How has it happened that certain religions have become missionary while others have never desired or been able to transcend the limits of the tribe or the home?

What attributes must distinguish a missionary from non-missionary religions?

These then were the problems which created this book, for they compelled the author to study his own faith in their light. He could not but feel that Christianity stood among the religions which must be historically investigated and philosophically construed ; and that no greater injury could be done to it than to claim for it exceptional consideration at the hands of the historical student or philosophical thinker. For he who advances such a claim practically surrenders either the truth and equity of his religion, or the integrity of the reason which was God's own gift to man. But it is further obvious that the mode of interpreting other religions, especially as regards the fundamental point of the origin and warrant of the ideas which are as the heart or basis common to all, has the most serious possible significance for Christianity. For if our primary and original beliefs be but the glorified survivals of certain "mistaken inferences" deduced by savage man from the phenomena either of his own dreams or of a nature he did not understand, then it is clear that every religion will be made to suffer from the inherent and inherited sin of its remotest ancestor. And, again, if great historical religions which innumerable millions of men, as rational as we, have professed through thousands of ages, be resolved into systems of error and delusion that only the blind deceitfulness of the human heart could tempt man to believe, then it is evident that we dare not use the reason or the conscience which we have so discredited either to believe or to attest or to justify the truth of our own. In other words, the philosophy that misreads the origin of religious ideas and the history of any religion will not, and indeed cannot, be just to the Christian ; while he who would maintain the Christian must be just and even generous to all the religions created and professed of men.

This book, then, is neither a philosophy nor a history of religion, but it is an endeavour to look at what is at once the central fact and idea of the Christian faith by a mind whose chief labour in life has been to make an attempt at such a philosophy through such a history. The Son of God holds in His pierced hands the keys of all the religions, explains all the factors of their being and all the persons through whom they have been realized. And this means that the author would not, if he could, take the religion he loves out of the cycle of the historical religions. On the contrary, he holds that Christianity must stand there if it is to be really known and truly honoured. The time is coming, and we shall hope that the man is coming with it, which shall give us a new Analogy, speaking a more generous and hopeful language, breathing a nobler spirit, aspiring to a larger day than Butler's. It will seek to discover in man's religions the story of his quest after God, but no less of God's quest after him; and it will listen in all of them for the voice of the Eternal, who has written His law upon the heart in characters that can never be eradicated. And it will argue that a system whose crown and centre is the Divine Man, is one which does justice to everything positive in humanity by penetrating it everywhere with Deity. The Incarnation, as here read, is the very truth which turns nature and man, history and religion into the luminous dwelling-place of God.

In sending out this book the author must record his gratitude to two friends: Mr. P. E. Matheson, M.A., Fellow of New College, Oxford, for his patience in reading the proofs, and for the many emendations in style and expression he has suggested; and the Rev. R. S. Franks, M.A., B. Litt., formerly of Mansfield College, now of Birkenhead, for his labour in drawing up the Table of Contents and preparing the Index.

CONTENTS

INTRODUCTION

	PAGE
THE PROBLEM OF THE CHRISTIAN RELIGION	3–19
§ I. *The Person of Christ as the Mystery of the Christian Religion*	3–7
1. The Jesus of the Gospels and the Christ of the Creeds; the place of mystery in religion	3
2. Mysteries of nature and mysteries of art	5
§ II. *Need the Person be a Mystery*	7–12
1. Dialectic analysis of the doctrine of the Incarnation	7
2. Literary and historical analysis of the same	10
§ III. *Why there is a Problem of the Person*	12–19
1. The common defect of the foregoing dialectic and literary analyses is neglect of the place of Christ in history	12
2. It is the divine Christ who has entered into history	14
3. The problems raised by the person of Christ are both literary and speculative. Christ is in history as God is in nature. Reason must construe the doctrine of His Person	16

BOOK I

QUESTIONS IN THE PHILOSOPHY OF NATURE AND MIND WHICH AFFECT BELIEF IN THE SUPERNATURAL PERSON

CHAPTER I

THE BELIEF AS A PROBLEM IN THE PHILOSOPHY OF NATURE	23–60
§ I. *The Ideas of Nature and the Supernatural*	23–27
1. The incompatibility of the doctrine of the Person of Christ with the scientific view of Nature	23
2. Hume's argument against miracles criticized on the basis of his own philosophy	24

CONTENTS

	PAGE
§ II. *Nature and Thought*	27–37
1. Nature does not interpret man : man interprets Nature	27
2. Nature and Personality : What thought gives to Nature and what sense perceives in it	30
3. Energy known in Nature because freedom is in man	33
4. Nature a visual language ; the intellect and the intelligible expressions of one Intelligence	35
§ III. *Mind and the Process of Creation*	37–55
1. The problem of Evolution not organism, but the Reason that organizes	38
2. Methods of solution	40
A. The Regressive Method	41
i. Man and ape in natural and in civil history. Why do their histories differ?	41
ii. Darwin's *petitio principii*	46
B. The Egressive Method	48
i. Matter cannot originate Mind : speculative paralysis of the school of Hume : speculative passion of Science	48
ii. Granted the speculative conception of matter, can the creative process be explained ? Intelligence in Evolution	53
§ IV. *Conclusions and Inferences*	55–60
1. A. Nature must be conceived through the supernatural	56
B. (α) The real creation of God is spirit	57
(β) He remains in active relation with the spirits He has made	58
C. God's creative action never ceases	58
D. This is the meaning of the doctrine of Evolution	59
2. The key of all mysteries is man	60

CHAPTER II

THE PROBLEM AS AFFECTED BY THE PHILOSOPHY OF ETHICS 61–93

§ I. *The Problems raised by Man as an Ethical Being: Moral Judgements imply a Moral Standard.*	61–63
§ II. *Empiricism in Knowledge and in Ethics*	63–68
1. Intimate connexion between the metaphysics of knowledge and of ethics	63
2. Moral systems of Hobbes, Hume, and Bentham	65
3. These imply man's transcendence of Nature ; but fail to relate the individual to society	67
§ III. *Ethics and Evolution*	68–74
1. The inherited social interest	68
A. Darwin's theory of accidental variations	70

CONTENTS

	PAGE
B. Spencer's principle of conservation of life	70
2. i. The question of time not vital	72
ii. The transmission of acquired characters dubious	72
iii. Differences more important than similarities	73
iv. The end not the adjustment of the individual to society, but of both to the ideal	74
§ IV. *What do Moral Judgements Involve?*	74–83
1. The question of Freedom	75
2. The idea of the Right; the Right as happiness	78
(α) What is happiness?	79
(β) What sort of happiness is the measure of the Right?	79
(γ) Whose is the happiness?	80
3. Duty or conscience	81
§ V. *The Ethical Man means an Ethical Universe: Butler and Kant*	83–89
1. Butler and Kant compared	83
2. Butler on the moral law and its Giver	85
3. Kant's categorical imperative and his deductions of Freedom, Immortality and God	87
§ VI. *Deductions and Conclusion*	89–93
1. Moral evil transcends Nature because creative	89
2. Self-realization the law of human progress	90
3. Man cannot be measured by Nature	91
4. Moral good is realized in persons	92
5. A supreme Personality the fitting vehicle of the highest good	93

CHAPTER III

THE QUESTION AS AFFECTED BY THE PROBLEM OF EVIL.

A. Historical and Critical	94–131
§ I. πόθεν τὸ κακόν;	94–99
1. The problem appeals to the finest spirits	94
2. Moral evil the gravest problem	96
3. The problem intensified by belief in God	97
§ II. *Optimism and Evil*	99–111
1. Optimism of Plato and the Stoics, of Augustine and Nicholas of Cusa	99
2. Leibnitz and Pope	103
i. The *Theodicée*	104
ii. The *Essay on Man*	106
3. Criticism of Pope: Voltaire: problem of the survival of the fittest	107

CONTENTS

	PAGE
§ III. *Pessimism Ancient and Modern*	111–117
1. The causes of Pessimism	111
2. Pessimism Uncongenial to the Greek mind : compared with Mediaeval Asceticism	113
3. Pessimism in Goethe and Byron : in modern politics .	114
§ IV. *Eastern and Western Pessimism*	117–131
1. Philosophical Buddhism : its origin and aim . . .	117
2. Western Pessimism. Schopenhauer : influenced by Kant, Fichte and Buddha : compared with Buddha. Von Hartmann	121
3. Appreciation and criticism of Pessimism : Gain or loss?	127

CHAPTER IV

THE QUESTION AS AFFECTED BY THE PROBLEM OF EVIL.

B. Some suggestions towards a solution . . .	132–168
§ I. *The Limits and Terms of the Discussion* . .	132–136
1. The Responsibility of God	132
2. Distinction of physical and moral evil : the painfulness of experience	134
A. Physical Evil : its kinds and functions . .	136
§ II. *Man in the Hands of Nature*	136–141
1. Evils arising from the inter-relations of man and nature classified	139
2. Functions of physical evils	137
i. Education in the arts	137
ii. Education in humanity	138
iii. The motherhood of Nature	139
iv. Nature inexorable that she may be beneficent .	140
§ III. *Evils Peculiar to Man*	141–146
1. Death man's tragedy	141
2. What life gains through death	144
§ IV. *Evils Man Suffers from Man*	146–152
1. Classification : the problem raised	146
2. The physical constitution of the race morally educative : immortality and the problem of evil . . .	147
B. Moral Evil : its Nature, Origin and Continuance .	150
§ V. *Moral Evil and God*	152–158
1. God as conditioned in creation	152
i. External conditions	153
ii. Internal conditions	154
2. Conditions defining the character and states of the creature.	155

CONTENTS

i. A creature necessarily limited in knowledge.	155
ii. The end of the creation God's glory and human good. God reflected in a creature	156
(a) Moral	156
(β) Free	157
§ VI. *The Permission of Moral Evil and the Deity*	159–163
1. Law and freedom necessary correlatives: involve possibility of evil	159
2. Interference no remedy	162
§ VII. *Why Evil has been Allowed to Continue*	163–168
1. How moral and physical evil are related. God views the race as a whole	163
2. A state of suffering not one of probation, but of recovery from lapse, the last word not Nature's	166

CHAPTER V

THE PHILOSOPHY OF HISTORY	169–185
§ I. *The Significance of History*	171–175
1. Man denotes the race, history its articulated mind.	171
2. The growth of consciousness: its problems personal and collective	172
3. These problems of interest only when man realizes the idea of his unity	173
§ II. *The Ideas of Unity and Order in History*	175–181
1. What the idea of unity signifies	175
2. The unity as an immanent teleology	176
3. Order in history a late idea, nevertheless necessary; distinction from the order of Nature	178
§ III. *The Cause of Order in History*	181–185
1. Mind the maker of order	181
i. Man its vehicle	181
ii. Action of Nature on Man	181
iii. ,, of Men ,, ,,	182
iv. ,, of God ,, ,,	182
2. How does the idea of order arise in Man's life	183
i. An ethical substituted for a cosmic process	183
ii. Primary passions	183
iii. Their regulation	184
iv. An ideal authority	184
v. The ideal must be immanent	185
vi. Does it exist?	185
vii. Religion the answer	185

CONTENTS

CHAPTER VI

THE PHILOSOPHY OF RELIGION 186–226
    A. Religion: its Idea and Origin . . . . .
§ I. *The Phenomena to be Studied: the Religions* . . . 187–194
    1. The outfit of man, savage and civilized 187
        (α) Material: 188
        (β) Spiritual 189
    2. Vision of the Religions in history 190
    3. Religion the mother of order, and creator of law and custom 192
§ II. *Religion as Universal is Native to Man* . . . 194–200
    1. The science of Nature and man incomplete without religion: man more than his environment . . . 194
    2. Man cannot escape from Religion 196
    3. Religion as architectonic idea: the problems of Religion 197
§ III. *The Idea and Origin of Religion.* 200–208
    1. Religion subjective and objective 200
        i. Religion an exercise of the entire spirit of man . 200
        ii. Religion a mutual relation between man and God 202
    2. Man the interpretation of the phenomena of Religion; ethnography not a philosophy; Spencer's anthropological theory stated and criticized 203
§ IV. *Ethnographic and Historical Religion.* . . . 208–215
    1. The ethnographic method subjective: the historical objective 208
    2. Religion no superstition 209
        (α) Religion rooted in reason, but conditioned by Nature 210
        (β) Ethnographical religion unreal: savage religion less significant than civilized 213
§ V. *The Causes of Variation in Religion; Conflict of its Ideal and formal factors* 215–226
    1. Race as factor of change 216
    2. Place as formal factor of ideas: transcendence and immanence 218
    3. Influence of ethnical relations 220
    4. Influence of history: the gods conceived after the fashion of men 221
    5. Influence of the social ideal on the conception of Deity. 222
    6. Influence of creative personalities: the Divine purpose in history 223

CONTENTS

CHAPTER VII

THE PHILOSOPHY OF RELIGION

  B. The Historical Religions 227–257
    As speech to dialects, so is Mind to the Religions . 227
§ I. *Religions as National and Missionary* 230–235
  1. The classification and its limits: universal empires do not beget universal religions 230
  2. National religions which are missionary. . . . 232
  3. Missionary religions which are racial: Christianity seems western to eastern peoples. 233
§ II. *The Idea and the Institution in Religion* . . . 235–240
  1. The universal and the local in religion; custom in Greek religion and reason in Greek philosophy . . . 235
  2. Opposed action of custom and of thought in religion . 238
§ III. *The Idea of God in Religion*
  A. Buddhism 240–244
  1. Whether a Theism 240
  2. Apotheosis of a moral ideal 242
§ IV. *The Idea of God in Religion*
  B. Hebraic monotheism 244–253
  1. Monotheism begins as a tribal cult . . . 244
  2. But soon reveals its intrinsic character:
    Hebrew history of creation, man and religion . . 246
  3. Action of the idea and the institution within the religion 248
    (α) Jehovah transcends Israel: becomes ethical in character: man holy as God is holy . . . 248
    (β) The tribal instinct controls the worship . . 251
§ V. *Judaism at Home and in the Dispersion* . . . 253–257
  1. How Greek life and thought made Hebraism Hellenistic 255
  2. Judaism as the victory of the local cult, yet as the vehicle of the universal idea 255

CHAPTER VIII

FOUNDED RELIGIONS AND THEIR FOUNDERS . . . 258–288
§ I. *Religions, Spontaneous and Founded* 258
  1. Spontaneous religions apotheoses of Nature: founded apotheoses of personalities 258
  2. Personal religions rise out of natural, and need . 259
    i. An historical substructure 260
    ii. A creative religious genius 262
    iii. A congenial society, in which to live . . 264

CONTENTS

PAGE

§ II. *Impersonal Religions Classified as Personal* . . . 265–270
    i. Confucius a statesman, but not the founder of a religion 266
    ii. Monotheism not the creation of Moses, but of Israel 267

§ III. *Religions, Founded and Personal* 270–286
    A. Buddha and His Religion 270
      1. Buddha the creator of a religion missionary yet Indian: the India of Buddha 270
      2. His philosophy and discipline 273
      3. His apotheosis through the Church: his humanity humanizes the ethics of Buddhism 274
    B. Mohammed and Islam 277
      1. Mohammed compared with Buddha: his character and education: the vision of Abraham 277
      2. Islam and the sword: severity and mercy of the Prophet 280
      3. His religion and state: ultimate ideas of Islam . . 283
      4. The man incarnate in the word: the miraculous in the history of the Koran 285

§ IV. *Canons of Criticism or Regulative Ideas for the Interpretation of the Christian Religion* 286–289
    i. The Founder and His Religion a unity . . 287
    ii. He has both an ideal and an historical significance 287
    iii. His historical Person determines the form of His Religion 287
    iv. His ideal significance determines its value for man 287
    v. His word never ceases 288

BOOK II.

THE PERSON OF CHRIST AND THE MAKING OF THE CHRISTIAN RELIGION.

IN THREE PARTS.

                                                           PAGE

1. The Founder as an historical person; or Jesus as conceived and represented in the evangelical history   311–433
2. The interpretation of the Founder; or the creation of the Christian Religion through the Apostolical construction of Jesus as the Christ 435–514
3. The comparison of the elements and ideas in this interpretation with those most constitutive in the ideal of Religion as conserved and exemplified in the Historical Religions 517–568

INTRODUCTORY

RECAPITULATION AND STATEMENT OF THE NEW QUESTION 291–309
§ I. *The Old Problem* 291–295
    1. The common ground of the intellect and the intelligible in a creative intelligence 291
    2. The ethical in man involves an ethical God . . . 291
    3. Evil owes its being to man, but increases the responsibility of his Creator 292
    4. God as active in history 292
    5. Importance of religion 293
    6. Religions natural and universal: the achievement of Christ 293
    7. Christianity a founded religion 294
§ II. *The New Problem* 296
    Its questions and their ancillary studies . . . 295
§ III. *The Criticism of the Literature and the Person* . . 296–302
    The Gospels and the Apostolical writings; speculation prior to history 296
        i. This is according to the laws of thought . . 297
        ii. Does not imply neglect of the history . . . 298
        iii. The sources of the Gospels; contemporary history in the Gospel 298
        iv. The eye-witness and the histories . . . 299
        v. The historian as an interpreter 300

CONTENTS

	PAGE
§ IV. *The Religion and the Literature*	302–307
1. Schmiedel and the Gospel history. The teacher a sovereign personality	302
2. The Gospels interpret Jesus as the Christ . . .	305
§ V. *The Founder and the Religion*	307–309
1. False antithesis of natural and supernatural : problems raised by the Person and the history	307
2. Three main questions :	
i. The historical Jesus	309
ii. The Christ of Faith	309
iii. How Christianity came to be a religion . .	309

PART I

THE FOUNDER AS AN HISTORICAL PERSON, OR JESUS AS HE APPEARS IN THE SYNOPTIC GOSPELS

CHAPTER I

How His Person is Conceived	311–330
§ I. *The Natural View of Jesus in the Gospels* . . .	311
1. Natural factors of character : and the natural view of Jesus	311
2. Caiaphas governed by it ; his statecraft . . .	314
3. Pilate also governed by it ; the Roman touched with pity ; his vision and his awakening	317
4. An immiraculous Passion becomes a mean and sordid riddle	322
§ II. *The Supernatural View of Jesus*	323–330
1. The hypothesis of the Gospels common and prophetic ; its embodiment in a personal history . . .	323
2. The miraculous Person a rational and conscious unity. Jesus no mythical creation, but a study from life ; the natural and supernatural in Him	327

CHAPTER II

The Historical Person and the Physical Transcendence	331–355
§ I. *A Sane Supernaturalism*	332–337
1. Acts and character correspond ; the mythical imagination unhealthy ; extravagance of Jerome and Gregory	332
2. Jesus embodied beneficence ; intellectual sanity of the Evangelists	336

CONTENTS

	PAGE
§ II. *The Physical Transcendence is Moral Service* . .	337–343
1. The Temptation a subjective process ; its ethical significance	337
(α) Conflict of the ideal of dependence with the ideal of pre-eminence	338
(β) Conflict of a reasonable against a presumptuous dependence	339
(γ) Jesus ethical in means as in end . . .	341
2. The temptation continuous and signifies that Jesus is governed as is man	341
§ III. *Supernatural Power as a Moral Burden* . . .	343–348
1. Absolute power depraves man unless he be as good as God ; it does not deprave Jesus	343
2. Supernatural power alienates man from man ; but does not estrange him from Jesus	346
§ IV. *The History of the Supernatural Person as a Problem in Literature*	348–355
1. (a) The Supernatural Person elevates the idea of God .	348
(b) How should we write the history? The Supernatural Person. How the Evangelists do it . . .	350
2. The Gospels as literature. As the world is embosomed in the Infinite, so is Jesus in God	353

CHAPTER III

THE ETHICAL TRANSCENDENCE OF JESUS	356–379
§ I. *The Ethical Ideal of the Gospels*	357–361
1. The ideal of the imagination and the real figure of the Gospels	357
2. Difficulties of portraying the ethical ideal . .	358
i. The subject must be an unconscious sitter, as was Jesus	358
ii. The writers must be as unconscious of their art .	356
iii. Light and shade in the humanity of Jesus .	360
§ II. *The Sinlessness of Jesus*	361–367
1. The external testimony	361
2. The internal evidence	363
i. Jesus has no consciousness of sin . . .	363
ii. The Sinless forgives, yet is Friend of sinners .	364
3. Jesus perfect ; yet without the mechanism of religion .	365

CONTENTS

	PAGE
§ III. *Qualities of this Ideal of Sinlessness* ; its	367–373
1. Originality	367
2. Catholicity	368
3. Potency creates	370
(a) The idea of conversion	371
(β) Fear of sin and love of sanctity	372
§ IV. *Sinlessness and the Moral Person*	373–379
1. Sinlessness applies both to nature and conduct. Sinless nature not explained by one immaculate conception. Sinlessness distinguished from infallibility	373
2. The Sinless still a man; but man ideal, imitable and Godlike	378

CHAPTER IV

The Religious Personality Interpreted by Himself

A. The Teaching and the Person	380–400
§ I. *The Teaching and its External Characteristics*	381–390
1. The mind of Jesus as the ideal and universal mind	381
2. Simplicity and spontaneity of the teaching of Jesus: Nature and man as reflected in it	382
3. i. The real world involves the reality of the history	386
ii. Jesus no abstraction	387
iii. His teaching timeless and placeless	388
iv. The sovereign idealism of the world	389
v. What it has achieved	390
§ II. *How Jesus Conceives and Describes Himself*	391–395
1. The reserve of His early ministry	391
2. His claims	392
i. He fulfils law and prophecy	393
ii. He saves the lost	393
iii. "Follow Me"	393
iv. His personal sovereignty	394
v. His unique relation to God	394
§ III. *The Person and the Passion*	395–399
1. The "Galilean Springtime"; the harbinger of the Passion	395
2. His prophecy of the Passion; His death a sacrifice	397

CONTENTS

CHAPTER V

THE RELIGIOUS PERSONALITY INTERPRETED BY HIMSELF.

		PAGE
B. Significance of His Death		400-433
§ I. Growth of the idea		400-411
1. The disciples estranged from the Master		400
2. His death " a ransom for many "		403
(*a*) Different interpretations of the term "ransom"		403
(*b*) The term interpreted by the context; contrast between the kings and kingdoms, their means and ends		405
3. Results of the analysis		408
(*a*) Death free, not compulsory		408
(β) His motive		409
(γ) His end		409
(δ) Worth of the ransom		411
(ϵ) Its uniqueness		411
§ II. *How Jerusalem Helps to Define the Idea*		411-418
1. The entry into Jerusalem is the King coming to His own. Which yet does not know Him		412
2. Teaching of the Jerusalem period		415
(*a*) Exoteric: the parables spoken in Jerusalem explain the nature of His Death		415
(β) Exoteric: His anointing for the burying		417
§ III. *The Significance of the Supper*		418-425
1. The different accounts: the underlying idea the same		418
2. What Christ meant by the words of institution		421
(*a*) The antithesis of the Covenants		421
(β) What the Paschal Sacrifice signifies		422
(γ) Christ the Sacrifice, because the Head of the Race		424
§ IV. *Gethsemane and the Cross*		425-433
1. Death as idea and experience; joy in the death before Him; agony in the experience		425
2. Interpretation of Gethsemane		426
3. The Evangelists do not represent the agony as caused by the fear of death, but by the thought of its means and agents		428
4. The horror of sin to Jesus; sin made more exceeding sinful by grace. The Passion not to be analyzed; its infinite reality; the Cross creates the sense of sin, while the symbol of grace		430

PART II

THE CREATION OF THE CHRISTIAN RELIGION BY THE INTERPRETATION OF THE PERSON OF CHRIST

INTRODUCTORY

PAGE

The Facts to be Interpreted as Factors of Religion; Limits of the Discussion 435–437

CHAPTER I

The Person in the Apostolical Literature . . . 438–451
§ I. *Paul and the Pauline Literature* 439–443
   1. His epistles autobiographic 439
   2. His many-sided personality; a consistent unity, yet an epitome of his day 440
§ II. *The Person of Christ in the Pauline Epistles* . . 443–447
   1. History in the Epistles and in the Gospels . . . 443
   2. Christ's ideal majesty 444
     (a) He unifies the Race 444
     (β) He reveals God 446
§ III. *The Idea in Hebrews and the Apocalypse* . . 447–451
   1. The Person of Christ interpreted through the Alexandrian philosophy 447
   2. The might of Rome and the King of kings . . . 450
§ IV. *The Idea in the Gospel of John* 451–457
   1. The Prologue, its theology and relation to the history . 451
   2. The Logos translated into the Son, who becomes the Ideal of man and true tabernacle of Religion . . 454

CHAPTER II

The Genesis of the Idea 458–479
§ I. *The Idea and the Apostolic Literature* . . . 458–460
§ II. *Whether Paul was the Father of the Idea* . . 460–467
   1. The psychological interpretation of the Pauline theology; manifold sources of the same 460
   2. (a) Factors in Paul's education hostile to the belief . 464
     (β) Forces and circumstances prophetic of it; where psychology fails and where it succeeds . . . 465
§ III. *Whether the Idea is the Product of a Mythical Process* 467–474
   1. The process transfigures the Person and the Death; defects of the Mythical Theory 467

CONTENTS

	PAGE
2. Historical Laws which the Mythical Theory offends	470
(α) The mythical construction should precede the speculation; here the reverse is the case	470
(β) Speculation in general construes history: here a Person	472
(γ) Speculation must be germane to the soil out of which it grows: here its product seems alien. For	
i. It grew up under strict Hebrew monotheism	473
ii. And apotheosis was abhorrent to the New Testament writers	474
§ IV. *The Historical Source of the Idea*	474–479
1. The mind of Christ	474
2. The interpretation of the Person creates the religion	476
3. The Incarnation the Epitome and Mirror of all the mysteries of Being	478

CHAPTER III

THE DEATH OF CHRIST AND CHRISTIAN WORSHIP	480–514
The ideals of theology expressed in worship	
§ I. *Christ as Idea and Institution*	481–485
1. The Cross the centre of Christian worship; contrast with other religions, especially Buddhism	481
2. The Death of Christ in Apostolic thought more an institution than a doctrine	484
§ II. *The Levitical Legislation and the Christian Idea*	486–492
1. Christ in the new religion takes the place of the Temple in the old	486
2. The Temple as an ideal of worship	487
3. The Apostles and the Temple	489
§ III. *The Christian Idea as Interpreted through the Levitical Categories*	492–500
1. The sacrificial idea in Paul	492
2. Priest and sacrifice in the Epistle to the Hebrews: the transitory and the eternal	494
3. Conclusions of the Epistle	497
i. The Son obedient to the will of the Father	497
ii. Worth of the sacrifice: efficacy of the priest	498
iii. Eternity of His priesthood	498
iv. Its universality	499

CONTENTS

                                                                      PAGE

      v. The sacrifice vicarious 499
     vi. Significance of the substitution of a person for an
         institution 500
§ IV. *The Christian Sacrifice as Interpreted through the Prophetic Idea. Peter and the Apocalypse* . . 500–503
§ V. *The Christian idea as Interpreted through the Rabbinical Law* 503–507
    1. Levitical and Rabbinical Judaism; Paul's sense of
       defect in the latter 503
    2. His antithetic principles 504
      i. Redemption from the curse of the law . . . 504
      ii. Christ made sin for us 505
      iii. The new life 506
        (α) The condemnation of sin in the flesh . . 506
        (β) The constraining love of Christ . . . 506
        (γ) Crucifixion with Christ 507
§ VI. *Love of Christ the New Law* 508–514
    1. Love native to man; poets sing of a love that is dead;
       but the love of Christ never faileth 508
    2. It is as sufficient for its work as are the forces of Nature
       for theirs 511
    3. The love of Christ necessary to the service of man . 513

PART III

THE RELIGION OF CHRIST AND THE IDEAL OF RELIGION

INTRODUCTORY

    i. Nature of syncretism 517
    ii. Christianity not a syncretism, but the result of an architectonic idea 518
    iii. Action of this idea upon the religion 519

CHAPTER I

THE PERSON OF CHRIST AND THE PEOPLE OF THE RELIGION 520–535
§ I. *The Problems to be Solved* 520–523
    1. The people through which the universal religion must
       live; how are local forces to be overcome?. . . 520
    2. The people must be created, though out of virgin soil . 521
§ II. *The Social Ideal of Jesus* 523–526
    1. His Ideal the Kingdom of God 523
    2. The ideal ethical, yet religious 525

CONTENTS

III. *The Social Method of Jesus and its Impersonation*	527–532
1. The method discipleship; the vision of Jesus still potent after His death	527
2. Possible alternatives	529
3. His person His embodied ideal; His society His articulated Person	531
§ IV. *Positive Religions and Christ's Religion*	532–535
1. Christianity a personal, not a positive religion	532
2. Christ's spiritual sovereignty	533
3. Characteristics of His social ideal	534

CHAPTER II

THE IDEAL RELIGION AND THE IDEA OF GOD	536–550
§ I. *The Idea of God in Religion*	536–539
1. Summary of the previous argument	536
2. Immortality of religious beliefs; difficulty of the advance to ethical monotheism	537
§ II. *God Interpreted through Christ*	539–541
§ III. *The Christian Idea Makes for Universal Ideals*	541–547
1. The idea of God dissociated from a tribe and attached to a Person	541
2. The correspondent change in the idea of God; His universal Fatherhood	542
3. Change in the idea of man; the value of the unit and unity of the Race	544
§ IV. *The Condition of Realization*	548
1. The idea of Christianity appropriated by Faith	548
2. The idea of Faith specially characteristic of Christianity; what Christ has done for religion	548–550

CHAPTER III

THE IDEAL RELIGION AND WORSHIP	551–568
§ I. *Place as it Affects Worship*	551–557
1. Holy places; how they externalize and localize worship	551
2. Religions universal in idea limited by place; Judaism and Islam	554
3. The emancipation from place achieved by Christ; how the ideal may be carnalized	555
§ II. *The Institution as it Affects Worship*	557–560
1. The Institution and the idea of God	557
2. How it affects religion	558

CONTENTS

	PAGE
§ III. *Christ the Only Institution for Christian Worship* .	560–564
1. His Person conceived in the New Testament as an institution	560
2. i. Christ's sole sufficiency the cardinal fact of the Christian religion	561
ii. The Eucharist not worship, but a means of communion	562
iii. Preaching in relation to worship	563
iv. The new institution founded by God not man . .	562
v. The institution defines the worshipper . . .	563
vi. Its ultimate end the glory of God	564
§ IV. *Conclusion*	564–568
1. The failure in the ethical interpretation of Christ the Church's gravest heresy	564
2. The place of Christ in universal history corresponds to the belief in His Person	566

INTRODUCTION
THE PROBLEM OF THE CHRISTIAN RELIGION

καὶ αὐτός ἐστιν πρὸ πάντων, καὶ τὰ πάντα ἐν αὐτῷ συνέστηκεν.
—*Col.* i. 17.

Tolle deum a creatura, et remanet nihil.—NICOLAS OF CUSA.

Gott ist das Herz oder Quellbrunn der Natur, aus ihm rühret alles her.

Du musst nicht denken, dass der Sohn ein andrer Gott sei als der Vater, dass er ausser dem Vater stehe, wie wenn zwei Männer neben einander stehen. Der Vater ist der Quellbrunn aller Kräfte, und alle Kräfte sind in einander wie eine Kraft, darum heisst er auch einiger Gott. Der Sohn ist das Herz in dem Vater, das Herz oder der Kern in allen Kräften des Vaters. Von dem Sohne steiget auf die ewige himmlische Freude, quellend in allen Kräften des Vaters, eine Freude die kein Auge gesehen und kein Ohr gehört hat.—JACOB BÖHME.

Glaube ist die Abschattung des göttlichen Wissens und Wollens in dem endlichen Geiste des Menschen.—JACOBI.

INTRODUCTION

THE PROBLEM OF THE CHRISTIAN RELIGION

§ I. *The Person of Christ as the Mystery of the Christian Religion*

1. EVERY reader of recent theological literature is familiar with the remarkable contrast between the image of Jesus in the Gospels and the conception of Christ in the œcumenical creeds. It represents a change which time cannot measure or place explain. The Council of Nicæa stands as nearly as possible at a distance of three hundred years from the death of Jesus, while the interval between the Council of Chalcedon and the latest of the Gospels is at most three centuries and a half. But years and even centuries cannot describe the difference between the simple lines in which the Evangelists draw the historical portrait of Jesus and the metaphysical terms in which Nicæa defines the person of the Son and His relation to the Father, or Chalcedon distinguishes the natures and delimits their provinces and relations. On the one hand we have the Son of man "meek and lowly in heart"; humble in birth, obscure in life; "despised and rejected of men," disbelieved by the priests and rulers, companying with publicans and sinners; "crucified under Pontius Pilate"; forsaken in death by His disciples, and followed to the grave by only a few women, who were too mean to be heeded by His enemies, and who but loved Him the more that He had suffered so much. On

the other hand we have the Son "consubstantial with the Father," "begotten, not made," "very God of very God"; we have a Person composed of two distinct natures, which must neither be divided nor confused; for how could convertible natures be opposed? or how, if they were separable, could there be a real and enduring personal unity? If we attempt, first, to look through the eyes of the Evangelists, and, next, to think in the categories of the Councils, we shall feel as bewildered as if we had been suddenly transported from a serene and lucid atmosphere to a land of double vision and half-lights, where men take shadows for substantial things.

Yet the two moments are too organically related to be characterized and dismissed in a series of contrasts. They are bound together by a dialectical process which has only to be understood to turn their antithesis into a synthesis; and in this synthesis the opposed elements appear to coalesce and become indissoluble, the later conserving the earlier belief, the earlier vivifying the later. For if we may reason from the processes of collective experience to law in history, we may say that two things are certain, viz. (a) that without the personal charm of the historical Jesus the œcumenical creeds would never have been either formulated or tolerated; and (β) without the metaphysical conception of Christ the Christian religion would long ago have ceased to live. Clear and sweet as the Galilæan vision may be, it would, apart from the severer speculation which translated it from a history into a creed, have faded from human memory like a dream which delighted the light slumbers of the morning, though only to be so dissolved before the strenuous will of the day as to be impossible of recall. The religion which makes its appeal to the sense of the beautiful, and speaks to the fancy in legends, or to the imagination in symbols, may do well for a season or while a special mood continues; but only the religion which addresses and exercises the reason will continue to live. To say that the article of faith which the intellect finds the hardest to construe may be the most necessary to the life of the religion, is to state a sober truth and no mere paradox. This does not mean that the heart has to be satisfied at the expense of the head; it means the very opposite, viz., that unless religion be an eternal challenge to the reason it can have no voice for the imagination, and no value for the heart. The symbol is only a thing of sense, most valued where it has displaced the ideal and become the sole reality; but the mysteries which compose the atmosphere in which all truth lives, are too inseparable from thought to be absent from religion. The pure reason has its antinomies, but the very ideas it so describes may be said to be the laws which bind together mind and nature, which make a rational experience possible, and which set the personal intellect in the midst of an intelligible system. The faith, therefore, that had no mysteries would be an anomaly in a universe like ours; and would suffer from the incurable defects of being a faith without truth and without the capability of so appealing to reason as to promote man's rational and moral growth. For in the degree that a religion did not tax thought it would not develop mind; it is the problems which most imperiously appeal to the reason for solution which open those glimpses into the secret of the universe that most fascinate the heart and awe the imagination. And the Person of Christ is exactly the point in the Christian religion where the intellect feels overwhelmed by mysteries it cannot resolve, yet where Christian experience finds the factors of its most characteristic qualities, and the Church the truth it has lived by and is bound to live for.

2. But mysteries are of two sorts: they may either be things of nature, or creations of the art of man. The mysteries of nature are universal, and are known to man in every place

and in all stages of his culture, though their forms are many and most varied ; but the mysteries of art are a vaster and more mixed multitude, occasional in origin, partial in distribution, living and increasing at one stage of culture, diminishing and dying at another. The faculty which sees and feels the mysteries of nature is the reason, and the more rational or conscious it grows the more does it realize their burden and their impenetrability to mortal sight. But the art which makes mysteries is not so much conscious as spontaneous in its operation ; and shows itself in the skill with which it blends the fantastic with the real, and out of the impossible weaves the very texture of life. The mysteries of the reason are the problems of philosophy : this world, who made it, and how was it made ? Our rational experience, how is it possible ? Is it created by what man brings to nature, or by the action of nature upon man ? What are Space and Time ? Are they forms of perception or are they outside things, which, through association and sense, impress themselves upon the mind ? What is Mind and what Matter ? Are they two, or are they one, in aspect different, in essence the same ? Is there such a thing as Will in the universe and Freedom in man, or does fixed fate govern all ? If Necessity reigns, how is the illusion of Freedom to be explained ? If Freedom reigns, how are the uniformities of Nature and the order of History to be understood ? These are questions man cannot escape : art has had nothing to do with their making, or time with their origin or end ; for they are involved in the very processes of the intellect, and they grow at once more imperative and more complex with the progress of knowledge.

But the other order of mysteries bears rather the tool-marks of made or manufactured articles, and have not the stamp of the inevitable which belongs to the work of nature. They may be the creations of Tradition or of the Schools, made by the hand which reveres the past too much to change the forms of its beliefs even where their substance has perished ;

or by the master whose skilful subtlety has shaped formulæ which later men may accept but dare not question. They may be but the fantastic shapes of an old mythology frozen and sterilized by the cold breath of the understanding, which loves to deal with the fluid forms of poetry as if they were stiff and pedantic prose; or they may be speculative interpretations of historical persons and events, translating them into figures in a new mythology which is all the more audacious that it is a creation of the logical intellect, and not, like the old, of the concrete imagination. Of this sort are mysteries which all religions have been rich in, and which none seems to be able to live without. Hinduism transmutes the epic hero Krishna into an incarnation of deity; Buddhism makes out of its founder a being with more infinite capabilities of change and action than any god; Zoroastrianism turns the phenomena of day and night into the terms of an ethical dualism and personalizes eternity; Islam so magnifies its Koran that it experiences a kind of apotheosis and becomes an uncreated Word, which had no beginning and can have no end, and which found manifestation but not origin through the mouth of the prophet. These are examples of the mysteries which art makes in religion, and which are in their own order more intricate and invincible than any of the creations of the mythical imagination.

§ II. *Need the Person be a Mystery?*

1. Now, to which order of mystery does the doctrine as to the Person of Christ belong? Is it a thing of nature? or is it a made or manufactured article, a myth, which the logical intellect has woven out of the material offered by a simple but beautiful history? It were certainly easy so to represent it, and to urge that by so doing we should relieve religion from an oppressive dogma, and religious thought from a problem which always perplexes, and even bewilders, the

intellect, if it does not provoke it to disdainful denial. There is, as we have said, in this case, a sort of infinite incommensurability between the historical person and its theological construction; the one is so simple, so natural, so like a child of His time and people; while the other is such a mass of intricate complexities, as it were a synthesis of all the incredibilities with which religion has ever loved to shock and offend the reason. The spontaneous impulse of the intellect, therefore, when it first comes face to face with the modest premises and the stupendous conclusion, is to attempt to divorce them, and to conceive Jesus as real, and the deified Christ as the product of idealization. And this attempt may be cogently justified by both thought and criticism. If we begin with thought, we may represent its process of analysis and argument somewhat thus:

'The doctrine that affirms that Jesus was "God manifest in the flesh," or, in other words, that in Christ the natures of God and man were so united as to form a single and indivisible person, is the very apotheosis of the inconceivable. God is a Being too transcendental to be either known or rationally conceived; but man is a child of nature and experience: how, then, can we attach any idea to the words which affirm a union of these two?—of the God who transcends our experience, and of the Man who is its most familiar factor and object? But suppose it be granted that both ideas are alike real, is it any more possible to conceive them as so united as to constitute an historical person? The incarnation of God in all men, the manifestation of the Creator in the whole of the race He had created, might be an arguable position; but not its rigorous and exclusive individuation, or restriction to a single person out of all the infinite multitude of millions who have lived, are living, or are to live. God and man are too incompatible in their attributes to be conceived as co-ordinated in a Being who appears on the stage of history as a human individual, and who has the experiences and suffers the fate proper to one. The man cannot become God, for man is mortal and finite, God eternal and infinite; and it does not lie even with the Almighty to invest temporal being with the attributes of the eternal. Nor can God become a man any more than His eternity can be annihilated or His infinitude cancelled or curtailed. To attempt to conceive God creating another God, or ceasing to be the God He is, were to attempt a feat which is impossible to reason. Then if the union is effected by God remaining God, and the man a man, what sort of being is the resultant person? Nay, is he, in any tolerable sense, a person at all? Is he not rather a mere symbol of contradictory ideas, as it were qualities which thought refuses to relate, and is therefore unable to unite, personalized and made into an everlasting enigma?

'The matter is not illumined, but rather darkened, by definition and explanation. The union has been defined as personal, and again as between a concrete, i.e. a divine person, the Son of God, and an abstract, i.e. human nature before it had taken shape in a personal man. But what is union in a person save a conscious unity, being realized and made homogeneous in the unity of a rational consciousness? But is not the very note of this case the double consciousness where the person knows himself now as God and now as man; or, what is still less rationally conceivable, as living a veiled and double life, where he speaks and acts as man, while he consciously possesses the omniscience and power of God? To a life lived under such conditions, what reality, what integrity or veracity, could be said to belong? And as used here, are not the terms "nature" and "person" simply the catch-words of a juggler? When the speech is of God, He is described as three persons in one nature; when it is of Christ, he is represented as two natures in one person. In the former case the persons are plural, but the nature singular, and the argument is based on the position that unity belongs to nature and difference to person. But in the latter case the person is singular and the natures plural, and the argument proceeds on the premiss that unity belongs to the person and difference to the natures. Apply to Christ the conception of nature or substance as it is predicated of the Godhead, and the unity is dissolved, because the natures become personalized; apply to the Godhead the idea of person as used of Christ, and the argument for the divinity loses all its force, because unity of nature is no longer necessary to the personal integrity. It is evident, therefore, that a doctrine which can so little stand the criticism of the reason is a manufactured mystery, made by the art and craft of man, not by the solemn and inexorable necessities of thought, as conditioned and confronted by a universe which it must interpret in order that it may continue to be.'

2. In some such manner, then, the understanding, by means of its keen and dexterous logic, might argue that the Incarnation was a mere fictitious or artificial mystery, significant only of the extravagances of the ecstatic or dogmatic mind, without any significance for the saner reason. And if we proceed from the destructive dialectic of thought to the analytic process of literary and historical criticism, we may find the fatal cycle completed somewhat thus:

'Literary analysis enables us to discover a primary and a secondary stratum in the Gospels. Jesus, as he is presented in the primary or original document, is a real and tangible enough figure, capable of easy and complete historical explanation. He is the last of the prophets of Israel, ethical as they all were, but sweeter in character and in speech than they had been, larger and more reasonable in mind, as became one who lived under the influence of Rome and its universal ideas. This gives the source of His most distinctive teaching. Hebrew literature—Canonical, Apocryphal, Talmudical—supplied the matter; the spirit of the time determined the form. His God is the Jehovah of the Old Testament, though sublimed and subdued to the likeness of his own genial nature. His idea of the kingdom of God is the common prophetic belief, though adapted and enlarged by the genius of humanity within him. His notion of the Son of man comes, partly, from Daniel, and, partly, from Enoch. His conception of the suffering Messiah was directly suggested by Isaiah's Servant of God. In the Psalms can be found his ideas that the true worship of the Father is to be not by sacrifice and ceremonial, but in spirit and in truth, by men of clean hands and contrite hearts. His notion that God's people are the pure and holy in spirit came from Jeremiah. His doctrine of repentance was Ezekiel's. His idea of God's forbearance with the wicked and desire to save them only repeated and expanded Hosea's. His ethical temper was inspired by the Books of the Hebrew Wisdom and their Apocryphal successors. Some of his individual and most characteristic precepts, such as the love of one's neighbour, or the law of reciprocity, were commonplaces in the Jewish schools, certain to be frequent on the lips of men who loved learning and revered the rabbi. And as he has his antecedents in Israel, so has the literature which preserves his memory. The Gospels are the creations of men who knew the Old Testament, and found again its most miraculous histories in the life of him who had in their eyes fulfilled it. The things that were possible to Moses, the wonders that had been worked by Elijah, the translation of Enoch, the deliverance accorded to Jonah, were occurrences which the regretful admiration of simple-minded disciples could not refuse to ascribe to him whom they had come to conceive as the most marvellous and winsome of the sons of men.

'The secondary stratum in the Gospels has thus been formed by the very same influences that shaped the figure which is embedded in the primary. The associations created by the only literature which their authors knew, made at once the atmosphere through which they saw Jesus, the attributes in which they arrayed him, and the categories under which he was conceived. Hence came the miracles which they ascribed to him, his supernatural birth, his sacrificial death, and the ascension which translated him from a guilty world to the right hand of God. In a word, their imaginations, touched by the enthusiasm of an all-believing love, became creative; and, losing the very power to distinguish between the things that had happened and the things that might, or rather that ought to, have happened, they saw Jesus as if he had been the Messiah they had hoped he was. They dreamed in the language of the Messianic hope, and when they attempted to describe him, their dreams so mingled with the realities that the realities partook of the idealism of the dreams, and the dreams absorbed the realism of the realities. Thus by a perfectly natural process one who had been in actual life a Hebrew peasant, though indeed a peasant of superlative genius, supernal goodness, and ineffable charm, came to wear to the imagination a divine hue and form; and once this had been achieved for him it needed only the fearless logic of a metaphysical but unscientific age to identify him with Deity and resolve his humanity by the incarnation of the son of God.'

§ III. *Why there is a Problem of the Person*

1. But now what precisely is this double argument of rational logic and analytical criticism worth? Is it not cogent simply because it is narrow? The conclusion of the dialectic is invincible for the reason that it started from an inarticulated premiss. The rational problem is not so simple

THE PROBLEM OF UNIVERSAL HISTORY 13

as the argument assumed, for the facts to be co-ordinated and the ideas to be construed are infinitely more complex than the premiss was allowed to state or to suggest. The dexterous logician is not the only strong intellect which has tried to handle the doctrine. The contradictions which he translates into rational incredibilities must either have escaped the analysis of men like Augustine or Aquinas, or have been by their thought transcended and reconciled in some higher synthesis. It is a wholesome thing to remember that the men who elaborated our theologies were at least as rational as their critics, and that we owe it to historical truth to look at their beliefs with their eyes.

And as with the dialectical, so with the critical process: the two are related by having a common premiss; and if it be insufficient or invalid in the one case, it cannot be beyond question in the other. Thus it is possible that the secondary element in the Gospels may be due rather to intellectual prevision than to imaginative reminiscence. We have not solved, we have not even stated and defined, the problem as to the person of Christ when we have written the life of Jesus, for that problem is raised even less by the Gospels than by Christ's place and function in the collective history of man; or, to be more correct, by the life described in the Gospels and the phenomena represented by universal history viewed in their reciprocal and interpretative inter-relations. If the Gospels stood alone, the problem would be comparatively simple; indeed, there would hardly be anything worth calling a problem, for they are concerned with events which happened in time, and with an historical figure whose antecedents, emergence, circumstances, behaviour, experiences, fate, words, are exactly the sort of material biography loves to handle. But the very essence of the matter is that the Gospels do not stand alone, but live, as it were, embosomed in universal history. And in that history Christ plays a part much more remarkable and much less compatible with common manhood than the part Jesus plays in the history of His own age and people. And we have not solved, or even apprehended, any one of the problems connected with His person until we have resolved the mystery of the place He has filled and the things He has achieved in the collective life of man.

2. We have granted that it were an easy thing to construe the life of Jesus, isolated from its historical context, in the terms of a severe naturalism; indeed, the ease with which it can be done makes it the first temptation of the intellect, which is as naturally indolent as it is instinctively audacious. But suppose our rigorous naturalism has done its work, what then? Why, we have come face to face with a new problem, which may well seem all the more mysteriously insoluble that our naturalism is courageous and complete. For Christ has to be fitted into our scheme of things, and we have to explain (1) How He whom we have resolved into a mere Jewish peasant, came to be arrayed in the most extraordinary attributes which were ever made to clothe mortal man; (2) how His historical action has corresponded to His fictitious rather than to His real character; and (3) what sort of blind accident or ironical indifference to right can reign in a universe which has allowed to fiction greater powers than have been granted to truth. The question does not relate simply to the apotheosis of Jesus; that is a process which the indolent intellect, if it be also ingenious, can facilely describe. We admit that the process may be stated in terms of such amazing verisimilitude as to turn it into a cogent probability. The question becomes urgent only when the deificatory process has been completed. The deification, if we may so call it, though the term is radically incorrect, has all the effect of the most finely calculated purpose formed after all the needs of man and the whole course of his history have been considered. There is nothing in nature or art that can so well illustrate design or adaptation to an end.

And though it be illusory, yet it works not as illusion, but as truth, and for it, in a most miraculous way; true men receive it, are made truer by it, so use it as to build the world up in the love and pursuit of the truth as it had never been built up before. As unconscious fiction it is as void of substance as a dream, yet it acts upon humanity as if it were the most substantial good which had ever descended upon it out of heaven. And how, by what right, at whose instance, did this thing, the apotheosis of the obscure, happen? For it is the apotheosis which has proved the real or substantive factor of change. It is not Jesus of Nazareth who has so powerfully entered into history; it is the deified Christ who has been believed, loved, and obeyed as the Saviour of the world. The act or process of apotheosis, then, created the Christian religion; and who was responsible for it? If the imaginative peasants of Galilee, they were doing a deed no less wonderful than the creation of the world, and the power or providence which allowed them to do it was consenting by fiction and make-believe to govern reason and form character.

But what kind of reflexion is it upon the Maker and Master of the universe if we conceive Him as consenting to do this thing? Nay, in what sort of light does it set reason if we imagine it capable of being so deluded and deceived, seduced to martyrdom or compelled to enthusiasm by a mistake? Indeed, if the doctrine of the Person of Christ were explicable as the mere mythical apotheosis of Jesus of Nazareth, it would become the most insolent and fateful anomaly in history. For it could not stand alone; it would affect all thought and all objects of thought. "Here," men would say, "a mere chapter of accidents has made one of the meanest figures in literature the most potent person of all time, the source of a series of illusions which have exercised the most transcendent influence upon the life and destinies of men. If accident and illusion have played such a part in history, what character must we attribute to the power which rules the world? Order in nature is an insignificant idea compared with the idea of order in history; but how can there be an order if the persons who create it be, in the very degree that they are potent, themselves the mere creatures of chance, or of worse than chance, fiction and pure phantasy?"

3. We may say, then, that the doctrine of the Person of Christ is no mere theory concerning an historical individual with whose biography we are all familiar. On the contrary, its attributes are those in an even higher degree of a symbol than of a fact, though of a symbol which owes all its reality to its being fact transfigured and sublimed. In other words, Christ's person is even more intellectually real than historically actual, i.e. it does not simply denote a figure which once appeared under the conditions of space and time, but it also stands for a whole order of thought, a way of regarding the universe, of conceiving God and man in themselves and in their mutual relations. Its interpretation, therefore, is not a problem in mere formal logic or limited literary criticism; but touches at once facts of history and the ultimate mysteries of being. We may, then, make here a perfunctory distinction, and say that it raises two series of questions: historical or literary, and speculative or philosophical. The historical problem is threefold, concerned, first, with the life of Jesus of Nazareth; secondly, with the process by which the thought of His people regarding Him developed from the synoptic Gospels into the conceptions that needed for their expression the formulæ of the œcumenical creeds; and, thirdly, with the mode in which the Person as represented in the history and interpreted in the doctrine has created a religion which has absorbed the noblest elements out of the past, and been the most potent factor of moral and intellectual progress that has ever entered into the life of man.

But the speculative problem is at once more simple and less soluble, viz., in what terms must we state our idea of the order in which He stands, of His place within the order, and of the qualities or right by which He holds it. Now, it is evident that every attempt to solve the former problem must be incomplete without some attempt at the solution of the latter; for a person who fulfils universal functions cannot be described and dismissed as if He were a particular individual. In other words, the secret of such a personality is not explained when historical science and literary art have combined to tell in the most adequate and exhaustive way the story of the life He lived at a given moment in a given place, and of how He was conceived in ages of imaginative faith and metaphysical enthusiasm; but only when such a coherent conception of Him is reached as shall show Him in organic relation to the whole system of things. Now, whatever we may think of the œcumenical formulæ, we must acknowledge that their purpose was to make Christ represent in His person the natures, relations, inter-activities, community and difference in attribute and being, of God and man. They may have in many respects done violence to both speculation and logic; but one thing we must confess: if the idea they tried to express as to Christ's person had not been formulated centuries since, we should have been forced to invent it, or something like it, in order that we might have some reasonable hypothesis explanatory of the course things have taken. And this, we may add, means that the problem is neither dead nor concerned with the recovery of a world of dead ideas, but one of living actuality, concerned with all that is most vital and characteristic in the thought of to-day.

Now, this defines our purpose, which may be stated thus: to discuss the question as to the Person of Christ, what He was, and how He ought to be conceived, not simply as a chapter in Biblical or in systematic theology, but as a problem directly raised by the place He holds and the functions He has fulfilled in the life of Man, collective and individual. The principle which underlies the discussion we may further state in these terms: the conception of Christ stands related to history as the idea of God is related to Nature, i.e. each is in its own sphere the factor of order, or the constitutive condition of a rational system. The study of nature has been the means of unfolding, explicating, and defining the contents of the idea of God; the study of history has developed, amplified and justified the conception of Christ. We hope that this statement may in the course of the discussions which follow become something more and better than a paradox.

Of course, a too timid faith may doubt whether it be pious to regard the Person of Christ as in any proper sense a fit subject for philosophical discussion; and it may urge that, as the knowledge of it came by revelation, it is only as a revealed truth, attested and authenticated by inspired men, that it ought to be accepted and understood. The only proper method of elucidation and proof is the exegesis of the sacred Scriptures, while the precise sense in which it is to be construed has been defined by the great councils of the undivided Church. The Incarnation is a mystery which transcends reason, and it can enter into the categories of metaphysical criticism only to be mishandled, profaned and misjudged.

But to this it may be sufficient to reply : it does not lie in the power of any man or any society to keep the mysteries of faith out of the hands of reason. Nature and history, the very necessities of belief and its continued life, have combined to invite reason to enter the domain of faith. The only condition on which reason could have nothing to do with religion, is that religion should have nothing to do with truth. For in every controversy concerning what is or what is not truth, reason and not authority is the supreme arbiter ; the authority that decides against reason commits itself to a conflict which is certain to issue in its defeat. The men who defend faith must think as well as the men who oppose it; their argumentative processes must be rational and their conclusions supported by rational proofs. If it were illicit for reason to touch the mysteries of religion, the Church would never have had a creed or have believed a doctrine, nor would man have possessed a faith higher than the mythical fancies which pleased his childhood. Without the exercise of reason we should never have had the Fourth Gospel or the Pauline Epistles, or any one of those treatises on the Godhead, the Incarnation, or the Atonement, from Athanasius to Hegel, or from Augustine to our own day, which have done more than all the decrees of all the Councils, or all the Creeds of all the Churches, to keep faith living and religion a reality. The man who despises or distrusts the reason despises the God who gave it, and the most efficient of all the servants He has bidden work within and upon man in behalf of truth. Here, at least, it may be honestly said there is no desire to build Faith upon the negation of Reason; where both are sons of God it were sin to seek to make the one legitimate at the expense of the other's legitimacy.

BOOK I

QUESTIONS IN THE PHILOSOPHY OF NATURE
AND MIND WHICH AFFECT BELIEF IN
THE SUPERNATURAL PERSON

Il n'y a point d'autre nature, je veux dire d'autres lois naturelles, que les volontés efficaces du tout-puissant

Dieu est très-étroitement uni à nos âmes par sa présence, de sorte qu'on peut dire qu'il est le lien des esprits, de même que les espaces sont en un sens le lien des corps.—MALEBRANCHE.

Quid enim est natura nisi iste ordo, secundum quem Deus suas creaturas regit?—LA FORGE.

Nec sineret bonus fieri male, nisi omnipotens etiam de malo facere posset bene.—AUGUSTINE.

Von der Idee entfremdet, ist die Natur nur der Leichnam des Verstandes.—HEGEL.

Die wahre Philosophie der Geschichte besteht nämlich in der Einsicht, dass man, bei allen diesen endlosen Veränderungen und ihrem Wirrwarr, doch stets nur das selbe, gleiche und unwandelbare Wesen vor sich hat, welches heute das Selbe treibt, wie gestern und immerdar: sie soll also das Identische in allen Vorgängen, der alten wie der neuen Zeit, des Orients wie des Occidents, erkennen, und, trotz aller Verschiedenheit der speciellen Umstände, der Kostümes und der Sitten, überall die Selbe Menschheit erblicken.

Was die Vernunft dem Individuo, das ist die Geschichte dem menschlichen Geschlechte.—SCHOPENHAUER.

Gleichwie die mancherlei Blumen alle in der Erde stehen und alle neben einander wachsen, keine beisst sich mit der andern um Farben, Geruch und Geschmack, sie lassen Erde und Sonne, Regen und Wind, Hitze und Kälte mit sich machen was sie wollen, sie aber wachsen eine jede in ihrer Eigenschaft, so ists auch mit den Kindern Gottes.—JACOB BÖHME.

Es liegt wesentlich im Begriffe der wahrhaften Religion, d. i. derjenigen, deren Inhalt der absolute Geist ist, dass sie geoffenbart und zwar von Gott geoffenbart sei.—HEGEL.

CHAPTER I

THE BELIEF AS A PROBLEM IN THE PHILOSOPHY OF NATURE

§ I. *The Ideas of Nature and the Supernatural*

THE real and initial difficulty the modern mind feels in the face of the apostolic doctrine as to the Person of Christ is its radical incompatibility with the scientific view of Nature. It was an easy thing to men who had no conception of natural order or law, and who habitually thought in the terms of the miraculous, to say, "We believe in a supernatural Person." Their view of the universe was not, in our sense, normal, but was rather a compound of the extraordinary and exceptional. Natural things were explained by supernatural causes; gods were as numerous as men; dreams had more significance than observation or experience; the commonest events were ascribed to Divine interference; while to seek a physical reason for disease or health, or states of ecstasy or trance, was regarded as highly profane. But the instinctive faith of the modern temper may be expressed in the formula, "I believe in an order that admits no miracle and knows no supernatural." Nature is to us the realm of law; we suspect the abnormal, and tend to deny promptly whatever postulates for its being a force we cannot analyze or measure. The creed common to modern man we might describe by the word "Naturalism," were not the term so illusory and so incapable of a fixed meaning. In a sense, we are all Naturalists; we speak and think as those who live and move and have their being in a nature which represents to us all we know of reality and life. For the Nature we describe as dead is a mere abstraction, without any being in our conscious experience. Spinoza distinguished "natura naturans," from "natura naturata": the former was causative, creative, efficient nature, the latter nature as caused, created, produced. But the distinction was subjective and arbitrary; it represented no objective reality. We do not know this "natura naturata" by itself; it is the "natura naturans" viewed as a realized or embodied order. Nor are we able to separate the "naturans," from the "naturata," for it is only the system we know conceived through the causal idea, a system charged with the energies which as efficient are the sufficient reason for its continuance. But whether we think of "Nature" as causative or as caused, what we mean is a system whose reason is in itself, which would be disturbed or broken up by the intervention of any higher power or will, superseding its forces and accomplishing something beyond their capacity or scope. So universal and instinctive has this notion become that we feel as if a supernatural Person—especially in so exaggerated a form as we have in Jesus Christ—were an idea we could as little conceive in thought as represent in imagination.

2. This is too great a question to be argued as if it concerned the old and exhausted commonplaces as to the possibility and credibility of miracles. There never was a more unreal discussion raised in any School, or by men who had less right to raise it. Hume was a dexterous dialectician, and in nothing was his dexterity so apparent as in the way in which he concealed, if not from himself, at least from his opponents, the incompatibility of his argument against miracles with the first principles of his own philosophy. That philosophy was the purest and most consistent of all modern scepticisms, and Hume was the most subtle and logical of all modern empiricists. His apparatus was simple, his analysis of the material contained in Locke's two sources of knowledge was

thorough, and his deduction complete. The originals of all knowledge were two—impressions and ideas. Impressions denoted the direct and vivid appearance of Nature in and through sense ; while ideas were remembered impressions,—as it were their faint echo or image. 'Now,' Hume argues, 'since these two are the sources and only realities of knowledge, and since we never find ourselves without an impression or idea, we have no independent existence, and are nothing but the series of our impressions and ideas. It follows that as we—or the succession of images we mistake for ourselves—can never have impressions of more than single things, we can never have any impression of self, which, so far from being a single thing, is an infinite multitude of things existing in either arbitrary or determined relations. It further follows that as we perceive only external occurrence and not internal causation, we can never have any impression of cause or perceive anything more than antecedence and sequence or the coexistence and association of contiguous things. But where we have no impressions we can have no ideas; and therefore we cannot speak of causation or causes as real things. Nor, for the same reason, can we have any impression or any consequent idea of so vast a thing as space, or of so multitudinous a thing as time. The ideas of self, causation, space, time are, therefore, all unrealities, begotten of the tendency to feign, i.e. they are mere fictions of the phantasy. All the knowledge that comes to man is given in individual impressions, and all that legitimately remains is the echo of these in single or associated ideas.'

Now let us take the principles supplied by this method and apply them to the ideas or beliefs which underlie Hume's famous argument against miracles. Miracles, he says, have two things against them : (*a*) they are impossible, for they imply a violation of the order or the laws of nature, and (β) they are incredible because they contradict our human experience. Well, then, could the first argument stand against Hume's own method of criticism? Let us begin with the idea of Nature. Where did we get it? and what does it mean? Had we ever an impression of Nature? How could we have it? We may have an impression of single things, say, of cold, of heat, of taste, of smell, of light, of sound. But Nature is not a single thing, but rather the vast, multifarious, complex aggregate of all real and possible perceptions; it is, therefore, not capable of being the object or occasion of an impression, and so it can only be by an entirely illicit process that we form the fictitious idea of Nature as a connected and coherent whole. How then can we say that Nature is? Still more how can we tell what Nature is? Can we even by analysis tell the immense number of things which the term Nature means? It is (a) the total infinite multitude of those impressions which make up the world without us, whose cause no man can discover; (β) the whole army of associated ideas within, which we mistake for ourselves, but which is only a stream, or series, or succession of units in perpetual flux, moving and changing with inconceivable rapidity; and (γ) it is all these unresolved but associated units bound into a system by some unintelligible principle in some inexplicable mode. There can be no such thing, therefore, as an idea of Nature, for of Nature we can have no impression, and what is so named is only an accidental aggregation of ideas. Hence, all reasoning based upon the notion of Nature as a known thing or system of things is illicit.

But let us see whether the idea of Order will fare any better in the hands of this criticism: can we have any impression of it? Here difficulties of another kind meet us: for order implies time and its sequences. And so to have a notion of order we must be ourselves continuous; but we are on Hume's premisses without any permanent personal identity, nothing indeed but a momentary taste or fragrance, an affection of heat or cold, a sensation of colour or resistance; in a word, only a series of impressions and ideas, with no existence save such as they can give. If, then, we are to receive an impression of order, we must have the whole infinite series summed up in one single sensation, which would imply a sensory as vast as the universe. As the thing is so manifestly impossible we can have no conception of order, and, therefore, cannot reason as if we had. Again, take another term in Hume's argument, Violation; but how can we have a conception of violated order if we have no notion of the order said to be violated, any more than we can have any conception of Nature or Self, when both nature and self have been dissolved? Therefore, to argue that miracles are a violation of the order or laws of Nature, is to assume a multitude of ideas which experience has been proved incapable of giving, and psychology unable by any analytical process to discover, leaving as the only possible conclusion the assumption that man first gave them to Nature. The result is that Hume's argument is so fundamentally opposed to his own first principles in philosophy as to be broken, split, and ended by the very criticism he himself brought to bear upon personal identity, upon causation, upon space, upon time, upon the very ideas on which his argument against miracles rests, and which gave to it all its apparent validity.

§ II. *Nature and Thought*

1. But it were altogether inconsistent with the gravity of the discussion on which we are entering, to conduct it as a mere *argumentum ad hominem* against a man who confessed that he did not live up to his own philosophy. It is evident, indeed, that a position so *a priori* and final as this, that we live under an order or system which has no room for a supernatural Person, must be discussed as a principle involved in the most fundamental of all questions, viz., in what terms must we interpret this order or system? What does Nature mean and what include? Does man make it, or does it

make man? Is thought the product of experience, or is experience made possible by factors which transcend it? These are radical questions, as old as the attempt to explain all that we mean by the term Knowledge, its genesis and conditions, its limits and reality; and they may seem as insoluble as they are ancient. But it does not follow that the more fundamental a problem becomes the less soluble it grows, or that, though perhaps beyond a final speculative solution, it is incapable of a rational answer. And the fundamental character of these questions is seen in the way in which they determine all our thinking, our attitude to what is termed Nature, our interpretation of the phenomena we call History. For what they really mean is this—whether we are to find the ultimate factors of knowledge in personality or in the impersonal forces we co-ordinate under the phrase "system or order of nature." The intellectual result will indeed be very different as we make Nature or Thought the ultimate term in our logical process. If "Nature," taken in the sense of the system of forces that surround us, be conceived as the method and the measure for the interpretation of man, it means that he is to be construed as part of a universe which knows antecedence and sequence, but not rational causation, i.e. it is a universe of co-ordinated phenomena, not of connected and intelligible being. In such a system man may be conceived as a succession of similar or dissimilar states of consciousness, but not as a concrete and coherent person, i.e. a continuous and self-identical being. The successive conscious states which he may identify with himself, will be governed by forces operating from without and independently of what he may call himself, i.e. the conscious states which he is pleased to regard as constituting the only personality he knows, will represent the action of forces he does not know. He thus becomes in the strict sense not a cause, but an effect or result; his concrete and conscious being, his character and mind, appear as the creations of powers and circumstances which he can neither discover nor name, though he must conceive them as necessitating; yet to say that they were necessitated would be to transcend experience. His thoughts, his feelings, and his actions are thus regulated by laws as absolute as those which determine the ebb and flow of the tides, the movement of the planets or of the stars, the moulding of the tear or of the dewdrop.

But if Nature be thus used for the interpretation of man, two things follow. First, the man who emerges from this speculative process is not the man we know, i.e. he is not a free and conscious reason who can act from choice and for an end he can state in terms now moral, now intellectual, now emotional, and who even distinguishes himself as a person from the things, events, and circumstances amid which he moves. And, secondly, the Nature which is invoked to explain him ceases herself to be intelligible, is without any explicable relation to the intellect, and has nothing rational either in her order or in her phenomena. There is, indeed, no single idea on which science prides herself which could be received from Nature alone; for even if mind were regarded as a simple receptivity, a mere *tabula rasa* or sheet of white paper, it would be necessary to invest it with the power of reading the things that are written upon its clean or figured surface; and the power to read implies what we may term the whole grammar of natural intelligence. For the thing written is something which conveys thought to thought; i.e. it is a language which one mind speaks and another mind understands.

But to a language three things are necessary: it must express reason, contain reason, and speak to reason. If thought did not make it, thought could never interpret it, for nothing but the work of thought is intelligible to thought. But thought is the most distinctive attribute and exercise of personality; only in a person does it originate, and only by a person can it be understood. For how an intelligible can be without an intelligence, both creative and receptive, is a thing which experience does not know and thought cannot conceive. If, then, we eliminate Personality from Nature—either objectively, as interpretable; or subjectively, as interpreted—we are left without a nature we can regard as intelligible. Personality thus becomes the very condition through which Nature, as known to science, is, while it is also the factor through which all the sciences which explain Nature have come to be and are able to continue in being. But the organ through which all natural forces are known cannot be itself a mere unit of force; i.e. the co-ordinating genius cannot be one of the co-ordinated atoms. In other words, the Personality which makes Nature was not made by the Nature it makes.

2. But in order that the position so summarily stated may appear to be not without reason, and that the drift and purpose of the argument which is to be built upon it may be made more apparent, it will be necessary to attempt a more detailed discussion of the relations between Personality and Nature as factors of the intelligible which Nature constitutes and Personality interprets. We are accustomed to distinguish Nature as the realm of necessity from Personality as the seat of freedom. We conceive uniformity to be the note of the one, but reason and will to be the notes of the other. What is termed causation reigns in Nature, where the law of antecedence and sequence is held to be invariable; but Personality is itself a cause; i.e. it has the power of initiative or of breaking into the sequences which Nature follows, but can neither interrupt nor evade. Now what relation exists between the Personality which is conceived as thought or reason, as freedom or will, and the Nature which is conceived as uniform and necessitated? Or, to express our question otherwise, Can what we term Nature exist without the Personality which construes it, and, in a sense, constitutes it?

Now certain things may here be said to be perfectly

obvious, for it will be conceded that they are due to the modification of the senses through which we hold intercourse with the outer world. We refer to the psychology of those qualities which are regarded as peculiarly secondary, like colour. The eye distinguishes objects by their special colours or distinctive hues, and we speak as if these colours inhered in the things themselves, and were quite independent of the spectator. But subtract the man who looks at the objects, and what would become of their hues and colours? Here, for example, stand three men; in the centre is one with the eye of the artist, sensitive to every shade and delicacy of hue, finding variety where men with a less sensitive organ can see only sameness. But on his right hand stands a man whose reds are all green, whose yellows are all browns, or to whom all colours appear only as a sort of yellowish white; and we ask, why Nature wears such a different complexion to him from what it possesses to the artist, and we are told that he is colour-blind. Again, on the left hand stands a man who can take no part in the controversy, for he is blind, and to him colours are not; and were we to ask him what scarlet is like, he might reply in the language of the blind man in Locke, that it is like the sound of a trumpet. Colour then does not inhere in things; Nature by herself is without it. It is there because man is there, possessed of the sense by which it is not simply perceived, but, in a sense, constituted.

But what is true of colour is no less true of sound. We may think of it as the result of purely natural causes, concerning in an equal degree the physicist who speculates about energy, and the physiologist who studies the senses in relation to the external world. If we ask the physicist, he will explain the mode of its transmission; he will draw a parallel between the movement of light and of sound, and theorize as to the length of the wave by which they travel, or the rapidity by which the waves of sound move from the place of origin to the tympanum on which they break. But how far can he carry us? How much does he explain? Here again stand three men. One man has the sensitive ear of the musician. He listens to the oratorio and can detect each separate instrument in the orchestra, tell whether it be well or ill played, and what it contributes to the collective harmony; he can note the tones of each singer's voice, and, as he hears the wonderful march of the music, he can combine into a whole the world that had moved in the master's mind. He sees, through his hearing as it were, the mortified anger and shame of the defeated priests of Baal and the mocking laughter of the prophet; the mustering of angelic hosts; the tramp of disciplined armies; the gathering of the dead to the sound of the last trump; the agony and infinite yearning of the soul that cries to God out of the depths; and the jubilant and exulting speech of the spirit that stands justified before the Eternal Judge. Not a sound escapes him, and out of their harmonies come visions and dreams such as only the master can create and the soul of the sensitive disciple can see. But on his right hand stands a man who listens with impatience or doubt or bewilderment. These instruments to him make but a jangling of confused sounds; the voices that rise and fall and tremble in song have less significance than if they had been lifted in prosaic speech. The enthusiasm of his neighbour is to him extravagant and foolish; his call for admiration seems sheer impertinence; the whole thing is utter weariness and distress. What is the matter? In current phrase, the man has no ear. He knows sound, he can interpret speech; but music has for him no charm, or even any being. While the man on the right hand so feels, what of the man on the left? His face is a blank; he looks round curiously but without any sign of intelligence; he watches faces that teach him nothing, and he only knows from gesture and action that there is proceeding between the other two a discussion in which he can take no part. Their controversy concerns a point on which he cannot adjudicate, for he has heard no sound ; he is deaf. And what does this total difference of attitude to what we regard as the physical phenomena of sound mean but this—that sound is not without but within man ; that he can educe sounds from the waves which have been set in motion by the vibrating body, and can weave them into harmonies such as Nature never made, speaking of things more glorious than the heart of Nature could have conceived or imagined? And he is able to do this and to compel Nature to lend him the means of doing it, because it is only through him and his power to interpret and to combine them that all the factors and conditions of sound are realized.

And we could go from sense to sense, from ear and eye to taste and smell, and by analysis enlarge and confirm the conclusion that the qualities which our senses perceive are not things merely of external Nature ; but that either they could not be or could not seem to be without the constitutive faculty or the interpretative Personality of man. In other words, Nature in her own right is, if not a void, yet at most a mere aggregate of mechanical properties ; her pomp and beauty, her voice and all her harmonies she owes to Mind. We receive from her what we have given to her, and without us she would not be what she is.

3. But it must not be supposed that this argument avails only as regards the qualities we term secondary. There is no conception so necessary to the modern idea of Nature as that of Energy, for without it no change and no continuity would be possible. For Nature would be simply an inert, unmoved, and unmovable mass, if indeed, to our modern way of thinking, these terms do not denote ideas too contradictory to be placed together. Energy is the cause, and its convertibility the form, of all physical changes. It is held to be constant in quantity, indestructible and persistent in essence, but infinitely

varied in mode: while ever changing its form, it yet never ceases to be capable at once of a permutation which knows no rest, and a continuance which knows no break. But there is a question which underlies all our reasoning concerning the behaviour and permanence of energy; to wit, how do we come by the idea of it? This does not simply mean, what evidence have we for the existence of force? but rather this: how can we think, nay, why must we think, that there is in Nature that power of doing work which we name Energy? If we explain it by our experience of resistance,—i.e. by our knowledge that whenever we exercise effort there is something without that resists us, presses against us, overcomes our effort, or is overcome by it,—what does this theory as to the origin of the idea mean? Does it not signify that in order to the knowledge of energy without we must posit free power within? If we could not put forth effort we could never meet resistance; the energy that resists would therefore remain unknown. But is not this to argue that we know causation, because we are ourselves causes; and that it is through our own power of acting that the notion that Nature has power to act is gained and formed? It means that we derive the notion of energy from our own conscious freedom,—that the idea of causation in Nature is a clear, or even inevitable, deduction from Will? In other words, a world of necessitated beings could not form or conceive the notion of energy; for the very experiences that make the notion of it possible, the faculties to which it could be presented, and in whose terms it could be represented, would be absent; and such thought as there was would be too purely mechanical—i.e. too unconscious of any power that could be exercised within and resisted without,—to be able to conceive a universe whose surest datum was the consciousness of "Matter, Motion, and Force." If, then, we speak of Energy and attempt to interpret Nature through it, what are we doing but constituting Nature in the terms of Personality, using what is given within as the key to open the mysteries or reveal the realities which exist without? We conclude, therefore, that Energy in Nature is the correlate of Freedom in man; and were he not free, he could neither think nor speak of energy, for he would be without the intellectual powers needed for its recognition or discovery.

4. But secondary qualities like colour and sound, or special and definite conceptions like causation, whether represented by physics as energy, or by metaphysics as will or cause, are not the only sort of terms which Personality supplies for the interpretation of Nature; it supplies also what is even more fundamental—the forms under which we perceive the phenomena which, we may say, constitute the many-featured face it turns towards our senses, and the categories through which it becomes intelligible to our thought. We have already argued, in effect, that the intelligibility of Nature implies both an intelligence through which it is, and an intellect to which it is, the one creative, the other interpretative, of the thought embodied in Nature. The real world of the intellect is, of course, the intelligible, and neither could exist without the other; i.e. there could be no intellect without an intelligible; no intelligible apart from the intellect. We may expand this proposition into a series of inferences which may be stated thus: (1) since the intellect can interpret Nature, Nature is intelligible; (2) since Nature is intelligible, there must be some correspondence or correlation between its laws or methods and the rational processes in us; (3) since there is this correlation between the intelligible world and the interpretative intellect, they must embody one and the same intelligence. What these terms respectively mean and what the argument aims at proving may be made obvious by an illustration. Language is capable of translation or interpretation by reason just in the degree that it expresses reason. The speech of the mad is ridiculous to the sane, the speech of the sane has no meaning to the mad. The traveller or missionary who discovers and settles among a hitherto

unknown tribe, may learn its tongue, however rudimentary and formless, may get to understand its beliefs and customs, its views of nature and life, however barbarous and uninformed; but he can do so only so far as he finds in the savages a reason so akin to his own that he can stand, as it were, within the tribe's consciousness, and look out at the world through its eyes. Scholars of this century have, by the help of bilingual or trilingual inscriptions, recovered to historical and literary knowledge several long-forgotten languages; but no ingenuity could have deciphered into literature or worked into history figures that were mere fortuitous scratchings, freaks of Nature, or accidental lines drawn by some wandering horde. So the very fact of the intelligibility of Nature, or the possibility of its interpretation by mind, means that it embodies or expresses intelligence,—is the medium or vehicle of ideas which the human intellect can discover and think as if they were its own.

But this argument admits a further development. The human intellect could not live unless embosomed by a universe which was in its constitution and contents as rational as itself. Reason could not live in a world where no reason was. If the world became mad, if its physical forces were now conserved and now destroyed; if continuity governed one day and accident the next; if gravitation now ruled, and all rivers flowed to the sea and all lighter bodies fell towards the heavier; if, again, levitation reigned, and the sea turned itself into the rivers, and rose above the mountains, and the heavier bodies flew away from the lighter—what would the effect of this mad world be on the sane mind? Could mind in its presence maintain its sanity? Or, to reverse the supposition, if the world were beautiful and orderly, a scene of grander order and higher law than we now know it to be, but if all the men within and upon it were mad—would it be to them a sane world? Would not their madness make its very sanity more mad and more vain than the worst insanity

THE INTELLECT AND THE INTELLIGIBLE 37

would be? And does not this signify that we must have the correlation of the intellect and the intelligible before we can have either a rational mankind or any science of nature? But it signifies one thing more, viz., that the Intelligence which is embodied in this intelligible Nature, is in kind and quality one with the intelligence embodied in its interpreter. The Reason that lives in Nature, speaks a language that the reason personalized in man can understand and translate. The mathematics which have controlled and guided the Builder of the heavens, are identical with the mathematics which the astronomer in his study deduces from the idea of space given in his own thought, and which he proves by the processes of his own reason. If he looks at this fine correspondence from the subjective or dialectical side, he may say with Plato, "The Creator in His act of creation has geometrized"; but if he regard it from its objective or observational side, he will say with Kepler, "In reading the secrets of Nature I am thinking the thoughts of God after Him." But whether he speaks with Plato or with Kepler he means the same thing: there is such a correspondence between the mind and the universe, between the intelligible we think and the intellect we think by, that their relation can only be explained by identity of source, i.e. by both being expressions of a single supreme Intelligence.

§ III. *Mind and the Process of Creation*

The principle then which underlies the discussion so far as it has proceeded may be expressed thus: The problem of personal experience is one with the problem of universal existence; and from this principle we have attempted to deduce the conclusion: the only postulate from which we can derive an intelligible Nature or a rational experience is thought. In other words, since we can conceive Nature only through the forms and in the categories supplied by the interpretative Personality, we are bound to infer that the Nature which none but a personal Intellect can interpret, none but a personal Intelligence could create.

1. But this conclusion supplies us with a premiss for a new discussion, and this discussion will as much concern the nature that the biologist interprets as our past discussions have concerned the nature that the physicist conceives. We may state the new premiss, which follows from the conclusion of the previous argument, thus: The real Nature that needs to be explained is not the phenomenal, but the noumenal; not the world which appears to reason, but the reason which organizes, into an intelligible whole, the world of appearances, making it real to experience through its reality to thought. The meaning of this principle is that the real problem of Evolution in the organic kingdom is the genesis and the development of mind as it is realized in the individual and has been exercised by the race. Certain masters of scientific exposition have written as if the serious problem of evolution concerned the origin and succession of living forms. They have thought it enough to prove the mutability of species, the parts played by the factors of organism and environment in the development of the powers that best fitted for success and survival in the struggle for life. It has been imagined that we could, by the comparison and correlation of forms, exhibit the process of their evolution, or the mode and the order in which our planet came to be peopled with the busy tribes of flesh and blood. I raise no question as to the mode or as to the order; what I do question is, whether a theory as to the evolution and the succession of biological forms has any claim to be regarded as a theory adequate to the explanation of the facts of the case; i.e. to be considered a scientific hypothesis as to how the whole of nature, inclusive of every form and quality of life, came to be.

The theory may indeed be described as essentially concerned with the creational mode rather than with the creational cause; but the mode cannot exist without the energies or the forces that—operating either in the organism or the environment, or in both—accomplish the evolution. Indeed, the theory expressly proceeds upon the principle that the only forces it knows or reckons with are those called natural, though it conceives Nature in a strictly limited and exclusive sense. While, then, evolution, so far as it is a scientific doctrine, is a theory of the creational mode, yet where it is represented as an adequate account of the history of life upon this planet, it becomes also a theory of the creational cause. The theory is thus philosophical as well as scientific; and though the philosophy may be implicit, yet it never ceases to be both active and determinative in the science. The degree in which this is the case will become more obvious as we proceed.

We may say that we understand evolution in the field of organic life to mean the emergence of such new organs or such a modification of old organs in the struggle for existence as secures the survival of the fittest, and through it the development of new species. We need not too curiously describe or consider the changes in Darwin's hypothesis by later and younger men of science like Weismann. It is enough to say that the more the process is simplified the more complex does it require the cause or the sufficient reason of the movement to be; and the more urgent does the demand become that the action of the cause be immediate, continuous, universal. The less we insist on the transmission of acquired characters, the more do we insist on the sufficiency of the more strictly natural and impersonal causes that are at work; the less emphasis we lay on the achievement of the individual for the good of the whole, the more emphasis are we compelled to lay on the operation of the whole, and of the forces it represents on each and every individual.

So far then as concerns our present discussion, there are in the theory three ideas or positions that must be noted—Cause,

Process, End. These terms may here be distinguished thus: "Cause" expresses the sufficient reason alike for the result achieved and the means necessary for its realization; "Process" denotes the way or method in which this cause does its work; while "End" means the collective result, not nature as it terminates in biological forms, but nature as it culminates in mind, and as it lives in the intelligence of man, with all its experience and all its history. The problem, therefore, that arises is this: Are we able, by the process of an evolution, conducted strictly within the terms of Nature and by purely natural forces, to account for the origin of human reason and the history of all its achievements? In other words, what evolution has to explain is not nature and life but Man and Mind and History.

Now one thing is evident: the more severely natural the process is, the less can we allow anything to emerge in its course which is not really contained within the terms of the Nature which inaugurated the process, forms the bosom within which it proceeds and the energies which move it onward. What Nature *e*volves, Nature must have *in*volved; and to emphasize as natural both the process that leads to the end, and the end to which it leads, is to bind ourselves to find in the primary or causal term of the process the sufficient reason for all that follows.

2. In working out the problem which has just been stated we may follow two methods which may be termed respectively the regressive and the egressive. The regressive method starts from the completed process and proceeds backward step by step in search of the factors and the forces which have produced the completion; and this regressive movement cannot terminate till the sufficient reason or the ultimate cause be reached. If we follow the egressive method, we simply reverse the procedure, and reason downward from the beginning or assumed cause through its successive achievements to its ultimate issue. Let us take each method in succession.

A. The Regressive Method

Here we must note the starting-point or premiss of the argument: it is the term which Nature, in the process of her long development, has reached—the final page, which now lies unfolded before us, of her vast and varied history. That end is not represented by the inter-relations of plants and animals under domestication, nor is it represented by the organisms that exhibit the highest forms of structural excellence. The point from which we have to start is Man, and man is Mind. And it is not individual man. He is a small being, even though he be a universe in miniature; he is a simple problem, even though he be the measure of all things. The man we mean is vaster and more complex—collective man, with his arts, his letters, his empires, his intellectual achievements, his ethical ideals, his laws and his religions. It is man with all the qualities that mark him as a race, which, though made up of an infinite multitude of units, is yet a great organic unity.

(i.) If, now, we are to apply evolution as a theory descriptive of the strictly natural process or method of creation, we shall have to explain everything that has come to be through what was before it and what is around it. Let us begin, then, by going backwards from man one single step and coming to the animal. And here our question is as large as it is direct:—Is evolution, as a theory of the creational process moving within strictly natural lines and appealing to none but natural forces, able to account for man by the upward struggle of those beneath him? Some years ago we had eager and even angry discussions as to man's place in Nature. It was argued that "man was separated by no greater structural barrier from the brutes than they are from one another"; and it was further argued that "if any process of physical causation can be discovered by which the genera and families of ordinary animals have been produced, that process of causation [and we note the term 'causation'] is amply sufficient to account for the origin of Man."[1] And this process was said to have been discovered in the theory which will ever be honourably associated with the name of Darwin. A still more audacious thinker with a wider outlook than Huxley had, like him, argued from the structure of the man-like ape, from similarity in the greater organs, from the skull and cranial capacity, from hand and foot and teeth, from texture and size of the brain, that the ape might be called the older form of the man, and that there was no insuperable barrier between the man and the ape.[2]

Now let us understand precisely what an argument of this kind amounts to. There are, on the one hand, when man and the ape are regarded simply as organisms, similarities and differences of structure; but, on the other hand, when the persons or beings organized are taken into account, there are between them specific differences of history and achievement without any corresponding specific similarities. Now, the organic or structural affinities are obvious enough, and the consequences they involve may be drawn without any recourse to a too heroic logic. What is more flagrantly apparent, and more in need of adequate explanation, are the historical and personal differences. Is it argued that the structural similarities imply such a genetic relation that the man must be regarded as the descendant of the manlike ape? If so, is it also argued that the structural differences which make the man a new species, are the causes of his superior excellence? If not so, it is obvious that the real point at issue is not simply a question of structure, but of personality and its history. For let us see the facts that have to be explained. Here is a man-like ape. He is, as far as history is concerned, an older being than man; he can boast a more venerable ancestry; he is a more ancient inhabitant of our

---

[1] Huxley, *Man's Place in Nature*, p. 146.
[2] Haeckel, *Hist. of Creation*, cc. xxii. xxiv.—*Anthropogenie* (Vierter Abschnitt); cf. *Confession of Faith of a Man of Science*, p. 38.

planet, and has had, therefore, the greater opportunities a longer course of time have supplied, in which to develop the resources that are in him and achieve his man-like apehood. But how stands the case? He stands to-day precisely where his most ancient ancestor stood; he cracks his nuts and feeds himself in the ancestral manner; he practises the old arboreal architecture; he lives in the old home in the old way, swings himself from tree to tree by the same organ and with the same dexterity; he emits sounds of alarm or ferocity or affection, cries of defiance or of solicitation, which men may try to imitate but can only understand by ceasing as much as possible to be men and becoming apes. In a word, he began as a brute and a brute he remains.

But what of man? He may have begun by dwelling in caves and holes of the earth, but he has not continued to dwell there. He has built for himself the hut and the wigwam; he has designed and erected the stately pleasure-house; he has reared the palace and has embosomed it in beauty; he has dreamed of temples for his gods and cathedrals for worship, and he has realized these in stones which seem even more lordly than his dreams. His earliest essays in art may have been rude pictures on the walls of his cave, or on the bones of some animal he had slain and eaten, or on his own limbs or face, to make him beautiful to his friends or hideous to his foes. But he has not stayed at the stage where he first used tools; on the contrary, he has disciplined and trained himself in art until there has arisen under his chisel the shape of a man so passing fair that it seemed to need only speech to be the man it seemed, or an image of his deity so sublime, so godlike and august, that men who have looked upon it have said, "Lo! we have beheld God face to face"; or he has trained himself so to mix his colours and so to handle his brush as to make flowers bloom and landscapes to unfold their beauty on canvas, until men have seen through his eyes and from the work of his hands more in Nature than they had ever discovered for themselves. Man's social life may have begun in a state of savage war, where the strong man reigned and the weak man went to the wall; he may then have lived as the animal that devours its foes, even though of its own kind, and lives by plunder, by rapine, and by a killing that is no murder. But out of that savage state he slowly and painfully emerged into social and political order, built him up states governed by laws which judges impartially interpret and magistrates administer with justice—laws which protect the weak, punish the criminal, secure freedom to those who love it and safety to those who have known how to multiply the wealth and increase the graces of life. He has created great empires that have lived through centuries, developed civilization, broadened culture, and made history. Then his speech may have begun in rude cries, mere interjections, now of alarm, now of enjoyment, now of discovery, even as brute may call unto brute, sounding the note of danger or the signal for prey found; but he, by-and-by, learned to weave words into language—the most marvellous of all man's creations—and language into tales, to represent it by pictures, to create for it symbols and signs that made the transient word a thing imperishable. From his rude tales have come great literatures: the epic, with its heroes and its battles, its march of armies or its wandering sages, its pictures of grand shapes that have been or of terrible fates yet to be; the lyric, with its cry of love, man yearning after woman, woman after man, and both after God; the tragedy, with its tales of will in conflict with destiny, of character at war with circumstance. And this literature he has made thousandfold, mysterious, immortal, in many tongues and in many times. He may have started on his new career as a being with a capacity for religion, one who feared powers invisible impersonated in a blasted tree, a rude stone, a whitened bone, or a running stream, but he has not stood fixed in that rude faith; he has made him religions to comfort and to uplift his soul; he has believed in gods who could do gracious or awful things; he has come to think of a God majestic, sole, holy, ineffable, who inhabiteth eternity; to think of man as one who looks before and after, and who follows his thought into the eternity towards which it has ever aspired. Man has been a wonderful creator, and his creations have only just begun. No day dawns that does not see some new wonder added to the wondrous history of the race; the century which has just ended being for invention, for discovery, for its marvellous enlargement of knowledge and increased sovereignty over Nature, the most extraordinary of all the crowded and glorious centuries of his existence.

In the face, then, of their contrasted histories, let us now put man and the man-like ape together and ask, What is the problem they offer to science? Do the eloquently minimized differences which we find in the structure of the man as distinguished from the man-like ape, explain the differences in their histories? If they do, then we ought to be told how such small differences in structure have become causes of effects so wondrously and vastly opposite. If they do not, then why speak as if man and the man-like ape stood in the same system, and were in any tolerable sense related as ancestor and progeny? When their respective histories are viewed together and honestly compared, is it true that man is in faculty as in structure one with the brutes? Must it not rather be affirmed that man starts with some endowment which the brute has not? If Darwin needed his first form before he could trace the genesis of species, so no less is it true that we must have mind before the history of man becomes possible or capable of intellectual realization. But if it be mind that constitutes the differentiation of man from brute, then to imagine that the distance between them is reduced by the discovery of similarities in their organic structure, is a mere irrelevance of thought.

But we have come by another way to the very conclusion which was reached by our previous argument: the reason or mind which distinguishes man from the brute, relates him to the heart or secret of the universe. The same intellect which separates him from the animal, binds him to the intelligible in Nature and to the Intelligence which is above both and explains both. Where he is distinguished from the lower he attains kinship with the higher; and so our premiss, changed in form but unchanged in essence, emerges as the reasoned conclusion of the discussion, viz., the noumenal and not the phenomenal explains man, and shows the substance of his being to be one with the essence of the universe which he perceives and construes.

(ii.) But we have as yet taken only a single step in the regressive process, and so must further proceed with our backward search for the sufficient reason of the Nature we know. The stages would indeed be many and our progress both slow and toilsome were we to pause over each and there pursue our analytic quest—the birth of consciousness, the dawn of sentient life, the advent of the animal and the vegetable. But instead let us at once step across the successive periods and down the descending species of the organic kingdom until we enter the inorganic. Our question now is, whether it be possible to find in the physical energies or forces which science supposes to have preceded life, the cause of life, with all its forms, its infinite possibilities and multitudinous activities? Can we imagine anything within the terms of Nature as Nature was before life or mind were, or as we must conceive it to have then been, which would be a Sufficient Reason for the history that was to be? Darwin, as we have just seen, asked to be allowed to assume a first or a few forms in order that he might show how the earth, as it pursued its silent way through space, was tenanted with living beings and became the arena of all their works. But simple as his request seemed, it was a tremendous assumption that he asked leave to make, for it meant that he wanted to start from an unexplained Something, a mystery, a miracle—originated life, though how and why it had originated, what cause adequate to its production was lying behind, he did not know and did not presume to enquire. He asked, in short, no less a gift in the form of a premiss than the old theologian asked when he meekly took for granted the creation of Adam, in order that he might deduce from him mankind and all their works. For Darwin asked permission to posit not only the few forms whose being had just begun, but also the environment within which they lived, i.e. the whole conception of created forms and a creative Nature already at work upon them. He thus, under this explicit *petitio principii*, smuggled in two of the largest conceptions which can be formed by the mind of man, the very conceptions which have perplexed the race into belief in all the cosmogonies. But it enabled him to do another and no less important thing, viz., conceal from himself the distinction between a simplified cause and a simplified process ; and this was the more to be regretted as the rigorous simplicity he intended to illustrate in his natural process of creation enormously increased the complexity of the cause he so quietly assumed. For let us attempt to imagine the vision that might have come to a prescient mind watching those parent forms in their first blind struggles for a hardly discernible life, while yet foreseeing all that was to be. The vision would start with the spectacle of a steaming earth waiting to become the fruitful mother of all living things, with the simplest germs of organic being bedded deep in her hot and hardening slime. As the earth cooled and the moisture folded the minute organisms in its damp but fertilizing embrace, new and higher forms were seen to multiply, vegetation became abundant, gigantic trees and vast forests stood rooted in the rich soil and raised their branches into the warm and liquid air; while there moved through deep lagoons immense reptiles, which Nature, in her first endeavours at protection, clothed in coats of mail, seeming to think that they would not die because their enemy could not reach the centre of their life. But climatic changes come. The huge creatures vanish, the mammal appears, and the process of evolution goes on till Nature teems with myriad forms of organic life. And then the supreme moment approaches, man steps upon the scene and forthwith begins to modify the nature which has been so creative, to subdue the animals that have been so mighty, to build himself cities, to form states, to speak with tongues, to develop arts, to create literatures, to formulate laws, to realize religions,—in a word, to create the society and the civilization that we know so well. Now what in the inorganic mass which it surveyed could the prescient mind discover capable of accomplishing these things? Nothing; unless he conceived the mass as, though inorganic, yet capable of creating organic being, of thinking like himself so as to create thought. But how could he so conceive it without changing it from a mass of conserved and correlated forces into the seedplot or seminal garner of all that was to be? But how could that womb which was thus pregnant with all the organs, all the organisms, all the minds of the future, be described as dead? Was it not rather quick with all the germs of all the forms that were waiting the touch of time to live, laden with all the potencies and all the qualities and all the lives of the future? If, then, we attempt to conceive what was before life and mind as the condition or cause or factor of their being, we must invest it with the qualities which enable it to do its work. And what is this but turning it from dead matter into living spirit?

B. THE EGRESSIVE METHOD

(i.) But the question which has just been raised as to the relation of the primordial inorganic forces to the creation and development of organic forms, can be better discussed under the head of the egressive than of the regressive method. How shall we conceive, how define or describe, the stuff which was before life and was the father of all living things? It would be hard to set man a severer or less soluble problem than this: to imagine or discover within Nature as known to him a physical substance, or any concourse or combination of physical elements or qualities, that could, within a universe that knew no life, cause life to begin to be. The frankest terms are here the soberest and the truest: the thing is inconceivable. It is not simply that the primary generation would have to be spontaneous, i.e. self-caused, i.e. miraculous in the superlative degree,—for spontaneous generation is a thing unknown to experimental science, and to biological observation, and is, at best, but a form under which the operation of an unknown cause is disguised; but also because matter cannot be defined save in terms that imply mind. Whether mind may be conceived without matter, is a point that may be argued; but matter can be represented in no form which does not imply mind. And this may be stated in the form of what may be described as a curious and instructive law in philosophy, whether ancient or modern. The highest speculations concerning the ultimate cause have been expressed in the terms of the intellect or the reason, while those which have ventured to use physical or material terms have had all the rarity of the exception which proves the rule. And this law is made the more impressive by the fact that the exceptions apply mainly to the childhood of speculation, but the rule to its manhood or maturity.

One of the most characteristic things in modern thought is the history of the ultimate causal idea in the school whose fundamental principles forbade them the use of transcendental terms. It would be traversing too familiar and well-beaten paths to trace the genesis and examine the basis of Hume's scepticism; but this may be said: within the circle which accepted his first principles and followed his method there happened what can only be described as a paralysis of the speculative faculty, and the reduction of philosophy to the limits and the problems of a more or less conjectural psychology. Its members assumed, not willingly but from sheer logical compulsion, an attitude of ignorance or impotence towards the problems, which had, by simply though imperiously demanding solution of the reason, been perhaps the most potent educative agencies in the history of our race; and confined themselves to the question as to how our ideas came to be associated, and so to bear to man the appearance of a reasonable order. Thus we have the elder Mill attempting an "Analysis of the Human Mind," in its essence a confession that a psychology was the only possible philosophy; and that concerning the relations of thought and being, or of the cause and end of being, "nothing whatever could be known." Comte, too, had, if not a speculative soul, the hunger of the true system-builder, satiable only by an order that could be formulated, ambitious to classify and organize knowledge, to demonstrate the laws of human progress, and to create the only real and possible conditions of human happiness. But he understood the empirical philosophy he inherited from Hume, and knew well the iron lines it had drawn, the blank impenetrable walls it had built round the spirit, and he loved logic too dearly to seek to escape into a freer air. So he declared phenomena to be all that man could know, proclaimed the search after a First Cause vain, placed the very word "cause" under a rigorous ban, dismissed psychology from the circle of the sciences, and planted physiology in its stead. And his early English interpreters were here specially emphatic. One brilliant scholar, G. H. Lewes, wrote a History of Philosophy, expressly to prove that metaphysics was the search after the illusive, that their reign had ceased, that the birth of Positivism was the dawn of a millennium when barren problems should cease to trouble and only fruitful facts and phenomena occupy mind. The subtle and assimilative intellect of John Stuart Mill felt the same paralyzing influence. He loved to be constructive, and was so, though in a less degree than he desired, in politics, in economics, and in formal logic; but when he came to metaphysics, he was content with mere analytic criticism and inconclusive psychology. And even before he could get to it he had to postulate three great things: the mind, the tendency of the mind to expectancy, and the laws of association; and then on this vast assumed and unreasoned basis he attempted to explain the relation of mind to the outer world. Yet he did not, like Kant, frankly recognize that these assumptions of his were transcendental principles, *a priori* forms of perception, categories of thought or factors of knowledge which he had no right to use. But he hid meekly—as it were under a proposition he need not argue— the most fundamental of all possible questions: What was mind? Why had mind expectancy? How was it that in mind the laws of association worked? And higher and more transcendental still was the question, Whence did the idea come, and how was it that it came to mind, and was by thought turned into something absolutely different from the Nature that sent it? And when he proceeded to define matter as "the permanent possibility of sensation," what did he define it as being? Something subjective, dependent on mind. If matter be "a permanent possibility of sensation," how, without the sentient consciousness, could we have matter? And when, later, he resolved mind into "a permanent possibility of feeling," he carefully forgot that he had assumed mind, its expectancy and associative laws, in order that he might explain matter as "the permanent possibility of sensation." In a word, Mill's analysis was too purely governed by the old empiricism to allow him to reach either subjective or objective reality. He would have been more consistent had he, with Berkeley, confessed spirit to be the one solid and enduring entity, and matter a mere idea. This was what he meant, but what he could not say without being forced to the theistic conclusion of his great predecessor. And so instead we had both the subject and the object of knowledge reduced to the permanent possibilities of things unknown.

But science was suddenly seized with a speculative passion, begotten of two great doctrines—the Conservation of Energy and Evolution. Sleight of tongue is a more illusive art than even sleight of hand, and metaphysics do not become physics by being stated in the terms of "matter, motion, and force," nor do they turn into biology by being expressed in the formulæ of natural selection. So impelled by the speculative passion which made physical terms the vehicle of metaphysical ideas, thinkers like Mr. Lewes forgot their paralyzed nescience, and began to lay the "foundations of a creed." Men of science became adventurous world-builders; awed us by natural histories of creation, overawed us by visions of our long descent, and the easy elegance with which they could leap the boundary which divided the organic from the inorganic kingdom, and find in matter "the promise and the potency of every form and quality of life." Their difficulties and our perplexities began when they tried to define matter, or to find it without assuming the mind it was to explain, or to leave it in any sense the matter known to science and yet deduce from it a living and organic Nature. Goethe's words were gratefully recalled: "Matter can never exist and be operative without spirit, nor spirit without matter." So were Schleicher's: "There is neither matter nor spirit in the customary sense, but only one thing which is at the same time both." Then we had the despairing but descriptive phrase of the late Professor Clifford, "mind-stuff," and Professor Bain's, "One substance with two sets of properties; two sides, the physical and the mental; a double-faced unity." But what is this save carrying back into the beginning the dualism of the living consciousness? It did not define or describe the primordial stuff which constituted and created the world, but only expressed a distinction which came into being with the conscious Self. "Two sets of properties" imply a mind through whom they are perceived; "a double-faced unity" implies eyes to which the faces appear; and these are but attempts to get the effects of mind out of the primordial matter without conceiving the matter as mind.

(ii.) But suppose we abandon all logical reservations and make a present of the conception of matter to the venturesome thinker who would deduce from it the Nature we know, are his difficulties ended? Nay, they are only about to begin. He is at once faced by the questions: When and why did the creative process commence? What moved the atoms toward their miraculous work? What had they been about before? Why did they begin then? Why not earlier? Why not later? Matter on this hypothesis has always been; it is eternal, it is indestructible, and in its existence that of its properties is involved. Now however far back the primary movement is carried, eternity lies beyond it. Why in that eternity did not the eternal matter work itself into a world? Why at this specific moment was it started on its creative career? We may, with Democritus, imagine atoms, quantitatively but not qualitatively different, falling through the void, the heavier by colliding against the lighter causing a lateral movement that results in their aggregation and combination, and in the generation of the heat without which we can have no life. But to conceive atoms tumbling for ever through infinite space, meeting, and by impact causing heat and changing direction or form, yet ever acting according to their mechanical properties, is not to come one whit nearer the understanding of how this inorganic mass became the parent of all organic being. It is significant that neither modern physics, perhaps the most audacious in speculation of all the sciences, nor chemistry, possibly the most skilled in the secrets of Nature, has advanced us here a single step beyond Democritus: instead of his $\dot{\alpha}\nu\alpha\gamma\kappa\acute{\eta}$, men may use the terms "chance" or "unknown," but they all mean the same thing: to matter, as science must conceive it, causation of life, not to speak of mind, is a sheer impossibility.

But now suppose the transition is made from a world of inorganic force to a world of living forms, how are we to explain their increase and development? For one thing, it is impossible to imagine that the power which produced the first form exhausted itself in the effort and thenceforward ceased to act. The growth, the multiplication, and the differentiation of organisms are but the forms under which the original creative energy continues to operate. The inexplicable element in the origination survives through all the later processes, though hidden away in the ample folds of the immense mantle which our ignorance names the environment. And here one instructive fact deserves to be noted: in order that the struggle for life may be attended with survival, attributes and acts of intelligence are ascribed to unintelligent creatures, processes, or things. Thus Mr. Alfred Wallace praises Darwin because of the brilliant generalization he gives in his work on Orchids, viz., "that flowers have become beautiful solely to attract insects to assist in their fertilization." But this generalization implies the capacity in the flower to feel, if not to observe, what pleases the insect; the ability to appeal to this pleasure, the desire to use it for personal ends, and the instinct or intuition that can turn personal into altruistic acts. If it were not for the metaphors he borrows from mind, the biologist would never be able to make his processes seem natural. And this means that Nature is to him alive with intelligence; that it is able to accomplish its end—the increase of life and development of living forms—only because it appears, when all its parts are taken together, a sort of incorporated Mind.

But though organic life has been produced, Nature is not yet: before she can be a further step must be taken forward into Mind. But this last, the most inexorable step of all, is the most completely beyond our rational capacity. For there is nothing that physiology has been so little able to do as to discover the relation between organization and consciousness. As Tyndall once said, a man can as little prove any causal relation between these two as he can lift himself by his own waistband. The phenomena may be parallel, but they do not stand respectively in the relations of cause and effect. We are left, then, with a natural process that leaves, as regards explanation, the main thing precisely where it was found. Mind, in its action and its origin, is a great enigma. How it emerges is as insoluble a mystery as what it has achieved. But one thing seems evident, that it can be got out of Nature only by being deposited in Nature; that what constitutes Nature has constructed Nature, that what makes her capable of interpretation is one with the condition that makes the process of knowledge real and actual.

§ IV. *Conclusions and Inferences*

The issue of this discussion, then, seems to be that we cannot conceive either Nature or its creative work otherwise than through Mind. The metaphysic of knowledge is one with the metaphysic of being. We may therefore express our conclusion thus: The transcendental cannot be excluded from our view of the universe, but the transcendental in philosophy is the correlate of the supernatural in theology. The former uses abstract speech, the latter employs concrete terms; but it is only when the abstract becomes concrete that it receives application and reality. To affirm the transcendence of thought is to affirm the priority of spirit, for spirit is but thought made concrete—translated, as it were, into a personal and creative energy; it is mind as opposed to matter, a known as distinguished from an unknown, conceived as the cause of all dependent being. And how can we better express this thought in its highest concrete form than by the ancient name God?

But now what is the bearing of this discussion and conclusion on the question with which we started, Whether the idea of a supernatural Person be compatible with the modern conception of Nature?

1. Let us attempt to state what seem the fair and logical deductions from our argument.

A. Nature takes a larger and richer sense than is known to the physical sciences; it includes thought, the whole mysterious kingdom of the spirit through which it is and for which it is. From this point of view the distinction between the natural and the supernatural ceases, or becomes thoroughly unreal. For the supernatural, as commonly taken, denotes a cause or will outside as well as above Nature, opposed to it and supersessive of its laws; but here it denotes a cause which is as native to Nature as reason or thought is to man. Withdraw or paralyze this cause, and Nature as its effect ceases, i.e. without the supernatural the natural can neither begin nor continue to be. But how can we conceive Nature without the idea which is necessary to its very being as a complete and self-contained whole? And as it is only when our view takes in the whole that Nature is rationally conceived, we can never regard that as a scientific interpretation of Nature which applies mathematical processes or laws to the behaviour of bodies in space, but forgets the mind that compels man to think the pure ideas of his reason; which speaks of energy or force but ignores the will through which man knows it is; and which imagines it sufficient to exhibit the genesis of a form without feeling it needful to find a sufficient reason for that process of continuous creation which we call the history of man. Nature, then, is not rationally conceived when the supernatural is excluded, but only when it is viewed as standing in and through the supernatural, i.e. when Nature is conceived as constituted not by forces that can be measured or by energies that struggle for life, but by the thought which makes it and which finds it intelligible, that is, organizes and articulates it into a coherent and rational Idea.

B. As the only concrete term which can adequately describe the creative Mind or Intelligence is God, and as the created intellect is man, two things follow: (*a*) the intrinsic character of the creation to which God is related, and (β) the quality and nature of His relation.

(*a*) The real creation of God is Spirit; and if we attempt to conceive His creative action simply under physical categories, or to state it in the terms of physics, we shall never either truly conceive or rightly describe it. In the strictest sense matter has no independent being, but spirit has, for independence is made by two things—the ability to know and the capacity of being known. Neither attribute belongs to matter *per se*. It is a mere abstract till mind has, by investing it with qualities, made it concrete; and thus were mind withdrawn, there would be no matter. But while mind may be necessary to the concrete being of matter, for matter mind has no being; neither can share the other's life; for where knowledge does not meet knowledge there can be no fellowship, no reciprocity or correlativity of being. And where there is no knowledge the highest, if not the sole, reality is absent; for what does not know does not really exist; it may have being for another but has none for itself. It follows that God and man both are, since both are capable of knowing and of being known, i.e. each is real both to himself and to the other; but neither is real to the matter which owes all its actuality to mind. Hence the real presence of God must be stated not in physical but in spiritual terms; it belongs to the sphere of rational experience, and not to the field of mechanical energies. The latter may be an arena within which the Divine will may operate; but the former, as accessible to spirit, can receive and feel and realize the Divine presence; in other words, matter may be through God's will and to His reason, but mind is open to Himself.

He can fill, possess, and live within it just because He can be for it; and this intercommunal life is the beatitude of God in the creature and of the creature in God.

(β) What then constitutes the universe a reality to God are the spirits He has created to inhabit it, exactly as a house is a house to a man by virtue not of its rooms and its furniture, but of the persons who there live in and through and for him, though the more he cares for the persons the less will he be indifferent to the furniture and the rooms. But if this be so, we may fairly infer that God will not become a mere curious spectator of their ways and works, as a man may be of the architecture and industry displayed by a hive of bees; but that He will remain in positive and active relations with them, all the more present that He may be totally unperceived. For only thus can He complete His creation, since, according to its very nature, Spirit cannot be made all at once, but only by such a continuous process of discipline and instruction as will bring it under the law and fill it with the illumination of God.

C. God, then, as the Perfect Reason and Almighty Will through whose action and by whose energy Nature was and is, cannot be conceived as otiose or inactive; omnipresence is not an occasional, but a permanent attribute of Deity, omnipotence is not incidental or optional. He must be everywhere, and wherever He is He must be operative. Omniscience simply means the omnipresent intellect in exercise. God is the thought that is diffused through all space and active in all time. And this involves the consequence that the form under which His relation to Nature ought to be conceived is immanence, though not as excluding transcendence; for the very reason that requires the interpretative intellect to be transcendent, requires also the causal Intelligence to be the same. But it is the active intercourse of these two that constitutes Nature as an intelligible whole. For the Divine immanence in Nature is inseparable from the same immanence in mind. There is, so to speak, a constant process of intercommunication, God with man and man with God. And this means that His beneficence becomes a universal and continuous activity. We could not imagine a Being with any grace of character creating for any motives save such as could be described as good, still less could we conceive Him proving unstable and in the course of His providence changing to another and lower will than He had in the beginning. If He were moved to create, it could only be that He might through creation find a richer beatitude; and if the creature was needful to His blessedness, He must be still more needful to its. But if this be so, it can only mean that His creative action never ceases: the sabbath of the Creator is found in an activity which is ever beneficent and never tires.

D. Creation, then, is here conceived not as a finished but as a continuous process. The will of God is the energy of the universe: uniform and permanent in quantity, yet expressing itself in modes of an infinite variety. Nature without the supernatural Will were a vaster miracle, or rather an infinite series of vaster miracles, than Nature realized through it; but a concluded creation would be more miraculous still, for it could only signify an exhausted universe and a dead Deity. What do the theories of energy and evolution mean but the continuance of the creative process? But if new forms in biology have emerged,—if from however mean an origin, in a mode however low, Mind once began to be, why may not new and higher types appear in the modes and forms of being known to history as politics, ethics, religion? In other words, may not the very Power which determined the appearance of the first form, and the whole course of evolution from it, determine also the appearance of creative Persons in history and of all the events which may follow from their appearance? Might we not describe the failure of the fit or the needed man to appear at some supreme moment as a failure which affects the whole creation? And would not the work he did for God be the measure of the degree of the Divine Presence or quantity of the Divine energy immanent within him?

2. It seems, then, fair to conclude that so far from the idea of a supernatural Person being incompatible with the modern idea of Nature, it is logically involved in it. That idea lives and moves and has its being in the mysterious or, let us frankly say, the miraculous. We begin in mystery; we live in mystery; and in mystery we end; and what are we but symbols or parables of the vaster life of the whole? But yet the key of all mysteries is man. The first and last, the highest and the surest thing in Nature, is the thought which explains Nature, but which Nature cannot explain. And the thought which Nature embodies has been progressive, has moved upwards to Mind, and a mind that feels its kinship with the Source, the Secret, and the End of all this mysterious system. Would it not be absolutely consistent with the whole past history of the creative action as written in the living forms which have dwelt and struggled on our earth, that the Creator should do for the higher life of man what He has done for the lower,—i.e. first not in the chronological but in the logical and essential, or typical and normative, sense—the form after and from and through which the higher life may be realized? Whether He has done so is a question which must be investigated and determined like any other reputed matter of fact. It is enough if our argument here has prevented it being decided by a high and rigorous method of *a priori* logic or presupposition.

CHAPTER II.

THE PROBLEM AS AFFECTED BY THE PHILOSOPHY OF ETHICS

§ I. *The Problems Raised by Man as an Ethical Being*

THE argument which has so far been pursued has proceeded on the principle that man is the interpretation as well as the interpreter of Nature. What is most characteristic of him is thought, and thought is exactly the reality which no physical theory of creation can explain. He is not only an object of knowledge, but he is the person who knows; and there is no science which does not implicitly posit him as intelligence and Nature as intelligible. But man is more than a being whom the metaphysics of knowledge may attempt to explain; for he is not summed up in the category of intellect. He is a doer; he can and does act; and his actions have specific qualities which are judged approvingly or disapprovingly alike by himself and the society within which he lives. The judgment, whether by the spectator or by the doer, as to the specific quality of an action is largely affected by its being regarded as the man's own. He believes himself, and is believed by others to be able to act or not to act. If compulsion determines conduct, then judgment does not so much concern itself with him as with the power that compels him. Approval or disapproval of conduct is thus conditioned by the belief in freedom of choice, in the ability to will freely. But this capability to do or refuse to do, with the judgment it conditions, further implies that there is a standard which ought to govern the man's conduct but which may not be allowed to do it. In other words, there is a law which he ought to obey, though he may not do as he ought.

Nor is this all. The man is not simply an isolated unit; he is an integral part of a social unity. He is a member of a family, which is a sort of organism whose varied organs stand in relation to each other as well as to a wider whole; and the family is liable to be judged in the same way as the man, its character and collective conduct falling into similar categories of good and bad, right and wrong, virtuous and vicious. The family in its turn stands within the larger society of a city or a tribe; and the city or tribe stands in the still wider society of the State. And law, written or unwritten, again appears as regulating the relations and actions of these persons and communities,—the conduct of the units in the family, and of the family as a whole, to the city, to the tribe, or to the State, and also the acts and relations of the city, tribe, or State to both individuals and family. The State regards certain actions as noxious, certain others as innocuous. It protects both itself against the noxious and the individual in the performance of the innocuous act; and if it has to judge of certain overt actions done by one citizen or family to another citizen or family, it bases its judgments upon some positive law or principle of equity as between man and man or citizen and citizen. The standard by which the individual judges may be termed "moral"; the standard by which the State judges, may be termed "civil" or "criminal" or "natural" law; but in every case the standard of judgment is rooted in moral ideas which affect or condition the sentence pronounced. We thus find that judgment on the acts of men and communities implies the qualitative character of their actions: they are praised or blamed according as their qualities are judged to be good or bad.

Then men, tribes, cities, societies, and States exist in almost every possible condition of culture, from the most savage to the most highly civilized; but amid all the differences which distinguish these varied conditions there is a single unifying idea—a certain similarity in the essence, if not in the form, of their moral judgments. It is easy indeed to indicate degrees in the laxity or elasticity of moral standards, to notice how at certain stages of progress or among certain peoples lying may be regarded as almost a virtue, stealing as a necessary if not a natural thing. But this has to be noted—that the lying which is held to be better than truth is the lie that is not found out; the theft that is applauded is that which is so cunningly conducted as not to be discovered. In other words, the favourable judgment depends on the thing being taken for its opposite; if found out, it is judged according to its true quality. Public law nowhere endorses the lie or condones the theft; when it speaks, the judgment it expresses is moral. In order to be approved law must be just when it judges, though it cannot always command the evidence that enables it to be what all men feel it ought to be.

We may say, then, that in universal law, universal custom, and universal language we have witnesses to the fact that when man, whether he be an individual or a community, judges actions, whether those of a person or a State, he does so according to a standard which must be characterized as moral.

§ II. *Empiricism in Knowledge and in Ethics*

This brings us to our primary and fundamental problem. How are we to explain the origin of these moral judgments? What is their basis? Where is the reason for the unity in moral idea which pervades all communities in the several stages of their social being?

1. There is an intimate connection between the metaphysics of knowledge and the metaphysics of ethics; they represent

different sides of the same thing. If we need the *a priori* elements of the understanding in order that knowledge may be conceived as possible, we need no less in human nature transcendental moral elements in order that the genesis of our moral actions and the reason of our moral judgments may be understood. And so if a metaphysic supposes the mind to be a sheet of white paper on which Nature writes her marvellous story, then it must also suppose that all our moral ideas and judgments are creatures of experience, due to what man suffers rather than to what he has the faculty to achieve. There is, indeed, a difference between the process of knowledge and the evolution of morals. The process of knowledge is conceived as due to the action of Nature through sense upon what must still be spoken of as mind. But moral ideas must be represented as acquired not so much directly from Nature as indirectly through society, or from the action of man upon man, *i.e.* the interaction of the individual who struggles for life and the society that either struggles against him as a noxious force, or struggles to use him as an atom in its organism that may increase the energy needed for its own larger and more eventful movement. If the individual be thought to acquire his moral ideas through the experiences he undergoes in his social medium, they will be conceived as ideas that contribute to his fuller being, to the maintenance and development of his energies, to the use he can get out of life, or, in a word, to his pleasure or his happiness. If, on the other hand, the factor of his moral ideas be construed as the society in which he lives, then its function will be to implant itself within him, to get him to judge as it judges, to become, in a word, an epitome of its mind, a minister to its wealth, an agent of its well-being. According as the one standpoint or the other be adopted, the regulative standard of judgment will differ. In the one case it will be self-interest, in the other case it will be the communal interest—the greatest happiness of the greatest number.

2. Various attempts have been made to combine these points of view with greater or less success. In Hobbes we find the theory in a courageously individualistic form. Pleasure is the standard of right; the action that most conduces to present happiness is best. Men call the actions that please virtues; the actions that displease vices. Action depends on the will; the will depends on the opinion of the good or evil which the act or its omission is to bring: therefore all action has its cause in the appetite for pleasure. The highest form of pleasure is glory, or to have a good opinion of one's self, or, more decently expressed, it is to love and to have power. Charity is but a form of this, for it consists in a man "finding himself able not only to accomplish his own desires, but also to assist other men in theirs." Yet so far is Hobbes from thinking that we are bound to contribute to another's happiness that he regards our own conscious pre-eminence as the condition of the highest enjoyment. Hence he describes wit or laughter as enjoying "the sudden imagination of our own odds and eminency," or, what is its correlative, "another man's infirmity or absurdity." It "proceedeth from a sudden conception of some ability in himself that weigheth," or "in the elegant discovering and conveying to our minds some absurdity of another." The pleasures of memory consist in remembering some happy thing that occurred to oneself, or some miserable fate that befel a neighbour or a rival. This is a sort of colossal egoism, born of the idea that the strongest man is the best, that might is right, and that he who can impose his will on others, and make them serve his ends, simply because they are his, is the lawgiver and king.

Hume, with more subtle skill, and a greater sense of what was needed to make a doctrine agreeable to the average man, endeavoured to reconcile the two points of view, the individual and the social, by saying that while the act that promotes pleasure is right, it is pleasure seen, as it were, from the standpoint of society. "Whatever produces satisfaction is denominated virtue," "everything which gives uneasiness in human actions is called vice." If "the injustice is so distant from us as no way to affect our interest, it still displeases because we consider it as prejudicial to human society." Hence duty is the action promotive of happiness as it appears not to the narrow self, but to his larger environment; or, in a word, personal conduct viewed as society views it. Interest and sympathy are thus the sole sources of our moral obligations. When an action, seen as society sees it, tends to promote happiness, it gives pleasure, and is right. If, seen as society sees it, it tends to promote unhappiness, it gives pain, and so is wrong. The sense of duty is, therefore, the social feeling implanted in the breast of the individual. Conscience is the judgment of society expressed as self-judgment.

Jeremy Bentham put the matter in a franker way. "Nature has placed mankind under the governance of two sovereign masters, Pain and Pleasure." They tell us "what we ought to do, as well as determine what we shall do." To their throne the standard of right and wrong on the one hand, and the chain of causes and effects on the other, are bound. "The community is a fictitious body"; its interest is but "the sum of the interests of the several members who compose it." And interest means the thing or action which in the case of the individual "tends to add to the sum total of his pleasures, or to diminish the sum total of his pains." Here, then, is the final as well as the efficient cause of man's actions, and the standard by which they are to be judged. Those actions that make for pleasure are right; those actions that make for pain are wrong. To men, therefore, as moral beings there exist only two things—agents and instruments of pleasure. The man himself is the agent, other men are the instruments; and their value to him is their power to contribute toward this end, though the end is taken not as personal simply, but as the greatest happiness of the greatest number. This being his standard of right, Bentham was, quite consistently, anxious to get rid of the too absolute sense of duty which had come into English ethics under the name of Conscience; and so he held that the evil thing in morals, the mark of the pedant, "the talisman of arrogancy, indolence, and ignorance," was the word "ought," "an authoritative impostor," which might be tolerated in the other sciences, but ought to be expelled from the science of ethics. Yet even he was compelled to concede something to this imperious moral sense. We may say of an action "conformable to the principle of utility" that it "ought" to be done: in such a case the word has a meaning; otherwise it has none. Bentham's disciple, James Mill, argued that the agreeable and pleasant were the same thing, and that all actions done for the agreeable, approximately or remotely, were right. But his illustrious son introduced a famous distinction, the full significance of which we shall see by-and-by, between the qualities of pleasures; and he proposed by this qualitative distinction to enable man to determine which actions were the more and which were the less excellent and obligatory.

3. Now these systems suggest two remarks. First, while they proceeded on the principle that man is a natural being governed by natural impulses—especially the impulse to seek happiness, in order to a larger and richer life—yet as systems of ethics they were attempts to moralize nature, i.e. they conceived man as if he were other and more than a mere natural being. For they were not simply theories explanatory of conduct, but they were even more schemes regulative of life ideals of a better and more happily ordered being than Nature knew. They were not merely hypotheses of a science which tried to co-ordinate phenomena, but they were intended as guides to life, explaining principles and ends of action in order that they might be more easily and completely realized of men. Thus they did not deal with hunger in the man as if it had been the same in quality and character as hunger in

the tiger. The instinct to satisfy appetite exists in both, but no code of ethics would have any significance for the tiger, and no body of men would judge concerning his attempts to satisfy his instincts and to escape famine as they would judge concerning the acts of a man. The very attempt, therefore, to interpret man ethically implied that he was more than a natural being, that he transcended nature, that his transcendence ought to be progressive in its quality, and that a completely moral state was one where laws proper to man governed men: creatures merely natural could not be governed by such laws.

But, secondly, these earlier ethical thinkers had to remain individualists even when laying most emphasis on the social sanction. The experience they thought of was personal; each man had to acquire his own. The result was that the only form in which society could operate on him was by its positive forces and institutions, its methods of education, its systems of law and penalty; and the only way in which he could realize the influence of society was by imaginatively occupying its standpoint and judging himself according to its standards. This involved so limited an experience, and so arbitrary a method of acquiring and exercising moral judgments, that the system inevitably broke down in the very hands of its builders; for it could not but fail to establish any real continuity or organic relation between past experience and the living man, or between the organized society and the unit that it had to deal with, and that lived within its bosom.

§ III. *Ethics and Evolution*

1. But even more in ethics than in metaphysics the new scientific speculation has made itself felt. The theory of evolution in particular has radically affected our question. For it has supplied two important factors of our rational and moral experience—the idea of transmission and inheritance,

and the idea of unlimited time. Before two incommensurables had faced each other: (*a*) the ephemeral individual without any experience behind him, who had to acquire moral ideas, exercise moral judgments, and realize moral character within the limits of a brief existence; and (β) the permanent society, which had in its continued being energies and an experience that left its units helpless in its hands. All that was needed was for the society so to impress itself by means of its sanctions on the transient individual, that he should, even for the brief season of his present existence, become a vehicle of its spirit, or a means to its end. But the doctrine of evolution, at any rate in its older and, possibly, still more orthodox form, made experience a thing more or less transmissible, and turned acquired characters into a species of heritable property. And so the individual, though transient, became through his inheritance in a sense as permanent as the society around him. He had within him tendencies, tempers, passions, traits that descended to him from innumerable ancestors, running back into immemorial time, and made him, as it were, the sum of all their experience, the embodiment of what they had by action and experiment learned to become. And as the time during which the process went on was without limit, the result corresponded to what was beyond and before personal existence, rather than to what was around and within himself. The experience that he thus inherited from his vast ancestry became in him a sort of intuition, the correlative in man to instinct in the brute; and his acts, while those of an ephemeral individual, yet proceeded from one who was the resultant of all his ancestors, and the vehicle for the transmission of their qualities to all his descendants.

There are two forms in which this relation of evolution to ethics has been presented: one where it represents the view of a modest naturalist, the other in which it represents the dream of a more venturesome metaphysician.

(*a*) Darwin saw that his theory must be applied to man as well as to animals, and assumed a law of continuity that required our whole nature, social, moral, and intellectual, to be derived by a process of variation and development from the rudimentary forms discoverable in the lower animals. Their instincts were compared with the faculties of man, especially as he exists in the savage state; and it was argued that the social instinct which made the approbation of the tribe act as a law to its members, was the mother of the moral faculty or sense. But the social instinct could more easily explain uniformity than difference, while it was upon difference more than uniformity that growth depended. Hence these variations in development had to be conceived as due not simply to the two factors of organism and environment, evolved and guided by natural selection and the struggle for existence, but also, in the last analysis, more or less to what may be termed accidents. There was no point more happily or extensively illustrated by Mr. Darwin than the arbitrary character of the fancy or the taste which in the lower races guided selection, whether sexual or natural; and where the selection is arbitrary it is under the rule of chance or circumstances. Yet he recognized no greater or more potent factor of the social framework, and therefore of the moral sense. We may say, then, that he so applied the principle of accidental or occasional variations to the growth of moral ideas or feelings as to leave them incidents that happened in the course of things rather than products of any reason, personal or collective. The accidents indeed to which they were due were conditioned by the operation of Nature; but still they were things that observation could not explain otherwise than by saying they might or might not have occurred.

(β) But a philosophical theory of evolution cannot allow a place within it to the accidental, and so Mr. Herbert Spencer has attempted to eliminate the notion of accident by enunciating the principle—which, by the way, was cogently stated in almost identical terms by Hobbes—that the "conduct which conduces to life in each and all" is good; that "pleasure somewhere, at some time, to some being or beings, is as much a necessary form of moral intuition as space is a necessary form of intellectual intuition"; that it is so because pleasure makes for the conservation of life, and the tendency of every organized being is to conserve its life; and that the struggle to conserve life during the long periods of evolution has resulted in the discovery of those acts which, by begetting pleasures, most tend to its conservation. In this theory, then, two things have to be noted: (a) the objective end which governs the process; and (β) the subjective faculties and judgments which the process creates. The end is contained in Mr. Spencer's notion of the life for which all beings struggle, and towards whose fuller realization the conduct qualified as good conduces. Life consists in "the continuous adjustment of internal relations to external relations," or, in the terms of the more familiar formula, the adaptation of organism to environment. Hence the conduct which promotes this adjustment is good, and the more it promotes it the better the conduct becomes. Moral progress is thus movement towards the "ideal congruity," which is the life of "the completely adapted man in the completely evolved society." But the struggle towards this end is a process which creates the moral sense. "Experiences of utility, organized and consolidated during all past generations of the human race, have been producing nervous modifications"; and these, "by continued transmission and accumulation," have become in us instincts or intuitions which discern the fit action, and create the feeling of obligation. In this process, of course, actions which differentiate pleasures are qualitatively distinguished, the higher being the more conservative of life, the lower the less; and so the total result is an evolution of ethics that are in a sense at once intuitional and empirical, showing the moral experience of the race realized and articulated in the character and conduct of the individual and in the organization of society.

2. On the relation of evolution to ethics as thus stated it may be remarked:

(i.) The question of time is not so vital as it seems. The past into which we are taken is not living but dead; it is largely the past of organisms that were, as imagined by minds that are. The problem concerns mind, but by no process can we out of petrified bones get a mental psychology. The past we recreate is made in our own image; it is turned into a stupendous man, individualized, personified. And when that is done, what is brought out of it is only what we have put into it; it is a past read not as it lived in fact, but as it lives in the mind of the speculative thinker. In other words, the length of time during which the creative process endures does not make the creation less miraculous, especially as the mind which dreams the process is not explained by its dreams.

(ii.) We have to take evolution here with the important modern qualification that the transmission of acquired characters or qualities is a very dubious hypothesis. The younger evolutionists argue that you have no right to call into operation more causes than are necessary to explain the facts. The phenomena which the enormous apparatus of heredity is invoked to explain, can, they say, be explained without it. If heredity were true, then what would be the result? If acquired characters survived and were transmitted, what manner of beings should we be? The most marvellous thing in evolution is not what we do inherit, but what we do not, the fact being that it is only the most infinitesimal part of all that distinguished the parent which descends to the child: in other words, the thing which most needs to be explained is not the possibility of acquired characters being transmitted, but the certainty that the major part of them will perish. It is pathetic and significant that the thing the child most needs and would most profit by, the experience of the parent, is the very thing it does not receive, but has to gain for itself in the bitter way common to all its ancestors.

(iii.) It has to be noted that throughout the whole process we apply a standard of judgment that involves a theory of values. For what permits the theory of evolution to be applied to man and society? It is increased differentiation. Now in this case to what are we to affix the value? To the origin? To the process of differentiation? To the thing differentiated? or to the inheritance? If, for example, a new organ appears differentiating one member of a species from all the others, and if this organ becomes the parent of an entirely new species of organisms, what is the significant thing? It is not the points in which the new and the old species agree, but the points in which they differ. To apply this to the case in hand: if we have to measure man's ethical ideas by any reasonable standard, it should be not by their affinity with the instincts of real or imaginary creatures below him or of imagined ancestors behind him; but rather by the qualities which distinguish his character and conduct from theirs. In other words, it is the point of distinction, not of similarity, which is the great thing. Love of offspring is common to a man and a lion. The feeling that compels the parent to seek food for his offspring exists in both; but in the man the obligation to maintain his offspring is qualitatively different from what it is in the lion, involving duties educational, social, ethical, which belong to a world higher than the animal. The lion is not bound to perish rather than not find food; the man may be so bound: the lion's duties are bounded by his den; the man's by humanity. The differentiation in this case is the important point and as here, so throughout. And this means that the difference in what the man creates from what the man inherits may be more and greater than all his inheritance. It is evident, therefore, that man does more to interpret the process that is behind him than the process has done for the interpretation of man.

(iv.) The end or law which governs the process, the need of adjusting internal to external relations, of adapting organism to environment, inverts the order of thought and nature. The obligation that lies on moral beings is not to adjust themselves to their environment, but to adjust their environment to the higher ideal which they bring to it. Harmony between the social medium and the social unit is not the ultimate measure of conduct; to argue as if it were is to turn circumstances into the master as well as the maker of conscience. And this means that before we can speak of this adjustment as good we have to adjust the society or the medium to an idea of the good which was before it and is distinct from it; i.e. we judge both the environment and the organism, because we apply to both an ideal standard which expresses our notion of what both ought to be. This ideal is native to us, lives inseparably in us, and is developed from the reason we are. It compels us to seek the amelioration of society as well as the improvement of self, and so aims at the adjustment of the two not simply to each other but to a more absolute law. Mr. Spencer's doctrine thus leaves us with an end which neither explains the beginning nor brings us face to face with the forces that have carried men so far towards it. The mystery of the moral ideal and moral obligation lies in man rather than in his environment.

§ IV. *What do Moral Judgments Involve?*

Let us now, in the face of these discussions and distinctions, go back to our problem, and see precisely what are the points that need to be explained. Man is a doer of deeds which are distinguished by their ethical qualities. They can be tested by moral standards; they are subjects for moral judgment. What do these judgments mean? What is their source and basis? Why among all the creatures that live is a moral standard applied to man alone and everywhere and always by man to men? The questions involved may be reduced to three. First, is man capable of directing his own conduct? is he able to do actions which have moral qualities? Secondly, what standard have we to apply in order to the differentiation or qualification of his actions? Thirdly, why is he bound to do acts of a certain quality, and to leave undone acts of other and different qualities? In other words, our questions concern Freedom, Right, and Duty: whether man is or is not a free agent; whether he has or has not faculties or standards which qualify him to use his freedom; and whether he has or has not any feeling or sense of obligation as to their use.

1. We begin with the question as to his power; this is fundamental. Where there is no ability there can be no obligation; what lies outside a man's power does not lie within a man's duty. Nay, more, without this freedom or ability man becomes a mere natural being, no more a subject of moral judgment than the brute. It is by virtue of his power to determine his own choice or to elect his own lines of conduct that he is to be praised or blamed for the thing he does. Now it is remarkable and characteristic that those who have made ethics the creation of experience, who have attempted to resolve them into the acquired instincts of the organism that has had to struggle for life, have done so on the explicit or implicit ground that man was without moral freedom, a creature of circumstances, a child of motive, governed by his love of the agreeable, which conserved life, or his dislike of the disagreeable, which threatened it. In the endeavour to maintain this position, a distinction has been drawn between freedom of will and freedom of action. Freedom of will has been denied; freedom of action has been affirmed; but freedom of action without freedom of choice is only a form of necessity. It means the capability of a thing to be moved, rather than the ability of a person to move; it belongs rather

to the field of physics than of ethics. The motive is a cause which exacts its equivalent effect in the choice. Freedom in this sense does not mean that man has the power of initiation, but only that he has the capacity of responsive movement, can act if he is acted on. Now we must here distinguish what is necessary as an occasion for choice from what is sufficient to cause it. Freedom has been denied to will on the ground that motives are necessary to choice; but while motives may be necessary they need not necessitate. Jonathan Edwards, indeed, argued that the will always is as the strongest motive is; but he did that on the express ground that will is the same as desire, inclination, the most agreeable,—that motive is, in short, emotion. But it is of the very essence of the argument that the will selects motives, motives do not select the will. If the will always is as the strongest motive is, then man has no choice to be other than what the motives which come to him make him. The responsibility for himself is not his, it belongs to the motives that surround and find him. If so, amelioration of character must depend upon amelioration of circumstances. Thus as the man is he must remain, unless he be re-made by the maker of his motives, or, in a word, his environment. For only through a change in his circumstances can any change come to him; and so the way to effect conversion will be to place the bad man where no evil motives can reach him, and the good man where only bad motives can find him. But this way is an impossible way, for the man carries his motives within him; they go where he goes, for they are part of his very self. For, as Coleridge said, it is not the motive that makes the man, but the man the motive. Granted a good man, a bad motive cannot sway him; granted a bad man, a good motive will not find him. Thus it is not true that the will always is as the strongest motive is, but it is true that the motive is as is the man, and what the man is is more a matter of will than of circumstances.

The bondage of the will were indeed fatal to the judgment that holds man responsible for his acts, and approves or disapproves according to their special quality. If motives determine action, the fable of Buridan's Ass ceases to be fabulous. It is possible to conceive alternatives where the motives are so equally balanced that the will would be compelled to remain in a state of complete equilibrium, incapable of inclining either to the right hand or to the left. But while will is not necessitated by motives, motives are necessary to choice; for it is the very essence of rational freedom to demand a reason why it should act. If there were no reason, choice could not be rational; it would be an accident or a chance. But there is nothing so little arbitrary as a rational will; where it is not the arbitrary must be; for the free will acts in view of reasons, and would not be rational if it could choose without them.

Still the reality of freedom lies deeper than argument. Nature witnesses to it; man blames himself when he does wrong because he believes himself to have voluntarily chosen the worse when he could have taken the better. Law judges a man most severely when it holds him to have freely committed the crime with which he is charged. Responsibility is not a vicarious thing, where a necessitated victim bears the blame of ancestral or social sins; but it means that man is to be judged for a thing or act he himself willed to do. He is tried alike by God and man upon the principle which each individual conscience authenticates—that he whose action is in question did it when he could have done otherwise; and he was then bound to do as he could have done.

But while freedom is a *sine quâ non* of moral action and implied in all moral judgments, it has here a further significance:—it qualifies the argument from the transmitted experiences of the past. For what a man inherits leaves him still a free man; the judgment he has to bear is for his own act, and not for the acts of his ancestry, even though they may have created in him tendencies which are not easily resisted. These tendencies do not cancel freedom, only condition it; they define the limits of responsibility, but while they may qualify they do not annul it, for its ground stands unbroken. But in doing this his freedom does much more; it lifts man above the chain of physical causation, and makes him the symbol of a being higher than the forces that are governed by mechanical necessity. For since he is free he stands in conduct in the same transcendental relation to the forces and laws of Nature as he does in knowledge to her qualities and objects. His freedom is the correlate of his thought; and as the man who knows phenomena is not one of the phenomena he knows, so the will that can initiate action is not a mere event or link in a series of antecedents and sequents, where each follows the other either without perceived connection or in a rigorous order of physical causation. Thought is transcendence as regards the phenomena of space, Will is transcendence as regards the events of time; the double transcendence involves the complete supernatural character of man.

2. But we come next to the idea of the right. What is it and whence is it? We have seen that those who would give a strictly naturalistic account of ethics have attempted to explain the right as the agreeable, or, to use the very precise and definite language of John Stuart Mill, "Actions are right in proportion as they tend to promote happiness, wrong as they tend to produce the reverse of happiness. By happiness is intended pleasure and the absence of pain; by unhappiness pain and the privation of pleasure."[1] A sentence like this is quite without significance until the terms "pleasure" and "happiness" be defined, and until we have determined whether pleasure or happiness be one and uniform, or varied in kind and quality. There are really three questions which

---

[1] Mill, "Utilitarianism," *Ethics*, p. 91 (Douglas' ed.).

such a sentence directly suggests: what is happiness? what sort of happiness? whose happiness?

(*a*) What is happiness? It is an infinite thing, so infinite that no man can tell its forms, enumerate or measure its varieties. There is happiness which is mere sensual indulgence, and happiness which is intellectual enjoyment. There is the happiness of the savage, who lies and suns himself, gorged, on the bank; of the serious student, who lives in the study and among his books; of the speculator, who gambles in stocks and shares; of the strenuous athlete, who feels as if his soul were in his muscles or his limbs; of the *nouveau riche*, who feels as if recognition by Society were admission into heaven. Unless we define happiness, how can we speak of it? And if we qualify it, we introduce distinctions not contained within the idea itself, but drawn from another and higher sphere. For Happiness, unqualified, is the most absolutely insignificant term in the whole vocabulary of philosophy or of literature; and it is therefore signally unsuitable when made to play the part of ultimate arbiter as regards the qualities which make actions right or wrong.

(β) What sort of happiness? Is it sensuous? Is it intellectual? Is it ethical or social? Is it "comfort" which seems to so many Englishmen the only real paradise? As we have seen that quality is a needful element in the definition of Happiness, we find it to be also needful in the differentiation and appraisement of its kinds. For the sorts of happiness are innumerable, just as the persons who may be happy or miserable represent not only in number but in grade all degrees of capacity. Is then happiness a thing we can quantify as well as qualify? If we use it as an ethical measure or standard, must we not in our reasoning add mass to quality? Is the greatest quantity of a lower quality of happiness to be preferred to a smaller quantity of a higher quality, or, on the contrary, is quality to be preferred to quantity? Then what or who is to determine the sort of happiness to which superior and determinative excellence belongs? Is it the man? Is it the fashion of the passing society? or is it some standard apart from both, and more permanent and universal than either? In other words, it is impossible to begin to distinguish between sorts of happiness without introducing a standard by which happiness can be measured. But where a standard is introduced, it is distinguished from what it measures, and is held to be higher than it; and so happiness, as something which is itself determined, cannot be determinative of the quality of the action whose character it was thought to decide.

(γ) But suppose we have found and agreed upon some method of differentiating or testing the quality of pleasures, we are at once met by the question, Whose is the happiness that I am to promote? My own? My family's? My country's? My kind's? If these be inconsistent, who is to decide between them? If I am to promote my family's happiness, it may be at the sacrifice of my own. If I am to promote my country's happiness, it may be at the expense of my family's. If I am to promote the happiness of my kind, it may be by turning against my own country, and playing what would be by many described as a treacherous or an unpatriotic part. How are these things to be determined, or the particular persons whose happiness I am to promote to be found out? But further, if I give up my personal pleasure to promote that of any of those just named, what guarantee have I that theirs will be promoted, or that in doing so I am not reducing by the sacrifice of my own or my family's or my country's the sum total of happiness in the universe? If I so serve this generation as to increase its pleasure, may I not be doing it at the expense, say, of my own health, or the health of generations that are to come after me, especially those that may spring from my own loins? And the matter may become very urgent, for the question, Whose plea-

WHENCE THE SENSE OF OBLIGATION? 81

sure? blends also with this other, What sort of pleasure? Is it the Queen's in the palace? Is it the peasant's in the hut? Is it the greatest happiness of the capitalist or of the workman? Nay, is it the greatest happiness of the greatest number? But who is to estimate the number? Who is to tell the happiness? Is the greatest number to tell me what it is, or am I to tell the greatest number what its happiness is or ought to be? And how am I to find out the acts that will either fulfil my notions of what the greatest happiness of the greatest number is or ought to be, or what they conceive their own happiness most distinctively to consist in?

It seems then as if pleasure were a completely impracticable standard of the right, and as if we must find one more capable of application to all the varieties of human action and conduct, or abandon in despair the effort to discover what is right or good.

3. But there is not only the power to do the right and the right to be done, there is the obligation to do it. The word Duty, or, put into its concrete form, Conscience—how do we come into the possession of this? Whence the feeling of obligation, the idea represented by that imperious word "ought"? Suppose that the happiness of the greatest number is the standard of right, the question remains, Why am I bound to promote it? We may be told that the sense of obligation is, as it were, the social sanction worked into our consciousness and woven into feeling; the authority of society translated into a personal judgment. Suppose this were so, how or by what process is the social sanction got into the man? The process of incorporation may be represented in some such form as this: the social sanction, it may be said, is implanted in us because society educates us; and having found out what was most for its own good, it instils into us by law and education, by convention and custom, its idea of what acts are suitable or appropriate to its needs or conducive to its well-being. This process of instillation is

so subtle and so completely carried out that the man cannot separate the judgment of society within him from himself. It has been made a part and parcel of his own being, and so he judges himself just as if he were collective society personalized.

Well, now, suppose we grant this, and grant also another thing, that society has by an extraordinary exercise of arithmetical genius so worked out the terms of the ethical calculus that it can tell which among all possible acts most makes for its happiness, and which acts most make for its misery, what then? Is the phenomenon of duty, are the phenomena of conscience, explained? On the contrary, wherein consists their permanent and pre-eminent peculiarity? In this, that man feels, when most bound by conscience, most independent of society,—bound to do the thing which duty imperiously commands, even though society may imperiously forbid. If the man be a religious man and the society also in earnest about its own view of religion and against his, his defiance of its judgment and its sanctions may involve his going to the stake. And how does his conscience show its quality? In compelling him to go to the stake rather than submit to society. If he is a statesman, and society prescribes a policy which he disapproves, what is he bound to do? Accept the authority of his own conscience or of society? Would he gain or lose respect by publicly professing to regard the voice of the State, in opposition to his own moral judgment, as the voice of God? Is not the distinctive peculiarity of conscience this:—that if it commands a policy or mode of conduct or expression of opinion that may make a man a social outcast and bring upon him in their severest form all the penalties which the social sanction may be able to enforce, yet there is expected from him, all the more rather than the less, full and unqualified obedience to its behests?

But though this is a point which we may leave as a

problem to the hedonist, let us proceed a little further, and suppose that the man has been got to occupy the standpoint of society, to look at himself through its eyes rather than his own, and that society has succeeded in incorporating its judgment in the feeling which he calls his conscience, how is that judgment to become to him a law? How is that to be translated into a categorical imperative? Fear of the social sanction cannot do it, for we have just seen how easily and how often in the highest and most imperious cases that sanction may be defied. And may not a man of lower quality than the martyr or the sufferer for conscience' sake reasonably argue thus?—"Society is an immense and continuous organism, while I am a humble and ephemeral unit. My happiness is a far greater thing to me than society's can ever be to it, for it is impossible that the whole of society can by a single act be made miserable as I may be, not only for this moment but for all the moments that are to come of my ephemeral being. How then is it possible for me to contribute better to the sum total of happiness than by increasing the amount of my own?" And would not that man's argument, whether regarded from the standpoint of the most enlightened self-interest or from that of social interest, be valid and invincible? And so we are left by this philosophy as completely without an authority to enforce duty as without a good to be realized or any ability to realize it.

§ V. *The Ethical Man means an Ethical Universe: Butler and Kant*

1. If now Freedom, Right, and Duty cannot be construed as creations of experience, whether individual or collective, it follows that they either represent or are integral elements of human nature, involved in its very idea and evolved in its evolution. But that which is integral to man is

no less integral to his universe. What is in him is not independent of what is without him, but repeats and reflects it, lives in him in active intercourse with what is above and around him, just as his organism lives within and through its environment, absorbing into itself the elements without that are needful to growth and health within. The same law holds in the ethical as in the physical region, and, as we have seen, also in the intellectual. As the intellect implies the intelligible medium in which it lives, so we can conceive a personal conscience only where it can express a universal law, and moral freedom only where there is a supreme ethical Will to govern. Without this correspondence of man's nature with the constitution of the universe in which he lives moral life would not be possible to him, nor would obedience bring the harmony between personal will and imperative law which is the very notion of beatitude.

Two great ethical thinkers—Butler and Kant—may be taken as exponents of certain deductions which follow from the ethical position here maintained. They are instructive alike in their agreements and in their differences. They agree, first, that there is a law ultimate and absolute incorporated in the nature of man: ultimate, because it neither asks nor gives a reason for its dictates, but simply commands; absolute, for while it speaks in the individual its tone is that of the universal, of a sovereign endowed with perfect right and manifest authority. They agree, secondly, that this law is immediate; nothing comes between it and the man; it speaks with him face to face, enforces duty and allows no intermediary to qualify or repeal its authority. Thirdly, it is so intrinsic and essential in its character that without it the person is not a man, through it he becomes human; by obedience he achieves humanity.

Both of these eminent thinkers, then, saw that the conception of the intrinsic and essential morality of man involved similar elements in the universe; but each works out the principle with characteristic differences. Kant is the more formal and scholastic in method, Butler the more cautious and suggestive in statement. Kant combines with his critical doubts as to the competence of the pure reason in the region of transcendental dialectic, a rigorous dogmatism in the conclusions of his ethical logic; but Butler so feels the range and reality of our ignorance that he insinuates rather than draws his more certain or assured inferences. Kant's interests are intellectual, and even where he is most the moralist he does not cease to be the philosopher; but Butler's main concern is religion; and when he is most the philosopher, he still remains the divine. Kant's philosophy is critical because he feels at every moment its antithesis to the old dogmatic rationalism; Butler's theology is apologetical, for he never forgets the deism which is the fashionable belief of his day, or the men who have found their way through a relaxed faith into laxity of morals. These differences of method and mental attitude are reflected in their respective arguments.

2. Butler's argument exists in two forms, a positive or didactic, and an apologetical or polemical. We find the former in the Sermons, the latter in the Analogy. In the Sermons his philosophy is a Christian Stoicism. Men ought to live according to Nature, which is not acting as we please, but doing as we ought, obeying our legitimate sovereign, the Conscience, making it the whole business of our lives, as it is absolutely the whole business of a moral agent, to conform ourselves to it. "This is what the ancient precept means, *Reverence thyself*. It is the essence of a system to be an one or a whole made up of several parts," but the parts can be a whole only as they form an one. A watch is a whole composed of many parts, yet made a unity for the measuring of time by the all-pervading and controlling mainspring; and men and societies are multitudes which are reduced to system, or units made into unity by the com-

mon yet individuated empire of the conscience which regulates life and defines its end. And they have been so constituted by the Creator, for Butler conceives that "following Nature" and "obeying the voice of God" are not two things, but one and the same. In the Analogy these ideas are elaborated into a defence of those religious truths which teach belief in a future life, the providence and government of God here and hereafter, the life that now is as a scene and period of probation, and the need of a revelation to make this life what it ought to be in view of the life to come. We may therefore represent the argument as having unfolded itself before the mind of the English divine in terms somewhat like these: "The law which is everywhere incorporated in man implies a Lawgiver. While it lives and speaks in the individual, it is yet distributed through the whole; and this universality is only the more distinctly expressed in the severe individualism under which it is realized. For it signifies that the law is so essential to human nature that it must be incorporated in the unit in order that it may be the more completely and universally evolved from him into the unity; but it could not be complete and universal were it simply incorporated in the whole in order that it might be impressed from without upon the unit. The order that is made by external pressure may be mechanical, but is not organic; it may be political, but it is not moral. The highest order springs from the harmony of all the units, which means that the outward and inward so correspond that the individual can be worked into a system that completely satisfies every personal and realizes every collective end. The essential unity of a State is not secured by the sovereign, but by those remarkable unities incorporated in each individual that we term blood, descent, language, tradition, belief. It is an ideal thing which custom may express, but legislation cannot create. The alphabet is in every educated man; it lies at the root of his knowledge of his own tongue.

His knowledge of that tongue lies at the root of his enjoyment of its literature, his appreciation of its poetry, its history and its science. Without that knowledge its literature would speak to him in vain. Similarly, the moral law of the universe is impersonated in its moral units. It is over all men because it is in all. There has therefore been a common Lawgiver; and this Lawgiver must have also been Creator, for He who made man made also the law in and with the man; and He who made both law and man administers the law by judging the man. He is therefore sovereign; the system we live under He instituted, and the life we live under it is one of probation, lived that we may give in an account to Him who rules His universe by enforcing His laws."

3. Kant's argument differed considerably from Butler's especially as it made Deity one of several deductions from the moral law—the highest in a trinity of consequences from its supremacy. The stress he laid upon duty in his Practical Philosophy was a sort of compensation for the argumentative impotence of his Speculative. The intensity of Kant's moral convictions, the severity of his doctrine, the force with which he preached duty to an age that did not love it, entitles him to something more than the regard we give to the father of that critical and transcendental philosophy which has done more to educate and uplift Mind than any purely speculative school the world has known since the days of Plato. Kant starts from the position that the only thing good without qualification is the good will; and that will is good which acts from duty and not simply from inclination, duty being respect for law and obedience to it. This law as moral is absolute in its authority. It is a categorical imperative expressed in an unconditioned "thou shalt." The categorical is distinguished from the hypothetical imperative in not being consequential, or something dependent on a prior principle or condition. It simply speaks the thing that man is bound to do, every individual act being the expression of a universal principle or duty.

From this absolute categorical imperative three things followed :—(*a*) freedom ; where the obligation is absolute the power possessed must be equal to its performance. The being it commands could not, in respect of what is commanded, be under the control of any merely natural or external force. Only where "thou canst" may be said is "thou oughtest" possible. But though the will be free it is not blind ; its choices are not arbitrary. Hence every moral act must have an end—the highest good. This good consists of two elements—virtue and felicity or happiness. If either be absent, the good is not realized. But the two are inseparable ; virtue is a necessary condition of felicity, felicity the natural crown of virtue.

But now (β) this cannot be realized within the terms and under the limitations of our empirical existence. Hence immortality follows as the second deduction from the ethical postulate. The moral law demands perfect virtue or holiness; but a mortal being cannot realize moral perfection or a holy completeness of nature and conduct within the bounds of his mortal life. If, then, there is to be virtue, there must be immortal existence. The law that demands perfect virtue guarantees immortality as a condition for its realization.

But (γ) to freedom and immortality God must be added. For if there is to be happiness, the felicity that crowns virtue and turns it into the supreme good, there must be conditions favourable to its being. But these conditions can be realized only where nature and will work together in harmony ; i.e. while the moral law is independent of nature, nature in all its conditions must serve the moral law if felicity is to be complete. But this service man is unable to compel ; the only being able to compel it is Deity; for He alone is Master of Nature. He then is as necessary as freedom and immortality to man's highest good. These, then, are the necessary postulates of the practical reason, the logical implicates of the categorical imperative : Freedom, Immortality,

God. They may be no objects of speculative knowledge, but they are objects of the rational faith, whose being is grounded in the categorical imperative and guaranteed by it. And the faith they warrant is that the ethical man lives in an ethical universe; the moral nature which is essential to man moralizes his universe.

§ VI. *Deductions and Conclusion*

The difference between the two arguments is perhaps more formal than substantial, a matter of formal logic rather than metaphysical principle. Butler does not emphasize freedom as strongly as Kant, but he holds it as firmly, while he conceives immortality and God to be necessary to probation here and beatitude hereafter; and, therefore, to be clear and indubitable implicates of his moral interpretation of Nature. And with Kant the subordination or argumentative dependence of Deity upon the categorical imperative is more logical than real. The system as a whole hangs together. Subjectively, the ultimate, the thing of which we are supremely conscious if we are conscious of ourselves at all, is the sovereignty of conscience; but objectively, the reality which is the correlate of our ultimate consciousness, is a universe in which God is Sovereign. We may then deduce from this ethical dialectic principles that ought to carry us to conclusions of the first importance for our present discussion.

1. Man as moral, and therefore free, stands above nature, even while he seems within it. The will involves another order of transcendence than belongs to the intellect; for it is a much higher and more complex transcendence to stand in act and character above the order or succession of mechanical sequences than in the act of cognition to unify phenomena. Man, in short, is no mere physical or natural effect; he is a moral cause. As a moral cause he possesses the power of initiative. He is not simply made by the past; he is the

present, and he helps to make the future. The increase of moral good in the world is as possible as the increase of energy is impossible, and moral good is the direct creation of moral will. Physical forces, so far as they are conceived as causes, pass into their effects; the change produced is the exact equivalent of the energy expended. But there is no such exact equivalence between moral causes and their effects. The will is a permanent force, not exhausted by a single choice or any number of choices, but ever creative, ever re-creative, making conditions which not only allow, but promote and demand the existence of higher things. The correlative of the indestructibility of matter is, if we may so phrase it, its increatability; it can be as little made as destroyed, but remains a stable quantity, though with infinite instability as to mode. But these terms cannot be used of either good will or moral good. There may be an indefinite multiplication of good wills, and in moral good an infinite upward progression. In this region every person of higher excellence than the society into which he is born, every nobler ideal realized, every new virtue or finer type of old virtues achieved, every grace added to humanity,— is an increase of the good stored in the world and the direct outcome of the moral will. This will stands, therefore, as an initiative force, a centre of creative action, able not only to effect or suffer changes, but even to augment in quantity and improve in quality what it found in existence.

2. Man further transcends nature by carrying within himself the law he is bound to obey. The code of ethics which he makes for himself out of himself differentiates him from every merely natural being; and it signifies that it is by transcending nature that he becomes himself. He progresses by self-realization. This self is not empirical, does not grow out of experience, but is transcendental, makes experience; and is never satisfied with the experience gained, but ever strives after the unrealized. Hence there is something uni-

versal in the Ego; it is never a mere enclosed or shut-in individual, but a person of one substance not only with the race of man, but with the whole of reason everywhere. Hence man, within the physical conditions that limit him and seem to reduce him to the hue and mode of his environment, creates conditions—intellectual, ethical, social—which contend against those imposed upon him by nature. Over against its pitiless struggle for life he creates a passion for well-doing, the mercy whose quality is not strained, the "truth that worketh by love," "the hope that maketh not ashamed," "the love that rejoiceth not in iniquity, but rejoiceth in the truth." And the qualities that do most to perfect his personality contribute most to the creation of the higher ethical conditions; so much so that the degree in which he transcends nature tends to humanize even her most brutal forces.

3. Since man as active will and immanent law transcends nature, he cannot be measured by it. Generalizations based upon the study of nature ought not to be used to determine what is or is not possible to him. The laws under which phenomena may be grouped do not apply to persons who are more than phenomenal, who are the noumena through which all phenomena are. The natural law of the Roman jurist was not an actual thing, nor was the perfect man of the Roman Stoic an actual person. They were ideals, but they were not unreal because they were not actual; rather they were all the more real that they were so ideal. Natural Law meant the abstract justice and right, the ideal equity of the human reason, which could be so applied to the concrete and positive Law as to make it less cruel in its enactments, less severe in its judgments, less barbarous in its modes and instruments—in a word, more just and more humane. The Perfect Man was an ideal of goodness, which was so presented to actual men as to tempt them to live more worthily and to aspire more wholly after better things. So man transcendent is man ideal, above nature while within it, able to ex-

plain it, incapable of explanation by it. And if we find the ideal of the Perfect Man realized, must we not conceive him in whom it is impersonated as essentially supernatural in quality, and in intrinsic worth of being above anything which nature can produce?

4. Since the moral law is immanent in man and realized by his will, it follows that all moral good is personal in its source, originates with persons, is realized in persons, and is by means of persons incorporated in the laws, institutions, and agencies which protect, preserve, and develop it. There is, indeed, no factor of change or cause of progress known to history or human experience equal in efficiency to the great personality — the man who embodies some creative and causal idea. It is not nearly so true that great movements or moments produce great men as that the men create the moments. The wars of the world bear the marks of their leaders; and each has been glorious or ignoble, brilliant or disgraceful, just as its captain has been. What is the history of art but the biographies of great artists? Where would Greek sculpture have been without Pheidias, or modern painting without Raphael, or music without the Masters? Has not science been made by certain supreme minds, discoveries by certain daring explorers, political order and ideas elaborated and embodied in politics by genius in the form of statesmen? It is personality that counts in all things, and most of all in that concentrated form of moral good which we call religion. For religion has at once this distinction and value: it is moral good under its most august and sovereign aspect, as it affects man's inmost being and ultimate relations. It is good *sub specie æternitatis*, enlarging mortal into immortal being, and reconciling man to himself and to the whole infinite order, which dignifies him by making him needful to its completeness. In this realm there is no great and no small, for all the categories are infinite and all the ends are divine.

5. If, then, man, by his moral being touches the skirts of God, and God in enforcing His law is ever, by means of great persons, shaping the life of man to its diviner issues, what could be more consonant, alike with man's nature and God's method of forming or re-forming it, than that He should send a supreme Personality as the vehicle of highest good to the race? Without such a Personality the moral forces of time would lack unity, and without unity they would be without organization, purpose or efficiency. If a Person has appeared in history who has achieved such a position and fulfilled such functions, how can He be more fitly described than as the Son of God and the Saviour of man?

CHAPTER III

THE QUESTION AS AFFECTED BY THE PROBLEM OF EVIL

A. HISTORICAL AND CRITICAL

§ I. Πόθεν τὸ κακόν;

1. THE doctrine that man's nature embodies a moral ideal which he is bound to realize, is more easy to believe and to vindicate when stated in the abstract than when set face to face with the facts of life. For, as a matter of experience, man has not realized the moral ideal. If theology knows depravity, history is acquainted with cruelty and wickedness in high places and in low; ethics are as familiar with vice as religion is with sin; and philosophy has no harder or more obstinate questions than those connected with the origin and the existence of evil. Indeed there is no problem that has so perplexed our finest spirits, reducing some to silent despair, rousing some to eloquent doubt, and forcing not a few into unbelief; while probably a multitude no man can number have saved faith by forcing their reason to sit dumb and blind before the mystery it could not penetrate or unravel. One of the most beautiful and pious spirits it has ever been my privilege to know, was a man who had been trained to the office of the preacher, who had distinguished himself as a scholar and as a thinker, and who had become the hope of his college, his professors, and his Church. One day it fell to him to proclaim in public what he had tried to learn in the study and in the classroom; but, as he stood and faced the upturned eyes of men, there came such

a vision of the evils that filled life and the impotence of the Will which seemed to rule the world, as well as of the preacher and of the word he preached either to mend or to end them, that he vowed unto the God in whose goodness he still believed, that were he only allowed to escape with his reason from that appalling place, he would not again lift up his voice in a pulpit until he had a message better fitted fo the supreme crisis of the soul sojourning amid scenes so confused and perplexing. That message never came to him, and he retired into a silence that nothing could tempt him to break, vanquished by the potency of evil.

Another and more distinguished thinker has charged nature with perpetrating on the most stupendous scale every crime and cruelty man has ever been guilty of: " Nature impales men, breaks them as if on the wheel, casts them to be devoured by wild beasts, burns them to death, crushes them with stones like the first Christian martyr, starves them with hunger, freezes them with cold, poisons them by the quick or slow venom of her exhalations, and has hundreds of other hideous deaths in reserve, such as the ingenious cruelty of a Nabis or a Domitian never surpassed." And he has made out a dread catalogue of the deeds which " Nature does with the most supercilious disregard both of mercy and justice," ending with " the hurricane and the pestilence " which overmatch " anarchy and the Reign of Terror " " in injustice, ruin, and death."[1] That indictment by John Stuart Mill may, as was long ago noted, recall the famous stanzas of Tennyson on the man—

> "Who trusted God was love indeed,
> And love creation's final law—
> Tho' Nature, red in tooth and claw
> With ravin, shrieked against his creed."

But while there is in both an equal feeling of the savagery of nature, there was not in Mill any sense of the " love

[1] J. S. Mill, *Essays on Religion*, pp. 29-31.

indeed." It was the conflict of nature's way with man's sense of justice that compelled him to judge her so terribly; it was not its contradiction to a heart of infinite pity in the God who had made man.

2. But the evil that perplexes most is not physical or natural; were it only this, man might bear it with patience or fight against it with courage, or at least refuse to let it vanquish his better manhood. The evil which perplexes his reason, enfeebles his will, and confounds his conscience, is moral, not physical. Crime, vice, sin, the lusts that in their search for pleasure make pain, the passions, the lecheries, and the brutalities that possess man and desolate men, are the evils that create astonishment and dismay, for they do not simply inflict suffering, they waste what is the most god-like thing known to time—the soul and its happiness. The darkest of all the visions that can appal the imagination is that of the wasted manhood of the world; the savage peoples that, on dark or fertile continents or beautiful sun-lit islands, have lived and died hardly men; the wasted men and women, possibly a vaster multitude than all the savage peoples in the heart of Africa and in the Southern Seas, who in civilized lands and in Christian cities have lived to be little else than the causes or instruments or victims of sin. And the vision, if it be that of a religious imagination, will not be confined to time; it will range into eternity as well. The thought of a man who has been base enough to seduce, or of a woman wretched enough to be seduced, and to avenge her seduction by becoming in turn a seducer; the thought of the miseries and the diseases that have gone on multiplying themselves at an almost incalculable ratio through generations of mortals who are, or who ought to be, on their way to immortality, is, in all soberness and truth, a thought oppressive and painful beyond what the most solid reason can calmly bear. And if consolation be sought in the faith that God has no pleasure in the death of the wicked, but will have all men to

be saved, then out of that very comfort new perplexities come —Why then is His will so impotent? Why do so many perish as if the Maker cared for them no more than the slaver cares for the slaves he carries in his hold? That old mystery of evil is still a new mystery—most invincible of all the obstinate spectres which haunt human thought, and which will not be exorcized. To face it and to feel its force is to taste to the full that misery which Pascal said "proved the grandeur of man," the misery of a being who knows himself suspended between the abysses of nonentity and infinity; a nothing as compared with the universe, a universe as contrasted with nothing. In the moment when that misery is keenest and the knowledge it brings most vivid, the words of the ancient poet speak to us as if they voiced the truth—the happiest thing would have been never to be born; the next in happiness is for the living to return as quickly as possible to the place whence he came.

3. Our perplexity is further increased by the fact that this mystery is made more mysterious by those high and sacred beliefs which ought to be its full and final explanation. The shadow that Theism so feels and fears Theism deepens and darkens, if, indeed, it does not altogether make the shadow. For if men did not believe in a good God, or if they had not the mood or disposition that this belief has created in humanity, they would not feel evil to be so insoluble a mystery. To a man who believes in mechanical necessity, or a fixed fate, every fact of life, including its evil, will remain as it is; but then his conscience will not be burdened, nor his heart afflicted, nor his reason perplexed, as they will be if he believes in a free and beneficent Deity. If he imagines that the only sovereign in the universe is the force which holds every individual in its iron grasp, and necessitates every act he does, every thought he thinks, and every event that happens to him; if he believes that man can only do what he must, that there is for him no pity anywhere in nature, and that

there is no higher will to which his miseries can make their dumb appeal for mercy,—then he may, perhaps, regard evil, and with it existence, as a thing intolerable to him as an individual, but he will not feel compelled to pronounce judgment against the almighty Energy which produced both him and it. For where there is no choice and no morality, there can be no responsibility and no condemnation. But if a man believes that there is a powerful and righteous God, the Creator and Ruler of the world, he is, in the very degree that he is thoughtful, certain to be perplexed by the problem, 'Why has He allowed evil to exist?' And he may fall a victim to some swift and dexterous piece of logic like this: 'Either He could have prevented evil, but would not; or He would have prevented it, but could not. If I accept the first alternative, then I must conclude that He is a being of imperfect goodness; if I accept the second, the conclusion must be that He is a being of imperfect power. In either case He is less perfect than the God I had imagined myself to believe in. It is inconceivable that a perfectly good being could have allowed so much evil to enter, and to devastate the world.'

Evil, then, when viewed in relation to existence and to its Author, formulates the gravest problem that a man who believes in a personal God can face. But whether he believes in Him or not, it remains a problem, acute in the degree that his view of life is moral. Two antithetical systems of thought—the one either personal and theistic or impersonal and pantheistic, and the other either mechanical and non-theistic, or conceiving creation as the work of an irresponsible and unconscious, though motived, cause—have attempted to deal seriously with this question. The one which it is customary to term Optimism, conceives existence as good in spite of its evil, or even, in certain cases, because of evil and through it. The other, which as its antithesis bears the name of Pessimism, is a philosophy which gives scientific expression to the view that life is hateful because of its attendant evils, and it may even conceive existence as in its essence so bad that it had better never have been.

§ II. *Optimism and Evil*

1. Optimism is, in a sense, implicit in Theism. The more perfect we conceive God to be, the less can we predicate evil of His works. As Plato said, "the deeds of the Best could never be or have been other than the fairest"; and so the world He created was "by nature fairest and best,"[1] "as far as possible a perfect whole and of perfect parts,"[2] and could be described, in terms that become the Maker rather than the thing made, as the "visible God, the image of the Intelligible, the greatest, best, fairest, most perfect, the one only begotten heaven."[3] But this is nature interpreted through God, while the very essence of the problem is the interpretation of the character and ways of God through nature. The Stoic was even more certain than Plato that the creation was, in its kind and measure, as perfect as the Creator, but he had to maintain his belief in the face of an acuter moral sense and a more emphasized moral law. And he did this by affirming, in spite of his belief in an invincible fate, that there were limits to Divine power which could as little keep man free from moral evil as from physical disease;[4] that it was as irrational to think that God could connive at wickedness as that law could be guilty of crime;[5] that like the vulgar jest in the play, evil might be offensive, but, blended with the whole, it heightened the general effect;[6] and that it was here to train character and to be, therefore, finally transmuted into good.[7] But the difficulty became

---

[1] *Timæus*, p. 30. [2] *Ibid.* 32. [3] *Ibid.* 92.
[4] Cleanthes, *Hymn*, 17 ff.; Plutarch, *De Stoic. Repub.*, 21, 44; 36, 1.
[5] Chrysippus in Plut., *De Stoic. Repub.*, 33, 2.
[6] Marcus Aurelius, vi. 42, with the reference to Chrysippus, Plut., *Adv. Stoic.*, 14.
[7] Chrysippus in Plut., *Adv. Stoic.*, 13; cf. *De Stoic. Rep.*, 35, 3.

vaster and more acute to Christian than it had been to Hellenic thought, for to the Christian mind God was more personal, more august and beneficent, while sin was a subtler and more terrible conception than evil, a power more destructive while less destructible. For sin was conceived as a sort of impersonal and diabolical counterpart of God, able to maintain itself against Him, with a kingdom of its own, propagating itself and multiplying its effects by means of the order He had instituted, compelling His very justice to encourage its growth and continue its being by making the habit of sinning the supreme penalty of the act of sin. And so it was no mere ironical Nemesis, but an inexorable law of logic, that laid upon Augustine, the Father who was mainly responsible for this doctrine, the duty of vindicating the Providence whose ways it seemed so seriously to impugn. His apology followed several distinct lines, some of which were more germane to the notion of evil than of sin, having been suggested by the Greeks themselves, who had chiefly influenced him. Thus he argues, after Plotinus, that evil is nothing real, but is simply negative, a negation of being, and especially of God, who is the most real of all beings. Hence he boldly formulated the position, "in quantum est, quidquid est, bonum est."[1] There is but one God, one supreme essence, from whom whatever is holds its existence. As He is good, all His works, i.e. all created being, must be the same; and so evil ought to be conceived as negative, an attempt to deny or abolish the works and the acts of God. The more being abounds, the more abundant becomes the good; the more it is restricted or encroached on by the unreal, the more evil prevails. But Augustine knew that metaphysics of this sort could do little to comfort those to whom misery was an actual experience and sin a profound reality. So he argued, as the Stoics had done, that evil is

[1] *De Vera Rel.*, 9; cf. *De Civ. Dei*, xii. 6, 7; *De Ord.*, ii. 20.

GRACE THE ANTITHESIS OF SIN

needed to enhance the beauty and the glory of the world.[1] It is like the barbarisms which the poets love to use now and then as a foil to their own elegance.[2] Time is like a picture which needs the shadows as well as the light for its loveliest effects.[3] Even the eternal fires of hell, however penal to the sinner, tend to magnify the beauty of the whole, and exalt the glory of the mighty Artificer.[4] But Augustine's own contribution as a theologian to the solution of the problem was of a nobler and more satisfactory order. Over against the potency of sin he placed the omnipotence of God; over against its power to ruin he set the grace that saved. Sin must be conceived through an antithesis, without which it never could have been. Christ was not because of Adam, but Adam because of Christ. Man had not been allowed to sin that God might be free to punish, but that He might have the opportunity to save. Sin entered that grace might abound. Through sin as occasion, though not by means of it as cause, God was brought nearer to man, suffered with him, endured sacrifice for him, and lifted him out of his evil to a higher glory than he could without it have attained. But it was a dangerous, if a daring, feat to raise evil into a means of good: it invited a damaging retort as to the bungling character of the workman who had to mar his work in order that he might find some way of perfecting it. As a matter of fact the retort was given, for the thought which so lightly touched evil could not bear to feel the shadow of sin. But ancient philosophy in all its classical forms had been struck with decrepitude, and the criticism of the decrepit is more querulous than creative or illuminative. On the other hand the eclectic speculations which Augustine had so largely absorbed, made no notable contribution to the discussion, while in theology the reign of dogma was at hand, and thought moved from the

---

[1] *De Civ. Dei*, xiv. 27.
[2] *Ibid.* xi. 18.
[3] *Ibid.* xi.; *De Ord.*, i. 18.
[4] *De Civ. Dei*, xii. 4.

problems of the reason to the more pressing and practical questions of ecclesiastical organization.

The mediæval schoolmen were, on the whole (there were certain conspicuous exceptions), faithful to Augustine, lived in his intellectual world, faced his problems, and acutely discussed such questions as, Whether all things, in so far as they really exist, are good. But the hour came when the ancient world awoke, and mind, hearing its voice, awoke with it and tried to look at life in the light of the common reason ; but though the classical literatures helped to open the eyes, yet they could not silence the conscience. And so while the thinkers of the Renaissance learned to speak of evil, they still thought of sin ; but sin was less amenable to the categories of ancient thought than evil. The first Teutonic scholar to be renewed by the knowledge of antiquity, Nicholas of Cusa, is also here the finest exponent of the new mind. While Greece awoke in him the feeling for nature, it did not take from him his inherited passion for God ; rather, as he himself tells us, it begot in him the ambition of uniting the two in a single conception.[1] God is superessential, and can be expressed in no category.[2] He is the eternal Unity which is prior to all variety, and the ground of all change.[3] He is the synthesis of all being, all is in Him, and He is in all.[4] Nature is an organism whose soul is God,[5] and whose organs are the infinite multitude of persons who live and move and exist in Him. The world is nothing but the apparition of the invisible God ; God is but the invisibility of all visible existences.[6] Since the two are so related, each must be as the other is ; disharmony can neither mar its life nor disturb His ; He is the absolutely perfect Being, and it is the most perfect world possible.[7] The philosophical successor of

---

[1] *De docta Ignor.*, iii. *ad fin.*   [2] *Ibid.* ii. 8.
[3] *Ibid.* ii. 5.   [4] *Ibid.* iii. 4.
[5] *Ibid.* ii. 13. Nicholas' phrase is *mens mundi* ; cf. *De Poss.*, 175.
[6] *De docta Ignor.*, i. 11 ; cf. *De Conjecturis*, ii. 10.
[7] *De docta Ignor.*, ii. 4 ; *De ludo Globi*, i. 154.

Nicholas was Giordano Bruno, who developed the notion of God as the Unity of all difference into an explicit and conscious Pantheism.

2. But our concern is not with the logic that made men pantheists; it is with the modes in which the ideas of God and evil affected each other in minds that had ceased to believe in Christian theology while living face to face with the Christian religion. Now the remarkable thing is that just as thought became less Christian, the problem of evil grew at once more mysterious and more imperative. Christianity is the only religion that has dared to articulate a theology from the premiss not simply of God's sole sovereignty, but of His direct responsibility for man; and has had at the same time the courage to conceive man as capable of alienating himself from God and of making evil his deity. For centuries the Christian notion of sin had held man in its burning hands, magnifying his power, but darkening his state and his destiny; for many centuries he had believed in a God infinitely good and gracious, the Maker of a race that had chosen to become bad, the Redeemer of the race from the evil its own choice had made. These things stood indissolubly together: man's act, or the sin that alienated; God's action, or the grace that saved. But the denial of the Christian redemption left men standing face to face with two ideas they could neither deny nor relate and reconcile, God and evil. This antithesis stood at its sharpest in Deism, which loved to describe itself as a system of natural religion, but which we may describe as an attempt to conceive God in the manner of the Christian religion without any of the experiences, beliefs, and associations that had made it possible so to conceive Him. God was good, and evil was the grimmest of all realities. He had made the world, and had allowed sin to enter it, yet He would not touch the world He had made or do anything to save it from the evil He had allowed. Hence came a stupendous problem, which Deism did its best

not to see; and the easiest way not to see it was to say, and keep on saying, "Everything which exists is according to a good order, and for the best." The "perfect Theist" was defined to be the man who "believed that everything is governed, ordered, or regulated for the best by a designing principle or mind, necessarily good and permanent."[1] This is the optimism of the eighteenth century, and it has two classical representatives—Leibnitz and Pope. It is hardly fair, indeed, to bracket two such men together, for Leibnitz was the most original speculative intellect of his day, an orthodox Protestant, while a rational theist; but Pope was, while a Catholic, a very conventional and derivative deist, who proudly acknowledged that the views unfolded in his rhymed argumentation were borrowed.

(i.) Leibnitz expressed his view, philosophically, in his *Théodicée*,[2] and its formula has passed into general literature—"This is the best of all possible worlds." He emphasized the word "possible." Nature did not exist by necessity; it might or it might not have been, and it was because God had so willed. A better world might be imagined, but no better could have been made. Leibnitz's idea had a positive and a negative basis; the positive was the goodness and wisdom of God. Since He was what He was, He could be satisfied with nothing less than the best attainable. The negative basis may be termed the limitations which thought must set to the Divine power. God could accomplish only the possible, and a moral world without evil was beyond the resources even of Omnipotence. The only perfect being was the Infinite, but the Infinite could not be made; the created must be limited, and where limitation is, there evil, in one form or another, must be. Leibnitz distinguished evil as of three classes—metaphysical, physical, and ethical.[3] (*a*) The metaphysical

---

[1] Shaftesbury, *Characteristics*, vol. ii. pp. 4, 5.
[2] *Essais de Théodicée sur la Bonté de Dieu, la Liberté de l'homme et l'Origine du Mal*, 1710.   [3] *Ibid.* p. 85, § 21.

evil was primary; it was limitation of being, it belonged to everything less than God. Whatever had its being in time, whatever had less than infinite being, suffered from metaphysical evil; i.e. was forbidden by the very terms of its existence to possess within itself the beatitude, the absolute knowledge, the power, experience, and benevolence of the Deity. (β) Physical evil was due to metaphysical; wherever an essentially limited being existed there was not only the capability but the necessity of suffering in some form, either privative, because the limited being was without the beatitude of the divine; or positive, from the operation upon the finite or limited of the infinite multitude of causes that make up the created universe. (γ) Ethical evil was the free and voluntary disobedience of a moral being. The ability to sin, nay, the certainty of sinning, was rooted in the original or metaphysical imperfection of the creature.[1] Where there was limitation of knowledge and experience there could not but be subjection to an outer and regulative or higher Will. But since moral obedience could not be necessitated, moral disobedience was certain; for inexperience could not but be unstable, and where experiment was needed failure might be the surest way to success.

These three kinds of evil so co-existed in the very idea of a moral universe that one could not possibly be framed so as to exclude them. This was obvious to the Divine Intelligence. An infinite multitude of possible worlds lay before the vision of God. Evil was involved in every one which He conceived as possible, but out of all this infinitude of possibilities He selected for realization the best possible. As absolutely good and wise, He could select no other. And this world He selected, not because of its evil, but in spite of its evil, resolved to overrule the evil, which was inseparable from created being, to its greater good and His own greater glory.

[1] *Ibid.* p. 199, § 156.

The only alternatives, therefore, which Leibnitz allowed were not between a more and a less imperfect world, but between the best possible and no world at all. If there was to be no evil, there must be no creation; if God chose to create, He had no choice but to create the metaphysically imperfect, i.e. those capable of suffering and of doing evil. And here he introduced two important modifying ideas : (*a*) Creation was not a completed event, but a continuous process;[1] if God ceased to act, nature and man would cease to be; and He acts freely, ever willing and working the creature's good. And (*β*) this good is progressive; as man improves evil decays, the improvement being the work of God, the deterioration, or delay in realizing the good, the work of man. God is related to the world of actual forces as the stream to the boat which floats upon it. If the progress of the boat is hindered, it is not by the stream, but by obstacles on the banks or in its course. "And God is as little the cause of evil as the current of the river is the cause which retards the movement of the boat."[2] He so guides and controls the world, which His creative action ever renews, that even from its evil we shall yet reap a large harvest of good.

(ii.) Pope's view was expressed in his "Essay on Man," which crudely, though poetically, summarized the deistic optimism that had in Bolingbroke its elegant and prolix exponent. His optimism had its formula in the familiar words—

"Whatever is, is right,"

and it had, in effect, three principles. First, the sovereign will was cosmical rather than ethical; its absolute might made all its deeds and decrees right. Hence he did not so much explain how moral evil came to be as deny that it was.

"If plagues or earthquakes break not heaven's design,
Why then a Borgia or a Cataline?"

The Creator

"Pours fierce ambition in a Cæsar's mind."

[1] *Théodicée*, pp. 375–378, §§ 382–385.   [2] *Ibid.* p. 91, § 30.

And it was as little natural to expect

> "Eternal springs and cloudless skies,
> As men for ever temp'rate, calm, and wise."

He so works out the parallel between nature and man, between physical events and moral characters and acts, that the moral becomes even as the physical; and his right is too much the product of might to be the equivalent of Augustine's "good" or Leibnitz's "best possible." Hence, secondly, he is as unjust to suffering as to sin, and sacrifices without scruple the individual to the universal. The principle that "partial evil is universal good" is construed to mean that the person who suffers ought to be content to bear the evil he suffers from because it serves great universal ends. He should not rebuke nature for enforcing her laws, even though it be at his expense, for only by such enforcement can harmony be secured. And all the evil that disturbed and distressed us was harmony not understood. It was, as it were, the discord in the universal symphony which made its music more majestic and more complete.

> "Respecting man, whatever wrong we call,
> May, must be right, as relative to all."

And, thirdly, there was the principle that evil ought not to be judged simply from this life, but also from man's relation to the future, which had to be invoked if the present was to be comprehended. The balance of our judgment needed, in order to its perfect equilibrium, to have time counter-weighted with eternity. And so we were bidden to

> "Hope humbly, and with trembling pinions soar."

We might not know the future, but hope could make its blessings a present experience.

> "Hope springs eternal in the human breast;
> Man never is, but always to be blessed."

3. We may frankly confess that Pope's optimism seems to us of the shallowest. It was but the smug content of the well-

to-do, praising in polished metres the Providence which had been wise enough to make him comfortable. He rejoices to find his happiness set off by the abounding misery. The God he so often names does not live; He is a mere abstract term adjusted to suit now the premiss, now the conclusion of a rhymed syllogism. What is true of English Deism as a whole, is true of this its most brilliant production: it "was only a particular way of repudiating Christianity. There was as little of God in it as could well be."[1] *Candide* is a satire on optimism; but though it was a piece of insolent impiety, I would rather have Voltaire's attitude to this question than Pope's. For he showed that he could be moved by suffering, and could feel as intensely about the calamities man endured from the forces of nature as about the injustice he experienced at the hands of man. The earthquake of Lisbon stirs him almost as much as the tragedy of Calas, and one respects him the more for the passion he shows, for the indignation with which he rejects the idea that eternal law can justify the massacre of the innocents. Was Lisbon more wicked than London or Paris? Yet

> Lisbonne est abîmée, et l'on danse à Paris.

In this moral fury there was an unconscious Theodicy; if the Sovereign of the universe be moral, it would be infinitely more agreeable to Him than the epigrammatical eulogies of a poet more intent on refining his numbers than touching the heart of things. The optimism which has not gravely faced the immensity and the intensity of the world's misery has no claim to be heard. And Pope's claims are the fewer that he so played with the greatest of human hopes and the deepest of human facts; for if time cannot be justified without eternity, then, as time is all that is known to our experience, the result is a serious impeachment of the divine rectitude. We may be quite unable to judge a complete work until the

[1] Mr. John Morley, *Voltaire*, p. 95.

EVIL AND THE LAW OF EVOLUTION 109

work be completed, yet it is mischievous logic which seeks to make the universe we know a thing incapable of vindication without the help of a universe we do not know. If Butler's plea—that most of the difficulties of faith are due to a system imperfectly understood, were valid, then, it might fairly be argued, so would its converse be, viz., that a system which stood embodied in our own experience could not be justified by a system which was so far beyond it as to have no real being for it. And what could two such opposites do save neutralize each other? Time, therefore, ought to have within itself its own apology and ought not to require to depend for justification on an appeal from itself to eternity.

It may be of more interest to remark that Pope's plea for " partial evil " as " universal good " has almost an equivalent in the speculative physicism of to-day. It is wonderful how our intellectual and moral thought has been so penetrated by the doctrine of the struggle for existence and the survival of the fittest that we almost feel as if it were an eternal law, even though the fittest be so often the strongest rather than the wisest or the best. But in this law of survival there are two sides—one affecting the victor, another affecting the vanquished. It may be an excellent thing to the survivor to survive, but this does not sweeten the lot of the victim who has had to succumb. And the vanquished, as much as the victor, belongs to the whole of life; he is as integral a part of the universe, and has, therefore, such rights as the fact of being may carry with it. And it is the whole of being that needs to be vindicated. It is possible to purchase the continuance of the elect few at too high a price; and it is so purchased when it means the sacrifice of the infinite multitude of the rejected, each unit of which had all the possibilities of happiness or misery, of sensitiveness to suffering and susceptibility to joy which the survivor himself possessed. And if we are to vindicate the law or order of the universe, it must not simply be in the eye and judgment of him who has survived—the fact of his own survival is to him justification enough—but in the eye of him who has been vanquished. It is the sufferer who needs to be consoled. It is not the man who never had a son who needs to be comforted when a mother mourns beside the bier of her dead boy. We cannot, therefore, exclude from consideration the weak who suffer, and only magnify the strong who survive. If there be partial evil, we are not to say that it is made righteous by the existence of universal good, which is the very point in dispute; we must tell those to whom partial evil has been the whole of life what their evil means, why their evil is, and how it stands related to Him who, as the Author of their being, has sent them where they have had to suffer so severely.

4. With what many would regard as pantheistic optimism we do not need to concern ourselves. It has two distinct types—one with a specially ethical temper, represented by Spinoza; another with a more intellectual or logical mind, represented by Hegel. Neither of their systems is indeed properly pantheistic; both may better be described as simply speculative or philosophical theisms. Spinoza held evil to be a thing natural; vice to be something not to be condemned, but to be explained. All that is he conceived as a mode of the infinite Being or Substance, and evil as a necessary element in the infinite modes which, as modifications of the Infinite or God, were inseparable from Him. Evil was necessary because it was privative, imperfection being mere negation of being, therefore proper to every mode in the degree of its remoteness from the whole of being. He thus affirmed that he could not concede sin and evil to be anything positive, still less could anything be or become contrary to the will of God.[1] The optimism of Spinoza was thus due to his inability to recognize vice as voluntary, wrong as optional; all was part of a necessary system, and justified by its necessity. The Hegelian view was formulated in the principle

[1] Ep. xix., *Opera*, ii. p. 66 (Van Vloten et Land).

that the actual was the rational. Find a reason for what is, and what is will be found to be reasonable. Hegel's was the optimism of a universal logic which attempted to represent the whole of time as a dialectical movement, and conceived life under the categories of thought ; and which, therefore, by its constant need of theses and antitheses and syntheses, could find no place for that which ought not to have been. This, of course, is a vague and general statement as to Hegel's position, truer in the abstract than in the concrete. It is hard, nay impossible, in any rational philosophy to find a place or a reason for an irrational thing, which evil essentially is. While no man ever argued more cogently than Hegel to the negative character of evil, no man ever stated more emphatically its incompatibility in the concrete with the moral ideal. Evil, speculatively construed, was "a negative which, though it would fain assert itself, has no real persistence, and is, in fact, only the absolute sham existence of negativity in itself" (*der absolute Schein der Negativatät in sich*).[1] But moral evil could not be otherwise conceived and described than as the incongruity (Unangemessenheit) of what is with what ought to be.[2]

§ III. *Pessimism Ancient and Modern*

1. From Optimism in its several types Pessimism stands distinguished thus : Evil is not an incident capable of an explanation which justifies either God as the Author of existence, or existence as the handiwork of God ; but it is, as it were, the whole of being ; it composes and constitutes the whole picture, occupies the eye and prospect of the soul, which cannot see life save through evil. Pessimism thus makes evil as of the very essence of being, and so conceives the universe that it does not seek the preservation of being by the expulsion of evil, but rather the expulsion of evil by the

[1] *Encyclopädie*, vol. i. p. 73 ; Wallace's *Logic of Hegel*, p. 71.
[2] *Encyclopädie*, vol. iii. p. 364 ; Wallace's *Hegel's Philosophy of Mind*, p. 94.

abolition of existence. This means that it cannot regard the actual as the rational, but as the irrational; or the good as universal and evil as partial, but, on the contrary, evil is universal, and there is no good. It is so far from conceiving this as the best of all possible worlds that it describes it as so bad that no-world would have been better. Pessimism knows no creator whom it can hold responsible for evil, nor any sovereign through whose benevolence or wisdom it can be removed. Hence it is a philosophy which aims not only at explaining how existence happened to arise, but how it may most surely and utterly cease to be.

But perhaps we shall make its real meaning more intelligible if, instead of confining ourselves to the exposition of a single term, we attempt to present it in certain of its historical forms, and in relation to the mood or temper which they express. It is peculiar neither to Western thought nor to our own century. It did not owe its being to Schopenhauer nor its vogue to Von Hartmann; it expresses a temper which is too near the surface, and too ready to express itself in poignant speech to have been so late of birth. It has arisen in different countries and at different times, though always under similar conditions; and it implies the operation of similar causes, general and personal. We find it emerging wherever great wealth, luxury, and refinement co-exist with want, famine, and the savage mood which these beget in civilized men. It belongs to times when the forces that work for evil overpower the individual will, and undertake to command masses of men. And it springs from the feeling, whether in a few or in many minds, which may be described as an attitude either of despondency, or of despair, or the contempt of life. It is not a normal or a healthy feeling. The normal healthy man does not ask, " Is life worth living?" He lives his life, or he may try to live it, worthily, and to fill it with such worth as he himself possesses. It is the man who despairs of life who feels it a burden, doubts whether it be worth his while to go through with it, and concludes that if it be worth the trouble to do so, it is only in order that he may benefit man by helping him to bring his existence to a final and more utter end.

2. Pessimism was not a mood very congenial to the classical mind, especially as it expressed itself in Hellenic philosophy. The nearest approach to it we can find is in Cynicism, but Cynicism was in many respects the converse of Pessimism. It was marked not so much by a contempt for life in the abstract as a contempt for men who did not live worthily. It believed that life was good, and that it became bad only when its accidents were taken for its essence. It believed in a law that bound all men to be virtuous; and it despised those who claimed to be men of worth, yet did not observe or obey the law they claimed to embody. It may be described as a cruder, a more primitive, and, in a sense, a more savage Stoicism. Greek Stoicism and, in an even higher degree, Roman was positive, an attempt to realize the idea of manhood implanted in the nature of man; but Cynicism was negative, a criticism of the lives of men in the light of the ideal. Yet the Cynic was not simply a critic; on the contrary, his criticism rested on a doctrine of human nature as ethical as the Stoic, though he had not worked out as genial a method of perfecting character. In his scorn of those who made the accessories into the essence of life, he tended to dispense with even what was good in these, and to despise refinement as well as the luxuries in which it imagined it seemly to be clothed, in order that the nakedness of the natural man might be the better hidden. He made his protest against the conventional habits which suggested the shameful and stimulated the sordid they were professedly used to conceal, by attempting to live as a barbarian. Thus the element of Pessimism in his thought was due to the clearness with which he saw the evil in existing tendencies, societies, characters, and persons; but so far was he from

identifying the shams which he hated with the whole of being which he loved, that he conceived evil as a contradiction of that law of right and duty or virtue which was the highest of all laws, written in the heart and soul of man for realization in his conduct and in society.

Again, mediæval Asceticism had certain principles and features in common with Pessimism. It thought the world wrong, too unclean to be a fit home for a holy man; therefore a place to be forsaken of him who would save his own soul. The existing order of society was conceived to be evil, and it was thought better that the good man should take himself out of that order than endanger his own soul by remaining within it. On its personal side it was a doctrine of salvation, but on its social side it was a doctrine of annihilation, so far at least as its attitude signified that the world was so bad that the pious man could neither desire its continuance, nor do anything to promote it. It was in this latter aspect that it agreed with Pessimism, for it conceived secular society as so under the power of evil that the happiest thing for it was to pass away and perish. But here the similarity ended, for Asceticism cultivated the hope that One who was more potent than the world might be persuaded, through the penance and self-denial it practized, to save the poor soul of man, and to replace the dissolved secular society by the new and higher spiritual order called the Church.

3. These classical and catholic tendencies are typical of the pessimistic mood which is never very remote from any of us. The first impulse of the man angry at the emptinesses and unrealities of human life, is to rage at it as all vanity and vexation of spirit. And the quick overmastering passion of the man who has just been seized and possessed by belief in the reality of spiritual and eternal things, is to forsake a world which is absorbed in the enjoyment of things temporal, and to retire to a solitude where he may cultivate his fears and watch from a distance sure-footed fate overtake those

who are too blind to see its approach or too sodden to care for it. But common tendencies have many forms besides the ethical and the religious; and some of these the modern pessimistic mood has readily assumed. In the first decades of our century it took an imaginative and emotional or sentimental shape, and had, in the poetry of revolt, extraordinary vogue. Goethe, in his earlier period, passed through it, but he cultivated contempt of life only that he might the more enjoy it. He loved the bitter because it helped to flavour the sweet. With Byron there is more of the genuine pessimistic spirit—the feeling that made him love to think of himself as a kind of martyr, sacrificed by a too conventional society because of his own too conventional vices. He had a vanity that only sang the more that it sat in the cold shadow of criticism, though the song into which it broke was one of vehement satire and vicious denial. He had the sense of being an outcast from his country and his kind.

"With pleasure drugg'd, he almost longed for woe,
And e'en for change of scene would seek the shades below."

But even in him it was a mood, a temper, now petulant, now imaginative, expressing personal feeling rather than reasoned conviction. He had a pessimistic hatred of life, not unmingled, as far as his vanity allowed it, with contempt of himself; and this, of course, was only the obverse of his dislike to the society which would not indulge him with the praise his temper imperiously claimed. How much it was mood and how little it was reasoned belief may be seen from its vivid contrast to the jubilant imaginative idealism of Shelley, who so feels the joy of existence that he carries, as it were, his own skylark singing within his breast, making him feel as if the only true philosophy of life was a kind of divine intermingling of being with love and of love with being. But we must distinguish the imaginative temper, which is strictly personal, from the philosophical, which is intellectual and universal; and Pessimism is not the poetic expression of a mood, but the dialectical explication of an idea which seeks to cover and comprehend the whole of life.

The Pessimism in politics which is known to us as Anarchy or Nihilism is as significant of the close of the nineteenth century as the poetry of revolt was of its opening. Nihilism does not, like Socialism, express the belief that there is an ideal order which not only may be, but which ought to be, realized; on the contrary, it expresses, in the true pessimistic vein, the precisely opposite belief—that the social system is so bad that it had better cease to be, i.e. that society should be resolved into its primitive elements. Socialism may be described as Utopian, i.e. it is a form of ideal Optimism, the belief that though the best of all possible societies has not yet existed, it may be made to exist; and indeed the whole effort of human society and the sole function of legislation is to turn as quickly and as painlessly as may be practicable this possible best into a beneficent reality. But Nihilism springs from the despair of beneficent change, and simply proposes the total abolition of things as they are without any scheme for their amelioration or any suggestion of a better or a worthier order. It is instructive to note the conditions under which Nihilism springs up. It is a native of countries where absolute authority reigns, which are governed by a despotism that will not allow free speech, or the distribution of the literature that may educate and enlighten the mind, or the expression of the opinion that, by telling of social discontent, reveals its causes and shows how it may be changed into contentment. We may take it as a certain law of history and society that where mind feels unable to modify the system under which it lives, it will seek good by the dissolution of the order which dooms it to impotence. The system that has no room for reason, reason can neither respect nor spare. On the other hand, in the political conditions where speech is free, where combination is allowed and where the main factors of amelioration are in the hands of those who feel the hardships of life, the tendency will be to seek help from constructive ideas in social politics. Hence in free countries dissatisfaction with an existing order becomes either, if political, the dream of a broader freedom; or, if economical, the dream of a more ideal society, where the units are to be equal in wealth and in well-being. But Nihilism expresses the awful impotence of the individual in the face of an absolute power; while Socialism implies the competence of those who have power to change the existing system from one that works to the benefit of a class or classes into one that works for the equal benefit of the whole. The significance of Nihilism as Pessimism in politics for our present discussion is that it illustrates the conditions which produce the pessimistic mood, and make inevitable the pessimistic idea. Men may well think that where being cannot be improved, even when it works disastrously, it is better that it should be destroyed than continue to destroy.

§ IV. *Eastern and Western Pessimism*

1. But poetry and politics are here only incidental and illustrative; the theme that concerns us is philosophical Pessimism. It may be described as the sense of evil turned into a theory of being and formulated in a law for the regulation and conduct of life. Speaking in the most general terms, we may say that, both as a mood and as a philosophy, it is more native to the East than to the West. In the East it has had its completest expression not exactly in popular Buddhism, which is too ethical, too eclectic, and too wishful to help where it pities to be properly described as pessimistic; but in philosophical Buddhism, the speculative theory which may have been at the root of the Master's mind and certainly was in the mind of his disciples. It has characteristic analogues in certain types of Hindu philosophy, in the fatalism of Islam, and in at least one of the great sects of China. If this Pessimism is to be understood in its basis

and in its essence, it ought to be studied in and through the conditions which created what we have termed its most perfect expression—the Philosophy of Buddhism.

Let us distinctly conceive the conditions under which the system arose. It stood in a two-fold antithesis to the speculative tendencies it found in India, even though it was a dialectical evolution from them. The philosophy that made it was that of the ascetic communities, or the forest schools, where men cultivated the meditation by which they hoped to escape from the conditions of their mortal being. In these schools there was a kind of aristocracy both of blood and of idea. The scholars sprang from the castes of the twice born, i.e. they were men of Aryan descent; and the ideas on which they meditated had been born of the Aryan mind, and were rooted in its experience and history. They conceived man as an emanation from the great abstract Being whom they had evolved from their old and simple theistic beliefs. This being was not personal and masculine, but abstract and neuter, a Substance or Essence rather than a God. They called him now Brahma, now Atman or Paramatman, Soul or Supreme Soul, now the One or the That, which breathed breathless,[1] within whom had somehow arisen a sort of dim desire to realize himself, whence had come creation and all the souls of men. These souls were like so many atoms singly and collectively imperishable, each capable of conversion, but incapable of destruction; all issued from Brahma, all were destined to absorption in Brahma; but from the moment of origin to the moment of absorption—points infinitely remote from each other—there ceaselessly revolved the wheel of existence, and they with it. And this wheel, to which all being was bound and with which all moved, carried the individualized soul, or the separated atom, round and round in cycles and epicycles of incalculable change till the supreme moment arrived when he could escape from it back into the

---

[1] *Rig Veda*, bk. x. 129.

undifferentiated and undistributed Brahma. In one age he might be born a man, in another a wild beast ravening in the forest; in his human cycle he might move downward from king to beggar, or upward from low-born fool and sinner to high-born sage and saint, or he might fall from the seraphic to the demoniac state; in one existence he might live like a god, in another he might be humiliated to the lowest ranks of the brute creation. But rest, the end he was bound ever to seek and to crave, was of all things the hardest to attain; and here the cruel and inexorable partiality of the conditions which regulated these changes appeared. They were made to depend on acts done in states of existence prior to the one in which the man for the time found himself—states of which he had no recollection, and acts whose consequences he bore, but whose performance lay outside his consciousness. These acts were the thongs which bound him to the wheel of existence as it ceaselessly revolved, now lifting him to the summit, now plunging him to the depths, but never allowing him to escape from the life which was destiny. The theory was, therefore, not simply metaphysical or philosophical, but also intensely practical because applied, in the most ghastly way, to character and conduct. It had been worked into a social order, sanctioned by a religious system, guarded by ceremonies and sacerdotal sanctions of the most ubiquitous and imperious kind. The misuse of ritual, offences against caste, neglect of observances belonging to the ceremonial of religion, violation of the customs, order, or organization of society, might have effects on souls living here that could not be exhausted by ages of downward, upward, or dubious change. And this social system was administered by men who were neighbours, but could not be relations; men who as priests held the approaches to God, and in right of their divine descent regulated human affairs with a higher authority than belonged to kings. And as Buddha stood face to face with this system of eternal change, conditioned in its operation, in its good or ill, by external acts, he said: "What is life on these terms? Can it be called a good? Is it not rather a misery? And can there be any benevolence in continuing an existence which must be either in idea or experience miserable? The existence which possesses such eternal possibilities of sorrow, nay, such dreadful temporal certainties, cannot be good; its very essence is evil; instability marks it; birth introduces to a world of suffering; death is departure to a world of greater suffering, if not in actual experience at least in possible event. And where the possibilities of evil are in number and in duration so nearly infinite, can existence be other than an agony to him who contemplates it with a serious and sober eye?"

Existence, then, seemed to Buddha to be in its very essence sorrow; sorrow for misery that either had been, or was being, or was to be, endured, whether by ourselves or by others or by all combined, the whole creation which groaned and travailed in pain together. Now sorrow is not good, but where it is inseparable from being the only possible escape from sorrow is escape from existence. But how can we escape it? Buddha's answer sprang out of the philosophy which he had learned in the ascetic communities, but its conclusion, the negation in which it ended, was due to the negation from which he started, the denial of Brahma and of the soul with which he was identified. With the Hindu schools, Buddha said: "If we live to-day, it is because we have in some past existence accumulated the merit that calls for reward, or the demerit that cries for punishment. Merit is only a less evil than demerit, for it maintains in being, and by means of this continuance perpetuates the eternal possibility of some downward change through some act of conscious or unconscious sin." And then he added: "in order to escape from being we must escape equally from merit and demerit; but to do this we cannot live among men, where we must do the things which entitle to penalty or reward. We must retire from the world and cultivate the suppression of the very desire to live, the surrender of the capability to act, the quenching of the thirst that by goading us into action binds by merit or demerit to the wheel of life. When we have ceased to desire, we shall cease to will, cease to act, to acquire, or to lose merit. The law that maintains being and enforces change will then cease to operate, and released from the ever revolving wheel, we shall attain Nirvana and return no more."

Buddha's theory was pessimistic, for it conceived being as sorrow, and the discipline he enforced was a method for the cessation of personal existence; but it was a pessimism which could be so justified and construed as to be translated into its contrary. On the principles which he assumed, and under the conditions in which he lived, it may almost be termed an Optimism. For if personal being is an endless cycle of change, now upward, now downward, conditioned on acts seldom ethical and still more seldom evitable, then certainly the noblest conception we can form of it is that it is bad, and the most benevolent thing we can propose to do with it is to abolish it. If to be is to suffer, if to continue in being is to be confronted with the eternal possibility of ever darker and deeper suffering, then being is a thing better ended than mended. Buddhism measured by the purpose of Buddha, and the principles which were the assumed basis of all his thought and of the thinking of all India in his day, is only formally pessimistic, in spirit and design it is an Optimism.

2. If now we turn from India and Buddha to Europe and Western Pessimism, we shall see what material differences lie within their formal agreements.

Pessimism first received conscious philosophical expression in the West at the hands of Schopenhauer, who was born in 1788 and died in 1860. I have no intention to enter into any details of biographical criticism, though no philosophy owes more to its author's peculiar psychology or more faithfully reflects the collision of the forces which now lifted him to heaven and now cast him into the dust. His life was rather mean and sordid than noble, the life of a man who never knew how to live in harmony and peace either with himself or with men, who quarrelled, spitefully, now with his mother, now with his sister, now with his publisher, now with his landlady, now with the obscurest and least reputable of the neighbours about him, and quarrelled ever in the meanest and most implacable way. It is too undignified a life to be alluded to further than to say that in judging a system we must ever remember its author's personal equation, reckon with his character, his intellectual and ethical qualities. He had moods when he reverently studied "Plato the divine and the marvellous Kant," and moods when his hatred of Hegel broke into virulent and scurrilous speech. He had a temper that now gloried in depicting "the utter despicability" of mankind in general and great men in particular, and now so pitied man that he could not admire the beauty of nature for thinking of the human suffering hidden within it.

Now, though this peculiar temper and mood may not explain his philosophical principles, yet they help to explain the use to which he turned them, the spirit he breathed into them, and the form they assumed in his hands. So far as his system owes its being to external causes it was the result of two tendencies—one specifically German, the other distinctively Oriental. The German tendency supplied his thought with its philosophic groundwork, but the Oriental, though it came from an East ill understood, gave the impulse that built into a system of Pessimism the principles he had inherited. He had philosophical antecedents in Kant and in Fichte; but the impetus which determined the direction he took was given, though mediately, by Buddha. His thought stood rooted not so much in the transcendental as in the practical dialectic of Kant; or rather, to be more accurate, the transcendental dialectic gave him his critical idea, but the practical suggested, if it did not already contain, his positive doctrine.

He learned from Kant's speculative system to affirm the subjectivity and limitations of knowledge; to argue that the realities of science and vulgar experience are only appearances, mere ideas of the mind, and that if we are to find reality we must seek it in man rather than in nature. And in the search for reality Kant was again his guide, though it was the Kant that Fichte had made known rather than the Kant of Schelling and Hegel. Fichte started from the ethical philosophy, especially the idea of the categorical imperative and the freedom that was necessary to it. In his hands the Ego became the creative idea; it not only organized and constituted, but it made the world. The categorical imperative and the Will that obeyed it represented the ultimate reality, the law that fulfilled itself in the Ego, and became through its acts and by its means the divine force in history and religion, the true moral order of the universe. And it is significant, as indicating an unsuspected unity in the two main sources of Schopenhauer's system, that Fichte's idea of moral order as deity had a curious kinship with Buddha's *karma*, which represented the inexorable concatenation of act and result, merit and reward, demerit and penalty. Will thus, as the Ego in action, became the chief factor of life, its qualities, and the order within which it was lived; in other words, it was the Providence that governed the lives of men. Schopenhauer took this idea, and made Will the supreme reality and the cause of existence; by it being was realized. The idea is the object which exists for a subject, things as perceived, but the force which objectifies is the Will, which may be described as causation interpreted in the terms of psychology or volition rather than of physics or energy. It is more a motived than a mechanical force; it is one and universal, lies outside time and space, yet is ever objectifying itself in the things that arise therein. As individuated in man, it is noumenal, and is inseparable from the person, distributed through the whole organism, acts in it and through it; the organism is the incorporated Will. It is therefore because of this Will that we live, and willing is living; we create life by willing to live. This function of the Will, while it grew out of Kant as interpreted by Fichte, was the correlative of Buddha's *Upadana*, or the grasping at existence, which is the cause of continued being. The Will, which was the essence of the Ego, became thus the symbol of the universal cause; it was the root alike of individual and of universal life. It was because of the Will to be that we had personal being; this Will was indeed unconscious, it acted with purpose, for it willed to live, but without design. It held a sort of reason in it, for all will is reasonable, and so could not be conceived or represented as force, which is mechanical but not rational. This universal Will to live, as everywhere distributed, was a passion for being, a struggle to live, a yearning towards realization; but this passion was blind, save in so far as its end was being, and the maintenance of being. Schopenhauer agreed with Spinoza in conceiving thought as essential to the ultimate Being, though the thought which was to Spinoza an attribute of his infinite Substance was to Schopenhauer involved in his rational Will; but he differed from Spinoza in recognizing a sort of teleology. Spinoza's thought was conceived in the terms of mechanics, Schopenhauer's in the terms of transcendental metaphysic; and so he could never accept the coarse materialism which seemed its only alternative. He said, "I am a metaphysician, though I do not believe in metaphysics," and he turned scornfully from men who argued as if organization could explain thought. That he said was the philosophy of the barber's man and the apothecary's apprentice; it was not the philosophy of reason which conceived that since thought as Will explained organization, it was incapable of explanation by it. Will, as he conceived it, was therefore a kind of reasonable though unconscious struggle towards being and towards its continuance.

But the existence which the Will struggled to realize was misery; it was sorrow. He said that if creation as we know it, life as we possess or undergo it, were the work of a conscious creator, then he was the greatest of all wrong-doers. He must have been an ill-advised god, who could make no better sport than to change himself into so lean and hungry a world. Consciousness, therefore, he denied to the creator; the existence that was misery could not have been designed, or its designer would have been guilty of an unpardonable crime. He did not say, imitating the phrase but reversing the sense of Leibnitz, "This is the worst of all possible worlds"; but he said, "This world is so bad that no world would have been better; it is something that had better never have been." What then was to be done with it? Since it could not be mended, it ought to be ended; since the only way of escape from sorrow was by escaping from existence, then the best thing to do was to make this escape. And so he preached a doctrine of resignation or abdication of will, praised the action by which man gave "the lie to his phenomenal existence," and suppressed "the Will to live, the kernel and inner nature of that world which is recognized as full of misery," and which excites in us when we really know it a feeling of "horror." Men were, by the suppression of the personal, to suppress the universal Will. Since all being was due to Will and the world was as we willed, it was by extinction of the Will that extinction of being was to be attained. "Voluntary and complete chastity is the first step in asceticism or the denial of the Will to live."[1]

In this exposition of Schopenhauer we have found in how remarkable a degree he repeated or echoed Buddha; but it would be a mistake to conclude that their systems were either identical or parallel. While they may have agreed in certain metaphysical principles, in ethical spirit and intention

---

[1] *Die Welt als Wille und Vorstellung*, § 68, p. 449. English Translation, vol. i. 491.

they differed absolutely. Where men are so utterly unlike their thoughts cannot be the same. The heart of Buddha's Pessimism was pity; he loved man, and because of his love of man he hated the existence that was sorrow. The heart of Schopenhauer's pessimism was more contemptuous than pitiful; his scorn was not so much for life as for the men who lived it. There was nothing so alien to Buddha as Cynicism, nothing more native to Schopenhauer. The Hindu was moved by compassion for his kind, he wished to strike the fetters from off the enslaved soul; but behind the thought of the German was a colossal vanity. And when vanity measures the worth of men, its judgments tend to be as falsely low for others as they are fabulously high for self. Then Buddha was a rare and beautiful personality—tender, the ideal of all that was attractive and gracious to his people, who did not so much believe in his pessimistic Nihilism as in his ethical transcendence and the beneficence of his will. It was as the ideal of human grace, the realization of human loveliness that he was followed. But no process of idealization could have made the character of Schopenhauer admirable; and as a beautiful mythology could not gather round him, as worship of himself could not redeem his system from its native hopelessness, so his Pessimism remains an unadorned abstraction, appealing to the intellect without any fascination for the heart. Buddha, by his personal transcendence, raised his system into a religion; but Schopenhauer's personal qualities made it necessary to divorce the man from his thought, which became therefore a matter for rational criticism rather than imaginative appreciation.

But perhaps this contrast would convey a false idea if we did not add that Schopenhauer was not without disciples. He indeed lived long an unbefriended man, for he was a man hard to befriend, and ceaseless warfare against things that commonly awaken enthusiasm may be due even more to the unamiable than to the heroic in character, and the unamiable is never an attractive man. But in his later years disciples began to gather round him; and though his system never obtained, like the old transcendentalism, the sovereignty of the academic chair, yet he secured from men who loved to apply philosophy to life recognition and even acceptance.

Von Hartmann is the best known of his disciples, and he has attempted at once to qualify and to develop his master's system. He has attempted so to unite the idea of intelligence with that of unconscious Will as to be a speculative theist, who speaks of the "Unconscious" when he really means the "Over-conscious." He is penetrated, as his master was not, with the idea of evolution, though he has criticised its Darwinian and scientific forms in very drastic terms; and he has endeavoured to apply it at once to history and religion. In his historical theory he has made mankind the victim of successive illusions; as one illusion vanishes another comes, leaving the process of final disillusionment, as its supreme problem, to the philosophy which, by preaching the vanity of human expectations, hopes to promote the beatitude of the future. The first illusion, belonging to the childhood of the race, was the dream of happiness in the life that is, which was soon discovered to be a vain illusion. It was followed by the dream of happiness in a life to come. That, too, has proved empty; and in its place there came the dream of happiness for the race in another age, in a great future for humanity. That too has proved an illusion; and now man, disillusioned or in process of disillusionment, has before him the problem of how to bring this march of misery consoled by illusion to its final close, when misery will end with the ending of existence.

3. Now Pessimism has certainly various elements of worth. It takes a serious view of the evils of life, and that is a matter on which too serious a view is hardly possible. There is something admirable in moral passion against suffering, and in no respect do we more feel the superficiality of a

thinker like Strauss than in his smart but unworthy retort: "Von Hartmann says that this world is so bad that none would have been better; Von Hartmann's philosophy is part of the world; and as such it is so bad that it would have been better if it had never been." We feel the question to be too grave to be so lightly handled and so cavalierly dismissed. We recognize, too, that Schopenhauer was not simply indulging his own cynical mood, nor imitating in the West the temper and the speculations of the distant East, but representing a deep underlying tendency of the time. Our idea of the necessity of things, our belief in physical law and order, and the inexorable connexion between cause and effect, has seriously affected our view of life and of evil. It is an instructive as well as a most serious and significant fact, that the more a merely mechanical notion of nature and of man prevails, the less hopeful and the less cheerful becomes the outlook upon life. The individual is lost in the universal, and in losing freedom he loses the power to contend against circumstances, and becomes the mere victim of chance. If the miseries that happen to us must be, and if we too must be, then they and we are equally integral and equally necessitated parts of being; amelioration is impossible to us, change is impossible to them, and what remains but hate for what we can neither avoid nor change? If in the midst of this necessity man is conceived as only the highest organism in the universal struggle for existence, then there is added a peculiar element of pathos to the situation; for in a nature where only the strongest survive it means that the feeble have no function save that of perishing, and that the system under which we live reserves all its mercies for strength and cunning. The system where the individual is nothing and the whole is all in all, is the system of all others most provocative in the individual, especially when he is at once conscious of feebleness, and ambitious of pre-eminence and strength, of the most pessimistic theory. In other words,

Pessimism is of the nature of a philosophical protest against the idea that an unethical force can be the sovereign and ultimate arbiter of ethical existence, personal and social. And in making this protest it speaks for the common reason and heart, which cannot bear to be the tools or the playthings of an unheeding mechanical energy. But where Pessimism errs is, on the one hand, in making its appeal to an unconscious will, and in assuming, on the other hand, that the creative Will has done its last and best with existence. For the fact that evil exists, so far from lessening, really augments the need of an ethical Will in the universe to contend against it and in behalf of good, and for the rescue of life from the dominion of sorrow or suffering. Let us grant that evil is, and then let us subtract from man his faith in God, and what have we gained—or rather, what have we lost? We have lost, first, a thing that is above all others needed for the amelioration of life, to wit, hope. Hope cannot live if the individual feels that he stands possessed of a being that is misery, helpless, in the face of a mechanical order, to which he is no more than an atom or an aggregate of atoms, or in the face of an unconscious creator, to whom he is less than nothing and vanity. We have lost, secondly, the faith through which hope lives, for it would be void of energy and inspiration were it without the belief that man is part of a system which incorporates a mighty moral Will, able by its inexhaustible power of initiative to work towards the higher moral ends. When he stands in such a system, he feels that he can help to create the conditions of amelioration, and take part in the struggle needed to secure the expulsion of evil from the realm it would fain rule. And, thirdly, we have lost love as a motive to service, and have gotten in exchange the emotion of pity, which is more beautiful as a feeling than strong as a helper. And pity, when it takes counsel of despair, ceases to be beautiful and becomes either indignation against the doer of the wrong it cannot redress, or scorn of him, or it grows cynical in the face of suffering or it turns sentimental, shedding tears that both emasculate itself and exasperate the patient. Pessimism may spring from pity, but it does not produce philanthropy or benevolence ; and in what respect does a will that is not goodwill differ for the better from a mechanical energy or a physical force ?

But Pessimism is not simply ethically unsuited to the temper and mood of the time, its notion of being is unsatisfactory to the common reason. Existence is not an evil, though evil exists. Life is not simply something which is capable of being enjoyed, but something capable of being improved, and the greatest of all pleasures is to work for its improvement. It is all the more to be valued that it is not perfect, only capable of perfection. The normal attitude of man to life has something infinitely more healthy in it and truer to the truth of things than the attitude of the man who identifies negative evil with positive good. To speak of non-existence as better than existence, or to speak of the world as so bad that it had better never have been, is to say what no man of healthy mind can be got in the heart of him or in his higher and better moments to believe. Let us try to give the notion concrete form, and, in contrast with our sunlit, star-filled space, to imagine an infinite void,—though the very attempt to imagine it will prove its impossibility, for non-entity can only be conceived by being translated into some form of being. Still let us think we can do it, and attempt to make the bold essay to represent in our fancy nothing but vacant space where now circle the worlds that shine to each other as stars—nothing but darkness, no sunlight to make the day, no starlight to break or beautify the night; nothing but death where now there is life ; no glad, swift-darting fish in the waters of river or sea ; no river or sea for them to be glad in ; no green earth for flocks to feed on or flocks for the green earth ; no fragrant and lovely flowers,

EVIL NOT THE ALL OF EXISTENCE

no laden bees to hum, no lark that, like a blithe spirit, soars as it sings,—

> "In the golden lightning of the sunken sun,
> O'er which clouds are brightening,
> Thou dost float and run
> Like an unbodied joy whose race is just begun";

no man to think great thoughts, to do battle for the true and right; no woman to love, to grow strong and happy by loving; no race to weave the wreath that crowns it with beauty out of the pale lilies of death and the warm red roses of life; nothing but utter, absolute vacancy, a dismal, dark, dumb infinite, where now lives and moves and abides a vivid and vocal and reasonable universe, peopled by minds that look before and after, and read in things visible the mysteries and the presence of the Eternal God. And then, when we have fairly envisaged the two alternatives, let us try to compare them,—if, indeed, a glorious reality be comparable with an irrational impossibility,—and let us ask soberly, whether the negation of being can stand in thought alongside the idea of a world which is radiant in its very shadow, and, in spite of all its evil, is good, because capable of being made ever better? What the answer would be does not lie open to doubt: the normal man loves being by the compulsion of his rational nature, and not simply by the force of an irrational Will; and it is not his own existence that he loves,—did it stand alone he would hate it,—but he loves being as a whole, for as a whole it lives in him, and in the whole he lives.

CHAPTER IV

THE QUESTION AS AFFECTED BY THE PROBLEM OF EVIL

B. SOME SUGGESTIONS TOWARDS A SOLUTION

THE criticisms in which the previous chapter concluded only emphasize the philosophical difficulties that beset Pessimism; they do not answer the intellectual and ethical difficulties that create it. The belief in God is an excellent thing when we face evil as something to be vanquished; but when we face evil as something to be explained, the belief is itself surrounded with serious difficulties. If evil is such as, if not to justify Pessimism, yet so far to explain it as to compel us to say that it is not without reason and ought therefore to be heard,—then we must farther admit that the higher our conception of God, the holier, the more benevolent, we conceive Him to be, the greater and the graver become the difficulties concerned with the creation and government of the world. In a word, we are faced with the venerable problem—How has it happened that, under the rule of an infinitely good, powerful, righteous Being, evil has come into existence and still continues to exist? This is a question that our criticism of Pessimism but compels us the more seriously to consider and to discuss.

§ I. *The Limits and Terms of the Discussion*

1. Let us begin then our attempt at suggesting some factors towards the solution of this problem by frankly expressing the idea which gives it all its gravity: although it be granted

THE RESPONSIBILITY OF GOD 133

that man is responsible for the introduction of moral evil (and we here recognize the fact that many would refuse to grant so much), yet we must conceive the Creator as responsible for the system under which it was introduced, which made it possible, which allowed it to become actual, and which now follows it with moral penalties and physical sufferings. We ought not to shrink from affirming what we have called the responsibility of God; we do not think, if we may reverently so speak, that He Himself would deny it; certainly it is an idea that lies at the root of the New Testament, and especially of its doctrines touching redemption and grace. It may, indeed, be argued that responsibility implies a higher authority, a judge to whom we must give an account, and whose award is final; but this is a juridical rather than an ethical view of the matter. The tribunal in moral responsibility is personal and real, but in legal responsibility it is judicial and formal. The sovereign is as responsible to the citizens for good order in the state as the citizens are responsible to the judge for obedience to the law. The father may be said to be morally responsible to his family, while he is legally responsible to the common law for its maintenance and education; but the two responsibilities are neither identical nor coincident, the moral being higher, subtler, more comprehensive, and imperious than the legal, asking qualities of character, forethought, prudence, forbearance and courtesy, which the law is powerless to demand. And we may, with all humility, speak in somewhat similar language of God. The older theology, with its emphasis on God's indignation and horror at sin, needs to be supplemented by a thought which affirms His responsibility for the sinner. The guilt of man does not by itself justify God, for the order under which it happened He instituted, and the system under which it continues He upholds. Hence the vindication of God must come from some other principle than His hatred of the evil which theologians define as the violation of the divine law.

2. We recognize, then, that we are here concerned with a problem which gravely affects our belief in the goodness, the wisdom, and the justice of God; and that it were better to deny His existence altogether than to believe Him to be less than infinitely perfect. We acknowledge, too, that the beauty of nature, which has been so much emphasized and so often appealed to by both classical and Christian theists, is, for many reasons, here an irrelevant consideration; for it represents only one side of nature, and that the least obvious and the least helpful of the sides, which she turns to the vast multitudes of our race. Our concern, then, is with evil, which is the sad and tragic fact that looks out at us from man everywhere and refuses to be ignored. It may be said to be of two kinds—evil that may be suffered, and evil that may be done. The evil that may be suffered it is usual to term physical; the evil that may be done, moral; and though it is impossible in actual experience to disjoin them, yet it will be better that they be considered apart. They belong, indeed, to entirely distinct categories: physical evil is incidental, occasional or relative, and may be termed negative or privative; but moral evil is positive, and may be termed actual or real. The phrase "physical evil" is not indeed used as the equivalent of "bodily suffering." Were it, the usage would raise an even vaster question than the one we are attempting to discuss, viz., the ethics of creation as regards the whole animal kingdom, where the animal suffers as well as the man, and disease and death reign, and the strong prey upon the weak, and ferocity gluts itself with the blood of the feeble and inoffensive. The principles that underlie and guide our discussion may apply even to this question, but the application is not to be directly made. Our question concerns man, for in him the physical shades into the moral problem, and physical evil means all the sufferings he may have to endure, whether bodily or mental, nervous or sympathetic, alike as a distinct individual and a social unit, alike as a natural being,

fleshly and mortal, and as a human being, sharing in the special history of a people and in the collective fortunes and immortality of the race.

Taken in this large sense, then, physical evil may be endured or suffered either by an innocent or by a guilty person, and its being and function may be in both cases, though for different reasons, equally natural and necessary. To acquire experience can never be a wholly agreeable or painless process; if it were, the experience would have no educative or expansive value. If happiness consisted in being set in a perennial stream of agreeable feelings, it would soon become the most wearisome of states; for into a state of mere enjoyment there would soon come nauseous monotony, which would be fatal to ultimate pleasure. We have need here to clear our minds of cant, and to recognize frankly that even heaven cannot be the mere synonym of the agreeable, and ought not to be conceived as if it were. If men in beatitude are to know discipline, they must put forth effort; and if there is to be effort, there must be strain; and if there is to be strain, there must be emulation; and if there is to be emulation, there must be the divine rivalry which finds pleasure in excelling and in the endeavour to excel. The man who has thought deeply has also doubted severely, and doubted not merely whether there be a God, but whether there be any moral good, or any worth in any being. The state of doubt may have meant to him misery or even despair, but it was the necessary and strictly natural though transitional condition of a man realizing at once the limits, the resources, and the possibilities of his own intellectual and moral being. It may be described as an evil, just as partial knowledge is an evil as compared with omniscience; but it is more excellent than its complete negation would be; for a higher beatitude of thought is realized through it than could be realized without it. What may thus be called the pain or suffering intrinsic in a created intellect feeling its way towards the Uncreated Light, may stand as an example of evils involved in the very terms of created and therefore limited being, but so involved as to be the condition of higher good. We may not, then, think of all physical evil as either calamitous or even mischievous in character and action; whether it is either or neither will depend upon its reason or cause, upon its seat and tendency: nor till it be viewed in relation to moral evil can we really judge whether it be positive or negative in its nature, a real or a privative thing, the suffering that simply makes sorrow or the sense of want that is the condition of all activity and attainment.

It will therefore be convenient, for the purposes of our discussion, that we should deal with the two classes of evil as distinct, yet as essentially related.

A. Physical Evil: its Kinds and Functions

We may divide physical evils into three classes: 1, those that arise from man's relation to nature, and nature's to man: 2, those that are native to his own being: 3, those inflicted upon him by men, whether ancestors or contemporaries.

§ II. *Man in the Hands of Nature*

1. The evils that arise from the inter-relations of man and nature are an innumerable multitude, and fall into a variety of classes. (*a*) There are those wholly due to the destructive or terrific forces of Nature herself. They may be represented by the storm, the hurricane, and the earthquake. These indeed are forces that work appalling disasters; and we may not forget that a single calamity like the earthquake at Lisbon raised more painful doubts as to the wisdom and the goodness of God than all the speculative and anti-Christian criticism of the eighteenth century.

(β) There is the class of evils which Nature works by failure to respond to the labour and the skill of man. These may be represented by the famine, whether caused by the drought which has allowed the seed to die in the ground, or by the flood that has rotted the roots of the grain or of the fruit which man has been patiently waiting for, or by the locust, the caterpillar, and the cankerworm, which devour what he had painfully been rearing for food.

(γ) The third class may be represented by the disaster which Nature brings upon man through the destruction of the works he has invented, in order that he might turn her forces to his own service. Here is the storm which brings shipwreck, the tempest that lays waste his cities, the lightning that smites his proudest buildings into ruin.

(δ) We may find a fourth class in the evils that spring from man's neglect of Nature, and the revenge which she takes for the neglect. Here we have the pestilence and disease in its hundred forms of slow or swift death.

2. But it is hopeless to attempt to classify the infinite forms of the suffering which Nature inflicts upon man, though what has been sketched is enough to show that Nature seldom acts alone; and before we burden her with the blame we ought to attempt to discover how far Nature or how far man is the more responsible factor of the evil. The two, indeed, are so curiously intermingled that we may say, the evils accomplished by Nature alone are but few; those wrought by Nature and man in conjunction form a multitude which no man can number; while those caused by man's own ignorance or neglect of natural forces constitute an infinite, a never-ending series. But if we cannot exhaustively classify physical evils, and trace them to their causes in Nature alone or in man alone, or in the two combined, we may say certain things concerning their functions.

i. The natural forces that now and then work so disastrously for man are among his most beneficent educators; he has to study them that he may master them, and the more he studies their secret the greater the mastery he attains. It is marvellous what limits he has set to the destructive power of Nature; and in setting these limits he has learned the most beneficent of all lessons—that he conquers by obedience, and commands by obeying. Nature and her forces must be known if they are to be controlled or turned into servants. It is a moral lesson, though it comes in a physical form. Man acquires the wonderful art of reaching his end by following a way that is not his own, but a larger and better way than his. The educative force of Nature exceeds our capacity to acquire. We have all learned of her in total unconsciousness more than we have learned consciously from all other teachers. We have imitated her methods, and we have calculated her forces. At her bidding the farmer has learned how to till and sow and reap; the fisherman how to ply his craft upon the great waters; the mechanic how to generate force and how to build the engine to use the force he has generated. The navigator has learned from stars and sun how to steer his ship, and has compelled the currents that run through the earth so to point the hands of his compass as to indicate the way in which he should go upon the sea. Study of Nature has thus educated man, and out of her school he has issued wiser than he could have come from the hands of an earth-mother who had nothing to teach him of obedience and self-control.

ii. But the suffering which Nature can inflict on man has helped to educate him even more in humanity than in the arts. She has, so to speak, by her very inhumanity, made man humane. The awful use which he himself can make of her destructive forces for his own ends, is putting a bit and a bridle upon his more brutal powers, his lust for blood, his love of battle and conquest. But still more has it taught him to see that the men who suffer at Nature's hands, are men he is bound to help. The shipwreck calls for the lifeboat, and the hardy men who stand safe on shore can brave the terror of the storm in pity for those who are threatened by the devouring sea; the famine that sends gaunt death into the homes of one people touches another with pity, and helps to create among those who are alien in blood and speech the feeling of kinship, the gracious and kindly sense of brotherhood. In the darker ages pestilence was dreadful, for it roused, by the fear of contagion and the horror of death, the fiercest passions that can burn in the breast of man; but the more men have penetrated into the secrets of Nature, the more have they learned their community of interests, and the more have they been moved by a feeling which has turned into the passion to fight disease, even though they themselves might enjoy immunity from it. Nature has indeed been here a great educator in human pity and helpfulness; the very suffering she has inflicted has disciplined man in mercy. The time was when natural calamities divided men; the time is now when calamities evoke the sympathy that hastens to help; and the time will be when the sympathy, anticipating the calamity, will restrict its reign, reduce its proportions, and, by the amelioration of Nature and the lot of man, tend if not to eliminate famine and pestilence from his life, yet to lessen all their attendant miseries and fears, and to educe at the same time those higher humanities which had otherwise remained latent within him.

iii. And so man, in the presence of the forces that seem in Nature to dominate his life, is learning to organize it on a higher level and after a humaner sort. They who have learned most of the secrets of Nature, especially as to how to keep her wholesome, to make her healthy and to turn her into a kindly minister to man, feel themselves compelled to impart the secrets they have learned to less forward or less favoured peoples. It is a curious but instructive law of human progress that we learn by the evil we inflict not only to cease from inflicting it, but also that we are in humanity akin with those we may have wronged. The people who enslaved the negro learned through the penal consequences that followed to themselves from their own act the humanity of the men they had enslaved. We slowly discover that the secrets of Nature are not the property of the men who discover them, but of the whole race. Since we are all children of the one mother and suckled at the one broad bosom, we come to feel that the mysteries of the motherhood of the earth are not for those who think themselves the elder-born or the favoured sons, but for the whole brood, the collective human family. Our common dependence upon Nature becomes a bond of unity between all the sections of mankind; the life we live is one, though its forms and modes are as multitudinous as the units of the race.

iv. But experience slowly teaches us that by far the larger proportion of the suffering that man endures at the hands of Nature is not due to Nature at all, but to man. It is the result of neglect, of improvidence, of carelessness; it is due to the ten thousand causes which turn things preventible and innocent into things inevitable and injurious. Nature exists for man, not man for Nature; but if she exists for him, it is to teach him to transcend her, to make him ever more of a man, raising each generation above its predecessor. To do this she must awaken the energy and forethought that are in him, compel him to study that he may know, to imitate that he may prevail. And for this reason Nature, in order that she may be beneficent, must be inexorable in her laws. The greatest calamity that could happen to men would be the grant of supernatural aid whenever they had by negligence or ignorance, or any act of wilfulness, involved themselves in straits. The very miracle that was worked to stay Nature in a destructive course, or calm her in a tempestuous mood, would arrest the progress and the amelioration of mankind; for by teaching man to depend upon external help it would take from him the desire to improve, to trust his own intelligence, to obey the law of his own conscience and reason, and to amend by effort his own life and the lives of men. If the stormy sea had been subdued whenever it threatened to engulf him, or if the hurricane, when it promised to overwhelm him, had been softened into the zephyr that blows gentle and sweet upon the violet, or if the lightning had been arrested in its swift and lurid course as it approached the orbit within which he moved,—we might never have had any dreadful tales of shipwreck or other disasters of the deep; but still more surely we should never have had the marvellous engineering and the brave enterprize which have built the big ships, bidden them traverse the mighty ocean, and turn its once dividing waters into the crowded highway of the nations across which they carry their wealth to the exchanges that enrich and federate mankind. We all know that there is nothing so fatal to the manhood of a people as the charity that pauperizes. Were we so to relieve the improvident as to make him as well off as the provident, so to protect the thoughtless from his thoughtlessness that he would suffer as little as the thoughtful, so to fill the squanderer's hand, whenever he had emptied it, that he would know less of want than the industrious and the careful—would not the result be to set the highest possible premium on the shiftless and retrogressive qualities of men? And so, were men, whenever they provoked Nature, or challenged her to use her forces to destroy them, to be saved from the consequences of their own folly; were they, whenever they invited calamity, to be miraculously lifted out of it, they would,—in the very degree of the frequency and efficiency with which the supernatural power interfered on their behalf,—have their manhood injured. Nature must be faithful to herself if she is to do her best for man. In her severity lies the education which is the last thing that man could afford to lose.

§ III. *Evils peculiar to Man*

1. But there is a second class of evils—those native to man's own being—which are also an infinite multitude in

themselves, while dismal and distressing in their causes, consequences, and incidents. They imply man's community with Nature, his participation in the ebb and in the flow of her life. There is disease, hunger, thirst, the struggle to live in the face of a hard and ruthless order; there is birth in pain, there is life in toil, there is death in agony or despair. Indeed, the whole of the evil native to us may be summed up in that one word, mortality. Here is man, a conscious being, able in imagination to retrace the ages behind him, to look into the issues of the life around him, to forecast the future when there shall be for him no earth, no sea, no sky; here he is a creature able to think of the eternal God while conscious that he himself is only mortal, and has had measured out to him only his pitiful threescore years and ten. Is it not a shameful and a painful thing to be doomed to so brief a life, which must be lived under conditions so narrow, to be like a steed fit for the chariot of the sun, yet forced to bear the dreary drudgery of dragging behind him the tumbril of death? This is a hard matter to explain; it comes so near our own experience, it appeals so urgently to heart and imagination as well as to reason; for the awful cruelty of death lies in its not only ending one's own life, but in so often making desolate innocent and helpless lives that would otherwise be happy. If it were one's own loss only, it would be possible to die like a Stoic without a murmur and without a tear. It is the desolation of the living that is so painful to thought, turning death into the sum of all our miseries. But when all has been thought and said, why should death seem an evil? Birth is not, and surely death is but the complement and counterpart of birth. The one is because the other is; it is because the grave is never full that the cradle is never empty. Then how without death could man realize the meaning of life? How feel the immensity, the possibilities, the god-like qualities, the capability of endless gain or loss contained within the terms of his own being? The picture of man before and after he knew death in the "Legend of Jubal" is as true to experience as to imagination. In the old, soft, sweet days before men knew death, when all that was known of it was the single black spot in the memory of Cain, his descendants lived in gladsome idlesse; they played, they sang, they loved, they danced, in a life that had no gravity and no greatness; but when the second death came, and men saw that there had come to one of their own race a sleep from which there was no awaking, a new meaning stole into life. The horizon which limited it defined it, and made it great. Time took a new value; affection, by growing more serious, became nobler; men thought of themselves more worthily and of their deeds more truly when they saw that a night came when no man could work. Friends and families lived in a tenderer light when the sun was known to shine but for a season; earth became lovelier when they thought the place which knew them now would soon know them no more. The limit set to time drove their thoughts out towards eternity. The idea of the death, which was to claim them, bade them live in earnest, made them feel that there was something greater than play; for death had breathed into life the spirit out of which all tragic and all heroic things come.

Death has thus added to the pomp and the fruitfulness, to the glory and the grandeur of life. Without it we should have had no struggle of will against destiny, of the thought which wanders through eternity and beats itself into strength and hope against the bars and the barriers of time; without it man would have had no sense of his kinship with the Infinite, for the finite would have been enough for him. And if a soul made for eternity were to be withered by time, would not that, in another and darker sense than attends the end of our mortal being, be the death of all that is worthiest to live? And has not time, by her successive generations, been enriched, enlarged, made varied and wealthy as she never could have been by a race of immortal Adams, unchanged and deathless? It is a poor and a pitiful dream to imagine that it were a happier than a mortal state were man to know no death, but to endure in characterless innocency, untouched by the shadow feared of man, never feeling the light within made resplendent by the darkness death shed without. Instead of a single generation we have a multitude of successive generations, each fuller of humanity than the one which went before. Instead of one individual we have an endless series of mortal persons on the way to immortality, each a miniature deity, each in time yet destined for eternity, each with inexhaustible potentialities within him, each realizing himself under the conditions which a measured existence affords, and all contributing to make the wondrous and varied life which we call the history of man. Who will venture to say that the dream of an innocent Eden, a single paradise of immortals, is comparable to this majestic procession of mortals moving as to the music of a celestial dead march through time towards immortality?

2. As to the desolation that comes to those who lose, who would dare to make light of it? Yet must we not recognize that even this is not without a beneficence of its own? The thought of possible loss touches with tenderness all the relations of life. It explains the watchfulness of the mother, the ungrudging labour of the father, the solicitous care of the wife, the affection and forethought of the husband. Those who love the living feel life to be all the sweeter and dearer because it is so transitory. And if death brings loss, does it not mean that before creatures could be lost, they had to be possessed? Here, let us say, is a young man full of promise. He had been a bright and happy boy, the pride of his mother's heart, the light of his father's eye; he had been an earnest student, the joy of his tutors, the hope of his school and his college, raising high expectations even in the withered breast of his professor. He had

been the centre of a brilliant circle of friends, who talked with him, walked with him, disputed and argued with him concerning high things, ever stimulated by his brilliant thought and vivid speech. And he comes to the threshold of life, with school and university behind him, high hopes and fair visions before him, and noble purposes looking out from his radiant face. And just then a fatal disease claims him as its own, and he dies, while men whose hearts are dry as summer dust linger on in what they call life. Discipline had been gained, weapons mastered, and skill acquired; time and opportunity alone were needed for him to achieve great things. But death denied him what he needed and what all men desired him to have. And was not the act ruthless, and can it be counted anything else than evil? Was not a good life lost? and could the loss be anything but a sore grief to some, an injury to many and a calamity to all? But even here there is another side to be looked at: he had not lived in vain; his life had been a large good. For more than twenty years he had made a home richer than without him it could ever have been. In school and college he had made ideals realizable that apart from him would never have been dreamed of, and by doing this did he not enhance in the men he touched the value of life? And did not his death compel them to feel that they must live his life as well as their own? He who writes these things once knew a man who was to him companion, friend, and more than brother. They lived, they thought, they argued together; together they walked on the hillside and by the sea shore; they had listened to the wind as it soughed through the trees, and to the multitudinous laughter of the waves as they broke upon the beach: together they had watched the purple light which floated radiant above the heather, and together they had descended into the slums of a great city, where no light was nor any fragrance, and had faced the worst depravity of our kind. Each kept hope alive in the other and stimulated him to high endeavour and better purpose; but though the same week saw the two friends settled in chosen fields of labour, the one settled only to be called home, the other to remain and work his tale of toil until his longer day be done. But the one who died seemed to leave his spirit behind in the breast of the man who survived; and he has lived ever since, and lives still, feeling as if the soul within him belonged to the man who died. And may we not say, this experience is common and interprets the experience of the race? Death has to be viewed not as a matter of a single person, but of collective man; and it works out the good of collective man by doing no injustice to the individual, but rather using him to fulfil the highest function it is granted to mortal men to perform. So let us say that however men may conceive death, it belongs to those sufferings by which mankind learns obedience, and is made perfect.

§ IV. *Evils Man suffers from Men*

1. The third class of physical evils are the sufferings that are inflicted on man by men. These are indeed infinitely vaster, darker and more terrible than the sufferings inflicted on him by Nature. The sufferings caused by want of heart, by want of thought, by ambition, by greed, by passion, by pride and vanity, by neglect and presumption, by all the lusts that ravin and devour, are in number, in kind, in intention, and in effect, the transcendent sufferings of the world. And while they may be physical in form they are almost uniformly ethical in source, and also in their consequences. It were vain to attempt to classify evils so infinitely varied in character and in quality, but their types may be determined according to their more common sources. (1) **There** are evils that spring from the constitution of the race, the law of descent and inheritance

(2) Evils that come through the very affections that create the home and the family, which includes the problems raised by the nature and relations of the sexes. (3) Evils that spring from the social constitution and civil relations of man, or man as organized into communities and classes, into nations and states. (4) Evils that spring from economical or industrial causes, from man as a being that must work in order that he may live. (5) Evils that come from international rivalries, the jealousies, conflicts, and collisions now of uncivilized tribes, and now of colossal civilized powers.

With only certain of these evils, those which, as involved in the very constitution of the race, raise grave questions as to the power and wisdom of the Creator, are we here specially concerned, though we may later have to deal in more detail with others. The law of heredity is a serious problem for any one who regards Nature as moral in source and in purpose. How has it happened that a wise and beneficent Creator so constituted the race as to place in the hands of individuals enormous powers which they are, from the very necessity of the case, totally unfit to exercise? How is it that He has wedded together the purest affection with the basest passion, and made it possible for man to feel and act like a brute to one who feels and acts like an angel? And how is it that He has so formed the highest of all His creatures that this brutish person may not only sacrifice to his lusts the chastity of the living but also destroy the virtue, the happiness, and the health of the unborn? Does it not argue some signal ethical incapacity or moral indifference in the Creator first to create natures in which the angel and the devil so intermix, and then to endow them, even when they are most demoniac, with such power to control the plastic and productive forces of life?

2. Now, while we ought to distinguish in this problem the elements which concern man from those which concern

Providence, yet it is necessary to see how intimately and inextricably they are interrelated. So far as man is a factor of evil, especially in those functions which involve the good of posterity, it is evident that we judge him not as if he were a mere natural being, but as one who stands in a higher order, who has duties he ought to fulfil, and duties which may forbid him to indulge his natural instincts. That the constitution of the man is what it is, and that man has sexual and sensual passions which impel towards licentious living, is not allowed, then, to extenuate the evil he may do. On the contrary, he is held bound to obey a law which would turn Nature's way in his hands into an instrument of immense good; and, if he neglects it, he is charged with guilt odious in the degree that he has made Nature the partner and servant of his offence. Now this means that we conceive Nature to be good in herself, evil only when she falls into evil hands, and is made a minister of sin; that her Author designed her, as appears from the higher law under which man lives, to serve moral ends by being in the service of moral beings. But we cannot so think without being forced to go much farther. Nothing has contributed more to the moral education of the race than its physical constitution; through it the feeling of responsibility and obligation in the individual to the whole has been evoked and defined. The sense of the harm man could do to man has possessed the individual conscience with fear, and has armed the social conscience with all its sanctions and almost all its terrors. The knowledge of the power for mischief incarnated in a reckless man, has made society surround him with restraints; and the appeal of the silent unborn generations to the latent fatherhood in man, has induced him to bind himself about with the obligations that help to make and to keep him moral. Growth in civilization may be measured by the limitations progressively laid upon man's power to harm man, just as growth in religion is marked by his increased will to help. Law is meant for the lawless and disobedient, and in it we may see expressed man's feeling that the order of the race is rooted in justice and that its life ought to be regulated by duty. And could we conceive what Nature would be in the hands of a wholly moralized mankind? The constitution which now works in a way so mixed of good and evil, would then work wholly for good. The law which now transmits so much misery and disease and vice from parent to child, would then bequeath virtue and truth. The inheritance of the race would be a cumulative good; it would represent the stores of health and sanity, wisdom and knowledge, acquired in one generation and transmitted to its successor in order that they might be made into a worthier and richer heritage for those who were to follow after. We are not to judge what is as if it were the ideal and the eternal. It is neither, but it has been designed for both; and though evil may use for its own ends what was designed for good, yet good will reclaim its own and reign the more securely that reason has learned through experience that Nature is holy and just.

In this discussion we have tried to deal with the question as it affects the system under which we live here and now; yet at no moment have we thought of man as if this life were the whole of him. If it is a poor philosophy which calls in the rewards and penalties of another life to redress the wrongs caused by the unequal distribution of pleasure and pain in this, yet no argument which attempts to justify the ways of God to men can afford to forget the full measure and duration of God's relations to man. Time and Eternity are one; he who is and he who is to be are one and the same person; and his life, its meaning, purpose, discipline, can never be understood if he be regarded as a mere mortal being, with no existence save what begins with birth and ends at death. The scale on which an immortal being is planned is not commensurate with any measure of mortality; and what to a mortal might well seem unmitigated evil may appear to the immortal only a discipline the better qualifying him for his immortality. We might well imagine that were his mortal life to be his whole and sole existence, then it ought to be like a sweet pastoral melody; but an immortal life is so vast that the prelude to it may fitly reach the proportions of a mighty epic, or be distinguished by the tragic situations that beseem an immense drama.

B. Moral Evil: its Nature, Origin, and Continuance

In the course of this discussion it has become evident that the two classes of evil so shade into each other that it is impossible to draw a clear boundary line between them, and say, "On this side moral evil lies, and on that side physical." As a matter of fact they are inextricably interwoven. Sin determines an infinite number and variety of the forms which suffering assumes, whether as regards action, quality, character, tendency, or function. Yet, vague as it is, in the last analysis the distinction holds; physical evil is the evil men suffer, moral evil is the evil they do. The one falls under the categories of choice and action, the other under those of result and consequences. And this means that moral evil is due to the act of the personal will, but physical is conditioned by the operation of fixed laws, or an established order. The moment the will has chosen, the fixed law begins to operate; and so, though the act may be transient, the consequences are permanent. In its essence the act creative of moral evil is, to use a juridical phrase, "a violation of law"; to speak with the Stoics, it is a refusal to "live according to nature"; to employ the language of Butler, it is the failure to recognize "the authority of conscience," or in that of Kant, it is to decline to obey "the categorical imperative." In these cases "law," "nature," "conscience," "categorical imperative," are but impersonal names for the ethical sovereignty of God; and the denial of this sovereignty means the alienation in will and character of man from his Maker. It is this denial and consequent alienation that creates and constitutes moral evil in its two ultimate forms, act and character, or choice and habit, or will and nature.

On account then of the origin and essential quality of moral evil as the revolt of the personal will against the sovereignty under which it was constituted to live, we cannot describe it as disciplinary; but only as absolute and unrelieved evil. It is bad as seen in the individual; it mars the god-like beauty which is native to the soul; it steals away the charm which made it seem to the eye of its Maker very good; it isolates it from the source of life; it removes it from the breast of the Almighty who breathed it into being. It grows by what it feeds on, for in sinning there is no cure of sin, there is only increase of the evil. But if it be bad in the individual, it is worse when incorporated in families and turned into a sort of inheritance; and worst of all when it possesses and dominates the collective race. And so far from dying as civilization advances, it grows subtler the more civilized the race becomes. The man who is naked and unashamed is not depraved by his nakedness; it is the knowledge that he ought to be clothed which begets shame, and it is shame that begets depravity. Unconscious sin does not brutalize, it is conscious sin which corrupts the nature and wastes the whole man. And what is growth in civilization but increase of the knowledge that makes us conscious of sin? And so our modern city is depraved in a sense that no primitive community ever was. There is more hope of the conversion of the unclothed savage than of the clothed and skilled and inured wrong-doer of our East-end dens or of our West-end clubs. Hence out of both our personal and our collective experience comes the problem—How is it that the Creator has allowed all the fair promise and all the divine potentiality of man to be falsified by the rise of sin and the cumulative wickedness of all the generations of men?

There are, then, two main questions to be discussed, one as to the origin or introduction of moral evil, the other as to its continuance and consequent diffusion.

§ V. *Moral Evil and God*

As to the origin or introduction of moral evil it may be argued:—" Man has indeed done evil, and may, in a sense, be described as its author, but this does not exonerate God. For man could not have sinned unless he had been made capable of sinning. Why was he so made? And having been so made, why was he not so watched and superintended as to make this evil deed of his impossible? To say that he did it is but to saddle him with the secondary responsibility; the primary responsibility is the Creator's, who so made man that he could do this thing, and so neglected and forsook him at the critical moment as to leave him no choice but to follow his inclinations and hasten to do it." The answer to this argument will compel us to enter a more speculative region than any we have as yet attempted to penetrate. For the question, why God permitted moral evil, or rather, why He made man capable of doing it, requires, before it can become either intelligible or soluble, the exposition and analysis of certain underlying and regulative ideas. These relate, chiefly, to our modes of conceiving the Deity and the creation in themselves and in their mutual relations.

1. Well, then, it is not possible to think of the Creator under the categories of an abstract Absolute or an isolated Perfection. We must, if we think of Him in relation to the universe, bring Him more or less under the conditions of a

related being, one to whom space and time are not abstract forms of thought, but modes of activity and terms of real existence. For Deity as Creator is not a mere Abstraction, an unconditioned Absolute; but He acts and He produces, and to act is to be conditioned, and to produce is to be related. Now conditions, as they affect action, are of two kinds, external and internal.

i. External conditions are such as these—impossibilities must exist to God as well as to men; possible things Omnipotence may achieve, impossible things not even Omnipotence can accomplish. To be Almighty is not to be able to perform what is, in the nature of the case, incapable of performance; and this inability does not in any respect limit the might, it only helps to define its province. These inabilities or impossibilities may be said to be of three kinds: physical, intellectual and moral. The moral inability may be stated in the familiar phrase: " It is impossible for God to lie." The intellectual may be represented either under the category of thought: It is impossible for God to conceive the false as if it were the true; or under the category of knowledge: It is impossible for God to know things that are not as if they were real things. The physical impossibility may be expressed in various forms: It is not open even to God to make a part equal to the whole; to make the same thing both be and not be; to make a circle at once a circle and a square, or to make a square out of two straight lines. Or, to express the same inability in a different form, we may say: God could not make another God infinite like Himself, for two infinities could not co-exist; nor could He create a being who should start as if he had a long experience behind him or an acquired character within him. He could only make a being capable of gaining experience and realizing character. The power of making monstrosities is not divine, and God, even where most god-like, will be conditioned by the very terms of the work He seeks to do. As the most rational and the most moral of beings, all His acts will be reasonable and all His ends moral.

ii. But the internal conditions are even more determinative of the scope, the quality, and the purpose of the Divine action than the external. Omnipotence is not the synonym of God; if He is perfect, He must not be conceived simply under the category of an Almighty Will. If He be conceived simply as substance, or as a mere *Ens Infinitum*, then we may, with Spinoza, reduce His attributes to two—extension, which denotes His behaviour in space, and thought, which describes His action in time; or if we conceive Him, with Schopenhauer, purely as unconscious Will, then we may express His activity in terms which have no more rational value or moral significance than matter, motion, and force. But if we conceive God as a Subject, i.e. as a conscious centre of thought and volition, then, in the very degree that we think of Him as infinite, we must interpret His attributes and action under the categories of moral reason and ethical will. And this means that in our conception of God the qualities of will and potency are secondary and determined, the qualities of goodness and truth are primary and determinative. The Deity is not divine to us because He is almighty,—for an omnipotent devil could never be the god of any moral being; but because we conceive Him as the impersonated ideal of the Absolute Good. And this signifies that we regard the external attributes, i.e. those which are physical and pertain to the maintenance of physical relations and the exercise of physical energies, as less divine than those that denote ethical qualities, and the exercise of spiritual and intellectual power. Wisdom is more and greater than omniscience; righteousness is more and higher than omnipresence; love is vaster and diviner than omnipotence. Now we can only conceive an absolutely Perfect Being as one whose whole nature is harmonious in all its actions and activities; for might without love were mere violence; presence without righteousness were only energy; omniscience without wisdom were but intellectual perception,—the reflection of things in a mirror which had the quality of being conscious of the things it reflected. But if we so conceive the Divine Perfection, then all the physical attributes will be under the control of the ethical, and must be conceived as only means, while the others denote sovereign motives and ends. Power may forbear to do many things possible to it as power, because they would be alien to love; and the forbearance would not argue defective but effective will, not imperfect but perfect might, because exercised in obedience to qualities and for ends higher than any which could belong to it simply as power.

Now, the moral of the argument is this: if we conceive God as thus conditioned in His action, we shall not ask of His might what would be alien to His love, nor of His presence what would be opposed to His righteousness, nor of His knowledge what would be contrary to His wisdom. In other words, we shall think of God, not under the category of energy, but as a Being of such absolute perfection that He governs all His attributes and is governed by none.

2. But corresponding to the conditions which affect the action of the Creator, are those which define the character and status of the creature.

i. Leibnitz's notion of metaphysical evil expresses the most obvious of truisms. No created being can possess the attributes or the beatitude of the Creator, or have His outlook on life. To begin to be, is to be possessed of being without the experience needed for its control; and no measure of seclusion, as in some imagined paradise, or supersession of responsibility for personal conduct, could ever teach the man how to rule himself. To be a new created being is to be nothing more than a potentiality; and it is as such, a being compounded of infinite capabilities, that man is of transcendent worth for his Creator, and of incalculable value to His moral system. The primitive state of innocence represents the inexperience of the man just arrived on the scene. He is not good, he is not evil; he is simply in a negative or privative state; what he is to be must wait on his earliest experiments in living.

ii. What is less obvious than the necessity of metaphysical evil, but is more important for the question at issue, is the relation of the Divine Perfections to the character, quality, and rank of the created being. We can only conceive God as moved to create by ends determined by His own nature; for as His character is in an infinite degree nobler and more generous than the aggregated nobility and generosity of the created universe, it follows that the only ends capable of satisfying Him must, in order to be worthy of Him, be found in Himself. If, then, He is moved to create by an end that may be described, on the divine side, as His own glory, its correlate will be, of course, on the created side, the creature's good. And this will be, alike as regards intensity and extension, a more pre-eminent good than could have been conceived or attempted had the good been accommodated and proportioned to the creature's deserts. But the good-will of the Creator, while in itself a will of absolute good, must be, in action, conditioned by two things, (a) the capacity, and (β) the capability of the Created.

(a) Now, the only capacity capable of moral good must itself be moral; love in the strict sense can only be where love has been or may be reciprocated. Things may be admired or praised, and they may even excite wonder, but they cannot evoke love. The very admiration they awaken is not for themselves, but for their author. Art means creation, a mind and hand behind the thing admired; and it is the mind in the thing we praise, not merely the thing in itself. But the only kind of creature that could satisfy a Being of absolute goodness would be a creature capable of the highest form of good, the being loved by the Best, and

GOD SEES HIMSELF IN MAN 157

therefore able to love the Best in return. Now, these distinctions will help us to determine what qualities will make the creature acceptable to a moral Creator. It would be the unworthiest of all possible conceptions to imagine God as a mere infinite Mechanic or Artist creating a system simply for Himself to admire, a marvellous mechanism, cunningly contrived like the watch of our familiar apologetic; or like the engine strongly built and well stored with fuel imagined by the deists; or a picture skilfully painted and proportioned which should show the most wonderful blending of colours; or an oratorio which should exhibit the most unexpected and sublime mingling of harmonies. In our serious and thoughtful moods we confess to ourselves that a God who passed His eternities only in the contemplation of His own workmanship would not seem to us worthy of the only worship fit for the Deity. If this be true, it signifies that Creation, to be agreeable to Him, must be of creatures like Him; spirit as He is Spirit, intellect as He is Intelligence, love as He is Love.

(β) But this involves the second and correlative quality in the creature—capability, freedom, the power to give or to withhold, to welcome or to cast out, to obey or to refuse obedience. The capacity for God is not mere physical space, but moral capability; and moral capability has two attributes—freedom or spontaneity, and educability or the faculty of continuous amelioration. When the freedom is ordered, moral growth will follow; where the will obeys, there the nature attains progressive enlargement, which can only mean that the more capability widens moral capacity, the more pleasure God will have in the creature, in the increased room made to receive the gifts which He loves to pour into the soul that craves His presence. Moral freedom, therefore, must belong to the only creature capable of being regarded with complacency by the Creator. If we could conceive a universe of automata, or of reasons purely mechanical, which would be as if nature had become the storehouse for an infinite multitude of logical machines, what would they be but a universe of mere contrivances, the diversions of a curious mechanic, no creatures of a moral Creator? If, further, we were to imagine a universe of such automata equally responsive to impact from some moving body without and to logical processes started from within, but absolutely without power to vary either the logical formulæ or the direction in which the external impact would drive them; and were we then to ask, whether they would be able to satisfy the soul of their Maker, what could the answer be but this? Were He only an architect, a skilled builder, or a cunning maker of watches, which once adjusted and wound up could go on for ages, He might be satisfied with a universe of this sort; but if He were so easily satisfied, then the very depth of His satisfaction would be the measure of His imperfection, for it would argue Him void of those moral qualities which we conceive most essential to goodness.

We may say, therefore, that the external and internal conditions which qualify the divine actions, and the attributes that determine the divine character, must have something correspondent in the capability, the quality, and the status of the creature; i.e. the more morally perfect we conceive God to be, the more must we conceive Him incapable of satisfaction from any save moral creatures. And they are creatures who must make their own experience, form their own characters, govern their own conduct,—in a sense, determine their own destiny. If God were, on some critical occasion, by direct action or interference, to supersede the choice of the will or the tendency of the heart, then He would, in the same degree, undo His own creation, annihilate or abolish its moral and responsible being. We come, therefore, to the conclusion that the only creation worthy of a personal God is a universe of persons; and persons born as potentialities who can be educated by experience, awakened to reason, won to love, and persuaded to obedience.

§ VI. *The Permission of Moral Evil and the Deity*

1. Now it is evident, from the principles which have issued from this discussion, that the more we conceive the Creator through His moral attributes, the less can we reduce Him, by means of physical and logical categories, to a mere abstraction; and as we think of Him at the beginning we must think of Him throughout. The immutability of God is a fixed and fundamental principle; but immutability does not mean immobility. God is in nature, character, and purpose unchangeable; but in attitude and modes of action He is as varied as the infinite needs of changeful man. For He could not be invariable in mind and end unless He were variable in the use and application of His energies. Hence the act and fact of sin, while they could have caused no change in the principles which determine His choices and ends, may yet have effected a distinct change in the things He chose to do or in His mode of doing them. This means that the laws of thought and being which had conditioned the action of the Creator, did not cease to condition Him when providence followed upon creation, and man was apostate instead of obedient. But the significance and bearing of the principle thus stated will become more apparent in the attempt to deal with the question which has so long waited for an answer:—How can the permission of the evil that has so depraved man be reconciled with the being and character of an infinitely good and powerful God?

Now, it may be well to note here that "permission" is not a very happy word, and may imply consent to the doing of an action, though not moral approbation of the action itself. But under no form can it be allowed that God consented to the introduction of evil. We conceive that He used every means short of recalling His own creation to prevent it. Let us change the term "permission" for the terms "non-prevention of the evil," so as to indicate that there was no moral consent, only abstention from the use of physical force or restraint. But even as thus changed, the question does not raise the precise issue, which may be more positively and explicitly stated thus—Is the exercise of obedience or the cultivation and practice of righteousness compatible with an order which the infinitely good and holy and powerful God has instituted? The reply would be instant and emphatic:— "Nothing is more certain than this compatibility; His order must exist expressly for the purpose of promoting obedience, holiness, happiness." But now let us honestly ask, Could there be obedience where disobedience was impossible? or could there be righteousness if wickedness could not be done? The person that could not disobey would be quite incapable of obeying. If there was no power to do evil, there would be no ability to do good. Where the will has no alternatives, its choices can have neither merit nor demerit; where only one path lies before the traveller, error may be impossible, but so is discovery; where there is no vice to allure, there is no virtue to be won. The very notion of a moral nature under a moral law involves, therefore, an order that can be broken. Where there is no law that can be violated, there may be necessity, there may be a conversion of forces, or a phenomenal sequence of events, but nothing which can be termed law. We use a metaphor when we speak of the law of gravitation; for it knows neither precept nor sanction, but only describes a mode in which things are observed to behave. Where no transgression can be, there is no law, and it is impossible to predicate obedience or disobedience of a planet, a river, or a stone. But the very essence of the law which rules man is that it can be obeyed or disobeyed; both obedience and disobedience must be possible, or both impossible. Hence if a universe is to be created where moral good shall be, it must also be a universe where moral evil may exist. The essential quality of moral law is repeated in the essential character of the moral being.

If such a being were necessitated, he could be neither moral nor under moral law; he could be neither holy nor wicked, but he would remain simply as he was made—without character and without will.

If, then, it was good to have moral beings under moral law, evil must be possible. Even God could not, however much He might will it, cause it to be otherwise. Things that cannot be conceived or related in thought are in the region of realities impossible things; and so as His reason and ours are akin, the things ours will not think His cannot achieve. It is, therefore, no more derogatory to the majesty of God to say that He could not create a moral being without the power of choice than to say that He could not make another infinite, or cause a being who began to be at a definite moment to have all the experience of one who had been from eternity. If, then, a moral must be a free creature, with the faculty and opportunity of choice, a new question arises : Was it good that God should make moral beings? That question has been by anticipation answered. If it was good for God to create those who could share His own beatitude, He could do so only on the condition that He made them capable of rejecting that for which they were designed. And who will say that he would apply another law to the universe and its Author than he would apply to himself? There is no man with an honourable manhood within him who is not enlarged and ennobled by both the idea and the fact of fatherhood; but every man who wills to become a father faces the problem which God faced when He made the universe. In the home and in the family the father is disciplined by the child as much as the child is disciplined by the father, but to the father belongs the responsibility for the child's being; and on him lie duties of self-restraint, of providence, of the daily concern to make all things that happen bear upon the formation of the higher moral qualities in his child. May we not say, then, that what justifies the responsibilities man dares to undertake when he becomes a parent, justifies God in making a universe which shall be the home of reason, vocal with the harmonies of love and the dissonances of life? And we may be certain that the evil we now feel is to us more darkly real, and more nearly coincident, if not indeed identical, with the realm of being than it is to Him who sees the end from the beginning and each fraction in its relation to the whole.

2. But at this point a question we have long foreseen and anticipated may be asked :—Could not God, when man's will inclined to evil, have intervened and changed its inclination or even prevented its choice? But intervention would have been destruction. A will suspended in its choice were a will destroyed. It would only be a masked form of annihilation for God to give a will and then to withdraw it, leaving the man standing before his alternative choices a will-less automaton. Only on the supposition that God were double-minded, and so unstable in all His ways, would it be possible to believe that, having first created man as a being capable of acquiring experience, He, in fear of his acquiring it as a man rather than as a god, went back on Himself, uncreated His own creature, and refused to leave him to act and to learn by action as He had meant him to do. But, it may be urged, the change or intervention could have come at an earlier point. When the vision of God ranged through all the infinite multitudes of possible worlds, He must have foreseen what would happen in the ideal He actually selected for realization. And when He foresaw evil, could He not have arrested His purpose, or have stayed His creative hand? But who then would have been victor?— God who turned aside from His purpose because of possible evil, or the possible evil that caused God to turn aside? The scheme that involved no difficulty were not worth realizing; the Creator who because of difficulties abandoned His plan could surely not be reckoned as either courageous

or wise. The anthropomorphic language dismays and even revolts me, but, in the absence of a more perfect medium, it must be used in the question which concludes this section :— Was it not better that Deity, instead of turning aside because of evil, should go on, create the existence where evil was to be, and then deal directly with the evil when it had become?

§ VII. *Why Evil has been Allowed to Continue*

1. The question which has just been put brings us to the next stage in our discussion : the continuance of evil. And here we begin by simply formulating the principle : it is impossible to conceive the good and holy God as ever conceding to evil the right to be ; for by its very idea it is a denial of His sovereignty and a challenge of His claim to be the First and the Last and the All in all. And this principle enables us to place physical and moral evil in their true reciprocal relations as integral parts of a single system, elements in what we may call the method of the divine government. For though the two evils are different in fact and distinct in thought, yet unless physical evil have a moral reason and function, it can have no justifiable existence in a moral universe. While, then, we conceive moral evil as man's act, we conceive physical evil, so far as it has its roots in the nature of man and springs out of the organic relations or social and historical constitution of the race, as belonging to the consequences which the order established of the Creator has caused to follow upon the act. I do not like to use juridical terms of God and His relations to man, but there are occasions when they are the only terms that can be used. If, then, such terms may be used here, we might say that Law is implied in the ideas of both moral and physical evil, but in the two cases Law is used with a totally different both extension and connotation : in the one case, it is Law as preceptive and prohibitive which is broken in respect of what it enjoins or forbids ; in the other case, it is Law with its

retributory sanctions, enforced and punitive, that is active. The precept may be wholly moral, but the sanction, whether held to be penal, disciplinary, incidental, or vindicative, must be largely physical. Law as it forbids man to steal, or to bear false witness, or to commit murder, is a precept enjoined by the lawgiver, perceived by the reason, and fulfilled or broken by the man's own choice; but law as it punishes the man who has stolen, or borne false witness, or committed murder, is a sanction enforced by a power which need not depend on the approval of the man's reason or the consent of his will. Now, this means that the law which appears to us twofold,—as moral, a precept we can obey, a command we can resist, and, as physical, a penalty or a consequence we must suffer, may appear as a unity, i.e. as a law wholly moral, to the Creator, who must see and read our complex life in its context, with the physical penetrating the moral, the moral affecting the physical, both reciprocally active and inter-dependent. Hence the distinction that is so obvious to us may have no being for God. Where the moral attributes are sovereign the view of the universe will be imperatively moral; and so what we regard as physical suffering may seem to Him, who sees the whole as a whole, altogether ethical in function and in value. This variety of aspect is not unknown even to ourselves; our laws, whether civil or criminal, are many-sided, and the face they turn to different sections of the community is never quite the same. The legislature will see the law which it makes as a whole or a unity, though probably the emphasis in its mind will lie on the end to which the law is a means; the judge who has to administer the law will read it with the emphasis thrown on the sanction by which order has to be vindicated and justice maintained; the lawbreaker who has to suffer at its hands sees in it a penal instrument, and feels it as a physical force; while the body of the citizens feel only that they may dwell serenely and securely under its protection. So we who suffer may distinguish our physical pains from our moral deserts, while He who made the physical for the moral may steadily see the means through the end and in it, both alike moral and alike good.

But this principle involves another, which is its correlative or counterpart. For what is true of the law must also be true of those who are under it, i.e. while its subjects are to us single persons they may appear to the Creator as a unity, co-ordinated as a collective mind, or incorporated in the organism of nature and the race. In other words, man is to God a whole, a colossal individual, whose days are centuries, whose organs are races, whose being as corporate endures immortal amid the immortality of its constituent units; and this unity has at once an ethical and a physical character. Hence there must be a divine judgment of the race as a race, as well as of the individual man as an individual; and the severer the judgment on the race the more leniently will the individual be judged. For while the race may cause suffering, it is the individual alone who can suffer; and the measure in which his sufferings are just can be determined only after the responsibility has been equitably proportioned between himself and the race. It was this idea which in the older theology made the doctrine of original sin so cognate to the doctrine of grace, while here it shows the need of a standard too absolute to allow justice to be lost in pity or pity to be sacrificed to justice. For evil is by its very nature personal, but law is by its nature universal, and it is through the universal that the personal must be judged. And this limits and defines both the responsibility of the individual and the province or function of law. On the one hand, he stands at once above and within nature and the race, above them as a distinct person, within them as an inseparable unit and integral part, giving to both, receiving from both, and amenable to the law according to the measure or the merit of his giving and getting. On the other hand, his mind or will may choose to do evil, or augment the evil he has suffered from nature and the race. And it is here where the law enters, as ideal or preceptive to determine his merit, as disciplinary or vindicative to apportion the penal consequences which will best suit his case and express his deserts. And as the choice is the act of the man as a whole, so the consequences must affect the whole of him, natural or corporeal as well as spiritual.

2. On grounds and for reasons such as these we argue, then, that, however moral and physical evil or moral and physical law may appear to us, they stand organically related in the mind of Him who made and who governs nature and man. And it is this organic connexion of the two laws and the two evils (which, it ought to be observed, is a very different thing from their identity) that makes it possible to vindicate both the justice and the goodness of God in the face of continued moral evil and universal physical suffering. Were there no suffering, moral evil would live a sort of unchallenged and authorized life; were suffering an end in itself, it would imply the ferocity of him who either allowed it to be, or himself inflicted it. Were it even only penal, it would signify his injustice, his failure to discriminate between sinners not simply by causing all to suffer, but by often dealing more severely with the innocent than with the guilty. While, then, the connexion is positive, it may be termed disciplinary or educative rather than punitive or retributory; i.e. the purpose of physical evil is not so much to uphold law or vindicate justice as to change and instruct man and form character. The older apologetic used to argue from the existence of suffering that this was a state of probation. Both the idea and the phrase were borrowed from Deism, and were alien to Christian theology. To it this was not a state of probation, but a fallen state, within which redeeming grace was active. God was conceived not as trying men, but as seeking to save them; and this idea represented a higher

and more generous belief. Physical evil may be coincident with moral, the sign of a fallen state; but it signifies that the state is not final, that the man is recoverable, that ameliorative forces work around him and within him, detaching him from evil, attracting him to good, showing him in the mirror now of his heart, now of his imagination, now of his social or domestic experience, the miseries that follow from a lustful will, what calamities lurk in want of thought, how ages of poisoned existence may flow from the brief indulgence of vicious selfishness. The most remarkable thing in suffering is not its extent or duration, its intensity or immensity, but its educative, regenerative, and propulsive force, its power to make man conscious of his enormous responsibilities and to awaken in him the desire to fulfil them. So conceived, physical evil may be described as a divine energy for moralizing man and nature. This is, if not its main function, yet its chief result. It has been the motive of all our beneficences, though their source has been the heavenly Grace.

But the argument which has defined the action and the function of physical evil has vindicated the goodness of God in maintaining the conditions which allow moral evil still to continue to be. It continues to exist not as a rightful or permanent inhabitant of the universe, but as one whose very right to be is denied, and for whose expulsion all the energies of nature have been marshalled and trained to fight. And this is, as we conceive the matter, the only conduct which would have become the Deity; certainly we could not conceive the annihilation of the creature to be seemly to His majesty, or withdrawal from all care or concern for him to be congenial to His grace. On the contrary, if we may so express ourselves, evil was the mute but potent appeal of the creation to the Creator not to forsake the work of His hands; and was it not an appeal His own very honour bound Him to regard?

In this chapter we have laboured to keep our thought

strictly within the lines of a natural and rational theology, but the point whither the argument has been tending is clear: Nature cannot here speak the last word; we must wait the revelation of the Son of God. To allow evil to become and to continue without any purpose of redemption—i.e. to leave it as an ultimate fact and the final state of created existence—were to us an absolutely inconceivable act in a good and holy and gracious God. And so we may conclude this chapter with two questions: (*a*) May not the existence of evil explain and justify the event which we call the Incarnation? and (*β*) How can we conceive the justice and the goodness of God in relation to evil if His continued and final action towards it be excluded from consideration?

CHAPTER

THE PHILOSOPHY OF HISTORY

THE positions we have reached may be described as too purely abstract to be of any scientific significance; but if so, they will not be correctly described. For, in attempting to discuss the principles which are involved in the interpretation of the concrete, we have been helped to a more definite idea of the concrete itself. (*a*) We have come face to face, not with a nature which is but an aggregate of chemical elements and physical energies, or a mere succession of living forms that are ever struggling to live, yet ever succumbing to death; but with a nature which is veiled spirit, which speaks of mind to mind, and which, as an intelligible order, is a medium of intercourse between the Intelligence it embodies and the intellect by which it is studied. (β) And Man completes the lesson of Nature. He is not a mere fortuitous aggregation of atoms or an organism made by his environment, whether conceived as nature or as circumstances, but a person who embodies a moral law so imperative in its terms as to imply that the universe in which he lives is also moral. (γ) And the life he lives corresponds alike to the nature which enfolds him and to the nature which he realizes. It is not the life of a mere physical being or animal automaton, but of a moral person, standing within nature, yet rising above it, gifted with freedom, yet without either the knowledge or the experience that could at once use it for ends becoming the ideal of his personality; with the eternal law written on his heart, yet with fleshly passions or inherited tendencies or defects of temper that obliterate the law or bewilder him who would read it. And so there arises in his nature a conflict which is only too well expressed in the contradictions of his conduct. But out of his struggles with himself and his environment, with his habits and his conscience, with the nature around him, the law within him, and the God above him, come sufferings that educate and ennoble. From life he so learns to know evil and good, sorrow and happiness, that it may well be described as a discipline for immortality.

But we must now pass from what some may still conceive to be the region of abstract metaphysics to the very concrete region of the history which shows man living his common and collective life. Now, it is not my purpose either to sketch this history, which could be done here only in an outline too shadowy to have any significance, or to expound a philosophy of its course, its stages, and its goal, but simply to indicate what may be regarded as some of the principles needed for its interpretation and to state one of the great problems it raises. This chapter is, indeed, but transitional; it is meant to connect the discussion of fundamental questions in religious thought with a discussion concerning historical religion.

§ I. *The Significance of History*

1. The point where the new discussion joins hands with the old is here: the man who is at once the interpreter and the interpretation of nature, who is embodied reason and incorporated law, and who looks at the perplexities of life with an eye suffused and dim from the troubles of his own soul, is not a particular but a typical person. What we conceive to be his mind does not mean the psychology of this child or that individual, the philosophy of a school or a period, but the mind of generic Man; and so man here denotes a Race with a history behind it which helps to explain the mind that is

within it. And this history, construed as man's articulated mind, signifies that the science of nature without the science of history is an incomplete and an indecipherable fragment.

Now we have already argued that nature and man are so related that it must be read through him and he be read into it if it is ever to be more than a mass of unintelligibilities. Without him it would be as unfinished as a literary fragment which never got beyond the preamble to the story, and which, indeed, knew nothing of any plot, and less than nothing of any *dénouement*. But the parallel goes much farther than this, and means that the creative process whose beginnings can be traced in nature is continued in man; that his acts and achievements, the states and customs, the laws and literatures, the arts and sciences, the philosophies he has elaborated and the religions he has believed, are as real things and as integral parts of the universe as any of the forces, elements, or organisms which physical science is accustomed to think it handles; that the tendency to educe higher from lower forms reigns in human as well as in natural history, and was, indeed, seen in the former long before it obtained recognition in the latter; and that the true method of interpretation is to proceed from man to nature, for the highest holds and knows the secret of the lowest, while the lowest neither holds nor knows the secret of the highest. If, then, the history of man be the continuation of the record of creation, it follows that the creative energy has not ceased to operate, and that its character, qualities, tendencies, modes of working and relation to the forms developed, can be better studied here than in the field of nature. This position is fundamental to our argument, and follows from the parallel between the immanence of God in nature and in man. He dwells in both and He works through both, though always in methods agreeable to the medium employed. What is energy in nature is reason and will in man, but they are no less ours that they are inspired by Him, and no less His that they appear in us as conscious and voluntary activities. These may seem but cryptic utterances; we must try to make them more intelligible and lucid.

2. The experience of the individual has an instructive counterpart in the life of the race. The significance of his own history dawned but slowly upon the mind of man. It is a curious but certain fact, with something much more than a psychological interest, that Nature was at first a much more urgent problem to him than he was to himself. His earliest and most urgent intellectual need was to adjust himself to his environment, to make out the meaning of the world he lived in, the objects he handled, the food he lived on, the river that flowed past his cave, the sun that shone by day, the moon that walked in beauty by night, the stars that came out of the darkness and hid themselves at the breaking of the dawn, the powers that worked him good or ill, the birth in which his life began, and the death in which it ended. He could not but puzzle himself about these things. What did they mean? who had caused them? and whence had they come? what did he himself mean? why were the scenes around him and he so short a time together? what had been before him? and what would be after him? These were the questions his curious intellect asked of itself and of Nature, refusing to be satisfied without some more or less rational response, and this in time worked itself here into a science, and there into a philosophy, now into some act of worship, and again into an article of religious faith. But in the long and slow course of development man became a greater problem to himself than ever Nature had been to him, though he did not even then discover that his problem involved a vaster and more colossal Man than was contained within his own personality. For the human individual is no atom, without a history and without a name. He begins to be generations before he is born; then he is born into a family, he resumes the family he is born into, and is the

sum of all his ancestors. The family dwelt in a village which lived in a state; the family epitomized the village, and the village epitomized the state, while the state embosomed the village and the village absorbed the family and the family the individual. The state, in its turn, was subsumed under a people, was heir to all its acquired qualities, the organ of its peculiar genius, a form under which that genius lived, and through which it accomplished its work. The people, again, was a member of a still wider organism, belonged to a given species, a white or black, a tawny or yellow race, speaking a given kind of language, nasal or guttural, monosyllabic or polysyllabic, inflexional or syntactical, or both. And, finally, the species was absorbed in the genus; individuals, families, states, and kinds were comprehended under the generic Man, the collective Race, the sum total of Humanity. What then was Humanity? How were its parts related? Had it any reason, any end? Whence had it come, and whither was it going? Had it a common life, or was life an attribute only of the units composing it? How were the periods of its history connected, and what was the value of its several ages—ancient, middle, modern—for each other and for the whole? And without any solution of these questions could man, even as a solitary individual, be said to be explained?

3. But these questions were for long the problems and speculations of an elect few; even now they are to the vast majority of mankind unknown and inconceivable. For they become of intellectual interest and urgency only when certain ideas emerge which bind the unit consciously to mankind. These ideas may be represented by the terms:—the unity, the continuity, and the community of human life, order and purpose in human history. Man had to be conceived in all his families, races, states, and times, as even more a unity than the nature which enfolded him, while his unity included a variety unknown to nature. For this unity was not a mere term of co-ordination, but denoted continuous being, a

race immortal through the mortality of its units, and with a life which every moment grew out of the life that was or that had been. And the life as continuous was common, possessed by all, shared by each, communicated and communicable through the reciprocity of the unit with the whole, and the whole with the unit. And so this unity involved an order pervading all the tumults of men, harmonizing all their dissonances, and making at once their storms and calms, their alliances and their enmities, their jealousies and friendships, the horrors of their wars and the victories of their peace, work out the end towards which Humanity, as a mass moved by its units, ever tended and struggled.

But these ideas, though native to what may be termed the ideal in man, were unwelcome to much that was actual in him. They represent the supernatural rather than the natural elements in his life; and, odd as it may seem, man's ear has ever been quicker to hear external sounds than the inner voice. And these were not ideas that rose unbidden, demanding entertainment and refusing to be dismissed; but guests to whose entreaties the natural mind and passions of man could offer a stout resistance. For the very conditions that made Nature speak to man, turned man himself dumb. Thus the idea of unity has proved to be an offence to what we may term the natural human mind in all the stages of its culture. Savage man was proud of his family and his tribe; other families were there to be robbed, other tribes were there to be slain; what he cared for was not to know his kinship with them, but his differences from them, alike as regards origin, fortunes, and destiny. And this pride of race or blood was even more a note of civilized than of savage man; and, strange to say, drew its inspiration from causes that ought to have been its death. Thus his culture made the Greek scornful of the barbarian, his religion made the Jew insolent to the Gentile, his law made the Roman citizen jealous of the provincial. And this is not an individual, it is an even intenser political and social feeling. For what are states in their relation to each other but embodiments of that industrial jealousy and exclusive pride which has made so many of them like colossal personalities inspired by greed, ambitious for conquest, full of the lust of battle with feebler tribes and peoples, ready to find fame and even happiness in annexing the wealth of those they subdued, and to use the very strength of the vanquished as if it were their own? It was therefore not by any easy process of Nature, but by a high and supernatural grace, that the unity of man became first a possible, then a tolerable, and finally a victorious idea.

§ II. *The Ideas of Unity and Order in History*

1. But what does unity as here applied mean? The idea is so complex, and contains so many and so varied elements, that it may well break while being stretched wide enough to comprehend them all. The term does not denote unity of origin either as regards time or place or mode; but it does denote unity of source or cause, the equal and cognate relation of all to the one Creator who is the common Father of men. It also expresses unity of nature, a oneness of spirit or of reason, which shows itself in all minds being subject to the same laws and conditions of thinking, and which makes thought simply as thought intelligible to every mind, and every mind capable of knowing and being known to every other. The metaphysical idea of unity differs from the physical, for the conscious unit who lives within the organic unity called the human race is divided, as by the whole diameter of being, from the unconscious atom which is a convertible moment in a physical universe it can neither know nor be known to. It, further, connotes sameness of value, not adventitious, but essential, not as actual or realized, but as real and realizable; and makes the savage the equal of the sage, not in extrinsic and attained, but in intrinsic and potential worth. The substantive thus becomes an ethical

unity, for the most refined has duties to the coarsest; the man who leads the van has in his keeping the life of him who brings up the last rear guard. It is therefore a unity which has nothing to do with the accidents of existence; indeed it finds in these—the differences of colour, climate, custom, language, laws, religions—the supreme hindrances to its outward realization; and so it tends to grow into a unity of interests, a communion of responsibilities, a law of solidarity which makes the good of any a common good, and the injury of one a harm to all. As in physics the unity of energy is expressed in the correlation and convertibility of forces, so the unity of man is authenticated by the capability of men to become each like to the other. And if we seek a name for the common essence or character which constitutes this unity, what better one need we desire than Humanity, a name which so felicitously combines the ethnical and the ethical, the real and the ideal elements in the conception? For the term expresses a process as well as a fact, since wherever unity is believed, unification begins; and attempts are made to realize the dream of the one humanity which is yet to stand up and build upon the earth the city of God.

2. Out of this unity, with its correlative community and continuity of life, comes what we may describe as the immanent teleology which makes man's progress in civilization a progressive realization of reason, the incorporation in the societies and states he creates of the qualities intellectual, ethical, æsthetic, and religious by virtue of which he is man. If his customs and institutions, languages and religions, arts and literatures, stages and degrees of civilization be studied in themselves, they will appear to present an infinite variety; but if they be looked at in relation to the mind which has been their source, it will be seen that there have been at work certain uniform causes which express a certain unity in the causal nature. For it could only be in obedience to some immanent tendencies or laws of being, though educed

and exercised by external needs, that men have everywhere grouped themselves into families, families have formed themselves into tribes, tribes have aggregated into nations, and nations expanded and consolidated into states. It is due to no accident that in every community systems of legislation have arisen whose affinities can be explained only by factors of origin which are common in nature and invariable in action, though their differences imply the dissimilarity of the conditions, outer and inner, under which each community has lived and tried to order its life. Industries, too, and arts have risen and grown as if they were spontaneous things, though they are products of will and creations of reason, affected indeed by climate and geographical situation, but determined as regards being by the character and quality of the race. Commerce and exchange, economic states and conditions, may also be brought under the categories of law and reason; and so represent the operation in human nature of common and stable factors. Literature is as universal in its being as it is varied in its forms, existing here as the rude or savage story, there as the classic poem or elaborate romance; but wherever or whatever it may be, it embodies the ideas by which some people lived and were moved. Religion is the greatest and most distinctive of all the creations of the human spirit, in form the most infinitely diversified, but in substance, in ultimate ideal constituents, the most invariable. The essential unity of these products of the reason, and, consequently, of the reason which has created them, is seen in their communicability, their being in the most perfect degree exchangeable and transmissible things. Nation can borrow from nation; the later is the heir of the earlier age. And so no state creates a good for itself alone, and no empire can do an evil that is not an injury to the race. The life of humanity is one, and its goods are common. The uniformities of Nature have their counterpart, and, as it were, intellectual equivalent in the unities of History.

3. But if unity was a late and hard idea to acquire, order was, though for different reasons, still later and harder. For what is the conflict of forces, the tempestuous strife of elements in Nature, compared to the collision of will and passion in man and between men? "He loved the better, he did the worse," represents a fact of collective as of personal experience. If a single state, nay, if a single city, be taken as a type of man, what can his history seem but the chosen arena of wilfulness or lawless accident, the field where an infinite multitude of choices, each under the guidance of a reason which does not show itself reasonable because bent only on petty aims and mean ambitions, meet daily in forceful antagonism? How is it possible to discover order in history when all that can be discovered, if man be studied in his actual life, is a mass of colliding units, every unit being a centre of force which cannot be changed by expenditure into some other mode of existence, because where the soul is concerned, the fiercest impact against other souls makes each only the more distinctly personal? The state of war in the savage tribe is a state of kindly humanity compared with the mass of latent or open violence in the modern city, where nothing but the overmastering strength of the law, which is sovereign, can hold down the explosive energy stored in thousands of sullen and discontented wills. And if, when life is studied in the concrete present, we can see only this conflict of lawless wills, how, when the whole is regarded, can there be any room for the ideas of law, or progress, or purpose? And without these what could history seem save a chaos less rational and more disordered than that which the ancient imagination conceived as heaving tumultuous in the abyss, before the broad-bosomed earth, or the starry heaven, or "the golden-tressed sun" rose to call out of the confusion a radiant and ordered cosmos?

But here the doctrine of the connexion and the continuity of nature and man asserts itself. For if no order or law can be found in history, the collective life of man will represent only a mindless chance; and if law be left out of human life, can it be conceived to reign in nature? And if we conceive it to reign in the lower, but not in the higher realm, what completeness or consistency can there be in our view of the universe? Mind surely cannot stand within an ordered Nature with this as its sole distinction—that it is the home of all disorderliness. To find physical laws inviolable, and then to allow no historical laws to exist, would be to act like a man who should find the alphabet significant, but no significance in the literature created by the reason of the philosopher or the imagination of the poet. And so thinkers were driven to seek in history the law and order which they had found in Nature, though their search was slower and less successful in the one case than it had been in the other. It was characteristic that the idea had come to theology long before it dawned on philosophy, and while as yet science had no dream of it or care for it. Men who had conceived the Divine Will as the cause of Nature could not, with any show of logical consistency, allow that in the higher realm of mind God had, by leaving the whole course of time to the mercy of an infinity of blind and aimless wills, deposed Himself and enthroned Accident. Hence it became a necessity to belief to introduce some idea of law in history; and the form under which this was attempted to be done was by making the will of God the sole efficient factor of movement and change. His was affirmed to be the one free will, and He foreordained and executed all things according to His good pleasure. While Freedom reigned in heaven, Necessity governed on earth; and men were but pawns in the hands of the Almighty, who moved them whithersoever He willed. This was the principle common to theologies like those of Augustine and Calvin, and to philosophies like those of Spinoza and Leibnitz; but while it made of God the highest reality, it also made illusions of our most real experiences, and turned the most invincible of human beliefs —the belief of man in his own freedom—into the unveracity of a nature which could not choose but lie. Such a theory had not, therefore, the secret of continued life within it, and died before the emphasis which came to be progressively laid on the truth of human nature and the reality of human experience.

But though the idea of order be necessary to the scientific views both of nature and of history, yet the order is not in the two cases identical in kind and character. The order of nature is a rigorous uniformity, but the order of history is veiled in an infinite variety. In nature there is a uniform energy, incapable of exhaustion by expenditure or of destruction by change; but in history the cause of movement is though one yet not uniform, and is so highly and variously conditioned as to appear often arbitrary or accidental in action rather than simply contingent. In nature the operative cause necessitates, but in history there are forces that lead as well as forces that drive; and it is here no paradox to say that the power which does not persuade will be unable to compel. Indeed, we may affirm that what appears in the vicissitudes of states or the careers of persons now as fate or necessity, and now as chance or luck, will be found on analysis to be beliefs translated into facts by the energy of some rational will or wills. And this means that the factors of order in history must be stated in the terms of mind rather than of matter, i.e. as reasons and motives, as needs and desires, as beliefs and aims, rather than as forces, static and dynamic. But if mind be the main maker of order in history, then its movement will be progressive, the struggle of mind to realize itself, to be emancipated from the dominion of what is not mind; and, therefore, from the restrictions, physical political, social, which hinder the development of its immanent ideal, personal and collective. If order be so conceived, then we may define it as the tendency which the reason institutes and governs, but nature and passion now condition, now limit, and now impede, towards the realization of its idea as reason, i.e. the attainment of the highest freedom, or the right of man to be himself, a free man in a free state.

§ III. *The Cause of Order in History*

1. But so to conceive the order is also to determine how its cause must be conceived. The cause is mind or reason or thought, which, whether it be impersonated in man, embodied in nature, or operative in the forces and tendencies which govern human affairs, is one in essence, cognate in all its forms, and kindred in movement, though varied in manifestation. What is involved in this statement may be briefly thus exhibited.

i. Man is the vehicle of the order; through him as mind it is realized. This does not mean that he is or has always been a being of high or developed intelligence; but only that he must, in however germinal a form, be rational to be man. He may be but potential intellect; but whatever he may be, the energy which compels all life to grow forces the potential to struggle into the actual. In other words, reason must act according to its nature; and its nature is to express and to enshrine itself in forms, customs, laws, institutions, which reflect it and correspond to the stage of growth, culture, or development it has reached. As it is the nature of the normal reason so to behave, this behaviour is not the characteristic of one person, but of all persons; their affinities make their collective action contributory to a common end, though the line along which they act may be indefinitely extended and may here and there bend into the most curious and tortuous curves. The person is thus, by the very idea of him, a social unit, and all his action contributes to modify or develop the social unity.

ii. The man who is reason lives within a rational system and in intercourse with it. The intelligible which is without operates upon the intellect which is within, evoking its energies and stimulating its thought. The action of nature upon mind represents the action not of mere physical forces or material qualities upon the senses of some more or less passive percipient, but of one reason upon another reason. It is a movement in which the subjective reason which is an, and the objective Spirit which weaves the appearances we see Him by, alike participate. The nature which is visible Mind speaks to the man who is embodied spirit.[1]

iii. Nature, though the earliest, is not the sole Intelligible which acts upon man; man is another. The individual is impossible without the society, and the longer the race lives the more potent grows the power of the past over the present; persons affect persons, who are, in an ever progressive degree, healed, helped, or harmed more by them than by Nature. This means that moral forces are cumulative as well as regulative. It follows that personalities become factors of progress marking man's movement towards civilization; and the philosophy which does not reckon the potent personality as a great generative ethical force will never fully and really render a rational account of human life.[2]

iv. The race which is conceived to be so constituted does not live in isolation from its Source. The forms that struggle for life can never be separated from their environment. The visible environment of man is twofold, an intelligible nature and a rational and a moral society; but the invisible Environment, the common background of both, is the Spirit whose thought has been aiming in each and through each at ever fuller and more adequate expression. There is nothing so inconsequent and hateful as the atheism which finds God in nature but not in man, in creation but not in history. If we believe that God never ceases to govern, we must conclude that His activity will find a large field for its exercise in

---

[1] Ante, pp. 35–37. [2] Ante, p. 92.

human affairs. And if His will be active there, then it is not simply as a directive, but as a creative will, and His peculiar creations are the ideas and ideals that most make for freedom and righteousness. Of course His action is mediate, but it is none the less His that it is through another, by men that it may be for man. It is, too, limited by the intelligence and conditioned by the freedom of the agent, and has in its results all their infinite degrees of capacity and attainment, but still He is the impulse that moves, His the fraction of truth or equity, perhaps infinitesimal, which their elaborate structures have been organized to preserve.

2. Out of the idea, then, of history as a continued creative process due to the continued, though conditioned, activity of the original creative Mind rises the problem we desire to discuss:—By what method and through what agency have the ideas of order and law come into man's life and incorporated themselves first in tribal, then in national, and finally in universal forms? How has it happened that, in spite of the strong tendencies in human nature, personal and social, to selfish preservation and enlargement of being, there has yet been a development of the race towards a wider reason and a nobler mind? The problem, which may be said to be common to all modern speculations, philosophical or theological, concerning the cause, method, and end of human history may be stated in more detail somewhat thus:

i. The course of human society has been to create an order higher than the natural, to substitute an "ethical process," governed by altruistic principles, for the "cosmic process," where the weakest goes to the wall and the strongest survives. The course has not been uniform or rapid; but if we take the foremost peoples as the standard of the possibilities in man and in society, then the distance covered by them in the movements from the savage to the civilized state, is simply immeasurable.

ii. Among the most potent factors of human development there stand certain primary impulses, instincts, or passions which, as representing in the human individual and society the same order of facts and forces that create in the lower animals the struggle for life, we may call natural. These primary passions are apparently most potent in the more rudimentary stages of social evolution, where the strong man is the sovereign, and the only order obeyed is his will, while hunger and greed recognize no moral restraints; and they persist in the aggressive selfishness of individuals and the colossal selfishness of classes or States. These passions of ungoverned human nature, which is yet feeling after modes and principles of government, are, up to a certain point, efficient in developing both the personal and the social organism; but when this point is reached, they tend to become forces of disintegration and dissolution. For as forms of mere force their tendency is to evoke forms of countervailing forces, i.e. to beget the private and social vices which, as public injuries, first burden and impoverish the feeble, and then grow heavier burdens than the strong can carry.

iii. If, then, there is to be rational and moral progress, or movement towards a happier and better balanced state of being, it must be by some process or power which subordinates first the individual and then the whole to some higher law than the mere struggle to live, or the hunger that will not be denied food, or the passion that only indulgence can assuage. This higher law may be described as the emergence of an authority that can compel the will of the unit to seek the good of the whole, and the will of the whole to labour for the good of the unit.

iv. This authority must, in the ultimate analysis, be ideal, i.e. an authority which does not repose on mere strength or physical might, but makes its appeal to the reason, and rules by governing men from within, by the categorical imperative which speaks to the conscience, and by the persuasion which constrains the will to seek the better part.

The authority must be thus ideal in its nature, and ethical in its form, function, and scope: for force, whether natural or institutional in its origin, whether military, sacerdotal, or regal in its kind, can cure no moral ill; and is in its essence only a primary passion become colossal and victorious.

v. The only ideas capable of subduing man's primary passions and aboriginal nature, and creating an order higher than they knew, are ideas which are in harmony with the ideal he incorporates, and which he has evolved in the course of his historical existence. This evolution, though it is a natural, is yet not a purely self-determined process, but is moved from above as well as from within, by the creative will as well as by the creature's. But unless the ideas which are to govern man were germane to his nature, they could not be appropriated by him, or obtain ascendency over him.

vi. Hence comes the problem—Have any ideas of this order grown up at once in and out of the intellectual and moral life of man, i.e. ideas that had the power to master his natural impulses and passions, to penetrate, transfigure, and command the nature which needed to be subdued, and then, by means of the change effected in it, to organize a higher and more ethical society? If so, whence did these ideas come? and what gave them their authority?

vii. But if this be the problem, it is obvious in what direction we must look for a solution, for modern research has proved that the main factor by which the higher ideas and emotions are evoked for incorporation in human conduct, custom or institution is Religion. In it there is expressed a mind which transcends Nature, and reaches out to ideals which Nature alone could not realize. If, then, man and the powers that move him in history are to be understood, we must try to understand the religions. And so we are by the philosophy of history introduced to the philosophy of Religion.

CHAPTER VI

THE PHILOSOPHY OF RELIGION

A. Principles: The Idea and Origin of Religion

PHILOSOPHY, understood as reflexion on our ultimate ideas, is almost as old as religion, and began to be the moment man consciously enquired concerning beliefs that had unconsciously arisen, What do they mean? He had to live much longer, forget much and learn more, before he could ask, What do I mean by my beliefs? A yet vaster revolution of time and mind had to happen before he framed the questions: What do my beliefs mean to me? and have their many changes of form and setting since the days of my youth left them still the old beliefs and still mine? But all these might be discussed as problems in religious philosophy without ever raising the distinctive questions in the philosophy of religion. The two are distinguished thus: the former is concerned with religious ideas, but the latter with concrete religion; the one deals with beliefs, their basis, psychological genesis, and intellectual forms, but the other enquires why religion as an objective fact and living organism has appeared, and how it has behaved; what are its sources and elements, its ideas and customs; what its dependency on man and on environment; what functions it has fulfilled, and with what results, and for what reasons in personal, tribal, national, and collective history. It recognises religion as a universal fact which has to be construed through what is universal in human nature; and it seeks to discover the forces and the factors that modify the universal fact into the infinite variety of forms it assumes in time and place, and to determine the worth of these modifications. Its scope is therefore immense, and its problem intricate, but one thing it must never do, lose hold upon reality, the phenomena to be explained, or forget the obligation that lies upon it of finding for them a rational explanation.

§ I. *The Phenomena to be Studied: the Religions*

1. The philosophy of Religion starts with man, and sees that whenever and wherever he appears it is as a voyager between life and death, conscious of the mystery in which his voyage begins and the tragedy in which it ends. It never finds him without religious ideas or forms appropriate for their expression. These belong to his most solemn acts and the customs by which they are sanctioned. If we try to make the races of man, with their most transcendental ideals and governing enthusiasms, pass before the eye which sees in solitude, we shall find that what we have called up is a vision impressive above all others to the imagination. For we have summoned man in all his tribes and in all his ages to defile before us in ghostly procession, bearing his supreme hopes and fears, aspirations and agonies, dreams of deity, death, and bliss as they are incorporated in his religions. We may begin with what is esteemed their lowest and most primitive form, religion as interpreted and realized for us by the living savage. Anthropology has painted for us a picture of him which is as rich and complex as it is real and full; and has made us familiar with his weapons, his ceremonies, his ideas, his hopes, and fears. It may have tempted us indeed to exaggerate the rudeness, the audacious monstrosity of his thought and mythology; but one thing it has made conspicuously evident, viz., the place his religious beliefs occupied in his mind, and the space his religious customs filled in his life. How great these were may be discovered if we compare his total outfit for

life in two respects, the material and the spiritual, with our own.

(*a*) As to his material outfit. This is represented by a rude weapon or two, a piece of flint sharpened to act as knife or spear-head; and possibly, if he be very highly gifted, to these may be added a bow and arrow, a fig-leaf round his middle, or the fat of some slaughtered animal with which he has been wont to daub his body, the scalp of an enemy he has worn at his girdle, the skull of a beast he has slain and used either as ornament or as weapon. If he dwells on an island or by the sea, he may have fashioned and sailed some curious canoe; and if he has learned to love rhythmic sounds, he may have contrived to form out of a piece of wood and a skin some instrument from which he can produce them. These, or something less than these, represent the whole of his material equipment; all the property he has either to carry with him to the tomb, or to leave behind to his family or his tribe. On the other hand, civilized man is found clothed, housed, fed by the products of all lands; able to travel over earth and sea with the speed but without the fatigues of a winged creature. He dwells in cities adorned with art, enriched by commerce, absorbed in industries, governed by law, illumined by history, informed by literature, comforted by religion, pervaded by a thousand-handed charity and watched by an even-handed justice which will not allow the aggressor to go unpunished. He can look with eyes that see to the ends of the earth, and can listen with ears that hear the faintest murmur amid far-off peoples of war or disaster, prosperity or distress, the suspicion that alienates man or the trust that unites them. If now we compare the two, could more utter or more pathetic destitution than that of the savage be conceived? The multitude of things that have become not simply conveniences but necessities to the civilized man, be he rich or be he poor, which are completely unknown to the primitive, makes one feel the distance that lies between the simple state of nature and the wealth of the poorest rustic that ever followed a plough, or was carried unlamented to his grave.

(β) Let us now place, in contrast with their material, their respective spiritual outfits. Here, indeed, the wealth of the savage bewilders. His ideas as to ghosts and gods are so multitudinous that every object he handles, everything he sees, has within it a hidden deity. Life, death, and the future speak to him as to us; but, with a more sensitive imagination than we can boast, he guards his life by charms and rites from those last terrors which cast upon him so dark a shadow. Souls he finds everywhere and in everything; and so he can hardly speak without weaving the phenomena of Nature into poetry. We have only to recall some of the many forms employed to explain his beliefs in order to show how complex they seem to us, whatever may have been their cogent reasonableness to himself. We have his legends construed in the terms now of a solar, and now of a floral mythology. In the one case sun and moon and stars are made the ancestors of all his gods and ours; in the other case, these are displaced in favour of trees and plants. Then we have an animal mythology, with varied legends of animal ancestry, and theories of animal and human kinship. Then we have a cosmogonic mythology, theories as to how Nature came to be, what the eclipse signified, and how the earthquake was caused. And we have an historical or ancestral mythology, where the memory of the tribe has been turned into a chronicle of divine names and a calendar of persons worthy of divine honours. And though these schools and types of mythology may signify much more as to the ingenuity of the civilized man attempting to read the savage mind than they signify as to the world which the savage actually knows; yet the very fact that such theories have been possible shows the amount of material that has to be interpreted, and the space which spiritual beliefs fill in the savage life. For his customs are as full of belief as are his tales :—his institutions, the sacred persons, the rain-makers, the wizards, the doctors he trusts; the sacred things like trees and rivers, bones and stones he fears; the sacred places he frequents, like cairns and mountains, forests and wells; the cave which he turns into a tomb and the grove he rails off as a home for his dead; the charms on which he depends for help against the malign forces that dwell in nature or act in man, all express the same thing—the wealth of his spiritual outfit compared with the appalling poverty of his material possessions. This is the more remarkable as civilized man is marked by a contrast of the reverse order. His spiritual world—however rich in intellectual formulæ or æsthetic adornment, in ceremonial and musical expression—is like the wilderness, in which the rose does not blossom, standing over against the prodigal luxuriance of the material comforts that make up so large a part of his life. It were dangerous to draw too sharp an antithesis; but if we judge from the ethnographic evidence, we may say that the savage, in contrast to the civilized man, is more occupied with supernatural and ideal than with natural and material things. Nature to him is of spirit all compact, and even the life we think so low and brutal has in its dreams and fears and crude beliefs the stores of a large imagination.

2. This absorption of the primitive man in religion is no mere accident; on the contrary it means that the nascent mind in him feels its kinship with the divine, gropes after it, and the more it gropes rises the higher in its manhood; and that it can only begin freely and intelligently to handle matter when it has in some measure clarified its outlook towards spirit. But if we desire to see how little the increase of intercourse with material things signifies any growth out of religion, we have only to turn our eyes on the peoples who can boast

VISION OF THE RELIGIONS IN HISTORY

an historical and ordered being. Let us go back to our most ancient civilization, unbury the temples of Egypt, disinter her cities, rifle her tombs, unswathe her mummies, and read her hieroglyphs; and what do we find? That the thing that made her the mother of the arts, that bade her build her pyramids and her temples, that forced her to preserve her dead that the disembodied soul might on its return find again its ancient home, was belief: faith in the life that never died—her religion. Or let us take the greatest nation of merchants the world has ever known, the men who first learned how to navigate the pathless sea, to colonize for commerce, to weave the mysterious signs of the alphabet into written speech; and how do we trace their wanderings in search of gain? By the votive tablets which the Phœnician everywhere set up and left behind in the praise of his gods. Or let us move eastward till we enter the old Mesopotamian valley, dig into its shapeless and melancholy mounds and dig out its winged bull or its man-headed lion, discover and decipher its cuneiform inscriptions; and there read the history of its wars, the ambitions and the achievements of its kings, the myths and the legends of its people; and what have we discovered? That the thing all lived by and lived for was religion; kings ruled by favour of the gods, and delighted in the victories that did them honour. Or let us go further eastward till we reach India, and what is the idea that there penetrates everything, that fills all nature, that builds up and organizes all society, but the idea of an omnipresent Deity, who, though impersonal, is yet impersonated in all things, the bosom out of which all came, and into which all return? Let us move still eastward till we come to China, and there we find man held in the lean yet iron fingers of his dead ancestors; but all his ancestors—with the spirits that fill the heaven above, and people the earth below—speak to him of one thing—the religion which the people did not make, but which has made the people.

And if we think that by returning to the saner West and investigating its sanest and sunniest peoples we may escape from this all-environing belief, what do we find? That the poetry, the art, the philosophy of Greece live and move and have their being in its religion; and without it these could not have been either what they were to the Greeks or what they are to us. And did not Rome conceive her Empire to be so much the creation of the religious idea that her emperors came to be honoured as deities? The gods built and ruled the city, and the city achieved her greatness by the favour of the gods; nay, she was herself imperial and eternal because she was divine. And what does this ubiquity of religion, with its all-penetrative and commanding action, mean? Not simply that man possesses it, but that it possesses man, and is the mother of all his order, all his arts, and all his architectonic ideas. Till religion, therefore, is explained he is inexplicable, and only as it is purified and strengthened can he be made perfect.

3. To speak of religion as the mother of our architectonic ideas may seem to many only a form of vain and sounding words, yet what they state is the sober truth. The thing that anthropology has made most certain is this—that primitive religion is not the apotheosis of accident, the child of nightmare and imaginative terror, but the organizing idea of society, the force which holds the whole social system together, builds it up, and gives to it its character and unity. Order is created because customs are established as religious, and are enforced by sanctions too dread to be despised. Law is divine, the oath is made sacred, and certain acts are stamped as crimes that must be punished by being conceived as violations of a will too awful to be corrupted and too inexorable to be defied. The forms of early society which are denoted by the uncouth terms which we owe to anthropology—taboo, totemism, fetishism— are the names of so many chapters in the early history

of religion. By religious customs kinship is defined; through them kingship is established; by them the family, the clan, or the tribe, is delimited; and because of them the civil institution takes shape or finds its root and reason. And as it is in the most primitive societies, so it is also in the most stable, progressive and civilized. The marvellous continuance of China is the fit handiwork of the one religion which can be truly described as " ancestor-worship," which has saved the present by causing its indefectible loyalty to the past. The social system of India, the wonderful order of caste, so hateful and so little intelligible to the European, is but the articulation of racial pride, enforced by sanctions, preserved by customs, guarded by rites, consecrated by associations, which are all religious. The ancient empires of the East—Egypt, Assyria, Persia—were, in a sense, missionary associations, the victorious conqueror being but the potent apostle of his god. The greatest personal Empire was the shortest lived, it died with the man who made it, for with Alexander its only principle of life went out. The apotheosis of the Roman State expressed the idea that organized the Roman Empire; the tendencies that undeified the state dissolved its dominion. The societies that live longest and exercise the widest sovereignty are those which the religious idea has created and inspired. The Church of Buddha is a remarkable example of existence continued amid diffusion, unbroken by dispersal through peoples of alien blood and speech, unhurt by the downfall of friendly or the triumph of hostile states. The word of Mohammed laid hold upon the Arab tribes, divided by immemorial hates and centuries of bloody feuds, and fused them into a nation of a single passion and irresistible power. Translated into the soil of another and most ungenial race, the same word built the throne of the Turk in Europe and the Moghul in Asia. Religion remains thus, in all its forms and ages, a creative and architectonic force, a power all the more absolute that it is moral and intellectual rather than material, economical, or military.

§ II. *Religion as Universal is Native to Man*

From this rapid survey of religion, both in its primitive and historical forms, as of all facts the most universal and distinctively human, and as of all factors of movement and of social change the most potent and determinative, two or three important conclusions follow:

1. Science cultivates no field so necessary to the complete knowledge of man as that occupied by his religions. The circle of the sciences concerned with the interpretation of nature and man is immense, and it is all the fuller of knowledge and of meaning that no single science stands alone, but that each depends immediately or remotely upon all the rest. In their presence two things fill me with wonder—the immensity of the field they cover, and the inadequacy of them all combined, in spite of their coherence and their unity, to the interpretation of man as at once the interpreter and the interpretation of the universe. If we think of it, is not the point where these co-ordinated sciences stop even more remarkable than the point where they begin and the goal whither they tend? They start with those mathematics which are pure metaphysics, those ideas which the reason cannot think without or think away, and which underlie all its attempts at the interpretation of Nature as being in space. And then from this they rise through the more concrete sciences—physical, chemical, geological, biological—till they terminate in man as a social and economical being. The field is vast and crowded with marvels; but what is more marvellous than even its extent is its limitation. What is most cardinal and characteristic in man and his creations remains untouched, or is touched only at a point remote from the centre, and so distant from the enquirer that he cannot so see it as to bring it within

the terms of anything that can be called scientific knowledge or discussion. Science indeed attempts to touch religion where it appears as savage custom and belief; but, as we are about to argue, these are for all scientific purposes much less significant than the historical religions; while the material they supply is less capable of judicial sifting and verification than the material,—monumental, institutional, literary, artistic,—available in history. There are indeed special sciences that cultivate these and cognate fields; but it is one thing to study religious art and archæology, or historical and literary criticism, and quite another thing to study the religion that produced the art and made the literature. And apart from the religion its creations cannot be appreciated; but to understand religion man must be understood, especially as regards those faculties, real or potential, by virtue of which he is its organ and bearer. Now the only science which has seriously concerned itself with this question is anthropology, which, like a new and more formal comparative anatomy, or a sort of psychological palæontology, takes up the dried and broken and scattered bones of savage myth, ritual, and institutions; and then, with the benevolent condescension which marks the child of culture when he deals with those lower civilizations out of which his own was born, it attempts to discover for us the process by which spiritual ideas first entered the primitive mind, and then organized themselves into the customs and the myths which are the originals of our civilized religions. Yet when it has spoken its last word, does it not leave unexplained the mystery of thought within the savage that compelled him to make and follow the custom, to think and create the myth? The man is more than the environment; it never could have acted on him as it is supposed to have done, or he have drawn from it what he did, had he not been man. More wonderful than the rudeness of his tools was the need he felt for them, how he made them, and what in his hands they accomplished; more remarkable than the extravagance of his beliefs was their existence, and they, like the tools, existed because of him. He, by the marvellous alchemy of his thought, distilled them from his experience; and they became the strong drink of his mind, now intoxicating and now inspiring, yet ever signifying that he had, by transfiguring nature into spirit, humanized himself. And his maddest dreams have within them the reasonable soul of a potential manhood. It does not become us to marvel at the grotesque things he said and believed at the supreme moment when the reason within him awoke, and he looked with the eyes of a dazed and perturbed imagination at the world without. For our own speech even now tends to become bewildered when we stand in presence of the mysteries of being, but are we to cease to think because the expression of our thought is inadequate? And is the scientific way to belittle thought through the inadequacy of its vehicle, or to read the vehicle through the reality of the thought? For it must have been some strong instinct in the savage that moved him to the creation of these naïve beliefs and rites which we seek so curiously to explain. And this means that it was not the Nature without, but the nature within the man and behind the beliefs, that was the really significant and causative nature.

2. Religion is so essential to man that he cannot escape from it. It besets him, penetrates, holds him even against his will. The proof of its necessity is the spontaneity of its existence. It comes into being without any man willing it, or any man making it; and as it began so it continues. Few men could give a reason for their belief, and the curious thing is that when it is attempted the reasons are, as a rule, less rational than the beliefs themselves, and are but rarely possessed of a ratiocinative cogency. Its strength on the collective side lies in its institutions and usages; but on the personal side in its intellectual ideas and moral ideals. Men bear its institutions while they believe its

truth; and no social or political revolution is possible anywhere save by those who have revolted from the beliefs on which the society or the State has been constituted. In the hour of the revolt individual men may will to have nothing to do with religion; but instinct is stronger than will, and religion in some form both of idea and usage returns, be it as the memory of a dead woman, as with Mill or Comte, or as an abstraction like Humanity—*le grand Être*—loved of the Positivist, or as the Unconscious adored by the Pessimist, or as the Unknown affirmed by the logic and worshipped by the awe of the Agnostic. And what man is to religion he becomes to history. It is in his religion that he knows himself man, and through it that he realizes manhood. Like a subtle spirit it pervades his whole being, and controls both his personal and social development. His first attempts to interpret Nature are governed by religious ideas, and from his last attempts they are inseparable. He must, for he is rational, think, and what is the thought of a reasonable being but a factor which relates him to the Infinite and the Eternal? The society man creates, embodies his religious idea, and the same idea orders his history. Language in all its terms is instinct with religious feeling, and thought in its whole movement is governed by the religious problem. In theology philosophy begins, and in theology science ends, all the more that it may refuse to name the very notions which transcend its sphere and yet are implicit in all its premisses and will not be excluded from its conclusions. For what is the Agnostic but a man who confesses that there are ideas which he will not name but cannot escape from—ideas that he must disguise in order that he may reason concerning them? These ideas beget the ideals which have an infinite meaning for man, for they are born of religion and for ever cause religion to be born anew within him.

3. If religion be, as it were, so built into man as to be the heart of his being, it follows that the agencies which work

most for its amelioration serve man in the highest possible degree. Genius is varied, and can accomplish great things in all the provinces and spheres of thought and life. In art it can give us the things of beauty that are joys for ever, and that govern the taste of all later ages; but art is not the whole of life. Sensuous beauty and moral uncleanliness have before now lived together without any feeling of mutual dislike or disgust; but in the course of ages the moral uncleanliness proves mightier to harm than the sensuous beauty to bless. Genius in literature may create the classical forms that educate all later intellects, but the most cultivated literary societies have often been cursed by the most absolute selfishness. In music the imagination of the master can blend the harmony of sweet sounds in the *opera* or *oratorio* that speaks to man in the language of the gods. But the delight music may give is of the sense rather than of the soul. Religion, on the other hand, affects and controls all these. To it art, pagan or Christian, owes its noblest subjects and highest inspirations. For it is not to be forgotten that art has everywhere lived and moved and had its being in religion. This is even more true of classical than of mediæval art, for it was at once a more adequate and a more refined expression of the religious ideal. Pheidias helped to spiritualize the religion of Greece in a sense and degree that has no counterpart in the work of Raphael for Italy; and if we do not read Greek art through the Greek idea that the Beautiful was the most fit symbol, if not indeed the very synonym, for the Divine, we shall never appreciate its nature, or understand what it achieved. From religion, too, literature has received the problems which have given it dignity, the spirit which has breathed into it sublimity, and the soul which has been its life. Without his mythology Homer would have made no appeal to the imagination of all time. Æschylus would have given us no tragedy, Plato no philosophy, Dante no *Divine Comedy*, Milton no *Paradise*

Lost or *Regained*, without the motive and the material which religion supplied. And these are but typical cases, for to illustrate the point as it might be illustrated would be to marshal the masterpieces from the literatures of all peoples and times. And, finally, without religion music would lose most of its power to charm, for it elevates just as it breathes the soul of religion, and is the minister of the religious emotions. The religious is thus, as we have said, the architectonic idea of society, the commanding idea of conduct, the imperial idea of all our being and all our thinking, and he who can create its most perfect form is our supreme benefactor—the foremost person in all our history.

If, then, religion be to such a degree the force which makes for order in history, what are the philosophical problems it formulates for us? These are indeed a multitude, but they may be said to reduce themselves to three main classes: First, those connected with the nature, the origin, and the permanence of religion as such, i.e. the religious idea without reference to any of its specific forms. What is it? How did it come to be? Why does it continue to be? Secondly, those connected with the rise, the peculiar qualities and characters, and the distinctive behaviour of the special religions. How are we to conceive and explain the many forms the idea has assumed? To what causes do they owe their being? What forces,—physical, personal, political,—have worked for their modification? Thirdly, those connected with the historical action and generic significance of the particular religions; i.e. their merits, measured by some standard which philosophy may judge adequate, as systems embodying an ideal and working for its realization in the actual. What gives their worth to local religions? Is it enough that they have a history and serve their peoples? Is there such a thing as a universal or absolute religion? In what relation do the particular religions stand to each other and to the idea of religion in general? These are large questions, and we shall in this chapter confine ourselves to the two prior and fundamental points—(1) the idea and origin of religion; (2) the causes of variation in religions. The other point, as raising other issues, will be better discussed in a later chapter.

§ III. *The Idea and Origin of Religion*

1. Religion, so far as it is a matter of philosophical investigation, has a twofold sense—a subjective and an objective, or a personal and a collective, or an ideal and an historical. As subjective it denotes certain thoughts, ideas, feelings, and tendencies which belong to man as man. As objective it denotes the beliefs, the legends, the mythologies, the sacred books and creeds in which the thought is articulated; the ritual, ceremonial, acts or institutions of worship in which the feeling is embodied; the customs or laws by which the acts are regulated and sanctioned; and the practices, conventions, and social judgments by which the tendencies are developed and enforced. A provisional definition might therefore run somewhat thus:—Religion is, subjectively, man's consciousness of relation to suprasensible Being; and, objectively, the beliefs, the customs, the rites, and the institutions which express and incorporate this consciousness. But it may be necessary to say something more in explanation of both sides of this definition.

(i.) As to the subjective side, what is this consciousness? Can it be resolved into any single faculty or the function of any faculty, perception of the Infinite, intuition, or faith? Is it an intellectual, an emotional, or an ethical consciousness? Religion has, indeed, been conceived now as an act or state of knowledge, now as an act or state of feeling, now as an act or state of conscience. As thought or knowledge, it is a sort of provisional philosophy; as feeling, it is a more or less inchoate mysticism, a sense of dependence on Nature or natural forces or the Absolute; as a state of conscience, it

DEFINITIONS CRITICIZED

has been resolved into a high morality, again into morality touched with emotion; and still again, into a categorical imperative apprehended as a Divine command. But the religious consciousness is too rich to be represented by any single element in the conscious life of man. It is neither knowledge, whether described as intuition or thought; nor feeling, whether conceived as sense of dependence or admiration; nor conscience, whether as a sense of obligation or as an organized and externalized authority. It is no one of these, yet it contains within it all these, for it is a consciousness which includes the whole energy of man as reasonable spirit. There cannot be religion without knowledge, for faith and knowledge are rather a unity than a true antithesis. Faith is intellectual, involves thought; and it is only as man conceives an object that he can have any conscious relation to it. The Unknown, as outside man's consciousness, is an object neither of thought nor of faith; and so has for him no real being, nor any relation to his conscious life. There can, therefore, be no religion without thought, for not to think were not to believe—to have nothing that could be described as either object or article of faith. Nor can religion exist without feeling, for all thought implies feeling; and there can be no feeling without thought. To be conscious of emotion is to know ourselves as its subject, and something not ourselves as its cause or object; and the feeling will in its quality correspond to the qualities which thought has predicated of its cause. No man can have a feeling of dependence who has not conceived himself as dependent on something, or conceived Some One as existing on whom he depends. Nor can religion be apart from conscience, for conscience is the unity of knowledge and feeling, the knowledge of the difference between acts and the qualities of acts, and the feeling of obligation to do acts that are of a given kind or have a certain quality. And so a relation such as is realized in religion is exactly the kind that supplies conscience with its law or norm. The consciousness, therefore, which knows itself related to suprasensible Being represents not one faculty, but the whole exercised reason—the concrete spirit reaching upwards and outwards to a spirit as concrete as itself.

(ii.) Turning now to the objective side, it is clear that the relation of which man is conscious is conceived as mutual, and not simply as one-sided. The God he thinks of is one who speaks to him as well as one who can be spoken to. The mutual relation is therefore conceived as a mutual activity; there is reciprocity between the related persons. Man worships, but God hears and sees and responds. While man offers himself to God, God communicates Himself to man. If it were believed that God ceased to be related to man, man would feel as if he also were without relation to God. And this implies an important addition to the ideas both of the object who is adored and the subject or person who adores, viz., the idea of a law or will which unifies the two and governs the relations which man, by his usages, seeks to establish between himself and the Deity. That law or will is the God who, as immanent both in nature and in man, is their common principle of unity. The evolution of religion is not a mere subjective process worked by an unconscious dialectic; it is a process in which man's whole environment takes part. It is due, as it were, to the converse of the soul with Nature—impossible without the soul to speculate, to question, to argue, to infer; but impossible also without an order that impels the soul to ask, and that answers as much by silence as by speech. And the real respondent in this controversy or discussion which provokes the soul to the dialectic that becomes religion, is not nature but God, the transcendent Reason using the terms of experience to awaken the transcendental idea. The Maker of man does not cease from relation with the man He made, and He cannot be related without exercising influence over him.

This relation is one which every philosophy that seeks any ideal aim or rational process in this world has recognised. The reason that is in man is one with the universal Reason; his ideals must serve the order or stream of tendency which guides the systems of things to which he belongs. To conceive man and God as so related is to conceive the one as the form or vehicle in which the Other lives and through which He speaks. And so to complete the idea of the factors that work subjectively for the creation of religion, we must not forget the God who dwells in consciousness any more than the consciousness which knows of His indwelling.

2. But the distinction between the subjective and objective senses of religion will, by being translated into more concrete terms, bring us to a new stage in our argument. The equivalent of the subjective sense is man, conceived as reason or spirit, the ideal ego who cannot be without thought and cannot think without affirming Deity. And the equivalents of the objective sense are the phenomena, the personal, social and ceremonial forms which embody his ideas, or constitute outward religion. Now if the relation between these two be conceived under the category of causation, man may be regarded as the producer, religion as the produced; but this needs to be qualified, as man is not an absolute cause, but conditioned; he never acts in isolation, but ever as a creature who lives within the limits of time and under the stimulus of place. Yet the most conditioned cause retains its causal functions and character; and so the subject must be conceived as the generative agent in religion. If, again, the relation be construed under the category of time, priority of being must be claimed for the subject through whose consciousness religion is realized. But the distinction is unreal, for the moment man thinks, his thought is objectified, and it exists for him only as it is an object. The two things, subjective and objective religion, are then, as a matter of fact, inseparable, though it is also true that in the order of thought

the subjective is in being and in action the prior, the objective the later. In other words, man is before history; history is in consequence of man; i.e., it is the unfolding and expression of potentialities that were latent within him, and that have been evoked in the course of his personal and collective life. It is impossible indeed for history to reach the first man and describe him as he really was. He is, whether understood as person or as species, more or less symbolical, a creature of the imagination, made in order that he may be argued about. And this is as true of the idea of the primitive state as it is of the idea of the primitive man, whether with theology we speak of the one as Eden and of the other as Adam, or with science we describe the primitive as a savage state and name the person half-man, half-brute. Where we cannot investigate we must be content to speculate; and so all enquiries into the origin of early beliefs and institutions, however disguised in archæology or in history, are really philosophical. Our modern anthropologies are in heart and essence as speculative as mediæval scholasticism or as any system of ancient metaphysics. Indeed, the most barbarous metaphysical jargon which has ever been foisted upon patient thought, is that which uses terms like "taboo," "totem," "fetish," "ghost," to denote indiscriminated and even most dissimilar ideas, which are often, on the most unsifted and dubious evidence, attributed, first, to some scarcely known tribe; then, by an act of audacious generalization, to all primitive peoples; and, finally, to aboriginal man. There is no region where a healthy and fearless scepticism is more needed than in the literature which relates to ethnography. There is no people so difficult to understand and to interpret as a savage people; there is no field where competent interpreters are so few and so rare, where unlearned authorities are so many and so rash, or where testimonies are so contradictory, or so apt to dissolve under analysis into airy nothings. But what we deprecate is not the collection, the investigation, and the co-ordination of all facts connected with the habits, beliefs, state, and affinities of savage peoples; it is the philosophy they may be made to disguise. For the explicit and reasoned or implicit and inarticulated postulate of many ethnographically stated and illustrated speculations as to the earlier forms of religion, is a doctrine not simply as to the development of man and society, but as to the kind of being who was to be developed, what potentialities he had, and what forces made him the being he finally became. It is this doctrine which may both need criticism and repay it. For it does not follow that the anthropology which is an accurate description of man in his savage state is a good philosophy of religion.

3. The point of our criticism may become more obvious if we distinguish the question touching the subjective and objective senses of religion from two very different questions, those, viz., as to the source of religion, and as to its oldest and most primitive form. The question as to the source asks, Why did man begin to have a religion? but the question as to the form enquires, What sort of religion had he in the beginning? It is possible, indeed, to agree as regards the sort of religion man began by having, and to differ fundamentally as to why and as to how he came by it. We may hold that in religion, as in other things, the primitive were the rudest and the lowest forms; while we also hold that they owed their existence, low as it was, to what was highest and most rational in man, even as he then was, reaching out towards what was highest and most reasonable in the universe. If we so think, we shall see in the lowest form the promise and potency of the highest, just as we see in the savage himself the prophecy of reason and knowledge, culture and civilization. But if we conceive that not reason, but accident or ignorance, was the subjective factor of religion, then we shall regard his beliefs as a series of "mis-

taken inferences" or as a "system of superstitions" to be outgrown with the growth of knowledge, rather than as a soil rich with the germs of higher things. The phrase we have just used is Mr. Herbert Spencer's, but it is not a very felicitous phrase. A "superstition" is the belief of a lower stage of culture surviving into a higher, with which it has no affinity, and to which it adheres as a sort of fungus. Hence the belief in lucky days or magic formulæ, in witches or charms, becomes in an age of science a "superstition;" for it is a survival from a period when the notion of natural law was not into a period which conceives Nature as pre-eminently the realm of law. But the belief is not a "superstition" when it is part of a consistent whole, an integral element in the living view of Man and Nature. The term, therefore, is not applicable to the religions of lower races, which are entirely relevant to their stage of culture, and to use it of them is significant only as indicating the attitude of the enquirer's own mind. What it here expresses is Mr. Spencer's theory that the religion, or "system of superstition which the primitive man forms," is due to "mistaken inferences" or to "erroneous interpretations" of familiar phenomena. But in order that he may formulate his theory in a manner that proves it, Mr. Spencer has first to make his "primitive man"; and this man is, of course, a purely imaginary creature, made in the study and after the image of his maker. And the religion attributed to him is as imaginary as himself, for it is put together by a method that knows no order and follows no law. Time and place, race and racial relations, historical antecedents and conditions, degree of culture and moment of development, are in the matter of proof and method of treatment, utterly ignored. Thus Mr. Spencer will, in the same chapter, or even paragraph, cite the Tahitians, the American Indians, the New Zealanders, the Veddahs, the ancient Hindus, the modern Hindus, various African tribes, the Egyptians, the Greeks and Romans, the Hebrews, the Arabians, Semites in general, and "Europeans in the old times," whoever they may have been, whether Esquimaux, Finns, Basques, Kelts, Teutons or Slavs, and multitudes more,—to illustrate some particular statement or doctrine without the slightest regard to the cardinal point of their respective environments, and the no less cardinal point of the history and "experiences" of their antecedent organisms. He handles religions as if there was no such thing as chronology, or place, or genetic development, or historical evolution. Criticism, historical and literary, is for him as if it were not. He never distinguishes old and original from recent and foreign elements, but deals with the immensest systems as if they had had no history and had known no growth, at least none save such as could be determined by "the laws of mental evolution."[1] He cites[2] the Rig Veda and the Laws of Manu as alike veracious witnesses as to "what the original Aryan beliefs were," which is very much as if one were to quote the Epistles of Paul and the Decrees of the Vatican Council as equally valid testimonies concerning the most primitive elements in Christianity. With quite as delightful naïveté the Hebrews are proved to have had "rites like those of ancestor-worshippers in general," mainly by an appeal to Deuteronomy, Ecclesiasticus and the Book of Tobit.[3] The "Hebrew ideas of another life" are described in a few crude sentences,[4] and ideas of Persian origin and peculiar to later Judaism are regarded as distinctively Hebrew. The Greek and Roman religions are handled without regard to their origin or significance, and are made to illustrate Mr. Spencer's thesis either by an utter inversion or entire forgetfulness of their meaning. He is aware, indeed, that his interpretations will be called "Euhemeristic," but he does not see that

[1] *Principles of Sociology*, vol. i. p. 232.   [2] *Ibid.* p. 315.
[3] *Ibid.* 317.   [4] *Ibid.* 208.

the objection to Euhemerism is that it is radically unhistorical and unscientific, possible only where a developed mythology is studied through a philosophy; quite impossible where it has been studied in its genesis and development. It is significant, too, that he is as confident about his doctrines and theories when he cannot as when he can find evidence for them in the ancient religions. He finds in none but the Egyptian evidence of belief in a Resurrection, but he never seems to miss it. His case in no way rests on history or criticism; it is an evolution from consciousness, a theory transcendently deduced, ethnographically illustrated, but in no case historically proved. Allow a man to adapt the laws of logic and the method of proof to his own convenience, and give him the whole of time to range over for illustrations of his peculiar theory, and he will prove it; only the theory, when proved, will have but small scientific significance, since without any real relation to the growth of mind and the order of human development.

§ IV. *Ethnographic and Historical Religion*

1. Now this criticism of Mr. Herbert Spencer has, it is hoped, made several things evident. First, the difference between the ethnographic and the historical treatment of religion. Ethnography studies and sketches features, characteristics, customs, scattered, insulated, or separable phenomena; but history studies the organism as it lives and grows in its own home, affected by all the forces that surround and play upon it. In ethnography the writer selects the incidents, the customs, the beliefs, the qualities that interest him, groups and grades them in his own way, throws the emphasis where he thinks it ought to lie; in a word, states the problem in his own terms, and finds the factors that he imagines will solve it; but history allows him no such freedom, defines for him the time and the space within which he must move, the growth he has to measure, the variations he has to explain.

The only development ethnography can be made to exhibit is the one which the writer designs; it is like a picture painted on a flat surface by an artist who creates his own perspective, and by a skilful use of light and shade compels us to see just what his imagination has seen and as he saw it. But history presents us with a development which nature and man have combined to conduct, invites us to watch it proceeding, and to discover the factors by which it has been or is being accomplished. The ethnographic method is thus subjective, and either, if the man who uses it be an artist, simply descriptive, or, if he be a thinker, an illustrated dogmatic, i.e. a system speculatively deduced, though expounded in terms drawn from savage customs, real or imaginary. But the historical method is objective, and is possible only to a man who has an eye to see and to read, as if it were a living thing, the complex unity of thought and custom which man made for a religion to himself, and in making which he made himself man, and became a society, a state, and a people. It is not too much to say, that if Mr. Spencer had studied at first hand a single historical religion, we should never have had the theory which forms the basis of his sociology. And what is true of him may be said of many another ethnographer who has tried to turn his descriptive science into a philosophy.

2. But a second thing our criticism has made evident is the distinction and independence of the questions concerned respectively with the primitive form and the source or origin of religion. The question as to the form is historical, but there is no history that can resolve it. But the question as to the source is philosophical, and so admits of discussion. Yet there is a connexion between the two which may be thus indicated:—If we cannot trace religion to the hallucinations or dreams, with their suggestion of mysterious "doubles," of a gorged or a hungry savage, it will be impossible for us to describe its oldest or most rudimentary forms in such terms

as "superstitions" or "mistaken inferences." What this means will become apparent in the next discussion, which has to determine two points: (a) the relation between the subjective factor and the objective fact of religion, and (β) between the assumed primitive or ethnographic religion, and the religions of history.

(a) The subjective factor is Mind, or, more concretely, Man, conceived as nascent reason, and so constituted that he cannot become rational without realizing religion. The first effort of the reason is to distinguish itself from Nature, i.e. to become a conscious person; and the second is to transcend the Nature which it knows is different from itself, i.e. to create an order which is not an order of Nature, but of Reason. Now both processes are accomplished in the same way—by the evolution and articulation of ideas which are native to the reason, because the ideas by virtue of which it is rational. These ideas are not external things implanted in the mind by various cunning contrivances, but they are educed from within, the products of thought acting according to its own nature or laws. The most hopeless of all problems ever set to human ingenuity is this: Grant an organized being without reason, by what process of Nature can we get reason inserted within him? Man does not get reason from without; he is reason, and as reason awakens it speaks, and its speech embodies the ideas which reveal its nature, and which are at the same time the mirror in which it beholds itself. Thus it follows that the ideas which reason expresses must correspond in character and quality to what it is in itself, rather than to what can only be defined as the negation of itself. What these ideas are we may best express by saying that they are those of a being who cannot think without thinking God, or act without incorporating his thoughts in appropriate customs and institutions, i.e. as his thoughts are beliefs concerning Deity, his usages are forms which speak of his relations to the Deity and of the Deity's to him. This means that man can as little choose to be religious as to be rational; he is both, and both by the same necessity of Nature. For expression is a necessity to reason; if it is to live, it must by speaking create speech. And, similarly, expression is a necessity to religion; if it is to live, it must take to itself shape—make for itself a body; and this body will have a double correspondence, on the one side to the reason, on the other to the place which is its home.

And it is here where we may perceive the relation between the subjective factor and the objective fact. For religion, though its source be ideal, is yet not pure but embodied spirit, an expression of the reason conditioned by the environment in which it lives. Man can as little think as he can live in a vacuum, and the place he occupies will supply both form and colour to the thoughts he articulates. In other words, religion at its birth is an epitome alike of the spirit which bears it and the natural conditions within which that spirit lives. In it are mingled all the elements which compose the man and constitute his world. He can think of the gods only under terms intelligible to his intellect; still, however rude the form under which he thinks them, it is of gods he thinks. He may conceive the divine as the magic which dwells in some stick or stone, in some old garment or strange plant; or as the mysterious power which resides in some animal—a bull or bear, a dog or cat; or in some person—poet, medicine man, or chief; but however he may conceive it, what he conceives is to him as real a deity, and as truly supernatural, as Jehovah was to the Hebrews. The living heart of his belief is the theistic idea; the form in which he expresses it is the accident of time and place, marking the stage and quality of his culture, and connoting the conditions—climatic, geographical, ethnical, and political—under which he has lived. The form is, as it were, the double of the world he lives in—therefore the creation of experience; but the matter is the double of the spirit he is—therefore the product of his own transcendency. His religion is made up, then, of two constituents (i.) the substantive or ideal, i.e. the conception of the transcendental, the supernatural, or the divine, which is a product of thought working on the phenomena it perceives ; and (ii.) the formal or real, i.e. the terms or vehicles which embody his ideas, the stories, rites, and customs that come out of his own experience, both outer and inner. The ethnographic student of religion tends to emphasize the latter, and to select now one, and now another, of its features as the chief or essential element in religion. The emphasis has fallen now on the philological or literary expression ; and the mythology, the folklore, the divine names and attributes have been investigated and compared. Then the emphasis has changed to institution or custom ; and the totem, the sacrifice, the priest, the magician have become the fields of research and speculation. But these by themselves are more significant of the stage of culture than of the nature or character of the religion. For if man tells certain stories of his gods, it is only such stories as he could believe were they told of the more heroic men ; and if he believes that the sacrifice is a meal which satisfies the gods, it is because he knows that even such a meal would please men, and express or seal amicable relations between them. But the life and permanence of the religion do not lie in the elegance of the mythology or the persistence of the institution or custom ; they lie rather in the continued and refining activity of the thought. It would be hard to exaggerate the rudeness of the form which religion assumes in the lower stages of culture ; but this ought not to conceal from us the fact that the process which produced it was in its own order, if not as fine yet as rational and real, as that to which we owe the art, the poetry, and the philosophy of to-day. Man produced it because he was struggling to express or realize himself, within a system that forced him to be rational in order that he might be man while the system remained Nature. And the real continuity of religion lies in the continued activity of the creative process, the thought which is ever refining the forms it has inherited, and seeking fitter vehicles for its richer and sublimer ideas.

(β) The second question, as to the relation between ethnographic religion and the historical religions, is as important from a scientific as the first question was from a philosophical point of view. The generalities of anthropology may show how features persisted or customs survived; but they do not help us to see how the organisms called historical religions were built up, and quickened, and developed. To find a multitude of "survivals" is a thing as easy as it is insignificant; but what is much more difficult to explain, and much worthier of explanation, is how so many religious beliefs and customs have died while religion has survived, their death tending rather to its rejuvenescence than its decay. And what does this mean but the want of objective validity in what we have termed ethnographic religion as opposed to the religions of history? What is presented to us as the religion of primitive peoples is a mere abstract system stated and developed in the terms of generalized customs rather than of logical formulæ. The term *totem*, used by the North American Indians to denote one of their own customs, has been applied to Australasian tribes whose customs are too varied to be stated in identical terms, being indeed often, as the latest researches show, exactly the converse of the Indian; and the conveyance of the phrase has been naturally followed by the attribution of the thing and the whole order of thought it represented. But a particular fact stated as a general proposition is an argumentative proceeding whose worth can be easily appraised. As a consequence this product of the ethnographic method can be brought into organic relation with no single historical religion. Mr. Andrew Lang has plaintively bewailed that the strata in the field he has so thoroughly studied and so interestingly described, are not superimposed or even adjacent, but widely scattered. And the difficulty is to find the succession of the scattered strata; their sequence is a thing of imagination or conjecture, not of history. The fragments have to be collected, like the limbs of Osiris, from the most distant places, only Osiris has to be made out of the limbs, with no certainty that he ever was, or, if he ever were, that the limbs were really his. The image made of members collected from India, Australasia, America, China, Africa, and Europe, can hardly be expected to make a very homogeneous figure, though, indeed, it may well be a figure capable of being the parent of anything. But the impossibility of affiliating the forms or of finding any valid sequences in their order, makes the attempt to find the origin and roots of religion, or to define and determine its function in history and in the evolution of society through the study of its meanest and most barbarous forms, seem an altogether fallacious procedure. For religion is neither a peculiarity of the savage state, nor is it there that its social action can best be studied. Man does not leave it behind him as he leaves his stone implements, his cave dwellings, his nakedness, his polyandry, and the other accidents of his savagery. It is the one thing that can be described as his invariable attribute; and, like all things which do not die, its higher or more perfect forms are more significant of its real nature, and therefore of its actual source and cause, than any multitude of low forms or rudimentary types. This does not mean that the comparative study of the primitive religions is worthless; on the contrary, it is a discipline that no student of human nature and history can afford to despise. The more we know of savage man the better we shall know man civilized; but then civilized has even more significance for savage man than savage for civilized, especially if our purpose is to discover his possibilities and intrinsic worth

The meaning of childhood becomes apparent to us only in and through manhood; and though the psychology of the child may be a matter of inexhaustible interest to the man, and most instructive to him if he be a parent or a teacher, yet it is only in the man that the mind of the child stands revealed. So if religion be studied through savage custom and myth, some religions may be better understood, and some elements in all religions may be made more intelligible; but religion as the most potent, universal, and permanent of all human things will not be any nearer scientific explanation. For it can be explained only as it is traced to causes which are as common and as constant as itself, which operate even more powerfully in the civilized than in the savage state, and do so because the civilized man is a truer type of humanity, because he is more of a man, than the savage.

§ V. *The Causes of Variation in Religion*

Religion, then, is best studied as an organism living within its own special habitat, experiencing change even while it performs work, and developing new organs and functions because it is daily challenged to exercise new energies. But this brings us to a question concerning which something must be said, viz., if religion have a common and single root, why have we such a multitude of religions? Are there any natural causes working for variation? The fundamental principle here is: What is most generic in religion has at once its root and organ in what is most generic in man. He is religious not by chance but by Nature, not by choice but by necessity. He did not stumble into religion, but grew into it, and it grew in and with him. The true survival in religion is not the superstition or the custom which persists from a lower into a higher state, but the idea which undergoes transfiguration but not conversion. The persistence of the idea means the continuous activity of the creative factor, but the infinite variety of the forms it assumes are due to causes more or less local and occasional. There is a constant conflict between the ideal and the formal elements in religion. The spirit which created is never satisfied with its own creations, is ever returning on them, questioning, doubting, re-formulating them; and it is by being continually handled that they continuously live, outgrow their ancient forms, and effect changes even in the things they themselves had made. But the forms—creeds, customs, laws, ceremonies, priesthoods—represent the formal elements; and their invariable tendency is to impose themselves and their limitations on the ideal. Man is conservative by virtue of what in him is local and particular—what is his own in distinction not only from what is another person's, but what is man's; but he is progressive by virtue of what in him is universal and generic—what in him is his own because he is man. Hence, while the ethnographic student thinks that the custom and the institution, as the best conserved and least changeable element in religion, is the most characteristic and important; the philosophical student, aware that the institution endures only by virtue of the ideas read into it, seeks the secret of the religion in these ideas and their source. Without these the institution would die and the custom cease; it is the universal that keeps the local alive, while the local is ever threatening the universal with death. It is, therefore, in the local and occasional causes which create the outward forms that the factors of variation must be sought.

These are too many to be here analyzed and described, but they may be reduced to certain great categories, such as race, place, ethnical relations, history, social and economical needs, and special or creative personalities. Each of these affects religion on many sides and in many ways. We note only the most salient.

1. Race. It is easy to exaggerate both the fact and the function of racial characteristics, yet it is hardly open to doubt that such characteristics really exist. There is a psy-

chology of peoples as well as of persons, and communities exhibit on a large scale the distinctive qualities that particular persons show on a scale infinitely minute. The fact that the literature of one people can be translated into that of another, implies their likeness; the fact that no translation can be the exact equivalent of the original, implies their difference. When M. Renan, in his early work on the Semitic Languages, expatiated on what he termed the monotheistic instinct of the Semitic peoples, he gave poetical expression to what he conceived to be a racial characteristic. This instinct might have no more to justify it in fact than that the parent monotheism of the world issued from a Semitic people; but the theory forgot that no Semitic people has been able by its own act to make monotheism a reality. The Arabian, without the help of the Persian on the intellectual side and the Tartar on the political and military, would never have made Islam the great missionary religion it became, and has remained. The Jew would have cancelled his monotheistic ideal by his tribal enthusiasm, which allowed the Gentile to become a worshipper of Jehovah only on the condition that he became a Jew. Yet the passion that breathed the breath of life into the idea of the one God, and made it live to other races, was distinctly Semitic. The passion may have implied a deficiency of imagination and a simplicity of thought, both of which may have been due to early associations with a nature more severe and monotonous than fruitful and varied; but whatever the reason, monotheism was in its origin a Semitic faith. The Aryan, on the other hand, has never been spontaneously monotheistic, though often monistic. The unities he has striven after have been unities of thought, abstractions rather than concrete personalities. He has loved to make his gods either speak in forms more or less appropriate to the senses, or exist in formulæ more or less intelligible to the reason: according to the one impulse he has been a polytheist, according to the other he has been a pantheist; and the harmony of the tendencies has been seen in this, that where he has been most pantheistic his polytheism has been the most multitudinous. These tendencies may express influences flowing out of ancient years when the susceptible mind was impressed and worked upon by a nature that seemed alive, that blossomed into beauty, that burst into fruitfulness, and ever revealed to sense an inner energy of being that delighted to break out in life and growth. But whatever may be the cause of its special characteristics, race has its value in things both of the mind and the imagination; and so we but formulate an obvious conclusion when we say that blood counts in religion as a factor determining its special type.

2. Place acts variously upon a people, but there are two distinct influences it may exercise;—either, directly, a physical, or, indirectly, an ethnical, due to its power from its position or its configuration to hinder or to promote human intercourse. Thus the child of the mountains or the son of the desert has each had his beliefs directly affected and modified by his place. The nature which environs the two is so different that the ideas it begets in them as to the creative and conservative powers appear in very different forms and with dissimilar qualities. If the sun dispels the cloud around the mountain, thaws the ice in the valleys, and sends down the fertilizing streams into the plains, it will have one meaning for man; and if it beats hotly upon him by day, endangering by its beams his life, heating the sand under his foot, and drying the water in the springs, it will have quite another meaning for him. And as he will read through the great forces of Nature that which is behind it, the sun will in the one case become to him the name or symbol of a beneficent deity; in the other case of a demonic or of an actually or potentially maleficent power. And so the attitude of man's mind to the theistic idea, and the terms or forms he uses to express it, will be largely conditioned by his physical environment. Hence

races cradled amid a fruitful Nature,—where its vital force is the most manifest thing, compelling men to feel as if suckled at breasts of inexhaustible fulness—come to think of the creative life as something spontaneous and inner, an energy which struggles from within outwards. But races whose cradle has been the desert or the arid plain—where the forces without wither the feeble life that tries to issue from within, and where a man has to be strong if Nature is to be subdued—tend to think of the creative energy as outward, something which imposes its will on the reluctant wilderness. In the former case the tendency is to conceive Deity as an immanent energy, and life is deified as with the Egyptians, or the soul which dwells in all men and rolls through all things is made the sovereign god, as with the Brahma of the Hindus. In the latter case the tendency is to conceive Deity as outside and above Nature, a force which acts upon it rather than lives within it; and so gods are named masters, makers, lords, and described in the terms so familiar to the student of the Semitic religions. When the elements latent in each of these attitudes of mind are developed and unified, the conception becomes in the one case that of Divine immanence, in the other that of Divine transcendence. When the idea which had spontaneously arisen comes to be speculatively construed, the immanence will blossom into a Pantheism, the transcendence into a Monotheism. And as an indication of the long persistence of qualities which physical influences had tended to create, it deserves to be noted that while Pantheism is native to both Hindu and Greek thought, it has never appeared as a native product among any Semitic people, the cases which do occur having been due to the action of alien thought on special persons. And we may add, it is not without significance that the race which first learned the meaning of the Pole-star to the mariner, was one which came of a desert parentage. It applied to the trackless ocean the instincts that had been transmitted to it through fathers who had learned to seek in the heavens above guides for their way through the trackless sand below.

3. Ethnical relations, largely also affected by place, exercise varied influences. Their kind and degree and effect will depend on such things as whether the peoples meet as friends or foes, as cognates or aliens, as buyers and sellers, or as explorers and explored; whether they touch as it were only from a distance or mix and intermingle; whether their culture is alike or different in character and in stage; whether the one is of an established order with fixed laws and recognized usages, while the other is, in all similar respects, fluid and unformed; whether the one is conqueror and the other conquered, or both are equals. Thus the lower races are powerfully affected by the presence of the higher. It is doubtful whether the man who visits a new people that he may study their customs, does not cause or occasion some of the most characteristic customs he describes. The very attempt to render to a stranger an account of the thing he does, changes the attitude of the simple mind to the thing or to the mode of doing it. Wherever the foot of the white man touches, it works changes in the thoughts, blood, ways, and worship of the people. He may not mean to effect any change, but he effects one all the same; and his ubiquity has now made the discovery of a pure native religion a thing no longer possible. Then it has been often remarked, though not always with truth, that the gods of one race or tribe become the devils of another; and it is even more curious that the two things which people can most easily interchange are their vices and their gods. This is no new thing, but as old as man. It did not need to wait for illustration upon the action of our merchants and missionaries to-day; Egypt and Phœnicia, Babylonia and Assyria knew it, and ancient literature is full of it. The intercourse of peoples then as now worked for good and

evil, hastened civilization even where it changed religion. The races that were planted on the northern shores of the Mediterranean came early into contact with the older races on its eastern and southern shores, and learned from them arts and crafts, customs and beliefs that quickened their development, exercised their energies, and fitted them to play their great part in the history of the world at a much earlier period than their brothers who had remained in central and northern Europe. This ethnical intercourse made them, too, different in character and in destiny from the brothers who had wandered into India, and had become there such potent factors of religion and change. Man's influence on man, therefore, is as powerful as ever was the influence of Nature to modify worship and belief.

4. But history tends to modify religion even more than nature or ethnical relations. The longer man lives the stronger grows the power of the past over the present. For not only does memory become more crowded with images, but the images grow more defined and definite. Imagination comes to its aid, and the hero experiences apotheosis; deity is made in the image of man, and anthropomorphism enlarges the qualities and attributes of the divine. But the stage of culture at which the process of apotheosis begins, as well as the underlying idea of Deity in its relation to Nature and man, must also be taken into account as helping to determine the specific character of the religious ideal. Thus the notion of the Divine immanence was native to both the Hindu and Greek mind, but their respective pasts made a notable difference in the form it assumed. In India it was an immanence that was primarily one of nature and class, but in Greece an immanence in the man as a man. It was the Brahman who was to the Hindu the pre-eminent incarnation of his God, but in Greece it was the hero—the most manlike of men. Then, too, the stage of culture made itself apparent in the con-

struction of the Divine order. The Vedic mythology has been termed simultaneous, the Homeric successive, i.e. the Vedic deities stand together, independent, distinct, co-ordinate, but as it were uncombined and unsystematized; while the Homeric deities are reduced to system, and a principle of subordination has been introduced which reflects Greek society and the State. In the Homeric mythology there is a fine harmony between the worlds of gods and of men; neither is a reproach to the other, but each is wrought in the other's image. They do not differ in morals, lust, cruelty, love of friends, and hatred of enemies; the duties of hospitality and friendship reign in heaven as on earth. Zeus and Hera have their jealousies, quarrels, and inconsistencies even as Agamemnon and Clytemnestra, though Olympus does not know a love so pure and invincible as Penelope's. In the councils of the gods the same infirmities of temper, the same swift and satirical speech, appear as in the assembly of the Greek chiefs. The gods, like so many hungry warriors, love the smell of fat beeves, and go where they can most enjoy it. They are as envious as even men themselves can be of the happy or the prosperous man. In the upper world, as upon the earth, the under world is feared; and fate and death cast as thick a shadow upon Olympus as they do upon the homes of men. This complete anthropomorphization of the Greek god is the counterpart of the complete immanence of the idea of the divine in man; while in the Hindu mythology the pre-eminent incarnation of deity in a class or the instruments of a class, results in a notion of the divine so little man-like as to be now brutal, now physical, but never as human and ethical as we know the Greek gods tended to become.

5. But this action of history further shows itself in the influence exercised by the social or political ideal on the notion of the divine. We have very different conceptions of Deity and his relations to man in societies that are organized on the

patriarchal or regal, and in those governed by the social or communal idea. Thus amid the Semitic tribes we have very early the patriarchate. The family is the natural unit of society and has at its head the father, who is the natural monarch. And we have in consequence two parallel phenomena : the most absolute sovereignty is ascribed to God and also to the king. This is connected with the notion of the Divine transcendence, which means that God is a Will above Nature, and not within it; just as the king is at once in being and will above the state, creative of it rather than incorporated within it. On the other hand, amid the Aryan tribes of India the regal as well as the priestly class are conceived as evolved from the people; they proceed from below upwards, or grow from within outwards rather than constitute the state by a transcendent and external will. The immanent notion and tendency which in thought created Pantheism built up a society which, in its very classes, grades, and functions, represented an inherent order. The social ideal of the tribal polity thus becomes the vehicle and symbol of the tribal theology. As a consequence the social and the religious worlds helped to organize each other; the same idea was the architect of both religion and the state.

6. But now as a special form of the historical influence qualifying the political and social, the action of great personalities must be recognised. There is no region in which they are at once so powerless and so powerful—so powerless to annihilate or create, so powerful to modify or change. It does not lie with any human will to determine whether religion shall or shall not be; it is so much a product and decree of Nature that it will be whatever any individual may desire or decide. But its quality or character, its opportunity, form, or line of development may be powerfully influenced by the direct or indirect action of persons. To illustrate this would be to write the history of almost all

religions; but some remarkable phenomena may be simply noted. In religions which emphasize the immanent idea creative personalities have been rarer than in those which emphasize the transcendental. There is no land or people so steeped in religion as the Indian; all their hopes and aspirations move in obedience to its will; their literature has been made by it, their social order embodies it; but the really remarkable thing is that, while the religious person, now as teacher, now as reformer, is everywhere in the history of India, the creative personality has but rarely appeared, and in a transcendent degree has appeared but once in its whole history. On the other hand, peoples with less of the genius for religion have had persons of vaster influence on the world's history. The small tribe of the Jews produced the prophets of Israel and the apostles of the Christian faith; a small tribe in Arabia, shut off from cosmopolitan influences, produced Mohammed; China, at a remote period in her life, produced Lao Tsze and Kung Fu Tsze; ancient Persia had its great personality in Zoroaster. The reason at once of the more frequent emergence and the vital power of the creative personality in religions which are governed by the transcendental idea, may lie here—that they emphasize in so much higher a degree personal freedom and will, while where immanence is so construed as to depersonalize deity he becomes the synonym for necessity both in man and in Nature. The things that are must be, and there is no power in man to change their course. On the other hand, the transcendental idea is an expression not of force but of will; though all else may be necessitated, yet God is free. Hence, though in the popular judgment fatalism may mark Islam, yet it is not the fatalism of an inexorable mechanism or blind necessity, but of an irresistible will. Where God necessitates but is not necessitated, there must ever exist the possibility of personalities appearing which He creates and sends to accomplish large things for religion; where the cycle of life is a necessity tempered by the contingencies of a social or sacerdotal order, there is no room for the free personality and its creative and modifying work.

These are a few of the factors of formal change in religion. But within the local there lives and moves what may be termed a universal Spirit, a life we may feel rather than analyze. God has never left Himself without a witness. He has manifested Himself to men; has written His name in their hearts, and they have never ceased to be conscious of the name. The attempt to read it may have resulted in the strangest misreadings, in grotesque interpretations and applications; but from the name and the necessity of finding Him whose name it is, man has never been able, nor indeed has ever wished, to escape. And as the name is there, He who wrote it has never forgotten His own handiwork, and has moved in men and nations like the spirit which quickens the understanding. And now and then man becomes conscious of this quickening spirit, and a change passes over him; a vision of higher ideals than the mean greeds and ambitions of his secular life possesses his soul. On such occasions a tidal wave of change sweeps over the face of humanity, and by some mystic method moves from east to west, or from north to south, over peoples who had never heard of each other's existence. In one century we may find great prophets in Israel, a great religious reformer in India and another in China, and all humanity moving to new religious impulses; and there are seasons when one race seems to dominate all other races, to be for a season the master of the world, till, defeated by its very victories, it declines into a deeper obscurity than that from which it had emerged. Where are the skill and the wealth and the statesmanship of ancient Egypt? where the military prowess of Assyria and Babylonia? where the ethical passion and imperial ambitions of ancient Persia? where the art and poetry of Greece? where the statesmanship and military discipline and genius of ancient Rome? And yet do they not all live in the men and peoples who are alive to-day, and alive in a manner impossible without these earlier states and peoples? The ebb and flow in the life of humanity is a marvellous thing, and the special moment at which a man is born has, in relation to the great tides that mark the onward movement of society, a special and peculiar significance. And what do these things signify but that changes do not come unbidden,—that the inspiration of the Almighty is a factor in human destiny, and that the God who works in history fulfils Himself in many ways?

CHAPTER VII

THE PHILOSOPHY OF RELIGION

B. THE HISTORICAL RELIGIONS

THE analyses and discussions conducted in the preceding chapter may be said to have introduced us to the problems co-ordinated under the terms "the Philosophy of Religion." What is so named may now be defined as the dialectical or reasoned interpretation of the consciousness of man as expressed in his religions and unfolded in their history. As such its function is to study mind in religion, in order that it may the better explain religion through mind. Now the mind it studies is a much more concrete and real object than the abstract mind which the metaphysician tries, speculatively, to read; which the psychologist attempts, experimentally, to observe and analyze; and which the anthropologist, imaginatively, invites nature to insert or inscribe in his primitive man. For history may be described as the incarnation or externalization of this mind, and the events or acts it records as the steps and process of its self-revelation. For though these acts may have been done by persons, yet the persons have not been isolated personalities, but rather the concatenated and rational vehicles of a single and coherent power, which could operate in a multitude of forms without losing its essential unity. If then, we conceive the languages, the literatures, the institutions, the laws, the societies, and the beliefs of peoples as so much undesigned and spontaneous racial autobiography, it is evident that if these can be accurately interpreted they will enable us to live within the racial mind, and look at the world through its eyes. We have already argued that the problems of individual are one with those of collective experience; but though they be identical, yet it is no paradox to say that they grow more rather than less capable of solution by being extended in scope and increased in complexity. For while the universe does not become a mystery to man till man has become a mystery to himself, yet, though he does not cease to be mysterious, he becomes a more intelligible mystery when viewed through the whole than when regarded as a separate and independent atom. The very fact that it is those immense idealisms which we call the religions that have been the main factors in the organization of society, speaks volumes as to the intrinsic quality of the spirit which we call human nature.

We return, then, to the position, that there can be a philosophy of religion only when the religions are historically studied. Without history the philosophy would move as in a dream, attempting to grapple with the shadows of a world unrealized; while without thought history would have no vision in its eyes, would find no reason in what it saw, would simply aggregate matter whose atoms were, singly, insignificant and, collectively, an unordered heap. We may say, then, in terms suggested by one of Kant's most famous *dicta*, the philosophy without the history is empty, the history without the philosophy is blind; or, changing the figure for one more illuminative, the religions are like a multitude of dialects into which man's aboriginal speech or faculty of speech has broken. The concern of philosophy is with the speech, or the faculty that made the speech, for without it articulate and intelligible dialects could not have been. The concern of history is with the dialects, for without them speech could have had no actual or continuous life. The universal is realized in and by the individual; but the individual without the universal would be simply an uninterpretable unit. History, then, has to do with the religions as children of time and place, each with its own ancestry and kinships, its own accent and idiom, its own features and idiosyncrasies, its own antecedents and environment; but philosophy has to do with the causes which made all religion possible, and the conditions which turned the possible into actual religions. The two are thus necessary to a complete synthesis, for we can as little explain history by a method of isolation or individuation as we can interpret nature by a process of physical or metaphysical abstraction, which conceives force, but will not recognize any correlation of forces. Without the accurate knowledge of local forms, the character and behaviour of the universal cause could never be ascertained; and without the investigation of roots and reasons, the enquiry into why things are what they are and why they behave as they do, research into local forms would lose almost all its scientific worth. But the more we seek for religion some root in reason, personal and collective, the less can we conceive any religion as void or vain, an irrational chance or mischance, which has come, no one knows whence, to walk the earth with aimless feet and vanish, whither no one can tell. For if we hold with Bunsen that God, which is but another name for Reason, "and not the devil or his Punchinello—Accident—governs the world,"[1] then we must conclude that just as there is a divine thought in nature, so there is a divine idea in the religions; and could we find and express this idea, we should have the very vindication we most need of God's ways to men.

---

[1] *Christianity and Mankind*, vol. iii. p. 4.

§ I. *Religions as National and Missionary*

1. One of the most obvious and familiar classifications of the historical religions is into the local or national, and the universal or missionary. The local or national live within a defined geographical area, and are so bound up with the speech, the customs, the institutions, the special modes of thought, the social and political order of the particular peoples who inhabit it, that they could not exist apart from these conditions; while they are at once jealous of all foreign intermeddling or intermixture and void of the ambition to become the faith of the alien. The universal religions, on the contrary, refuse to be limited by a land or people, by any special speech or local usage; and are by nature expansive, seeking to comprehend man simply as man, and to live by being believed rather than merely observed. The local religions are an infinite multitude, while the universal are but three. Of these, two—Buddhism and Christianity—possess independently the missionary spirit; but the third, Mohammedanism, derived its idea from the second. The first is the product of the Aryan, the second and third of the Semitic race. The antecedents of the first lie in a religion whose keynote is monism and the immanence of Deity; the antecedents of the second, which are in a large degree also those of the third, lie in a religion whose keynote is monotheism and the transcendence of God. And each owes its special characteristics to the religion out of which it grew; the features of the parent faith are visible in the face of its offspring.

But this, like all obvious classifications, is neither accurate nor descriptive. For there are national religions that may be termed missionary, while no missionary religion either has been or can be independent of national forms and the service of particular nationalities. It may also be added that there are religions which have inspired universal empires, though without becoming universal themselves. It is, indeed, one of the curious facts of history that dreams of universal empire are older and more common than the vision of a universal religion; and it is instructive as well as curious that the peoples who dreamed of empire were never possessed of the vision, while those who had the vision were untouched by the lust of secular power. Thus the Egyptian kings subdued and plundered their weaker neighbours in honour of Horus or of Amon Ra; the mighty potentates of Mesopotamia conquered and enslaved states to the greater glory of Bel or Assur, Merodach or Nebo; Persia overcame Assyria, Babylon, and Egypt, and invaded Greece in the name of her great god; the Greek carried his language and his arts to farthest Ind, and the Roman legions bore the Roman eagles, and with them Roman law and order, throughout the civilized world. But these empires did not dream of establishing their religions where they imposed their wills. Their ambition was not to reign over mind and conscience, but simply to be sovereign in civil affairs. The peoples, indeed, were ready enough now to mock at alien deities, thus expressing their scorn or hatred of the states they defeated or were defeated by; now to borrow or propitiate them, and now to endow them with the names of their own gods; now to imitate alien cults or turn them into mysteries which should do for the initiated what their national worship failed to accomplish. But the wisest of all the world-empires most scrupulously respected all the legal rights of the religions native to the regions it conquered, and did not allow Jove to reign over any of the lands it governed. Instead the state itself underwent a species of apotheosis, the emperor became *divus*, and the citizens were, if not so tolerant, yet so devout as to naturalize in Rome the deities of other lands. And so it seems as if civil ambition were fatal to religious expansion, and to nurse a missionary empire were to cultivate a restricted faith.

2. But it was said above that a national might also be a missionary religion. The ideas do not constitute a true antithesis, for a religion may spread by a process as well of absorption as of diffusion, i.e. a religion may so assume new families or tribes into itself as to outgrow its original limits, yet without departing from its original type and home. Thus Brahmanism is so intensely racial that it may well be described as the apotheosis of blood, or as the pride of race deified. There is no law so inexorable or so pitiless as the law of Caste; it binds the Hindu peoples, even though split into a multitude of states, into a unity more absolute than the most imperious despotism has ever, or could ever anywhere have, achieved. The religion has not, indeed, any outlook beyond India; it does not love the sea; to cross it and mix with alien peoples is to lose caste; it is sufficient for itself, does not seek to be known, has no wish that the foreigner should know it; it told its meaning reluctantly, with many a protest that the secrets wrung from it were not its genuine and veritable mind, and that only the twice-born man could seek and know the truth. Yet, in spite of this deification of race, nay, perhaps because of it, Brahmanism is in India missionary to a degree and in a way that Islam is not. The latter has the strength and the severity of a system which has been knit together and forced into its place by a succession of imperious wills, creating a fanaticism as imperious as their own; but the former lives and grows like an organism perfectly adapted to its environment—plastic, elastic, invincible as the waves which break against the rock only to return unwearied, increased in volume, massed into rhythmic ranks, to break unbroken again and yet again. And so Brahmanism grows irresistibly, absorbs tribes, steals into the jungles, creeps up the mountains, modifies the Mohammedan, assimilates the hill-man, ever enlarging its numbers, yet never leaving its home. And as in India so in China, where the ancestral religion may be described as the

apotheosis of the family as distinguished from the race. Here, too, tribes have been absorbed, other cults and religions have been assimilated, the magic of Taoism has been allowed to stand beside the wisdom of Confucius, and the word and ritual of Buddha have supplemented the simple speech of both; but the ancient customs still live, observed by hundreds of millions where once they were followed by tens. These religions are national, yet they are missionary; though their increment comes by absorption, yet the absorbed are the converted, changed from heathen into children of the faith.

3. But it is no less true that the most aggressively missionary religion has a radius within which it lives most vigorously, races it commands and possesses most completely, and social or political conditions which it feels most congenial to its spirit and most favourable to its growth. Thus Buddhism moves within a well-defined area, which it has never been able to break through or live beyond. It spread very early to southern India; crossed the sea from Ceylon to Burma and Siam; in the north it pierced the passes of the mighty Himalayas, and moved eastward to China and Japan. But the enthusiasm of its missionaries failed to touch the free and wandering tribes of Central Asia, or the cold and more rational mind of Persia, though both were destined a thousand years later to put their stiff necks under the yoke of the stern Arabian prophet. We may say, then, that Buddhism is a missionary, but not a universal religion,—it is not even generically Asiatic, though specifically Oriental. Its intellectual basis and superstructure, the ethics it inculcates, the ideal of life it enjoins, and the type of society it would create or realize, are, while distinctive of the land of its birth and congenial to the peoples it has converted, yet so foreign and so offensive to the more strenuous Western mind that it could not persuade it to believe or awaken within it any sympathetic response.

And Western does not here mean European; it means to the West of India, and includes races which gave to Asia its oldest civilization and its most masterful empires as well as its last and most aggressive religion. It was not its white face that made Europe insusceptible to the eloquence of the dusky Hindu, but it was what the Hindu preached. His word was a gospel to his own people, but a meaningless mystery to minds with another history and a different outlook on life.

The missionary and universal features in Christianity will be discussed later; but here it must be noted that it seems to the Orient as distinctively Occidental as the religions of India or China seem Oriental to us. We may argue that intellectually it is of no place or time; that historically it is Asiatic in origin; that its founders were Semites, its first preachers and earliest disciples Jews; but this is to the Hindu or the Chinaman to speak ancient history, not living fact. It comes to India from the land and in the speech of its conquerors; to China in the ship and the raiment of the merchants who trade for gain, and who would for the sake of profit break up the most ancient civilization in the world. And it is not surprising that the peoples judge as they see, and hate because they so judge. It would be wonderful were it to be otherwise. Christianity comes to them speaking the tongue of Europe, thinking with its mind, baptized into its spirit, charged with its ambitions,—if not expounded, yet annotated, illustrated, and made lucid more by its soldiers, statesmen, merchants, and magistrates than by the missionaries whose office it is to speak up for the religion. The Eastern peoples cannot see it because the Western sunlight that streams through it has got into their eyes. And so they feel its missionary spirit to be offensive; it is part of the insolence which marks the raw aggressiveness of the young and inexperienced West. They identify the religion with the people most active in its service, and think of it as only a national faith which European vanity has, simply because the faith is Europe's, mistaken for the world's.

§ II. *The Idea and the Institution in Religion*

1. It is evident, then, that our analysis must be carried farther back until we reach principles of differentiation at once simpler and more determinative than can be expressed by terms like local and universal, national and missionary. And here we begin by drawing a distinction:—to use national forms and to be served by particular nationalities is a very different thing from being either dependent on them or identical with them. If a religion were incapable of assuming a national or local form, it would be disqualified from doing any good to the nation; but if it were incapable of assuming any other form than this one, it would be unfit to be of service outside the particular nation, or simply to man as man. A universal religion may be described as one capable of being possessed by any people, but incapable of being the possession of any one people; while the mark of a particular religion is fitness for one state or race and unfitness for any other. The universal addresses man as man, is able to speak his many languages, adapt itself to his many stages of culture, live within his many environments,—physical, intellectual, social, political,—even though it may be for the purpose of ultimately adjusting them to its own ideal; but the local can use no more than one tongue, live within but one body, and flourish in only one environment. In other words, the universal emphasizes the substantive, the ideal, the essential; while the local emphasizes the formal, the external, what we may term the provincial accent and the dialectal idiom. Now, the analysis of religion into the subjective or causal elements, and the objective or caused, revealed certain possibilities of emphasis in actual religions: they may accentuate the ideas, the truths, the beliefs which constitute their reasonable soul; or

they may accentuate the customs, the polity, the institutions, and usages which form their visible organism. Where the accent falls on the ideas and beliefs, the religion is more or less independent of place; where the accent falls on customs and usages, the religion is local, the only expansion possible to it is through the growth or diffusion of the people, the caste, or the order whose institution it is. The mere change of accent from usage to belief does not indeed by itself distinguish a universal from a local religion; that depends more on the quality of the ideas, the character of the ideals, and their power to command a suitable embodiment, personal and collective. The mere development of the intellectual contents of a national religion will not universalize it—may indeed dissolve it as custom without enlarging it as faith. Thus the action of Greek thought was as disintegrative of Greek religion as it was later re-integrative of the Christian. The ideals of the philosophical intellect and the realities of religious custom formed in Greece a contrast that soon became a conflict. What the religion was we know only in part. We have learned since Lobeck to think of the mysteries as shows or spectacles rather than as schools of secret wisdom; but we forget that to see is also to learn, and that what is true of the mysteries is largely true of the cults as a whole: they were spectacles, though not always edifying spectacles. The student who studies Greek religion in literature or in art may with Hegel speak of it as the apotheosis of the beautiful; but the man of cultivated reason and refined feeling who saw it as it lived, feared rather its power to deprave the passions and defile the imagination of the multitude. Of all the gods of antiquity the Greek were the most human: warriors and heroes, fathers and sons, husbands and brothers, magnified men all of them, no one immortal in his own right, pure by nature and good by choice. The poetry which describes their characters and lives was the only sacred history the people knew, yet to us it is the most secular poetry in all ancient literature. But the discovery made by philosophy, that the ideals of the reason were one with the ideas fundamental in religion, begot a sense which the worship of the temple and the mythology alike offended. With the vision that spared no illusion the Greek thinkers saw that two things were needful: religion must be saved by being purged from its coarser customs, and men must be got to think of the gods better than they thought of themselves. It was the necessity, yet impossibility, of doing these two things that forced the thought to dissolve the religion it could not refine. Yet what it failed to accomplish then it achieved later. The Greek thinkers bound once for all thought and belief, reason and deity, man's highest idea and his chief object of worship, indissolubly together. They made him feel that he could never think his best unless he thought worthily of his God, and that the truth which it was the function of the reason to seek was, when found, a law for the government of life. They coined terms that were to be used in building up a more universal theology than their own, and so evoked what we may term the religion latent in man as to make it the inalienable heritage of the race. To make a theology may be a smaller thing than to found a religion, but it is only through its theology that the religion can have any reality for the intellect or any authority for the conscience. Theologies apart from religion are but fields for the exercise of the speculative reason; religions apart from theologies are but sensuous arts, the sanctioned amusements of the vulgar. Hence, though Greek thought dissolved the consuetudinary religion of Greece, yet by laying the basis of every future theology it performed a service so eminent that it deserves to be described as the contributory creator of a religion qualified, by the degree in which the Deity it worships is one with the highest ideal of the reason and the supreme law of the conscience, to be at once missionary and universal.

2. But the principle which has just been stated involves another, its complement and counterpart: the religion that emphasizes the formal at the expense of the substantive element loses in moral quality just as it gains in local features or provincial character. Worship and belief stand to each other as language and thought; as man thinks of Deity, so he worships, but it is from the worship, and not from the schools, that the multitudes learn what to think or believe concerning Him, as well as the terms on which He will accept their homage and consent to be their friend. But worship is precisely the point where man is most potent, where his fears, passions, impulses of hope and despair have freest play; and where he finds it therefore so much easier to accommodate the usages he follows to his own weakness than to make or keep them worthy of the majesty of God. The very desire to stand well with God, when he knows he ought not so to stand, leads man to the use of means for appeasement or propitiation congruous to his own nature, and so more or less ignoble; and the use of the ignoble in worship by depraving the notion of Deity lowers both the man and the religion. As a simple matter of fact, which the scientific student of religions will be the last to dispute, the agencies which do most to deteriorate and demoralize religion are the usages, the sacrifices and the offerings designed to reconcile man to God. As a rule, when man attempts to do the greatest offices, he tends to do them in a way which he himself feels to be agreeable, just as if he argued, What is pleasant to me must be acceptable to the Deity. And as his worship, like his word, is the incarnation of an idea, the idea it incarnates is his interpretation of God, the kind and quality of the Being he wishes to please, and the sort of things that are conceived to give Him pleasure. A purely speculative idea of Deity does not constitute a religion; it is constituted by the idea which is realized in the worship, and

is by it judged or redeemed. Thus the speculative idea of ancient Egypt was refined and even noble: the ethics in the Book of the Dead are perhaps the most exalted ethics in ancient religion; but the worship of the ox, the ape, the cat, the crocodile, and similar beasts, with all the bestial ministrations it involved, stamped the religion with a character and made it exercise an influence which suited its worship rather than its speculative idea or its theoretical ethics. Greek thought laboured hard to redeem Greek religion from the worship that depraved it, but it laboured in vain. Xenophanes reproached Homer and Hesiod for attributing to the gods things men held to be dishonourable and disgraceful. Herakleitos condemned the men who prayed to images, or sang the shameful phallic hymns to Dionysos, and the priests, priestesses, and mystery-mongers who traded on men's fears. Plato described the popular mythology as "lies and bad lies," and proposed to blot out of Homer the stories that did not become the good, the images, acts and indecencies, unseemly in all, but most of all unseemly in Deity, which appealed to the more ignoble qualities in men—the fear of death, contempt of virtue, lust, irreverence, hate, treachery, cowardice, insensibility to the true and the beautiful. The Stoic, who consciously lived under the reign of an ethical ideal, tried to get rid of the immoralities in the popular beliefs, which the worship articulated, by allegorizing the mythology, turning it into an elaborate and finely articulated parable in which the ancients had stored their wisdom and out of which the moderns were to draw it like honey from the honeycomb. And did not the greatest of the Epicureans, the Roman Lucretius, because he so loved beauty and truth, hate religion, which had so much power to terrorize and deprave, but none to elevate and ennoble, and which could only lower with baleful eyes from the four quarters of the heavens upon the unhappy race of mortals? And as with ancient Egypt and Greece, so with modern India. There are Brahmans who think high thoughts, and dream sublime dreams, and conceive Deity as pure Being, whom to know is highest bliss. But they do not represent the religion which is known as Hinduism; with it their Supreme has only the remotest speculative concern. The god who is worshipped in the temple is not the Brahma of thought; but it is the wild and furious Kālī, or the mighty and excited yet ascetic Śiva, or the golden-haired and swift-moving and gracious Vishnu, or Krishna of the many loves and the invincible life, and the multitude of similar deities that the *pujari* waits on and the people pray to and praise. And the worship is as the gods are, and the religion is as the worship and the gods. The idea that does not penetrate, purify, and command these may be an object of thought, but is no part of religion; the religion which does not absorb the highest thought, at once refining it and refined by it, is divorced from reason and morals, and has ceased to guide and inspire man's better life. It may continue a worship or a usage, but it has ceased to be in the true and proper sense a religion.

§ III. *The Idea of God in Religion*

A. Buddhism

1. The ultimate principle, then, which determines the character and quality of a religion, is the object it worships, or, to use the old simple and concrete term, its idea of God. Worship is essentially an act and process of reciprocity, a giving and a receiving; in it man surrenders himself to God, that God may communicate of His grace to man and realize in him His will. But this reciprocity signifies that each term of the relation is a person, each conscious of the other, each seeking to find and know the other. On the one side is the person who admires and adores and implores; on the other side is the Person who can see the speaker, hear his voice,

and respond to his appeals. Hence no impersonal Being whether named fate or chance, necessity or existence, the soul or the whole, can be an object of worship, though it may be an object of thought. As a matter of historical fact no religion has ever been a pantheism, nor has any pantheism ever constituted a religion. The Hindu philosophies, for example—and this is especially true of the Vedantâ—are just as much and just as little a religion as are the speculations of Plato and Plotinus, of Spinoza and Jacob Boehme. They are of the nature of afterthoughts, hypotheses to account for things as they are, to be studied and criticised as products of the logical intellect rather than of the spontaneous and inspired reason. Pantheism, in all its forms, is on its ideal side the deification of the actual, or the apotheosis of what is, and its ultimate truth is the right of all that is, whatever it is, to be. Hence it can be quite consistently used to vindicate the most multitudinous polytheism as well as the grossest cults; but what it cannot do is to take the place of any one of the gods or cults it vindicates, and by inviting worship become a religion. The impersonal must be personalized before thought, which is a subjective activity, can pass into worship, which is a reciprocal action, or a process of converse and intercourse between living minds. But we cannot say of monotheism what has been said of pantheism; on the contrary, it was a religion before it became a philosophy, and its speculative problems and perplexities grew out of its power as a religious faith. The notion of a single and supreme God obviously involves a single religion, and so cannot be used to justify either a multitude of deities, or the legitimacy of their worship, or the existence of an actual which is in conflict with its ideal, the holy and gracious character of a God who must be personal to be worshipped, but who can be most easily conceived by having all His personal qualities translated into empty logical abstractions. And so monotheism has a much harder intellectual problem than pantheism, but it has a higher religious value and greater ethical force. For since what is does not satisfy it, it feels bound by obedience to the Supreme Will to create what ought to be. The historical significance of this idea for religion is, therefore, the question we have next to discuss.

2. But before we can proceed we must deal with a curious fact which may seem to invalidate both our argument and the conclusion which has been stated as the premiss of the new discussion: there are, as we have seen, two original missionary religions, and of these the one knows no God, while the other knows no God but One. Buddhism has been cited as an illustration of how a highly and potently ethical faith can exist not only without a personal God, but even without any deity whatever. Such citation, however, is essentially incorrect; for nothing could be farther than the soul or system of the Buddha from what we mean by atheism. He indeed denied both the pantheistic and the polytheistic Brahmanisms of his day, with the authority of the sacred books on which they were based, the social distinctions by which they were justified, and the customs by which they were guarded and enforced; but to turn this denial into the affirmation of an atheism is a feat of the most inconsequent logic. We maintain, on the contrary, that his denial was the expression of a thoroughly theistic consciousness. Buddha's relation to the thought and religion of his time has been already sketched.[1] He desired to escape from its unethical metaphysics and sensuous worship, and to come face to face with the moral realities of existence and life. This he did by insisting that a Supreme Soul which had no direct and helpful relation to the millions of souls that sorrowed, was but a supreme deceit; that gods who were void of moral qualities were but empty names; that a priesthood which did but observe ceremonies, perform sacrifices, or cultivate a self-regarding asceticism, and did not teach men who were

[1] Ante, pp. 118-121.

dying in ignorance, was but a master of make-believe; and that such a social system as caste was derogatory to the dignity of man, the harmony of society, and the end of existence. And so he became a preacher, persuading men to believe as he did; he praised virtue, practised charity and chastity, lived as one who had discovered that goodness was the secret of life and that its end was to be holy, and he showed men how to associate for its attainment. He could not free himself from the sub-conscious mind of his people; he thought as they did, used their logic to disprove their formulated principles, and to substitute for their egoistic metaphysics the noblest dream of altruistic ethics which ever broke upon the Oriental spirit. And if the idea of a sovereign moral order, too inexorable to allow the evil-doer to escape out of its hands and too incorruptible to be bribed by sacrifices into connivance at sin, be a theistic idea, then Buddha was a transcendent theist. But his people could not stand where he did; his philosophy could not become a religion without a person to be worshipped, and they, by a sublime inconsistency of logic, rose in the region of the imagination and the heart to a higher consistency, and deified the denier of the Divine. Buddhism, then, may be described as the apotheosis of the ethical personality, an apotheosis spontaneous and imaginative rather than rational and logical It could not be justified by the reason, but it was a vivid reality to faith. The deification was none the less complete that the religion knew no God, though it was a result that at once paralyzed the intellect and quickened and satisfied the heart. For on the speculative side Buddha was an anomaly in the universe, stood where no being could have been conceived as able to stand, invested with higher ethical attributes and enshrined in more reverent honour than India had ever ascribed to any deity, yet without having any of the physical qualities or functions which belong to a divine Being. But on the religious side devotion embalmed him in the richest and sweetest mythology known to man. Tales of his infinite tenderness became the soul of his religion, which lived not by the worship of his relics, or by meditation on the four sublime truths, or by the many attempts to stumble into the noble eightfold path, or by the subtle disputations of the doctors, but by the faith that he who impersonated its ideal was a person who had spoken, who could hear speech, and who would himself yet return to accomplish what was further needed for the complete saving of man.

§ IV. *The Idea of God in Religion*
B. HEBRAIC MONOTHEISM

1. We turn now to the question raised by the action of monotheism. What is here cardinal is the fact that it appeared as a belief creating a religion, not as a rational idea constituting a philosophy. And this means that while it rose amid a people to whom the transcendental idea was native,[1] it began to live, not as a speculative principle, but as a belief surcharged, as it were, with personality. It had none of the qualities of an intellectual concept, did not define or deny, but simply affirmed, as of a definite person, "The God of the people is a living God, and acts, loves, hates, thinks, wills as a Being must who has made a nation His special concern and care." And here another cardinal fact has to be recognized, that the belief, unlike a reasoned philosophical idea, had to be incorporated in local and social forms; that these could not be other than ancient and ethnical; and that therefore it could not fail to be governed in its life and growth more by these consuetudinary forms than by speculative or dialectical forces. In other words, in a world where all religions were only local and tribal cults, it was only as such a cult that mono-

[1] Ante, pp. 217–219.

theism could begin to be; and the only form in which it could be held by men who were neither speculative nor logical thinkers, but only sons of the desert, in consciousness incoherent, confused though convinced in mind, was as a belief in the superiority and sufficiency of their God, not as an articulated notion which denied reality to all other gods.

In itself, as handled by analytic thought, the belief signified that ideas which transcended the tribe or nation had come into existence; and that in due season, by the sheer pressure of its immanent logic, the ancient and hitherto invariable association of God with a particular people and its special forms of worship would cease. But as a matter of fact the belief had to live as an expansive and expulsive power within a twofold rigorously limiting medium; first, a tribal consciousness of colossal egoism; and, secondly, the institutions and customs of the tribe. The humane force in Greece was culture, or the thought which so interpreted nature as to refine man; the humane force in Israel was faith, or God so interpreted as to be incapable of restriction to any people or place. Culture was personal, and so independent of the customs it disliked or the laws it criticized; faith was collective, could become worship only by becoming social, and so stooping to tribal usages. Thus the idea which the faith expressed the polity tended to restrict, if not to deny. The impossibility of either surrendering or realizing his religious ideal is the tragedy in the history of Israel. The very majesty of the ideal waked the fanaticism of the tribe, and begot the consciousness that it had a treasure too singular and sublime to be entrusted to the hands of any other people. In theory Jehovah was the God of the whole earth, but in fact He was the God of the Jews only; and to share in His grace and covenant other peoples must become Jews, it was not enough that they should be men.

2. But even under these conditions, or possibly all the more because of them, the monotheistic idea revealed its intrinsic character. We may study its action first in the attitude of Hebrew thought to man and history. If we examine the conception which underlies the structure and narratives of the Old Testament, we shall find, as the peculiar and characteristic creation of the theistic idea, what we may without extravagance name a philosophy of history and of religion. The similarities of the Hebrew narratives of creation to the Chaldæan mythologies, with their days and stages of creation, the chaos and the void which preceded it, the division of the waters, of the darkness and the light, with the order in which the successive organisms appear, the coming of man and the dawn of the Sabbath, are too well known to call for either exposition or remark; but the genius of Israel contributes the idea which turns the mythical into a rational process, and which entitles his race to the praise Aristotle accorded to Anaxagoras: he walks amid the ancient peoples like a sober man among drunkards. We start with a beginning in which God is; He is the only uncaused Being; the vision that would pierce the eternal past sees Him alone, and beside Him stands no second; and His creative methods are those of the thinker rather than of the mechanic or artificer, and are as remote as possible from the monstrosities of the mythical cosmogonies, whether Babylonian or Greek. He speaks, and His language is nature; He commands, and the personalized forces obey His word. His spirit moves upon the face of the waters; He breathes into man the breath of life. And His relation to the creature is no less remarkable. Since man is His breath, he is His kin, with a dependent being, yet with an independence of will which fits him to hold fellowship with the God who made him. This dignity, which he can keep only by obedience, he receives but to lose; for on the very morrow of the creation, which, as it left God's hand, was so good, evil

HISTORY OF MAN AND RELIGION 247

enters because man, who had been made so much greater than he knew, was by his very innocence and inexperience so open to its enticements.

And from this point onwards the marvellous segregative and organizing faculty of the monotheistic idea shows itself with growing distinctness. The material it deals with is old, traditional or borrowed, expressing the common knowledge or beliefs of Israel and the cognate peoples; but the idea so acts as to build it into a new structure with a new life. Evil becomes the opponent without being the counterpart of God, and works against Him through man, in whom it becomes impersonated, while He works against it in man and in the course of his history. And here we meet in an implicit and more profound form the question so familiar to certain schools of Greek thought as to the origin of religion. Man has been so made that religion is native to him; but he has so acted that a multitude of religions have come to be. The instinct to worship springs from the nature he owes to the Creator; but the impulse to imagine counterfeit deities comes from the evil which desires a God lenient to sin. Man cannot escape his destiny, he must be religious; yet even in being what he must he indulges his self-will, and by multiplying religions grows alien from the truth. But man's misbehaviour does not relieve the Creator from responsibility for His handiwork; nay, it has rather increased it, and so sin is met by punishment. The guilty race perishes in the waters of the flood; but, as if to show that destruction is no cure, the saved family, the moment it touches the earth, again betakes itself to sinning. Since the severest and most exemplary penalties, so far from acting as deterrents, seem only to encourage evil to return as an unvanquished and mocking power, discipline is tried instead. If men will not retain God in their knowledge, He will neither accept their depraved ignorance nor abandon them to it. And so a people is chosen, and by special methods trained as the vehicle of His truth, that in them "all the nations of the earth may be blessed." In the literature this universalism within the election is never lost sight of; the people are not allowed to think themselves an end, God is not restricted to their borders, but in the Law a hedge is set round them that His name may be preserved for all mankind. The forms used to express this idea are as graphic as they are naïve. The man who appears as priest of the Most High God, blessing the father of the faithful and receiving tithes of him, does not belong to the selected family.[1] The forsaken bondwoman and her son are seen and specially cared for in the desert by the God of Abraham, who thus knows Ishmael as well as Isaac.[2] The "perfect man, who fears God and eschews evil," dwells not in Judæa, but in the land of Uz.[3] The anointed minister of His will is a heathen king, a Persian.[4] Out of the East comes a queen to admire the wisdom of Solomon.[5] In one prophetic vision all nations are seen bowing down to serve Him;[6] in another all empires, even those most violently opposed to His kingdom, are made to be the ministers of His will.[7] And these universal elements persist in the face of the rigorous tribal consciousness which ever tended to conceive God as Israel's rather than Israel as God's.

3. But still more instructive than the thought which applies the monotheistic idea to man and history is its action within the religion. Here there is a twofold movement, one which is proper to the idea itself, its immanent growth or personal history; and one which belongs to the worship and institutions in which the collective consciousness laboured to incorporate and realize it.

(*a*) The history of the idea shows its progressive amelioration and expansion, the coincident growth of higher moral

---

[1] Gen. xiv. 18–20; cf. Ps. cx. 4; Heb. v. 6, 10; vii. 1–10.
[2] Gen. xvi. 10–13; xxi. 12–20.   [3] Job i. 1.
[4] Isa. xliv. 28; xlv. 1.   [5] 1 Kings x. 1–10.
[6] Isa. lix.–lxi., lxv.   [7] Dan. vii.

BECOMES ETHICAL IN CHARACTER 249

qualities, and a wider and more sovereign universalism. At first strength or power and God are nearly equivalents. His names speak of might, of a force that can be neither exhausted nor resisted; and while He is so conceived He is but the strongest—and therefore the most majestic and awful—of the gods, who has selected a people for Himself. Since He has chosen Israel He cannot brook a rival; He is a jealous God, towards the faithful pitiful and slow to anger, but terrible to the faithless. Yet even in early times His moral quality appears; at the heart of the Mosaic legislation there stands a moral idea or law which governs His relations to His people and His people's to Him. These relations are conditional and not absolute; God can be theirs, and they can be His only as they believe and obey, and their obedience is to be personal and ethical, not simply collective and ceremonial. This was a wonderful innovation in religion, a thing so new and so strange that its significance and its possibilities were by no means obvious to those who saw it made. But this was only the beginning of change; the longer the people knew God and the better they served, the more they loved and revered Him. He had called them out of Egypt, founded their state, which stood in His strength rather than in its own. On this act He would not go back, for was He not faithful, bound by His acts, bound by His promises, though acts and promises alike implied that His people should be as faithful as He? But this strong and sovereign and faithful God was also tender and compassionate: had He not married Himself to Israel, and would He not be true to His vows even when Israel erred, and be patient, forbearing, forgiving, even as a noble husband to a faithless wife? But there was a nearer and a higher thought: the Maker was the Father; and though his child might rebel, yet would He not forget the fruit of His loins. And if He was a God of this order, did He not dwell apart from all gods, and from all frail and feeble creatures, holy in nature and in name? But the more moral He was conceived to be, the more moral man had to become in order to please Him. It was not enough that He should be honoured by fasts and festivals, by sacrifices and oblations, as were the gods of the Gentiles. What He required of man was justice, mercy, humility, purity of hands and heart; the only service fit for a holy God was the service of holy men. Hence the worship of the Good by the good was the only worship He could approve. And at this point the evolution of the idea introduced into the religion a twofold change; first, Jehovah ceased to be regarded by the great teachers as the God of one people, bound to them by peculiar ties of word and deed, and He came to be conceived as the God of the pious man everywhere, sought and worshipped by him, loving the search and approving the worship; and, secondly, He was to be recognised in a hitherto unknown degree as the God of the individual, the hearer of his prayer, the comforter of his life the object of his faith, and the hope of his salvation. And these were not opposed, but concordant tendencies, for what is most universal must be open to every individual, and what every person may appropriate must be accessible to all. The books which express these ideas are the sublimest, not only in Hebrew, but in all sacred literature. The great prophets of the captivity and the return, especially Jeremiah and the later Isaiah, express the monotheistic as a collective yet ethical faith, opening its arms to all the reverent, blessing all the obedient. And the Book of Psalms is the voice of the monotheistic faith as a personal religion, seeking with a passion that will not be denied the God who is the light and life of the soul. It needs Him in its joy and in its sorrow, in the face of death and in the midst of strife, when it goes to the house of God in goodly company, and when it pines alone, forsaken of all the men it trusted; when it dwells in the besieged city or watches on the lone plain the flocks by night, when it is uplifted by being cast down into the depth

THE TRIBAL INSTINCT IN WORSHIP 251

or humbled by being allowed to go its own way to disaster and shame; but, above all, it needs Him when it has sinned against Him, and can only ask that He would, according to the multitude of His tender mercies, blot out its transgressions. The Psalter is a great Book of Religion; it shows that devotion is most sublime when it is most personal, that the man who has never stood with his soul uncovered before God has never worshipped, or tasted the ecstasy of one who, though a mortal, has lost all sense of mortality by feeling round him the everlasting arms. The literature that can plant so majestic a life in the soul may well be known as the sacred Book of Monotheism.

(β) When we turn from the idea to the institutions, or the worship by which God was to be approached, and in which He was to be served, we come upon a history with a very different moral. Here we find the tribal consciousness at work, seeking to restrict God to Israel, to fix the terms on which the Gentile should be allowed to participate in His grace. It is a sad story, all the sadder because through so many ages the Christian read the Jew's legislation with the Jew's eyes and in his sense. But now that our eyes are opened we can see, as Stephen and as Paul saw, the strenuous labour of the Jew, running through many centuries, to limit the Holy One to his tribe. The institutions, which were the organism of worship, if not in intention yet in fact and in effect, contradicted and cancelled the monotheism which was the intellectual and moral soul of the religion. To say this is not to undervalue the ethical ideas that underlie the ritual. The people elected to serve God must be worthy of the God they serve. "Be ye holy, for I am holy," is the maxim on which their worship is founded. The people who are God's priests to mankind must be clothed in the beautiful garments of the priesthood. The idea is excellent, provided the symbolical sense be not forgotten; but here as everywhere the tribal instinct translated the symbols into substance. And as the ethical was lost in the ceremonial, the universal died in the particular. The more sharply the national consciousness expressed itself in national institutions, the more emphatically were tribal limitations placed upon the religion. The more they made the law they enacted the law of God, the less could they allow peoples who had not the law any share in their God. By building the temple they localized the worship of Him who knew no place; by drawing tighter the terms of the covenant, they confined to themselves the Father who loved every people; by forming an hereditary priesthood they attached His service to one family; by elaborating their ceremonies, they shut religion within the ritual which they alone possessed, though even here the ethical sovereignty which could not be denied to Jehovah made Him broader than their law. The writer of most significance here is Ezekiel, who is priest as well as prophet, and who stands between the Deuteronomic legislation on the one hand, and the Levitical on the other. Jehovah is to him pre-eminently the God of Israel and they are his people.[1] He makes with them an everlasting covenant, sets His temple in their midst, and dwells in their land.[2] The priests, like himself sons of Zadok, are the ministers who enter the sanctuary and approach God for the people;[3] and their independence is to be secured by a gift of land which is to be "holy," the portion of the priests, the ministers of the sanctuary[4] whose revenues are thus assured that they themselves, with their offices and rites, may be protected from princes and people. Ritual offences are grievous sins; and though he holds the individual responsible, yet the real unit before God is the nation, and the only goodness the nation can know or manifest is conformity to some external law. Hence Ezekiel represented the tendency that would restrict God to a particular place or definite temple, His ministry to a specific priesthood, His worship to special forms, and His

[1] xxxiv. 30.   [2] xxxvii. 26-28.   [3] xliv. 15, 16.   [4] xlv. 3-8.

servants to a peculiar people. The higher and more spiritual prophets struggled indeed to emancipate the religion from this tribal particularism, but they struggled in vain. They saw the impure idolatries which corrupted the nations; they described with passion and splendid irony the idol which the smith made and the carpenter fastened in his place, and the people bowed down before and called upon as their god; and over against it they placed the Eternal, the unmade Maker, who formed the light, who formed the darkness, who overthrew kings and set up kingdoms, who fainted not and never was weary, and they bade all states to come and worship Him. But their ideal remained a prophetic vision; it never became a reality. The real that was they hated only less than the heathen worships, if indeed they hated it less. For in the region of realized things the fanaticism of the tribe was mightier than the inspiration of the prophet. It is one of the supreme ironies of history that the last century in which the monotheistic people existed as a nation was also the period of their most frenzied particularism. In the heated imagination of the tribe the vessel became more infinitely precious than the treasure it carried.

§ V. *Judaism at Home and in the Dispersion*

1. But what Israel at home failed to do, the Israel of the dispersion more nearly accomplished. The men who escaped in some measure from the tribal institutions escaped also in the same degree from the tribal consciousness; and so could look at religion in the light of their universal theism rather than through the shadows cast by local cults and customs. Of the kingdoms that sprang from the empire of Alexander, two had dealings with Israel: the Syrian oppressed him at home, the Egyptian protected him abroad. The Seleucid kings so tyrannized over the elect people, so insulted their faith and worship, as to provoke the Maccabæan revolt; and

in the war for freedom religion became the symbol of the patriot and the seal of civil independence. As a consequence the tribal and the religious consciousness became more deeply interfused, the religious gave to the tribal its exaltation and its sanction; while the tribal defined, narrowed, and embittered the religious. But the Ptolemies, by befriending the Jews, who had by settling in their opulent cities increased their wealth and enhanced their importance, evoked a temper quick to admire the different and to assimilate the foreign. And the amelioration was most marked in the region of faith, for the immigrants soon discovered that even as regards religion the Gentiles could teach the Jews as well as learn from them. The very attempt to interpret their religion for the foreigner, interpreted it into a new and larger faith for themselves. The Scriptures were translated out of the Hebrew into the Greek tongue, and so became international or even cosmopolitan, a book for Gentiles as well as Jews. Then translation did not leave the matter unchanged; sacred history and discourse, read in the medium of a literary and philosophical language, not only lost much of their old simplicity and many of their old associations, but also gained with their new forms new associations and a new sense. The Jew who knew Greek but did not know Hebrew read his Scriptures more as a Hellenist than as a Rabbi; the traditions of the great synagogue fell from him, and the canons, critical and exegetical, of the Alexandrian schools took their place. With the knowledge of Greek came also the knowledge of another order of religious thought. To hear Moses and Plato, Jeremiah and Zeno, Isaiah and Euripides speak in the same tongue was rather to realize their kinship than to feel their difference. And there began to dawn upon the students of Alexandria what had been hidden from the patriots of Judæa, that the vision of Deity had been known to Greece as well as to Israel. The Attic sage and the Hebrew seer were of one spirit, fulfilled like functions, were inspired and instructed by the same God. The method of allegorical interpretation which the Greek had used to reduce his mythology to literary decency and philosophical wisdom, the Jew used to turn his sacred history into a theology; the creation, Eden, the fall, our first parents, the patriarchs and their acts, were all subjected to the metamorphic process which had expelled violence from Homer and reduced to respectability the most lascivious of the gods. But the theistic idea suffered the most significant modification. The Greek Logos was allowed to break into the stern solitude of the Hebrew Deity. It stood between Him and the world, separated Him from its evil and grossness, and relieved it from the oppressive weight of His almighty hand. The Logos was the intelligible which He had thought into being; but it was also the architect who had realized the actual. The All-holy did not stand face to face with the material and sensuous, but He saw them, if He could be said to see them at all, through the medium of His beloved Word. And this mediated relation allowed a kindlier attitude to man and his religions. They were studied not through the divisive properties of law and custom, but through the affinities of imagination and thought. The speech which had interpreted the religion made the religion more just to all who had used the speech. Greece as well as Judæa had known the true God; in the one as certainly as in the other the Logos had been active; men through contemplation of His beauty had learned to obey His will. And so a conclusion was reached which we may thus express: Where the thought is the same the religions may be distinct, but cannot be different, for the God who made the intelligible made all intellects akin to each other and to Him; and it is through the knowledge of the truth that He is most truly known, and in its contemplation that He is most purely worshipped.

What Judaism represents, then, is the issue of the conflict between the universal idea and the local cult as embodied in the localized race. Where the cult had behind it the traditions, the associations, and the patriotism of the home it proved stronger than the idea, imposing upon God, who was theoretically one and alone and supreme, the limitations of a tribal worship; but where the idea was emancipated from those domestic and ancestral associations, it tended to prove itself stronger than the cult. The triumph of the cult meant the nationalization of the religion, which would then be an abortive or unrealized monotheism; but the triumph of the idea meant the universalization of the religion, which could only become an absolute monotheism by the worship being loosed from the bonds of the tribe and realized in humaner forms. And the form which the process assumed in the dispersion was the modification of the religion into a system of philosophy, whose notes were eclecticism in thought and syncretism in worship. But the necessity of the situation was the consistency of idea and form, the homogeneity of the worship, the worshipper, and the God. And this homogeneity no syncretism has ever realized. Hence came a conflict which was not incidental, but essential; for it grew out of the imperious demand of the only thoroughly universal idea which had risen in the history of religion for a medium which should do justice to its universalism. In the nature of the case this could not be found in the institutions which were the symbols of national existence, as they were the creations of the tribal or national consciousness. To speak of the Jewish law and worship in these terms is to characterize, but not to depreciate, them. The universal idea could come into the thought and faith of humanity only through special persons, and such persons could be born and nursed only by a special people. The fitness of Israel to be the foster parent of such an idea does not lie open to question; it is writ large on the whole face of his history and of man's. He lived for his idea; his loyalty to it resisted all the absorbent forces of the ancient empires, and though the mightiest empire of them all broke up his state and threw his homeless members broadcast upon the world, yet the dispersed units have defied the assimilative energy of all modern peoples. And we may add that that energy has been inspired by every passion—hate, fear, greed, revenge, disdain, indifference, toleration, love of freedom in the abstract rather than of concrete men—by everything, indeed, save the only thing that could have helped and healed, viz., sympathy and appreciation. Such a people was the very medium needed for the birth and breeding, the nurture and development of an idea which man so required, and yet was so averse to receive; but the idea which could be begotten and nursed only by such a people could not continue their perennial possession. And the pathos of Israel's position lies in their invincible devotion to the national form of a belief which, in order that it might realize itself and become man's, required to lose all trace of its national origin and tribal history and live in a medium as universal as its nature and function. Whether such a medium has been found is a question which has yet to be discussed.

CHAPTER VIII

FOUNDED RELIGIONS AND THEIR FOUNDERS

§ I. *Religions, Spontaneous and Founded*

1. THE question as to the part played by Jesus Christ in the creation of the Christian religion is particular or specific; but it involves principles and problems which belong to the philosophy of religion and to its comparative history. Founded religions constitute a class or order by themselves; their qualities can be explained only through the relations between them and their founders, and the conditions out of which they both grew. The founded may also be described as instituted or personal religions, in distinction from those which, as without any single or conscious creator, may be classified as natural, spontaneous, or impersonal. The spontaneous are products of the common or collective reason, whose units work, though without defined purpose, yet instinctively and concurrently, combined in action because conditioned throughout by time and place; but the instituted run back into certain historical personalities, and are, if not their immediate and designed creations, yet the clear outcomes of personal reasons and conscious wills. The impersonal religions are not the work of any one man or any special body of men, disciples or apostles, but rather of our common nature; and they have come to be by a process as natural and as much regulated by law as that which produced language, custom, society, and the State. But the founded or personal religions have their source or spring, if not their sufficient reason, in some particular man and are in-

separably connected with certain specific beliefs as to his person, office, or work. The one class as collective live in, for, and through the tribe or people, grow with them, and form an integral part of the national order; but the other class as personal are rooted in the active reason, appeal to it, live in it, and grow with it. Spontaneous religions may be termed apotheoses of nature, or the interpretation of spirit and the expression of its ideas in sensuous forms; but instituted religions may be described as apotheoses of personality, or the interpretation of man and the expression of his ideas in the terms of mind or spirit. As a first consequence the spontaneous religions tend to be in character more consuetudinary than ethical, more legal than rational, affairs of the community rather than of individuals or societies within it; but the instituted, as more nearly allied to spirit than to nature, tend as regards matter to emphasize the ideal, and as respects form to think more of mind and character than of observance and custom. As a second consequence the spontaneous religions are not capable of detachment from the nation or tribe; while the instituted addressing themselves to the individual, working from within outward, or using the outward only to get within, constitute societies out of the likeminded, and organize them according to some dominant principle. The distinction, then, seems to be here coincident with that between national and universal or missionary religions; but it really carries us a step farther, for it enables us to trace the most distinctive attributes of the missionary religions to their sources or roots. Man is more universal than nature; the system which has most humanity in it speaks to man most intimately and is most capable of satisfying him; while the higher the moral character of him who institutes the religion, or causes it to be instituted, the finer will be its ethical qualities and the more humane its spirit.

2. But though the spontaneous and the founded religions form distinct classes, they yet stand in historical relations and

appear in a determined order. Three things are indeed necessary to the creation of a personal religion : (i.) an historical background or a fit ancestry ; (ii.) a creative religious genius ; and (iii.) a congenial society or environment upon and within which the genius may operate.

i. The instituted religion needs a substructure on which to build. As a matter of fact no religion capable of being so described is primitive or, in the strict sense, a new or a pure creation. We have here, as elsewhere, first that which is natural, and afterwards that which is spiritual. If the impersonal did not already exist, the personal could not even begin to be; the one is the parent whose being the other as child presupposes and authenticates. To be the founder of a religion is not to be its inventor—for the invented would be artificial, manufactured, arbitrary and therefore local and ephemeral ; but it is to be the cause or occasion which developes a new species out of an old. Every founded religion implies therefore some ancient historical religion which it has transformed, on which it has built, and without which it would not have been possible ; but not every spontaneous religion is capable of becoming the foundation or parent of a personal religion. Growth does not always mean production, or development the creation of new forms ; for many religions have lived thousands of years and undergone infinite modifications without changing their nature or losing their impersonal character. Thus Hinduism and the Vedic religion are so different that they may be said to have hardly a single essential feature in common ; their pantheons, priesthoods, worships, sacrifices, ceremonies ; their social systems, ideals of life, personal and collective, as well as their ideas of death and the future, all differ, often radically and even diametrically. Yet if anything in history be certain, it is that Hinduism, with all it stands for, has descended without any break of continuity, though with cumulative accretions and ever increasing variations from the faith held and the order observed by the Vedic men. On the other hand, Hebraism and Christianity are much more alike than the two Indian systems and have an historical connexion even more intimate and organic. In their ideas of God, His character and His law, of man and his duty, of the prophet and his word, of life and its issues, in almost all those things in which the modern differs from the ancient Hindu, they fundamentally agree; yet they constitute not one religion but two, each incapable of fusion with the other, dissimilar in character and independent in being. The Jewish had no room for the Christian religion, the Christian has no room for the Jewish; and though they use the same name for God, speak of Him in identical terms, praise Him in the same Psalms, with equal reverence regard the same book as His inspired word, and alike enforce the need of clean hands and pure hearts in the men who would worship Him, yet one fact or belief so determines their respective qualities and relations that neither can be merged in the other. Hebraism is Christianity and Christianity is Hebraism in every respect save this one, the interpreted Person of Jesus Christ; what divides them is not the historical Jesus, the Man who was a son of Israel and lived in time, but the theological Christ, the Person who has been construed into the Son of God, whose Deity is equal to the Father's. Without this we should have had no Christian religion, but only a Jewish sect the more; with this we have a Jewish sect the less, but the largest and most missionary of religions. Yet though this belief more than any other thing divides and distinguishes the religions, the younger owes its peculiar form and quality to the elder. For it is because the antecedent religion was so essentially a religion of the Divine unity that the passion for it was so native to its successor that it could never be tempted to think of Deity as other than one; and it is because the successor not only had a new teacher but was a peculiar belief concerning Him that it became a new religion essentially distinct from the old. The revolutionary and creative power did not lie so much in the person as in the belief; and what gave the belief its power was that, so far from dissolving the monistic and exclusive quality of the theistic idea which it inherited and after which it was framed, it only helped the more to intensify and define it. And here we may see why the belief is so offensive to the Jew and so unintelligible to the Hindu. The Jew cannot conceive how his God could become incarnate in any man; the Hindu cannot conceive how any one man should be the sole and exclusive incarnation of God. He thinks of deity as incarnate in every man and in all forms of life; in so thinking he makes incarnation in the Christian sense impossible, for by deifying everything he undeifies all. The only possible form a revolt from Hinduism can assume is that of negation—a denial of the idea by which it lives, explains man, and organizes society. Buddhism was this, and because it was this, while it lived in India long enough to show that in a system that knew no deity there could be no permanent or real apotheosis of the founder, yet its inevitable fate was to perish by being absorbed into the religion it had repudiated. But an absolute monotheism is a principle of absolute coherence and individuation; it can allow no deity to stand alongside its God and share His worship and dignity. And if the idea of incarnation ever finds a foothold in connexion with such a Deity it must, unless His unity and personality are broken up, involve a unity and be expressed in a personality as absolute as His own. Hence the unity which constituted Hebraism was continued in Christianity, whose Founder became as solitary in deity and as pre-eminent in His solitude, as the Jehovah He realized rather than superseded.

ii. *The founder must be an historical person of creative genius.* Unless he be "an historical person" there can be no continuity in the religion, nothing to bind it to the past, connect it with the present, or transmit it to the future. A system which is without antecedents can have no consequents,

THE FOUNDER NO MERE REFORMER 263

but is a mere isolated, and therefore inexplicable phenomenon. To be without father and mother is to be also without descendants, a being man can neither understand nor construe, neither believe nor imitate, neither obey nor follow. The historical reality of the founder is thus a condition antecedent to the historical being of the religion which is to bear his name. "Creative genius," again, is a term denotive of the force which enabled him to be what he was and perform what he did. It means more than intellectual, ethical, or social eminence; it means such a transcendence of local conditions as cannot be explained by the completest inheritance of the past, a personality that so embodies a new ideal as to awaken in man the imitative passion and the interpretative imagination. Thus the founder must here be distinguished from the reformer; every founder may be a reformer of religion, but not every reformer is a founder. The reformer may arise, preach a new or revive an old doctrine, call to a higher life and institute a society for its realization; and this type of man has been known to every historical religion, has appeared in some an innumerable multitude of times, though he has risen only to create a new sect or a new order within the old. To this class belong Benedict, Francis, and Dominic, and their great and saintly kinsmen in all the historical religions. What changes the reformer into the founder is not so much his own act as his people's, the creative action of his personality on their imagination forcing them to invest him with attributes and functions supersessive of the authority and worship of the ancient gods. No teacher simply as a teacher ever created a new religion, for a religion is made not by discussions but by beliefs, not by abstract principles but by a concrete object of worship, not by the quickening and cultivation of the intellect but by the operation of an authority which commands the whole man, and organizes his life on a more spiritual basis and according to a higher ideal. It is, then, not simply in what the founder was and did, but in what he was conceived to be, that the forces creative of a new religion lie ; but even though his historical personality be thus transformed, it does not cease to be operative; on the contrary, it becomes, by being idealized, more potent. For it is made the interpretative and normative term of the highest religious ideas ; the universe, its source and meaning, its course and end, are read in the light of his personality, and God is interpreted through the man.

The founder, then, has a twofold value for the religion, an historical and an ideal. Without the historical he would have no connexion with humanity, standing outside it he would be unable to act upon it, absolved from all relations he would have no more worth than belongs to a dream or vision of the mind. Without the ideal he would have no transcendental significance, no meaning for the mystery of the universe, nothing to say to man touching the ideas by which he lives. The historical character of the founder determines the ethical quality of the faith he founds ; his transcendental signficance defines its higher beliefs. The two must be combined before knowledge of him can constitute a religion.

iii. The function and the need of a congenial society or medium within which the founder may live and operate will now be apparent. Its function is the interpretation of his person, the practice of his worship, the imitation of his character, the study of his thought, the realization of his ideals ; in a word, it is to make the religion called by his name a reality. The society may thus be defined as, on the one hand, a contributory cause, and, on the other, a condition necessary, to the being of the religion. As the founder embodies for it the ultimate truth of the universe, so it embodies for mankind his mind and life ; and it is by these in their union that the religion is constituted. And there is a parallel between the creative process in the personal and in the natural religions. These latter arose from the intercourse of mind with nature ; but the former from the intercourse of mind with certain historical personalities. Nature in the one case, the personality in the other, represent the objects to be interpreted; in both cases mind brings the regulative ideas and interpretative categories to the object. Those ideas and categories which are, in the one case, latent in mind, are educed, explicated, and verified in the course of its endeavour to interpret nature and comprehend itself; but in the other case, these ideas and categories which have become explicit for thought through its being exercised on the ancestral religion and the problems it has raised receive expansion and, as it were, concretion by application to the historical person. This does not mean that the parallel processes justify the very dissimilar results, but it means that as the processes are rational the formulated results must be judged by analytic and comparative criticism. But the time for applying this canon is not yet.

A founded religion may be defined, then, as a religion whose ultimate truth is an historical person speculatively construed. This definition, with the discussion which has led up to it, will help us to determine what religions fall within this category.

§ II. *Impersonal Religions Classified as Personal*

We must exclude three religions, which are often reckoned as founded or personal, those of ancient Persia, of China, and of Israel, which are, respectively, ascribed to Zoroaster, to Confucius, and to Moses. Of these, Zoroaster is a person known only by the aid of dubious documents, late in origin, imperfectly understood, uncertain in date and in worth, and representing a religion whose history, broken and discontinuous, it is impossible critically to construe. Taken at the best Zoroaster is a teacher and reformer, not a founder, and his religion has an archæological rather than an historical and living interest. But of the other two something more positive may be said.

1. Nothing could be less correct than to describe the classical and imperial religion of China as the Confucian. Confucius did not create it, did not mean to do more than maintain it in its integrity, or, to use the term which best expresses his mind, "transmit it," just as it had been loved and observed by the fathers before him. He studiously avoided saying or doing anything which the ancients would have disapproved; in their maxims and customs he found the wisdom which he, illumined by experience, applied to the regulation of life, public and private. He stayed within his own province, a counsellor of kings, a guide of States, an instructor of statesmen; and discouraged as needless all inquiry touching what was before birth, after death, or above and behind the visible. As a son he illustrated reverence; as a citizen he exemplified obedience, though to sovereignty rather than to any person as sovereign; as a magistrate he cultivated virtue, tempering justice with mercy and making the people's good his chief concern; as a teacher he never forgot his disciples, but loved to open their eyes to the lessons and the duties suggested by common things. The heaven he thought of and believed in was a happy kingdom; his saints and sages were the persons who could create and administer its laws; his religion was the way by which it could be made to come. He loved and observed the ceremonies that turned the peasant into a well-mannered gentleman, and made the king a man while a ruler. He collected and edited the songs of his people, for he believed that they were the best allies of law and formed in men the law-abiding mind. He recorded the words and the acts of the wisest chiefs, and described the contentment which came from a virtuous reign. He made literature a mirror into which kings and peoples alike could look, see themselves and their times, and learn to admire the good and despise the evil. But he intended only to conserve what was old, though it was an idealized age, the creature of the imagination rather than

NOT THE FOUNDER OF A RELIGION 267

the reflexion of experience; and the last thing he dreamed of doing was to establish a new religion. And his people, who have loved him well, have understood him perfectly. He is to them the ideal embodiment of a religion at once domestic and civil, without a priesthood but with duties defined by the home and the State. They have built temples in his honour, but to him as sage, not as God. Their worship, properly so called, is reserved either for the heaven which is above all and enfolds all, or for the ancestors who have made the family and love the families they have made. In the former case the worship is conducted by the emperor as head of the State; in the latter, by the father as head of the household; for the most common of all beliefs in China is this, that the spirits of the dead can never be happy without the sacrifices and progress of their living descendants.

But this simple religion existed ages before Confucius; his words and acts may have interpreted it, his wisdom have sanctioned it, his example enriched it and stamped it with the approval of the greatest immortal of his race, but he loved it too well to wish to see it changed, especially by or because of himself. His character is best described in his own words of true yet proud humility; he was "simply a man who in his eager pursuit of knowledge forgot his food; who in the joy of its attainment forgot his sorrows, and who therefore did not perceive that old age was coming on." He who could so speak of himself might be a sage, but he was not the founder of a religion.

2. What the religion of Israel owes to Moses is a point criticism finds it hard, if not impossible, to determine; and to attempt to determine it here would carry us into a field of discussion alien to the problem and purpose of this book. But, happily, we are not specially concerned with the literary questions as to the rise of monotheism, or as to the mode and time of its origin, but with the discovery of a cause sufficient to explain it and constant enough in operation to show how

it overcame a multitude of hostile forces subtly and ceaselessly active. Now the more we conceive its rise to have been gradual the less can we attribute it to any single man. And there are two significant things here: (*a*) the religion, when we get to know it, and so far as we do know it, is national rather than personal; and (*b*) the idea that governed its history was the God who gave the law and not the man who received it.

The first of these positions signifies that the constant cause which produced monotheism and never ceased to operate till it had been perfected, was more racial than individual. What used to be termed "the monotheistic instinct,"[1] the peculiar endowment of the Semitic race, became in Israel the passion to conceive God as one, and Jehovah as the only God. The belief in its earliest form may have been crude, and the theistic idea may have been so loosely conceived as to be predicable of a multitude of beings of varying ranks and differing powers; but all the more is there needed for the emergence of an absolute and exclusive unity, the operation of a permanent cause like a race. Polytheism was in the air; it represented common and spontaneous beliefs; it had flourished under the older and higher civilizations; it was the faith of all the dwellers in Canaan, of all the cognate families and tribes: why, then, did Israel alone escape it? Much has been made of the fact that he is often polytheistic in idea and feeling and act, in custom, in speech and inclination; but we forget what the English civilian in India could illustrate out of his own experience, how impossible it was for Israel, situated as he was, wrestling with the poverty of speech and against strong tendencies in human nature, to be anything else. The fact we have to reckon with is the persistent growth, in the face of the mightiest adverse forces, of this monotheistic idea. And the persistence is the more extraordinary that the idea stood

[1] Ante, p. 217.

alone in a sort of naked simplicity, unsupported by the fellowship or countenance of kindred ideas. It was not made by any system of thought, but had to make its own system. And here the significance of the second position will appear; the history of Israel did not so much produce the monotheistic idea as the idea produced the history. It made him; it is his sole claim to remembrance: but what a claim it is! How it places this rude, fierce, and intolerant people in the forefront of the benefactors of mankind! And throughout it appears as the work of the family, rather than of any single man. Moses may have been the legislator of the family, yet he was not its sole or sovereign authority in religion; others stand by his side, come after him, rise above him, even supersede him. His name subsumes the law and he becomes the synonym of rules that bind but do not govern. The note of the founder is that he is indispensable, he without whom the religion could not have been. And monotheism could have been without Moses but not without Israel. Yet the legislator, alike in what he did not do and in what he did, perfectly impersonates the idea. If we conceive him to have lived in Egypt and to have been acquainted with its worship, it is marvellous how little of its religion he brought away with him—nothing of its ideas of the future, of the fate and treatment and judgment of the dead, of its sacred animals and signs, of its symbolism, its temples, its priesthoods, its nomenclature and its mystic lore. Yet if it suggested to him the idea that the law of God was a moral law which the state that took Him for its Sovereign was bound to obey, then it was the mother of the most potent and fruitful of all the beliefs that have worked for the amelioration of religion. For by this idea both God and religion have been moralized, and monotheism saved from falling into a monism, which must always conceive deity under physical or metaphysical, rather than under ethical categories. I then, Israel was the organ and vehicle of the religion, Moses may be described as not only its law-giver, but, as the later literature conceived him, as its prophet, as indeed the greatest because the first of the prophets, the type of the ideal servant of God whose voice men were to hear and obey. And a higher achievement than this no reformer or legislator could perform.

§ III. *Religions, Founded and Personal*

There remain to be considered as in the strict or proper sense founded religions, Buddhism, Islam, and Christianity the three which have already been described as missionary.[1] How did they come to be religions, as distinguished from sects or schools? What part did their respective founders, Buddha, Mohammed, Jesus, play in their creation? What reciprocal significance in each of these cases has the founder for the religion and the religion for the founder?

A. Buddha and his Religion

1. The significance of Buddha as a philosophical teacher[2] and a religious personality[3] has already been sketched. What we have now to do is to show the process by which he became what is termed the founder of a religion. We begin by noting his undisputed supremacy in his own church; it lives by faith in him and in what he stands for. There is no image so familiar to the East as his; he sits everywhere, in monastery, pagoda, and sacred place, cross-legged, meditative, impassive, resigned, the ideal of quenched desire, without any line of care or thought to disturb the ineffable calm or mar the sweetness of his unsmiling yet gracious face; a silent deity who bids the innumerable millions who worship him become as blessed by being as placid as he is. And the belief which the image symbolizes is not of yesterday;

---

[1] Ante, p. 230.   [2] Ante, pp. 118–21.   [3] pp. 240–44.

it is as old as Buddha's church. The ancient formula of discipleship confesses the sufficiency of the Teacher, his doctrine, and his order for all the needs of man. The council which met on the eve of his death knew the formula, spoke of him as the exalted, the enlightened one, whose word saved and with whom was the secret of a holy life. The second council, held about a hundred years later, proves the existence of sacred texts, definite doctrines, and an operative order. And these carry us near enough to the founder to make us sure that, however much his history may have been embellished by the retrospective imagination, he was no subjective ideal or mere lay figure arrayed in the worn out garments of the old solar mythology, but a real being of flesh and blood, though in genius ancient and Indian rather than modern and European. The world he moves in is too actual to allow us to dissolve him into unreality. It is very different from the Vedic world, but no less concrete and coherent, with men and women tempered by climate and changed by experience, but as true to type and time. Instead of the song we have the epilogue; instead of the hymn, with its clear speech and praise of a God who has never been doubted, we have minds that have speculated till faith has failed and they have been compelled to ask, Who will show us any good and tell us whether there be any God, what we may call and how we may find Him? Yet this India of the fifth century B.C. is as real as the Vedic India of five or even ten centuries earlier. It is a land where kings are powerful, chiefs are rich, priests influential, and peasants diligent; where castes are strong and jealous of privilege, and the out-casted the most pitiable of men. Religion is the great concern, and men love it too well to allow it to become an affair of the priesthood, and conceive it to be a mother of truth and thought rather than custom and ritual. And so they feel the priest's forms to be tedious and divisive, while his sacrifices seem too cruel to be acceptable to the gentleness that ought to be the soul of all things. The seekers after a more excellent way fill the land, ascetics who have renounced all worldly pleasures that they may attain a beatitude without lust or desire; mendicants who have ceased to toil and spin that they may begin the quest of the supreme good; pious men who torture themselves that they may win the applause of a deity who loves self-inflicted pain; disciples who seek a master; itinerant sages who offer to teach wisdom in the places where the consciously ignorant congregate.

In the eastern region of this land, a region imperfectly Brahmanized, which may be described, in comparison with the sacred and ancient Vedic country lying to the westward as "Galilee of the Gentiles," the man who is to be the Buddha is born. The priest has not as yet here completed his usurpation, nor have the king and noble lost their ancient functions in religion; while the spirit which compels man to conceive himself as made for eternity rules the selecter minds. By his birth the man has in him the blood of kings and warriors, but by instinct and temper the love of eternal things. He inherited the faith of his people, believed that he was fated to move through the immense and awful cycle of successive births and deaths, and he desired early and complete emancipation. The priestly method of attaining it seemed to him too slow, circuitous, and uncertain; and was he not of the race of men Nature had made priests before art or custom created Brahmans? And so he enquired of many teachers, but they did not help; he tried many methods—asceticism, self-torture, renunciation—but in vain. At last meditation showed him how through suppression of desire to escape from sorrow and enter into the Nirvana which is perfect peace. When he had attained this knowledge he became Buddha, the enlightened; and after he had overcome the temptation

HIS PHILOSOPHY AND DISCIPLINE 273

to keep his secret he began to preach it, leading men through discipleship and his order into the way whose end was everlasting peace.

2. Buddha thus became a teacher of a kind as common in India then as now. There the man with a message never wants a hearing, nor, if his message has promise or helpfulness, does he ever want a following. The history of post-Vedic religion is but the biography of teachers, now ascetic, now scholastic, now social, now mystic, now rational, who have formed schools and founded sects, without ceasing to be Hindus; on the contrary, only the more expanding and realizing Hinduism. And Buddha so acted in the way of his people as to exhibit evolution rather than revolution. And he himself could not do otherwise; the logic that changed development into revolt came from his society. Yet the premises on which it argued and acted were his. His philosophy was not orthodox; it did not build on the Vedas, it denied the reality of Brahma and the persistence of the soul. It agreed indeed with the older schools in affirming that salvation was by knowledge rather than by priestly sacrifice and ritual; but, unlike them, it did not seek the knowledge in a priestly service, or call its object by a priestly name. The Brahmans were to him like a chain of blind men, none of whom saw anything, and whose faith and discourse were alike vain. Their sacrifices were at once foolish and ineffectual, cruel and profitless. The only sacrifice that became a king was the repair of all injustice; that became a man was the cessation from lying and deceit, from the lust that coveted and worked unchastity, from the passion that killed to increase fleshly pleasure. Self-torture was no sacrifice, had no merit, and gained no good. In an unknown tongue there was no sanctity. Truth did not become truer, nor did excellence grow better by being stated in Sanskrit; the speech the people knew was the fittest medium for the teacher. And the more people knew the truth the greater the number that

would be saved. But truth involved duty; by obedience the knowledge was proved to be real, and the measure of perfection was the degree of their harmony. Hence Buddha's society was twofold: an inner circle—a church or order, and an outer circle—the adherents. The former were made up of the called or chosen, men and women who renounced everything and became mendicants, monks and nuns, persons who had the vocation to a holy life. Celibacy and chastity were fundamental principles in a system which seeks to end the existence which is misery. The adherents were the devout, those who believed in the Buddha, but were not strong enough to make the great renunciation, and break the fetters that bound them to the sensuous world. The cardinal idea of the system is an individualism which is best when realized in the social medium that promises to make an end of the individual. This individualism governs it throughout. Its one authority is an individual beside whom no second stands. Every individual is a self-sufficing unit, charged with the care and the control of his own destiny, who has the right of his own free will to make the last surrender, but on whom no other has any right to lay a violent hand. The happiest being is he on whom the love of the only life he has power over—his own—has died; the next in happiness is he who so loves all being that he will inflict suffering on none. The first has become a saint and attained Nirvana; the second has entered upon the path, and will in due season reach the goal.

3. But do the narrative of Buddha's life, and the interpretation of his mind, taken by themselves, explain the rise of the religion called Buddhism? There is a teacher, a school he founds, scholars that revere him, multitudes that admire him, and a message he delivers concerning the knowledge that saves, but these things, even more in India than in Europe, do not found a religion, they only constitute a sect. Now what turned the school or sect into a religion? It was the

event or process which we may term, all the more fitly that the system knows no god, the apotheosis of Buddha. The process was twofold, though the result was one, an imaginative and a speculative, or a mythological and a philosophical. The starting point was the master or teacher, the man, the Buddha, the Illuminated, who revealed to the ignorant the way of life. His manhood was not denied; on the contrary, its reality was the primary assumption which made the creative process possible. Deities are too common and too easily discovered in India to have much significance; they appear everywhere in everything, and can be made to become anything. Incarnations are as common as deities, and as insignificant; and to them it is more natural to assume an animal or a monstrous, than a human form. Hence to have conceived Buddha as a deity or as the incarnation of a deity would have been to deprive him of all distinction, to have made the fall of his school into a sect inevitable, and the rise of a religion bearing his name impossible. Individuality, then, is his attribute; he is himself, and not simply the form of another. He has incommunicable properties, has a will of his own which performs duty and shapes character, and is not the mere mask of an unknown and irresponsible power. Hence comes the belief that he is an ethical being, that his chief qualities are moral, that his virtues, his grace and wisdom, his goodwill and kindness are his, and are real, and that out of his intrinsic qualities all his beneficent acts have issued. This was a new notion in India; it was substituting an ethical for a metaphysical conception, and reaching the universe through the idea of a moral man rather than through the abstract idea of soul or substance. And here the mythological process began; the Buddha it transformed was a living being, for the moment the imagination touches death and the abstract they are quickened and personified. He was, therefore, not allowed to begin to be with birth, or to cease to be at death; he became the personified beneficence of the universe, doing good in all worlds and in all ages to all kinds and classes of suffering creatures; and the people that meditated before his image, or spoke of him to the multitudes, clothed their faith in the forms that their imagination supplied. What the process achieved we may learn not simply from the "Birth Stories," but from the sober and often prosaic narratives of the Chinese pilgrims. Hiuen Tsiang, a doctor learned in the law, skilled in all the subtilties of what we foolishly call Nihilistic Buddhism, gravely tells how at this *stupa*, or that sacred place, the Blessed One had descended and confounded a sinner, or helped a saint, or built of precious stones some tabernacle for men to pray in. And as the imagination clothed him in a suitable mythology, so the speculative reason resolved him into " the eldest, the noblest of beings," and surrounded him with an army of "exalted, holy, universal Buddhas," though he alone remained the author of eternal salvation. And as on the one side he personified the moral energies of the universe, so on the other he became the governing ideal and example of human duty, the humanity of the standard making the ethics humane. And it was this transcendental interpretation of its founder, his apotheosis as we have termed it, which made Buddhism a religion. The process may or may not have been legitimate, but it was here the only possible method of creation. Unless Buddha had been man, we should never have had his system or his influence; unless he had been conceived as more than man, we should never have had his religion. The elevation and beauty of his humanity, when applied to the supreme object of worship, marked an immense advance on all prior notions of deity in the Orient; but its want of a theistic basis left it nebulous and void, save for the pious imagination, which can be legitimately and finally satisfied only by the satisfaction of the reason.

B. Mohammed and Islam

1. Mohammed divides with Buddha and the Brahman the religious sovereignty of the Oriental mind, yet the sovereignties are in idea, in type, and in form worlds apart. All three are rooted in religion, but the faith of the Brahman is a polytheism so multitudinous and tolerant as to include everything that men may call deity, if only the deity will consent to be included and to be respectful to those who dwelt in the pantheon before him. The sovereignty of Buddha is that of the ideal man and the idealized pity, which, without concern or care for any god, draws humanity toward the dreamless beatitude he has himself attained; while Mohammed's is strictly derivative and representative, due to his being the one sufficient and authoritative spokesman of the one Merciful and Almighty God. The Brahman's sovereignty is social and heritable, came to him by the blood which defined his place and function in society as well as his office before the gods and on behalf of men; but both Buddha's and Mohammed's may be described as in a sense personal, though it was acquired by the one through his own efforts, achievements, and merits, and granted to the other by the will and deed of his God. The sovereignty of the Brahman is expressed in the society he has organized, the system, at once natural and artificial, of caste; while Buddha's is expressed in a society whose orders correspond to his theory of merit, and Mohammed's in a brotherhood where all are equal before a God too great to know any respect of persons. The image, or the symbol, of his god which the Brahman loves is to Mohammed but a shameful and empty idol, while the statue which the Buddhist reveres speaks to him of a still more graceless idolatry, the supersession of the uncreated God by the created man he had appointed to be his minister. But though his sovereignty is not represented to the eye by any image, it yet has a fitter and more imperious symbol,

a book which reveals the mind of God and proclaims the law which man is bound under the most awful and inexorable sanctions to obey. The worship it enjoins is one of stern yet majestic simplicity; it concerns God only, and there is but the one God who has made Mohammed his final and sovereign prophet, and declared through him that all idols are " idleness and vanity."

> They have not any power ; no, not over the husk of a date.
> If ye call upon them, they hear not your calling.[1]

But though no image of God or man is to be tolerated, yet the tomb of the saint is to be visited by the foot of the pilgrim, and over it may rise the mosque where God will be all the more devoutly praised that the dust of a servant waits beneath till the resurrection of the just.

Now Mohammed is of all religious founders the most intimately known, and Islam is the only religion of which it can be said it was born in the open day. There is no book more autobiographical than the Koran, more capable or more in need of being interpreted through history. This makes it peculiarly difficult to a stolid and unimaginative Western mind to be just either to the man or the religion. Instead of standing in the workshop amid its perplexing cross-lights, lurid fires, blazing furnaces, ringing hammers, torrid heat, and perspiring craftsmen, we sit in our cool study, analyze, criticize, award, praise, and blame as if the religion had been forged in an atmosphere as undisturbed and luminous as our own, and by men as detached and cultivated as we assume ourselves to be. And so Voltaire, who knew Paris excellently, but knew nothing of Arabia, little of religion and less of man, conceived Mohammed as a lustful hypocrite, who pleaded inspiration in order that he might gain a freer and fuller licence for his vice ; while

[1] Koran : Sura xxxv.

Gibbon, who disliked fanaticism, whether embodied in a Julian, a Mohammed, or a Calvin, described Islam as compounded of an eternal truth and a necessary falsehood, the truth being the unity of God, the falsehood that Mohammed was His prophet. And as if to keep us humble and the balance true, we have one modern and Christian scholar tracing his inspiration to Satan, and another resolving his religion into hysteria. But in history it is a useful canon never to assume that great effects can have mean causes. In matters of faith and the Spirit nothing fails like duplicity and make-believe ; nothing is so necessary to success as integrity and conviction of mind. The splendid sincerity of Mohammed's early disciples sufficiently testifies to the reality of his own ; but he was sincere in the manner of an Arab and an unlettered visionary. We must imagine this Arab as a delicate, posthumous child nursed by the Bedouin, early left without a mother, first to the care of a grandfather, then of uncles kindly disposed but critical. He grew into a boy who loved to commune with nature and gather the wild berries as he tended his flocks; he became a youth with few companions, with a soul that sickened at the coarser vices, meditative, sensitive to suffering, susceptible to the finer emotions, shrinking from pain, and destitute of the physical courage which easily turned into ferocity, and which the Arab admired as the bravery proper to a man. In his solitude great thoughts came to him ; travel and intercourse with men brought glimpses into a larger world than Arabia knew of. Marriage, bringing wealth, supplied him with the opportunities for silence, solitude, and visions, which reflected his richer experience. He had heard of the Jewish patriarchs, and the story of Abraham, the friend of God and the father of Ishmael ; it touched his imagination, and he saw the Arab tribes unified, their sacred places purged, themselves made the heirs of the promise, and their deities, Lat and Ozza and

Manat, cast out by the one supreme God. He heard of Moses, and he learned to think of God, the lawgiver, calling His people into the wilderness, forming them into a state where idolatry was forbidden, and the prophet was the voice of God. He thought of these things in the way of an imaginative man till they took hold of him, possessed, inspired him, forced him into speech.

> Cry! in the name of thy Lord who created—
> Created man from clots of blood.[1]

In a passage of amazing beauty and majesty, which may well be read as a chapter from his own experience, he pictures Abraham[2] called from his idols to the faith in the one God. The evening falls and the stars come out one by one in the lustrous evening heaven, and he cries, "This, indeed, is the Most High"; but the moon rises, and they fade, and he thinks, "Here is the Being I must worship." Then the dawn breaks, the moon pales, and the sun rises out of the bosom of night, and he bends before this all-glorious luminary as the light which is God; but the day ends, night and darkness return, and Abraham thinks the Eternal can never pass and be eclipsed, and he says, "I turn my face to Him who hath created the heavens and the earth."

2. The monotheism of the Semite, simple, inflexible, sovereign, had at last found a fit organ, and from the call of God there could be no turning back. But though Mohammed must speak, he could not always convert; a few, his wife, a slave, a friend believed; some hesitated, many doubted, the vast majority denied and hated as only the untutored mind can hate when it sees its ancient gods

---

[1] Sura xcvi.
[2] Sura vi. Cf. the Jewish prototype in Geiger, *Was hat Moh. aus dem Judenthum aufgenommen?* pp. 123–125. It will help us the more to feel the beauty that may be conferred by the touch of genius.

scorned and dismissed for a God it does not see. Hence came years of conflict, force pitted against faith, strength against weakness. Exasperation, pain, and death confronted the prophet and his religion. Then Medina opened her arms, and called, and, helped by what has ever seemed to the imagination of his people a series of miracles, he stole out of Mecca, and by his flight saved himself and founded Islam. And what he founded was not only a religion, but a State, the two being one. The ideas were there, the omnipotent God, the mortal man; heaven for the faithful, hell for the unbeliever. But the institution was there also, the prophet, who was the voice of God, his word which was God's truth, the law which could not be broken but must be obeyed. And this law created a State, which lived, as States must, by the sword, but a sword wielded, as none had hitherto been, by the hand of the Almighty. It is not indeed, true to say "Islam is founded on the sword"; it is founded on the prophet's word, and it preaches and teaches with a zeal and a fanaticism no religion has ever surpassed. Yet the sword was used by the prophet and has been used by his successors in a way unknown to the other founded religions. Asoka, the Buddhist, may have subdued India, and Constantine may have conquered the Roman Empire in the name of the Cross; but these were acts of violent disobedience and usurpation, for Buddha did not love the battle, and Jesus expressly deplored war and condemned the sword. It is impossible, then, to acquit Mohammed of the charge of spreading his religion by the sword, although he did not found upon it. For two things of incontrovertible historical truth may here be said: (*a*) Without the sword he never would have converted the Arab tribes and made them the apostles and warriors of his religion; and (*b*) his use of the sword has sanctioned its use by all his successors. Wars of religion may be even more desolating than those of military or political ambition;

but wars by religion encourage, above all others, ferocity and blood-madness. And the history of Islam, unhappily, abounds in proofs of this fact. But even in his wars Mohammed did not forget his religion, though his mindfulness but showed the old Arab alive within him. The spoils taken from the enemy enriched the brotherhood, being divided according to principles of merit and equity. If the nearest kinsman was an unbeliever, he was shown no more pity than the most complete alien; if the bitterest foe became a convert, he was at once taken to the bosom of the prophet and the faith. Of an unbelieving uncle, he said:

> Blasted be the hands of Abu Lahab! and let himself be blasted!
> His riches shall not profit him, nor what he has earned;
> He shall be cast into the broiling flame.[1]

When he had fought and conquered Mecca, and had thrown down her idols, for

> Truth had come and falsehood gone;
> For falsehood vanisheth away,[2]

his magnanimity reached even to his most implacable foe, who now submitted, and was bidden "Hasten to the city, and say that none who taketh refuge in the house of Abu Sofian (the man himself) shall be harmed this day." But another and no less significant change happened at Medina. Before, Jerusalem had been his holy city, thither Gabriel had borne him on a winged steed, and he had met and been welcomed by a council of ancient prophets. Thence he had been carried into heaven, and the lips of God had commanded him and his people to pray five times daily with faces towards the holy Temple. But now Mecca was idealized; ancient memories made her beautiful in the prophet's sight. "Thou art the choicest spot upon earth to me, and the

---

[1] Sura cxi.   [2] Sura xvii. 82.

most delectable," he cried; and the city of his love became the sacred city of his faith. The Divine voice said: "Turn thy face towards the holy temple of Mecca";[1] and so it henceforth was the true *kibla*, the goal of pilgrimage, with its once heathenish black stone and holy well sanctified for evermore. But these ways signified a radical change in the mind of Mohammed. The prophecies he now delivered were occasional, and served the occasion; some were intended to hush scandal, others to reconcile estranged friends or despoil enemies, to proclaim wars or celebrate victories, to enhearten after defeat, to regulate worship, or even to justify the prophet in taking a new wife to his home. While he lived the law was alive, grew daily, and daily was modified and applied. When he died it was closed, became a *corpus* which had to be interpreted, but could itself suffer neither increase nor diminution. His death saw the Koran finished, the State constituted, and Islam founded.

3. Islam as just described may be conceived to be a State rather than a religion, but it would be wrongly so conceived. For it is both a religion and a State—a religion by virtue of its ideas and ends, a State by virtue of its forms and means. As a religion it is Semitic rather than Arabian; as a State it is Arabian rather than Semitic. As a religion it is secondary and derivative, with sources partly Jewish and partly Christian; as a State it is original though not independent, a dream of universal dominion conditioned by the local customs, tribal polities, and social order of Arabia. The force which fused these elements together and made them into the civil religion or religious State we call Islam, was Mohammed. He did not discover the ideas, for they existed before him, but he translated them into the tongue of Arabia, he made his beliefs live in forms so vivid, so picturesque, so full of poetic charm and spiritual passion and the conviction which may not be questioned, that the imagina-

[1] Sura ii. 146.

tions and consciences of all who believed his word became as potter's clay in his hands. The Koran is indeed a marvellous book, which speaks with tremendous force to men who can and do believe it. Its God is a consuming fire in a sense quite unknown to the Old Testament. There the future has but a feeble or shadowy existence; the scene where Jehovah reigns is more this world than the next. But in the Koran if God is eternal, man is immortal, and death is no escape from His hands. In no religion is the other world so real as in Islam; heaven is described in terms most alluring to the oriental imagination, hell in words that scorch and blacken. And God holds man and his destiny in His inexorable hands, awards heaven to the believer, hell to the infidel, no one being able to escape His terrible decree. The idea is one of transcendent power, so simple, so intelligible, so commanding, especially to those who feel that there is nothing between them and this sovereign will. Polytheism leaves man the master of the gods, they are his creation, and if he despairs of one, he can find help and hope in another; but a rigorous monotheism offers no alternatives, allows no concealment, sets man as it were naked before an eternal Face whose smile is life and whose frown is death. And the duties based on the idea were as simple as the idea itself. They were prayer and fasting, which had reference to God; almsgiving, which was duty to the brotherhood; and the pilgrimage to Mecca, which was a sort of homage to the birthplace of the religion, an outward and visible sign of unity, and a witness to the power of Arabia over the founder. But above all, authenticating all, stood the prophet. The God to be believed was the God he revealed; to deny Mohammed was to disbelieve God. His authority was ultimate, for through him God had freely and finally spoken and only through him could God be really known. The primary belief, then, in Islam is not the unity of God, but the apostolate of Mohammed. The beliefs do not simply stand indissolubly together, but the greater is built upon the less. Without the prophet God would still be One, but the one God would not be believed and known of men.

4. Here, then, we can see in what sense Mohammed can be conceived as the founder of the religion. Without him it could not have been; he is not simply the medium of its realization but of its continuance. Islam is the one absolute book religion of the world, and may be most properly defined as the Apotheosis of the Word. The Koran is the mind of Mohammed immortalized for his people, speaking to them, being questioned by them, making their laws, governing their lives. His God is theirs, conceived in his terms, worshipped in his manner, obeyed in his spirit. And this means that an Arab's consciousness of the sixth century A.D. has determined the deity and governs the faith of Islam. The connexion between the man and the religion can thus be dissolved only by the death of both. It has often been said that Islam is of all the great religions the nearest a pure naturalism. Its earliest history has few miracles, perhaps none, and but for certain incidental customs the most strenuous believer in natural law might be a devout Moslem. The saying is as superficial and inaccurate as any saying of ignorance could well be. The supernatural and the miraculous are the very atmosphere which Islam breathes. Mohammed himself is to it a supreme miracle. He stands alone among men, God's apostle, without a rival and without an equal, and to question his authority is to doubt the truth and veracity of God. So cardinal is his pre-eminence to the theology of Islam that how to conceive the prophet and yet to keep him man, has been at once its most inevitable and insoluble problem. On his supremacy, as not simply personal but transmissible and hereditary, the greatest of all the Mohammedan schisms is based. And as with his person, so with his word; it is his incarnation, himself made immortal, universal, articulate. And here also we come upon a fundamental problem of the

Schools: how did the Koran begin to be, and when? Truth is eternal, and the Koran is the truth. Eternity is thus its note; and though God showed it in vision to Mohammed, and he told his vision to men, yet it had ever been in God, the light of his bosom and the love of his heart. The most rigid Christian theories of the sacred canon and inspiration are but nebulous dreams compared to the dogmas which have defined and enshrined the Koran. And this brings us to the miraculous in its early history; the whole story of its coming is a miracle—the visions of the prophet, the angels that speak to him and that carry him whither they will, the God in whose name and at whose bidding he speaks, are all miracles, as full of supernatural ideas and incidents as the most credulous mind could desire. The very collection of the Koran under Abu Bekr, the destruction under Othman, fifteen years later, of all versions but one, and the consequent formation of a single authoritative text, signified that the book was held to be so miraculous that it must be preserved as their book of life, and so preserved that there should be but one form of the prophet's words, these and no other being the truth of God. And here we touch the point where the ideas of the religion and the State coalesce. Both are positive creations, i.e. are founded and built up by positive laws. Positive laws are expressions of a personal or communal will, the rules it makes and the precepts it formulates for the guidance of the individual and the ordering of society. Islam then, whether conceived as religion or as State or as both, is a creation of positive law, the work of a personal will, of the man we know as Mohammed.

§ IV. *Canons of Criticism or Regulative Ideas*

The relation of Jesus to the founding and formation of the Christian religion is too immense a subject to be discussed as a subordinate head in a single chapter; but we may here

RELATION OF RELIGION AND FOUNDER

formulate certain regulative ideas or critical principles that seem to have emerged from these discussions.

i. The Founder and the religion stand so related that neither can be considered without the other. His historical being precedes and conditions its historical origin, and exercises a permanent effect on its development. In him its qualities lie implicit; in it his immanent character and mind are evolved. This means that the religion not only begins with or starts from him, but perpetuates and propagates the ethical type he impersonates. Moral character is thus a matter of fundamental importance to the religion.

ii. The Founder has an historical and an ideal significance both for his own religion and for philosophy or thought in general. The historical significance concerns not only the part he played in making the religion first possible and then actual, but also the influence he has exercised on its earliest behaviour and its later developments. The ideal significance concerns not only the part he has played and been the means of making his religion play in the history of man and of religion, but also the relation in which he stands to the ideal cause, process, and end of human life, individual and collective.

iii. The historical person of the Founder determines the outward character of the religion, its institutions and civil form, the means it uses to fulfil and develop its function as a factor of social order and ethical amelioration as well as to cultivate the persons it enlists and commands and relates to the Eternal. The order of Buddha and the State of Mohammed are their personal creations.

iv. The ideal significance of His person determines the permanent and essential value of the Founder to man and religion. For as the person is conceived to be supreme in history, in mind, and in the universe of actual being, he is the symbol of all that the universe is on its most real yet mysterious side: the side it turns to man as he seeks to know why he is and for what end. The theology of the person becomes then the religion's philosophy of nature and man, of mind and history.

v. If the Founder is to be known, he must never cease to speak; if he is to be a universal authority, his mind must never taste death, but be so immortalized as to be always and everywhere accessible to those who would inquire of him. This explains the need and defines the function of revelation as it exists in a personal religion; it turns the moment of the Founder's historical being into an everlasting now. To be complete the revelation must enable us to know the Founder, his personal history, what manner of man he was, how he took himself and caused himself to be taken, what he taught and what men thought concerning him, what he intended, achieved and suffered. In other words, it must enable us to judge not only as to the Founder's person and history, but as to the entire process that created the religion. It is only thus that we can discover what it really is, and conceive it according to its place and worth and work in universal history.

BOOK II

THE PERSON OF CHRIST AND THE MAKING OF THE CHRISTIAN RELIGION

IN THREE PARTS

I. THE FOUNDER AS AN HISTORICAL PERSON; OR JESUS AS CONCEIVED AND REPRESENTED IN THE EVANGELICAL HISTORY

II. THE INTERPRETATION OF THE FOUNDER; OR THE CREATION OF THE CHRISTIAN RELIGION THROUGH THE APOSTOLICAL CONSTRUCTION OF JESUS AS THE CHRIST

III. THE COMPARISON OF THE ELEMENTS AND IDEAS IN THIS INTERPRETATION WITH THOSE MOST CONSTITUTIVE IN THE IDEAL OF RELIGION AS CONSERVED AND EXEMPLIFIED IN THE HISTORICAL RELIGIONS

Πάντα ὑμῶν ἐστίν, ὑμεῖς δὲ Χριστοῦ, Χριστὸς δὲ Θεοῦ.
—PAUL, 1 *Cor.* iii. 23.

Humanum genus bene se habet et optime, quando secundum quod potest Deo adsimilatur. Sed genus humanum maxime Deo adsimilatur quando maxime est unum ; vera enim ratio unius in solo illo est.—DANTE, *De Monarchia*, I. cap. viii.

Igitur, qui innocentiam colit, Domino supplicat ; qui justitiam, Deo libat ; qui fraudibus abstinet, propitiat Deum ; qui hominem periculo surripit, optimam victimam caedit. Haec nostra sacrificia, haec Dei sacra sunt ; sic apud nos religiosior est ille qui justior.—M. MINUCIUS FELIX, *Octavius*, cap. xxxii.

Alle Erscheinungen des religiösen Lebens auf Erden, auch das Christenthum, sind nur in der Idee der Religion wissenschaftlich zu verstehen, zu würdigen, und der Idee gemäss, nach ihrem Musterbegriffe und Musterbilde, reiner, höher, und lebenreicher auszubilden.—K. C. F. KRAUSE, *Die absolute Religionsphilosophie*, p. 1013.

> Eine nur ist sie für alle, doch stehet sie jeder verschieden,
> Dass es Eines doch bleibt, macht das Verschiedene wahr.

An die alttestamentliche Religion hat das Christenthum angeknüpft und sich als seinen Schluss, als seine Erfüllung und Vollendung dargestellt, dem Judenthum aber ist es entgegengetreten. Und das Christenthum ist nur eine neue und letzte Stufe dieser selben Offenbarungsreligion : auf ihr ist der Heilige selbst erschienen, und das Ideal, welches die alttestamentliche Stufe im Volke Israel vergeblich darzustellen suchte, eine heilige Gemeinde, ein Reich Gottes auf Erden wird nun verwirklicht durch die, welche mit ihm in die Gemeinschaft des Glaubens treten und die Kraft der Heiligung aus ihm ziehen. -A. DILLMANN, *Ursprung der Alttestamentlichen Religion*, 1865, p. 35.

> Alles hat seine Zeit,
> Der Herr der Zeit ist Gott,
> Der Zeiten Wendepunkt Christus,
> Der rechte Zeitgeist der heilige Geist.

INTRODUCTORY

RECAPITULATION AND STATEMENT OF THE NEW QUESTION

§ I. *The Old Problem*

THE principles elucidated in the past discussions have now to be applied to a problem which is all the more philosophical that it is so historical and particular, viz., the interpretation of the relation between the Founder of the Christian religion and the religion He founded. What is involved in this new discussion may become more obvious if we resume the successive stages of the argument which has led up to it.

i. The argument started with an examination into what is meant by the idea of Nature, and whether it can be used to deny the being and action of a supernatural Reason. What may be termed the primary premiss may be stated either thus :—the interpreter of nature is also its interpretation ; or thus :—the problem of individual is one with that of collective experience. The fact of knowledge was found to imply a transcendental factor which justified the inference as to the ultimate and causal reality of thought. From the correlation of the intellect and the intelligible, or of rational man and an interpretable universe, it was argued that they must have had as their common ground a creative Intelligence, who had used the visual language we call nature to speak to the incarnate reason we call man.

ii. This primary premiss was next expanded into the position that man was not simply a being who knew, but a person who acted, that his actions could be qualitatively distinguished, that he felt the obligation and possessed the power to choose the good and avoid the evil; and that as the intellect implied an intelligible, so man as a moral person involved a moral universe, while the two in their concordance and concurrence justified the belief in a moral order. According to the first argument God was to be interpreted in the terms of the reason; according to the second, in the terms of moral sovereignty or of conscience and will; while both arguments conducted to the conclusion that the relations between the Creator and the creature must be active, continuous and spiritual.

iii. The third step in the argument was a discussion of the gravest of all the facts which a believer in moral order can face—the fact of evil. The rational and moral creature had behaved as an imperfect and inexperienced being, which he was, and not as a perfect and eternal being, which he was not; and so his earliest attempts at using his freedom had been by the indulgence of self-will, whence had come evil and the suffering which disciplined. But while evil owed its being to man, it had only increased what was termed the responsibility of God; in other words, it was impossible to conceive that infinite goodness would cease to seek to help and heal the creature whose being it had willed, because that creature had been so misguided as to choose the evil rather than the good; and if divine action on behalf of man continued, how better could it be described than as continuous creation?

iv. The argument then moved forward from nature and man in the abstract to nature and man in the concrete, living together, acting and interacting on each other, nature as physical environment, man as the moral and social organism we speak of now as society and now as state. This carried us into the field of history, and it was contended that the ideas of law and progress which had made nature interpretable and had organized its interpretation into the collective physical sciences, must be valid here also, or they could have no validity anywhere. But though we were bound to conceive order and unity, co-ordinated movement and change in the common life of man as in universal nature, yet they must be conceived as operative under appropriate forms, i.e. forms proper not to physical energies, but to thought, to reasons, emotions, consciences, wills, or simply to man and mankind. But what history exhibits is a creative process rather incomplete than completed. Biology has to construct the succession and filiation of organic forms by an act of retrospective imagination ; but history, though it has to deal with an immeasurable past, yet can study the forces that make for evolution, producing the moral, the social, and the religious forms of the present. We may then distinguish the two arenas thus :—in nature where new organisms have ceased to appear, evolution may be said to have accomplished its work ; but in history the work is still only in process, and waits final accomplishment. Here, then, is the field where the Creator's continued activity finds its fitting sphere ; and its products are (1) the ideas creative of human progress and unity, and (2) the persons through whom they come.

v. But the ideas that do most to evoke and to organize the humanity latent in man are those embodied in his religions, and so here if anywhere the continued activity of the Creator can be studied. It is indeed a mediated activity, conditioned by the medium in and through which He works. And so its forms had to be analyzed, viz., the notion of religion, its sources, the method in which it does its work, the causes and conditions which affect the many shapes it assumes. In all religions men think of deity, and as they think they worship ; and in all they believe themselves to influence him and to be influenced by him. And the voice of Nature is here the voice of truth.

vi. From religion in the abstract the discussion moved into

the field of the concrete, its history; attempted to find what had made and kept religions national; and what had impelled, out of all the multitude of local or tribal religions, only three to seek to transcend the nation and become missionary. The ideas of a religion were, it was argued, more capable of translation and diffusion than its institutions, which tended as local and tribal to hedge off the people and to hinder the distribution of their faith. Analysis further showed that the national religion which possessed the most universal idea— the Hebrew—was as much limited as any by the usages which the fanaticism of the people jealously guarded and observed, as if they constituted its very essence; and was therefore, by being placed under rigorous tribal restrictions, prevented from realizing its idea. The emancipation of this idea, and its embodiment in a religion at once universal and missionary, was in a special and peculiar sense the achievement of Jesus Christ.

vii. But if the Christian religion is conceived as the achievement of Jesus Christ, it owes its existence to a person, and thus falls into the category of instituted or founded religions. Indeed, the three which have been described as " missionary' had all a personal origin; and each has had its special character or creative and constitutive idea determined by the person who gave it being. Hence the question as to the relation between the religion and its founder is not peculiar to Christianity, but is common to the class as a whole, and so belongs to the province of comparative history and philosophy. Approached from this point of view it was found that while an historical person and his creative acts were presupposed in the religion, yet it could not in any real sense begin to be without some form of apotheosis by the community. Institution or creation was thus a process due to the concurrence of two distinct factors, which may be described as, respectively, personal and communal. These gave to the founder a significance at once historical or real, and intelligible or ideal; while without the first the religion could have had no positive existence, without the second it could have no intellectual value, no moral energy, no continuous being as a social force appealing to the conscience and the imagination of man. Hence come regulative ideas, terms and standards of comparison which we must not shrink from applying to the connexion between Jesus Christ and the Christian religion.

§ II. *The New Problem*

If, then, we carry these categories with us, we may the better appreciate the questions we have now to discuss: How was it that Jesus of Nazareth, a Jewish peasant, became the Founder of the Christian religion? Was it as a peasant and as a Jew? Did He create the religion, or was He rather its creature? If He created it, by virtue of what qualities did He accomplish the work? If it created Him, by what process and impelled by what causes did it produce so remarkable an effect? In other words, How do His person and the religion stand related to each other? What does it owe to Him and He owe to it? May we say that He did not so much found it as cause it to be founded? And what does this causation imply concerning His person, its constituents, continuance, functions? If religion can as little be without worship as without belief, is Christian worship a mere exercise of the subjective spirit, or has it any correlative objective reality? What is this reality? Would the religion continue were Christ believed to be dead, or conceived as only a beautiful soul incarnated in His own rare words for the admiration and instruction of mankind? Can it be claimed for His Person that as interpreted in the apostolic writings it made an absolute and ideal religion possible? And can anything from the fields of philosophy and history be said as to the warrant or legitimacy of this claim?

These questions trench on the province of certain connected and cognate studies which it is impossible either to pursue here or entirely ignore. The most important of them is the literary and historical criticism of the oldest Christian literature. This criticism takes the literature as a *corpus* or body of scriptures which has to be studied and explained through its sources, historical and personal, through language and thought, through social and religious movements, antecedent and contemporary tendencies and events. Once it has showed us how the literature came to be, in what order it was written, at what date, by what men, in obedience to what impulse, for what end, its work is done,—its problem is solved. But our question is at once larger and more radical. The literature is to us the scheme of a religion and the story of its founding; and as such it is even more organically connected with the future than with the past. We have to study it not as a fact to be explained, but as a factor of events which without it would be without any explanation. What concerns us is indeed still history, but it is a history whose temporal and spatial relations have been so widened as to become universal and eternal. What we seek to gain is not simply the mind of a contemporary, or the knowledge of the exact conditions which produced each document and of the world it reflects; but also to discover the seeds and causes of the ideal world in which we dwell. We do not cease to use criticism, for by determining the nature and value of our sources it governs the degree and the certainty of our knowledge; but its canons do not measure for us the religion which the literature it handles at once describes and enshrines. For this we have to study it in the light of collective religion, or as it lives in the medium of the human spirit and answers to it, and as it stands on the stage of history, living and behaving as its creative ideas command.

§ III. *The Criticism of the Literature and the Person*

The literature, as related to our subject, falls into two main divisions,—one, the Gospels, concerned with the personal history of Jesus ; the other, the apostolical writings, including the Acts, concerned with the interpretation of His Person as the Christ. The former show us what manner of man the Founder of the religion was ; the latter what the thought of His people conceived Him to be and what they accomplished in His name. But the chronological relations of these divisions are not the same as their historical. In the order of time the person precedes the interpretation ; but the books which interpret Him are older than those that narrate His personal history. The most certainly authentic documents in the New Testament, contemporary with the events they describe or refer to, are not the Gospels, but certain Pauline Epistles ; and of these the first must have been written about 50 A.D., and the last could hardly have been later than 62. Of the non-Pauline Epistles the greatest and the weightiest, Hebrews, belongs probably to about the year 70, while near it in point of date stands a work of, possibly, inferior theological importance, the Apocalypse. In these we have what may be termed a completed Christology, though the only Gospel that existed in the year 70, if, indeed, it did then exist, was that of Mark. He is one of the Synoptists, the other two, divided from Mark by periods, probably, of from ten to fifteen years, being Matthew and Luke, who use the same material and present, with significant differences, the same view of the Person and His History. Now, it may seem a strange inversion of the natural order, and certain to involve perversions of fact, that we should have had the speculative construction before the actual and personal history ; but it can only so seem to a hurried and inconsequent thinker. For

i. The literature here follows the strict order of nature, or the laws of exact thought. There was at first no question as to the history of Jesus, His birth, life, doctrine, sufferings death ; but there was from the very outset the sharpest differences as to what He was, why He was, and what He did.

And this was a question that had to be settled in order that His Society should know whether it was to die or to live.

ii. The extraordinary activity of apostolical thought concerning the Person did not imply neglect of the history ; on the contrary, it involved continual occupation with it. So much, indeed, is this the case that it is quite impossible to understand the Epistles without the Gospels; the logic of the former assumes at every point the history of the latter. Were a scholar unacquainted with the Gospels to read the Pauline writings, with their references to the birth, descent, character, love, righteousness, grace, cross, death, and resurrection of Christ, he would find them utterly unintelligible, not only because he did not know who this Christ was, where He had lived, what He had been and claimed to be, but also because the very man who writes and the persons he writes to, with their special ideas, questions, and arguments, would be inexplicable without Him. And if the Gospels are so necessary to the reader of the Epistles, can the history they record have been less necessary to their writer? And if so construed, do the Epistles not authenticate the history they assume, though not perhaps the books that describe it in the form in which they have come down to us?

iii. Criticism has enabled us to analyze the Synoptic Gospels, to discover the documents that underlie them, the use they have made of common sources, narrative and didactic, their relation to each other, and their respective modes of dealing with the history on the one hand, and the *logia*, the notes or memoranda of addresses, parables, or conversations on the other. These things indicate the method of the historian : the men do not invent their material, but find, arrange, and set it in order. And here as the Gospels are needed to illuminate the Epistles, the Epistles are needed to supplement the Gospels and bring out their distinctive features. It is remarkable, indeed, how distinct their provinces are, how little of the oral or written material which the evangelists employ finds its way into the Epistles, and how few of the distinctive formulae or the special terms and problems which exercise the earlier apostolical writers are incorporated with the Gospels. And there is another and parallel fact to be explained. In 70 A.D. Jerusalem fell and with it the Jewish State. However much it signified to the Jew, it signified to the Christian no less. It meant that the city that had refused to hear, and cast out, mocked and crucified the Christ, had perished in its pride, that God had avenged its guilt and vindicated His innocence. It meant that the home of the influences most hostile to the Church had been razed to the ground. Yet in the two later Synoptic Gospels the event leaves hardly a trace on the history. It may be involved in certain texts or references in the apocalyptic addresses, but these can be removed without seriously affecting the narrative. The effect on contemporary Judaism we can study in the pages of Josephus; or, to cite a parallel case, we can see in Augustine's *De Civitate Dei* the influence which the fall of Rome exercised on both Christian and pagan thought. Yet the fall of Rome stood in no such obvious tragic relation to the church of Christ as did the fall of Jerusalem to His death; and had no such evident and immediate significance for the religion. That the Gospels were so little affected in texture and in matter by inner movements and outer events, is a point which students of cognate and contemporary influences in literature will be able to appreciate.

iv. History does not lose but gain in accuracy and truth by being mediately rather than immediately written. The last and most trustworthy historian is not the eyewitness, but the man who can question him, and who can through the issue read character, action, and event with greater intelligence than he. The most accurate and informing history is not the diary, but the discourse of the writer who sees not simply the salient feature of each person or occurrence, but sees also each thing as it is and all the things together. And when we come to study the Gospels together, we see how much time has done for the perspective which gives to each figure in the scene its due place and proportion. The sense of the causation and connexion of events has grown in the Evangelists. Mark is more of the simple narrator than either of the other two; he tells what he has heard rather than what he has seen, writes, as Peter was wont to speak, the simple yet picturesque words which describe Jesus " by the sea of Galilee,"[1] calling Peter and Andrew, " James the son of Zebedee, and John his brother," casting " the unclean spirit " out of the man, healing " Simon's wife's mother, who lay sick of a fever," sitting " at even, when the sun did set," with the sick and the possessed of devils around Him " and all the city gathered at the door." This is the thing an eyewitness, or the man who reports an eyewitness, can do, and Mark does it perfectly. His pen realizes the scene, and we see Jesus as He was, and as only a pen which followed the tongue of a speaker describing experiences too vivid to be forgotten, can show Him. With Matthew and Luke the atmosphere is different; Jesus is more an historical figure with roots in the past and relations in the present, and less a person loved for His own sake and with His reason in Himself. The antitheses are more sharply conceived; in Matthew he fulfils the law and opposes the Pharisees, in Luke He befriends the poor, the publican, and the sinner; and in both His world is, whether in retrospect or prospect, as large as the history of man.

v. And here we may observe how the enlarged and enriched thought of the apostolical writings has affected the atmosphere and the setting as distinguished from the matter of the Gospels. The author of Matthew has affinities with the Epistle to the Hebrews, though his affinities are those of a Palestinian rather than a Roman or Alexandrian Jew; but Luke's are more Pauline. Matthew, like Hebrews, reads the New Law through the old, though his symbolism is more historical

[1] Mark i. 16-34.

than institutional, more in things and incidents than in ideas and forms. Hence his genealogy begins with Abraham, and comes down through David to Joseph the husband of Mary.[1] The child is named Jesus, for " He shall save His people from their sins."[2] He " is born King of the Jews "[3] and every event of His childhood fulfils a prophecy.[4] And as then, so throughout. He begins His ministry like a new Moses proclaiming on the Mount a law which speaks in beatitudes rather than in curses,[5] yet He comes to fulfil the old and not to destroy it.[6] He forbids His disciples to go into the way of the Gentiles, for His mission is to the lost sheep of the house of Israel,[7] and His message tells that the kingdom of heaven has come.[8] Yet this particularism is only the prelude to a richer universalism. For many are to come from the east and the west and sit down with Abraham, Isaac, and Jacob in the kingdom of heaven,[9] while the sons of the kingdom are cast forth into outer darkness; and His final commission is to make disciples of all nations.[10] Luke is more distinctly Hellenistic, but his Hellenism is that of the Greek rather than of the Jew. He interprets Jesus and His history through the Pauline idea of the Second Adam, and construes Him throughout in universal terms. His genealogy runs back to Adam, " the Son of God."[11] He is born as it were a citizen of the Roman Empire.[12] The message of His birth promises glory to God in the highest, and peace to man on earth.[13] He begins His ministry by reading a prophecy which identifies Him with the Servant of God and the cause of the poor and the oppressed.[14] And the great parables peculiar to Luke repeat and emphasize these ideas. He impersonates in the Good Samaritan Christ's everlasting rebuke to the vanity and

---

[1] Matt. i. 1-16. [2] i. 21. [3] ii. 2.
[4] i. 22 ; ii. 5, 15, 17, 23. [5] v. 3-12. [6] v. 17.
[7] x. 5, 6. [8] iv. 17 ; x. 7 ; xiii. 24, 31, 33, 44, 45, 47.
[9] viii. 11, 12 ; cf. xxi. 43, xxii. 1-14. [10] xxviii. 19.
[11] Luke iii. 38. [12] ii. 1, 2. [13] ii. 14. [14] iv. 18.

heartlessness of the priest and the Levite.[1] He leaves the Pharisee speaking his own shame in the temple, while He sends the publican home justified.[2] He bids the everlasting Fatherhood in the man who had two sons, both graceless, yet both sons still, rebuke the caste of the scribe and the isolation of the sectary.[3] And in the story of the rich man and Lazarus he gives dignity to poverty and makes all wealth which is proud of itself as mere wealth feel vacant and vain.[4] The same ideas are embodied and made articulate in such incidents, also distinctive of Luke, as the woman of the city, a sinner, in the house of Simon the Pharisee, with its lesson pointed by the appended parable;[5] the conversion of the chief publican, Zacchaeus,[6] and the scene in the house of the sisters Martha and Mary.[7] These are all though peculiar to Luke, yet authentic and characteristic. Mark would hardly have seen their significance, nor would the original witness whose version he repeats. Matthew had no eye for them, because they did not help to unfold his leading idea. But Luke, with a finer imagination, a more skilful pen and a wider outlook than either, preserved acts and words whose loss would have made us appreciably poorer; yet because they are so germane to the mind and purpose of the historian, they but add an illustration to the point, that the more a man brings to a history the more he can find in it, and also the better help us to find more there.

§ IV. *The Religion and the Literature*

1. The criticism of the literature may, then, be necessary to the discussion of our problem, but it is not by itself sufficient for its solution. On the contrary, it may be so pursued as to make any reasonable solution impossible. Thus a recent critic has found in the synoptists only five "absolutely credible pas-

---

[1] x. 25-37. [2] xviii. 9-14. [3] xv. 11-32. [4] xvi. 14, 19, 31.
[5] vii. 36-50. [6] xix. 2-10. [7] x. 38-42.

HISTORY AND THE MODERN CRITIC 303

sages about Jesus in general."[1] These are His refusal to be called "good," for "no one is good save God only"[2]; the blasphemy against the Son of Man, which "shall be forgiven"[3]; His relation to His kinsfolk when they held Him to be beside Himself[4]; the profession of ignorance as to the day and the hour which were known only of the Father[5]; and the cry of desertion on the cross.[6] To these he adds four passages "on the miracles of Jesus." The refusal to work a sign[7]; the inability because of unbelief to do any mighty work at Nazareth[8]; the warning of the disciples to "beware of the leaven of the Pharisees and Herod,"[9] which is, as it were, the title of a parable turned into a miracle; and the message to the Baptist touching His miracles[10]; where Jesus is made to speak "not of the physically but of the spiritually blind, lame, leprous, deaf, dead."[11] These nine passages are called "the foundation-pillars for a truly scientific life of Jesus." But what claim have they to be regarded as a solid basis for any "scientific life" which must explain not only the life that ended on the Cross, but also the work accomplished by the Crucified in and for mankind? They are mainly negative; and it is only when viewed through a larger context and an atmosphere which they themselves do not create, that they gain any positive significance whatever. They show what Jesus was not, what He could not know or do, they do not show what He was or did. Yet of all real things the most positively real, the most efficient and continuous in its recreative action, is His Person; and to attempt to explain it by nine negatives, made the more absolute by appearing in one or two cases in a positive form, is only to resolve it into a more darksome

---

[1] Schmiedel, *Encycl. Bibl.*, pp. 1881-1883. [2] Mark x. 17, 18.
[3] Matt. xii. 31, 32. [4] Mark iii. 21.
[5] Mark xiii. 32. [6] Mark xv. 34; Matt. xxvii. 46.
[7] Mark viii. 12; Matt. xii. 39; cf. xvi. 4; Luke xi. 29.
[8] Mark vi. 5, 6; cf. Matt. xv. 38. [9] Mark viii. 14-18; cf. Matt. xvi. 6.
[10] Matt. xi. 5; Luke vii. 22. [11] *Encycl. Bibl.*, 1883.

mystery than before. And this is only a type of the illusion that mistakes critical ingenuity for historical science. Another and more common is that which seeks in the words of Jesus the entire truth as to Himself and His mission. Truth is there, but truth is conditioned by the medium it employs and the minds that hear it as well as by the mind that speaks it. We cannot indeed know too much of His mind and thought; but, let us frankly say it, it is not here that His sole pre-eminence or our main problem lies. His work and meaning as a religious Teacher belongs to exegesis and comparative literary criticism; but our discussion is philosophical and historical as well as theological, for it relates to the position and function of Christ as a sovereign personality in religion. As a teacher there are many men in many lands and times with whom He may be compared; but as a creative and sovereign personality there are in the whole of history only two or three, if indeed there are so many, with any claim to stand by His side. As a Teacher He is a natural person, with historical antecedents, a social environment, a religious ancestry, and a position honourable but not unique amid the great masters of mind; but as a sovereign personality He is a new Being, without father, or mother, or genealogy, separate, supreme, creating by His very appearing a new spiritual type or order. As a Teacher we can easily conceive Him as a Jew and a peasant, the lineal descendant of the prophets and near of kin to the rabbis of Israel; but there is no harder intellectual task than to relate the sovereign personality to the Jewish peasant, his antecedents and environment. But this correlation is the very thing which must be attempted if all the phenomena are to be explained; for if anything is certain, it is this:—the teaching of Jesus, however its qualities may be described or appraised, can never by itself explain the power of Christ, the reign, the diffusion, the continuance, and the achievements of the Christian religion. And these are the things which stand in need of explanation; not simply what Jesus thought and why He thought it, but why men came so to think concerning Him as to create the religion which bears His name. Can the religion be without the idea of the Christ which made it? And was this idea a mythical creation, a mystic dream, an ignorant superstition, the inference of an imperious but illiterate logic? Or if not, what was it?

2. There are, then, distinctions both of issue and of fundamental principle between our problem and the questions raised by the literary and historical criticisms of the New Testament. These may be said to move within a special period and to be concerned with its literature and its contemporary history. They have for their aim to show us what manner of person Jesus of Nazareth was, whence He had come, how and under what influences He had been formed, how He lived, behaved, thought, spoke; how He was handled, spoken to, judged; what character He realized, what fate He encountered, what evil He suffered. But in all this they enquire simply concerning an empirical person, whom they look at from the standpoint of empirical history. In the strict sense Jesus did not so much create the Christian religion as cause it to be created. When He died, the creative process had only begun. Though He had so exemplified the spirit and character of the religion as to be entitled to the name of the first Christian, yet it is one thing to embody an ideal and another to constitute the faith which is to secure its embodiment. What the men who had followed Him believed Him to have accomplished, is written in their history. They did not mean to cease to be Jews; their discipleship did not divorce them from their ancestral worship, its customs, its sacred places and seasons. They frequented the temple, observed the Jewish hours of prayer, the regulations as to meats, circumcision, purification, sacrifices even;[1] and seemed

---

[1] Acts of Apostles ii. 46; iii. 1; v. 42; x. 14; xv. 5; xxi. 26.

indeed to contemplate nothing more than to add another to the many sects which had made themselves at home in Judaism. What changed their outlook and action was the interpretation of Christ's person; and it was by something more divine than a sure instinct that it was made to occupy a larger space in the New Testament than even the words of Jesus. By the time the Gospels came to be written the religion had become a reality, the creative process was well advanced, if not completed. And what gives to the Gospels their peculiar significance is that they are Lives of Jesus by men who believed that Christ had created Christianity. The empirical person is, though without losing His historical environment, yet transfigured into a transcendental personality. The natural is neither abolished nor depreciated, but it is read in terms of the supernatural. The struggle of the modern spirit is the exact converse of this; it is to get behind the faith of the Evangelists, and read the history they wrote with the vision they had before their eyes were opened. Yet there is a history which the book has made as well as a history which it records; and it is doubtful whether it be the note of the historical spirit to take a book out of the history it has made and to study it as if all its significance lay in the history that made it. For it is the faith which the book embodies more than the facts it states, that has placed upon its brow the crown of an illuminative history. Only as we read it in this faith can we know it as a book of religion, and it is as such a book that we here seek to know it. We do not, indeed, forget that the book has a natural history of its own, according to which it must, like any other piece of literature, be rationally judged; all we here desire to emphasize is the fact that the very process which produced it created a religion, and the book is not justly or even critically studied if this double process is forgotten.

§ V. *The Founder and the Religion*

1. The point of view here occupied does not seem to us either unscientific or uncritical; on the contrary, it is the standpoint to which philosophy has driven us. We have already examined some of the assumptions which underlie the modern belief in the inviolability of natural law,[1] but with us it is a fixed principle that violation of law, properly so called, is a thing impossible to God. The distinction between the natural and the supernatural, as it meets us in the field of nature, we have also considered;[2] but now we must review it as it confronts us in the field of history. The terms, indeed, as used here denote no true antithesis, but express ideas that are rather complementary than opposed. The supernatural is not identical with the extraordinary, the abnormal, or the miraculous; nor is the natural synonymous with the regular, the orderly, or the uniform. Each may be said to be the other under a different or changed aspect. The supernatural is the ideal, the universal, the causal existence, the permanent reality, or however we may choose to name it, which binds nature and man together, and determines the tendencies that reign in history, as well as the ideas that govern men. The natural is the apparent, the phenomenal, the unit in its isolation and distinctness, the thing in its separateness as opposed to the organism which is a living whole. Hence the natural by itself, if by itself it can be conceived, is uniform, therefore unprogressive and uncreative; its changes can be expressed in the terms of physical equivalence, but not of moral motive or spiritual impulse. But when it becomes the visible image of the supernatural, the body to its soul, it grows creative, progressive, ceases to be uniform, and becomes as varied yet as orderly as a movement of the reason. And this relationship is most perfectly realized in history, for here the form the supernatural assumes

---

[1] Ante, pp. 23 ff.   [2] Ante, p. 56.

is the personal, and the person is by nature at once empirical and transcendental. As empirical the person is a unit; as transcendental he belongs to a whole, and thinks in the terms of the universal. As empirical he is a creature of time and space, comes of a given race, is born at a given time in a given place to a given family, inherits a given past, is fashioned by a given present, and is a factor of a given future; but as transcendental his affinities are all with the eternal, and all his work is for it. Yet these things are not opposites, they are the integral and constituent parts of a single being; but the factors are not always equal, or as forces in equilibrium. Now the one and now the other rules; and the more the higher rules the lower, the more is the person the vehicle of the universal, i.e. the larger is the part of God in the making of the man and in his actions. Without the natural the supernatural would have no foothold in history, no means of translating its ideals into realities, or of guiding and impelling upward the life of man; without the supernatural the natural would constitute no order and know no movement towards a moral end. Whether, then, there is anything supernatural in a history is not a matter to be decided by the play of critical formulæ on a literature, nor by the study of periods or events in isolation. It belongs to the whole, and is to be determined as regards any special person by his worth for the whole and by the degree in which he is a factor of its good. Applied to Jesus Christ this means that He is not a problem in local but in general history, not in a special but in all literature, not in one but in universal religion; and that if He is to be interpreted, it must be in the terms of humanity, and not merely in those of Judea or Jewish Hellenism. He is a natural Being, or He could not be historical; but He is also supernatural, otherwise He could not hold His sovereign position, or exercise His universal functions. And these, as matters of experience and not simply of speculation, must be enquired into as real things.

THE PROBLEMS THEY FORMULATE 309

2. If the problem, as now explicated and defined, be formulated for purposes of discussion, it will be found to fall into three main questions.

I. The historical person and action of Jesus: what He was, what He designed to be and to do, what He became, and what He did. The discussion will here be concerned chiefly, though not exclusively, with the representation of Him in the Synoptic Gospels.

II. The interpretation of Jesus as the Christ: or how His Society conceived Him, and what it became through conceiving Him as it did. In this case we shall be mainly occupied with the apostolical writings, under which is included the Gospel according to John.

III. How the religion which came to be through the union of the historical action with the theological interpretation of His Person, stands related to the idea of religion given in the nature of man and unfolded in the course of his history. This question will carry us back into the fields of the comparative History and Philosophy of Religion.

ἀρκεῖν γὰρ οἶμαι κἀντὶ μυρίων μίαν
ψυχὴν τάδ' ἐκτίνουσαν, ἢν εὔνους παρῇ.—SOPHOCLES.

Dans l'espace de temps qui s'est écoulé de la mort d'Auguste à la mort de Marc-Aurèle, une religion nouvelle s'est produite dans le monde ; elle s'appelle le christianisme. L'essence de cette religion consiste à croire qu'une grande manifestation céleste s'est faite en la personne de Jésus de Nazareth, être divin qui, après une vie toute surnaturelle, a été mis à mort par les Juifs, ses compatriotes, et est ressuscité le troisième jour.—RENAN.

Das haben vor Zeiten die höchsten Theologen gethan, dass sie von der Menschheit Christi geflogen sind zu der Gottheit und sich allein an dieselbige gehänget ;—ich bin vor Zeiten auch ein solcher Doktor gewesen, dass ich hab die Menschheit ausgeschlossen ;—aber man muss so steigen zu der Gottheit und sich daran halten, dass man die Menschheit Christi nicht verlasse.—LUTHER.

Christus konnte nur der Sohn der Jungfrau sein, er ist selbst eine Jungfrau im Gemüthe, gleich dem ersten Adam in der Schöpfung.—JACOB BOEHME.

Dass alle Lehren und Vorschriften, welche sich in der christlichen Kirche entwickeln, nur dadurch ein allgemein-gültiges Ansehn erhalten, dass sie auf Christum zurückgeführt werden, gründet sich nur auf seine vollkommne Urbildlichkeit in allem, was mit der Kraft des Gottesbewusstseins in Verbindung steht.—SCHLEIERMACHER.

Die Kräfte der ewigen Gottheit offenbarten sich in Christo nicht neben den Kräften seiner Menschheit, nicht als übermenschliche ; sondern eben in den Kräften seiner Menschheit, eben darin, dass seine menschlichen Kräfte übernaturlich, d. h. über die durch den Sündfall depravirte Natur hinausgehende waren und er dieser depravirten Natur schlechthin überlegen war, so dass sie, wo und wann er wirken wollte, für sein Können nirgends eine Schranke bildete.—EBRARD.

Hat es jemals einen schlechthin originalen Menschen gegeben, so ist es Jesus gewesen.

Vor Christo hatten wir von Gott gehört, in Christo haben wir ihn gesehen.—ROTHE.

Jésus est la plus haute de ces colonnes qui montrent à l'homme d'où il vient et où il doit tendre. En lui s'est condensé tout ce qu'il y a de bon et d'élevé dans notre nature.—RENAN.

PART I

THE FOUNDER AS AN HISTORICAL PERSON, OR JESUS AS HE APPEARS IN THE SYNOPTIC GOSPELS

CHAPTER I

HOW HIS PERSON IS CONCEIVED

IN the Synoptic Gospels, and here we may also include the Fourth, the two views of Jesus which we are accustomed to distinguish as the natural and the supernatural are alike represented. It is through their conflict that the simple story of a humble and beautiful life is turned into the supreme drama of history. The one view is worked out with conspicuous fidelity to its last logical consequences by men who honestly believed it; the other view is presented with ingenuous simplicity, though with varying degrees of conscious and consistent completeness, by the writers, who either out of personal knowledge or from collected and sifted materials, attempted to tell the story of His life. The views so stand together as to compel us to compare them as respects their adequacy and historical truth.

§ I. *The Natural View of Jesus in the Gospels*

1. What this view involves has just been stated:[1] it conceives man as an empirical unit, and may be said to emphasize six factors of being and character: race, family, place, time, education, and opportunity. *Race* denotes man's whole inheritance as a human being, the mental endowment which

---

[1] Ante, pp. 307-8.

belongs to his special stock, the experience that has through long ages and by ceaseless struggles for the means of subsistence and against the enemies that threaten them, been accumulated by a given people for transference to its sons. *Family* describes the man's immediate ancestry, the qualities that come to him by blood and birth, the class from which he springs, whether governing, servile, professional, or industrial, with all that these signify as to transmitted faculty and advantage or disadvantage in beginning the struggle to live. *Place* speaks of geographical and social environment, the atmosphere which the man breathes and which quickens or deadens the pulses of his body and mind. *Time* is but a name for a reigning spirit, a mood, which affects the man's temper and soul as the place affects his physical organism, and which makes him love freedom or fear the king, breathe high hopes or nurse despondency and despair. *Education* is that study of the past which gives mastery over the present, the development of faculty by skilled hands, teaching a man to make the most and best of himself by telling him what men in other ages have thought and achieved. And *opportunity* is the chance which comes to a man to use to the uttermost what he is, what he has inherited, and what he has acquired. The most that the natural view expects from a man is that he be equal to the sum of all the conditions concerned in his making. If he transcends them, then we are landed either in an insolubility or in the recognition of an unknown factor which may be named personal genius, but can hardly be described as normal or according to law. In any case this appeal to an undiscovered or incalculable cause differs only in name from the appeal to the supernatural.

Whether these natural factors of personality are equal to the explanation of Jesus may be appear in the process of the discussion. At present we have only to note that while He lived the natural was the obvious view of Him, taken as a matter of course by men of all classes and kinds. In His own city, where He had lived like any other child subject unto his parents (ὑποτασσόμενος αὐτοῖς, i.e. τοῖς γονεῦσιν),[1] the multitude (οἱ πολλοί) even after He had achieved fame, described Him as "the carpenter," the son of Mary, and refused to distinguish Him in any special way from either His brothers or His sisters.[2] He was but "Joseph's son," even as they.[3] To Himself Mary, when she found Him in the temple, said, "Child, Thy father and I sought thee sorrowing."[4] The very disciples did not at first think of Him otherwise. Philip named Him "Jesus of Nazareth, the son of Joseph,"[5] Peter rebuked Him,[6] Judas betrayed Him, and the rest appealed to Him as Rabbi, the Master,[7] most familiar of names to the men of Israel. Even His own family thought of Him as one they could claim and coerce; and justified their attempt to force Him by saying, "He is beside Himself."[8] To the scribes He was but as one who blasphemed when He spoke of forgiving sins.[9] The Pharisees explained His miracles of healing by demoniacal possession,[10] a charge as common and as natural then as witchcraft used to be in our own darker ages. The very notion that He could wake the ruler's daughter from the sleep which was called death, roused the crowd to scornful laughter.[11] Indeed, so rooted was this natural view of Him, that we need to remember it before we can be just to the men who opposed Him and who compassed His death. They judged Jesus to be a common man, holding that any who believed otherwise were deceived.[12] His very home condemned Him, for out of Galilee came no prophet.[13] He is to the Pharisees but an itinerant sophist, so little instructed that even the Herodians were expected to

---

[1] Luke ii. 51; cf. 41, 43. [2] Mark vi. 3; Matt. xiii. 55.
[3] Luke iv. 22; John vi. 42. [4] Luke ii. 48. [5] John i. 45.
[6] Mark viii. 32; Matt. xvi. 22. [7] Mark ix. 5, xi. 21; John i. 38.
[8] Mark iii. 21; cf. 31-35; Matt. xii. 46-49, xiii. 57; Luke viii. 19-21.
[9] Mark ii. 7; Matt. ix. 3. [10] Matt. ix. 34.
[11] Mark v. 39; Matt. ix. 24. [12] John vii. 47.
[13] John vii. 52.

ensnare Him.[1] He was despised as the friend of publicans and sinners,[2] watched that He might be accused as a Sabbath-breaker,[3] allowed to go at large simply from fear of the people.[4] The Sadducee, though he was not, like the scribe, a trained disputant, yet had a logical puzzle of his own concerning marriage in the resurrection, and with it he tried to perplex Jesus,[5] just as he was wont to confound the Pharisee. All these men judged Him by the standards they applied to one another; and as they judged, they handled Him, and He died at their hands just as any ordinary person would have died. In all this there may be matter that requires explanation, but nothing calling for either surprise or censure.

2. But the two men whose conduct is most completely governed by this natural view are Caiaphas and Pilate, for these two so believed it as to become the joint authors of the tragedy of the Cross. Their relation to this tragedy was indeed very different; the one was the author of the plot, the other the cause of the catastrophe. Caiaphas was a Sadducee, an aristocrat in family and feeling, head of the Jewish Church, and an authority in the State, with the instincts and habits of the ruler controlled by the mind and exercised in the manner of the ecclesiastic. In the Sanhedrim his characteristic qualities had room for the freest and most effective play, especially when it met in such confusion and alarm as followed upon the events at Bethany and the triumphal entry.[6] For it is evident that Jesus had, in spite of Himself, become a political personage. In Israel religion and politics were not two things, but one and the same; for the name that denoted the strongest faith of the people expressed also their highest hope, their yearning after freedom from the yoke of the alien. The Messiah was expected to vanquish Cæsar;

---

[1] Matt. xxii. 15 ff.; Mark xii. 13.   [2] Luke v. 30; xv. 2; Mark ii. 16.
[3] Luke vi. 7; Mark iii. 6.   [4] Luke xx. 19, 20.
[5] Mark xii. 18-27; Luke xx. 27-40.
[6] John xi. 47; cf. Mark xii. 13-17; xiv. 1-2; Luke xx. 17-26.

and expectancy easily translates itself into action, especially when it lives in the heart of a passionate race. Rulers who do not believe fear profoundly the people who do; the statesmanship that is calculation dreads the enthusiasm which is ready to sacrifice its all in order that it may attain its end, without being able, or indeed caring, to balance or to measure the forces which oppose it. And in this council two different kinds of unbelief sat facing each other in solemn and unmasked fear. There was the unbelief of the Sadducee, who knew Moses but not the prophets, who neither expected nor desired any other Anointed than the priesthood which stood to him as the finest blossom of his race. And there was the unbelief of the Pharisee, who preached the Messiah that was to come, but who thought it best that the Pharisee should believe in the preaching while the people believed in the Messiah.

And the circumstances of the moment made action by the multitude on the ground of their faith at once most probable and most inconvenient. The Passover was at hand, Jerusalem was filled by an expectant crowd, massed, as it were, into a colossal person, sensitive on the outside to the softest touch of national hope or fear, while within, like a fire in the bones, there burned the fierce passion for the religion of their ancient race. Through this crowd the sudden fame of Jesus swept, fused it, inspired it, moved it by the delirious hope that here, at last, was the Messiah come to break in pieces the heathen oppressor, and to purge the holy city from the defilement of his presence.[1] The Council knew the people, and also knew the procurator,[2] whom it seemed to see sitting in his palace, jealous, vindictive, watching as with a hundred eyes for an occasion to interfere. And it stood bewildered between the rival terrors: on the one hand, the uncalculating and incalculable passion

[1] Matt. xxi. 8-11; Luke xix. 35-40, 47, 48; John xii. 12-15.
[2] Luke xiii. 1.

of the crowd, and, on the other, the cold omnipotence of Rome, here so easily roused and so pitiless when provoked. Just then Caiaphas stood up, the one masterful spirit who could command the storm. He had the significant yet dark distinction of being "High Priest that fateful year," and was about to fulfil his office in a sense and manner he little dreamed of. He spoke with a certain imperious scorn words that may be paraphrased thus :[1] "Ye know nothing at all: the public safety is the supreme law, and must not be endangered by the passion which in the populace is a fitful madness, easily kindled, but only to be cunningly quenched. In this case it can best be quenched through its cause; smite the hero the populace admires, and their admiration will die into disgust." The words seemed those of gifted sagacity; Jesus was nothing, the mere creation of a fanaticism blinded by many disappointments; and, though He was guiltless of crime, yet it was the high expedient of statesmanship to save the people by making an end of Him. And if He were only the common person the priest and the Council conceived Him to be, who will say that the expedient was foolish or unfitted for its purpose? For what is the wisdom of statecraft but ingenuity in the invention, not of just, but of effectual means to desired ends?

It is from this point of view that the policy of the Council and the method of the chief priest ought to be judged. Grant that Jesus was the mere natural man they conceived Him to be, and we do not see how they could have acted otherwise. They were not heroic men, but they meant well to their land and State, and feared above everything the anger or suspicion of Rome; for they had daily to face a governor who was more imperious than his master, and to watch soldiers who cared for nothing save his commands. And while they knew and trembled, the people were ignorant and without fear. In the soul of Caiaphas concern for the nation, the

[1] John xi. 49, 50.

temple, the priesthood, the worship, was uppermost; and he was anxious to give the Roman no occasion to doubt his own or his people's loyalty. Possibly, too, he was not disinclined to read the Pharisaic opposition a needed lesson. He would say to them, as it were : "You see what danger lies in your theories, and how easily they may become explosive forces in the heart of the populace. You teach that Jehovah alone ought to be King over this people; that Cæsar is a heathen and an oppressor; and that when God pleases to send His Messiah freedom will be achieved. They think that this Jesus is the Messiah you talk of, and wait only a sign from him to revolt. And, though he seems a peaceably-inclined, well-meaning, and even innocent person, yet some event which they may take as a sign may happen without premeditation or warning. Chance may bring it, and we may any moment find Jerusalem in arms against Rome. There is nothing so safe as a sound conservatism, which, though not at all contented with what is, yet fears more what may be; and so does its best to maintain the actual lest the attempt to realize the ideal become a catastrophe which shall engulf the whole nation. Let us therefore do our utmost to prove our loyalty to Cæsar; charge this man with being an agitator, an enemy of order and of Rome, surrender him as a pledge of our obedience to the Emperor; and so out of our very trouble pluck the approval of our conquerors, the peace of our State, and the continuance of our authority. 'It is expedient for you that one man should die for the people, and that the whole nation perish not.'" On his own premises, there seemed to be statesmanship in his policy; on the Evangelists', his policy appeared a devil's counterfeit of the purpose and mind of God.

3. The same conception as to the status and nature of Jesus which governed the policy of Caiaphas possessed the mind of Pilate. He is an unconscious actor in the drama, with only the dimmest sense that anything extraordinary is pro-

ceeding, or that he is playing more than his ordinary part.[1] There is something fateful and pathetic in the position and action of this man; when we think of him, we feel that justice must be blind, or she would pity too much to be just. Here is the only Roman known to history who saw Jesus; but his eyes had no vision in them, and so he looked as one who did not see, or so saw as only to misjudge and mishandle. In him Rome was impersonated. Out of him looked her imperial strength, in him dwelt for a subject people her statesmanship. As he faced the Jews he thought of Cæsar, and ruled the subject race with his feet firm planted on an empire which stretched westward to the Pillars of Hercules, northward to the forests of Germany and the outermost coasts of Gaul. And what were the Jews to him? Turbulent men, intolerable for their intolerant superstition, a people that the imperial image on a banner provoked into madness,[2] who would not allow the shadow of a Gentile to fall on their temple, though, indeed, that temple was so poor a place as to be unadorned by the statue of any god. Still it was necessary, the people being conquered, to rule them considerately—if they behaved; but if they were disaffected at this high feast and showed themselves seditious, or even if they only threatened to be, then in Cæsar's name let their blood be mingled with their sacrifices.[3] And what did Jesus seem to this man as He stood before him? A Jew, only a Jew, though most unlike the typical Jew in the gentleness of His bearing, the mystery of His speech, and the glamour of soul which the Roman felt touch his heart, now waking him to mockery, now moving him to pity.[4] He knew the chief priest and the Council; and he had for them the sort of contempt the conqueror feels for those of the conquered who seek by excessive suppleness to keep themselves

---

[1] Matt. xxvii. 24; John xviii. 31, 37, xix. 6.
[2] Josephus, *Antiq.* xviii. iii. 1-2.   [3] Luke xiii. 1.
[4] Luke xxiii. 4-7, 13-22; John xix. 8-9, 12, 19-22.

in place, mollifying with the one hand the strong-willed victor, and soothing with the other the irritable impotence of the vanquished. Jesus was a being of another order than these men; and though Pilate, listening to His discourse, was so vividly, by contrast, reminded of Epicurus and his great Roman disciple, as to throw out the jesting question, "What is truth?" yet he turned away with the feeling that he would save Him,—unless, indeed, the obstinate unreason of this most excitable people made it too troublesome.[1] For Rome did not mind the shedding of blood when it was necessary; but it did not love too frequent bloodshed in any province, Cæsar being then prone to suspect some fault in the governor. So it might happen, if His death were needed to keep the turbulent quiet, that it would be easiest to let Him die— worse things were done daily in the amphitheatre under the Emperor's own eye.

The successive scenes of the drama are full of the incidents which are character, — the priests anxious to make out Jesus to be the political personage their policy required Him to be, Pilate wishful to regard Him as a religious person in whom Rome had no concern, though the Jewish law might condemn Him; while Jesus moves in the midst aloof from them all and within a world of His own. According to both the Synoptists and John, the chief priest asks Him as to His teaching in general, and specially touching the temple, His own person and claims, but nothing concerning any political aim or purpose.[2] Yet, when they bring Him before the Procurator, their only charge is political. Pilate at first declines to hear them : " Take Him yourselves, and judge Him according to your law."[3] But they deftly accentuate the political accusation which Pilate could understand, and was bound to take notice of: " He has claimed to

---

[1] John xviii. 38, 39.
[2] Matt. xxvi. 59-65 ; Mark xiv. 55-63 ; Luke xxii. 66-71 ; John xviii. 19-24.   [3] John xviii. 31.

be King of the Jews."[1] But the very gravity of the charge proved to the Roman its absurdity; he could not take it seriously, and suspected that some religious idea or sectarian spite lurked under its political form. He tried to make out the truth by questioning Jesus, who would not disown His ideal Kinghood in terms which would have falsified their charge.[2] The definition He gave only the more bewildered the governor, and tempted him to conceal under a question that jested a suspicion that was growing into a certainty.[3] He next tried, by showing the pitiful figure of the scourged and mocked King, to awaken them to the sense of the absurd in their charge, but they would not be turned aside. In their fear of Jesus they lost fear of Pilate, and assailed him where they knew he was weakest: "If thou release this man, thou art not Cæsar's friend," for had not Jesus, by making Himself a King, set Himself up as a rival over against Cæsar?[4]

And so we see Pilate standing in dubious and deliberative mood, now scornfully temporizing with the multitude, and now patronizing Jesus, befriending Him with a sort of lofty condescension which was touched with regret, looking Him, as he vainly thought, through and through, though never failing to read the mind and motives of His accusers. But even when most convinced of the innocence of Jesus, he is perfectly sure of His mere manhood, though it be of a type rare in the genus fanatic. So he believes himself to have power, though he thinks Jesus has none. But let us imagine that, in the very moment when he boasted his power to crucify or to release,[5] a lucid vision had come to him, and that he had beheld the centuries before him unroll their wondrous secret. In less than eighty years he sees in every city of the Roman world societies of men and women meeting in the name of this Jesus and singing praises to Him as to God; while so powerful has His Name

---

[1] Mark xv. 2; John xviii. 33; xix. 21-22. [2] Mark xv. 3; Luke xxiii. 3.
[3] John xviii. 36-38.   [4] John xix. 12.   [5] John xix. 10.

grown in some provinces that the very temples are deserted, and the most famous governor of the day writes to ask the Emperor what policy he is to pursue. Then he sees Rome, astonished and angry at the might of the Name, lose her proud tolerance, become vindictive, brutal, even turning persecutor, and making the profession of the Name a crime punishable with death. But all the resources of the Empire are powerless against the Name; the legions that had carried the Roman Eagles into the inaccessible regions lying round the civilized world, forcing the tide of barbarism back before them, here availed nothing. And he beholds in less than three hundred years the symbol of the Cross on which he was about to crucify this Jesus, float victoriously from the capitol; while the Emperor sits, not amid patricians in the Roman Senate, but in a council of Christian pastors, all without pride of birth, all without names the Senate would have honoured, many maimed, some even eyeless, disfigured by the tortures Rome had inflicted in her vain attempt to extinguish the infamous thing. In another hundred years he sees the very empire herself fallen, while in her seat sits one whose only claim to rule is that he represents the Crucified; and because he does so, he builds up a kingdom beside which Rome at her vastest was but as a hand-breadth, and the city that had been proudly called eternal was in duration only as the child of a day. And if Pilate had waked from his dream as suddenly as he had fallen into it, and looked at Jesus sitting before him mocked and buffeted, helpless in the face of the howling mob, deserted of man, manifestly forsaken of His God, what could he have said but this? "What foolish things dreams are! Their world is a sort of topsy-turvydom of reality; for were this vision of mine true, then the invisible kingdom of this Man would be the only real empire, and my claim of power either to crucify or to release Him a vain and empty boast! Happily the cross will soon restore us all to sanity, and show the vanity of the dream."

[1] Pliny, *Epist.* 96.

4. This much, then, and no more, Caiaphas and Pilate saw in Jesus; and as they saw they judged; and as they saw and judged, so did all the men of cultivated intelligence in their time and place. They were not unreasonable, nor without integrity, but honest after their kind; only, like all who are consciously and proudly men of the world, they made their experience the measure of other men and all their possibilities. I wonder how many of all the sagacious intellects who govern the modern State and meddle in politics, national and international, or how many of the disciplined minds who cultivate in our day the natural and historical sciences would, similarly situated, have judged differently; certainly not many—possibly not even one; for the modern idea of the limitations of nature is more positive than the scientific belief in its potencies or in the capabilities of man. And the idea of a miraculous person might well seem incredible even to men who were credulous as to miraculous events; for the events would happen without their consent, while the person they might have to control or resist and dispose of. But if anything is certain, it is that this Jesus represented forces vaster than these rulers could direct or command, arrest or annihilate. In its outer setting the Passion is as mean and sordid a transaction as ever passed before the eyes of men; in all the outward accessories of dignity and grandeur it has been eclipsed thousands of times. Similar tragedies have been all too common. The young enthusiast, in revolt against the tyranny and oppression, the formalism and make-believe of his day, dreaming of nobler ideals for men and society, and attempting in some way to realize them, is a figure every age and every country has known. And if the age has not conquered the enthusiast by changing him into the spokesman of expediency and convention, it has yet been able, without any dread of supernatural retribution, to bid death make an end of his power to trouble. And this seemed only an ordinary case of the social and

A MEAN AND SORDID RIDDLE

religious Reformer in conflict with an established order, a collision of the static forces which preserve a society against a dynamic force which threatened its disintegration. That force might be impersonated in a character of rare loveliness and potent charm, but revolution is not made agreeable to the men who hate it by the moral excellence of those who would effect it. It was enough that Jesus by word and action threatened the order of the temple and the doctrine of the synagogue; the guardians of law and tradition could only unite to suppress a man who by questioning their right to represent God and rule man, assailed the very foundations of society. And they acted exactly as men situated as they were, and believing as they did, were bound to act: explained the law they knew to the governor who did not know it in a form he was certain to understand; and then demanded that he who had the power of life and death should exercise his power in the interests of the law and of the people whose sole safety it was. If their reading of the person of Jesus was right, one might say that their conduct exhibited the violence which is born of panic, or the craft learned by men who would, while slaves themselves, govern an enslaved people as if they were free, but he could hardly say more. But, then, the plea which justifies them leaves us with a riddle which has no fellow in all history: How has it happened that a transaction so common and so unspeakably squalid should, alone of all the innumerable similar occurrences in time, have been attended by consequences so extraordinary and recreative?

§ II. *The Supernatural View of Jesus*

1. The mere necessity of asking this question is enough to suggest that there must have been in the person of Jesus elements which escaped the eye of priest and scribe and procurator, factors or forces of change which His death might strengthen but could not dissolve. And we know

that there were even then a few men who, for reasons they dimly felt rather than clearly perceived, ventured to differ from the scholars and statesmen who imagined that the duty of the world was to think their thoughts after them. These men were for the most part poor and ignorant enough, but their disadvantages were lost in one supreme advantage—they had known Jesus, and had learned of Him; and because of this learning they were soon able, by what I can only describe as an extraordinary act of faith, to read a meaning into Him which the men of cultivated intelligence had failed to find. They formulated a theory—or, more correctly, an hypothesis—of His place and person, which had this remarkable peculiarity: it was an hypothesis which did not so much explain facts that had been or that were, as facts that were to be. It was what we may term a prophetic and a creative hypothesis,—prophetic because centuries of history were to be needed, not to make it conceivable, yet to justify it; creative because it was to call into existence the very facts that were to be its justification. And what was this hypothesis? It was the idea embodied in our Gospels, common to all of them, though differently complexioned in each:—Jesus is conceived as the Messiah, sent of God, descended through the Jews, come to live and die for the saving of the world. For Him all past Jewish history had been; towards Him the hopes of men and the events of history had alike converged. From Him went out the light that was to enlighten—the life that was to quicken—the nations. Thus Mark, the oldest, the simplest, the most objective, yet the most picturesque of the Gospels, conceives Jesus as the Messiah,[1] prophesied of beforehand,[2] announced by John,[3] declared to be the Son of God,[4] the Preacher of the kingdom,[5] whose Gospel is to be proclaimed to all the nations,[6]

[1] i. 1.   [2] i. 2–3.   [3] i. 7, 8.
[4] i. 11.   [5] i. 14, 15.   [6] xiii. 10; xiv. 9.

the Founder of the new society who calls and instructs His disciples,[1] the Son of man and the Lord of the Sabbath,[2] the Forgiver of sins,[3] the Doer of mighty deeds,[4] who gives His life a ransom for many,[5] and establishes the new covenant in His blood.[6] Matthew, though he uses Mark, gives more of His words than Mark, enables us to see farther into His mind, and to conceive Him and His work more as He Himself conceived them. But though the conception is larger, it is not different. He is "the Son of David, the Son of Abraham."[7] Yet He bears the name Immanuel, "which is, being interpreted, God with us."[8] The Magi worship Him;[9] the devil tempts Him;[10] the Baptist hails Him;[11] the disciples follow Him.[12] He fulfils the law and the prophets;[13] His words are imperishable, they judge men; and as He judges so does God.[14] He is the Son who alone knows the Father and only through Him can the Father be known.[15] He is the Messianic king, whose reign is righteousness and peace.[16] Men who take His yoke upon them find rest to their souls.[17] Death ends neither His existence nor His authority; He reigns for ever, and His law is to be obeyed every whit.[18] Luke, in what a master of style thought the most beautiful book in all literature, has fitly enshrined the most beautiful character in all history. He has a wider outlook than Matthew, and places Jesus, the Son of Adam, which was "the Son of God,"[19] in the same relation to man that in the first Evangelist He had held to Israel; yet conceives Him as "the Son of the Most High," "the Holy One," supernaturally begotten, at whose birth the heavenly host sang, "Glory to God in the highest, and on earth peace

---

[1] i. 16-20. [2] ii. 28. [3] ii. 5-11.
[4] i. 23-28, 30, 31, 40-45; ii. 3-12; iv. 35-41; v. 21-43; vii. 24-37, et al. [5] x. 45. [6] xiv. 24. [7] i. 1.
[8] Matt. i. 23. [9] Mark ii. 1-12. [10] iv. 1-11. [11] iii. 13-15.
[12] iv. 18-22. [13] v. 17. [14] vii. 21-27; x. 32, 33.
[15] xi. 27. [16] vi. 33; x. 34-42. [17] xi. 30.
[18] xxviii. 18-20. [19] iii. 38.

among men of good-will."[1] The author of the Fourth Gospel, with more speculative audacity than the synoptists, explained His pre-eminence thus:—"The Word which had ever been with God, and was God, became flesh and dwelt among us; He, the only begotten Son, which is in the bosom of the Father, hath declared Him."[2] And this incarnate Word, this manifested and manifesting Son, the Evangelist identified with Jesus. His person, in a figure which described a significant fact, was said to be the tabernacle or tent of meeting for God and man; and they that could look within and bear the light saw the symbol of the invisible Presence, the living image which expressed the Eternal God. Jesus, in a word, was Deity manifested in humanity and under the conditions of time.

Now this is in itself an extraordinary conception, and it is made more extraordinary by the marvellous way in which it is embodied in a personal history. There never was a loftier idea, or one better calculated to challenge prompt and complete contradiction, than the one expressed in our Gospels, models though they be of simplicity in narrative and language. Their common purpose is to describe the life and record the words of a person they conceive as miraculous. Critics differ, and with good reason, as to the degree of the miraculous which the Evangelists severally attribute to His person. Mark does not, like John, speak of Him in the terms of Eternity and Deity. John and Mark do not, like Matthew and Luke, write of a supernatural conception and birth. And it may be argued, from the small place accorded to it and its presence in only two of our extant documents, that the idea of a supernatural birth was not held to be essential to the idea of the miraculous person. But what is common to all four Evangelists, and what is in their mind essential, is the idea not that the miraculous history proves the person to be supernatural, but

[1] Luke i. 32-35; ii. 13, 14. [2] John i. 1-2, 14, 18.

that the history was miraculous because it articulated and manifested the supernatural person. The Gospels may indeed be described as the interpretation of this person in the terms of history; and so regarded the Jesus of Mark is as miraculous as the Jesus of John. There is more than art, there is real philosophy, in the evangelical standpoint and method; for the supernatural personality is more able to make the supernatural in nature and history real and credible than the miraculous in nature and history is able to make the supernatural personality living and intelligible. But we shall be better able to understand the philosophy and appreciate the art when we have studied a few of the forms under which the person and the history are so interwoven as to constitute a whole whose several parts authenticate and illustrate each other.

2. Jesus is conceived and represented, under whatever terms His Person may be described, as a conscious and continuous Unity. The portrait of Him is consistent, the work of writers who feel themselves to be dealing with a real and rational being, whose words could be reported and whose actions could be narrated in language men could understand. They do not write as men who romance, or who know that they are relating marvels other men will find it hard to believe: on the contrary they write soberly, with the unperplexed consciousness of men who describe matters of fact which, though wonderful, are yet entirely credible, because in keeping with the person and attributes of Him whose acts they are said to be. There is nothing so difficult as to unite in a single person attributes which experience has never seen so associated, and which thought persists in conceiving as opposites; but what would be not so much difficult as impossible would be for a writer to betray no consciousness of invention, no feeling of the abnormal; and to maintain, alike as regards nature, character, and action, the integrity and concrete unity of his hero as a rational

and historical being. Yet these are the features which distinguish our canonical Gospels. The Evangelists, however simple, uncritical, and credulous we may conceive them to have been, yet knew the distinction between the ordinary and the extraordinary, the normal and the miraculous; and understood how little compatible miracles were with the persons of the men they met in daily life. Experience, therefore, could not supply them with any type to which they could conform the person they meant to portray. Two alternatives are thus alone possible: either the portrait was ideal, a product of the creative imagination, or real, a study from life, a picture which embodied personal experience and observation.

One of the forms under which the theory of an ideal portrait may be presented has already been noticed.[1] It is an unconscious creation of the mythical imagination, regretful and retrospective. The theory is eminently attractive: it saves the honesty of the writers, it does justice to their affections, it credits them with minute knowledge of Hebrew literature, it endows them with an instructed imagination, which it quickens by admiration and inspires by love. But one thing it fails to do: explain how a selective fancy could, out of so many borrowed and broken and unjointed fragments, weave so perfect a personal unity and place it in an historical environment so suitable and consistent. The ideal remains an ideal, do with it what we will. The more spontaneously and without design the imagination works, the less will it be under the control of the critical reason, and therefore the more independent of local colouring and conditions; and so will be the less heedful of any violent improbabilities in the prosaic matters of time and space. But these are the very matters in which the evangelical histories are so real, so natural, and so exact. They are full of the feeling for the time; they understand its men, schools, classes, parties; they

[1] Ante, pp. 10–12.

know the thoughts that are in the air, the rumours that run along the street; they are familiar with the catchwords and phrases of the period, its conventions, questions, modes of discussion, and style of argument. And all is presented with the utmost realism, so grouped round the central figure as to form a perfect historical picture, He and His setting being so built together as to constitute a single organic whole. Now this appears a feat which the mythical imagination, working with material derived from the Old Testament, could not have performed. It could not have made its hero mythical without making the conditions under which He lived and the persons with whom He lived the same. The realism of these conditions and persons is incompatible with the mythical idealism of Him through whom they are, and whose environment they constitute. The organic unity of person and history seems to involve the reality of both.

It appears, then, as if the legitimate inference from the histories themselves were that we have in Jesus a study from life—the portrait of one who actually lived and as He lived. And it is this which gives peculiar value to the fact that the authors of the Gospels use to describe their subject two distinct classes of terms, expressing ideas that must have been as opposite to them as they are to us, which we differentiate, though they did not, as "natural" and "supernatural." He appears in all four Gospels as the son of Mary, as known to the inhabitants of Nazareth, where he had been brought up, though all they tell us is that He was a citizen of that mean city, and a member of one of its humblest families. He is described as growing in stature, in wisdom, and in favour with God and man. The one glimpse we have into His boyhood shows Him as a child His parents could lose and seek sorrowing; and in His manhood and public ministry He is seen to share our common human weaknesses. He is represented as weary, as hungry, as thirsty, as angry, as suffering, as in need of sympathy, as seeking God in prayer, as shrinking from death, as dying, and as dead. The attributes and the fate of universal man are His as they are ours. But He also appears, as we have just seen, clothed in quite other attributes and doing quite extraordinary things. He is to all four Evangelists the Son of God, the Messiah, Lord of the Sabbath, and Saviour of men, with power on earth to forgive sins, to establish the kingdom of God, to found a new covenant in His blood, and to judge the people, acquitting or condemning them as they have or have not confessed Him. And He behaves as one to whom such acts and attributes can be ascribed. He calls disciples, and forms them into an eternal and universal society. He works miracles, heals the diseased, casts out devils, feeds the hungry, even raises the dead. He has miracles worked upon Him, is transfigured and appears in a visible glory which proclaims Him the Son of God, and, after suffering the death of the Cross and being laid in the grave, He is raised up and appears unto many.

Now the remarkable thing is not simply that these attributes and acts are represented as His, but that they are conceived as quite natural to Him, as not making Him anomalous or abnormal, but as leaving Him simple and rational and real,—a person who never ceases to be Himself, who has no double consciousness and plays no double part, but expresses Himself in history according to the nature He has and the truth within Him. There is nothing quite like this in literature, no miraculous person who is so truly natural, so continuously one and the same; and no writers of the miraculous who so feel that they are dealing with what is normal and regular through and through. These are things which have more than a psychological interest; they speak of men who have stood face to face with the reality, and are conscious of only describing what they saw.

CHAPTER II

THE HISTORICAL PERSON AND HIS PHYSICAL TRANSCENDENCE

THE art with which the Evangelists interweave into a congruous whole the person and the acts of Jesus is so perfect as to deserve detailed examination; and it is the more remarkable as it seems unconscious art, accomplished by men who know not what they do. They conceive Him to be supernatural, and they attribute to Him miraculous acts, yet with an undesigned discrimination more sure than the most highly educated sense they observe distinctions and limits which leave Him the most natural of beings, and cause His most extraordinary actions to appear normal. It has been customary to discuss the miracles of Jesus as questions now in philosophy, whether they are possible; now in historical criticism, whether they are credible; and now in literary interpretation, whether they can be resolved into myths or allegories, the records of misunderstood events or of marvellous coincidences, or must be construed as authentic narratives. But the problems they raise are religious and ethical as well as philosophical and historical, and, we may add, the former are profounder and more determinative than the latter. Here we shall be concerned with the acts as an undesigned exegesis of the person, the two being so related as to be complementary and mutually explanatory; in other words, the acts when construed through the person become intelligible, while the person interpreted through the acts grows more articulate and coherent, conformed in being to His place in history.

§ I. *A Sane Supernaturalism*

1. What we have to study, then, is the representation of a supernatural person in an historical framework; i.e. we have to study, in a literary medium which is amenable to the fixed canons of criticism, a Being who transcends nature even while He lives under the forms and subject to the conditions of the nature He transcends. Now, the first thing we have here to note is this :—The miraculous acts which are ascribed to Jesus have qualities which curiously correspond to His character, or, in other words, they so duplicate and reflect it that the moral attributes which are most distinctive of Him reappear in His acts. Where they seem most supernatural they most completely externalize His nature. The common quality which distinguishes them all may be described as sanity or sobriety. Those acts which we term miraculous are yet not marvellous; they do not move in the region of the weird or the uncanny, nor do they, like the feats of the witch, strike with fear, or, like the tricks of the wizard or magician, smite with surprise. There is nothing so alien to the feeling of the Gospels as the love of wonders for wonders' sake. This is the more remarkable as the religious imagination, when allowed to work freely in the region of the supernatural, does not work sanely. The mythical miracle, as a rule, reflects a morbid temper, for it is commonly the creation of a fancy grown fantastic and even childish. As genius is closely allied to madness, so there are types of piety near akin to disease. The temper is permanent, but the forms it loves vary from age to age, though they all have a common character. The morbid temper, in our age and country, has no temptation to dream of miracles, but it may dream of things quite as mythical and unreal. In Liddon's Life of the late Dr. Pusey, a book marked by rare truth and candour, there is a very painful yet illuminative chapter dealing with

THE MYTHICAL IMAGINATION UNHEALTHY

his personal attitude to "penitence and confession."[1] It introduces us to the innermost, and in some aspects the most secret, chamber of his soul, where understanding is difficult and misjudgment easy. There is nothing that so reveals the moral quality of a man as his sense of sin, and nothing that even his bosom friend can so little comprehend and share. It is a sense so commanding that it will not be reasoned with, and must be appeased before the man can know peace. But it is a thing infinitely varied in form, and it is the form it assumes which shows the intrinsic character of the man. Now the sense of sin in Pusey was more sensuous than spiritual, more a matter for himself to bear than for grace to remove. It harassed him more than the sense of God comforted him, and so he felt as one who must express his conscious desert of ill in pains and penances. Hence it was as "an unnamed penitent" that he built a church at Leeds. His suspension in 1843, his wife's death and his daughter's, his public anxieties and private sorrows, he regarded as "punishments for his sins." He implored Keble to act as his father confessor, and he confessed himself "scarred all over and seamed with sin," "a monster" to himself; he loathed himself; he felt as if he were "covered with leprosy from head to foot." He begged for "a rule of penitential discipline"; he wore "haircloth" next his skin; he scourged himself; he resolved to "use a hard seat by day and a hard bed by night"; "not to wear gloves or protect his hands"; "never to notice anything unpleasant in what was set on the table, but to take it by preference and in a penitential spirit"; "to drink cold water at dinner, as only fit to be where there is not a drop to cool this flame"; "never to look at beauty of nature without inward confession of unworthiness." Now to lay on these sayings, heavy as they are with the passion of unspeakable grief, a cold and analytic hand would be both cruel and profane; but what they illustrate is the morbid as distinguished from the moral in the sense of

[1] Vol. iii. chap. iv. pp. 94-111.

sin, i.e. the feeling that it is something that can be satisfied by physical penance, and not solely by the infinite grace of God. But where this morbid sense is, a sane imagination is sure to be afar off; the view of self supplies the colour under which we see the universe, and to an imagination so possessed strange dreams and unwholesome fancies easily become substantial things. In a credulous age it creates miraculous marvels, as easily as it creates in a rational and sceptical age forms of penance.

This morbid consciousness, then, is the real mythical faculty, and the miracles it generates are even as it is. In certain men and times it becomes the veritable master of the mind. The more ethical the religious imagination is, it is the more sane; but in the very degree that it is sensuous it is fantastic, and is certain to people history with creations which mirror and echo its own hopes and fears. We have only to turn to ecclesiastical history to find examples innumerable of the miracles the mythical faculty invents, unconsciously, of course, though all the more in obedience to its own laws. Thus, if we compare with the Gospels Jerome's *Life of Hilarion* or the *Four Dialogues* of Gregory the Great, the difference between sobriety and extravagance in narratives concerning the miraculous will soon become evident. The one is the most learned of all the Fathers, the other is the most sagacious of the early Popes; and so far as the culture that comes of letters and affairs, or knowledge and experience, are concerned, they are both incomparably superior to the Evangelists. Well, then, Jerome gravely narrates such things as these: how Hilarion by his prayers made a barren woman to bear; how a certain Italicus, whose horses raced in the circus, prayed the saint to give him, since he was a Christian, a victory over his heathen rival, and how, by water out of the cup from which he used to drink, the horses of Italicus were made to flee to the goal, while those of his competitor stuck fast to the spot; how the saint casts out a lascivious devil from a maid who had been bewitched by certain magic figures and formulas buried beneath the threshold of her house; how he dispossessed of another devil a gigantic camel, which thirty men with strong ropes could hardly hold; how he commanded a mighty serpent, which had been devouring oxen, to ascend a pyre and be burned to ashes before all the people; how, months after his death, his body was conveyed from Cyprus to Palestine as perfect as if alive, and fragrant with sweet odours; and how at the places alike where he had been and where he was buried great miracles were daily performed, in the one case as it were by his body, in the other by his spirit. Gregory's miracles are even more marvellous than those described by Jerome, for he tells how certain of his Italian fathers or monks could treat the water as if it had been solid land; how pieces of gold, fresh as from the mint, fell upon them from heaven; how floods which rose even to the roofs of churches did not enter in at the doors, though they stood open; how the arm of an executioner, uplifted to strike off a monk's head, remained erect and fixed, sword and all, in the air, but power over it was restored on the promise being made never again to use it against a Christian. And as here, so always; for the creations of the mythical faculty are everywhere curiously akin. The mediæval friar would tell his hearers how a robber, who had been always devout and regular in his prayers to the Virgin, was at length taken and sentenced to be hanged; but when the cord was round his neck he prayed to his heavenly patroness, and she, with her own white hands, held him up two whole days, and so saved him from death: or how a paper of Scriptural proofs which the good St. Dominic had written to confound his opponents, leaped out of the fire into which it had been cast, while their documents remained and were utterly consumed. The Buddhist monk, illustrating the benevolence of the Master, would tell how in an earlier mode of existence he had met a famished tiger, and, pitying the hungry beast, had kindly offered himself as a meal; or how, regretting that his people had no fit image of himself, he appeared as a poor workman, carved the image, and vanished from the sight of those who would have rewarded him. The mythical faculty speaks in all the languages of man, but the thing itself we can never mistake for reality: its very features show whence it has come.

2. If now we compare the miracles of the Gospels with these, we shall understand what is meant by their sanity or sobriety. They have a sort of natural character, and are neither violent nor abnormal; like Jesus Himself, they are, though supernatural, not contra-natural. For what are the miraculous acts ascribed to Him? He heals the blind, the halt, the lame, the sick of the palsy; He brings comfort to the widow who has lost a son, to the Gentile nobleman who mourns a child; He creates joy in the heart of the woman who had sought counsel of many physicians and only grew the worse for all their attempts at healing. He goes through life like a kind of embodied beneficence, creating health and happiness. He incorporates the energies that work against physical evil and for social good. In a sense, His miracles are but the transcripts of His character, the symbol of His mind and mission. Were we to imagine an incorporated grace or mercy, should we not conceive her path marked by similar deeds? These miracles are, in a word, the physical counterparts of Christ's moral character and ethical teachings. Without them our picture of His personality would be incomplete. They show Him as the enemy of disease, of bodily imperfection and suffering, as a factor of the outer conditions that make for happiness. Without them our image of Him would be incomplete, while their singular freedom from the qualities everywhere characteristic of the mythical miracle place them in a category by themselves. One thing is certain: they could not have owed their freedom from these customary mythical adornments to the Evangelists themselves. For they were men who stood alike as regards age,

culture, and country, exactly at the stage when we expect the mythical consciousness to be creative; their material may have come to them in forms and under conditions favourable to its exercise, but yet the miracles they describe have this altogether exceptional character of moral sanity and rational sobriety. It were indeed the simple truth to say that the Evangelists are the most modern writers of Christian antiquity; and we may add, without fear of contradiction, that with the most absolute and august idea of the supernatural to be found in the whole literature of religion, they have given it an expression so objective and realistic as to be without any parallel. If we compare them with Fathers like Tertullian writing on the "Spectacles," or describing the nature and ways of wicked spirits; or with works like those of Athanasius on Antony; or Gregory of Nyssa on his namesake of Neo-Cæsarea; or with Augustine telling miracles he himself had witnessed; or Sulpicius naïvely narrating those worked by Martin of Tours, we shall come to the conclusion that our Gospels are remarkable, above all other ancient Christian histories, for critical caution and intellectual sanity. Is it too bold an inference to argue that the very magnitude of their subject had suspersedded in the Evangelists the creative activity of the morbid and mythical imagination?

§ II. *The Physical Transcendence is Moral Obedience*

1. But a still more distinctive quality of the supernatural action ascribed to Jesus is its altruistic character. His miracles do not regard Himself. This quality is all the more significant that the Evangelists themselves seem hardly conscious of its existence. It is implicit in their narratives rather than explicit in their thought; but, while unexplicated, it is a most integral element of their history. Thus it comes out quite distinctly in the Temptation, which, we may assume, represents a series of events whose importance lies in their being

the symbols of a subjective process. It stands at the threshold of the ministry, i.e. just when the consciousness of His mission had become clear and imperative to Jesus; and it describes the crisis as more moral than intellectual, or as due to His struggle with conflicting ideals. The greater the mission the more certain it is to present alternative policies expressing incommensurable principles; and what is temptation but the struggle of the conscience in favour of the more ethical and against the more expedient policy?

If we assume, then, that what is so named represents a real experience, a transaction within the soul of Jesus, what would be its natural sources or factors?

(*a*) There would be the question of His place in nature, His power over it, its power over Him, especially as affecting His relation to men and the work He had to do on their behalf. This is the point which is emphasized in the first temptation: "make these stones bread."[1] If this be read in the light of His later history, what does it mean? Simply this: 'Do for yourself what you know that you have power to do for others; the energies with which you are entrusted will be best disciplined for the service of all by being first exercised in your own. What it is right to do for those who need redemption, it cannot be wrong to do for their Redeemer. You are to feed the hungry; begin by feeding yourself. Your own physical fitness for the work you are intended to do ought surely to be a primary care.'

Now why should this suggestion have appeared as a temptation? Does it not rather seem like the recognition of a fact; to wit, the pre-eminence which endowed Jesus with special means for the preservation of life, particularly His own? We may assume, in accordance with all human experience, that the potentialities in Him and the possibilities latent in His career would make their appeal to His imagina-

---

[1] Matt. iv. 3; Luke iv. 3. The order in which the temptations are taken is Matthew's, not Luke's.

tion first in a purely personal form. But here the appeal is shown to have been made only to be dismissed as if it were a suggestion of the devil. "Man," Jesus says, "does not live by bread alone." That is, He recoils from the temptation to affirm the pre-eminence of His person by supernatural energy expended on Himself; for if He had performed such an act on His own behalf, it would have signified that He took Himself out of the category of manhood; that He surrendered the act of sacrifice; and it would have declared that His function was not to practise obedience, but to exercise personal power. In other words, He would have removed Himself from the ranks of the created who live under nature, and through it depend upon the Creator; and He would have relegated Himself to a special dignity where physical law ceased to reign, i.e. He would have translated His work into the assertion rather than the sacrifice of Himself. He would also have separated Himself from man, have ceased to be like unto His brethren, have refused to share the common lot, and instead have preferred the solitary state of a being beyond and above it. But it would have affected His relation to God even more than His relation to man; for He would, by ceasing to be dependent upon Him, have become, in a sense, God to Himself, and so the precise contrary of man in his dependence upon God. The very root out of which religion grows would thus have been eradicated in Him; and He would have fallen from His high estate as the normal type of the soul's relation to God, and of God's to the soul.

(β) If, then, "man liveth not by bread alone, but by the word which proceedeth out of the mouth of God," it follows that not otherwise than by this word did it become the Son of man to live. The first temptation thus represents the conflict of the ideal of dependence with the ideal of pre-eminence, or the law of an ordinary with the privileges of an extraordinary manhood. The second stands for an exactly opposite conflict—that of a reasonable against a blind dependence. "Cast Thyself down," it says, "from this pinnacle of the temple; for it is written, 'He shall give His angels charge concerning Thee: and on their hands shall they bear Thee up, lest haply Thou dash Thy foot against a stone.'"[1] This may be said to express the sense of dependence turned into sheer presumption, challenging God to exercise sole care for His Son, and to make immediate intervention in His interest. It is as if the tempter had said: "If You will renounce all power for personal ends, and refuse to act as Your own Providence; if You have resolved to live as one who knows Himself to be always and everywhere in the hands of the Almighty,—then prove Your august eminency and the sufficiency of Your faith by throwing Yourself from this height into the court below, so forcing God to intervene directly on Your behalf. By so doing You will dispose men to expect great things of You, and to repose great trust in you. And I will add, that only such absolute trust is worthy of the Son of God; and only by such absolute Providence would the Father be fitly declared."

The ideal is thus a confidence in God so absolute as to have become contempt of nature. But what is the answer of Jesus to this second suggestion? "Thou shalt not tempt the Lord thy God." And what did this answer mean? Simply this—that if He had dealt with Himself as if He were an exceptional and pre-eminent object of divine care, two things would have followed: first, His complete isolation from man, who holds his being under physical as well as moral law, and is bound at every moment and in all things to deal with the physical as if it were the moral; and, secondly, He would have substituted for a life environed by nature, guarded, guided, fed by it, participant in its forces because subject to its laws, a life divorced from nature, hostile to it, finding in it no presence of God, realizing through it no fellowship

[1] Matt. iv. 5-7; Luke iv. 9-12.

ETHICAL IN MEANS AS IN END 341

with man, inheriting nothing from its past, bequeathing nothing to its future. The temptation thus, under the disguise of honour to God, aimed at alienation alike from Him and from the fellowship of man.

(γ) The third temptation is a subtle combination of elements derived from the other two.[1] It means that He may by the use of physical and unethical forces obtain the mastery over the kingdoms of the world. In other words, it signifies that a person who has pre-eminent power ought to exercise the power he has without regard to God, or to the rights and the souls of men. And if God be regarded, it ought to be only so far as He may be a factor, more or less efficient, for some personal end; or, if man be helped, it will not matter though his soul be soiled, his conscience perverted, and his will enfeebled and depraved in the process. The ideal that stands opposed to this affirms that God is the only being man ought to worship; and that He can be worshipped only in a spirit and way that at once glorifies Him and exalts man.

If, then, the experience so picturesquely presented in the temptation has been correctly read, we may express its meaning thus:—The supernatural potencies which move within Jesus leave Him neither an extra- nor a contra- nor a præter-natural person, but a person to Himself and for Himself strictly and surely natural, with powers which are to be understood and used as means to ethical and altruistic ends, to increase the duty of obedience, to limit rather than enlarge the sphere of man's independence of God.

2. But the Temptation is so significant because it is the pictorial embodiment of ideas which rise spontaneously in the mind whenever man thinks of one possessed of supernatural power. They are ideas which Jesus Himself must have conceived, if not entertained; and as a matter of fact, they are the very ideas which prompted questions He was

[1] Matt. iv. 8-10; Luke iv. 5-8.

required to answer, criticisms He had to bear, and even the mockery and bitter taunts which insulted Him on the cross. Thus "Let Him save Himself, if this is the Christ of God, His chosen,"[1] is just a variation of the tempter's words, "If Thou art the Son of God, command that these stones become bread." Again, "He trusteth in God, let Him deliver Him now if He desireth Him,"[2] simply repeats "If Thou art the Son of God, cast Thyself down." "Let the Christ, the King of Israel, now come down from the cross that we may see and believe,"[3] is only a changed reading of the temptation that promised Him the world's dominion if He would use the world's power. This priestly and popular scorn, then, may express the selfishness of a nature which has forsaken and forgotten God, but it does not at all represent Christ's mind or will. It was man explaining Jesus by himself, showing by a process of unconscious imputation what he himself would be and do were it only granted to him to be the Christ.

In His whole life, then, and in all His actions Jesus exercised His power always and only for man. The mystery of the life which so appealed to the heart and imagination of His people lies here—with the power to save He yet wills to lose Himself. The vision of God which He creates brings to man beatitude; the vision of sin which He suffers brings to Himself sorrow. The strength of His will is seen not in any immunity from calamity which He commands, but in the sacrifice He makes. And this touches a specific and distinctive quality of the supernatural element in the Gospels. There is nothing like it in the mythology of the miraculous. The mythical miracle is primarily personal; for what could be the use of a supernatural power which did not serve its possessor in his own hour of need? Among the founders of great religions no life

[1] Luke xxiii. 35.   [2] Matt. xxvii. 43.
[3] Mark xv. 32; Matt. xxvii. 42.

is freer from mythical wonders than Mohammed's; but when they appear, it is in his interest. Thus we are told that the Prophet, when fleeing from Mecca, was hotly pursued by his foes. He took refuge in a cave, but as soon as he had entered it God sent a spider, which wove its web over the cave's mouth. His pursuers, who were close behind, stopped, intending to enter; but when they saw the spider's web, they said, "He cannot have entered here, for this great web could not have been so quickly woven"; and so they rode on, leaving the Prophet to escape out of their hands. The tale has in the myths of all religions many fellows; for it is Nature herself which bids men think that he who has been endowed with extraordinary power will exercise it first on his own behalf, and only as a secondary purpose on behalf of man. But Jesus from first to last, in all His acts and in all His doings, is supernatural on man's behalf and not on His own. He was a moral wonder rather than a physical marvel.

§ III. *Supernatural Power as a Moral Burden*

But there is a third aspect under which the supernatural power which the Evangelists ascribed to Jesus must be viewed, viz., in its bearing on His own moral character and on His moral relations with men.

1. If we consider it under the first aspect, we shall see that there could be no more tremendous gift; for it would be, under the ordinary laws that govern human nature, a power working for immorality. Under the most favourable conditions it would tax self-control to a degree that no moral will known to us could bear. To measure its strength, we may compare it with forces that lie within our own experience or that have acted upon the stage of history.

The power which men may not challenge and cannot resist tends always to deprave and even brutalize its possessor. Without the criticism of men, man would have to suffer from the unqualified action of mischievous moral influences. The man who feels above the law for himself, while he is the source of the law which distributes life and death to other men, has in his own passions and ambitions tempters which beguile him into forgetfulness of all the fair humanities. Flatterers surround him, and where man never has the truth spoken to him by men he easily comes to act like a devil, for he feels so like a god. To be able to command and to compel obedience to his commandments while under no compulsion to obey them himself, is an attitude ruinous to a nature which was designed to be made perfect through obedience, and to learn it through feeling dependent. Neighbourliness, fellowship, is needful to humanity; and if by undue elevation or depression we are denied it, we are certain to suffer moral disaster. And so social extremes meet; the worst crimes are to be found among those who are either at the very top or at the very bottom of society. It is a grave and a terrible fact that in the long catalogue of Roman emperors we have only one Marcus Antoninus, and even he, though a saint, was not tolerant of saintliness; but we have a multitude who do more disgrace than honour to mankind—men like Tiberius and Caligula, like Nero or Domitian. Roman order might be a great thing for the Roman population; but it too often involved the moral sacrifice of the men who were its nominal guardians. The imperial family which stands in Europe for the purest form of autocratic power, shows also the most dismal examples of moral madness. The house of Romanoff has, above all other sovereign houses, been stained by the uncleanliest vices,—crimes explicable only through the insanity which seizes those who may command others, but who go uncommanded themselves. The most pitiful victim of despotism is the despot; for while his power may, like a glacier, grind and pulverize the rock in which he makes his bed and through which he forces his way, yet he himself is like the deadly ice which can never know the presence of kindly and beautiful life.

But now let us apply the principle which we have thus derived from experience and history to a person who is believed to possess supernatural power, and who believes himself to possess it. Such power would be a more dangerous possession, a heavier burden for self-restraint to bear, a vaster force for wisdom to direct, than would the most absolute political autocracy. The character of the man who had it would be more severely tried than were he penetrated by transmitted passions or enervated by acquired lusts. For were he a being of fine nature, would he not, when confronted by the infinite meanness of men, their duplicity, their insensibility to the higher ideals, their avarice, their selfish greed, be ever, under the provocation of a noble rage, tempted to execute upon them the swiftest vengeance? If he saw oppression victorious and freedom lying wounded and broken under its hoof, or if he heard lust vaunting the chastity it had violated and falsehood triumphing over the truth it had betrayed, how could he resist the impulse which bade him become the sword of God? But what is the justice that proceeds from impulse save a form of self-indulgence? And does not a moral indignation which is ever indulged, easily become a vengeance that will not be satiated? Such a power would therefore inevitably tend to disturb the balance or sobriety of the moral nature; and unless he who possessed it had a will so absolutely under moral control as to be proof against the tides and tempests of moral passion, he would soon become the victim of the thousand immoral forces that act upon spirit through sense. We may say, then, that only a being absolutely God-like in his goodness could be equal to the control of so awful and so tremendous a power.

Were, then, any being less than infinite in wisdom, righteousness, and grace to be invested with omnipotence, his might would soon overmaster his morality and turn him into the most unspeakable of devils. For what would ungoverned power in command of the universe be but Satan upon the throne of the Almighty? And were he, though only for a moment, to sit there, the devil transformed into an omnipotent god, would he not undo the work of eternity and reduce the universe to a chaos which would be a universe no more? Omnipotence without divine goodness would become a force working simply for destruction. The opportunity to use a might none can question needs for its control a goodness none can doubt. And what have we in the Gospels? The picture of a will uncorrupted by power, untempted by opportunity, beneficent in the exercise of the mysterious energy with which it was charged. Jesus lives His open and frank and natural life as simply as the child who takes no thought for to-morrow because he is in the hands of one who thinks for him. And so He dwells in our imagination as obedient, humble, gentle, and easily entreated, never as the Master of the mysterious forces which rule nature.

2. But now the second aspect of the matter—its effect upon His moral relations with men—must also be considered. How would men be affected by seeing a man possessed of what they thought supernatural power? We know how terrible a thing witchcraft seemed in the days when people believed in its existence. The witch was a person to whom men showed no mercy; their fear became a frenzy which nothing less than death by fire or water could appease. And we need not wonder at their conduct, for if we believed as our forefathers believed, we should act as they did, possibly with even blinder fury. For to feel that a given person has over nature a power we wot not of, and can bid it torment or insidiously kill an enemy, undermine the health of the strong or work vindictively against the innocent, is to feel in the presence of one whom common justice cannot deal with, for common laws do not control; and, therefore, of one who must be driven forth from life, if life is to be lived in peace.

Wherever there has been belief in the ability to exercise supernatural power, this has been the universal feeling; and if it has been tempered at all, it has been by the hope of bribing the mysterious person to use his power for the briber's ends rather than his own.

The only complete exception to this law of human nature is the one which appears in the Gospels. The recognition of Christ's miraculous will is universal. All the men who surround Him believe that He possesses it; they see Him exercise it; they crave, though they never attempt to bribe Him, that He exercise it on their behalf. But here there is an unconscious contrast between the Master and the disciples, who, as the incident of Simon the magian shows, could be regarded as men that might be bribed.[1] Yet the miracle is a more integral part of the evangelical than of the apostolical history. The messengers from John are bidden by Jesus to "tell the things which they do see and hear: the blind receive their sight and the lame walk, the lepers are cleansed and the deaf hear, the dead are raised up and the poor have the gospel preached to them."[2] The centurion asks that his servant may be healed,[3] the sick of the palsy are brought to Him as He sits surrounded by His very enemies.[4] These enemies question His right to forgive sins, but not His power to heal diseases. They have indeed a theory as to the sources of His power—He does it by Beelzebub, the prince of the devils.[5] But is not this the most remarkable tribute they could pay to His self-control? Would they have ventured to attribute to the devil in Him the power which they acknowledged that He possessed, if they had thought that His will was really devilish? Would they not have spoken softly, and called Him by the gentlest names they knew, if they had believed that He incarnated

---

[1] Acts viii. 18, 19. [2] Matt. xi. 4, 5.
[3] Luke vii. 1-10; cf. John iv. 46-54; Mark v. 22-24, 35-43.
[4] Mark ii. 6-12. [5] Mark iii. 22-30.

malevolence rather than benevolence? And this quality is illustrated no less by those who believe in the beneficence of His supernatural will. They do not feel that it divides Him from them; they never distrust Him or suspect His motives, or feel that the extraordinary power which He possesses will be used for any other than a gracious purpose.

It is thus remarkable that the terror which ordinarily follows belief in demoniac power is, even when He is maliciously credited with it, here entirely absent. Men think Him so possessed by a moral will that they do not feel fear in a presence they believe to be supernatural. He is even to His enemies, more marvellous for the grace He impersonates than for the miracles He accomplishes. And this is simply saying that He was higher as a moral miracle than as a physical power. While the power may be great, the grace is greater, and men peacefully trust where under other circumstances they would have profoundly feared. This is a feature in the evangelical narratives that marks them with distinction. The character which they portray is so morally perfect that supernatural power can neither deprave it nor alienate men from Him who possesses it.

§ IV. *The History of the Supernatural Person as a Problem in Literature*

1. But there is a literary question which deserves to be looked at: the Gospels are histories which aim at performing a most daring feat; they bind together a person conceived to be supernatural and the actual world, and they describe the life He lived within it. This involved literary difficulties of two kinds: (*a*) theological—How were the extraordinary nature and relations attributed to Jesus to affect their theistic idea? and (*b*) historical—In what sort of history was this nature and these relations to be unfolded?

(*a*) The Evangelists cannot be charged with possessing a

mean theistic idea. They inherited an august conception of Deity, the least anthropomorphic, the most untouched by human passion, weakness, or mutability, known to antiquity; and to represent this God as the Father of Jesus without degrading or undeifying Him, was a literary task of the rarest delicacy and difficulty. In the mythical age of Greece it had been easy to imagine men as the sons of Zeus, and Zeus as the father of gods and men; but the more the mythical age receded the more its crude images and grotesque dogmas grew distasteful to the Greek intelligence, which refined Deity by making Him too abstract to stand in real or concrete relations with men. And what philosophy had done for Greece the monotheistic passion did for Israel; with the result that the more Jehovah was exalted the greater became His distance from man, and the less could the sons of God be conceived as mixing with the daughters of men. The sublimest things are the most easily made ridiculous, the most sacred can be most utterly profaned. And if any one had been asked beforehand to describe the probable action of the idea of Jesus as Son of the Most High on the idea of God, would he not have drawn a dismal picture of Majesty lowered into the dust, spirituality coarsened and materialized, and reason humbled by being carried back into that twilight of intelligence when as yet gods were indistinguishable from men? But the result is exactly the opposite. The supernatural birth is touched with a most delicate hand, and has no essential feature in common with the mythical theogonies which earlier ages had known. The marvellous thing is not that we have two birth stories, but that we have only two; and that they occupy so small, so incidental, so almost negligible a place in the New Testament as a whole. What is still more extraordinary is the mode in which the Sonship of Jesus affects the conception of God, how it touches its majesty with grace, softens its rigour, turns its solitude into society, and changes it from a dead abstract into a living concrete. The Fatherhood, which is its correlate, made the God of the Jews into the God of the whole earth. The Evangelists so present Jesus that He appears as a Son so intensely individual as to impart a personality as concrete as His own to the God He addresses as Father; and yet as so truly typical in His humanity as to communicate to the Father a universality cognate to the manhood He embodies. To be able to say this of the simple history which stands written in our Gospels, and to say it not as a thing probably or approximately true, but as true absolutely and without any qualification, is to confess that their authors have performed a task of incomparable difficulty. To give a human portrait so gracious as to exalt and ennoble our very idea of Deity, is a feat which no other piece of historical literature has achieved or even approached.

(*b*) But the other literary difficulty may be described as even more insuperable. Jesus, as conceived by both the Synoptists and John, was no ordinary person; He was rather such a personality as had never appeared in history before, yet He had to be presented in a history. Let us attempt to understand their difficulty by putting it as a problem we have ourselves to solve. Suppose, then, we had to describe the character and career of a person possessed of the miraculous powers attributed to Jesus; suppose we had to make the history at once express the power and become the character, and yet be entirely real and credible to men with the common experience and critical intelligence of their race—how should we proceed? what sort of terms should we employ? what kind of incidents select? We are told that our hero is to be a person who has power to heal the sick, unstop the ears of the deaf, open the eyes of the blind, and even raise the dead; or, to make the case even more real, suppose we had these two texts given us as a thesis which has to be elucidated and illustrated by means of an appropriate history: "In the beginning was the Word, and the Word was with God, and the Word was

God"; [1] "And the Word became flesh and dwelt among us, and we beheld His glory, glory as of the only begotten from the Father, full of grace and truth." [2] Our initial difficulties would no doubt concern the relation of the natural and the supernatural in Him; the outer form must be made worthy of the divinity that dwells within, yet how can it be worthily housed in flesh? and if it be so housed, how could men bear His glory, forget, ignore, or misunderstand the sight, or live in His presence their commonplace, sensuous, mean, indifferent lives? We should thus have to surround Him with a fit and awed society, and ought not this society to be like a nimbus or translucent cloud penetrated by His indwelling glory? And the more we were driven in this direction the more violent and fantastic would the history become, in form more akin to mythology or fairy legend than to history. For we should not dare to make Him as regards Himself subject to those very laws of nature which He was able, on man's behalf, to transcend. That would be too flagrant a contradiction of the probabilities in the situation. Hence He must be represented as remote from commonplace humanity, and especially without liability to disease, weakness, suffering, death. And what sort of speech should we attribute to Him? How conceive the mind which the speech was to reveal? Ignorance, of course, would be entirely unbecoming in a person so endowed. The future must be open to Him; from Him the secrets of God could not be hid; the past would be as clear as the future, and every reference to nature and history, to man and events, would express a knowledge that could not err. It would thus be impossible for Him to accommodate Himself to the conventions of His time, use its language, accept its theories, and move amid its people as one of themselves. To do this would be to be false to the supernatural in His nature; yet, unless He did this, how could He appear in any historical narrative? We should be tempted, when we

[1] John i. 1. [2] John i. 14.

thought of the marvellous person, to represent all He did as gigantesque, and all He said under the form of the mysterious and the oracular. But the more stupendous the representation grew, the more abnormal, contra-natural, incredible, would the whole conception become, and we should be forced to abandon the task, confessing that a work more impossible to literary art had never been proposed to man.

And how do the Gospels deal with this problem? In the most surprising way. The highest speculation is embodied in the simplest history. He who is conceived as "the Word become flesh" is represented as the most natural character in all literature. In Him there is nothing obscure, dark, or mysterious; He seems to lie all open to the day. His words are simple and plain; His thought is always clear and never complex. He is the last person who could be described as a man of mystery. He does not study or practise any art of concealment. He calls His disciples, and they live with Him, and He lives with them as a man among men. He does not claim to know the secrets of nature or the forgotten things of history, or the day and hour of destiny, which the Father alone knoweth.[1] He does not stand on His dignity, or require men to observe the order of their coming and going. A Jew who comes by night is not refused an audience, for he has come in deference to his conscience, even though he comes by night in deference to the Jews; but Jesus speaks to him as if all men stood before Him in that one man, and as a simple matter of fact they did so stand. While He rests, tired and thirsty, by Jacob's Well, He speaks with the woman of Samaria and asks from her water to drink, and then He addresses to her words the world was waiting to hear. We see Him loved of man and woman, loving as well as loved, living the homely, natural, beautiful life of our kind. His is the common, every-day, familiar humanity, which suffers and rejoices, knows sorrow and death. But this humanity is all

[1] Mark xiii. 32.

the more divine that it is so natural; it is man become the child of God, embosomed in the eternal, a nature transfigured by the indwelling supernatural. The simple history may be said to clothe the Infinite, and it makes by its very simplicity the Infinite all the more manifest. Truth enters at the lowliest door, for only so can it come to all men. There is nothing so universal as nature, and the truth which would reach all must assume a form intelligible to all; and this means that man, who is the image of God, is the fittest vehicle for the revelation of the God whose image he is.

2. We may say then that were the Gospels inventions, whether mythical or conscious, spontaneous or purposed, they would be the most marvellous creations of literary art which we possess. The underlying idea is majestic, sublime, complex, but the history which embodies it is simple, sober, sane, while the person in and by whom it is realized is the most natural and human character in all literature. Present the idea to the mythical faculty, and it would weave out of it a gay and variegated web, as it were a tapestry crowded with the adventures of the faeriest wonderland; present it to the disciplined imagination, and it would feel that the theme was vaster than it had strength of pinion to carry. But the Evangelists are saved by their very simplicity; they tell their tale, they report the words of their Master, and then they leave their history and their *logia* to sink into the reason and wake the wonder of men. And what is the result? Stated in the soberest way, we may put it thus: The Gospels have done for Jesus—and through Him for man, and all that man signifies—what the imagination under the long discipline of science has attempted to do for the earth—viz., so placed our time in relation to eternity, our space in relation to immensity, as through the greater to explain the less, though only by the less can we know and understand the greater. Here we swim in the bosom of two infinities, and only through these infinities can the process, by which our finite has come to be,

be conceived. To our fathers earth had no mystery. It was but a narrow plain, bordered and washed by the inviolate sea. It could hardly be termed venerable; its whole history lay within the brief period of six thousand years. On a given day in a given month of a given year, God had spoken, and through His speech the earth had in six successive days become what we know it to be. But now inquiry has crept slowly back through the centuries behind us, pushing time before it as it crept, and the few thousands of years have lengthened into millions; and as man has in imagination ascended this vast avenue of ages, he has seen the successive generations of being slowly descend in the scale until organic being has disappeared; and he has stood in thought on an untenanted earth, a slowly cooling mass, with fire within, with vapour around, like a monster sleeping in its own thick breath; while the vapour, slowly condensing, forms the seas, and the mass, cooling, hardens into the rocks. And even here the imagination has not remained; it has travelled back, and has looked out into the void which is the womb of time, and seen the raw forces of things mustering for their creative career, the atoms falling through space, striking against each other, aggregating, combining, here solidifying so as to form a sun, there throwing off smaller masses which formed themselves into planets, though rigorous law so bound the severed masses together as to make them constitute one system. And then the imagination, unexhausted by its backward exploration through time, has crept out into space, pushing before it the walls that limit our immensity, and by the help now of the telescope, and now of the photographic plate, it has added realm upon realm of being to our known and observed universe, till we feel as if earth were but a mote floating in the midst of a measureless expanse, which yet is no wilderness, but rather a fair and fruitful land, peopled with innumerable worlds. But infinitesimal as seems the earth in this infinitude, it yet for us holds the secret which explains it. It is one of the mighty host amid which it swims and floats. It shares their being, it partakes in their life, it marches in their order, it belongs to their system. We, though but a part, are yet in and through and because of the whole; and so in us the problem of the whole is concentrated. Our existence, little as it seems, is big with the meaning of the universe, holds the only solution we can ever find of the overmastering mystery of being.

Now just as our earth becomes at once more majestic and intelligible through these infinities that bound its finitude, and as it yet is the key to all their secrets, so Jesus is conceived by the Evangelists as a mystery that must be read through the eternal God, and yet as a reason that makes all His mysteries intelligible, credible, lucid, and articulate. The secrets which were in the bosom of the Father are so manifested in Him as to be perceptible by our grosser sense. Hence, within the limits of the sensuous lives a spiritual, expressive of things the eye hath not seen, nor the ear heard, nor the hands handled. And the humanity which so reveals Deity could not be other than universal, embodied indeed in a person, but a person who is as essentially related on the one side of His being to man in all his phases and in all his ages, as on the other side to God. And so to the Evangelists He is at once the Son of Adam and the only Begotten of the Father.

CHAPTER III

THE ETHICAL TRANSCENDENCE OF JESUS

THE miraculous history is the most local and ephemeral thing in literature; it lives within a given geographical and ethnic area, and never outlasts an early stage of culture. Mythologies which were once believed because of their supernatural machinery are now, on account of this same machinery, credible no more. They may help the enquirer to see the human mind petrified, as it were, at a particular moment in its development, but they can never be regarded as permanent products of the mature reason or be taken for rational theologies or authentic histories. The standard of credibility is not indeed uniform, nor is belief in the marvellous restricted to simple minds; and when the subtle believe in the supernatural, they do it with surprising thoroughness. In this region the Orient easily excels the Occident, for narratives which offend the critical reason of the European scholar, speak agreeably to the speculative genius of the Hindu pandit. If, then, the Gospels had been simply miraculous stories, they might have lived a precarious life in the East, but in the West they would have died long ago and been forgotten. What has made them potent and credible, even in the face of belief in a natural law which cannot be violated, is that they have acted as the frame to the picture of a moral loveliness that can never grow old. Yet the idea this picture expresses may be more radically opposed to naturalism, whether physical or historical, than belief in all the miracles recorded in all the mythologies. For physical pre-eminence is by its very nature individual and transitory, but spiritual transcendence is immortal, with qualities that penetrate to the very heart of nature and cover the whole circuit of history. Now the Evangelists may be said to have conceived the essence of Christ's person to lie in its spiritual transcendence; and in this they but anticipated the mind of Christendom. It is, indeed, remarkable what a small part the belief in the miracles has played in the life of the religion; and even this part has been due not to themselves but to their moral significance. It is only when we turn to the character of Jesus that we begin to escape from the outer court of the temple.

§ I. *The Ethical Ideal of the Gospels*

1. Ethical perfection is a much more delicate thing to handle, as well as a much more difficult thing to conceive and describe, than physical transcendence. For literary art has never yet succeeded in embodying it in an actual person. It has given us many a theoretical ideal, which was indeed but a category of definitions or a synthesis of abstract virtues so adjusted as to look like the articulated skeleton of some ancient moral man. But such an imaginary impersonation has always suffered from a twofold defect: (a) it has, like the perfect man of the Stoics, so exaggerated sectional qualities and local features as to make its ideal unsuitable to other times, classes and places than those for which it was written; and (β) it has been without practical efficiency, for the unrealized vision is too impalpable to move men either to imitation or emulation. But the embodied idea of the Gospels is, while personal, so generic as to be universally imitable; and it has proved its potency by accomplishing the vastest, if the most silent, of revolutions. Jesus is not a creature of the religious imagination, but rather its creator, or superlative inspirer; for He has determined the form it has

assumed and the ends it has pursued in the personal and collective histories of Christendom. It is as He appears in the Gospels that He has lived in the faith of man, shaped his character and governed his destiny. He could not indeed have so lived unless His person had borne a supreme transcendental idea; but the idea without the real personality would have been a mere dead abstraction. It is this which makes the Gospels books of religion rather than religious biographies. In a particular person they represent universal man; He is so typical that what He was every man may be, and all men ought to become. To follow Him is to save the soul; to assume His yoke and learn of Him is to find in the highest duty the most perfect rest. To have His mind is to be perfect even as the Father in heaven is perfect. He is an embodied conscience, defining duty and executing judgment. To imitate Him is to be obedient to God; to be faithless to Him is to lose eternal life. Foresight of their function is evident in every line the Evangelists draw, and history has justified their belief that in Jesus they had discovered qualities too immortal to die, and too transcendental to be overcome by the lapse of time and the change of place.

2. The writer who would embody in a person dwelling in space and time a perpetual and universal ethical ideal, has to overcome certain initial difficulties that may well seem insuperable.

i. The subject must not be allowed to appear as a conscious sitter, a person who knows that he is being watched in order that he may be sketched as an example for all later men. Were he to conceive himself as living his life in the eye of the world and for its edification, his mental undertone would be that of the actor who plays his part upon the public stage, with this difference—that the actor by profession may preserve his integrity, but the actor who means his acting to be taken for reality is certain to lose it. Conscious holiness is foster brother to conscious sin; the goodness that knows itself to be good is but the inward side of the spirit that outwardly thanks God that it is not as other men. And this is a spirit which other men see nothing in either to admire or imitate ; but from Jesus as the Evangelists show Him to us this spirit is infinitely remote. His character appears throughout as natural, His conduct spontaneous, His motives simple, His thought and speech transparently sincere. He is without the literary consciousness; He did not write or command anything to be written concerning Himself; neither did He seem to think that the craft of letters had any concern in Him or He any concern with it. His field of action was in the open air, not in the study ; He was content to impress Himself on the minds of men, to live divinely careless in the present, without any thought of how He should seem to the future, yet so conscious of the all-seeing and all-enfolding God as to make of the moment He lived in an eternal Now. Of all persons who have made history no one has had so brief a public life as He, for it extended but little beyond two years ; and it was lived face to face with nature and in the society of simple men, who had no eye for æsthetic features or majestic bearing or any of the things the artist in colours or in style so dearly loves. He and they were alike in knowing no art but nature, and so their transcendent results were attained by nature and not by art.

ii. The writers must be as unconscious of their art as their subject is of its being exercised upon him. And the Evangelists did not know how great a thing they were doing : if they had known, they could not have done it, for that would have meant that they conceived themselves as working, with the whole world looking on, at a model for all men to copy. If an author attempted to compose a history with a vision of all the ages standing at his elbow and reading his words, he would lose the serene eye which reflects the truth and would see double. Now what the Evangelists give us is a real portrait which is yet an undesigned ideal. They were not, any more than their great original, literary men; their atmosphere was not the Athens of Thucydides or Plato, the Rome of Cicero or Horace. The art of biography was unknown to their race and class, and the only literature they knew—if indeed they could be said to know it—was in a language which men of the classic tongues held to be barbarous. There is indeed one Evangelist who may be described as a Greek, but he is confessedly not an eye-witness, and only "sets in order" material which already existed. They did not dream of deathless fame, or of producing a work which posterity would not let die. They wrote to tell what they most surely believed; but in telling their tale they created the only true κτῆμα ἐς ἀεί.

iii. There is unconscious but real art in the limits they observe, in the shadows they allow to fall upon the sunlight of their picture. The temptation of the artist would have been to make his hero calm and radiant. He would have conceived the sinless as a sorrowless state, untouched by frailty or infirmity, undarkened by suffering or sin. But the Evangelists are greatly daring: the Jesus they describe is too completely a man to be in any respect alien from humanity. He is tempted without being overcome of sin; He can be angry and fierce as well as kind and gentle; He can speak words that bite as well as truths that console. He feels the bitterness of death, the horror of its great darkness, the desolation of being forsaken of God. It is by a supreme struggle that He achieves resignation, and in the conflict with His destiny He craves human sympathy, though He does not receive it. These are things the conscious literary biographer would have toned down or hidden, but the Evangelists leave them standing, flagrant, in the reader's eye. Without touching here the profound philosophy which justifies these traits, we may note how near they bring Jesus to man, how much they increase His personal charm and the potency of His example.

We can think of Him as of our kind—one of ourselves. There are multitudes of the saintly less accessible than He, severe ascetics, martyrs to conscientiousness, rigorous devotees of virtue and self-denial, so remote from all weakness and so severe to self-indulgence that we dare not confess our sins in their presence, or hint that our humanity is frail. But we can do this before Him, yet in doing it we come to feel more ashamed of ourselves and of our sins than we possibly could in the face of a sanctity too complete to sympathize with our susceptibility to sin. This may seem a paradox, but it is a fact; and it expresses an adaptation of Christ's person to human experience which can hardly be explained by accident or the operation of any fortuitous cause.

§ II. *The Sinlessness of Jesus*

1. It does not surprise us as it ought to find in books which have been said to owe their existence to the untutored and unchastened oriental imagination, the history of a high religious personality written without adulation and eulogy, and with a severe and even austere moderation. It is significant that they never speak of Christ in terms of praise so ecstatic as Plato puts into the mouth of Alcibiades concerning Socrates,[1] or as unqualified as those Xenophon employs.[2] On the contrary, they allow Him simply to unfold Himself in the light. They seem to have cared little for external testimony to His character, judging, perhaps, that an eye-witness sees but a single moment in a life and casts upon it but a hasty and prejudiced glance. Still, there are a few significant witnesses. Pilate, who has the magistrate's eye for crime, describes Him as a "just person," in whom no fault or cause of death has been found.[3] His wife expresses a like judgment.[4] The penitent thief confesses that, while he

---

[1] *Symposium*, p. 215 ff.   [2] *Memorabilia*, I. i. 11.
[3] Matt. xxvii. 24; Luke xxiii. 22; John xix. 6.   [4] Matt. xxvii. 19.

himself dies justly, Jesus "has done nothing amiss."[1] The centurion who watched by the cross, and who saw the Crucified, described Him as "the Son of God."[2] His enemies bear involuntary testimony to His piety when they utter their gibe, "He trusted in God."[3] Judas convicts himself of sin when he says, "I have betrayed innocent blood."[4] Even before His public ministry the Baptist, the most jealous and outspoken of all contemporary critics of character, recognized His moral pre-eminence;[5] and Peter so sees himself in the light of the Master's purity as to cry, "Depart from me, for I am a sinful man, O Lord."[6] "I am not worthy to touch Thee, and Thou art too holy to touch me." And the reserve thus studiously cultivated is but a reflection of Christ's own. He does not speak like one who feels as if He stood or fell by man's judgment. His challenge to the Jews, "Which of you convicteth Me of sin?"[7] means, indeed, that He knows, and they too know, that the only answer possible involves the counter challenge. "Why then do ye not believe Me, who am true and speak the truth?" He describes Himself as "a green tree"[8] over against the "dry tree," which was fit for the burning. He is more explicit to His disciples, and says, "The ruler of the world cometh and hath nothing in Me,"[9] *i.e.* the master of the sinful finds Me sinless. And so He is not of the world,[10] but, like His kingdom, He is from above.[11] These high and transcendent claims are not compatible with the consciousness of sin, and His reserve makes such utterances the more impressive: He who so studiously conceals His soul is to be trusted all the more when His soul is surprised into speech. Nor are these sayings weakened by

---

[1] Luke xxiii. 41.
[2] Mark xv. 39; Matt. xxvii. 54.
[3] Matt. 43; cf. xxii. 16.
[4] *Ibid.* xxvii. 4.
[5] Matt. iii. 14; Luke iii. 16.
[6] Luke v. 8.
[7] John viii. 46.
[8] Luke xxiii. 31.
[9] John xix. 30.
[10] John xvii. 14, 16.
[11] *Ibid.* xviii. 36, viii. 23.

His reply to the Jewish ruler: "Why callest thou Me good? There is none good except one, God."[1] He would not accept a title out of mere courtesy or politeness, nor would He allow to be applied to one who was only a "Teacher" an epithet which properly belongs to God alone. And this was the more imperative as the ruler uses of the act he would do the very term he uses of the Master. He needed, therefore, to be reminded that there was but one absolutely good Being; *His* goodness is original, and all other is derivative, even the Son being but the express image of the Father. "There is none good but one, God," does not signify "I am bad," but rather, "think of My goodness through Him, and judge the quality of the acts you would do through what is pleasing in His sight."

2. But more impressive than the explicit is the implicit evidence as to the quality of the moral ideal which Jesus embodied.

i. He betrays no consciousness of sin, neither confesses it nor asks pardon for it, nor speaks as if He were in thought or being alien from God, or had been guilty of any act which could have made God alien from Him. His goodness does not begin in any change of heart; for though He commands man everywhere to repent, He nowhere implies that He has Himself experienced, or has needed, conversion. He speaks throughout as one who does not belong to the category of sinners, a thing the holiest men have been the least able to do. He is aware, indeed, that sin is common to the race, that nothing more becomes man before God than the language of contrition and confession, and that he who imagines himself to be so good as to be apart from the guilty multitude is guiltier than they. He judged sin as no man had ever judged it before, and spared it not, whether as incorporated in persons of reputed godliness, or as expressed in acts; whether it lurked in the secret sources of action, lusted

---

[1] Mark x. 17; Luke xviii. 18. Cf. Matt. xix. 16-17.

in the eye, hid in the thoughts, or sat behind the tongue that feared to break into speech. But to have been conscious of evil while so judging it would have been, measured by the standard He applied to man, to be guilty of intolerable uncharitableness and pride.

ii. What is even more characteristic, and would have been in any ordinary case a note of pride still more intolerable, is that He forgives while He has no conscious need of forgiveness. He said to the sick of the palsy, "Son, thy sins are forgiven thee;" and the scribes, who knew the law, charged Him with blasphemy, saying truly, "Who can forgive sins but God only?"[1] To forgive sins against oneself if such sins there be, is an affectation of superiority which it needs a generous man to overlook; but to forgive the sins which concern God, and which only God can know, is an act which implies a purity of nature equal to God's own, an unconsciousness of sin and a consciousness of holiness which we can describe as nothing less than divine. And alongside the act stands a most unexpected consequence: the men whose sins He forgives hate sin as the unforgiven never do. Forgiveness in His hands does not become a concession to human frailty, or an encouragement to evil, but an injunction against sinning; the man who receives it feels he must sin no more. And there is a parallel yet opposite fact, what the meaner critic thinks a suspicious inconsistency between His doctrine and His practice. He judged sin seriously; He was most severe to the offending eye or heart, foot or hand; it was to be plucked out and cut off rather than that the man should enter whole into hell. His conscience was sensitive to the shadow cast by sin, yet He associated with the outcasts of Israel. The very men who wanted to convict Him of blasphemy because He forgave sin, complained that He was "the friend of publicans and sinners."[2] They could not understand why He should seek the society

[1] Mark ii. 5-7.   [2] Mark ii. 13-17; cf. Luke xv. 2.

of the guilty while He was so severe to their guilt. But the sinners never mistook the root and reason of His friendship for they knew, though the scribes did not, why He not only ventured into their company, but felt bound to seek it, even while hating the things they loved. He sought it because He was their friend; and because of His very sinlessness He could move amid evildoers like one who bore a will charmed against their spell, too perfect in its love of purity to be seduced towards evil. The Pharisee was but studying his own safety when he held aloof from the publican; the consciousness of sin warned him against all dalliance with sinners. Our social conventions are the safeguards of frail virtue against potent vice, and the policy of isolation is the method by which a nature no longer pure fortifies itself against natures still remoter from purity. But Jesus knew neither fear nor shame, and needed not the protection of distinguishing custom or speech, for while their state moved His soul to pity, His very presence awoke within them the desire after higher things.

3. But over against His relation to sin and man stands His relation to God. There is no saint in the whole calendar less distinguished by what we may term the apparatus of religion. It was His deficiency in this respect that helped to make Him despised and rejected of men. It would be easy to find persons in every age and church since He lived more zealous than He was in special religious exercises or for single virtues. Stones have been worn smooth by the knees of His penitents; martyrs have died at the stake for His name, rejoicing amid the flames and insensible to pain; the poor have been served more assiduously than He ever served them, and the diseased have been ministered to with a care and a tenderness He never surpassed, if indeed He equalled. The hermit or the monk who forsook the world that he might give himself wholly to the worship of God, has in bodily mortification gone beyond anything that is

recorded of Jesus; while the nun who has hidden herself in the cloister that she may attain whiteness of soul, has surrendered herself to a severer discipline than He ever practised. Yet these are but the strenuous labours of persons who are miserable through their great desire to win by personal effort what He possessed by nature. He lived embosomed in Deity, filled, penetrated, transfigured by God, yet not by a God who was simply the fulfilment of desire or the infinite abyss which swallowed up the very personalities it had produced; but rather a God of transcendent ethical severity, whose truth could suffer no falsehood, who was the light which could bear no darkness, the good which could tolerate no evil, the life which overcame death, the love that cast out hate. The extraordinary thing is the co-existence in the same person of this total unconsciousness of sin with the complete conscious possession of an absolutely holy God. For Jesus so lived that He seemed to men the ethical perfection of God embodied in an ideally perfect manhood. And indeed He is most really man when He and the Father so interpenetrate that they become one, each so mingled in the other that He and we alike lose all consciousness of distinction, and they who hear or who see the Son hear and see the Father. Yet this is not absorption in the manner of the oriental mystic; the personal is not lost in the universal soul. The mysticism which the East has loved is a dream of man's disappearance into a deity infinitely absorbent, where he attains beatitude by escaping from the form Deity had given into the substance Deity is. And the result is a piety of languor and quiescence, of ethical lassitude and social isolation, which fears the burden of self and desires above everything the chance of laying it down. But in Jesus the perfection which God loves is one with the realization of personal manhood; it is the harmony of idea and being, of the governed character with the governing thought. Obedience was to Him a movement that did not tire, because it

ORIGINALITY OF THE IDEAL

knew no friction; beatitude was the vision of God, expressed not in voluptuous quiet but in beneficent activity. It was out of the conflict of the ideal He embodied with the actual He confronted, that the sorrows came which constituted His passion and delivered Him unto death.

§ III. *Qualities of this Ideal of Sinlessness*

1. It must be confessed that this moral ideal, drawn by oriental peasants innocent of literary art—for Luke but repeats and arranges what he had received—is a work of stupendous originality. It has no prototype in religion or in literature. The mythical theory owed, as we have said, its vogue and its verisimilitude to the idea that the Evangelists were deeply versed in the Old Testament, and clothed their hero in garments which they had borrowed from that vast and ancient storehouse. But at the very point where this theory, if it were true, ought to have found final verification, it finds explicit contradiction and disproof. For the most original thing in the New Testament is not the acts or outward history of Jesus, but His spirit or inner character. It is no doubt true that His historical and religious antecedents are in the Old Testament; there, too, are the ideas He transfigures, the hopes He fulfils, the institutions He supersedes; but what is not there is His moral image, the personality He becomes. For in the Old Testament there is no sinless man with a mission to men rather than to the chosen race. Moses indeed is meek and "faithful in all his house," but he so sins that he is not allowed to set foot within the promised land. David, the hero-king, is described as a man after God's own heart, but he is guilty of deeds abhorred alike of God and man. Elijah, the most impressive figure among the prophets, breaks down in the hour of trial, and confesses himself to be a man no better than his fathers. Isaiah, the seer of sublimest vision, feels himself to be too

unclean of lip to be a messenger of God. In the prophetic vision of the suffering servant of God, who did no violence, neither had any deceit in his mouth,[1] there are lines that foreshadow the evangelical ideal; but the vision remained a vision, symbolical, typical, an image of collective Israel, until He came who so lived as to turn it into a reality. And thus it but helps to define and sharpen an antithesis which reaches its logical climax in the contrasted creations which sum up the character of the two dispensations. The Old Testament ends not in an ideal manhood, but in a ceremonial institution, in a method for making man, whom it cannot make pure within, liturgically clean. The literature burns here and there with the noblest ethical passion, but the religion refuses to realize its ethical dream, and plants the official priest in the place designed for the saint. The New Testament, on the contrary, begins not in a sacerdotal order, but in a Moral Person; its ideal is a manhood, not an institution; a creative character, not a purificatory method. And in this its greatness and its originality alike lie. All religions had, like Judaism, found it easier to create the sacred institution than the holy man, though none did it with higher energy and greater skill. But Christ opened a more excellent way—created a religion by means of a moral personality, and so bound the two together that they could never more live apart.

2. Quite as notable as the originality is the catholicity of this moral ideal. Jesus of Nazareth is the least local, sectional, or occasional type of moral manhood in all literature. In their ideals race differs from race and age from age. The typical manhood of Greece, while under the spell of Homer, is the swift-footed Achilles or the crafty and far-travelled Odysseus; but when under the spell of Plato, it is the sage who loved truth, praised virtue, and studied how to know and realize the good in the state. The saints of

[1] Isa. liii. 9.

the East would not be canonized in the West, while the qualities which the cultured West most admires the civilized East holds in disdainful contempt. Few things, indeed, are more permanent or more prohibitive of moral sympathy and appreciation than racial characteristics. A good man in a black skin may be pitied and helped, or patronized and misunderstood, by white men, but he would certainly not be hailed as a saviour to be believed or as a master to be revered and followed. We may say, "beauty is only skin deep," but, as a matter of fact, there are few deeper things than skin; it represents not so much a physiological or racial difference as an intellectual, a moral, and a social cleavage between man and man. The fields of religion and history teem with illustrations. Confucius is a sage China worships, but the Hindus would despise his ostentatious ignorance of the only Being they think worth knowing and his indifference to the only life they consider worth living. The ascetic community which is Buddha's social ideal for his saints, a Greek would have conceived as the final apostasy from good of a person destined by nature to live as a free citizen in a free state. The status Mohammed assigns to woman is an offence to the domestic ideal of the Teuton; and the way he indulged his sexual appetite makes him more deeply distasteful than even the "necessary fiction" which he compounded with "the eternal truth," "that there is only one God." But the character of Jesus transcends all racial limitations and divisions. He is the only oriental that the Occident has admired with an admiration that has become worship. His is the only name the West has carried into the East which the East has received and praised and loved with sincerity and without qualification. And this power it has exercised ever since it made its appeal to human thought: it overcame the insolent disdain of the Greek for all things barbarian; the proud contempt of the Roman for a crucified malefactor sprung from a hated and conquered people; the vain conceit of a commercial race, which before the moral majesty of a moneyless peasant has almost wished to forget its passion for gold. And this catholicity endures because it is based upon nature. What seemed to His own day disastrous to His claims—the want of rank, of name and fame and honour—has saved the ideal from death, emphasizing the fact that His transcendence was due to nothing adventitious, but to Himself alone. If He had appeared as Cæsar, the majesty of the man would have been sacrificed to the ostentation of the Emperor; if as the Roman Augustus, He could not have seemed so sublime and kingly as He does as Jesus of Nazareth. But though all men may see this now, few saw it then. Their ignorance and simplicity saved the Evangelists from the temptation to make Him appear more royal than He was. If they had known imperial Rome, they could hardly have refrained from borrowing some of its purple and fine linen for His cradle or His grave. If they had known how the Gentiles would regard His birth and state, they might have tried to hide them under the shadow of the pomp He had despised. But knowing Him and knowing nothing else, they told what they heard and described what they saw, and so created the most immortal work of art in all literature,—a character so complete and catholic in its humanity that to it alone belongs the distinction of having compelled the homage of universal man.

3. But there is a final quality in the character of Jesus which we can, perhaps, better appreciate than even the Evangelists: its potency. It had, indeed, in a rare degree the attributes of gentleness and inflexibility. He described Himself as "meek and lowly in heart,"[1] and men love to speak of Him even yet as "the humble Nazarene." But if "meekness" be understood to mean compliancy, or "lowliness" the want of self-respect and personal will, or "humility"

[1] Matt. xi. 29.

THE IDEA OF CONVERSION

the surrender of conscience and reason before the conventions and imperious commonplaceness of society, or indeed any qualities resembling these, no one ever lived to whom such terms could be less fitly applied. He is, where duty or truth is concerned, the very impersonation of the unconquerable will; where dignity or right is at issue, it is vain to speak of silence or submission; where pride would overbear or justice turn into expediency, He stands up with a front that may be broken, but cannot bend or retire. The cross signified that man could kill but not subdue Him; desertion and denial came and awoke His pity, but they could not turn Him from His goal. The potency of His character is, however, best seen in its historical influence, in its being an immortal and inexhaustible recreative energy. Under this aspect its force may be represented by two facts.

(*a*) By acting as the Friend of the publican, who "came to call not the righteous, but sinners to repentance," He introduced the great idea of conversion, set it by His own conduct as a duty before His people, and showed how it was to be accomplished. His new way of dealing with transgressors stood over against the old way, which was the way of pride and punishment, of insult and indignity, of a society which did not know any better means of protecting its order than the destruction of the persons who threatened to disturb it. The method of Jesus was remedial, changing the sinner and forgiving his sin. He used friendship and affection instead of isolation and distrust; His love played round the man whom hate had scorched, waked the goodness lying dormant in the heart of guilt, called faithfulness into being in the soul of the faithless, out of the man who had been cast as rubbish to the void making a pillar for the temple of God. Man has been slow to understand what this means, but he is at last coming to appreciate the new attitude it created in the good towards the evil, the hope it introduced into the lot of the oppressed, the sense of duty it begot in those who have inherited virtue to those whose main inheritance is vice, and the way it has enriched humanity by bringing into its service multitudes who would otherwise have sullied its fame and marched in the army which fights against its peace. Infinite, untouched possibilities lie in this idea of conversion. Though to it the Church of Christ owes the most radiant of the luminaries that have made its militant night clearer than the day, yet we have a long way to travel before we can get close enough to His spirit to see it as it is, and to be the willing captives of its power. But even so, this new mind and attitude is only an incidental consequence from the knowledge of His character, hardly visible amid the host of His benefactions to mankind.

(β) By His transcendent moral purity He has created two things which seem opposites, but are correlatives and counterparts, the deepest consciousness of sin and the desire for the highest sanctity. Man knew sin before Him; Hebrew literature is full of it. Men, as they thought of God's majesty, and knew that they were searched by eyes which were too pure to behold iniquity, abhorred themselves in dust and ashes. Classical literature knew it, for it is one of the themes on which Seneca speaks almost like a Christian apostle. Yet it is true that there was before Christ no such consciousness of sin as He, by His very sinlessness, created. There were ritual offences which ritual could remove; there were lapses from virtue which repentance could wipe out; there were even transgressions against God which His mercy could cover and forgive; but there was no such thing as a sin which cast its shadow upon the life of God. And sin has become to us not a ceremonial accident which the only sort of sacrifices man could offer might atone for, but an offence so awful in its guilt as to involve the passion of God and the death of His Son. Hence comes the tragedy of Christian experience —the co-existence and conflict in the same soul of a double sense, a fear of sin that almost craves annihilation, and a love of holy being that yearns towards the vision of God. Yet these are both due to the action in us of the ideal sinless personality, and express the love by which He guides man into the light of life.

§ IV. *Sinlessness and the Moral Person*

But we here touch questions concerning the function of the sinless personality in religion and religious thought, and the cause or reason of His appearance in history, which properly belong to a later stage in our discussions, and which must be left till then. There are, however, two questions which, as implied in the evangelical Histories themselves, ought to be noticed here: (1) The idea of moral perfection or sinlessness, and (2) how it affects our conception of the person and His history.

1. Sinlessness, though a negative term, is here used in a doubly positive sense. It applies to both nature and conduct, brings both under the same moral category, and so denotes what a person is as well as what he does. The two senses are, indeed, organically connected, since the quality of the nature is expressed in the conduct; while the conduct reacts upon the nature, uplifting or depressing it, enlarging or diminishing its good. The ancient maxim said: " Good acts do not make a good man, but a good man does good acts; the good fruit is made by the tree, not the tree by the fruit." This signifies that moral nature is more radical than moral action, and, as the prior in being, requires earlier and more careful cultivation. But there is more here than a distinction of time; there is one of cause and ground. Man gets his nature, but he wills his acts; for the first, others are more responsible than he; for the second, he is responsible more than any others, though the responsibility is not unconditioned. A vast and mixed multitude of factors help to determine the coming and the character of the human being. He does not

begin to be as an isolated unit or a characterless individual; but he exists, as it were, before he is born. He starts on his career as an historical and social being, though his history is ancestral rather than personal, and he lives in society mediately rather than directly—in his family, not as and for himself. And this means that he steps into a medium for which he has been fitted beforehand, possessed of a nature which he has inherited. Now here we come upon the fundamental difficulty in conceiving the sinlessness of Jesus:—If it be a matter of nature before it can become a matter of will, how, in the case of one who has a human descent and even an historical genealogy, shall we get the nature good to start with, the unflecked personality, the undefiled will? Do we not meet here the need for assuming the creation by the direct act of God of a new type or species of man, a being without father and without mother? The belief in Christ's moral perfection seems thus to involve the occurrence of a miracle beside which those described in the Gospels sink into insignificance. For it is not enough to affirm the supernatural conception; the real difficulty is conception itself under any form. The man who is born of a woman is her son, inherits her past, and owes to what it has made her his nature and nurture. We may find here the reason that induced the Roman Church to supplement the doctrine of the supernatural conception of the Son by the dogma of the immaculate conception of the mother; for the dogma was even more a concession to timid logic than to pious veneration for the Virgin. But it was a concession to the curious though common logic that thinks it simplifies and safeguards one mystery by creating another and greater, forgetting that there are mysteries which are credible because they are solitary, just as the reasons that persuade men to believe in one God are all against their believing in two. And the logic that justified the Roman dogma ought, in order to full rational consistency, to have required an enormous extension of the process; and argued that not only Mary, but all her ancestors and ancestresses back to Adam, were immaculately conceived, and quickened miraculously by grace and against nature. And even then the doctrine would not have been safe, for the only safety for an incorrupt nature would have been existence and growth in an incorrupt environment. Innocence is no match for experience, and the battle can never be equal if innocence, in all the feebleness of infancy, falls into the depraved hands of a deft and experienced age. Hence an immaculate conception were useless without an immaculate family, and this without an immaculate society and state, which speedily brings us to the logical but here impossible conclusion that, in order to the existence of a sinless personality, we must have a sinless world.

Let us try, then, whether we can find, without recourse to so halting a logic, a more valid and applicable idea of sinlessness. The Evangelists appear to conceive Jesus to be good both in nature and conduct. He impersonates for them the moral law; He judges, but is not judged, and is beforehand described as "holy."[1] But holy in what sense? Not in any sense that excluded liability to temptation, which implies not only the ability to sin, but susceptibility to sin's seductions. There is a distinction between an impeccable and a sinless nature; the impeccable is incapable of sinning; the sinless has the capacity to sin, but has not sinned. It would be quite incorrect to use the term sinlessness of God. He is absolute, and cannot change; infallible, and cannot err; and so, to ascribe to Him whose attributes are all positive a negative quality would be a logical impropriety. But sinless is the proper term to use of a nature which, with the capability of erring, yet has not erred; it is free from sin, yet possesses a will that can be tempted and may fall. The terms that may be used of moral natures are these:—Good, holy, innocent, evil. "Good" is absolute and exclusive, fixed and stable,

[1] Luke i. 35.

untemptable and infallible; "holy" denotes a character achieved and defined, a nature which has learned obedience; "innocence" describes a being without positive qualities, which has attained nothing, but may become anything—a mere potentiality, all the possibilities of evil and good lying latent within it; "evil" qualifies a nature which has been tried and found unworthy, a will which has sinned and become depraved. "Good" is predicable of God only; He alone as good can neither be tempted nor sin. "Holiness" is the attribute of saints and angels, who have been sanctified by the truth and become Godlike. The "innocent" is the untried, who is capable of becoming either angel or devil; while "evil," as regards both state and character, is the man who has fallen from innocence, whether his mind be one of penitence or obstinacy. Now, sinless is a term which may be distinguished from all these. It is stronger than innocence, for it implies tested faculty—will tried, but not overcome. It is more comprehensive than holy, for the holy may, on the one hand, be men saved from sin, and, on the other, men who have attained beatitude; but the sinless has done no sin, and yet lives in deadliest conflict with it and in sorest trouble from it. Yet the basis or starting-point of sinlessness is innocence, as its end is holiness, which will be eminent and meritorious in the very degree it has been attained without lapse. And so sinless is the word which most fitly describes Jesus as He was in the days when it became God to make Him "perfect through sufferings."[1] He had a nature which did no sin, but He faced the sin which could show no mercy to His nature; and in trying to conquer His will, it caused His passion and compassed His death. His humanity was no make-believe, nor the temptation a mere docetic process—a stage drama which He played in the actor's sock and buskin—but a grim wrestle between the tempter and the tempted. And it did not end with the forty

[1] Heb. ii. 10.

days, for, as Luke significantly says, " the devil departed from Him for a season," [1] i.e., departed only to return at many times and in many forms, in the trouble of His soul,[2] the weakness of His flesh,[3] the agony of Gethsemane,[4] and the desertion of the cross.[5] The disciples continued with Him in His temptations,[6] and knew Him to be in all " without sin." [7] What He suffered proved Him to be of our kin ; what He achieved showed how much He differed from all who had been before Him. The humanity, and the sufferings needed to test its sinlessness, were His, but the fruits of His victory are ours.

Sinlessness as thus construed denotes a moral quality whose intellectual equivalent would be freedom from error, i.e. a knowledge that so saw all things as to permit no ignorance and admit of no mistake. But a being of whom this could be predicated could not be conceived as either created or dependent. He would require a memory and an experience that went back to the beginning of things, and an eye that while it saw everything misread nothing. But this is the attribute which we call in the Creator omniscience, and which has nothing in any creature to correspond with it. To affirm that a given person so knew what every day and every hour would bring forth, that ignorance of any thing or event was impossible to him, would be to say he was God and not man. But sinlessness is essentially the note of a being at once dependent and perfect ; for as dependent he is under law or authority, and as perfect he must have completely obeyed. In other words, the only condition that will save an intellect from error is the knowledge of all things that have been, are, or are to be ; but the one condition needed to help men to righteousness is the will to obey. Hence the nature that cannot err is infallible, but the nature that is obedient is sinless ; the one term denotes a quality

---

[1] Luke iv. 13. [2] John xii. 27. [3] Matt. xxvi. 41.
[4] Matt. xxvi. 38. [5] Matt. xxvii. 46. [6] Luke xxii. 28.
[7] Heb. iv. 15.

which the nature has in its own right, the other a quality which has been acquired by the exercise of its own freedom. Infallibility inheres in the person or society which possesses it, the sovereignty which sinlessness obeys inheres in another. Now it is significant that Jesus as expressly disclaimed omniscience as He claimed to do always the will of God. He left knowledge of the times and the seasons in the hands of the Father; but He Himself ever did what was well-pleasing in the Father's sight. The note of His person was sinlessness; it was not the omniscience of Deity.

2. We are now in a better position to consider how the idea of sinlessness affects our conception of Christ's person and history. For one thing, it is evident that it is an idea which suits the historical person—leaves Him the son of Adam according to the flesh, and the Son of God according to the Spirit. By virtue of the first He was, while innocent, peccable and temptable; by virtue of the second He endured in the face of temptation, remained sinless and became holy. What we call the Passion was a real agony—our name for the awful struggle of sin against a pure and obedient will, and for the resistance of the will to the sin. His was the one will sin failed to overcome; and in what sense its failure was man's victory we shall yet see. For a second thing, the idea shows how His humanity could be at once real and ideal. Man as a moral being was designed for obedience; through it and in it, and not otherwise, he could attain perfection. The man wholly obedient is perfectly moral—a human being as God meant him to be; and so he does not so much transcend as realize nature, though to be the only person in history who achieves it is to transcend empirical nature while realizing the ideal. For a third thing, He who achieves this end is not so much taken out of humanity as placed at its head, and so becomes "the Firstborn among many Brethren."[1] While the most eminent, He is also the most imitable, the symbol

---

[1] Rom. viii. 29.

of what obedience to the highest law of being can make the man who obeys. For a fourth thing, it shows how moral perfection realizes rather than disturbs the balance of man's powers. To be sinless is to be God-like, but it is to be man and not God. It is to realize perfectly all that is contained in the creature's dependence and the Creator's sovereignty ; it is to accept and faithfully fulfil the duties and the relations these terms denote and define. It is to be perfect in the sense, though not in the degree, that God is perfect—to be miniatures of Deity, visible images of the invisible God. And so the sinlessness of Jesus leaves us face to face with questions which may yet carry us into regions of high philosophical and historical discussion.

CHAPTER IV

THE RELIGIOUS PERSONALITY INTERPRETED BY HIMSELF

A. THE TEACHING AND THE PERSON

THE character and teaching of Jesus are so mutually elucidative that neither can be construed in isolation from the other. He could not have spoken as He did unless He had been what He was, nor being what He was could He have continued dumb. Their congruity is so complete and reciprocal that the character becomes more credible through the word and the word more potent through the character. It was insight into their connexion and organic unity that made the Evangelists so carefully incorporate the *Logia* and the history; they meant us to read them together even as they themselves did, and interpret the words through the acts, the acts through the words, and both through the person. Psychology as a science is young, but as an art is old; and it is an art without which no one can be eminent either as biographer or as historian. For it signifies the faculty that sees in character the reason of conduct and speech, and reads speech and conduct as the expression and counterpart of character. History and the drama are both alike children of the imagination; and the more constructive the imagination the more perfect will its products be. The dramatist *sees* a character, and through it and for its embodiment he conceives a history, in order that he may enable others to see what he has seen. The historian by a study of words and acts gets to know the men who constitute his history, and then he writes it in order that, by placing the events he narrates, as well as the ideas and motives he describes, in relation to their causes in the men he knows, he may make the moment it covers an intelligible, if not a consistent and rational, whole. Hence where documents and occurrences, literature and history are so indissolubly interwoven as they are in the Synoptic Gospels, the critic needs both historical imagination and philological knowledge. Without the former he cannot turn the latter to any real account. The Jesus of criticism easily becomes even more unhistorical and inconceivable than the Jesus of dogma, without coherence, without reality, too shadowy to be grasped, too subjective to be a real person in history. Hence it may be well if we substitute for the critical the psychological method and attempt to construe Jesus from within, i.e. look at His acts and achievements through His consciousness.

§ I. *The Teaching and its External Characteristics*

1. We are of course here concerned with Jesus under a special category, as the Founder of a religion; and what we have to discover is not simply what the Evangelists thought and meant us to think, but still more whether He Himself had any consciousness of the work He was doing, or was to cause to be done. And at the very outset we may be surprised at what may seem a serious paradox. While there is in no religion any proper parallel to the claims made by His church on behalf of His person, there are yet in most of the historical faiths parallels to His most characteristic sayings. But this can only surprise those who forget the catholicity of His manhood. What used to be known as the *consensus gentium*, or the agreement of all peoples and religions in certain beliefs, was held to be a cogent witness to the truth of these beliefs; and so it is but natural that He who is conceived as if He were universal Man should in a language understood of all men express ideas implicit in all. That Christ's teaching as to peace, humility, and forgiveness should

be anticipated by the Tao-teh King as well as by certain Jewish Rabbis, or that the Confucian classics should contain His Golden Rule, even though it be in a negative form, ought to be no more extraordinary than that the belief in Deity should be common to all religions. That the *Dhammapada* should contain precepts on self-denial, renunciation, discipleship, and the service of one's neighbour, or that the *Bhagavad-Gita* should speak of God's indwelling in the soul and the soul's thirst for God, in terms not unworthy of Jesus, is no more wonderful than that similar ethical ideas should have been incorporated in dissimilar natural religions. That Plato should have written of truth and beauty, Paul of charity, and John of love with a sublimity and a tenderness that would have become the Master, is what is to be expected of the soul that in its serener and saner moments knows itself to be the son of God. The fact, then, that the human spirit in its most exalted moods has uttered thoughts akin to His ought not to make us disesteem the truths the man in Him speaks to the man in us, but rather to esteem them the more highly. This consonance of His mind with the ideal in ours has its counterpart in the agreement of thought and being, speech and character, idea and reality in Himself; and these two harmonies signify that He possesses veracity of nature in its completest and most excellent form, realization of the idea of humanity and obedience to its truth.

2. As to its external characteristics, the teaching is so small in quantity, that sifted from the narrative in which it is embedded it could be written on a few sheets of paper and read in an hour. It was the product of a ministry so brief as to be confined within a period more fitly reckoned by months than by years. It is without elaboration, so much so that Pascal was justified in saying, that Jesus said the deepest things so spontaneously and simply that it almost looked as if He did it without pre-meditation. He was so careless as to its preservation that He never wrote anything Himself, or

HIS SIMPLICITY AND SPONTANEITY 383

commanded anything to be written, or selected any disciple because of his facility with the pen. His words are in the strictest sense spoken words cast into the air like seeds which the vagrant winds are free to carry whithersoever they list. And His teaching makes no claim to respect as literature, is without pomp of diction, elegance, preciosity, classicism, or any quality of style which betokens the influence of academy or school. He was but a rustic teacher, uneducated even to the unlettered men of Galilee, speaking on the hillside or by the seashore, on the village green or in some squalid synagogue, on the highway thronged by pilgrims or in the city where the reign of passion would not allow the people to hear with reason. And the men he addressed were even more rustic than Himself, sons of the soil and of the lake, whose speech was a dialect which the scholar had not touched or the man of letters polished. And the forms His discourses took were as simple as His language and His audience:—the parable which the Oriental finds so natural, so easily uses and so well understands; the quaintly humble tale which speaks to his imagination more clearly than the most luminous argument; the proverb which invites endless explanation and application; the sharp question or the unexpected retort which grew out of His controversies with the Pharisees and priests, or His discussions with His disciples; the reflection on nature and man, on the wayside incident, or the event in sacred history; the overheard meditation, where the soul is surprised out of the deep secret it thinks it speaks to God alone. Yet in all its forms His speech is living, swift and moving, condensed and pregnant, charged with the thought that cannot be shut up in the closet but must live in the minds and on the lips of men.

But His discourses have so marvellous a hold on reality that their place, their time, and their whole social environment may be seen reflected as in a mirror. Nature is there as she lies under the clear Syrian sky. The lily blooms in a beauty that Solomon in all his glory fails to rival, while the great trees spread their branches in the radiant air, the birds build their nests in them, feed their young, and are fed by the heavenly Father. The vines tended by the vinedresser grow on the hillsides; the fig-tree blossoms on the plain, and speaks now of the summer which may tarry long yet so surely comes, and now, laden with figs, of realized hopes, or, again, bearing nothing but leaves, of unfulfilled promises. The yoked oxen plough the fields; in the furrows they have made the sower walks casting his seed into the prepared ground; while later the corn, white unto the harvest, covers the dark earth, and men as they watch it ripening pluck the golden ears and rub them in their hands. The lake, like a living eye, looks out on the landscape, and the heavens, whether in sunlight or in starlight, look down into the lake, which now rises tossed and angry at the stroke of the sudden tempest, and now lies placid and fair inviting men to come and listen while He speaks by its brink. And man is there as well as nature. The fishermen, to His eye potential apostles, to other eyes but ignorant and unlearned men, sit in the shadow of their boats mending their nets, or fare forth upon the lake and cast them into the sea, drawing them in here empty, and there so full that they break with their burden, or, again, leaving them behind in despair of their own lives endangered by some furious squall. Women toil and spin and grind at the mill, draw water from the well, seek health of the physicians, sin in the city, or minister in the home, where sisters are jealous and differ from difference of temper, where the housewife lights the lamp, sweeps the house, rejoices or sorrows with her neighbours, and delights to call them in to share her own happiness and celebrate it with a feast. There is nowhere so fine or so pure a picture of eternal womanliness, the nature that is so swift to see, so keen to feel, so shameless in its sinning, so splendid in its penitence, so quick in its gratitude, so ungrudging in its service, and so absolute in its devotion. Infants come in their mother's arms to be blessed and to be pointed out as types of life within the kingdom. Children play in the market place, making games for their amusement out of the serious business of their elders; they sleep with the father in the bedchamber, or they sit at table, eat, and are filled while the hungry dogs watch for the crumbs. Brothers differ over their inheritance; sons are by their expectations made suspicious of their father, the rectitudinous fearing he may prove indulgent to the profligate; while fathers think that sons dear to them will be as dear to their neighbours and dependents. In the city the poor and maimed, the blind and lame, are crowded together; in the market-place where the children play the weary labourer stands waiting to be hired, and often waits in vain. The rich men live in stately houses, are clothed in purple and fine linen, "and fare sumptuously every day"; while servants wait at their tables, and guests come by invitation, each at once clad in fit raiment and expected to know his proper place. There are slaves that may be beaten, and to them the foreman is harsher than the master; and there are workmen who may be paid, and they are easily discontented with their wages. On the bench there sits a judge of a genuinely oriental type, terrible to the poor and the weak, for he neither "fears God nor regards man." On the road from the capital to the provinces priests travel absorbed in a pride that will not allow them to notice the man who has fallen among thieves. At the street corner the Pharisee carries himself disdainfully before men; in the temple he boasts his almsgiving and fasting, and bears himself proudly before God, while the publican tries to stand hidden from hard and curious eyes, and does not dare to look up into the face of heaven. The representative of Cæsar lives and acts like a Roman; the people hate him and fear him; the sects discuss, academically, questions concerning the tribute money, which their scrupulous consciences would fain refuse to pay, though they are not strong enough to withstand prudence prompted by compulsion. The whole Jewish world is there, a compact, coherent, living world, which we can re-articulate, re-vivify, and visualize, even though the magic mirror in which we behold it is the teaching which reveals the kingdom of Heaven.

3. But these characteristics though we have named them external have yet an intrinsic significance.

i. They have for the evangelical history a positive critical and constructive value. Where the world which surrounds a man is marked by so much actuality he himself can hardly have been a shadow. The mythical imagination clothes the figures it idealizes in forms supplied by its own experience, i e. its hero, though his attributes may be those of more ancient men, is placed in a world which is neither his nor theirs, but that of the men who write their mythological dreams. Hence it is certain to be a world full of anachronisms, incredible through the inconsistencies and mistakes of its makers. But the teaching of Jesus lives and moves and is evolved in a consistent and actual world. The men around Him are real, belong to their own time and state, and to no other; we can mingle with them, think as they thought, hear as they heard, tell their province from their features, their class by their manners, their race and rank by their tongues. The critic loves to test a document by the conditions of its time, or the authenticity of an obscure history by the public events with which it synchronizes. But here he has few sources that he can freely use. The Syrian province was too remote from Rome to excite much interest there; Roman writers were few; of all her pro-consuls and soldiers but one had the splendid good fortune to call a Tacitus son-in-law. The Jewish references to Jesus, Talmudic or Hellenistic, are either too late and polemical, or of too uncertain authenticity or date to be used as fixed standards of judgment. As a matter of fact, it is from Christian sources that we derive the fullest and most trustworthy knowledge of the events, the acts, and the persons that bring Jesus into relation with the written history of the time; but this does not mean that we are without sufficient tests of authenticity. Far more even than in Josephus, or the Jewish apocryphal literature, or the Roman publicists and historians, can we find within the Gospels themselves the material which constructive criticism can wisely trust and safely use. They do not so much narrate a personal history as incorporate a whole society; though they do it without intention and without design, yet they do it so completely that we may search ancient literature, not excluding the history of Thucydides, or the political treatises of Aristotle, without finding anything so exhaustively done. And the society they describe is so real, the men who constitute it so actual and all so group themselves round the central figure that their actuality becomes a guarantee of His.[1] It is not thus that either conscious or unconscious invention works. If fiction or idealization steals into the portrait of the hero, it cannot be excluded from the environment. The background and the figure in the front must be adjusted to each other, and where nature has so supplied the scene we may be sure that art has not been the maker of the person.

ii. But if Jesus becomes as actual as the society in which He moved, then it is evident that He cannot be conceived as a detached or separated being who lived in an abstract or ideal state. His humanity becomes as real as ours; He enters into our common lot, bears our name, feels our pains, knows our weakness and our greatness. He has fallen under the charm and the tyranny of Nature, has experienced the fascination and vexation of home, has felt on him the thousand plastic hands of society, and has known how much it can do to mould man and how little he can do to change it. All man has is His, and He has what is man's. The actual things of time are not to Him dreams or shadows in the imagination, but realities, matters of experience which have entered into

[1] Ante, pp. 328–329.

His soul as deeply as into ours. The Jesus who teaches in the Gospels is to the Evangelists the most actual being in the scene they describe.

iii. The teaching of Jesus, though embedded in a world of such severe actuality, is not made by it local or provincial; on the contrary, what we may call its timeless and placeless note seems only the more accentuated by its narrow medium. The social conditions amid which it was born, and the language in which it was delivered, do not stamp it with their racial character and limitations. The sacred books of the religions are, as a rule, preserved in sacred tongues; while translation diminishes their significance for the scholar, it tends to destroy their sanctity for the people. The Chinese classics must be written in the language and with the signs the Chinaman knows if they are to possess for him any literary and religious worth; done into English they have become books to inform the western man, and have ceased to be authorities for the native mind. The Sanskrit of the Rig Veda and the Upanishads, of the Epics and the Philosophies, is sacred to the Hindu people; to know it is to hold the key of wisdom and of truth; to discover it required all the tact and patience and courage of noted European scholars. Hebrew is the tongue in which the Jew praises God, and without it his soul would be deprived of the speech which is to him his religion. The Koran made the Arabic in which it was written classical; the dialect of the prophet became the standard of art and elegance. But the words of Jesus do not constitute a sacred language; we do not possess His teaching in the tongue He knew and employed. It came to us in a translation, and has lived in translations ever since, multiplying itself endlessly without ever seeming to lose its vital energy. And this means that it has the marvellous faculty of being at home everywhere, intelligible in every speech, comprehensible to every mind, without country or time, because so akin to universal man.

And it is more than curious that the teaching of which this can be said is so marked by the actualities of the hour and the place of its birth.

iv. But what is still more of a paradox is the substance and scope of the teaching which appears in this narrow and local and sordid medium. We may call it the sovereign idealism of the world ; and this would be the sober truth, yet not the whole truth. It would also be true to say, though compared with the whole it means little when said, that Jesus dignified and enlarged whatever He touched, and He touched all man's deepest beliefs, his most regulative and commanding ideals. God He translated into Father, and made man conceive the Being he most dreaded as the Being who most loved him and whom he must love. Man He interpretated by son, raised him to a majesty before which the accidents of birth and state were humbled when they thought themselves noble, and ennobled when they knew themselves mean ; and set him as a being of infinite worth face to face with the infinite God. Duty he lifted from the dust into which it had fallen, and turned it into the obligation to be perfect as the Father in heaven is perfect. Love He purified from passion, and qualified it to be the bond which bound man to God, united man to man, organized life into a body of obedience and a realm of reciprocal service. On the basis of love to God and man He built up a kingdom, out of which the wicked in His wickedness was excluded, but into which the most wicked could by conversion enter and become the most holy. In this kingdom all men were to be brothers and all sons of God ; their worship of Him was to be a service of love expressed in obedience and realized within the community of saints. Instead of outside rules an internal law was to reign ; men were to live in the Spirit and speak in the truth, governed by a love which would not allow any one to exult in another's evil or rejoice in another's pain, but which moved all to a universal beneficence. It was a new idea of God, of man, of religion, each of these singly, all of them together, and all conceived as man's and not as limited to any elect race or conditioned by any sacred class. It was wonderful that a universal idealism so immense and mighty should have so lowly an origin, and come to be in a world so prejudiced, pragmatical and divided.

v. The influence exercised by this teaching stands in significant contrast alike to its origin, to its quantity, and to its literary quality. While it did not begin to be as literature, it has done more to create learning and letters than all the sacred books of the world. More scholars are employed on it than on the literatures of Greece and Rome, while speculation, poetry, and everything that can be termed imagination in modern men have owed to it exaltation and inspiration. The art and civilization of Europe are its creation; it has this significant distinction, which it shares with the words of no other teacher known in the West—men study it as an ideal of life, which they personally, and the State collectively, are bound to realize. The most serious reproach to a Christian man or society is to have failed to obey the law of Christ. And the teaching is conceived to have authority because the Teacher is believed to live; its power to govern and to bind reposes on the idea of His personal sovereignty. But the external characteristics so regarded and construed, cease to be external and become invested with high critical significance; for they show that the teaching can be as little explained by the origin, the distribution, and the use of the *Logia* as the reason which is man can be explained by the anatomy of his body. Anatomy is a real science, but it is not a complete anthropology; were it to claim to be such, it would only become ridiculous; and the criticism which handles documents would earn a similar epithet if it were to speak as a sufficient philosophy of the Christian religion.

§ II. *How Jesus Conceives and Describes Himself*

From this discussion of the teaching in its external characteristics we must now pass to what is indeed the main question it raises: How did Jesus conceive Himself and His special function in religion? One thing is certain: the teaching by itself could not have created Christianity or achieved universal significance. It does not cover the whole of life, whether individual or collective, nor does it even profess to deal with some of man's gravest problems, intellectual, ethical, and religious. There have been crises in every State, nay, in every real personal history, where, if it had been the only guide, it would have to be described as "the light that failed." But the programme of the religion lies in the person of the Founder rather than in His words, in what He was more than in what He said. This may seem an anomaly, especially to an age accustomed to think that it believes "the truth for the truth's sake"; but it is natural that words conceived as the vehicle and mirror of a transcendental personality should become to the reason symbolical of all the mysteries and all the authorities that meet in Him. Still, if this be so, the function we assign to His person must not be inconsistent with His idea of Himself, with the nature of things, or the course of history. Hence what here concerns us is His idea of Himself and the part this idea played in the creation of the Christian religion.

1. And at the outset we have a most significant thing to note, the comparative reserve or even reticence touching Himself which He maintains during His earlier ministry. He is clear and emphatic enough when He speaks to His disciples of God, or the kingdom and its laws; but concerning Himself He speaks not so much in parables as darkly and suggestively. He appears to have desired that their conception of Him should be of their own forming rather than

of His communicating, a belief reached through the exercise of their own reason and not simply received on His authority. His method was to proceed through familiarity to supremacy, not through sovereignty to dominion. If the discipleship had been formed on the basis of His divine pre-eminence, it would have had no reality, for He would never have got near the men, and they would never have come near to Him; aloofness would have marked His way and they would have walked as if divided from Him by an impassable gulf. And so it was as a man of whom they could learn, addressing men who would learn of Him that He called them. And He forced nothing, stimulated but did not supersede the action of their own minds; and when He asked His great question, " Whom say ye that I am?"[1] it was as if He had inquired, " What conclusion have you as reasonable men been compelled to draw from the things which you have seen and heard?" This method of Jesus explains two things: (a) the relative lateness of the period at which He invited the confession. It was the issue of a lengthened process in slow and simple minds, and to have hurried the process would have been to spoil the issue. (β) The immediate and consequent emergence of a new type of teaching, which may be described as more concerned with Himself than the old, and especially with the work required of Him as the Founder of the kingdom of God.

2. But though we must recognize, because of the reasons that prompted it, this early reserve as to the interpretation of His person, yet we must also emphasize the fact that from the beginning He made on His own behalf the very highest claims. Over against the five negative and limitative passages which, according to Schmiedel, constitute " the foundation pillars for a truly scientific Life of Jesus,"[2] I would place as more entitled to this character the following authentic and characteristic texts :

[1] Mark viii. 27-29 ; Matt. xvi. 15-16 ; Luke ix. 18-20. [2] Ante, p. 303.

DEFINES HIS PLACE AND FUNCTION

i. He fulfils the law and the prophets.[1] The terms "law" and "prophets" denote what we should term the Old Testament, the collective revelation to Israel. This Jesus has come to "fulfil," i.e. to realize its idea, to actualize its dream, to accomplish what it tried but failed to achieve. He who so speaks conceives Himself as more than the law, as greater than all the prophets, and so He does not explain as the scribes,[2] but proclaims as a new ethical authority a new law[3] and a higher prophecy.[4]

ii. He comes "to call not the righteous but sinners to repentance."[5] This idea receives fuller and even finer expression in words we owe to Matthew:[6] "Come unto Me, all ye that labour and are heavy laden, and I will give you rest." The consciousness of sufficiency for the saving of the lost was never more beautifully expressed: it has sounded through the ages as an appeal more irresistible than any command.

iii. The command which He addressed to the disciples, "Come ye after Me,"[7] or, more briefly and emphatically, "Follow Me."[8] And some interesting contexts show the absolute authority implied in this command. Thus the scribe who professes himself willing to follow Jesus "whithersoever Thou goest," pleads, when he hears of the homelessness involved in obedience, to be allowed to "go and bury my father"; but the imperative words, pitiless to the pretence of affection, are spoken: "Follow Me, and leave the dead to bury their own dead."[9] Again, the young ruler, who has inherited "great possessions" and wishes to inherit "eternal life," asks what he is to do, and is told: "Go, sell whatsoever thou hast, and give to the poor,

---

[1] Matt. v. 17-18.
[2] Mark i. 22; Matt. vii. 27.
[3] Matt. v. 22, 28, 32, 34, 39, 44.
[4] Matt. xi. 9-11; Luke vii. 26-8.
[5] Mark ii. 17; Luke xix. 10.
[6] xi. 28.
[7] iv. 19.
[8] ix. 9.
[9] Matt. viii. 18-22; Luke ix. 57-60.

and come, follow Me."[1] Jesus will brook no rival; the thing man loves most he must surrender if he would obey. Finally, He states the terms of discipleship: the men who would follow Him must deny themselves and take up the cross,[2] for only so can the soul be saved; and though a man may gain the world, yet if he lose his own soul he will suffer infinite loss.

iv. He affirms in His charge to the twelve[3] His personal sovereignty in the most impressive forms and phrases. They are to be persecuted for His sake; but if they endure, He will confess them before the Father; to lose their life for His sake is to find it; to do the meanest service in His name is to win an everlasting reward.

v. And His pre-eminence towards man is reflected in His uniqueness towards God. He is the Son, all things have been delivered unto Him of the Father; as the Son the Father alone knoweth Him, and He alone knoweth the Father, and without His action as revealer the Father cannot be known.[4]

These texts form an ascending series; they begin with His relation to the past; the old religion He at once supersedes and fulfils; the person to whom its precepts and promises, its offices and institutions pointed, and in whom they ended, is greater than they. Then He defines His relation to the old mankind: His primary function is to save the lost; and this is followed by His attitude to the new mankind whom He calls, commands, and binds to Himself by an affection which grudges no sacrifice and is equal to any service. And these claims represent a sovereignty which only a singular and pre-eminently privileged relation to the Father could justify. These are claims that become the founder of a religion, and, admitted or acknowledged, they almost explain its founding. But claims

---

[1] Mark x. 17–22. [2] Mark viii. 34–37.
[3] Matt. x. 16–42. [4] Matt. xi. 25–27.

which are to rule the mind and the conscience must have as their ultimate basis not a spoken word, but an idea which appeals to the reason and satisfies the reason to which it appeals. Hence Jesus in asking, "Whom say ye that I am?" consciously confesses that His religion will be as His person is conceived to be. And so the essence or heart of the later or higher teaching may be described as the creation of the Christian religion by the interpretation of the Christ.

§ III. *The Person and the Passion*

1. But at this point there comes a most extraordinary and unexpected development in the teaching. Coincident with the new emphasis on His person is the new thought of His passion. No one could be less fitly described as "the Man of Sorrows" than the Jesus of the "Galilean springtime." The idea embodied in Holman Hunt's *The Shadow of the Cross* is false to nature and to history, for Christ's was too fine a spirit to make out of its own sorrow a shade in which those who looked to Him for love should sit cold and fearful; and we may reasonably infer that before the evil days came His customary mood would be the exaltation born of the splendid ideal He was to realize. The morning of His ministry was a golden dawn; in His early parables the sunny side of life so greets us that we may almost see the smile upon His face answering the smile upon the face of Nature. His spirit is bright, His words are serious without being sad, weighted with the ideas of God, and duty, and humanity, but not burdened with the agony or wet as with the sweat of Gethsemane. Yet even then He had thoughts that prophesied the passion. They were native to Him, not given or forced upon Him from without. Experience was indeed to Him, as to us, a teacher; and as He "learned obedience by the things which He suffered," so, apart from the same things, He could not have known

His meaning and His mission. But these were conditions rather than sources of knowledge. The notion of a suffering Messiah filled a small place, if, indeed, it filled any place at all, in contemporary Jewish thought, but He could not study ancient prophecy without finding such a Messiah there. History showed that the very people who built the sepulchres of the dead prophets had refused to hear or even to endure them while they lived; and John the Baptist, slain by a foolish king to gratify the malice of a wicked woman, stood before Him as evidence of continuity in history. And as He preached the Kingdom He found that those who seemed or claimed to be its constituted guardians were His most inveterate foes; the scribe waited to catch Him in His talk; the Pharisee watched to charge His good with being evil; the priests resisted Him in the temple, which they had made into a mart for merchandise. Opposition confronted Him at every moment and in every point; His idea of God's righteousness as distinguished from the law's was made to appear a grave heresy; His friendship for sinners was represented as affection for sin; His very acts of beneficence were explained as works of the devil, and His doctrine of the kingdom was handled as if it signified a reign of lawlessness. Such experiences could create only one feeling, that the enmity His ministry encountered must ultimately fall upon His person; and as He could not surrender His mission He must be prepared to surrender His life. Hence there emerges a double consciousness attended by conflicting emotions which now exalt and now depress Him. He sees the necessity of His death, and does not seek to escape from it; but from the forces which work it and the form in which it, comes He shrinks with horror and alarm. He perceives its functions and issues, and He rejoices to give His life a ransom for many; but, as His life is taken as well as given, He suffers agony because of those who take it, even while He feels in the act of surrender joy at doing His

Father's will. As a result, those elements of the sacrifice and death which appear as the first and most essential to us, appeared as the last and most incidental to Him. Yet to those who can follow and interpret His thought, the new Passion is but the old sovereignty seen through its issue, or in the method of its achievement.

2. The new development in His teaching occurs, then, at the moment when the disciples had come to conceive Him as the Christ; and it is of Himself as the now confessed Messiah, with distinct reference to the idea in their minds, that He speaks. The terminology He employs constitutes a sort of symbolism. According to Mark[1] and Luke,[2] the name He uses to denote Himself as the victim is "the Son of Man." Whence this name may have come does not specially concern us; but what does, is that He uses it to denote the person who had been termed "the Christ." The words of Peter, both before and after, show that the disciples understood Jesus to mean by "the Son of Man" Himself. It is so unusual for any one to speak of himself in the third person, that it has been argued that the name is not historical but apocalyptic in its associations, and denotes not Jesus, but another—a symbolical being. But the idiom is not peculiar to this name; in certain most authentic texts Jesus speaks of Himself as "the Son,"[3] and without this form of words it is impossible to see how He could have expressed His idea. The subject at certain supreme moments becomes an object to Himself; He is more than a unit, He is a whole; more than an individual, He is a race; more than an atom, He is a world. Any one who has studied Fichte's use of the term "Ego" ought to have no difficulty in understanding Jesus' usage of the third as well as of the first person. "The Son of Man" is the

---

[1] Mark viii. 31-32.
[2] Luke ix. 20-22.
[3] Luke x. 17-20; Matt. xi. 27; Mark xiii. 32.

universal form under which He conceives and denotes the specific Jewish notion of the Messiah. What the one term signified for a single people, the other signified for collective man; yet with a difference,—it was the Messiah conceived as the suffering Servant of God; the hope of the people become completely one with the people, afflicted in all their afflictions, redeeming them by death. As, then, the subject—"the Christ," as the disciples had named Him; "the Son of Man," as He had named Himself—is a representative person, so are those who are to be concerned in His death: "the elders, chief priests, and scribes" are symbolical of Israel acting in a collective and solemn manner. "The elders" are Israel as a State; "the chief priests" are Israel as a Church; "the scribes" are Israel as possessed of the oracles of God. When they are conceived as working together, their action is conceived as Israel's, the work of a civil, sacerdotal, and religious body corporate. These contrasted titles then—"the Christ," or "the Son of Man," on the one hand, and "the elders, chief priests, and scribes" on the other—can only mean that the acts in which they were to be respectively engaged, bearing, suffering, and enduring, causing and inflicting, death, have a more than mere personal significance; they realize the ends for which the Messiah stood by means of the ideas for which Israel was the symbol. Thus Jesus conceives His death as in form a sacrifice, a means for the reconciliation of man to God, though a sacrifice may have been the last thing it was intended to be by the men who effected it. And the rebuke to Peter shows how necessary Jesus thought this view of His death was. His words are remarkable: "Get thee behind me, Satan! for thou mindest not the things that be of God, but the things that be of men."[1] It is hardly possible to avoid the inference that there is here a reminiscence of the temptation. Jesus feels as if

[1] Matt. xvi. 21-23.

the tempter, disguised as Peter, was once more showing Him "all the kingdoms of the world";[1] and He once more resists him and casts him out.

Here, then, we have the culminating idea as to Himself and His function; yet it is an idea so extraordinary and unusual, while so distinctive of the religion, that we must attempt to understand it as it rises in His consciousness and is expressed in His teaching. It is so seldom that we have the opportunity of discovering the sources of a potent belief and analyzing its primary form and primitive elements, that one must not be neglected when it offers; and we must here the more jealously use the opportunity that we can compare the present with the later forms and examine its action as a factor in the making and in the continuance of the religion. Our immediate purpose, however, is to find out what the idea signified to Jesus Christ; its worth for the religion belongs to a later stage in the discussion.

[1] Matt. iv. 10.

CHAPTER V

THE RELIGIOUS PERSONALITY AS INTERPRETED BY HIMSELF

B. SIGNIFICANCE OF HIS DEATH

§ I. *Growth of the Idea*

1. VAGUE and general as were the terms in which Jesus stated His anticipation of death, it was yet at once unwelcome and unintelligible to His disciples. For from this point onwards a change which profoundly affects their mutual relations may be seen in process. Their agreement with Him as to the central matter—His Messiahship—only accentuates the radical difference between them as to what the Messiah is to be and what He ought to do. The "Christ" as Jesus conceives Him is devoted to suffering and death; but the disciples conceive the Messiah not in terms they had learned of Jesus, but rather under the categories of local tradition and personal interest. The more explicit His Messianic consciousness grows the more He emphasizes His death; but the more strongly they believe in His Messiahship the less will they permit themselves to think of His liability to a death which they can only construe as defeat. And so there emerges the most tragic moment in the ministry, the bewilderment of the disciples and their alienation from the Master. The conflict which had hitherto raged between Jesus and the Pharisees is now transferred to the innermost circle of His friends; but with this characteristic difference: while the old conflict was open, frank, and

audible, the new was secret, sullen, inarticulate. The signs of the estrangement are many. Their ambitions grew sordid, and they began to feel as if following Him were sheer loss. When He said, "How hard is it for them who trust in riches to enter the kingdom of God"—no strange truth in His mouth—they were "astonished above measure," and said to Him, "Who then can be saved?"[1] Feeling as if this doctrine threatened them with the lot of the uncompensated, Peter, as ready a spokesman of suspicion as of faith, said, "Behold we have forsaken all and followed Thee; what, therefore, shall we have?"[2] The natural result was that jealousy, envy, and mutual distrust wasted their brotherhood, and they disputed by the way as to "who should be the greatest."[3] Hence Jesus had to set the little child in their midst that he might teach the grown men how to live in trust and love. Even thus their greed of place and pre-eminence was not silenced, for the ten were moved to indignation by James and John—two of the most privileged disciples—seeking to beguile the Master into a promise to give them seats, the one at His right hand, the other at His left, in His kingdom.[4] So far did they fall that they attempted to do His works without His faith,[5] tried to hinder men doing good in His name,[6] and even when His face was towards Jerusalem so little had they knowledge of His spirit or His mission that they asked authority to command fire from heaven to consume a Samaritan village.[7] The picture of the alienation is most graphic in Mark: "They were in the way going up to Jerusalem, and Jesus went before; and they were amazed, and as they followed they were afraid."[8] He walks

---

[1] Mark x. 26; Matt. xix. 25.   [2] Matt. xix. 27.
[3] Mark ix. 34.; Matt. xviii. 1-2; Luke ix. 46-48.
[4] Mark x. 35-41; Matt. xx. 20-24.
[5] Mark ix. 17-19; Matt. xvii. 19, 20.
[6] Mark ix. 38-40; Luke ix. 49, 50.
[7] Luke ix. 51-56.   [8] x. 32.

alone, unheeded ; the words He speaks they do not care to hear, for they are confounded, and walk as in a vain show, feeling as if the voice which had created their hopes had turned into a contradiction of the hopes it had created. This was their mood, and it is doubtful whether they ever escaped from it while He lived. It helps to explain their behaviour during the passion, which was but the natural expression of their imperfect sympathy with the Sufferer.

Jesus' method of dealing with this mood enables us to read more clearly His idea as to His sufferings and death. He met the protest of Peter by a public reproof, for Mark here has a trait which Matthew overlooked : "When he had turned about and looked on the disciples, He rebuked Peter"[1] —an act which the apostle had evidently never forgotten. But much more significant than the reproof is the manner and the circumstances under which He repeats and enforces the teaching as to His death. All the Synoptists agree in placing after this incident the words in which Jesus affirms that those who follow Him must not shrink from the fellowship of the cross.[2] They must deny themselves, willingly lose life for His sake and the Gospel's, live as those who love the soul and fear no worldly loss. But not satisfied with indirect instruction, He, under conditions which speak of exaltation, returns to the idea which they so hated. He speaks of it as they were descending from the Mount of Transfiguration.[3] While men were wondering at the things He did, seeing in them "the mighty power of God," He bade His disciples let His sayings sink down into their ears, "for the Son of Man shall be delivered into the hands of men."[4] But one Evangelist is careful to add, " They understood not

---

[1] viii. 33. [2] Mark viii. 34-38 ; Matt. xvi. 24-28 ; Luke ix. 23-27.
[3] Mark ix. 9, 12 ; Matt. xvii. 9, 12. Luke makes "His decease which He was about to accomplish at Jerusalem" the subject on which Moses and Elias are said to have discoursed (ix. 31).
[4] Luke ix. 43, 44 ; Mark ix. 30, 31 ; Matt. xvii. 22, 23.

this saying."[1] His answer to James and John, when they wanted the Samaritan village consumed, was, "The Son of Man is not come to destroy men's lives, but to save them";[2] which means, read in its connexion, to save even by suffering at their hands. Then at the very hour when the alienation was most complete, He would not hide the offence of the cross from their eyes, but once more predicted His death and the part "the chief priests and the scribes" were to take in it,[3] though even yet, as Luke says, "this saying was hid from them, neither understood they the things which were spoken."[4] So far, however, Jesus has only repeated His thought in its original form, His purpose seeming to be to make it as clear and distinct to the consciousness of the Twelve as it was to His own. He could not attempt to expand or explain it to men who would allow it no entrance into their minds. But their mutual rivalries, which were the fruits of their alienation from Him, created at once the opportunity and the need for further exposition; and He added to His prediction of the fact and manner a word as to the function and end of the Messianic death: "The Son of Man came not to be ministered unto, but to minister, and to give His life a ransom for many."[5]

2. This saying marks a very clear advance in the expression of His consciousness, or the definition of His own idea as to His death.

(a) Baur argued that this saying is so contrary to the thought and habit of Jesus that we must suppose He either never said it or said it in quite another form.[6] The exhortation to the disciples is complete without it, and so, said the critic, these words were made for Him, not used by Him. But it is hardly possible to conceive a more gratuitous conjecture. The words will stand any test, critical or diacritical,

---

[1] Luke ix. 45. [2] Luke ix. 56.
[3] Mark x. 33; Matt. xx. 17–19. [4] Luke xviii. 31–34.
[5] Mark x. 45; Matt. xx. 28. [6] *Neutest. Theologie*, 101.

that can be applied to them. The heart of the narrative implies its conclusion, for what do the "cup" He has to drink, the "baptism" He is to be baptized with, signify? Not surely the mere idea of service, but the idea of suffering endured to its tragic end. Here, if anywhere, we have a λόγιον ἀληθινόν, spoken to jealous, unsympathetic, disputatious disciples, while He and they were going up to Jerusalem. It is something to have this fragment of authentic speech, which has, as it were, seized and preserved His articulate voice in the very act of defining Himself and His mission. It is easy to import into the clause too much of our technical theology, but it is still easier to simplify it into insignificance by attempting to keep all theology out of it. The key to its meaning has been commonly found in λύτρον, and in a measure correctly. In each of His formal references in the Synoptists to the death there is a special *terminus technicus* which may well claim to be a key-word. In the first it is Χριστός, in the last διαθήκη, here λύτρον. Now λύτρον is a term easy of interpretation by itself, but here the context in which it stands makes it peculiarly difficult: for while the persons ransomed are specified, He neither defines the state out of which, or the state into which, they are redeemed, nor the need for the ransom, nor the person to whom it was paid, nor the precise respect in which it is the issue of His surrendered life. Ritschl,[1] in an elaborate dissertation, argues that λύτρον here, as in the LXX., where it translates כֹּפֶר, signifies means or instrument of protection (*Schutzmittel*), which may in certain cases become means or price of release (*Lösepreis*). He examines various typical texts in the Old Testament, and comes to the conclusion that those which present the most exact parallel to the words of Jesus are Psalm xlix. 7 and Job xxxiii. 24, and he thence deduces three positions: (i.) that this ransom is conceived as an offering to God and not to the devil; (ii.) that Jesus did instead of the many, what no

[1] *Christliche Lehre von der Rechtfertigung u. Versöhnung*, ii. 69-89.

one either for himself or for any other could do; and (iii.) that Jesus in thus defining His work specifically distinguishes Himself from man, who must die, as one who dies freely, or who by His own voluntary act surrenders His life to God. So he finally defines λύτρον as "an offering which, because of its specific worth to God, is a protection or covering against death." The positions are interesting, and we see how they are reached, but what we do not see is any connexion between the method of reaching them and the words of Jesus. Wendt[1] is less elaborate and exhaustive. He argues that the term is used to express one idea—the deliverance of many, i.e. "all those who will learn of Him," by Christ's voluntary sufferings "from their bondage to suffering and death"; but he has nothing to say as to the person or power to whom the ransom was paid. Beyschlag[2] considers the ransom not a payment to God, but a purchase for God, and a being freed from the dominion of a power hostile to him, the bondage neither of death nor even of mere guilt but of sin.

(*b*) Let us reverse the order these scholars have followed, and instead of coming to the context through the term, come to the term through the context. The sons of Zebedee and their mother had made their request for the two pre-eminent seats in the new kingdom. Jesus in charity attributes their request to their ignorance, and then asks, Were they able to drink His cup and bear His baptism? And they said they were able. The question and the answer are alike significant. The question shows that His spirit was already foretasting the passion. We see that while they wrangled and schemed as to who should be pre-eminent, He was feeling the awful solitude of His sorrow, the suffering that was His alone to know and to bear. Their answer illustrates, more than any other utterance recorded in the Gospels, the ignorance which

[1] *Teaching of Jesus*, vol. ii. pp. 227-234.
[2] *Neutest. Theologie*, i. 153.

was the root of the alienation in which the disciples then lived. It expressed a tragic temerity, the courage of the childish or the drunken, who use words but do not know what they mean. If John ever recalled this moment, and looked at it through the memories of the passion, he must have experienced shame and humiliation of a kind which it is good even for saints to feel. But though it suggests to us the audacity of the child which now overwhelms and now amuses the man, what it must have signified to Jesus was the distance between His mind and theirs, the absence from their consciousness of what were then the most patent facts and potent factors in His own. So He gently calls to Him the disappointed two and the angry ten, though in the ten the very thoughts were active that had moved the two; and proceeded once more to explain His kingdom in its antithesis to man's. They had construed His kingdom through man's instead of through Himself, and so had been seeking parallels where they ought to have found contrasts. And these contrasts He indicates rather than develops. (i.) The fundamental difference was in the persons who exercised kinghood, and therefore in the kinghood they exercised. In man's kingdom lordship is founded upon conquest, authority is based upon might, and so the great are the strong who compel the obedience of the weak; but in Christ's the note of eminence is service, "the chiefest of all is the servant of all." This, however, requires the rarest qualities: for service of all without moral elevation degrades both him who gives and him who takes. Humility without magnanimity is meanness; the humbleness that glories in being down invites the contempt of all honourable men, for it can neither climb up itself, nor lift up the fallen, nor help up the struggling. The service must therefore here be interpreted through the ideal Servant, "the Son of man." "Lordship" of the heroic order *is* not a difficult thing to attain, for men of marked moral inferiority have attained it:

Alexander, who was a youth of ungoverned passions; Cæsar, who was a statesman more astute than scrupulous; Napoleon, who was but colossal obstinacy, loveless and athirst for blood. But the pre-eminence that comes of being "the servant of all" only Jesus has attained, and it is a pre-eminence which has outlasted all dynasties, because based on qualities that have ministered to all that was best, highest, and most universal in man. (ii.) Correspondent to this contrast in the authorities of the two kingdoms, is the difference in their ends. The "lord" governs as a ruler, persons to him are nothing, order and law are all in all. The violated law must be vindicated, the man who breaks it must be broken. But the "minister" serves as a saviour; persons to him are everything; law and order are agencies for the creation of happy persons and the common weal. The law which lordship enjoins is in its ultimate analysis force, and is, when violated, vindicated by the strength it commands; but the end or law which the ministry obeys is benevolence, or in its ultimate analysis love, and it is vindicated only when it can, by the creation of a happy harmony between the person and his conditions, overcome misery and its causes. The creative energy in this case is moral, not, as in the other, physical; and the created state is beatitude, or personal happiness within a happy state. (iii.) The contrast of authorities and ends implies therefore a correlative contrast of means. The "lord" prevails by his power to inflict suffering, the "minister" by his power to save from it; but the saving is a process of infinite painfulness, while the infliction is easy to him who has the adequate strength. The "lord" has only so to marshal his forces as to work his will, but the "minister" has to seek the person he would save, bear him in his own soul, quicken the dead energies of good within him by the streams of his own life, burn out the evil of the old manhood by the fire of consuming love. The final act, therefore, of the King whose kinghood is a ministry, is the sacrifice of Himself, giving "His life as a ransom for many."

3. From this analysis of the words of Jesus, several positions seem to follow, and these we may illustrate, not only from the Synoptists, but from John, which is here full of elucidatory material.

(*a*) There is a distinct change in the point of view from which the death is regarded. Before it was represented as inflicted, the Son of man was to suffer death at the hands of the "elders and chief priests"; here He lays down His life, spontaneously submits to death. The entrance of this voluntary element modifies the whole conception, changes the death from a martyrdom to a sacrifice. The martyr is not a willing sufferer, he is the victim of superior force. He dies because others so will. He might be able to purchase a pardon by recantation, did his conscience allow him to recant; but conscience is not the cause of this death, only a condition for the action of those who inflict it. He does not choose death; death, as it were, chooses him. But sacrifice is possible only where there is perfect freedom—where a man surrenders what he has both the right and the power to withhold. Now Jesus here speaks of His act as a free act; He came, not simply to suffer at the hands of violent men, but to do a certain thing—"give his life." The terms that describe the ministry and the death are co-ordinate, freedom enters in the same measure into both; as He came to minister He came to give His life, the spontaneity in both cases being equal and identical.

The two points of view—the earlier and the later—are not inconsistent, but rather complementary. In John the spontaneity is more emphasized than in the Synoptists. His life no man takes from Him, He lays it down of Himself.[1] But the same Gospel emphasizes more than any of the others the

---

[1] x. 18

malignant activity of the Jews in compassing His death.¹ Their action was necessary to its form, but His Spirit determined its essence. The significance it had for history came from the framework into which it was woven; but its value to God and man proceeded from the spontaneity with which it was undertaken and endured. In the freedom, therefore, which He now emphasized, Jesus lifted His death from an event in the history of Israel to an event in the history of Spirit; and at the same time changed it from a martyrdom into a sacrifice, i.e. from a fate which He suffered to a work which He achieved.

(β) But beside this change from the conception of His person as a passive to that of it as an active factor in His death, stands another: the expression of the principle that governs His action. The sacrifice is not unmotived; it is in order to service, an act born of benevolence. John here supplies an interpretative verse: "Greater love hath no man than this, that a man lay down his life for his friends."² And there is a still higher synthesis. What is done in obedience to love is done in obedience to God. And so the same act which appears as love to man appears as duty to His Father, doing His will or obeying His commandments.³ The voluntary act thus turns into the very end of His existence, the cause why He came into the world.⁴ And He is therefore the person whose function it is as the way to lead to the Father, as the truth to show the Father, as the life to generate, enlarge, and perpetuate on earth the Spirit which is of God.⁵ The death thus ceases to be an incident in the petty and distressful history of a small people. It assumes a universal significance, is taken into the purpose of God, and becomes the means for the realization of the divine ends.

(γ) The ends to which the death is a means are variously represented. In the synoptic passage the end stands in

---

[1] v. 18; vii. 19, 30; viii. 37–40; x. 31–32; xi. 50.   [2] xv. 13.
[3] x. 18; xiv. 31.   [4] xviii. 37; xix. 11.   [5] xiv. 6.

antithesis to that of the ethnic kingdoms, i.e. it is a state not of bondage but of ordered freedom, in a realm where the highest in honour and in office are the most efficient in service. This is in harmony with the Johannine word, "the truth shall make you free."[1] But the opposite of freedom is bondage, and in each case the state is in nature correspondent to its cause. "Where the Spirit of the Lord is there is liberty"; but "whosoever committeth sin is the bondservant of sin."[2] The sin which man serves may be incorporated in many forms: the world,[3] which is sin generalized; the devil,[4] which is sin personalized; the wolves that harass and devour the flock,[5] which is sin symbolized. These are but aspects of one thing: sin is each, and sin is all; but His death is the means by which God effects deliverance from each and all. By it the world is overcome,[6] the devil is judged,[7] and the sheep are saved.[8] Now there is no term that could better express the means that effects these ends than λύτρον, i.e. where the end is redemption, emancipation, deliverance from the dark powers which hold man in bondage, the means are most correctly denoted a "ransom." It is evident that Jesus is thinking of the fitness and efficacy of His death as a method of accomplishing a given purpose, and this determines the word He chooses. He does not think of buying off man either from the world or the devil, or of paying a debt to God, or of making satisfaction to law; He simply thinks of man as enslaved, and by His death rescued from slavery. To require that every element in a figurative word be found again in the reality it denotes, is not exegesis but pedantry—the same sort of pedantry that would find in the parable of the Prodigal Son a complete and exhaustive picture of the relations of God and man.

[1] John viii. 32. [2] 2 Cor. iii. 17; John viii. 34.
[3] John xv. 18, 19. [4] viii. 44. [5] x. 12.
[6] xvi. 33. [7] xvi. 11; xiv. 30. [8] x. 14, 15.

(δ) The death is "for many." The "many" is to be taken as = multitude, mass. We cannot think that "the Son of man" and the "many" stand in accidental juxtaposition. The one term denotes a person who stands related to collective mankind; the other term denotes those to whom He is related as the "multitude," the "many," not as opposed to the few, but as distinguished from "the One." The One has the distinction of the unique: He stands alone, and does what He alone can do. Of the "many" no one "can by any means redeem his brother nor give to God a ransom for him";[1] but "the One" can do what is impossible to all or any of the "many." His pre-eminence, therefore, is the secret of His worth; He does what is possible to no other, for He transcends all others, and His personality equals as it were the personality of collective man. Hence He is able to "give Himself a ransom for many."

(ε) "For many:" ἀντὶ πολλῶν = "in room of many." His death is not a common death, and Jesus does not here conceive it simply as suffered "for conscience' sake," but as "for many." In it He endures the tragedy of His pre-eminence. Though His grace concedes to those who follow Him fellowship in His sufferings, yet in the article and moment of Sacrifice He is without a fellow. It is "a cup" which He alone can drink; "a baptism" which none can share. And it is so because He stands where no one can stand beside Him, in a death which is "a ransom for many."

§ II. *How Jerusalem helps to define the Idea*

The ministry in Jerusalem is the supreme moment in the history of Jesus, and we have therefore to inquire whether it reveals, and, if so, in what degree it defines, His idea as to His death. We must keep clearly in view the positive features in the situation: He comes to the Holy City, the

---

[1] Ps. xlix. 7.

heart of the religion, the home of the temple, the throne of the priesthood, the one place where sacrifices acceptable to God could be offered. And He comes consciously as the Christ, for the prophet could not perish out of Jerusalem.[1] And so everything He was to do and suffer was stamped by Him and for Himself with a distinct Messianic character.

1. The triumphal entry can hardly be regarded as an accidental or even spontaneous outburst of popular enthusiasm. The Synoptists are agreed in ascribing the initiative to Jesus; He sends for the ass and the ass's colt in order that He may fitly enter the Holy City,[2] and though John is less detailed he is almost as explicit.[3] The disciples read the command as a public assertion of His claim to Messianic dignity, and proceed to inspire the multitude with their belief. And so Jesus is welcomed as the King come to claim His own by a jubilant people, crying, "Hosanna to the Son of David!" He does not rebuke their joy, or, as He had once done,[4] enjoin silence as to His being the Christ, but accepts their homage as His rightful due. Hence when the Pharisees said, "Master, rebuke Thy disciples," He answered that, were they to be silent, the very stones would cry out.[5] He thus endorses and vindicates their recognition. But He knows that while the people are trustful and waiting to be led, the rulers are suspicious and watching to crush the leader and—to fulfil His prophecy. For to subtle rulers nothing is so easy as to use a simple people as they will.

But for His judgment on these public events we must turn to words spoken in the intimacy of His immediate circle. On the morrow, as He returns to the city, He speaks the parable of the barren fig tree.[6] It has a double moral, one pointed at the Jews, another at the disciples. The first tells

---

[1] Luke xiii. 33.
[2] Matt. xii. 1 ff.; Mark xi. 1 ff.; Luke xix. 29 ff.
[3] John xii. 14.   [4] Matt. xvi. 20.
[5] Luke xix. 40.   [6] Matt. xxi. 18–22.

how in the season of fruition He came to Israel, and instead of fruit " found nothing but leaves." And what was the good of the fruitless tree save to be bidden " to wither away "? The scribes, who ought to have been the eyes of the people, saw not the time of their visitation, saw only that their own custody of the parchment which held the oracles of God was threatened; and so they made the great refusal. The chief priests, who ought to have been the conscience of Israel, had no conscience toward God but only to themselves; and so they could think of nothing but the happiest expedient for effecting His death. So read, the parable is a piece of severe prophetic satire. The second moral told the disciples to have faith; with it they could accomplish anything, without it nothing at all. They were to be the antithesis to the rulers, and exemplify not a faithlessness which the world overcomes, but the faith which overcomes the world. The two combined show the twofold attitude of Jesus, on the one hand to the men who were to erect the cross, on the other to the men who were to preach in His name to all nations. What is significant is the place and function which the parable assigns to Himself: to fail to receive Him is fundamental failure; to believe in Him is to be qualified to effect the removal of mountains.

What immediately followed the entry must also be noted. Jesus went straight to the temple, where, Mark significantly says, " He looked round upon all things," [1] and, returning on the morrow, " He cast out all them that bought and sold in the temple, and overthrew the tables of the money-changers, and the seats of them that sold doves." [2] This incident has been very variously judged: it has been regarded as an outbreak of passion, as a lawless act, as even an act of rebellion and revolution; as a desperate attempt to precipitate a conflict, and by a sort of surprise attack save Himself from defeat

---

[1] Mark xi. 11. [2] xi. 15; Matt. xxi. 12, 13.

by the priests and rulers.[1] These seem to us shallow views. We could not feel as if Jesus became sinful simply because He was angry; nay, the more sinless we think Him to be the more do we conceive indignation and resentment as natural and even necessary to Him. There are acts and states that ought to provoke anger, and not to feel it would argue a singularly poor and obtuse moral nature, without any power of recoil from the offensive and reprehensible. And from what He saw in the temple Jesus did well to be angry though it was anger without passion. Matthew[2] finely indicates this by two things, "the blind and the lame"—the two most timid classes—came to Him to be healed; and the children, who are ever sensitive to passion and instinctively shrink from hate, were attracted to Him and sang in His praise; i.e. the anger which was terrible to the guilty seemed tenderness to the innocent. And so the chief priests and scribes said, in suspicion and alarm, "Hearest Thou what these say?" But He justified the children thus: "Yea, did ye never read, Out of the mouths of babes and sucklings Thou hast perfected praise?" And His own action, how does He justify it? By comparing the ideal with the actual temple: the ideal was to be a House of Prayer for all nations, but the actual had been made a den of robbers, i.e. they had narrowed it, and had prostituted the pure house of God to their own sordid uses. And He claimed the right to raise up the fallen ideal and to open the door wide to the pure in heart, who could see God, but could not trade in the holy place.

He thus, in effect, said that as they had failed to understand prophecy, they had failed to realize worship. The counterpart of the dumb oracle was the defiled altar. And

---

[1] Keim, *Jesus of Nazara*, vol. v. pp. 118–23, for example, speaks about "His uncurbed anger," "His passion for rule and revolution," and describes His action as the "Nothakt eines Untergehenden."

[2] Matt. xxi. 14–16.

so He affirmed His right to govern the house of God, to declare invalid the authority of the men who claimed to stand in the Aaronic succession and to sit in Moses' seat, to abolish the old and institute a new order, and to introduce the hour when the true worshipper was to "worship the Father in spirit and in truth." But in order to see the full meaning of the act, we must turn to a saying found elsewhere. At the trial two false witnesses appear and testify: "This man said, I am able to destroy the temple of God, and to build it in three days,"[1] and the words were repeated by the mockers at the cross.[2] The saying, which was truly told, but falsely interpreted, evidently belongs here, and means that He had conceived Himself as the spiritual reality of which the temple was the material counterpart. What it was in symbol He was in truth—the medium for the reconciliation of man and God. In Galilee His controversy had been with the Pharisees touching tradition and the law, here it was with the priests touching worship and the temple; but the same idea lies behind both—His transcendence of the system which the Jew regarded as absolute and final: the Son of Man is greater than the temple,[3] and the Lord of the Law;[4] both are from Him, through Him, and for Him. In the background of His mind, regulating His speech and action, is the thought of the ideal temple, which was profaned in the profanation of the actual, and as the pure Sacrifice He purged the place where sacrifices were impurely offered.

2. But it is still more in the teaching peculiar to the Jerusalem period that His idea is defined. It falls into two divisions, which we may call the exoteric and the esoteric.

(*a*) In the exoteric, or outer, there is a new note; His words are graver, sterner, much concerned with His death, and the

---

[1] Matt. xxvi. 61; cf. John ii. 19. [2] Matt. xxvi. 40.
[3] Matt. xii. 6. [4] Mark ii. 28.

part in it the rulers were to play. Ideas and principles also appear, different from any He had expressed while He lived in Galilee. (i.) There is the parable of the husbandmen, who first beat and kill and stone the servants, and finally slay the son that they may seize on his inheritance.[1] What is this but a picture of the scene which was passing before His eyes and theirs? (ii.) There is His interpretation of the stone which the builders rejected, but which yet became the chief stone of the corner.[2] The builders are the rulers; He Himself is the stone, hastily set aside, but so terrible that it breaks whoever falls on it, and grinds to powder the man on whom it falls. No words could more clearly forecast their respective parts in the immediate future and in the subsequent history. (iii.) There is the parable of the Marriage Supper,[3]—full of the tragedy of the moment,—the bidden guests scornfully refusing to come, the servants spitefully entreated, even slain, though the slayers are themselves soon to be slain, and their city burned up, while the wedding is to be furnished with fitter guests. The meaning is obvious: He is the King's Son, now is the festival of the marriage, and the rulers, who in spite of their proud claims are yet only guests in the House, are rejected of God for the rejection of His Son. (iv.) There is the attitude of Jerusalem to Him and His to her. He has a marvellous vision;[4] on the one hand the city is as it were personalized, and stands pictured as a colossal persecutor, inheritor of the guilt of all past martyrdoms, and so charged with all the righteous blood which has from the days of Abel been shed upon the earth; and on the other hand He stands as Maker and Leader of martyrs, a colossal Person in whose veins flows all the blood of all the righteous; and by whose will the new prophets are fitly to be sent to deliver their testimony and endure the cross; i.e. He con-

---

[1] Matt. xxi. 33-41 ; Mark xii. 1-9 ; Luke xx. 9-16.
[2] Matt. xxi. 42-44.   [3] Matt. xxii. 2-10.   [4] Matt. xxiii. 34-39.

ceives the hour to be at hand when acts are to be done which will epitomize and embody all the martyrdoms of all the holy who have ever lived. But He who sees Himself and His thus suffer at her hands, is the very One whose mission and passion it was to save and shelter her. (v.) In the most authentic and sublime of the Apocalyptic discourses He affirms what we may call the vicarious principle. The good or ill of His people is His; they are one with Him and He with them. The smallest beneficence to the least of His brethren is done to Him; the good refused to them is denied to Him.[1] And, we may add, this idea implies its converse: if their sufferings are His, His are theirs; what He endures and what He achieves, man achieves and endures.

We can hardly misread the significance of these passages. They bear witness to this: that the moment when He foresees His death most clearly He conceives His person most highly; that He regards this death as a calamity to those who reject, an infinite good to those who accept, Him; that those who compass it participate in what may be termed a universal crime, which shall work their disaster while constituting His opportunity to effect everlasting good. The principle which explains these things is His complete identification with all the righteousness of time, or the unity in Him of the being of all the good who are hated of all the evil.

(β) But these are more or less external views, conditioned by the antithesis under which they are developed; for His more inward mind we must turn to His words to the disciples. What this mind was is evident from the incident in the house of Simon, the leper.[2] The conflict in the city and with the rulers is over; and He can speak to His own quietly and without controversy concerning the secret things of His own soul. As they

---

[1] Matt. xxv. 35-40, 42-45. [2] Matt. xxvi. 6-13; Mark xiv. 3-9.

sit at meat a woman, bearing "an alabaster box of very precious ointment," steals softly up behind Him, and "pours it upon His head." What followed shows how little the disciples had learned, and how much of their old spirit still lived within them. "To what purpose is this waste?" is their indignant question, while their sordid feeling is disguised as concern for the poor. But the reply of Jesus expresses His innermost thought: "She is come to anoint My body aforehand for the burying." His death fills His mind, and it is to be a death which will leave no chance for assuaging the grief of the living by the last tender ministries to the dead. And He rejoices to see His own acts of sacrifice reflected in the gracious act of the woman; the love that surrenders life feels comforted by the kindred love which covers with grateful fragrance the body so soon to be lifeless. But there is an even finer touch, showing the faith that lived in the heart of disaster. Jesus, while He anticipates death, anticipates universal fame and everlasting remembrance. His gospel is to be preached "throughout the whole world," and the woman's act is to be everywhere "spoken of as a memorial for her." This consciousness of His universal and enduring import is a note of the sayings which belong to His last days, and stands indissolubly associated with His approaching death. His words are to abide for ever;[1] His gospel is, like the temple of God, destined for "all peoples." And these things He speaks of as simply and confidently as He speaks of His death.

§ III. *The Significance of the Supper*

1. But the most solemn and significant of all His utterances concerning His death are the words spoken at the institution of the Supper. Their sacramental inter-

---

[1] Mark xiii. 31.

pretation lies indeed outside our present purpose; so does the interesting question which has been recently raised, whether we owe the change of the Supper into a permanent sacrament to Jesus or to Paul, and whether the suggestive cause of the change was Jewish custom or Greek mysteries. This question requires a broader and more searching treatment than it has yet received. The later action of the mysteries, and the tendencies that created the mysteries, upon the ideas of the Supper, of the elements, the conditions, the effects, and the modes of observance, may be established by various lines of proof; but we see no reason to doubt that the Supper had become a Christian custom before Christianity had felt the delicate yet subduing touch of the Hellenic spirit. This question, however, does not affect ours, which is simply, "What did Jesus mean by the words He used as to His own death at the institution of the Supper?"

In the several narratives the formulæ are not quite identical. As has been often remarked, there are two main versions—that of Paul[1] and Luke[2] on the one hand, and that of Matthew[3] and Mark[4] on the other; but even the versions which are alike significantly differ from each other, and as significantly agree with a representative of the independent tradition. Thus the formula for the bread is simpler in Matthew (Λάβετε, φάγετε· τοῦτό ἐστιν τὸ σῶμά μου), and Mark (who omits φάγετε), but more detailed in Paul (τοῦτό μού ἐστιν τὸ σῶμα τὸ ὑπὲρ ὑμῶν· τοῦτο ποιεῖτε εἰς τὴν ἐμὴν ἀνάμνησιν), and, according to the received text, most detailed in Luke (τοῦτό ἐστιν τὸ σῶμά μου τὸ ὑπὲρ ὑμῶν διδόμενον· τοῦτο ποιεῖτε εἰς τὴν ἐμὴν ἀνάμνησιν). The variations affect both the theological and the sacramental

---

[1] 1 Cor. xi. 24-25.
[2] xxii. 19-20. But as to the text here see Westcott and Hort, *Introduction*, §§ 240, 241, and *Notes on Select Readings*, pp. 63, 64. Cf. Zahn, *Einleitung*, ii. pp. 357-359.   [3] xxvi. 26-28.   [4] xiv. 22-24.

idea, the former in τὸ ὑπὲρ ὑμῶν, the latter in τοῦτο ποιεῖτε εἰς τὴν ἐμὴν ἀνάμνησιν. In the formula for the wine, the cross agreements and differences are still more instructive. Mark is simplest: τοῦτό ἐστιν τὸ αἷμά μου τῆς διαθήκης τὸ ἐκχυννόμενον ὑπὲρ πολλῶν. Matthew changes ὑπέρ into περί, and adds εἰς ἄφεσιν ἁμαρτιῶν. Paul says: τοῦτο τὸ ποτήριον ἡ καινὴ διαθήκη ἐστὶν ἐν τῷ ἐμῷ αἵματι: while Luke combines Matthew and Mark with Paul, thus: τοῦτο τὸ ποτήριον ἡ καινὴ διαθήκη ἐν τῷ αἵματί μου, τὸ ὑπὲρ ὑμῶν ἐκχυννόμενον.

These variations are easily explicable, and show, so far as the sacramental idea is concerned, that the validity of the ordinance did not depend on any uniformity in the formula used; for words so freely altered could not be conceived to possess some mystic or magic potency capable of effecting a miraculous change in the elements. As concerns the theological idea, the difference in the terms represents no contradiction or radical divergence in the thought. Paul and Luke say, "the new covenant in My blood"—i.e. the covenant which stood in the blood, or had therein the condition of its being. Matthew and Mark say, "this is the blood of the covenant"—i.e. the blood which gives it being and character, which is its seal and sanction. They agree in their idea of the covenant, though Paul and Luke think of it as "the new" in contrast to "the old," while Matthew and Mark think of it, absolutely, as sole and complete. Paul says nothing as to the persons for whom the blood has been shed; Luke says, "for you"; Matthew and Mark, "for many." But the difference here is formal. Paul means what the others say, while the "you" is only the personalized and present "many," the "many" the enlarged and collective "you." Matthew alone definitely expresses the purpose for which the blood was shed— "unto the remission of sins"; but this only made explicit the idea contained in the ὑπὲρ ὑμῶν and the ὑπέρ or even the περὶ πολλῶν: for what other idea could the consciousness of the disciples supply save that the blood shed "for them," or "in reference to many," was shed "in order to remission of sins"? The phrasing varies; the language is here less, there more, explicit, but the thought is throughout one and the same.

2. What, then, did the words which our authorities thus render mean on the lips of Jesus? We cannot be wrong, considering where it stands, in regarding this as the weightiest, most precise, and defining expression which He has yet used concerning His death. The form under which He first conceived it was as an integral part of His work as Messiah, yet as a fate He endures or suffers at the hands of the elders and chief priests. The next form under which He conceived it was as the spontaneous surrender of Himself "as a ransom for many." But here these two forms coalesce in a third, which is at once their synthesis and completion. His death has (a) at once an historical and an ideal, a retrospective and a prospective significance; it ends one covenant and establishes another; (β) it has an absolute worth irrespective of the form it may assume or the means by which it may be effected, for though inflicted by men, it is endured on behalf of man; and (γ) its express purpose is to create a new, an emancipated people of God.

(a) But in order that these ideas may be understood they must be interpreted through His experience, the facts and factors that had shaped and were shaping His thought. The covenant which He established stands as "the new" in explicit antithesis to the "old," and finds its constitutive condition and characteristic in "His blood." He dies at the hands of the old covenant, but in so dying He creates the new. This makes His death the concrete expression of the antithesis of the covenants, and at the same time represents the inmost fact of His own conscious experience. While possessed by the feeling of radical unity with His people, He was an alien to the actual system under which they lived. He consciously incorporated their most distinctive religious ideas, but He was as consciously in conflict with the men who claimed to be the official representatives and only authorized ministers of the old religion. The degree in which He embodied those ideas was the measure of His antagonism to the men, and theirs to Him. To be the Christ of prophecy was to be the Crucified of Judaism. This was the tragedy of the situation : the Jew had existed in order that he might produce the Christ, but once He was there the Jew did not know Him, would not love Him, had no room for Him, could do nothing with Him save compass His death. The words of Caiaphas[1] are but the official version of what Jesus Himself had foreseen and so often foretold. His reading of the religion was the direct contradiction of theirs ; both could not live together, and the only way in which they could effectually contradict His contradiction was by His death. But at this point, as to what was to be accomplished by His death, He and they radically differed; they thought that by the cross He was to die and they were to live, but He believed that they were through His death not to live, but to die. This idea fills His later teaching ; it is the moral, not simply of the Apocalyptic discourses, but of the parables already noticed,[2] of His words to the women of Jerusalem,[3] and of His lamentation over the city.[4] It was the supreme Nemesis of history. What fate save death could happen to the system whose reward to its most righteous Son was the cross ?

(β) But this is an indirect, and, as it were, negative result of His death; the direct and positive is the new covenant which is established in His blood. We need not concern

---

[1] John xi. 50. [2] Ante, pp. 418–419. [3] Luke xxiii. 28–31.
[4] Matt. xxiii. 38 ; Luke xix. 43, 44.

ourselves with the idea of "covenant"; enough to say, it is here held to denote a gracious relation on God's part expressed in a new revelation for the faith and obedience of man. But what does very specially concern us is what Jesus says as to His blood. It must be explained through the moment and all its circumstances. He had strongly desired to eat the Passover with His disciples before He suffered,[1] and He had sent Peter and John beforehand to prepare it.[2] Now this means that its associations were vivid both in His mind and in theirs, and through these associations His words must be construed. The feast was the most domestic of all the feasts in Israel; in it the father was the priest, the home was the temple. The lamb was not the symbol of any sacerdotal function, but of family and racial unity, especially in the eye and purpose of God. Its blood was not shed to propitiate a vengeful Deity, and induce Him to pass kindly over the family for whom it had been slain and the house where it was being eaten, but rather to mark them as God's own; in other words, the paschal sacrifice did not make Him gracious, but found Him gracious, and confessed that those who offered it believed themselves to be the heirs of His grace. It was the seal of a mercy which had been shown and was now claimed, not the purchase of a mercy which was withheld and must be bought. It signified, too, that since the people were God's, they could not continue slaves, but must be emancipated and live as became the free, obedient to the Sovereign whose supremacy could brook no rival authority. It was the symbol, therefore, of unity, all the families who sacrificed constituted a single people; Israel knew only one God, God knew only one Israel. Jesus translated these associations from the traditions which acted as the fetters of the past into the ideals which were to govern the future. He manifestly conceived Himself as the sacrificial lamb, for only so can we find any meaning in the

---

[1] Luke xxii. 15.   [2] Luke xxii. 8.

reference to His blood; and the figure was beautiful enough to apply even to Him. It was the symbol of innocence, meekness, gentleness, of one who was led to the slaughter, and was dumb under the hand of the shearer; but it did not speak of a victim whose blood was shed to appease a vindictive sovereign. On the contrary, the blood told of divine grace and denoted a member of the family of God, a man spared, emancipated, introduced into all the liberties and endowed with all the privileges of Divine sonship.

(γ) So far we have been concerned with the relation of the blood to the covenant, but we are now met by another question: In what sense could it be said to be shed "for you" or "for many"? We have seen that He spoke of acts done to the least and the neediest of men as if they were done to Himself; but the precise parallel of this is that the acts He does may be conceived as done by man; in other words, He is so the centre or keystone of family or racial unity that in a perfectly real sense His act is universal, even while a person performs it. His position is twofold: He conceives Himself as the Lamb sacrificed in order to mark and seal the people of God, i.e. establish His covenant; but He also at the same moment sits in the seat of the host or father, who sums up in himself the household, acts and speaks as their sole and responsible head. As the one He distributes the elements which symbolize the sacrifice; as the other He is the sacrifice which the elements symbolize. The ideas proper to these quite distinct relations, blend both in His consciousness and in that of the disciples. According to the one He is offered for the many; according to the other His act is their act, in Him they live impersonated. Hence His suffering at the hands of man is theirs, and theirs also is His surrender to the will of God. The outer letter which is abolished by His death, ceases to have dominion over them; the inner obedience which is accomplished by His spirit, becomes a fact of their history, and a factor of their

DEATH AS IDEA AND AS EXPERIENCE 425

new experience. In other words, by being made a curse for us He redeems us from the curse of the law; and by means of the new spirit of life which is in Him, He sets us free from the law of sin and death. And so Paul sums up the innermost meaning of His words when he said: "Christ is the end of the law for righteousness to every one who believeth."[1]

§ IV. *Gethsemane and the Cross*

1. So far we have been occupied with Jesus' prophetic interpretation of His death, but when He comes face to face with it and sits in its shadow, we have to note a correspondent and characteristic change in His mental attitude. From the idea of death He never shrinks; He contemplates it calmly, speaks of it with the serene dignity of one who knew that the most tragic moment of His life was at once His own supreme choice and the real end of His being. But when He knows its mode and thinks of the agents it needed, His feeling changes, and His speech is charged now with admonition and judgment, now with pity and regret. This difference is recognized both by the Synoptists and by John. By the Synoptists He is shown as speaking of the positive fact and function of His death only when His mood is most exalted, or when He is most moved by love and pity, or when He feels least scorched by human hate and most moved by the clinging trust of His disciples. But when He confronts the men and sees the means by which it is to be accomplished, His spirit vibrates to another tone; the men are the wicked husbandmen, or the foolish builders; they are "blind guides," "hypocrites," who crucify the living prophets, and build the sepulchres of those long dead. The city they rule so moves His compassion that at the sight of it He weeps. The traitor is a man of so woeful a fate that he had better never have been born. And so while of death in relation to

[1] Rom. x. 4.

Himself He thinks and speaks with benignant grace, the thought of its manner begets in Him something akin to dismay.

In John the difference is even more strongly accentuated. He speaks of His death in language that would on other lips suggest rapture. It was His own act, the thing He had come by command of the Father expressly to do.[1] It was the hour in which "the Son of Man should be glorified."[2] By death He was "to be lifted up from the earth," and would "draw all men unto Himself."[3] But the sanctity of the death does not sanctify the instruments by which it is realized. On the contrary the traitor acts by inspiration of Satan.[4] The Jews are like their father the devil, who was "a murderer from the beginning,"[5] and this was said because He knew that they "sought to kill Him."[6]

We have, then, even in the prophetic period these two very different, but not at all incompatible, elements in the consciousness of Jesus. His sacred joy or spiritual exaltation in the prospect of death, and His horror at the form in which, and the forces through which, it was to come to Him. But now we must advance a step further, and study His spirit as it suffers in the hands of those forces whose action He had foreseen. And here we shall have constant need to remember the distinction between experience and foresight; for the evil the intellect watches is sweet when compared with the infinite bitterness of the evil which the soul touches and feels. What we have then to attempt to describe is the transition of the Saviour's mind from the objective contemplation of the death He was to die to His subjective experience of the powers by which it was to be accomplished.

2. The incident which exhibits this transition is the scene in Gethsemane. Now, of all the events in the Saviour's life

[1] x. 18.   [2] xii. 23–27.   [3] xvii. 1, 33.
[4] xiii. 27.   [5] viii. 44.   [6] vii. 1.

AGONY IN THE FACE OF DEATH 427

this seems to me to demand the most reverent handling; for it is, as it were, the very Holy of Holies, the inmost sanctuary of His sorrow, which ought to be entered only at those moments when thought has been purged from the pride and impurities of life. But the scholar is often more curious than reverent, though in sacred things the irreverent is near of kin to the blind; and as it is so easy to be unfit to be an interpreter, few incidents have been more utterly misunderstood than this. It is not surprising that Celsus should have explained the scene as due to Christ's fear of death;[1] or that Julian should have pitied Him as a miserable mortal unable to bear His fate calmly;[2] or that a modern pagan like Vanini on his way to the scaffold should have pointed to a crucifix, and said: "Illi in extremis prae timore imbellis sudor: ego imperterritus morior."[3] Nor are we surprised that the older Rationalists should regard it as the effect of a purely physical cause—fear due to bodily exhaustion and indisposition;[4] or that Baur should see in it only an event that enabled him to play the Synoptists off against John and John against the Synoptists;[5] or that Strauss, holding the narrative to be more poetical than historical, should have mythically decomposed it in his first Life,[6] and followed in his second Baur's antithetical criticism to its issue in a prosaic naturalism;[7] or that Renan, true to his Parisian sentimentality, should conceive it as a moment when human nature reawoke in Jesus, and He felt enfeebled, if not affrighted, at the vision before Him of the death which was

---

[1] *Contra Cels.*, lib. ii., c. xxiv.
[2] *Apud* Theod. Mops., *in Ev. Lucæ Com. Frag.; Pat. Gr.*, t. lxvi. p. 724.
[3] Grammondus, *Hist. Gall. ab. ex. Hen. IV.*, lib. iii. pp. 211 seqq.; cf. Brucker, *Historia Philos.*, t. iv., pars 11, pp. 675-8.
[4] Paulus, *Das Leben Jesu*, ii. pp. 202–210.
[5] *Untersuch. über die Kanon. Evang.*, pp. 198 ff., 207, 265 f.
[6] *Life of Jesus* (4th ed.), §§ 125, 126.
[7] *New Life*, § 87.

to end all, and the vision behind of the clear springs of Galilee and the fair maidens who visited them.[1] But we are surprised that Keim should see in it the human dread of death holding Christ back from His destiny;[2] that Schleiermacher should lose all sense of its sublime significance in a hypercritical analysis of the possible sources of its details;[3] or that Neander should see Him here asking, as a man, to be spared the sufferings that awaited Him.[4] But bad as these explanations are, some of those we owe to more orthodox theologians are worse. Steinmeyer thinks that Jesus here may have taken upon His shoulders the sin of the world in order that He might, vicariously, make atonement for it on the Cross.[5] Long before him Calvin had here seen Jesus as our substitute, burdened with our sins, bearing the wrath of God with the judgment-seat before His eyes.[6] More reasonable was Ambrose, who saw Jesus sorrowful not for His own, but for man's state: "Tristis erat, non pro sua passione, sed pro nostra dispersione."[7] But possibly even more reasonable was the elder Dumas when he represented the agony as a second temptation, in which the devil tried to drive Christ back from His work by three successive visions, the last and most terrible being the persecution by the Church of the heretics, their heresy being often their higher saintliness. These selections from a multitude of elaborately argued opinions, are enough to show how hard it has been to seize the real significance of this awful moment in the history of our Saviour's Passion.

3. If we are to interpret the agony, we must assume the reality and the authenticity of the Synoptic narrative.[8]

---

[1] *Vie de Jésus*, p. 378 (7th ed.).   [2] *Jesus of Nazara*, vi. p. 12.
[3] *Das Leben Jesu*, pp. 422-4. Cf. Essay on the Gospel of St. Luke, pp. 300-1.
[4] *Life of Christ*, § 280.   [5] *Leidensgesch, des Herrn*, pp. 62 ff.
[6] *In Harm. Evang. Matt.* xxvi. 37.
[7] *Expos. Ev. sec. Lucam*, lib. x. § 61.
[8] Matt. xxvi. 36-46; Mark xiv. 32-42; Luke xxii. 39, 40.

Though John does not give it, yet the attitude and state of mind it expresses were not unknown to him.[1] Luke differs in certain details from Matthew and Mark—the angel which strengthens Him, the sweat " as it were great drops of blood falling down to the ground," and the omission of the thrice-repeated prayer; but the differences are mainly noticeable for this—Luke, by the angel and the sweat of blood, and Matthew and Mark, by the threefold resort to prayer, express the same thing—the intensity of the strain, the deadly nature of the struggle. Now, it is evident that the Evangelists did not regard the narrative as representing anything so common-place and even vulgar as the fear of death. They had told, with many a touch of unconscious truth, how the disciples had refused to see the approach of its inexorable front while He had looked upon it with serene and open face ; and, simple as they were, they could not have mistaken the meaning of so sudden a reversal of mental attitude. Not that horror at death in Jesus would have been either an unseemly or an inexplicable thing. Contempt of life is the obverse, indifference to death is the reverse of the same mind. The more excellent the good of life seems, the more terrible will appear its negation; and it might well have been that the soul which most possessed the good, should have most loved life, and most have feared its darksome ending. But the feeling, though explicable in itself, will not fit into the history. The death so often anticipated, so solemnly sanctioned, so formally blessed, could not be thus met. The higher we place its significance for Jesus, the less can we construe it as the cause of His agony ; for this agony must stand in organic connexion with His expressed mind, not in violent contra-diction to it. If so, then it is evident that the antecedent of the agony was not the idea of death, but the feeling as to its means and agents. His death was to be for sin, but at the hands of sinners, yet of sinners disguised as "elders and

[1] John xii. 27.

chief priests," as disciples and judges. In foresight the mode of death was subordinate to the idea, but in experience the idea tended to be lost in the emotions which the mode awakened. How this was the history tells. In Galilee the men who were to effect His death were mere names to Him; in Jerusalem the names became men. They were the priests, who stood for all that the worship of God signified; the elders, who were in symbol the people of God; the magistrates, who guarded freedom, enforced law, and typified right; the disciples, who had heard and followed Him, and

> Lived in His mild and magnificent eye.

Behind the actual persons He thus saw ideal figures stand; and if the ideal signified what ought to have been, it was the actual which, by its inevitable working, determined His all too bitter experience. To see it stand in the holy place was bad enough, it was worse to feel that it stood there to oppose all that was of God in Himself. And worst of all was the discovery that evil had found a foothold and embodiment in the society He Himself had selected and trained. We must not overlook the influence which the conduct of Judas would exercise on the mind of the Master. Jesus as He entered the garden carried a double memory: the gracious dream of the Supper, and the lurid image of the traitor. From the very nature of the case, the more bitter would for the moment be the more potent feeling; for where the soul is so susceptible and tense, the painful strikes more deeply than the agreeable. And Gethsemane represents the struggle of Jesus with the new problem which thus came before His imagination personified in Judas and the priests, and which he had to solve in the very face, if not in the very article, of death.

4. And what was this new problem? Jesus was holy, and felt as only the sinless can the stain of sin burn like a living fire upon His soul. He had conceived Himself as a Redeemer by the sacrifice of Himself, as a Saviour by death. But now,

when He comes face to face with this death, what does He find? That sin has taken occasion from His very grace to become more exceedingly sinful, to mix itself up with His sacrifice, penetrating and effacing it, transmuting it from a free and gracious act into a violent and necessitated death. His act of redemption becomes, so to say, the opportunity for sin to increase. The thing He most hates seems to become a partner with Him in the work He most loves, contributing to its climax and consummation. Or if not so conceived, it must be conceived under a still more dreadful form, as forcing itself into His way, taking possession of His work, turning it into "a stone of stumbling and a rock of offence," a means of creating sinners while it had been intended to save from sin. And there was an even more intolerable element in the situation: the men who were combining to effect this death were persons He was dying to save, and by their action they were making the saving a matter more infinitely hard, more vastly improbable, and changing the efficient cause of salvation into a sufficient reason for judgment.

Is it possible to exaggerate the suffering which such a problem at such a moment must have caused? He could not turn back without being defeated by His horror of this transcendent evil, and He could not go forward without feeling that He was almost compelling it to be. And so first seclusion, then solitude, become to Him a necessity. The society that had made the Supper sacred He must forsake, for at it He had something to give which made Him happy, while it consoled and satisfied the disciples; *now* He wanted to receive and could not, for they did not understand what to give and why He suffered. So he leaves them that he may pray alone, yet pauses, and turns to take Peter, James, and John, the three who seemed to know Him best and love Him most. But they are as irresponsive as the dumb soul which speaks no word the human ear can hear, because it has no ear which the human tongue can reach. So He turns to God in what we may almost describe as His despair. Thrice He prays in an agony of spirit which becomes an agony of body; but even in the midst of the anguish that will not be controlled, He remains master of His will, compels it, even while all His nature seems to resist, to be not submissive but obedient, to accept not its own impulse, but God's wisdom as its law. The thing He would not do, is what His own nature abhors; but the thing He will do because He must, is what God requires. He feels the position as it lives in the place and the moment, but God sees the universal and the eternal issues within it; and so in spite of the noble and justified resistance of the flesh, the spirit obeys the wisdom that cannot err. The conflict is over, and He goes to a death which is at one and the same moment the world's redemption and the world's crime.

I feel the temerity and presumption in so thinking, and still more in thus writing, for I feel as if the intellect, in analytically handling the Passion, tends to become little else than profane. I may say, however, that the very last thing I could bring myself to do is to apply legal fictions or judicial processes to the mind and state of the Saviour in Gethsemane. Everything here seems to me superlatively real, in the last and highest degree actual. And the reality in this stage of the Passion concerns His relation not to the Father, but to destiny and death. From death as such He does not shrink, but from its mode and agencies, from death under the form and conditions which involve its authors in what appears inexpiable guilt, His whole nature recoils. And this recoil compels us to see that we must divide asunder His part and man's; in what He contributes there is saving efficacy, in what man contributes there is a guilt which causes shame, and becomes a reproach to all mankind. And here one may find some small part of the reason why

His prayer for release could not be granted. The cross has in a perfectly real sense done more than any other agency to convince the world of sin; one may say it has created in man, both as person and as race, the conscience for sin. It stands not simply as the symbol of the grace that saves, but of the wickedness that dared attempt to extinguish the grace. And another thing may be added. While He had to drink the cup, it would not be quite correct to say that His prayer was not answered. For He did not pray in vain. The author of *Hebrews* says, " He was heard for His godly fear."[1] Jesus died on the cross, but not of the cross. He suffered crucifixion, but He was not crucified. The will which triumphed in the conflict broke the heart which could not bear to endure death at the hands of sinners. And this brings us to the conclusion that the death which redeems was all the work of the Redeemer; and not at all of the men who might sin against His grace but could not sin away His mercy, or deprive Him of the splendid privilege of giving Himself "a ransom for many."

[1] v. 9

Mors ad hominem pertinebat, resurrectio ad Filium hominis.—
AUGUSTINE.

Incarnatio Verbi est complementum et quies creationis ; nam in illo opere quiescit potentia in se ipsa. Deus uti in maximo atque ultimo complemento operum in Christo quiescit.—NICHOLAS OF CUSA.

Die leibliche Geburt Christi bedeutet allenthalben seine geistliche Geburt, wie er in uns und wir in ihm geboren werden.—LUTHER.

Nous disons que Dieu craint, que Dieu se courrouce, que Dieu aime,
Immortalia mortali sermone notantes :
ce sont toutes agitations et esmotions qui ne peuvent loger en Dieu, selon nostre forme ; ny nous, l'imaginer selon la sienne. C'est à Dieu seul de se cognoistre, et interpreter ses ouvrages ; et le faict en nostre langue improprement, pour s'avaller et descendre à nous, qui sommes à terre couchez.—MONTAIGNE.

Here was, therefore, an exemplary temple, the fair and lovely pattern of what we were each of us to be composed and formed unto : imitating us (for sweeter insinuation and allurement) in what was merely natural, and inviting us to imitate him in what was (in a communicable sort) supernatural and divine.—HOWE.

He took off those many superinduced rites, which God enjoined to the Jews, and reduced us to the natural religion ; that is, to such expressions of-duty which all wise men and nations used ; save only, that he took away the rite of sacrificing beasts, because it was now determined in the great sacrifice of Himself, which sufficiently and eternally reconciled all the world to God.—JEREMY TAYLOR.

Die Erscheinung des ersten Menschen constituirt zugleich das physische Leben des menschlichen Geschlechts ; die Erscheinung des zweiten Adam constituirt für dieselbe Natur das neue geistige Leben, welches sich durch geistige Befruchtung mittheilt und fortentwickelt.—
SCHLEIERMACHER.

Ce qui est hors de doute, quelque soit l'avenir religieux de l'humanité, c'est que la place de Jésus y sera immense. Il a été le fondateur du christianisme, et le christianisme reste le lit du grande fleuve religieux de l'humanité.—RENAN.

PART II

THE CREATION OF THE CHRISTIAN RELIGION BY THE INTERPRETATION OF THE PERSON OF CHRIST

INTRODUCTORY

THE questions discussed in the previous part may be stated thus: How did the Synoptists conceive and represent Jesus? and, How did He conceive and interpret Himself? These have been dealt with less as literary and exegetical than as historical questions; i.e. the meaning of the Evangelists has been read through the history they made as well as through the histories they wrote. This does not mean that the definitions and dogmas of the later creeds have been interpreted into the words of Jesus and His biographers; but that the men and their beliefs ought to be construed not simply through their antecedents and environment, but also through the changes and events they occasioned. In other words, our endeavour has been to discover causes as well as to ascertain effects; for the logic which compels us to seek a reasonable cause for nature will not allow us to be satisfied with a non-rational cause in history. The *facts* we have to interpret have proved themselves *factors* of order and progress; and while they have to be explained as facts they must be interpreted as factors.

As regards this inquiry, so far as it has proceeded, three things may here be noted: (*a*) The field of research has been as much as possible restricted to what it is the fashion to call the *Ur-Marcus* and the *Logia*, or the history which is common to all the Synoptists, and the collection of sayings which has been so largely used by two, Matthew and Luke. The discussion has not infrequently, indeed, wandered beyond these sources, but rather for illustrative or confirmatory purposes than for such material as could in any degree affect the course and the validity of the argument. (β) As a consequence of this emphasis on their common matter it has become evident that while the Synoptic Gospels are, as regards literary origin, later than the oldest Epistles, they show remarkably few signs of having been influenced by the Apostolical mind in either the history they narrate or the sayings they report. This is evident in minor matters like terms and incidents as well as in major matters like ideas and speeches. If we would test the truth of this statement, we have only to compare the large place which the Apocalyptic vision fills in the later discourses of Jesus with the small space it occupies in the earliest Apostolical literature. The special matter found in only one Gospel, like the parables peculiar to Luke, stand on a different footing. (γ) The conception of Jesus in the history and in the sayings is a unity. He is the same person in both. His words do not contradict His acts nor His acts His words. The character explicated in the teaching is evolved in the life. This unity of the ideal and the real is most significant. Modern criticism has failed as signally as the old dogmatism to construct a coherent image of the historical Jesus; in its hands He has become after years of labour and effort ever less credible and less possible. The idea that satisfies a consciousness governed by a more or less conventional idea of nature, will almost certainly offend a consciousness governed by the idea of the living continuity of history.

The questions to which we now pass are at once the converse and the logical sequents of those already discussed. What idea had the men who followed Jesus, the Apostles and the Apostolic writers, of His person? How did this idea come to be? In what sense and by what process may it be said to have created the Christian religion? And what were the essential and constitutive elements in the interpretation? These questions bring us directly face to face with the Apostolic literature, especially with those parts of it which represent distinct types of the idea and mark stages in its expression and determination.

We have, then, three main problems to discuss:—

I. The interpretation of Christ's Person, which was the source of the main ideas as to God and man that constituted the Christian faith.

II. The genesis of the interpretation, or how the remarkable idea as to the person of Christ arose, and why it found acceptance?

III. The interpretation of Christ's death, which determined the nature and form of Christian worship.

CHAPTER I

THE PERSON AS INTERPRETED IN THE APOSTOLICAL LITERATURE

IN the synoptic Gospels we have the record of a life distinguished by many miraculous acts, but we have no explicit philosophy of the Person who performed the acts; in the apostolical Epistles we have a doctrine of the Person, but no history of His life. In the former we have the representation of a real individual who lived, suffered, and died, and who, as regards His character, words, and acts, may be criticized and appreciated like any other historical person; in the latter we have this Person regarded *sub specie æternitatis*, interpreted according to His place and function in universal history and as the central term in a theology or system of religious thought. The name of the uninterpreted person, the hero of the spontaneous biographies, is Jesus of Nazareth, but the name of the interpreted person, the Being who exists to thought and for it, is Christ; and these two are as distinct yet as indissolubly related as the mathematical diagram on the blackboard and the mathematical truth in the mind, which is by the diagram made explicit and applied to the interpretation of nature. In other words, Jesus is a symbol which the Epistles explicate for human belief and apply to human experience, individual and collective. The local and transient supernaturalism of the Gospels becomes in their hands a supernaturalism universal and transcendental. But without the local the universal could not have been.

§ I. *Paul and the Pauline Literature*

1. We have already recognized a very significant fact: the literature which defines and determines the doctrine of the Person is older than the literature which tells the story of the life. The oldest Pauline Epistle is divided by little more than twenty years from the death of Jesus; and the latest by a still shorter interval from the Epistle to the Hebrews and the Apocalypse. Within a period which may be thus roughly defined the doctrine of the Person had been elaborated, and, in its main lines, fixed by minds which were at once varied in type and quite distinct in their tendencies. Nor does this fully state the case. The authorship of the Gospels is a pure matter of tradition or of critical inference. We do not know with any degree of certainty by whom, for whom, when or where they were written. But there is nothing more certain in ancient literature than the authorship of the more important of the Pauline Epistles; and we may add that the author himself is better known to us than any other writer in the New Testament, or probably even than any other person in antiquity. There is nothing so perfectly autobiographical as the expression he has given to his thought; or anything so unconsciously characteristic of the writer and descriptive of himself and his world as the literary forms he has employed and the allusions he has made. He has so written his thought as to write history; he has told us what churches he founded, what difficulties he encountered and what differences he provoked; who helped him and who hindered. He has described the morals of the time in language of unparalleled plainness and power; he has shown us the obstinacy of the Jew, the instability of the Gaul, the frivolous and disputatious temper, the intellectual subtlety and ethical obtuseness of the Greek; and the part played by the wandering merchant or mechanic in the intercourse of the peoples, in the distribution of ideas and the diffusion of

religion. He has informed us as to the kind of men that were made into Christians and the sort of Christians they made, the questions they discussed, the discipline they needed and the Churches enforced; the ideals they lived for, and their effect on their lives. He has made us understand the minds of the men who founded the Church, the fears, the jealousies, the tendencies that divided them, the faith and hope that united them and made them better and greater builders than they knew. He has told us how he himself was judged, what he was in appearance, in speech, in writing; how he suffered and what he suffered from; how he persuaded the Jew and the Gentile to live together and to help each other; how his converts and how the men who were "reputed to be somewhat" esteemed him. In a word the questions that lie beneath phrases he lets almost unconsciously fall, carry us right into the heart of the constructive historical criticism of the New Testament.

2. Now let us confess that Paul, as he lives before us in his Epistles, is a man who holds many men within him,— so many indeed that we may describe him as the most unintelligible of men to the analytical reason of a critic who has never warmed to the passion or been moved by the enthusiasm of humanity; but the most intelligible of men to the man who has heard within himself the sound of all the voices that speak in man. He is a Jew, proud of his blood, but ashamed of its hot intolerance; a Pharisee who has studied in the schools till he has learnt their formulæ; a convert who finds in his conversion the meaning of his own and his people's past; a lover of righteousness who fears his own sin; a believer whose will to obey God is crossed and weakened and thwarted by the passion which will lust; a brother who would die for his brethren, yet holds a faith which exposes him to sufferings worse than death at their hands; a kinsman disowned of his own kin, who could not then, and have never since been able to forgive his desertion

of their tribal banner and contempt for their racial vanity, though he has done more than any other son of the fathers to redeem their name from its worst vices, and shed upon it a more beneficent light than streams from the Ghetto or the Exchange. He is a man who despises life, yet endures all things that he may save men from death; a person without sentiment, yet of the most commanding affection, mixing with the most obscure and illiterate, yet speaking to them with the courtesy which ought to be cultivated by the sons of God; a man hated, hunted, persecuted, denied the comforts of home, the cheer and the joy of woman's love, the tenderness and trust of children he could call his own, yet writing the grandest words in praise of love which ever came from human pen; a man who was mean outwardly, yet inwardly endowed with such strength as to lift the solid earth of religious custom, prejudice, and convention from off its axis. He uses a tongue which is in its words Greek but in its most distinctive idioms Hebrew, an inchoate dialect spoken by mixed peoples, which his thought, too massive and molten to be easily articulated, burdens with technical terms, exceptional usages and broken sentences hard to be understood or subdued into grammatical continuity, but which his imagination so charges now and then with splendid images as to lift it into the highest poetry, breathing the hope that neither suffering nor death can shame, the love that is as high as God and vast as eternity. So potent is he that he makes out of the tongue he uses a sacred language, compelling, almost in spite of itself, the religion he has embraced to forget its native speech and speak the Gentile tongue he speaks, that it may be the more quickly communicated and become the more readily intelligible to the civilized world. In him the past of his faith is epitomized and its future is foretold. He starts as a Jew, a zealot in "the Jews' religion," becomes a disciple of the Jesus he had persecuted, an apostle of the Christ he had despised; and he is driven by a logic which is not so much his servant as his master to " preach among the Gentiles " " the faith of which he had once made havoc." [1] And he not only foresaw the end, but he even began to garner the fruits of the land towards which he was leading the Church. Among the last of his words these stand written : " All the saints salute you, especially they that are of Cæsar's household." [2]

Paul, then, is the greatest literary figure in the New Testament ; round him all its burning questions lie. Looked at as an historical question, say certain minor critics, Baur spared too much when he argued that the four great Pauline Epistles were authentic, for they leave all that is most supernatural in Christianity standing in its oldest period and attested by its oldest monuments. They leave also Paul in a position too large for any man, and force us to conceive him to be as large as his position. Hence a strained hypercriticism has of late attempted to reduce to intelligibility one who is not so much a single man as a multitude of men, though the multitude form only a many-sided personal unity ; and so they have analyzed the multitudinous unity into a number of atoms, each in size and shape convenient and comprehensible. And so we have had the Paul of our documents decomposed into three men, (a) the authentic portrait of the " We-sections " in the Acts, (β) the man of the fragments saved from the wreckage of the Epistles, and (γ) the man of the completed Acts, the creation of primitive harmonistic. And then the Epistles have to be so decomposed as to assent, as it were, to the decomposition of their author. But, happily, this criticism is sporadic and incidental ; the main body of critics who are also scholars holding that the authenticity of the greater Pauline Epistles is beyond doubt. And beyond doubt we may hold them to be. There are no writings so little capable of being explained by conscious or unconscious invention, or any trick of the pseudonymous imagination. They are filled

[1] Gal. i. 16, 17. [2] Phil. iv. 22.

by one mind, the personality is one ; so are the speech and the mode of argument. The attitude to friend, to foe, to beliefs held and renounced, to Church and world, to the brothers he had forsaken, to the brethren who had but half welcomed him, to the disciples who would have plucked out their eyes and have given them to him, remains throughout consistently one and the same. This higher consistency is only emphasized by the minor inconsistencies of mood and moment ; for these were certain to come to one who lived so strenuous a life, so changeful in those outward circumstances which most affect a man's heart and imagination, so unchangeable in those tendencies and inner convictions which most govern the mind. We must, therefore, content ourselves with simply affirming the point that there are no questions in ancient literature more certainly determined than the authenticity of the Epistles which first formulated the belief in Christ's supernatural person and their priority to all the written Histories of His life.

§ II. *The Person of Christ in the Pauline Epistles*

Now when we come to compare the Pauline literature with the Synoptic Gospels, we find, as respects the treatment of the Person of Christ, two remarkable points of contrast.

1. The biographical matter of the Epistles is, on the whole, simpler than that of the Gospels. The miracles which play so great a part in the latter have, with one conspicuous exception, no place in the former. Our reason is not perplexed by any narrative of the supernatural birth, or any incident like that of the Gadarene swine ; we do not read of hungry thousands being fed, or of fish being charmed into a net or money extracted from one just caught in the lake ; of this woman being healed of an issue of blood, or of that paralytic man being made whole ; of a widow's son raised from the dead or a buried brother called back from the tomb. In a word, no attempt whatever is made to array

Jesus in the garments of miracle or to make Him live and move in a cycle of wonders. On the contrary, He is set amid a sordid poverty of incident, and lives a life which is more remarkable for its humiliation and feebleness than for its majesty or manifest divinity. He is born of a woman, and born under the law.[1] He springs from Israel, and is, according to the flesh, from the tribe of Judah and the seed of David.[2] He lives in the form of a servant,[3] and is unknown to the princes of this world.[4] He is poor, hated, persecuted, crucified.[5] He is betrayed at night, just after He had instituted the Supper.[6] He dies on the cross, to which He had been fastened with nails, and is buried.[7] There is no attempt to idealize these things, to veil their squalor, or soften their harsher features; rather are they emphasized and magnified as if they added lustre to the Person and were matters in which His admirers found their proudest cause for glorying.

2. But this poverty of outward incident in the life lends all the more significance to the remarkable contrast between the local and particular supernaturalism of the histories and the universal and absolute supernaturalism of those apostolic Epistles which originated so soon after His death. What stands there is a miracle of act and incident; what appears here is a Person so miraculous as to change the whole face of nature and history, and make it as miraculous as Himself.

(*a*) He is so conceived that the race by His presence in it becomes a stupendous organism, with a continuous history, a common life, realized by its units yet incorporated in the laws, customs, and tendencies they all obey. But the life of the race is not simply physical, it is, though absolutely different in quality from His, yet as ethical as He Himself

---

[1] Gal. iv. 4.
[2] Rom. ix. 5; i. 3.
[3] Phil. ii. 7.
[4] 1 Cor. ii. 8.
[5] 2 Cor. viii. 9; Gal. vi. 14; 1 Cor. i. 23-25, ii. 2.
[6] 1 Cor. xi. 23.
[7] 1 Cor. xv. 3, 4; Col. ii. 14.

is; and indicates that man, as regards the constituent elements of his nature, falls under the law which in the case of Jesus made His character of the very essence of His being. And the character He bears is creative and normative; it institutes a type and propagates the type it institutes. While all men have sinned,[1] He alone knows no sin.[2] The sin which all men know entered the world by the first man, and death so came in with sin that the two reign together over mankind; but by Christ came righteousness and through it the life which cancels death.[3] And so over against the sinning Adam and his sinful posterity stands the sinless and quickening Christ with His household of faith.[4] The flesh of man is sinful and mortal, but He assumed flesh that He might condemn sin and create life.[5] While Adam, the first man, was but a "living soul," the second man was "a life-giving Spirit"; while Adam was of the earth, earthy, Christ is of heaven and heavenly.[6] And as He is His shall be. To be joined to Him is to be "one spirit" with Him.[7] To be "in Christ" is to be "a new creature"[8] "conformed to His image,"[9] and "to the body of His glory,"[10] for as "we have borne the image of the earthy, we shall also bear the image of the heavenly."[11] And these "new creatures" are not a multitude of disconnected grains; they are built into an organism and become "one body," "the body of Christ,"[12] the home of His Spirit, the agency by which He accomplishes His will and shows Himself unto men.[13] To be Christ's is to be God's, to enjoy liberty, and to see God face to face.[14] Hence collective man is represented as, apart from Him, alienated from God, sinful and dying because of sin; but

---

[1] Rom. iii. 23.
[2] 2 Cor. v. 21.
[3] Rom. v. 12-21.
[4] 1 Cor. xv. 21, 22; Eph. ii. 19-22.
[5] Rom. viii. 3, 11; 2 Cor. iv. 10, 11.
[6] 1 Cor. xv. 45-49.
[7] 1 Cor. vi. 17.
[8] 2 Cor. v. 17.
[9] Rom. viii. 29.
[10] Phil. iii. 21.
[11] 1 Cor. xv. 49; cf. Eph. ii. 5, 6.
[12] 1 Cor. xii. 12, 27.
[13] Eph. iv. 16, i. 23; Col. ii. 19.
[14] 1 Cor. iii. 23; 2 Cor. iii. 17, 18.

through Him men can be reconciled to God, learn obedience, and be built into a new humanity, exercised in righteousness, and ruled by love.[1] Now this was an idea without any parallel in the history of human belief; so it has the most manifest right to be called a new idea. No one in any prior philosophy or scheme of thought had been conceived as so affecting the notion and life of humanity, so determining its constitution, so defining its character, so giving value to each separate unit, unity to its whole being, community to its interests, and continuity to its history; in other words, as creating by his very being order and coherence in the chaotic and heterogeneous mass of conscious but unconnected atoms which we call mankind.

(β) But this is the least wonderful aspect of this audacious endeavour at the interpretation of an historical individual as a universal, i.e. as an absolutely supernatural and creative personality. For His relation to man has its counterpart and complement in His relation to God. Here the same singular and transcendental qualities are made to distinguish Him. He is to God what no other being has been before Him or can be after Him. He is the Son of God, the firstborn, begotten before all creation.[2] He is the image of the invisible God; He sits at God's right hand; He upholds all things by the word of His power, constitutes all things into order or system; in other words, His cosmical relations are as absolute and creative as His historical are directive and judicial.[3] And His work is one which is worthy of the highest God: it is to create a new humanity and to be its Head.[4] His appearance is no chance or happy accident, but fulfils an eternal purpose.[5] And His coming is His own act, for though rich, it is for our sakes that He became poor,[6]

---

[1] Rom. v. 12–21. [2] Rom. i. 2, viii. 29, 32; cf. Col. i. 15.
[3] Col. i. 15–17; 1 Cor. xv. 24, 25; 2 Cor. v. 10.
Eph. ii. 19–22; Col. i. 18. [5] Eph. i. 4, ii. 9–11.
[6] 2 Cor. viii. 9.

AND IN HIM GOD MANIFESTED

or, to use the graphic phrase of another Pauline text, that He "emptied Himself" (ἑαυτὸν ἐκένωσεν).[1] And so He is conceived, not as one who begins to be, but as one who has ever been and will ever be; He through Whom are all things.[2] The very dignity and prerogatives of Deity are claimed for Him. He is said to be so in the form of God as to be under no need of counting it a prize to be on an equality with God,[3] and does not this mean that to Paul He already possessed the divine nature and majesty? In all things He has the pre-eminence.[4] Even the unity which is the ultimate attribute of Deity is not denied Him. As there is but one God and Father, so there is but one Lord Jesus Christ;[5] in Him are hid all the treasures of wisdom and knowledge;[6] in Him dwells all the fulness of the Godhead bodily,[7] and His love can as little be measured as the love of God,[8] for He is indeed in very truth God's love towards man.

§ III. *The Idea in Hebrews and the Apocalypse*

But the interpretation of the person is not peculiar to the Pauline theology; if it were, it might be regarded as the illusion of a mind intoxicated with metaphysics, or accustomed to the dreamland of an ecstatic mysticism. But the idea, so far from being singular, pervades a whole literature, though all we can do here is to select its most representative types.

1. The Epistle to the Hebrews is not Paul's, but it has many Pauline affinities. It is the work of a man who knew Philo and Alexandria as Paul knew Jerusalem and Gamaliel. Its outlook is less wide and more special; it thinks more of the Jews and less of man. But its philosophy, if narrower,

---

[1] Phil. ii. 7.   [2] 1 Cor. viii. 6.
[3] Phil. ii. 6.   [4] Col. i. 18.
[5] 1 Cor. viii. 6; Eph. iv. 5.   [6] Col. ii. 3.
[7] Col. ii. 9.   [8] Eph. iii. 19.

is more reasoned in its principles and detailed in its application. The rhetorical style, the technical terms, the occasional preciosity of phrase, the love of analogies, the interpretation of history as allegory and of institutions as symbols or parables, speak of the school in which the writer had studied. But the marvellous thing is the way in which the new idea lifts the man above his school, enlarges his outlook, and completes his thought. The Epistle to the Hebrews may be termed the most finished treatise of the Alexandrian philosophy; it grapples more successfully than any other with the problems of nature, mind and history. And it does this in the strength of its new idea: what the person of Christ signifies for God, for man and for religion. On the speculative side it re-interprets God and makes creation intelligible; on the historical, it exalts man and turns his life into a process of growth and education; on the religious, it finds a unity of idea within diversity of form, and it proves faith to be universal and constant, for its object is "the same yesterday, to-day and for ever."[1]

The author was indeed no ear- or eyewitness of the Lord,[2] but he speaks as one familiar with His history on both its brighter and its darker sides. He knew of His descent,[3] of His preaching and the signs and wonders which accompanied it,[4] of the temptations He endured,[5] of the contradiction He had to bear from sinners,[6] of the agony in the garden,[7] of the death upon the cross,[8] of the hill "outside the gate" where He suffered,[9] and of His being raised from the dead.[10] His humanity is real,[11] and He is distinguished by being unblemished,[12] by "godly fear," docility, amenability to discipline;[13] by mercy, grace and fidelity towards men,[14] and by obedience, faith and patience towards God.[15] Jesus is "without

---

[1] xiii. 8.   [2] ii. 3.   [3] vii. 14.   [4] ii. 3, 4.
[5] ii. 18, iv. 15.   [6] xii. 3.   [7] v. 7.   [8] xii. 2.
[9] xiii. 12.   [10] xiii. 20.   [11] ii. 14, 17.   [12] ix. 14.
[13] v. 18.   [14] ii. 17, iv. 15.   [15] iii. 2, v. 8, ii. 13, x. 5–7, xii. 2.

sin";[1] He is "holy, guileless, undefiled, and separated from sinners."[2] The author so speaks of the historical person as to show that his knowledge was equal to his love, and his love of the intensest and most commanding order. And yet without any sense of incongruity, or of intellectual discord, or of rational violence, he speaks of this Jesus as "the Son of God,"[3] and of this Son as the Maker of the worlds, the effulgence of God's glory and the very image of His substance; as the heir of all things, begotten of God, His firstborn, to whom He said, "Thy throne, O God, is for ever and ever."[4] Jesus is indeed described as having been made "a little lower than the angels";[5] but though He becomes partaker of "flesh and blood"[6] He does not cease to be Son or lose His high prerogatives; nay, He becomes this only that He may on a new and higher plane carry out His divine creative and administrative functions. The Mediator of creation becomes "the Mediator of the New Covenant";[7] "the heir of all things" becomes the builder of God's house,[8] and so the architect of an edifice whose material is "living stones" and not dead "things." Hence new titles come to Him: He is "the High Priest of our confession,"[9] and as such He is "without father, without mother, without genealogy, having neither beginning of days nor end of life."[10] As such He is the essence or Spirit of all religious institutions, the Creator of the men of faith and sanctity under the old covenant, the inaugurator who is also the sum and substance of the new. His concealed presence in the old was the reason of its being; His revealed presence in the new is the cause of its life. In Him God and man, eternity and time, creation and history, the ancient and transient religion of sense and the perennial and permanent religion of the Spirit, find their unity. It is a high dream and a

---

[1] iv. 15. [2] vii. 26. [3] v. 5. [4] i. 2–8.
[5] ii. 9.   [6] ii. 14.   [7] xii. 24. [8] iii. 3.
[9] iii. 1. [10] vii. 3.

spacious philosophy, cast perhaps into a form congenial to minds which thought concerning the New Testament in the categories of the Old, but representing truths which the speculative reason has unweariedly felt after without being able to find. And the whole is the spontaneous creation of the new idea as to the person of Christ.

2. The Apocalypse is in form, occasion, standpoint, method, purpose, the very antithesis of both Paul and Hebrews. Under one aspect it is the most Jewish, under another it is the most anti-Judaic writing in the New Testament. It is possessed of the idea that the spiritual Israel is to supersede the Israel of the flesh, and that the new Jerusalem is to displace and supplant the old; but it holds the idea in the face of a recent and most imperious dread. In place of Paul's fear of the Judaizer, of the alarm which the author of Hebrews feels lest his kinsmen should draw back, there has come terror of Rome. The seer has watched the giant awaken from his sleep, and dye his hands in the blood of the saints. And it is not the majesty of Rome that has awakened, but the ferocity of her emperor. And a ferocious man is more terrible than any wild beast, most terrible of all when he sits on a throne which enables him to indulge his lust for blood. It is this fear of the brute who has reigned and is to reign that fills the Apocalypse; but over against it stands the hope that stills terror. Above the masters of the earth sits the King of kings, and He shall compel even the wrath of man to praise Him.[1] He, too, has shed His blood like a martyr.[2] His blood is real, for He is of the tribe of Judah and the house of David.[3] He died, but now He lives for evermore.[4] He redeems and governs the new Israel.[5] He is Alpha and Omega,[6] occupies the throne of God,[7] is worshipped and adored,[8] judges the nations, and is terrible

---

[1] Rev. xvii. 14, xix. 16.   [2] i. 5.   [3] v. 5.
[4] i. 18.   [5] i. 6.   [6] i. 17, 18.   [7] vi. 16.
[8] v. 8–14; cf. vii. 12.

to the kings of the earth.[1] We have so little sympathy with the Apocalyptic spirit, so feel its elaborate visions, its violent ecstasies, recondite metaphors, and mystic numbers to be alien to the modern mind, that we can hardly discover the imagination that penetrates and illumines it. But one thing is obvious: all it has of foresight and permanent worth it owes to its idea of Christ and the place it assigns to Him.

§ IV. *The Idea in the Gospel of John*

But the most significant and picturesque presentation of the idea is to be found in the history ascribed to the Apostle John. The Fourth Gospel seems in form, in style, and in tone a work of lucid and ingenuous simplicity, but in matter and idea it is, speculatively, the most audacious book in the New Testament. It ventures to do what neither Paul nor Hebrews had attempted—to bring the speculative idea of Christ into direct relation with the history of Jesus; yet without this their discussions wanted the touch of reality. For the ideal Christ represents a thesis comparatively easy to expound and defend; but the actual Jesus as the embodiment of the ideal presents a problem infinitely more complex and difficult. To conceive a transcendental ideal which is the unity of Deity and humanity, to seek a prophecy for it in history and a need for it in nature, to find in it the end towards which all religions yearn, and the latent thought which all philosophers have laboured to express—is simply to charge oneself with the elaboration of a system which is none the less intellectual that it is dedicated to a religious purpose. But the Fourth Gospel essays a mightier problem, viz. to connect the person and the history of Jesus, on the one hand, with the inmost being of God, and, on the other, with the course and end of the universe.

1. The idea and purpose of the writer can best be understood through the prologue which introduces the history.[2]

---

[1] ii. 26, 27.   [2] i. 1–18.

He begins at a higher altitude than the ancient seer who saw God "in the beginning" create the world, for he attempts to define the sort of God who created. Eternity was not to him a solitude, nor God a solitary. God had never been alone, for with Him was the Logos, and the Logos was at once God, and "in the beginning face to face with God." (Οὗτος ἦν ἐν ἀρχῇ πρὸς τὸν θεόν.) And He was organ of the Godhead in the work of creation: "all things were made by Him." And the life He gave He possessed; in Him the creation lived, and His life was its light. But this light was confronted by a darkness which would not be overcome, though it was not possible that the Logos should consent to have His light overcome of the darkness. In brief but pregnant phrases the author describes the method and means which the Logos used in this supreme conflict. His relation to the creation never ceased; at every point and every moment He was active within it. In this way he stood distinguished from the prophet or preacher, who had his most recent type in the Baptist. John was a man sent from God for an occasion; before it he had no being, after it he had no function; his sole duty was to be a witness, to testify concerning the Light "in order that all men through him might believe." Over against this ephemeral witness-bearer, who appears, lives his brief day, does his little work, and then departs, stands the true, the Eternal Light. He shines for ever and everywhere; illumines all men, even though they be held to be heathen. With threefold emphasis the idea is repeated: "He was in the world," did not enter or come to be within it, but abode in it, was as old as it, is as young as it, unaffected by birth, untouched by death. He was, and had always been, for "the world was made by Him"; Man—no selected people simply, but collective Man—was made by Him, and how could He desert the work of His own hands? But it had deserted Him: "the world knew Him not." The peoples loved the darkness and knew not the Light. Even those who claimed to be the elect were blind. " He came unto His own, and His own received Him not." The children of the covenant, the heirs of the promise, had been no better than the heathen : the Logos who lived and worked in their midst they did not know. But in one respect they had greater excellence : sight was granted to some, a remnant saw and believed, and He of His grace gave them the right to " become children of God." And this adoption came not of blood or descent or act of man ; it was " of God." It was a vain boast to say, " We have Abraham to our father " ; the only title to divine sonship came of divine grace. And now there arrived the supreme moment in human experience : the Logos, who was Creator and uncreated Light, who had never ceased to be related to all men or to be without His own even among the Jews, " He became flesh." The phrase is peculiar ; he does not say, as in the case of John, ἐγένετο ἄνθρωπος ἀπεσταλμένος παρὰ θεοῦ, " there came a man sent from God " ; but he says, ὁ λόγος σὰρξ ἐγένετο, "the Word became flesh." There is no break in this continuity; it is the same Word who was with God, who was God, who made the worlds, who was the true Light, who shone in the darkness, who continued to shine among the heathen, who visited His own, and graciously made those who believed sons of God, who now becomes flesh. And what He becomes (σάρξ) emphasizes the visible mortal man, man not in contrast to animal, but in antithesis to God, the invisible, eternal, impalpable Deity. Paul loved to express the sacrifice or renunciation of the Son—" though rich, yet for our sakes He became poor," " though in the form of God He emptied Himself " ; but John here expresses the unity of the Being within the difference of the acts and relations. He who did all these high things is the self-same Logos, as He who now becomes flesh. And in this form, in contrast to His previous invisible though illuminative universality, He dwells among men, lives face to face with them even as in the beginning He had been with God. But lest the intellectual term Logos should be resolved into an abstraction or mere figure of speech, a significant change is made in the terms employed. "The Word become flesh" is described as "only-begotten from the Father," the bearer of "grace and truth" to men. And as such He is identified with Jesus Christ. And this marvellous conception is finally explained and justified by a principle of widest reach: "No man hath seen God at any time; the only-begotten Son which is in the bosom of the Father, He hath declared Him." This principle we may paraphrase and explain thus: "Monotheism has failed because men have found the invisible to be an inaccessible God; they feel after Him, and want to handle Him; but one who is simply the negation of all their experience they can neither conceive nor believe. And so He has stooped to their need, and has sent out from His own bosom, clothed in palpable flesh and blood, His only-begotten Son, that He might declare Him, make Him actual, visible, tangible to the dwellers in the world of sense." That was the principle the gospel was to illustrate; whether it has been confuted or confounded by collective experience, is a matter of too common knowledge to need to be here discussed.

2. But the remarkable thing in the gospel is not so much the Prologue as the History which it introduces, and by which it is explicated. Analytical criticism has much to say as to the Hellenic and Hellenistic sources of the terms and ideas which the Evangelist makes use of. Λόγος is one of the dark terms we owe to Heraclitus; from him it passed into the school of the Stoics, and was there stamped with their image and superscription. In the Hellenism of Alexandria it played a great part, and was made by Philo a mediator between God and the universe, with a vast variety of names and functions: He conceived it now as abstract, now as personal; described it now as archangel, now as archetype; here as the *Idea idearum* which is ever with God, there as "the

everlasting law of the eternal God, which is the most stable and secure support of the universe." Philo's logos is now the image of God, now His eldest or firstborn Son, and again the organ by which He made the world. Here God is light, and the Word its archetype and example ; and there God is life, while all who live irrationally (ἀλόγως) are separated from the life which is in Him. It is not to be doubted, then, that John neither invented his transcendental terms nor the ideas they expressed. But he did a more daring and original thing—he brought them out of the clouds into the market-place, incorporated, personalized, individuated them. He distinctly saw what the man who had coined the terms had been dimly feeling after—that a solitary Deity was an impotent abstraction, without life, without love, void of thought, incapable of movement, and divorced from all reality. But his vision passed through the region of speculation, and discovered the Person who realized his ideal. Logos he translated by Son, and in doing so he did two things—revolutionized the conception of God, and changed an abstract and purely metaphysical idea into a concrete and intensely ethical person. And then he made this person take flesh and become a visible God ; but with the most singular audacity he restricted this incarnation to a single individual whom he identified with Jesus of Nazareth, and then straightway proceeded to tell His history. And he told it simply, directly, as one who was only concerned to place on record things he himself had seen. It is significant that he does not descend from his transcendental to his historical idea, but, conversely, he rises from the historical to the transcendental. It is because he has heard with his ears, seen with his eyes, handled with his hands that he knows the Word of Life.[1] The thing he most fears is the denial that Jesus Christ has come in the flesh.[2] The personal name Jesus is the one he most loves to use ; and His human qualities—sympathy, tenderness, simplicity,

[1] 1 John i. 1.   [2] 1 John ii. 18, iv. 2, 3.

courtesy, friendliness, love—are those he most emphasizes. He likes to think of Him as "Jesus Christ the righteous," sinless, yet our example, who constrains us to purify ourselves even as He is pure.[1] The Fourth is, indeed, the most human of all the Gospels, whose hero is the veritable Son of Man.[2]

Yet within the biography John skilfully enshrined his transcendental idea. The Person was to him a symbol as well as a fact, His history was at once allegorical and real. His purpose is expressed in one of his most distinctive terms, "true" ($\alpha\lambda\eta\theta\iota\nu\acute{o}s$), "true light," "true worshipper," "true Bread," "He that sent Me is true"; "My judgment is true," "I am the true vine," "the only true God." The term denotes not simply the true as opposed to the false, but the real as opposed to the apparent, the original as distinct from the derived, the genuine in contrast to the counterfeit. And these antitheses help to define each other, and to make the history articulate the author's thought. Hence he sees Jesus not merely as a man, or historical person, but as a form under which the eternal ideal has been so realized as to turn the scenes and shapes around Him into shadows that now hide, now outline, and now counterfeit the reality. Thus the supreme need of the created order is, because of its ignorance and evil, reconciliation with the Creator; and this reconciliation is conceived as coming through the light which illumines, the life which quickens, the love which saves. And these are incarnate in Jesus. The Word who became flesh is as it were the tabernacle of a universal religion; in Him God came to men, and men met God, and the glory which they beheld was His very visible presence.[3] As the one real place of meeting He is the ladder which connects heaven and earth, keeping open God's way down to man, man's way up to God.[4] He is the genuine temple, which men will seek to destroy,

---

[1] 1 John ii. 1, iii. 3–7. [2] Ante, p. 326.
[3] i. 14. [4] i. 51.

AND TRUE TABERNACLE OF RELIGION

but He will reconstruct;[1] and over against Him stands the local temple, which is the shadow of the real and universal, good if taken as a type, but bad if regarded as sufficient in itself, and still worse if conceived as a final and abiding reality. And as He is the true Temple, He is also the true Sacrifice—" the Lamb of God which taketh away the sins of the world."[2] Other sacrifices are of man's providing and offering; He alone is of God. And so from Him comes life, through Him streams light; the light is the shadow of His truth, the life the fruit of His death.[3] And He who is at once the true temple and the true sacrifice is also the true Priest, the Mediator through whom the "righteous Father" reaches the world, and the sinful man finds his way to God.[4] The priests around Him are, like their temple and sacrifices, shadows—good if they speak of another, but bad exceedingly if they attempt to become the very form and being of the Eternal, and seek to suppress the manifested God as if He were the semblance and they the supreme reality. And so the Fourth Gospel may be termed a tragic parable narrated of God and His universe under the form of an actual transaction in time and space. There has come within the experience of man the most transcendent of all mysteries: the mind of God is translated into his speech, the life of God assumes his shape; and in a history which is all the more terribly real that it is so supremely ideal we see the characters, relations, and behaviours of God and man explicated by being realized.

[1] ii. 19-21. [2] i. 29.
[3] iii. 16-21; x. 7-18; viii. 12. [4] xvii. 25.

CHAPTER II

THE GENESIS OF THE IDEA

§ I. *The Idea and the Apostolic Literature*

THE idea of the person of Christ may, at this point, be best described as an idea generative of a whole literature. Without it the Apostles would have remained silent, mere craftsmen of the lake, the workshop or the school; but from it there came an impulse which drove them into speech. And the speech into which they were driven was an attempt not simply to portray a person but to articulate a system of religious thought. If it had not been for two reasons which, though they look like contraries, are yet essentially complementary, its religious significance and its want of literary distinction, the New Testament would have seemed to us the greatest speculative achievement of antiquity, all the more extraordinary that its authors were men unversed in literature and philosophy, without any knowledge of the problems with which human thought had wrestled or any of the argumentative skill which comes from long discipline in the dialectical art. By a sort of divination, the intuition which a new faith can create in the most simple, the apostolic men saw ideas which the most gifted minds had wished to see but had not seen:—The unity of God so realized in a universal religion as to unite all the families of men; the unity of man in blood and spirit, in source and destiny, the reign in him of a natural law which was good, and of inherited tendencies which were evil; the dream of a development which conceived the race as a magnified individual and the individual as an epitomized race, each repeating the stages of growth and the process of education marked and observed by the other; the vision of a sovereignty that never ceased to govern in nature and history, the eternal power and Godhead of the Sovereign being clearly seen through the things that are made, and His beneficence shown in never selecting men and nations for their own sakes alone, but only as agents for the common good; the idea of a humanity of the Spirit, a household of the elect, created by faith in the Eternal and creating obedience to His ends; the conception of a person who is an embodied moral law, with this to distinguish Him from all ethical standards man had ever imagined, that He not only humanized duty but supplied the motive that determined its fulfilment; the notion of this same person, who is the sum of mankind as also the image of God, accomplishing in a moment of colossal existence for all mankind what the election of grace had been attempting to do for each successive generation; the belief that the God who had made all men was so good that He could not be alienated by evil from the men He had made, but suffered on account of their sin and saved them by His suffering; the conviction that all men were amenable to this God, that they must appear before Him, see His awfulness, hear His judgment, and share His immortality, so that His eternity embosomed and enlarged their hour of mortal being and gave to it and to them a dignity almost divine—these, and a multitude more of cognate ideas, all too immense and too novel to be at once appreciated, or even understood, entered the world through the men who attempted to interpret for us the person of Christ; and because of this attempted interpretation, the intellectual system they created was not so much the child of the old world as the mother of the new. It formed the mind which disintegrated the ancient order and organized another on the lines and in the forms we conceive as specifically modern. The source to which the ideas that distinguish society as it now is from society as it once was can be traced back, is a source which has an indefeasible claim to eminence in reason as well as in religion. It were but an idle fancy were we to ask what would have happened had this idea fallen into the hands of Plato and Aristotle rather than into those of John and Paul; only this much is certain, it would have done even more for them and their immortality than they could have achieved for it. If Plato would have clothed it in a pomp of diction more congruous to its innate grandeur, if Aristotle would have analyzed it with infinite subtlety and explained it with incomparable lucidity, it on its side would have enabled the one to delineate a richer, a more humane, and a more practicable society than he has imagined, and the other to define a higher good and find a more potent and palpable ethical motive than he was able to discover. But the absence of the sage and the scholar from its exponents enables us the better to see that the very incompetence of the men it inspired to do justice to the idea exalts its meaning and its power. They by their own art could have done nothing for it; it by its native majesty did everything for them.

But is not this to assume the very issue in dispute, whether they were or were not equal to its production? If they were, there is no question : if they were not, whence did the idea come? Whose was the beneficent hand that started it on its creative career?

§ II. *Whether Paul was the Father of the Idea*

1. The really significant fact for our discussion is this: While the idea receives what many think its most finished expression in the latest of the apostolical writings, it yet appears in a form quite as transcendental in the earliest and most authentic of them. With it these writings are concerned from first to last; and any differences in detail, in the connexion in which it stands or the purposes to which it is

put, and the tendencies that determine these things, only accentuate this fundamental agreement. Now, it is evident that since the idea is articulated in our oldest authorities, which are the great Pauline Epistles, our present enquiry must begin with their author, and we must ask, whether there is in his temper, mind, or history anything that could be regarded as adequate to its causation. One thing is indeed remarkable, the rational sobriety of the writer. If intellectual sanity marked the miraculous narratives of the Gospels, it distinguishes in a still higher degree the Pauline dialectic. It may be impassioned, here and there too sharply antithetical in style, and its sequences may now and then be difficult to follow; but no argument could be more rigorous, no thinking more under the command of reason and logic or more free from the extravagances of the visionary, or the tendency which marks the fanatic, to confuse the imagined with the real, the ephemeral with the permanent. Now it is a question of more than common interest: By what process did Paul come to conceive and formulate his idea of Christ? What was its psychological source? and in what terms may we describe the factors of its origin? The subjective sources, the personal roots, the biographical and historical causes of the Pauline theology, are matters that in recent years have been minutely and curiously investigated. (i.) It has been argued, on the basis of certain narratives and phrases of his own, that he was a man of nervous temperament, prone to see visions and dream dreams; that he was a subject of epilepsy, which was his thorn in the flesh, the messenger of Satan that buffeted him. What he thought a sore burden and sorrow was the very source of his inspiration; whence came, on the one hand, his vision of Christ, his belief in Him, in His death for sin, in His resurrection and session at the right hand of God; and, on the other, his doctrine of the flesh, of the natural man, and of the body of death. (ii.) It has been argued that his personal history as a Pharisee who believed in the law, convinced him of the weakness of the law he believed in. It imperiously commanded "Thou shalt not covet"[1]—the point is significant—but did nothing for the suppression of covetousness; and the union in it of the imperious and the powerless made it seem that most intolerable of all dead things—an authority that could not be obeyed yet would not be denied. (iii.) It has been argued, on the one side, that he came to his views suddenly and completely, that by what we may call intuition and he called revelation[2] he saw them at once and saw them whole; and, on the other, that he grew into them, taught by experience, by controversy, by seeing how they affected the minds of men in many lands, by the way in which he himself was regarded, and his preaching was handled here by Jews, there by Apostles, in this church by Judaizers, and in that city by Greeks and Barbarians. (iv.) It has further been argued that his idea of Christ expressed the belief that his new life was God's work in him, effected by one he could not conceive as less than God's own Son; and that his theology was his theory as to his own conversion objectified, articulated, made into a system of the universe. Now these may all be interesting speculations, but what impresses one is their inadequacy as causes to produce the facts they would explain. The man is too large to have himself and his beliefs cast in a single mould, or shaped by a single circumstance, or resolved by a disabling constitutional peculiarity which may explain a mood, but cannot explain a history and a character maintained in consistency for a generation amid distracting labours and controversies. Historical and literary criticism has need to sit at the feet of science and learn the lesson that nothing can be accepted either as the sole cause or as the adequate reason for an event which cannot explain either it or its effects.

Paul, then, seems too wide and too complex a person to

[1] Rom. vii. 7. [2] Gal. i. 16.

be reduced to the terms of a single process in a simple and prosaic psychology; and his thought is as manifold as his personality. If we doubt this, we have but to review the attempts which have been made so to analyze the constitutive or structural elements of his mind and theology as to discover their sources. (i.) It has been argued that he remained as he was born and bred and educated, a Jew, especially in his attitude to the Old Testament; but this fails to account for the remarkable fact that, while he used it in argument and as evidence, as he used the light of nature in reason and in conscience, and the lessons of observation and experience, yet he did not find in it the cause of his salvation or seek in it the law of his life. (ii.) The theology of the synagogue has been pressed into the service of explaining his method, his cardinal terms, his forensic ideas, his eschatology and angelology; but this theory is urged in curious oversight of the facts that the synagogue was his most inveterate enemy and that his most enthusiastic disciples were those least distinguished by the Jewish mind or learning. (iii.) The Apocalyptic literature has been made to contribute to the formation of his thought; but its contributions have been illustrative of single points, and these so little distinctively Pauline as to be mainly in epistles of doubtful authenticity. (iv.) It is remembered that he was a son of the Diaspora, and the influence of Hellenism has been traced in his mind. Philo and his school have explained his love of allegory and the allegorical interpretation of events and persons in Old Testament history;[1] but this touches only an outer fringe of method and style, not the substance and structure of his thought. As a child of Israel in exile he must have known Greek life, and in a measure Greek thought, in a degree which the older scholarship—which mainly studied his classical quotations—utterly failed to recognize; and so we have had exhaustive analyses of the ideas and terms and

[1] Cf. Gal. iv. 21–31; 1 Cor. x. 4.

even usages he may have owed to the mysteries; the ethical impulse and teaching that may have come from the Stoics; the Hellenic outlook on life and thought which may have come from his birth and upbringing in a Greek city; the ideas of law, the feeling for liberty, the sense of dignity that may have come to him from his Roman citizenship; and the conception of a universal church which he may have acquired through his experience as a traveller within the Roman Empire. But what does this quest after sources, which turn out to be only outer and partial influences, mean? That the man was large enough to have found room in his nature for all they could bring to him; but that he was too strongly and too distinctly himself to be capable of explanation either by any single influence in particular or by all the suggested influences combined. His personality has to be reckoned with before their action can be understood.

2. As to the whole subject, then, we may say this: while it is not easy to over-estimate the interest of these questions, it is very easy to over-emphasize their worth. The psychological theory which helps us to understand the tendencies which predispose him to believe may do nothing whatever to explain the cause and ground of his beliefs, their intrinsic rationality, their intellectual coherence and cogency, their value to man and their function in his history; and yet it is by these tests that they must be finally judged. Looking, however, at what we may call its natural history, we may note that there were factors which made for the belief as well as against it.

(*a*) There are those which concern the man himself; and here we have to recognize forces which were distinctly hostile. It is extraordinary indeed that a doctrine of such stupendous novelty arose on such a soil in so short a period through such a man; and so tenaciously rooted itself in a mind that was by tradition, inherited prejudice, education or the want of it, so little qualified for its inception or its reception. What is evident is this: the man who elaborated the doctrine was a man who had been trained in Jewish schools, educated in the Jewish Law, and so bred that the passion of the Jew for monotheism and against any intermixture of God with man was woven into the very texture of his thought and speech. He had therefore no natural or acquired predisposition to the belief, though, indeed, he never conceived that by embracing the new he had been false to the old. On the contrary he believed that his monotheistic faith was clarified, enlarged, and preserved more effectually by his doctrine as to Christ than by any form it had yet assumed or any agency that had hitherto worked on its behalf. Faith accomplished that which the law had been intended to do but had failed to achieve—made the God of the Jews the God of the whole earth. He had then a most exalted idea of God, and a most intense abhorrence of the notion that there could be more gods than one. The idea of Christ prevailed only because he conceived that through Him the one God was made the only God of universal man.

But (β) there were certain forces in his mind and circumstances that were prophetic of change. Thus his very passion for the law of his God tended to estrange him from the law of his people; for the people's law demanded an obedience which it could not empower the will to render. It asked so much and gave so little that it filled the man in the very degree of his conscientiousness with doubt and despair. But what the law could not do Jesus as the Christ had done; the power the law withheld He had imparted. And it was this sense of the power which lived in Him that found expression in Paul's theology; and it was an expression which did not proceed from ignorance of what Jesus had been, but was rooted in the fullest knowledge as to the life He had lived and the death He had died. Paul says that he had known "Christ after the flesh,"[1] which does not mean that he had

[1] 2 Cor. v. 16.

had personal intercourse with Jesus while He lived, but it means that he had taken the same external or ceremonial view of the Messiah as the Jews had done, i.e. he had conceived Him as a sort of impersonated ritual rather than as the Spirit that quickened. Yet though he does not say that he had known Jesus in the flesh, we may infer that he had had opportunities for such knowledge. He must have been in Jerusalem, if not at the crucifixion, yet immediately after it. He must have heard in the school of Gamaliel the stories connected with the betrayal and the crucifixion. He must thus have come to know Jesus, not through the fond affection of the disciple or the admiration of the man who had believed and loved, but through the criticism of the man that doubted, the prejudices of the man that despised, the hatred of the man who had persecuted. And, as he himself tells[1] us, he had acted towards the Church as one whose knowledge was of this cruel and distorted kind. But in the very struggle to obey the law which commanded him to trouble and waste the Church, he discovered two things, (*a*) its ethical or spiritual impotence, i.e. its power to forbid but its inability to inspire with the spirit that obeyed; and (β) the potency of Jesus, as shown in the men he persecuted, to command obedience and to inspire with the love that was willing for His sake to endure the loss of all things and even of life itself. And this discovery involved a change of relation to Jesus, and therefore a changed attitude to the law. He saw that Jesus had introduced a new kind of obedience, a new ideal of righteousness, a new mode of finding acceptance with God, and that He had, by redeeming man from the curse of the law, achieved his salvation.

This may represent in an approximate degree the psychological process by which Paul came to his view as to Jesus being the Christ. As such it may have real biographical value, and even much critical significance; but it fails to

[1] Gal. i. 13, 14.

explain the only four things worth explaining; viz., (i.) how he came to conceive Jesus not simply as the Messiah, but as the Son of God, not officially or figuratively, but essentially, i.e. as Himself divine; (ii.) how it happened that a theory which had so arisen could so profoundly modify the man's whole conception of the universe, and take such possession of his intellectual nature; (iii.) how it could create the religion that has been the most important factor in the higher history and better life of the race; and (iv.) how it was that the idea was not peculiar to Paul but common to the apostolical society as a whole, including those men from whom he is conceived to have differed so widely and so strenuously.

§ III. *Whether the Idea is the Product of a Mythical Process*

While, then, it may be needful to recognize how much the experience and the peculiar psychology of Paul helped to create his attitude of reverence to the person of Jesus, yet we must also recognize how little they can explain either the genesis or the form of his idea. But there is an older and more radical hypothesis as to its rise, what used to be called the mythical theory. The change from mythology to psychology is significant of the new historical method; but the change is more formal than real. The one attempts to get at the subjective cause of what the other studied as a more or less objective process. Historical psychology is an analysis of the personal source, whether morbid or normal, of the ideas or beliefs which, when woven into a system or a history, constitute a mythology.

1. The theory of a mythical and imaginative origin for the idea may be stated thus: The death of Jesus was a complete surprise and disillusionment to His disciples. They had believed Him to be the victorious and immortal Messiah; they found Him to be a frail and mortal man; and in the first

shock of the discovery they forsook Him and fled from their own past beliefs. But these beliefs were not so easily renounced; they had begotten hopes too precious to be abandoned even at the bidding of fate; they were endeared by affections too tender to die in the presence of disaster. And so while experience tempted the disciples to acquiescence in the accomplished, which was but the end that Nature has in store for all, the imagination and the heart pleaded for another and more splendid issue. If the death was not to extinguish Jesus, He must be made to transfigure it, and change it into something quite other than the lot common to mortal men. This was the supreme achievement and victory of faith, which could not cease to regard Jesus as the Messiah, but could do a sublimer thing—invest Him and His death with eternal significance. The vision that created the belief in the resurrection made this transfiguration possible; yet the one was a harder and slower process than the other. All at once, as is the way of visions, the resurrection became a credited fact, which the visionaries on every possible occasion affirmed that they themselves had witnessed; but the death had come in an inexplicable, accidental, violent mode. So the one was conceived as God's action, but the other as man's. God had raised Him from the dead, but it was by wicked hands that He had been "taken, crucified, and slain."[1] The Jews had "killed the Prince of Life," demanding His death even when Pilate "was determined to let Him go."[2] But this crude theory could not long endure, for if "wicked hands" could prevail once, why not again and finally? So a second stage is marked by the acceptance of the customary Jewish explanation of the detested inevitable —it was the Will of God. While Herod and Pontius Pilate, the people of Rome and of Israel had appeared to act, the real Actor had been God; they only did what the hand and counsel of God had determined before to be done.[3]

[1] Acts i. 23. [2] Ib. iii. 13-15. [3] Ib. iv. 27, 28.

But this position had too little reason in it to satisfy the imaginative intellect of the young society. It read with new eyes the Old Testament, found that Isaiah's servant of God was a sufferer for human sin, and all his attributes and experiences were forthwith ascribed to Jesus.[1] As this sufferer was "led like a lamb to the slaughter," so Jesus became "the Lamb of God," with all the sacrificial ideas of Judaism aggregated round His person and His death. The process once begun, needed for its completion only a constructive genius, and instead of one such, three soon appeared: Paul, who argued that Jesus as the crucified Christ was both the fulfilment and the abolition of the law; the author of the Epistle to the Hebrews, who made Jesus and His sufferings the antitype which had their type in the elaborate ritual and worship of the old economy; and John, who found in the person, history, and death of our Lord the means by which the world was illumined and redeemed. And so by a perfectly natural, yet purely mythical and imaginative process, His death was transfigured from the last calamity of a blameless life to the act of grace by which God saved the world.

But this theory, however ingenious and plausible, has three great defects: it lacks proof, it is intrinsically improbable, and it fails to explain the facts. (i.) Its proofs are drawn from sources which its advocates have in other connexions, and for what they deemed adequate reasons, discredited. It is not open to the same criticism to prove by analysis at one time the early speeches in the Acts to be late compositions, and at another to use them as authentic evidence for the oldest Christian beliefs. And here the most primitive tradition is specially explicit. When Paul states that it pleased God to reveal His Son in me,[2] and that he preached "first of all that which also I received, how that Christ died for our sins, according to the Scriptures,"[3] he can only mean that at the moment of his conversion the belief had been not simply

[1] Acts viii. 30-35. [2] Gal. i. 16. [3] 1 Cor. xv. 3.

formulated, but elaborated into a system in harmony with the Old Testament. (ii.) As to the intrinsic improbabilities, we have to consider both the men and the theory; it was a belief of stupendous originality; they were persons of no intellectual attainments and small inventive faculty. So far as the Gospels enable us to judge, they were curiously deficient in imagination, and of timid understanding. They were remarkable for their inability to draw obvious conclusions, to transcend the commonplace, and comprehend the unfamiliar, or find a rational reason for the extraordinary. Such men might dream dreams and see visions, but to invent an absolutely novel intellectual conception which was to change man's view of all things Divine and human, was surely a feat beyond them. (iii.) And the improbabilities involve the inadequacy of the theory; it makes Christ, with all He has accomplished, not simply the creation of accident, but it also turns the beliefs and the religion which have so governed the course of history into phantoms of the rude and sensuous imagination.

2. But the mythical theory as here applied offends against certain of the laws which govern human development. It will be enough if three of these be here noticed.

(*a*) The concrete and historical, or the imaginative and the mythical stage of thought, in both the personal and the collective life, precedes the abstract and the speculative, or the dialectical and logical. In every society, as in every person, the order or succession of mental states is this: the imaginaation which loves the personal is active and creative earlier than the reason which loves the metaphysical. When mind is fresh and passion strong and the light of love looks through the eyes upon wonders the sobered understanding can never see, the mythical fancy has its creative hour, and weaves for its hero a history which corresponds to its own mood rather than to his achievements. But when experience has subdued emotion and damped the heats of youth, thought awakens, asks for reasons, and begins to speculate about the forms and shadows which looked so beautiful and so substantial in the vision the fancy made. Criticism, in its impulsive and wayward youth, learned this law from philosophy, and, assuming the Gospels to be the oldest documents, analyzed them as works of the mythical imagination, which had, out of a few mean facts, unconsciously created all their pomp of miracle and mystery. But it was soon discovered that the oldest Christian literature was not history but philosophy,—speculation as to Christ, not narrative concerning Jesus. While miracles, as single acts, have in this dialectical literature, if we may so name it, no place, yet in their stead, filling the whole space, stands a person so miraculous that in His presence the most miraculous narratives are subdued to tame prose. There was no doubt imagination in the dialectic, for simply from the point of view of its marvellous vision backward into history, forward into the future with its infinite possibilities of good, upward into the mysteries we denote by the term Godhead or God, and downward into the nature which we name man,—so compounded of the divine and the demoniac, yet so continually riven asunder by their strife—the speculative structure we owe to Paul stands for its imaginative qualities foremost among the dialectical creations of the world. But this only adds to the significance of the fact here emphasized: brief as is the period which divided the oldest Pauline Epistles from the death of Jesus, there has yet grown up in the interval not a mythological but an intellectual system,—the conception of a Person who is at once the interpreter of God and the interpretation of man, the centre of the finely articulated system which has drawn into its diamond network the whole order of history and all the forces which work for or against the good which is its end. And this conception cannot be explained as due to a blind mythical impulse acted on by a reminiscent and regretful love, which sought compensation for the loss of the loved by the eminence of its imaginative creations; for the man who formulates and articulates it did not know Jesus, and so was without the ardour of personal love and the sense of personal loss.

(β) A second law regulative of the formation and interpretation of mythical material is this: Since speculation is later than history, it is the historical incident or event that it most loves to construe. Mythology is the unconscious poetry of nature and history; while philosophy is the attempt of the conscious reason to translate the products of the unconscious imagination into rational theory. But what is peculiar in this case is that the dialectical explication is concerned with the Person and not with the history. It would not have been so extraordinary if the dialectical construction had begun after the lapse of a century or more, i.e., when His figure had grown nebulous and the exaggerative fancy had played its wizard tricks with His memory. Without the exuberant mythology which hides Buddha so completely from the eye of the historical inquirer, the Buddhist schools would have been deprived of the material out of which they have woven their wonderful metaphysical dreams. Without the Persian mind and imagination, looking through a medium of glorifying legend at the figure which had moved across the Arabian desert some generations before, we should never have had those mystic speculations as to the prophet, his word and family and heirs, which go so far to redeem Islam from bondage to the letter that killeth. Not till men had ceased to believe that Greek mythology was true, or that the Greek gods could be what it said they were, did they attempt its speculative interpretation; and ask, whether it was misunderstood history or hidden wisdom, natural science or moral truth disguised in allegory. But here, before the myth has had time to rise, or the legend to become current or the imagination to transmute base metal into fine gold, the speculative change has been not simply begun but accomplished. In other words, it is not Jesus in His environment of miracle who is interpreted, but it is the Person in His specially historical and religious, ethical and intellectual, significance. The idea seeks to represent and explicate Himself, not His acts and the incidents of His career.

(γ) The third law we wish to note is this: between the speculative construction and the soil on which it grows there must be close and intimate agreement. But in this case the remarkable thing is that the plant seems so totally alien to the soil on which it sprouted and grew. While Paul is an intensely Jewish thinker, and uses forms of thought, figures of speech, and methods of interpretation which he must have learned in the Jewish schools, the idea which he elaborates is the very contradiction of what he must there have been trained to believe. Our first impulse, when we come to understand the doctrine of the Person, is to seek for hints or intimations of it in the Old Testament, and these have been, both by apologetic and exegetical theology, most deftly and exhaustively handled. But the idea has no real parallel in the Jewish Scriptures, for they may be said never to have transcended the notion that God and man formed an absolute antithesis. The affinities of the idea appear rather to be with Greek religion. Indeed, were we writing of a process which that religion recognizes, we might describe it as one of apotheosis. But the term is inapplicable here for two reasons:

(i.) The process happens under a religion which knew nothing of gods who begot men or men who became gods. It was a monotheism, and the man who first shows us the completed process not only never at any moment abandoned in the smallest degree this faith, but he became by the change he effected in its terms its most victorious expositor and missionary. Indeed, it is one of the most remarkable facts in this most curious history—and were we dealing with an abstract question we should call the position an incredible paradox—that the idea of the Son of God who was equal with God, though it seemed most seriously to threaten the divine unity, has yet been the supreme means of its conservation. And this relation to the idea of one God makes the Christian incarnation a belief at once singular and original. In Greece apotheosis meant for both gods and men such a community of origin and such a communicability of nature and status, that the process of descent from the gods or ascent into their society was in the strictest sense natural and normal. But in Israel eternity was the attribute of God and mortality of man, and so, because of the distinction in their natures, Deity could not be communicated to man or humanity to God. And as a curious but instructive fact this difference was not so much reduced as emphasized by the place accorded to Christ.

(ii.) He is not conceived as the subject of a deificatory process—indeed, both term and idea would have been abhorrent to the apostolic writers, who thought that God was as incapable of change as of any beginning of being. Hence they would not have described as divine any one they did not believe to be essentially God; and so they never represent Christ as attaining Deity or achieving a rank which He had not known before. This makes their idea a contrast rather than a parallel to those transmutations of gods into men and men into gods so common in the Greek, the Latin, and the Hindu mythologies.

§ IV. *The Historical Source of the Idea*

1. The idea seems thus to be too speculative and too original to be explained by a theory which places the imagination before the reason, postulates as already existing the forms to be used, and requires for their growth into organic unity a congenial soil and a suitable environment. How, then, are we to conceive the genesis of this common and

creative idea of the New Testament, this constitutive and regulative idea of the Church? Its source must have been one acknowledged and revered by all tendencies and all parties, for only so can their agreement in this and their difference in other respects be understood. And this source could be but one: the mind of Christ. His teaching can explain the rise, the forms, and the contents of the Apostolic literature, but this literature could never explain how His teaching came to be. Postulate His mind, and we may derive from it the Apostolic thought; but postulate this thought, and we could never deduce from it His mind and history. In other words, He is the historical antecedent and the logical premiss of the Epistles, and it is open to no intellectual strategy to invert or change their relations. In His teaching lie principles they develop, but also elements they miss or misconceive. Yet it is exactly as regards His person that the connexion is most close and consistent, the development most precise and logical. He speaks of Himself as the Son who alone knows and alone can reveal the Father; and to this idea Paul traces His conversion, in it Hebrews finds the constitutive truth of the Christian religion,[1] Peter the quality by which the Christian Deity may best be defined,[2] the Apocalypse the image that makes the Head of the Church most sovereign,[3] and John the name he most loves to use.[4] Jesus speaks of the Messiah as Son of David,[5] so does Paul.[6] "The Son of Man" of the Gospels appears nowhere in the Epistles, but its interpretative equivalents "the second Adam" and "the second man," are determinative of the Pauline thought.[7] The best commentary on the claim that He had come to fulfil the law and the prophets is Hebrews; the most impressive representations of His functions as Redeemer and Judge are to be found in the

---

[1] i. 1.   [2] i. 2, 3.   [3] ii. 18.
[4] 1 John i. 3; iv. 9, 14, 15.   [5] Mark xii. 35–37.
[6] Rom. i. 3.   [7] 1 Cor. xv. 45–47.

Apocalypse. It has been argued that there are differences between His and the Apostolic idea; of course there are, but these are notes more of continuity and independence than of contradiction and isolation. Wendt argues[1] that the conception of the personal and heavenly pre-existence distinguishes the Pauline idea from Christ's; and Gloatz[2] well replies to him that this can be maintained only by one who excludes all reference to the discourses in John and places the most prosaic interpretation on some of the most characteristic Synoptic sayings. If, then, we view the idea as the creation of Jesus Himself, the expression of His own consciousness touching His own being, the Apostolic literature, thought and life may be explained; but if we seek for it some alien and accidental source, bewilderment—literary, historical and biographical—will be the sure result.

2. We have yet to show how the idea as to the Person of Christ created the Christian religion. It is enough that we repeat here, that that religion is not built upon faith in Jesus of Nazareth, but upon the belief that He was the Christ, the Son of the living God. Without this belief the religion could have had no existence; the moment it lived the religion began to be. And the process of interpretation was a creative process; every stage in the evolution of the thought marked a stage in the realization of the religion. In the synoptic Gospels, we have what may be termed the personal and subjective religion of Jesus, i.e. the modes under which He conceived His relation to God and fulfilled His duties towards man; but had they stood alone, we should have had only one picture the more of the ideal man, a Being to admire and imitate, not to worship and obey. In the apostolical Epistles the Person is interpreted in relation to the religion, and as the interpretation proceeds

---

[1] *Die Lehre des Paulus verglichen mit der Lehre Jesu*, p. 45.
[2] "Zur Vergleichung der Lehre des Paulus mit der Jesu." *Stud. u. Krit.* 1895, pp. 778 and 792–794.

the religion becomes more clearly defined, distinct in quality, real in character, absolute in authority. We see it become, first, different from Judaism, next independent of it, then absorbent of all that was permanent in it as well as in other religions, and, finally, when Christ is conceived in His divine dignity and pre-eminence, the religion appears as the alone true, as universal in its unity as the one God in His sole sovereignty. In the Fourth Gospel a final step is taken: this interpreted Person is made the key at once to the history of Jesus and to the purposes and the ends of God alike in creation and in redemption. By this means what was actual and personal is wedded to what is ideal and universal, and each is seen to have been a necessary factor of the concrete result. Without the historical Person the ideal would never have existed; but without the ideal the historical would never have been the source of a universal religion. The historical Person may be described as the primordial and creative or parent form. He defined the religion as essentially ethical, by exhibiting the type of man and character it was intended to realize. Men were to be as He was—sons of God; as gracious and beneficent, as blameless and gentle, as faithful and brotherly towards men; and as reverent and lowly, as pure and obedient, as sinless and holy, towards God. And the religion was to live and grow in the manner He instituted—by making disciples, by creating, through the methods of fellowship and friendship, out of the evil and the neglected, the publicans and the sinners, a society of the like-minded—men who loved God supremely, and their neighbours as themselves. Without the historical Person we should never have known what the religion ought to be, the sort of man it conceived as acceptable to God, the kind of worship it wished to cultivate, the mode in which it proposed to change the old order, and the new society it desired to form. He thus, as it were, determined the quality and inner essence of His religion, fixing for ever its special character and peculiar type. But if the historical Person had stood alone, i.e. if He had been conceived and regarded as a common man, though a man of rare dignity and a teacher of pre-eminent power, we might have had a school, a sect, or a philosophy, but we could not have had a religion. What made the religion was the significance His Person had for thought, the way in which it lived to faith, the mode in which it interpreted to reason God and the universe, man and history. It was this that saved the disciples from becoming the sect of the Nazarenes, and made them into the Catholic Church. It is by virtue of this idea that we have the Christian religion, and that it has lived and reigned from the moment of its birth till now.

3. But this analysis of the historical relations existing between the idea of Christ's person and the creation of the Christian religion has introduced us to a region at once of speculation and criticism. It is not enough to see that in the period of formation every change in the idea of the Person was attended by a parallel modification or transformation in the religion; it is necessary that we inquire whether the idea be in itself essential to religion, whether it has behaved in it like an arbitrary creation of religious emotion, or like a doctrine that is all the more rational to human thought that it so speaks concerning the mysteries of God. We confess, indeed, that the person of Christ is a stupendous miracle, in the proper sense the sole miracle of time. In it the mystery of being is epitomized and externalized. For there is no problem raised by the incarnation which is not raised in an acuter and less soluble form by creation, whether considered as an event in time or as an existence in space. If creation be an event or process, it is something which had a beginning, and in however remote a past the beginning may be placed, yet behind it stands a silent eternity; and though reason may ask for ever what was before the creative process began, what caused it to begin, and when was the beginning, it will for ever ask in vain. Again, if creation be conceived as being in space, then it is from its

very nature existence within bounds ; but how can the same space hold at once bounded and boundless Being ? How can any Being be boundless if once He be confronted by the bounded ? Can there be any room in a universe that knows the finite for the Infinite ? Does not limited existence, so far forth as real, cancel the very possibility of the unlimited ? In short, there is no problem raised by the idea of God manifest in the flesh as to the relation of the divine nature to the human in the unity of one person, or as to the historical origin of such a relation, i.e. its beginning in time ; or as to the action of the limited manhood on the illimitable Godhood, which is not equally raised by the inter-relations of God and nature. For in a perfectly real sense creation is incarnation ; nature is the body of the infinite Spirit, the organism which the divine thought has articulated and filled with the breath of life. But while the problems are analogous, the factors which promise solution are more potent in the case of the incarnation than of creation. For in nature the idea of God demands for its expression no more than physical and logical categories, but in Christ the categories become rational, ethical, emotional, i.e. they involve personal qualities and relations rather than mere cosmical modes and energies. And so, by investing God with a higher degree of reality and higher qualities of being, it makes all His attributes and relations more actual, all His actions and ways more intelligible and real.

CHAPTER III

THE DEATH OF CHRIST AND CHRISTIAN WORSHIP

THE new beliefs created by the interpretation of the person constituted the Christian religion on its ideal side; but to become actual it needed a worship, or the means of expressing and cultivating reverence and of inculcating piety and obedience. Worship is a function at once individual and social, not possible in the individual without the influences that make men devout, or in society without agencies that organize and control. The relation which the ideal and the institutional or consuetudinary elements in a religion sustain to each other, has been already indicated [1]; and we only need to add here that the very law which compels the idea to express itself in the institution and the institution to justify itself by means of the idea, forces upon them a policy of mutual adjustment. Neither can healthily separate from the other. The reasoned idea without the worship is theology; the worship without any reasoned idea is superstition; but the two in wholesome and corporate union make religion. What theology is to the speculative reason, worship is to the popular consciousness, a form under which deity is conceived and described. Each is a language which articulates some governing religious idea; and of these two languages worship, as the more frankly symbolical, addresses the imagination through several senses at once, and is, therefore, the less capable of being contradicted, while also the less sensitive to

[1] Ante, pp. 202–203, 238–240.

criticism. Its acts and observances may from constant repetition grow as stale as any common task, yet even where most stale they can lift the susceptible man out of and above himself till he feels as if he and God had joined hands and stood face to face. If indeed God be conceived to stand but a few degrees above man—and this never happens without bringing Him in some respects several degrees below him—the worship will easily fulfil its function, though it will signify little when fulfilled; but the higher and purer the conception of God is, the more difficult and the more necessary the worship becomes. For while it enables religion to overcome the incapacities of human nature, and by incorporating its ideals in persons to bring about their realization in society and history; yet it involves as a dangerous possibility that the observance or the custom may prove stronger than the idea. And if it does, God will be lowered rather than man uplifted. Speculation may refine thought, but this matters little if God be coarsened and debased by the means taken to approach and please Him. And in the long run worship is more powerful than speculation, for while the one may entertain the reason of the few, the other by its appeal to the imagination of the many commands the conscience and regulates the life.

§ I. *Christ as Idea and as Institution*

1. Now this is the point at which the founders of the Christian religion performed their most original and creative act. They so made a person into an institution, a mode and way of worship which at once exalted God and dignified man, as to make the religion incapable of being localized. They acted without conscious design, but in obedience to an instinct or experience which governed their thought; and their action changed the event which threatened their faith with extinction into the condition of its immortality. There is no other religion which has a crucified or slain person as the sole and suf-

ficient medium through which God approaches man and man approaches God. This surprised ancient as it has perplexed modern thought, but, considered simply as a matter of fact, without the Cross the religion could not have been. Christ is in the apostolical records conceived as a Saviour who saves by the sacrifice of Himself, as "the Lamb of God," without blemish and without spot, " slain from the foundation of the world," yet offered at the end of the ages that He might redeem men by His precious blood.[1] "He is our passover sacrificed for us,"[2] "whom God set forth as a propitiatory" (person), in order that He might "be just and the justifier of him who is of the faith of Jesus."[3] This mode of conceiving His death is so integral alike to the history and thought of the New Testament as to deserve to be termed its organizing idea, but it is so singular as to be without any parallel in the ideas and customs either of those natural religions which make most of sacrifice,[4] or of those which we are accustomed to compare as historical with the Christian. Thus to Israel Moses was a lawgiver who commanded and threatened, exacting obedience by the hope of reward or the fear of punishment, but he was never conceived as one who "appeared to put away sin by the sacrifice of himself." Confucius is a sage whose authority is based on his wisdom, or his power in revealing to persons and states the secret of a happy life; but death, whether his own or another's, is to him too great a mystery to be understood; the wise man can only sit dumb before it. Mohammed is a prophet who denounces hell to the disobedient

---

[1] John i. 29; Rev. xiii. 8; 1 Peter i. 19; Heb. ix. 26.
[2] 1 Cor. v. 7.   [3] Rom. iii. 25, 26.
[4] This is not the place to examine Dr. Frazer's learned and ingenious argument to the contrary. (*Golden Bough*, 2nd ed. vol. iii. pp. 186 ff.) His discussion of this subject seems to me a conspicuous example of conscientious but uncritical learning. He mistakes coincidence in things accidental for contact and causation in things essential, and forgets that there is nothing so easy as to prove the former, but nothing, when it has been proved, so entirely insignificant as regards the latter.

and promises heaven to the faithful; but he is more distinguished by the will to inflict suffering than by the heart to endure it, even where it may bring good to others. Buddha is the nearest approach to Christ; he makes the great renunciation, surrendering regal might and right and wealth for poverty and humiliation, and he makes an end of the ritual, the sacrifices, the priesthood, and the various deities of Brahmanism. For this reason his people revere him, love him, and seek to follow in his footsteps. But here the similarities are superficial, while the differences are radical. (i.) Buddha is a pessimist; he does not love life, for to him being is suffering, and his desire is to escape from sorrow by escaping from existence. But Christ is never a pessimist; His very passion is the expression of a splendid optimism, the belief that existence is so good that it ought not to be lost but held fast and rescued, and that when purged from the accident of sin it will become altogether lovely, a thing to be wholly desired. (ii.) Buddha is a leader, a man to be followed and imitated; what he did men must do that they may partake of his illumination and enter into his rest. But what Christ does no other person can do. He offers Himself a Sacrifice that He may win eternal redemption for men. (iii.) Buddha is an Indian ascetic, whose highest work is to break the bonds of life and all the forces which make for its continuance and for the social perfecting of the race. But Christ is in the strict sense a Redeemer and a Sacrifice, one whose sorrow is curative, who restores our nature to personal and social health, that it may attain individual and collective happiness, personal and general immortality. (iv.) The basis of Buddha's salvation is a metaphysical nihilism. In a world without God and immortality, but crowded with men of teachable moral natures, redemption is not difficult, instruction can accomplish it, the meditation which found the way can be followed until the goal is reached. But in a world where God cannot cease to be pure and man cannot will himself out of existence, to make the guilty man fit to be reconciled with the pure and eternal God is a work which may well cause suffering to the holiest and most blessed Being. The world which Christ redeems is one of infinite reality, man being in his own degree as real as God. The Passion, then, has a singular character and unique worth; it stands alone, without any parallel in the other religions of history. Why it holds the place it does, and what it does in that place, are the questions we have now to discuss.

2. What here concerns us, then, is not the doctrine as to the death of Christ, but its function in the Christian religion. How doctrine and function differ yet coincide we may see as we proceed; but at present we note that any critical discussion as to the process which made His death the basis of our redemption, usually starts with Paul and the need he felt to resolve the antithesis presented by the fact of the Cross to his idea of the Messiah. Now this procedure is for two reasons unhistorical: (i.) Paul tells us that he did not invent the belief, but found it in possession.[1] (ii.) Jesus was the historical source of the idea;[2] though experience and history were needed to make His meaning plain. The apostolical experience was a kind of educational dialectic, and its environment was like a school where the intellect was exercised by means of theses and antitheses. The school had, as it were, two departments or sides, the sacerdotal and rabbinical, or a school for priests and a school for scribes. The home of the one was the Temple, the home of the other was the Synagogue. Both were religious, though in a totally different sense: in the one case the religion was more personal, more rooted in conviction, concerned with thought and the government of life; in the other case the religion was more collective, consisted more in ritual and the regulation of worship, the acts which expressed it and the persons who were its celebrants. Both schools were

---

[1] Ante, p. 469. [2] Ante, pp. 395-431, cf. 475.

concerned with Deity, though under distinct aspects and in contrasted relations. The God who occupied the Temple was an object of worship; the God who was studied in the Synagogue was the Giver of the law. The law had indeed created both the Temple and the Synagogue, but the law did not mean to the two Schools exactly the same thing. To the one it signified the Levitical legislation, which had instituted the priesthood, organized and regulated its ministry, described and sanctioned its sacrifices; to the other it signified the ethical precepts and the ceremonial customs which gave to the State its theocratic character and to the individual the rules which governed his conduct. These two schools appear in the apostolical writings, and their very different tempers are represented by the sects described in the historical books. Thus in Hebrews the term has its distinctly Levitical meaning : " the law appointed men high priests " ;[1] priests " offer gifts according to the law " ;[2] " according to the law all things are cleansed with blood,"[3] and its sacrifices are " a shadow of good things to come."[4] But in Paul, though the term has an almost indescribable variety of meanings, yet its prevailing sense is the rabbinical, the law is the commandment which enjoins or forbids, which says " Thou shalt do this " or " Thou shalt not do that," promising reward to the obedient, threatening punishment to the transgressor.[5] Now both these types or schools of thought and policy affected in the way of antithesis the Christian synthesis ; Christ appears in contrast to the one as the eternal Priest and Sacrifice, and to the other as the Redeemer of man from the law which killed, and the Bringer of the Grace which gave life. And it is because He so appears that we can say that the function which apostolic thought assigns to His death can be better described as an institution than as a doctrine.

[1] vii. 28.   [2] viii. 4.   [3] xi. 22.   [4] xi.
[5] Cf. Rom. ii. 12, 17-27 ; vii. 7, 12, *et passim.*

§ II. *The Levitical Legislation and the Christian Idea*

1. The position here may be thus stated: Christ took the place in the new religion which the Temple had held in the old, and as a single Sacrifice and eternal Priest He superseded the multitudinous sacrifices and priests who had stood and mediated between God and Man. The substitution was a revolution, for the Temple was not a mere incident or aspect of the religion, but the symbol of man's whole conscious and expressed relation to the Deity. It typified, therefore, (i.) the presence and accessibility of God, His abode among His people, His desire to commune with them, to speak to them and to hear their speech. (ii.) The duty of His people to worship Him. He was their God and they were His people, and their right to the Temple meant their freedom of access to Him. (iii.) This limitation involved on their part a double relation to Him, a collective and a personal. The collective was primary, for the man must be of Israel before he could worship Israel's God; but the personal, though secondary, was essential, for the man who was an Israelite knew God and was known of Him. (iv.) The worship prescribed was such as became the character of God and expressed the state of man. The character of God was holy, the state of man was sinful, and the worship was designed to reconcile the holy God to the sinful man. (v.) Since man was sinful he could not come directly into the presence of the Holy, but needed a representative to stand before the Lord and speak in his name and on his behalf; hence came the priest. And since he had sins to confess and be forgiven as well as favours to ask or acknowledge, he could not allow the priest to enter the Divine presence empty-handed, but supplied him with the blood of atonement drawn from the sacrificial victim, or with the gifts which his gratitude prompted. (vi.) The stability of the Temple and the continuance of the worship signified that the intercourse was

constant. The people obeyed God's voice, and He heard their prayers.

2. The Temple, then, stood for an ideal of worship regulated by the law, whose seat was not the Synagogue or school, but the national sanctuary; whose ministers were not Scribes or rabbis, but priests and Levites; whose acts were not reading and preaching, but sacrificing and sprinkling of blood. It signified a legislation not so much recorded in books as incorporated in a living order. The Synagogue was provincial and sectarian, but the Temple was metropolitan and collective; the one spoke of difference, but the other was sacred to the unities of family and faith. In the Synagogue a man might be a Latin or a Greek, a Cilician or an Alexandrian, a pupil of Hillel or of Shammai; but in the Temple he knew himself to be a son of Abraham, an Israelite, who believed Jehovah alone to be God and who observed the customs of the fathers. Dispersion might occasion an enlarged use of the Synagogue, but it also increased the significance and the fascination of the Temple. The motherland is to the imagination of the colonist transfigured by a romance which the eye accustomed to the hard realities of the life within it does not see; and so he who dwelt far from Zion idealized the holy place, as he did not who sat in its lengthening shadow and watched the jealousies and plottings of its sons. It is almost certain that the man who wrote the Epistle to the Hebrews and the men who received it were all the more under the spell of the ideal that they knew so little of the actual Temple and its ways. But to all, whether near or remote, it was the living heart of the religion, an epitome of the people and their history. No other appeal to the present was so irresistible because none so perfectly embodied the past. In its earliest and simplest form, as the tabernacle which went with the fathers through the wilderness led them into the promised land, and helped them to build their cities and their state, it spoke of the God who had called them out

of Egypt, chosen them out of all the nations of the earth to be the people of His covenant and His grace. And when the kings came David felt it a reproach that he should dwell in a house of cedar, "while God still dwelt within curtains";[1] and so his ambition was to be found worthy to build Him a house. This though denied to David was granted to Solomon, whose wisdom designed, whose power erected, whose wealth adorned the first and stateliest temple. In the most glorious of all prophetic visions Isaiah had beheld it filled with the train of the Lord; in the most pathetic of all prophetic histories Jeremiah had described the anarchy and desolation in which it and the state alike perished. Yet towards the Temple the Exiles in Babylon did not cease to turn tearful and longing eyes, and Ezekiel had pictured it springing anew from its ashes in splendid yet measured proportions, and opening its courts to resurgent and restored Israel.[2] They came back a peeled[3] and suffering remnant, who built the house of God amid poverty and in the face of dangers unspeakable, yet cheered by the visions of the later Isaiah and the mighty music of his speech; and so they crowned the second Temple with a glory which the first had never known. What began in weakness lived in power, and gathered to it the sublimest memories of the people. Within it the Levitical legislation and ritual were realized; its courts had been built and its sacrifices were offered according to the law; psalms written in praise of God and for His service were sung in its worship; it was the symbol of His name, the seat of His visible presence, the home where He showed Himself to His people, conversed with them, and proved Himself to be their God. Its priests were sons of Aaron, who still seemed fragrant with the oil that had consecrated

---

[1] 2 Sam. vii. 2.   [2] Ante, pp. 251–253.
[3] Isaiah xviii. 2, 7, A.V.; cf. Milton, *P.R.* iv. 136. Speaking of the Romans "who conquered well but governed ill," "Peeling their provinces, exhausted all by lust and rapine."

him, and who, all the more that they were vowed to God, had played the part of heroes and taught the people how to win freedom by braving battle and enduring death. The Temple thus made an irresistible appeal to the imagination ; the Jew, wherever he lived or whatever language he spoke, ceased the moment he stood within it to feel as if he were an alien, and became consciously one of God's elect, who could speak to God and hear God speaking to him. Without it or otherwise than through it he could not think of his religion, and without his religion where were the Jew ? Even when the Temple had fallen, he could not believe that it had perished ; for the priestly race survived, and so long as it did not die the hope lived that Israel would yet praise God in the midst of the holy city.

3. Now the Apostles were Jews who thought in the manner of their race, yet as regards the Temple and its worship they had been forced to think otherwise than their race thought. Experience had made them conscious of the contradiction between its actual state and its ideal significance. They knew that it was the priests and not the Pharisees who had crucified Jesus ; that up to the entry into Jerusalem the latter had been His chief opponents, but from then onwards the former had become His irreconcilable antagonists ; and that while the rabbis had argued, the priests, who were a ruling as well as a sacred caste, had acted, and acted, as rulers will, with more regard for order than for right. It was in the court of the high priest that counsel was taken against Jesus.[1] He is betrayed to " the chief priests." [2] They send the multitude who seize Him.[3] He is conducted to the palace of the high priest,[4] where He is tried and declared guilty of blasphemy.[5] "The chief priests" bind Him, deliver Him up to Pilate, accuse Him,

---

[1] Matt. xxvi. 3, 4.   [2] Matt. xxvi. 15 ; Luke xxii. 4.
[3] Matt. xxvi. 47 ; Mark xix. 43 ; Luke xxii. 50.
[4] Matt. xxvi. 57 ; John xviii. 24.   [5] Mark xiv. 63 ; Matt. xxvi. 65.

demand His death,[1] and extort it from the hesitating governor.[2] They stiffen the purpose of Pilate by raising the cry, "Crucify Him,"[3] and wish the cynical inscription "The King of the Jews" changed to the personal charge, "He said 'I am the King of the Jews'";[4] and while He is in agony they mock His impotence.[5] And they dealt with the disciples as they had dealt with Him. The "priests and the captain of the temple" are sore troubled because the Apostles preach Jesus.[6] The judges of Peter and John, on account of "the good deed done to the impotent man," are Annas and Caiaphas and "the kindred of the high priest."[7] It is the same persons who, being "filled with jealousy, laid hands on the Apostles, and put them in public ward,"[8] and who charge them "not to teach in this Name."[9] While the priests seem to increase in vigilant severity [10] the Pharisees seem to become dubious, hesitant, double-minded, like men who temporize in action because they halt in thought.[11] In the Synagogue, where the Pharisees reigned, the Apostles were allowed not only to sit but to speak and dispute;[12] but in the Temple, which the priests controlled, they were not permitted to worship, Paul's attempt to do so provoking the riot that led to his imprisonment and the appeal to Caesar.[13] Exclusion from it was thus the sign and seal of their alienation from Israel, and forced upon them the questions, Why had it been built? What was its function and purpose? The question raised by the conflict of the local cult with the universal idea was as old as the prophets of Israel,

---

[1] Mark xvi. 5 ; Matt. xxvii. 1, 2, 11–14 ; Luke xxiii. 1–3.
[2] Luke xxiii. 13–19.   [3] John xix. 6.   [4] John xix. 21.
[5] Mark xv. 31.   [6] Acts iv. 1, 2.   [7] Acts iv. 5, 6, 23.
[8] Acts v. 17, 18.   [9] Acts v. 28.
[10] Cf. vii. 1 ; ix. 1 ; xiii. 2 ; xxiv. 1.
[11] Cf. the attitude of Gamaliel (Acts v. 34–39) and the conduct of the Pharisees at the trial of Paul (xxiii. 6, 7).
[12] Acts ix. 20 ; xiii. 5, 14, 15 ; xiv. 1 ; xvii. 17 ; xviii. 4, 26.
[13] Acts xxi. 26–30.

and as new as the sect of the Essenes, who forsook the Temple and cultivated piety in separateness and seclusion. Men of a Hellenistic temper, like Josephus, explained it as a mirror of the universe, while Philo found in it an allegory concerning the things sensible and things intelligible which made up his whole of being. Ideas of this order were not unknown to the earliest converts; we see them struggling with the Christian problem in the mind of Stephen. He conceives the Temple as alien to monotheism;[1] the universal God cannot be confined to a single place, the Builder of Nature to a house built by human hands. But though logic may prove that it is possible to worship anywhere a God who is everywhere, yet there are deeper questions than any exercise in dialectics can solve. Are not the people more than the place? Are all men equally fit and free to worship? Do sin and guilt matter nothing to Deity? As He has no respect of persons is He also without respect for character? Are there no terms to be observed, no obstacles on man's part which call for a priest or other mediator? These questions the Hellenistic speech of Stephen did not touch, nor did the early Apostles think that they had any connexion with the person and death of Christ. In his earliest discourses Peter speaks of Jesus as having been crucified " by the hands of lawless men,"[2] who had " killed the Prince of Life,"[3] and " set themselves against the Lord and His Anointed,"[4] " whom also they slew, hanging Him on a tree."[5] In curious forgetfulness of what he had been taught he seems to have conceived the cross as the symbol of victorious evil, which was only defeated by the raising of Christ from the dead. But light came from an unexpected quarter; the Ethiopian Eunuch put a question which effected the orientation of the Apostolic mind: did the prophet describe himself or some other as a sheep led to the slaughter?[6] In

---

[1] Acts vi. 14; vii. 46–50. [2] ii. 23. [3] iii. 14.
[4] iv. 21, 22. [5] x. 39. [6] viii. 30–35.

this there was a fine fitness; prophecy had created and organized the Hebrew Temple, preached the idea that made it necessary, declared against the local cults, urged the creation of a central sanctuary where the elect people could collectively meet the holy God, and offer Him a cleanlier and seemlier worship. But time had demonstrated how easy it was for an institution founded for the worship of God to supersede the God in whose honour it had been founded, to impose upon Him its own limitations, and invoke His authority to sanction and to sanctify its sins. And now the spirit of prophecy, reincarnated, substituted a person for a positive institution, a worship which knew no place and no sacred caste, for a worship which was bound to a special race and its peculiar customs.

§ III. *The Levitical Categories interpret the Christian Idea*

1. Apostolic thought starts, then, from a positive belief, "Christ died for our sins," and proceeds to construe this "according to the Scriptures." If the books we now call the Old Testament had then canonical existence, they yet had not a uniform authority. The Sadducean priests believed strongly in the Levitical legislation, which they termed the law of Moses, for it was the charter of their privileges, the basis of their rights; and their usage affected the apostolical literature, though with significant differences. Thus Paul never uses the terms priest or priesthood, but in Hebrews they occur thirty times. Paul speaks rarely, if at all, of sacrifices in the Levitical sense, but in Hebrews this sense was fundamental. The sacrificial idea was indeed too germane to the Pauline mode of thought to be entirely ignored.[1] And so he says, "For our passover has been sacrificed, even

[1] A. Ritschl (*Rechfertigung u. Versöhnung*, ii. pp. 161–163) argues against Richard Schmidt that Paul construes the death of Christ through the Old Testament idea of sacrifice. But he forgets that there are

Christ"; [1] but two things are here significant, (a) the passover was older than the Levitical system and independent of its priesthood; and (β) it was above anything in Judaism suggestive of the last supper and the passion.[2] Still it is used here to enforce a duty and not to define a doctrine. Since the lamb is already slain, the old leaven ought to be cast out, the house of the soul purged from its sin. A second illustrative usage occurs in Ephesians: "Even as Christ gave Himself for us, an offering and a sacrifice to God for an odour of sweet smell."[3] He here enjoins a love like Christ's by inviting consideration of His sacrifice. But the comparison was probably more literary than ritual in its origin; he was thinking of the sacrifices God delighted in rather than of those the priest loved to offer.[4] But one famous Pauline text owes its importance to what we may term a Levitical category: "Whom God set forth (as) propitiatory through faith in His blood."[5] There are here two sacrificial terms, (a) $\iota\lambda\alpha\sigma\tau\eta\rho\iota\rho\nu$ = "propitiatory," and (β) $\dot{\epsilon}\nu\ \tau\hat{\omega}\ \alpha\dot{\upsilon}\tau o\hat{\upsilon}\ \alpha\ddot{\iota}\mu\alpha\tau\iota$ = "in His blood." As to (a) the term is difficult whether taken according to its classical or its Hellenistic usage, and it is not easy to determine its sense exegetically. For reasons impossible to enumerate it is here regarded as an adjective qualifying ὅν, "whom," i.e. Christ Jesus. He is set forth as a propitiatory person, one able to perform the things the verse goes on to describe. As to (β) the phrase is characteristically Pauline, and occurs in contexts which emphasize its sacrificial quality.[6] The

many views of sacrifice in the Old Testament. With the Levitical view, properly so called, no writer had less affinity than Paul, and no one was less influenced by it; but it would be hard to overestimate the influence exercised on his mind by the suffering servant of God in the later Isaiah. For a severe and not quite fair criticism of Ritschl, see Seeberg, *Der Tod Christi*, pp. 201-203.

[1] 1 Cor. v. 8.   [2] Ante, p. 423.   [3] Eph. v. 2.
[4] Cf. Ps. xl. 6; Heb. x. 5, 6.   [5] Rom. iii. 25.
[6] Rom. v. 9; 1 Cor. x. 16; Col. i. 20; Eph. i. 7; ii. 13.

stress laid on it being "His" is manifestly intended to differentiate it from the blood of beasts, whether of the paschal lamb or the Levitical animals. If, then, these terms be so understood, what does the sentence taken as a whole affirm? (i.) That the person of Christ as propitiatory is a means by which guilty man can be reconciled to the righteous God. (ii.) That it owes this character to the express and public act of God, who of His own will and from His own initiative, unmoved by anything which man had done, set forth for all eyes to see this propitiatory person. (iii.) To this public act of God there is needed a responsive and correlative act of man—"through faith." This, too, is characteristically Pauline; for he is most mystical when most doctrinal. Where God wills and man believes the two coalesce in a unity which yet dissolves the personality of neither. (iv.) The aspect under which faith sees the propitiatory person is sacrificial—"in His blood." (v.) While the person and the death had a history in time His propitiatory quality is as timeless as the act of God, i.e. it explains why He passed over "the sins done aforetime," and "demonstrates His righteousness in the present," proving Him for all time to be "just while the justifier of him who is of faith in Jesus." We may say, then, that Paul in this text conceived Christ as having fulfilled for all time, by the gracious act of God, all the functions which the Levitical legislation proposed to perform for Israel. His person was an institution erected by the will of God, with whom the initiative remains, for the saving of man. In Christ, then, the elaborate mechanism of the priestly worship is done away; faith sees the inner purpose and the outer ways of God as God Himself knows them, and the justified man lives in love and peace with the just God.

2. But it is in the Epistle to the Hebrews that we find the Levitical categories most exhaustively used. Christ is there conceived as at once priest and sacrifice, in each case

in the later and liturgical rather than the older and domestic sense. The priest is defined as a mediator designated of man and called of God, "that he may offer both gifts and sacrifices for sins."[1] The two ideas stand, therefore, together: no priest without a sacrifice, and the sacrifice ever is as the priest is. Hence he is the determinative idea; if he is changed, the law or religion is also changed.[2] But in the twofold aspect of his office correlative ethical qualities are involved: towards men he ought to exercise a measured sympathy ($\mu\epsilon\tau\rho\iota\sigma\pi\alpha\theta\epsilon\hat{\iota}\nu$ $\delta\nu\nu\acute{a}\mu\epsilon\nu\sigma\varsigma$), and before God he must stand purged from sin.[3] Now in these respects Christ was qualified pre-eminently for the high priesthood. He was "without sin," and in eternity God said to Him: "Thou art My Son, this day have I begotten Thee."[4] While by origin, nature, and rank, He stood before men the image and representative of God,[5] yet He so partook of flesh and blood, and was so made in all things like unto His brethren, as to be able to stand in their name before God.[6] And He was qualified in character as well as in nature, being so "touched with a feeling of our infirmities," as to be able to succour the tempted.[7] Hence both the vocation of God and the designation of man were His.[8]

But how could Jesus, who was of Judah and not of Levi, the priestly race which alone, according to the law, could offer sacrifices in the Temple, be in any proper sense a high priest?[9] Here the writer boldly transcends the Levitical categories, in order that he may prove the old covenant to be provisional and transient, while the new is final and permanent. And he does this by an argument which has an instructive parallel in Paul. The latter says the promise is the older, the law is the younger, and it was introduced not as an end in itself, but as a means towards the end con-

---

[1] v. 1, 4.   [2] vii. 12.   [3] v. 2; vii. 27.
[4] iv. 15; v. 5.   [5] i. 2, 3.   [6] ii. 14, 17.
[7] iv. 15; ii. 8; vii. 26. [8] v. 5; vii. 28.   [9] vii. 14.

tained in the promise.¹ The promise therefore can never be superseded by the law, and comes to life again in the gospel. The writer of Hebrews uses personal names, but he intends the same thing. There was an older priesthood, one independent of the descent and succession which were of the essence of Aaron's, viz. Melchizedek's, "who abideth a priest continually."² His office did not owe its being to any father or mother, or its continuance to any child, for it was constituted by the vocation of God, and had neither beginning of days nor end of life. So the Levitical objection to a priesthood unauthorized and contrary to the law is anticipated and answered thus: "I do not claim for Christ an Aaronic priesthood,—that were but to affirm that He was made 'after the law of a carnal commandment'; but I do claim that He belongs to an older, a higher, and a more unchangeable order, made 'after the power of an endless life.'³ And He was so made by the act of God, who said unto Him: 'Thou art a priest for ever after the order of Melchizedek.'⁴ The superiority of this order to yours is manifest; for did not the lower priest do homage to the higher when Levi in Abraham paid tithes to Melchizedek?⁵ The old priests were instituted 'without oath'; but to Christ 'the Lord sware and will not repent Himself, Thou art a priest for ever.'⁶ In the old order there was a multitude, ever issuing from birth, ever devoured by death; in the new order there is but one, who 'abideth for ever.'⁷ He, as sinless, has no need like the old high priests 'to offer up sacrifices for His own sins'; nor is He like them a man 'having infirmity,' but He is 'the Son perfected for evermore.'"⁸

The comparison which has thus become a fundamental contrast is not simply personal and official but also ob-

---

¹ Gal. iii. 17-19.   ² vi. 20; vii. 1-3.   ³ vii. 16.
⁴ v. 6; vii. 17.   ⁵ vii. 4-10.   ⁶ vii. 21.
⁷ vii. 23, 24.   ⁸ v. 3; vii. 26-28.

jective, relates to the system or religion as well as to the priesthood. The note of time is stamped upon the Levitical institution; eternity and immutability are the attributes of Christ, who is "the same yesterday, to-day, and for ever."[1] He has "become the surety of a better covenant,"[2] while that which has been "groweth old and waxeth aged and nigh to vanishing away."[3] He "is able to save to the uttermost them that draw nigh unto God through Him";[4] but though the old priest stood day by day ministering, he offered sacrifices "which could never take away sins."[5] And it is at this point, where the objective comparison becomes most acute as a contrast, that the argument as to the abolition of the old by the new covenant becomes most emphatic and conclusive. The law had a multitude of sacrifices, the new faith has but one; yet its one is of infinitely more worth than all the multitude offered under the law.[6] They were bulls and goats and calves, and though repeated without ceasing they yet gave God no pleasure, nor did they cleanse the man's conscience, or qualify him to serve God.[7] But Christ's sacrifice, which He offered "once for all," was Himself;[8] the very reason of His coming in the flesh was that He might offer Himself to God, whose will He delighted to do, and who was weary of "whole burnt offerings and sacrifices for sin."[9]

3. The transmuting of the priest into the sacrifice without losing the identity and the reality of either—on the contrary, only making both more sure and their unity yet more absolute—is a striking audacity of thought, and enables the writer to bring his argument to a remarkable synthesis which we may represent thus:

i. The Son accomplishes what He does in harmony with the will of the Father, who appoints Him to the office, calls

[1] xiii. 8. [2] vii. 22. [3] viii. 13.
[4] vii. 25. [5] x. 11. [6] ix. 11, 12, 25, 26.
[7] ix. 13; x. 4. [8] ix. 26. [9] x. 5–10.

Him to the priesthood, approves the sacrifice which is prompted by the delight to do His will, and is offered through the eternal Spirit.

ii. The unity of the priest and the sacrifice secures to the sacrifice all the worth, the dignity, the grace and the power which belong to the person; and secures to the priest all the virtue, the merit, the redemptive efficacy which inhere in the sacrifice. Hence He is said to have made purification of sins,[1] to have destroyed him that had the power of death and delivered those who lived in bondage to it.[2] He is the author of eternal salvation, brings in a better hope, remits sins, perfects the sanctified, and wins eternal redemption.[3] The blood which He shed in sacrifice speaks better things than that of Abel, purges the conscience from dead works, and because of it God remembers our sins and iniquities no more.[4]

iii. His eternal priesthood signifies His eternal existence; i.e. His power to save is without beginning and is everlasting. This has, so to say, a temporal and a spatial expression. (*a*) The temporal expression shows that though the sacrifice was made at a single point of time, yet it ranged backward as well as forward, "else He must have suffered often since the foundation of the world."[5] And this finds splendid illustration in chapter xi. Those who are there named are men who have believed "unto the saving of the soul."[6] They did not live by the Levitical priests or their sacrifices, but "by faith"; and faith signified that as Moses "esteemed the reproach of Christ greater riches than all the treasures of Egypt,"[7] the secret of their strength was with Him. In this historical and personal form we find the same permanence ascribed to Christ that Paul states in the more abstract terms of the mystery and hidden wisdom which God had before the worlds determined to reveal, or of the Providence

---

[1] i. 3.   [2] ii. 14, 15.   [3] v. 9; vii. 19; ix. 12.   [4] xii. 24, 17; ix. 14.
[5] ix. 26.   [6] x. 39.   [7] xi. 26.

which has continued since the creation of this visible order. (β) The spatial expression is quite as characteristic. The writer cannot think of the priest and the sacrifice without the Temple; and he is Alexandrian enough to allegorize or spiritualize without personalizing the place. Christ has passed through the heavens, has indeed entered heaven itself, appeared before the face of God for us, and sat down at the right hand of the Majesty on high.[1] Hence the throne of God has become "the throne of grace,"[2] which we can approach with boldness, and "enter into the holy place by the blood of Jesus." He, therefore, abides "eternal in the heavens," "the Mediator of the new covenant," a being as imperishable as His home.[3]

iv. The unchangeable is also a universal priesthood. He says indeed that Jesus suffered "that He might sanctify the people through His own blood"; but "the people" here does not mean Israel, but "the spirits of just men made perfect";[4] for, as the author says, Jesus "tasted death for every man" ($ὑπὲρ\ παντός$),[5] and became "the Author of eternal salvation unto all them that obey Him." The correlate of perpetuity is thus universality; the sacrifice that knows no time can show no respect of persons. The man for whom He died is all mankind.

v. Our discussion has been concerned not with the doctrine, but with the religious function of the death; yet it is necessary to say a word as to one theological question. Is the sacrifice here conceived as vicarious? This has been met with a very decided negative; and it has been argued that substitution was unknown to the Levitical sacrifices, which were gifts to God rather than expiatory sufferings; that "the scapegoat" which bore the sins of Israel was a symbolical act, but no proper sacrifice, for it was not offered to God, but driven away into the desert.[6] This may or may not be true

---

[1] viii. 1.   [2] iv. 16.   [3] viii. 6.   [4] xiii. 12; xii. 23, 24.   [5] ii. 9.
[6] Ménégoz, *La Théologie de L'Epitre aux Hébreux*, pp. 118-120.

but it does not determine the question. For Christ's sacrifice, like His priesthood, stands in an order by itself. Christ offered Himself to God. Why? For our sins. Wherein was He distinguished from the Levitical high priests? He was sinless, they were sinful, and so while they needed to offer for themselves, He did not. How, then, shall we conceive a sacrificial act, which was purely for others, and in no respect for the offerer Himself? We may be too fastidious to use the terms "vicarious" and "substitutionary," but it is easier to object to the terms than to escape the idea they express.

vi. This exposition, then, leaves us with the principle already formulated: a person is substituted for an institution; one uncreated and immortal Priest supersedes all mortal and visible priesthoods. The full significance of this has yet to be seen, but one point may here be emphasized—the change in the priesthood signified a radical change in the relation of God to sacrifice. In the Levitical, as in other religious systems, the sacrifice was offered to please God, to win His favour, to propitiate Him by the surrender of some object precious to man. But in the Christian system this standpoint is transcended: the initiative lies with God, for in the fine phrase of the writer, " it *became* Him, in bringing many sons unto glory, to make the Author of their salvation perfect through sufferings."[1] Whatever the death of Christ may signify, it does not mean an expedient for quenching the wrath of God, or for buying off man from His vengeance. This was a gain for religion greater than mind can calculate.

§ IV. *The Christian Sacrifice Interpreted through the Prophetic Idea*

With Hebrews the attempt to draw a formal parallel between Christ and the Levitical system may be said to end; and so, with the exception of a possible and figurative refer-

---

[1] ii. 10.

THE NEW SERVANT OF GOD 501

ence in the Apocalypse,[1] He is never again described as "the high priest of our confession."[2] But this does not mean that the idea of His person as the new and purer institution was dropped or forgotten; on the contrary, the tendency was to increase the emphasis on its reconciliatory function. He became more and more the sole ground and means of worship; but He was construed more through prophetic ideas than through Levitical customs. This is most apparent in 1 Peter, which we may describe as an exposition of Christ in the terms of the Second Isaiah. So it is said that He "did no sin, neither was guile found in His mouth"; that He "bare our sins in His own body upon the tree," and suffered "the righteous for the unrighteous";[3] and that the Spirit of Christ "in the prophets testified beforehand the sufferings of Christ and the glories that should follow them."[4] More distinctly prophetical still is the picture of Him as "a Lamb without blemish and without spot,"[5] "foreknown before the foundation of the world." The latter phrase suggests the lamb in the Apocalypse, which, in the picturesque speech of the Seer, is said to have been "slain from the foundation of the world."[6] Both books thus represent the timelessness which belongs to the sacrifice, which, though to us it occurs at a given moment, yet stands to God's eye above and outside time, as real before as after man saw it happen. The lamb is, indeed, the most tender and the most terrible figure in the Apocalypse, at once august and winsome to those who love and worship, awful and intolerable to those who despise. Twenty-nine times does the Seer refer to Him; in His blood the guilty are cleansed and made saints, who praise His name for ever and ever;[7] before His throne the wicked stand, and call upon the mountains to fall and hide them from His wrath.[8] The same figure, interpreted through the same prophetic category, appears in

[1] i. 13. [2] Heb. iii. 1. [3] ii. 22–24; iii. 18; cf. Isa. liii. 4–9.
[4] i. 11. [5] i. 19–20; cf. Isa. liii. 7. [6] xiii. 8.
[7] vii. 14; v. 9. [8] vi. 16; cf. xx. 11.

John's Gospel,[1] and is expounded and explained in his first Epistle. He is "the propitiation for our sins," and "His blood cleanses from all sin."[2] And alongside the idea of His complete efficacy as a sacrifice or institution which qualifies man for the worship of God, there stands an attitude of indifference to the Levitical system. It has become a question about which Jews may dispute, but in which the Christian has no concern,[3] for he is purified by other agencies and in a more perfect degree;[4] and as if to show how all that the old symbols had struggled to express had now become intelligible and accessible realities, Christ appears as "the tabernacle of God with men," as "the temple of God" in the New Jerusalem.[5] He is the image of the Invisible, and in Him "all the fulness of the Godhead" dwelleth.[6] The Divine presence which Israel once found in tabernacle and temple, man is now to find in Christ; He lives in the heart of history as God manifest in flesh, that all men may see His glory and share His grace.[7] And the gate of this Temple stands open day and night, the pilgrim does not find it closed against him, nor need any child of the city mourn that he cannot scale its walls, for no stone was used to build it; and no buyers or sellers can traffic in its courts, or moneychangers sit at their tables in the sacred precincts, for its privileges are without price, and they that come to worship must come as the consciously poor who but seek to be clothed and fed. And within no proud or greedy priest can bid the broken in spirit depart unpitied, or claim from the destitute what his poverty cannot give; for the only high priest of God's making is there, and His grace is free and is too precious to be sold of heaven or bought of man. And still translating a symbolical idea into an eternal truth, the unity of man in the worship of God replaces the old unity of the elect people. Where men worship in Him the

[1] i. 29; cf. ante, p. 457.
[2] iii. 5; ii. 2; iv. 10.
[3] Gospel of John, ii. 6; iii. 25.
[4] 1 John iii. 3.
[5] Rev. xxi. 3, 22.
[6] Col. i. 15; ii. 9.
[7] John i. 14.

partitions which the ancient laws and ordinances of religion built up to divide race from race fall down, and show man standing face to face with man, one family before the one God.

§ V. *The Christian Idea Interpreted through the Rabbinical Law*

1. The atmosphere and the ideals of Rabbinical were very unlike those of Levitical Judaism, and were even more characteristic of the people and the religion. While the Levitical system perished with the Jewish state, the Rabbinical law survived it, as indeed it had the better historical right to do. For the decalogue represents the most fundamental and creative ideas in Israel; and the most pious men did not cease to believe that a regulated life was more agreeable to God than an elaborated worship. They conceived Him to be righteous rather than holy in the Levitical sense, a moral Sovereign who governed men and States and approved only those who obeyed His will. Their law was instruction rather than institution, and their sphere more the school than the temple. But though their ideas and ends were ethical, their means were legal, and they imagined that they could make man moral by defining and enlarging the rules by which he ought to live. And as these rules were based on two notions, that Israel was God's people, and that God was Israel's God, so their function was to keep the people for God and God for the people. Their ideal became, therefore, on the religious side, an intense particularism; and on the moral an obedience according to statutory regulations, though the statutes were those of the school rather than of the State. Now a morality which lives by rule ceases to be moral; its root may be piety, but its fruit is formalism; the more complex life grows the more numerous and vexatious become its regulations, more emphatic as to the details and

oblivious as to the major motives and principles of life. And this describes the Rabbinical school and the Pharisaic sect of Christ's time; they showed how a moral religion, juristically construed and enforced, ceases to be either religious or moral. So certainly it seemed, after due experiment made, to Saul of Tarsus. He had the feeling for conduct which had distinguished the most pious of his people and the most eminent of their prophets; but he found the law, which, as God's, was intended to make man Godlike, unequal to its work. Though he so lived that "as touching the righteousness which is in the law,"[1] he was "found blameless"; yet this righteousness, which was too unreal to satisfy himself, he could not conceive as approved of God. So driven by his imperious conscience for conduct, he turned to Christ, and there he found what he wanted—deliverance from the law, a righteousness which the law had prescribed but could not give, and a spring of action which made him a new man before God. In other words, the Person who had been made the sole religious institution he translated into a sovereign and sufficient divine law.

2. The principles which determined his thought have been formulated by himself in certain axiomatic phrases and sentences.

i. "Christ redeemed us from the curse of the law, having become a curse for us."[2] There is here a personal experience and a universal principle. The law had been to him a burden too heavy to be borne, but the death of Christ upon the cross had taken it away. Jesus was sinless, yet the Jews had said: "We have a law, and by that law He ought to die"; and the cross to which they condemned Him made Him in its eye unclean, "for it is written, Cursed is every one that hangeth on a tree." But the law which condemned the holy was itself condemned; for a ceremonial offence, which was in the last analysis its own infinite wrong against

[1] Phil. iii. 6.   [2] Gal. iii. 13.

a righteous person, was judged as if it were His guilt. And did not the law that so judged Him prove by its very judgement that it had forgotten its moral character and function, and so could no longer bind the conscience or claim to govern the conduct? And so Christ, by submitting to the cross and the curse it involved, redeemed Paul from the law and made him for ever the enemy of juristic and statutory religion. This personal experience defined, under its negative form, the positive function of His death; for it meant that the law was superseded, not in the interests of lawlessness, but of a more absolute obligation and higher ethical ideals. As to the principle it is too purely theological to be here discussed, but it may be stated that so far as law, taken in its most universal sense, is forensic and positive, Christ, by having once become a curse for us, redeems us from its curse.

ii. "Him who knew no sin, He (God) made to be sin on our behalf, in order that we might become the righteousness of God in Him."[1] The Pauline principles that meet in this verse, and are necessary for its interpretation, are fundamental and far-reaching; but its significance for Christianity as a religion lies on the surface. All worship, even where it most seeks to honour God, is designed to reconcile Him to man, or to make man more acceptable to Him. What makes reconciliation necessary is man's sin and self-will; what is needed to his acceptability is a righteousness God approves. Out of the desire for reconciliation all the sacrifices by which man has striven to win the Divine favour, have come; and out of his search after an acceptable righteousness all the rules and orders and penances by which he has laboured to make himself agreeable to Deity, have issued. Now Paul here says, in effect: "In the work of reconciliation, God has taken the initiative, though in a fashion which becomes a Being too holy to tolerate sin. He has dealt with the sinless as if He had been sinful, allowing Him to bear 'the contradiction of

[1] 2 Cor. v. 21.

sinners,' to feel forsaken of God, and even to taste death; and He has done this in order that we who are the sinful might become possessed of the righteousness which God gives to all who are in Christ." The act is absolute, but the result is conditional. God makes Christ to be sin, and in this action, though it is done on his behalf, man has no part; but he becomes the righteousness of God only provided he is so incorporated with Christ, and Christ with him, that they stand before God as one being. It is the function of faith to establish this unity, which is spiritual; while the unity by virtue of which He could be made sin belongs to the nature which embodies the will of God.

iii. The Christ who by His Cross "redeemed us from the curse of the law," and who was "made sin" in order that "we might become the righteousness of God in Him," creates also in us a new life which He supplies with motives and guides towards a divine end. This function Paul presents under three different aspects in three most characteristic texts.

(*a*) "What the law could not do in that it was weak through the flesh, God, sending His own Son in the likeness of sinful flesh and for sin, condemned sin in the flesh, that the righteous demand of the law (τὸ δικαίωμα τοῦ νόμου) might be fulfilled in us, who walk not after the flesh but after the Spirit."[1] Paul is no libertine, no lover of licence; he renounced the law because it had failed to make man righteous, and he embraced Christ because through Him the requirements of the law can be fulfilled. God is throughout the active subject; He sends His Son, He determines the likeness the Son is to bear and the reason for it; He "condemns sin in the flesh"; and His is the end to be realized, which is one with the purpose of the law and due to the law's failure to fulfil its purpose.

(β) "The love of Christ constraineth us, because we thus

[1] Rom. viii. 3, 4.

THE PERSONALIZED IDEAL A LAW 507

judge that one died for all, therefore all died; and He died for all, in order that they who live should no longer live unto themselves, but unto Him who died for them and rose again."[1] The love of Christ is said to "constrain," i.e. so to shut up and confine the stream of life as to determine it and all its energies towards a given end, because of a twofold judgement—(i.) the identity of Christ's death with our death, His as unmerited being undertaken on our behalf, and ours as merited being realized in His; and (ii.) the purpose of His death, not that we may be relieved from penalty, but that we may live unto Him, i.e. He as end was to be the new law governing life. The doctrine of the text is here neither explained nor defended nor criticized, though it is obvious that no criticism based on the atomism or rigorous individualism of the race could here be relevant. Paul does not write as one who thought that the race had no responsibility for the individual, or the individual no existence in the race; but as one who conceives man as a unity, and this unity as impersonated and realized in Christ. He is the personalized ideal of humanity; what He does or suffers man does and endures. To live unto Him is, therefore, to Paul to live for the service of man, to work and suffer and, if need be, die as He did for the saving of humanity, actual and ideal.

(γ) "I have been crucified with Christ, and it is no longer I that live but Christ liveth in me."[2] This illustrates the first text, and states in the form of a personal experience the idea expressed in the second. The old man, the man who lived under the law and realized through the flesh all its weakness, who hated, persecuted and killed in its name, is dead, "crucified with Christ." And this dead man knows no resurrection, his death is eternal; and the new life which dwells in the old form is not his own but Christ's, "who loved me and gave Himself for me."

[1] 2 Cor. v. 14, 15.   [2] Gal. ii. 20.

§ VI. *Love of Christ the new Law*

1. Paul thus, by means of his larger philosophy, assigns to Christ a much greater place in religion than the writer who construed Him through the Levitical categories. He is not only an institution for worship, but a law for the government of man; He creates at once the right relation to God and the true spirit of worship, evokes the humanity latent in man and realizes the proper order of society. The ideal He is He inspires man to become. There is nothing so remarkable in the whole history of human thought as this interpretation of a person not only into a universal religious institution but also into an absolute law at once moral and religious; and there is something miraculous in the way in which the interpretation has been realized, the simplicity of the means forming such a contrast to the immensity of the achievement. Enthusiasms seldom outlive the generation that sees them born, and a dead enthusiasm, save as the affectation of a sect or a set, returns to life no more. But to one enthusiasm which appeals to no earthly or sordid passion, man has for sixty generations been faithful; it is the enthusiasm which Paul terms "the love of Christ." Love is as old as man, and so Christ did not make it, but by consenting to become its object He gave it a new character and new qualities, a new function and new ends. Love indeed is more native to man than the air he breathes, for he breathes the air in common with the animals, but the love he knows is the distinctive note of his humanity. It waits his coming into the world, it weeps his leaving it; it ministers every moment to his most common and crying needs. Through the gates of its glorious romance we all enter into the larger day; at its touch the youth blossoms into the man; the maiden blushes into the woman; the sorrows of the mother are transmuted into a ministry of joy; the labour of the father

ceases to be a burden and his very toil grows sweet. Before Christ, as since, poets sang of its pleasures and its pains, its divine madness, its delirious delights, its infinite longing, its lasting bitterness or its abiding peace. In its honour or to its shame tragedies have been written telling of the lives it has made or marred, the struggles with destiny it has provoked, the deaths it has braced men to die, the lives it has persuaded men to live. And it was this love, so common and large, so pitiful and tragic, so commanding the destiny which brings ruin or glory to the man, that Christ took and lifted into a transcendent ethical power. The love which the poet had praised was sensuous in its form and personal in its character and aims; it was a passion for possession; it might desire to merge one's being in another's, or rather another's being in one's own, but it was in all its forms a passion to possess. But out of this love Christ made the most self-forgetful of forces, a law that moved man towards righteousness and all benevolence. We call it by many names, but no name is equal to all its activities and attributes. It is an enthusiasm for humanity, for the redemption of the fallen, for the rightening of the wronged, for building up the ruined, for beautifying the wasted; but however named, it remains a passion to serve man for love of Christ. And He invested this love with the qualities that made it not an occasional and fitful but a constant energy, an invariable moral dynamic. It did not die on the Cross, but became immortal with Him, a permanent factor of amelioration which had its continued being guaranteed by His. Hence it is a love which, like the priesthood of Melchizedek, stands in an order by itself. The love which is as old as man is embalmed in his literatures, but we embalm only the dead. At the dawn of Greek letters we see Penelope sitting in her hall in rocky Ithaca surrounded by the hungry and urgent wooers, while the husband of her youth tarries, wandering through many lands and learning from many men. The wooers she cannot love, and none of them will she wed, for her heart is with the far-travelled Odysseus who comes not, though well she knows that he is sure to return. To calm the strife of the suitors she promises to wed when the web she weaves so openly by day is woven; but by night she unweaves what she had woven by day that the end may not be till the day breaks which shall bring the wanderer home. But though the love of Penelope for Odysseus touches the imagination of the living, yet it is but a dead love. We love the poetry that speaks of it, the stately measures that linger in the ear like the music of a celestial voice; but what is loved is literature, not a passion that so holds the heart as to command the conscience and regulate the life. And Homer stands here for all Greek, nay, for all ancient literature; it is but a splendid tomb which Genius has built as a monument to love, that the memory of it may survive death and that it may become the admiration and joy of later men. And as with ancient so with modern literature; it begins to be when the stern and solitary soul of Dante breaks into responsive music at the touch of the most gentle lady Beatrice. We descend with him the circles of his "Inferno"; we struggle up the steep and arduous mount of the "Purgatorio"; we look through his eyes and behold afar off the great throne of light, the home of the blessed, to which his eyes and ours are drawn; and what compels him to go and us to follow is the hope that he may catch a glimpse of the most gentle lady in the paradise where she dwells in eternal peace. But while we suffer with Dante the pangs of a love that though it cannot be told yet will not be denied the comfort of speech, still the story he tells and we hear is of a love so dead that no will can revive it. The literature which is its shrine appeals to the imagination that seeks culture, but the love within the shrine is but dust and ashes which no voice can ever charm back into life. But the love of Christ is not a dead love, entombed in a classical literature, it lives and quickens and creates as no human thing can do. Age does not wither its ineffable charm, nor does the lapse of time exhaust its exuberant energies. It has created many literatures in many tongues; lyrics that express a passion that only loss of self in the eternal love can satisfy; epics that express the apostasy and departure of the soul from God, its wandering through many deserts of sin, where its thirst is deep and its pains severe, until it returns humbled and penitent to the Father's feet; tragedies that describe the struggles of the will that would fain have followed the lust of the eye and the pride of life, but could not for the grace that hedged it round and drew it back to the home it had forsaken but could not forget. Twenty centuries have passed since " they took Jesus and laid Him in a new tomb," but love of Him they did not bury, for it never died; and every day between this and then it has proved itself alive by the conquests it has made, compelling men to renounce loved vices and sending gentle women into the loathly slum, the deadly camp, or wherever man needed the hand of gracious helpfulness. This is the one love which abides while the lovers die, for it is possessed of immortal youth and the inexhaustible energies which are born of God.

2. But the love which is thus immortal has also the quality of sufficiency for its work. There is an ethical counterpart to the correlation of the physical forces. The vision which rises before the imagination of the physicist, when he sees his atoms falling through a space which he thinks of as otherwise vacant, and which knows no light of sun or star, is impressive. He sees them marshalled in their innumerable hosts, not as an unordered heap, but as a disciplined army, with its laws given in the form and weight of every separate unit. In obedience to these laws he sees them pass through infinite evolutions and involutions, now massing, now dissolving their

columns, yet ever marching breast forward across limitless fields of space and through unmeasured periods of time to the creation of the heavens and the earth. And if the eye of the seer of science be not weary, he may note how the cycle of change continues, and how the same force, unhasting, unresting, one, manifold, in form transient, in essence permanent, working through incalculable ages, appears now on the cooling mass as rock and vapour, as land and water, as plant and animal, or now as all that makes the endless panorama of earth and sea and sky, and now as the succession of organs and organisms that constitute our living world.[1] But more marvellous than this correlation and ceaseless conversion of physical forces are the correlation and the persistent permutations of the ethical energy which we call the love of Christ. It began to be in Him and with Him, and without increase or decrease it took shape in the men He made apostles; then, without any loss of momentum or intensity, changed its form and appeared as sub-apostolic men, apologists, fathers, and churches which rose round the shores of the tideless Mediterranean; then as missionaries who wandered through many lands, creating new peoples in the Syrian desert, in central Europe, on the bleak shores of the northern seas, and in furthest Asia. And dispersion did not dissipate it, for the lapse of time has not exhausted its energy; on the contrary, expenditure has only seemed to increase its potency and the capacity for conversion into forms still more infinitely varied. New peoples it has made have replaced the old, have colonized unknown continents, and made them as fertile as their own, building up societies and States, which illustrate anew the power of this marvellous love. And so it seems as if this gracious ethical energy is a force as incapable of perishing as it is capable of accomplishing the work it has been charged to perform.

[1] Ante, p. 354. A similar figure is employed, though for a different purpose.

3. And without this love man is unfitted for the service of his kind. For man to be served must be loved, but the supreme difficulty is to love the men who most need our service. Hate is easy, and where we hate it is both agreeable and natural to wish to injure. Where we do not love we feel no need to pity or to spare. Milton's Satan knew sin, knew how terrible it was to himself, making of him a hell, from which he saw no way of escape. But though he knew sin as the most terrible of all possible miseries, yet he had so little pity for man, and he so wished to spite God, that he crossed chaos, passed sin and death, and assumed forms disagreeable to his proud spirit, that he might tempt man to become even as he was—a hell with hells beneath so low and deep, as to make the hell then suffered seem a heaven. Hate of God made Satan pitiless to man, and his ruin a thing from which it was foolish to shrink. And all seduction is devilish because it is pitiless; it never springs from affection, ever from the lust that is self-indulgence. It has no imagination to see the misery it causes, has only the brutal passion which must be gratified that the baser self may be pleased. On the other hand the love of Christ creates not simply the pity that dare not harm, but also the grace that must save. It is here indeed that we discover the most characteristic quality in the love of Christ. To love Him is to love man. This is a function as unique as it is high, for he who despises cannot bless, nor can he who is despised be blessed. Hate is not a thing that need be spoken; it is understood without words, discerned without acts. It has only to be felt in order to be known, and to disqualify the man who feels it from serving the man who knows that it is there. And so love is necessary to the service of man. But then there are multitudes of men it is impossible to love. An abstract sin need provoke no passion, but concrete sin, which means the actual sinner, cannot fail to breed dislike. Hypocrisy is what every honest soul hates, but love of the hypocrite is less possible

still. A lie no man can love, and a liar is worse and less lovable than his lie. But Christ makes possible what these necessitated antipathies most sternly forbid. For to love Him is to love all mankind. He is not a single person; He is to those who know Him collective man, who is loved in the love of Him. Yet the man who is loved in Him is loved, in spite of his actual and radical evil, as a man capable of conversion, with this capability made everywhere and always possible of realization. And it is this love, not of the sin, but of the hidden and possible saint in the sinner, that makes the love of Christ so essentially ameliorative, a passion to seek as well as to save. And what does the immortal necessity and sufficiency of His love prove save that the experience of man has come to confirm the truth discovered by the experience of Paul, that the love of Christ was the law of God compelling men to obey Him and serve mankind?

> Ed io udi': "Per intelletto umano,
> E per autoritadi a lui concorde,
> De' tuoi amori a Dio guarda il soprano.
> Ma di' ancor, se tu senti altre corde
> Tirarti verso lui, si che tu suone
> Con quanti denti questo amor ti morde."
> Non fu latente la santa intenzione
> Dell' aquila di CRISTO, anzi m' accorsi
> Dove volea menar mia professione.
> Però ricominciai: "Tutti quei morsi;
> Che posson far lo cor volger a Dio,
> Alla mia caritate son concorsi;
> Chè l'essere del mondo, el'esser mio,
> La morte ch' ei sostenne perch' io viva,
> E quel che spera ogni fedel, com' io,
> Con la predetta conoscenza viva,
> Tratto m' hanno del mar dell' amor torto,
> E del diritto m' han posto alla riva.
> Le fronde onde s'infronda tutto l'orto
> Dell' ortolano eterno, am' io cotanto,
> Quanto da lui a lor di bene è porto."
>
> —DANTE.

We read in our Books of a nice *Athenian*, being entertained in a place by one given to Hospitality, finding anon that another was received with the like courtesie, and then a third, growing very angry, " I thought," said he, " that I had found here ξενῶνα, but I have found πανδοχεῖον ; I looked for a *Friend's house*, but I am fallen into an *Inne* to entertain all Comers, rather than a lodging for some private and especial Friends." Let it not offend any that I have made Christianity rather an Inne to receive all, than a private house to receive some few.—JOHN HALES.

Why measure we God by our selves, but because we are led with gay shews, and goodly things, and think it is so with God? *Seneca* reports, that a *Pantomimus*, a Poppet-player and Dancer in *Rome*, because he pleased the *People* well, was wont to go up every day into the *Capitol*, and practise his Art, and dance before *Jupiter*, and thought he did the god a great pleasure. Beloved, in many things we are like unto this Poppet-player, and do much measure God by the People, by the World.
—JOHN HALES.

The Divinity alwaies enjoies itself and its own Infinite perfections, seeing it is that Eternall and stable Sun of goodness that neither rises nor sets, is neither eclipsed nor can receive any encrease of light and beauty. Hence *the Divine Love* is never attended with those turbulent passions, perturbations, or wrestlings within it self of *Fear, Desire, Grief, Anger*, or any such like, whereby *our Love* is wont to explicate and unfold its affection towards its Object. But as *the Divine Love* is perpetually most infinitely ardent and potent, so it is alwaies *calm and serene*, unchangeable, having no such ebbings and flowings, no such diversity of stations and retrogradations as that *Love* hath in us which ariseth from the weakness of our Understandings, that doe not present things to us alwaies in the same Orient lustre and beauty: neither we nor any other mundane thing (all which are in a perpetual flux) are alwaies the same.—JOHN SMITH, the Platonist.

Dem gegenüber eröffnet sich uns durch den jetzt gewonnenen Begriff des Anfangs auch der Einblick in die Möglichkeit eines Fortgangs des Processes der Menschwerdung, eines solchen Fortgangs, welcher sich, wie die Idee der Sohnmenschheit es fordert, nicht in einem einzelnen Zeitpuncte der Menschengeschichte, sondern in allen Zeiten, nicht an einer einzelnen Person, sondern an dem gesammten menschlichen Geschlecht vollzieht.—WEISSE.

ὁ μὲν δὴ Θεός, ὥσπερ καὶ ὁ παλαιὸς λόγος, ἀρχήν τε καὶ τελευτὴν καὶ μέσα τῶν ὄντων ἁπάντων ἔχων, εὐθείᾳ περαίνει κατὰ φύσιν περιπορευόμενος.
—PLATO.

'Εκ Διὸς ἀρχώμεσθα, τὸν οὐδέποτ' ἄνδρες ἐῶμεν
ἄρρητον, μεσταὶ δὲ Διὸς πᾶσαι μὲν ἀγυιαί,
πᾶσαι δ' ἀνθρώπων ἀγοραί, μεστὴ δὲ Θάλασσα,
καὶ λιμένες, πάντῃ δὲ Διὸς κεχρήμεθα πάντες·
τοῦ γὰρ καὶ γένος ἐσμέν.—ARATUS.

Such a sort of deity as should shut up itself, and be recluse from all converse with men, would leave us as disfurnished of an object of religion, and would render a temple on earth as vain a thing, as if there were none at all. It were a being not to be worshipped, nor with any propriety to be called God, more (in some respect less) than an image or statue. We might with as rational design worship for God what were scarce worthy to be called the shadow of a man, as dedicate temples to a wholly unconversable deity. That is such a one as not only *will not* vouchsafe to converse with men, but that *cannot* admit it; or whose nature were altogether incapable of such converse.—JOHN HOWE.

For whatsoever the wisest men in the world, in all nations and religions, did agree upon, as most excellent in itself, and of greatest power to make political or future and immaterial felicities, all that, and much more, the holy Jesus adopted into his law: for they receiving sparks or single irradiations from the regions of light, or else having fair tapers shining indeed excellently in representations and expresses of morality, were all involved and swallowed up into the body of light, the sun of righteousness. Christ's discipline was the breviary of all the wisdom of the best men, and a fair copy and transcript of his Father's wisdom.
—JEREMY TAYLOR.

Christianity has materially contributed to call forth the idea of the unity of the human race and has thus tended to exercise a favourable influence on the *humanization* of nations in their morals, manners, and institutions. Although closely interwoven with the earliest doctrines of Christianity, this idea of humanity met with only a slow and tardy recognition, for at the time when the new faith was raised at Byzantium, from political motives, to be the established religion of the State, its adherents were already deeply involved in miserable party dissensions, whilst intercourse with distant nations was impeded, and the foundations of the empire were shaken in many directions by external assaults. Even the personal freedom of entire races of men long found no protection in Christian states from ecclesiastical landowners and corporate bodies.
—ALEXANDER VON HUMBOLDT.

PART III

THE RELIGION OF CHRIST AND THE IDEAL OF RELIGION

INTRODUCTORY

WE have reached the point where our two main lines of analysis and argument coalesce. The First Book, which was concerned with the mind and purpose of God as expressed in Nature and in the history of Man, culminated in a discussion as to religions, local and universal, and as to the relation between those founded and their founders. The Second Book has been so far occupied with the persons and processes concerned in the founding of the Christian religion; but its argument is still incomplete. We have yet to see how their ideal became actual, to ascertain whether it has qualities or attributes by virtue of which it may claim to be the only really universal religion. But before this can be attempted we must refer to certain introductory questions.

i. Terms like "founder" and "founded" need to be employed with caution. Strictly speaking, religions are not made, they grow; for growth is the process which life follows when it builds up an organism for its own inhabitation and enlargement. Opposed to growth is the process we may call contrivance or manufacture, which is represented in religion by Syncretism, or the attempt by the conscious selection and adjustment of old materials to create a new cult or system. Now this process has been known in both ancient and modern times, the age in which Christianity was born being particularly familiar with it. There were Romans who affected to think of the East as religious and wise, of Egypt as venerable and mysterious; and it became a Roman fashion to seek from the strange deities and rites of the orient replenishment for the exhausted native sources of inspiration. But Syncretism in religion, like eclecticism in philosophy, is a sign of decadence, for it creates nothing that outlives the age or the coterie that gave it birth. It signifies that mind, fallen into conscious impotence and hopelessness, has turned its back upon the future and its face to the past; and, despairing of producing or achieving anything, has begun to call upon vanished men and systems for principles which may help it to live. The mood is, as a rule, self-conscious and cynical as well as despondent, and so the formulae it borrows it builds, usually, to the music of a little disdainful and finical criticism, into a house of consolation and amusement rather than a temple of truth and worship.

ii. The last religion we could describe as a Syncretism is the Christian, and that for many reasons, though it will be enough to mention here two: (a) its founders were too completely ignorant of other theologies and philosophies to be affected by them; and (β) it was not an articulated skeleton but a living organism, carrying within itself the principle of life. This does not mean that it was without relation to the past, for without the persons, ideas, customs and influences it inherited, it never could have been; nor that it was isolated from the present, for if it had been untouched by living forces, it could not have reached living men. But it means that it behaved as a living being behaves, who, while the issue of a long ancestry, yet grows by transmuting into his own substance the matter his environment supplies. In other words, the religion grew because it lived, and it lived because it carried within it an immanent and architectonic idea, which governed it and yet was essentially its own. That idea was the belief it held concerning Jesus Christ, which double name denoted at once the historical person who was the first Christian and the transcendental ideal which had transformed God and religion, man and history.

iii. The action of this idea upon the religion may best be discussed under three heads : (*a*) the people, or the medium in which the religion had to live ; (β) the beliefs that made it, especially the belief which determines all others, the conception of the Deity it worships ; and (γ) the worship it offers Him, or the methods it follows to please Him and do Him honour, to cultivate the obedience and the virtues He approves.

CHAPTER I

THE PERSON OF CHRIST AND THE PEOPLE OF THE RELIGION

§ I. *The Problems to be Solved*

1. THE problems here are most complex. (*a*) The religion could not become an historical fact, still less a social force in the bosom of humanity, without a people, and a people was exactly what did not exist and what had, therefore, to be created. But creation is not a process which art can accomplish, and in this case there was nothing in the past experience of man to show how it could be done. (*β*) If the religion was to be universal, the people must not be local or capable of being localized; for if it were, the very degree in which it was identified with one family or tribe would make it alien to other races. (*γ*) If a people is to have a single religion, they must have the homogeneous consciousness which not only allows, but demands for its expression, identity of beliefs and worship; but this had not as yet been realized, save under the magic influences of a common home and place. (*δ*) A religion that would belong to all men must be without family customs, tribal institutions, or a national polity; for unless it could live without these things, it had not learned to transcend the limitations of kinship and caste, language and colour.

But while the immanent potentialities that create religion are universal, the forms it assumes, whether in belief or in worship, are determined by the empirical causes,—physical, ethical, intellectual, political, and economical,—which govern the social evolution as a whole. Thus the history of a religion is but a special branch of its people's history, not to be construed unless they are conceived as a sort of colossal personality, continuous in being, though multitudinous in experience. The forces that evoke the energy to live develop the will to believe; and where the forces are uniform the beliefs constitute a unity. Hence the agencies that tend to make a state local, tend to make its religion the same; and so rigorous has the relation between these two ever been that while no being has been more migratory than man, no religion born with or within a nation has been either able or willing to change its home. For outside the place of its birth it would lose not only its historical continuity, but its personal identity. Hence the migration of customs, beliefs, and myths is one thing, and the migration of religions is a different thing altogether. Men, or even tribes, may borrow a term or imitate an institution, but a structure which has been built up by a multitude of local agencies, operating through more generations than man can reckon, must stand where it has been built, and can be removed only by being taken to pieces. And so the religion a people has made must remain that people's, and cannot become another's, for the simple reason that its transference would involve the uprooting of the whole historical order and consciousness of one race and their implantation in the soul of another.

2. But these were not the only difficulties which the Christian religion had to overcome; of a different but still more radical order was this: it had to create the people it needed out of old materials, ancient races, who had lived in every kind and variety of state, who had been born in countries distant from each other and reared under different climates, and who had been accustomed to religions ranging from the most austere monotheism to the most indulgent polytheism. It found no virgin consciousness in which to

sow the seed of its ideas and usages, but had to form its people out of men who had no national unity, no common ancestry, no affinity of blood, speech or experience; in a word, nothing in their past to lead them to live together and think alike. On the contrary, each man who entered the new society was a focus of centrifugal energies. The Greek, acute, speculative, fastidious, metaphysical, had endeavoured to think of God either as He was in philosophy, as an abstract substance or a law of reason; or, as the plastic arts had represented Him, as an idealized man, godlike because beautiful; or, as the imaginative mythology conceived Him, as protean and stupendous in shape, but mixed in character and achievement. The Roman, civil in temper, political in genius, military in ambition and by habit, had conceived the Deity through the imperial idea, as typified in the Emperor and as defined and sanctioned by the State. The Persian or the Phrygian, touched with the oriental mysticism which construed existence as a kingdom under the rival forces of light and darkness, spirit and matter, good and evil, had been wont to divide the functions of God between a Creator who formed, but did not love man, and a Father who redeemed him and was not always able to save. The barbarian, who confounded ecstasy with inspiration and religion with exhilaration, could best appreciate a God who liked the oblation and the exuberant fertility of man. The Jew, who knew himself to be a son of Abraham, wished, even after his conversion, to believe in the God who had established the law and spoken through Moses and the prophets, who loved the circumcised, hated idols and condemned the ways and thoughts of the heathen. The men who constituted the people of the religion were thus varied in type and without any of the unities of thought and mind which come from centuries of organized co-existence and the cumulative effects of a long and jealously guarded inheritance. Hence came the problem: How out of the mixed families of man, the multitude of tongues he speaks, the strongly marked societies and castes, the opposed States and kingdoms, the rival religions and civilizations which at once make up the human race and isolate its parts from each other, could a people be evolved and organized into the social unity or the homogeneous society needed for the expression and realization of a universal religion?

§ II. *The Social Ideal of Jesus*

1. We have said that this was a new and peculiar problem, and we may add that it was one which no statesmanship could have solved. The solution, if it was to come at all, could only be effected by the energy of some constitutive idea acting in the mind. The inseparability of the religious and civil provinces and customs was, indeed, an ultimate axiom of thought to the societies and States of antiquity. Philosophical sects were common, and so were private and family cults, but these were conceived not as supersessive or prohibitive, but as supplementary of the public and legal worship. Indeed, the notion of a religion which appealed to man as man, and had no regard to racial, social, or class distinctions, was quite alien to ancient thought. Rome, in extending her empire, had spread her law but not her religion; she was, indeed, here more inclined to imitate older States than to require of them acceptance of her deities and observance of her rites. The ideal city of the Greek thinkers was a Greek State, incapable of realization by any other than Greek men. And so the last thing Greece and Rome could have imagined was the possibility of realizing a religion without some State, with its national customs and sanctions, as its basis. But the ideal of Jesus was altogether unlike these. He had lived so modestly within His own little world, He and it so corresponded, it so occupied His activities, and He found it so sufficient as an arena for His career, that we can hardly

think of Him as nursing vaster ambitions than had ever dawned on the imagination of any statesman or warrior of antiquity. And we do not so think of Him, for ambition is not a word that can with any propriety be used to characterize anything He designed or conceived. But the more we study the more we admire what He proposed to do, and the way in which He proceeded to do it. For Jesus had both a social ideal and a social method; the ideal was expressed in His notion of the Kingdom of God, and His method was the way He took to realize it. The ideal may be defined as perfect obedience towards God, embodied in perfect duty towards man. Obedience signified that man knew God as Jesus knew Him and had made Him known, loved Him as Jesus loved, and therefore obeyed as He obeyed. Apart from this attitude—i.e. unless God was pleased with man, and man was reconciled to God,—obedience was not possible; and the relation to God determined the duty towards Man, for God could not be loved and the creature He loved be hated. Thus love to one's neighbour was but active and applied love of God; and this love was the law of the Kingdom. It was a universal law, knew no distinction of caste or country, Jew or Samaritan. It was a law possessed of inexhaustible energies; it could never live as if it had said the last good word and performed its final good act, but must ever impel man forward. It was an imperious law, for it could never allow a man to suffer or to perish which the soul by dying might save. And it was necessary, for without it no help could be effective nor could any effort be restorative. This germinal and governing principle developed into a multitude of special laws, as (i.) the law of beneficence: men were to return not evil for evil, or even good for good, but good for evil; no one was to have the awful right of sitting in the judgment seat of God, or the devilish power of compelling us to harm him by being harmful to us. (ii.) The law of reciprocity: we were to do unto others as we would have others do unto us: our soul was to stand in their soul's place, and we were to act as if they were we and we were they. (iii.) The law of charity: we were not to judge lest we should be judged. Judgement was the function of God; the Pharisee over against the Publican showed how pitiable man became when he tried to appraise himself and his neighbour. (iv.) The law of forgiveness: man was to forgive his brother, not once or twice, but as often as he needed to be forgiven, certain that where all offended no one could be blameless. (v.) The law of ends or motives: the real sin is not the outer act, but the mind that wills the act, and the end that moves the will. Adultery is not a deed, but the lust to do it. (vi.) The law of self-denial: man is to surrender himself and all he thinks he rightfully possesses, that he may have nothing of his own, but may hold all of Christ, and hold it for Him and for the service of man. (vii.) The law of redemption: man is not to live as one who is to be ministered unto, but as one who is the servant of all, bound to save even by the sacrifice of himself. These are but a few of the laws of the Kingdom, which is a society of mortal men living as sons of the eternal God, with all their relations realized in time, yet all conceived as eternal. Men are neighbours to each other, but God is the one and absolute Sovereign; and all that they do to each other they do unto God.

2. Now this ideal may seem ethical rather than religious, more concerned with duty to man than with the worship of God. And without question it has some omissions that appear the more extraordinary that we cannot think them to have been undesigned. Jesus seems to conceive the cultus as the least part of religion, most abused when taken for the whole or for the most essential part. He teaches man to pray, but for Himself He prays apart. He visits the Synagogue, reads the Scriptures, and speaks to the people; but He prefers to teach on the mountain, or in the fields, by the wayside or at the seashore. He speaks of the altar not as if it consecrated the

gift, but as if the consecration depended on the spirit of the giver.[1] He makes prayer avail not because of the place where it is offered or the person who offers it, but because of the offerer's own heart.[2] For the priest as priest, the temple as temple, the ritual as ritual, He had no respect; but only for the mercy that was greater than sacrifice, the piety that was better than ceremonies. What His people came to regard as their supreme religious act was a social observance, a supper which recalled an event in the life of Israel in which the priesthood, as such, and the temple as temple, played no part, but where the worship was domestic and the father was the priest. Yet it would be to misconceive His whole spirit and purpose to say, "The ideal of Jesus is not so much religious as ethical"; on the contrary, it is so intensely ethical because so essentially religious. What concerns Him is that man should think rightly of God and do justly to man. If they so think and do, they will worship as they ought; if they refuse so to do and think, no worship they can offer will be agreeable to Him, and no regulations of it will be good and efficacious. There is nothing so certain as that the good man will worship; for him the most expressive form is the one most congenial to his spirit; and there is nothing more certain than that a bad man may scrupulously observe every ritual prescription without being any the better for all his observances. Jesus, in harmony with His own mind and practice, laid emphasis on the Spirit, what the man is to God and does to man, certain that where there is concern for the weightier matters of the law, the lighter will not be neglected.

[1] Matt. v. 22-24. The argument in xxiii. 19—cf. whole context 13-24—is *ad hominem*, and has no force if the Pharisaic thesis and attitude be taken away.

[2] Luke xviii. 10-14.

§ III. *The Social Method of Jesus and its Impersonation*

1. The social method corresponded to the social ideal; Jesus created a people for His religion by teaching men to become like Himself. He called them into His society, made them His disciples, which simply means men who could learn of Him; He lived with them, threw over them the spell of His character and influence, opened their eyes by His words and example, woke them to admiration, roused them to love. Discipleship did not mean attainment, but the capacity to attain, the fidelity that could follow, the sympathy that could appreciate, the susceptibility that could imitate. But this method depended on His personal being and presence: without Him it could have no existence, with Him it was of necessity. Now the fact we have to deal with is this:—the method continued in operation after the Crucifixion, and men became Christians by becoming disciples of Jesus. He called, and their response was termed conversion. And so His society did not die when He died, and what kept it living was the belief in His continued and active existence. This is the fact that stands out clearly amid the confusions of the first days. Peter preached that Jesus had not seen "corruption," but was exalted to the right hand of God as "a Prince and a Saviour."[1] The resurrection was not a mere physical miracle but a spiritual experience; it meant that Jesus lived and reigned as "both Lord and Christ." The belief emboldened Peter and John to refuse, on the ground that they must obey God rather than men, to be silenced by the priests and rulers;[2] and in its strength the Church stood the test suggested by the prudent diplomacy of Gamaliel.[3] The men who saw "the Son of Man standing at the right hand of God" believed that, since His presence had ceased to be local and visible, it had become universal and spiritual; and so they awoke to the duty of commanding in His name all men to repent, of calling

---

[1] Acts ii. 31-36; v. 31. [2] v. 29. [3] v. 38-39.

all into His discipleship. In the belief that He still lived Stephen died; it was a vision in which he saw the Lord that converted Paul. When persecution came and compelled the disciples to choose between Jerusalem and Christ, they chose as men who saw the invisible. The choice drove them out of Judea, and forced them either to be dumb or to preach His name to the Gentiles. They believed and therefore preached; and this raised questions as to His authority which they answered by placing Him high above Moses, and by so modifying, in spite of themselves, Jewish customs as to suit non-Jewish men. Soon the sole note of their society came to be faith in His Name; yet they did not by escaping from Judea escape from persecution. The rabble in the Greek cities proved even more intolerant than the Jewish priesthood; but the preachers only the more openly "placarded" Jesus Christ crucified before their eyes.[1] Municipalities, anxious to keep the peace, threw them into prison without trial; "lewd fellows of the baser sort" gathered together against them and set cities in an uproar[2]; philosophers argued as if they were ignorant men and dabblers in matters too high for them; tradesmen whose crafts were in danger became enthusiasts for the goddess whose shrines they made and sold; but love of the invisible Sovereign proved mightier than fear of all visible powers. In short, the idea organized a people for the religion in the face of difficulties both inner and outer, those within being even more insurmountable than those without. Racial temper, for example, is one of the most obdurate and invincible things in man, and in no man more than the Jew; but this idea so changed and humanized the strongest son of that strong race, that he declared there were in Christ neither Jew nor Greek, neither barbarian, Scythian, bond nor free, but only the family of saints, the household of God. It so overcame the antipathies of blood and culture and speech that Greeks and Jews became kinsmen, and the richer sent to the

---

[1] Gal. iii. 1. οἷς κατ' ὀφθαλμοὺς Ἰησοῦς Χριστὸς προεγράφη ἐσταυρωμένος.
[2] Acts xvii. 5.

poorer saints the help they needed. Newer ideals never work without friction, and wherever an old order is dissolved confusion reigns before a new one can be built up. We see in churches like Corinth how this happened; but we also see how the spirit of potent love worked like a healing grace, begot ethical ideals that rebuked ethnical customs, and was silently making a society that had been indifferent to good, careful of virtue. The people who accomplished these things had no arms in their hands, yet they faced without dismay the mightiest of all armed powers, and when it proudly commanded them to worship its gods as well as their own, they said: "Command us as a civil sovereign in civil things and we will dutifully obey, but speak to us as a religious authority and we will not listen to you. You may kill, for you have the power of life and death, but here you cannot command and shall not control. To our own Master we stand or fall, but that Master is neither the Emperor nor the Senate of Rome, He is Jesus Christ."

2. But before we can fully appreciate this ideal and method we must compare them with what may be conceived as actual or possible alternatives. Buddha had founded a church as well as a religion; indeed, in his case these may be termed one and the same. His ideal was an ascetic and celibate community: monks who, as weary of the world, took refuge with the Buddha and his order; and nuns who, though as women disliked and distrusted, had still as human beings established their right to consideration at his hands. In no point is his want of originality so apparent as here; he simply borrowed the idea of discipleship from the Brahmanical schools, made it express the ideal state, and framed the regulations which their and his experience had proved to be necessary. His community was to be vowed to poverty; his saint was to be a mendicant without worldly goods or ambitions, industrial energies or occupation. He was to cease to be a father or brother a husband or son a citizen or neigh-

bour; he was to wear a special dress, to abstain from many vices, but also from many duties; to live the profitless life of one whose sole end was to seek beatitude, and whose function was to show how it could be attained. What we should call the lay world was held to be only nominally and potentially of the religion, being needful to the maintenance of the mendicant community and the source whence it could be supplied with celibate members. But essentially, the man who had not made the great renunciation stood only in the outer court, where he waited the illumination that was to lead him within. If he was reverent, he was judged worthy to have the bowl passed to him; if impious the bowl must be withheld, i.e. he was not fit to contribute to the support of the monks who preached to him concerning the vanity of all human things. Now if Jesus had been no more original than Buddha, there were sects or schools enough for Him to imitate. There were the Essenes, pious men, ascetics, cultivating purity and poverty, "honouring God most of all," and after Him Moses, whom no man must be allowed to blaspheme. They believed in the rigorous regulation of life; in avoiding the touch of the uncircumcised; in bodily washings; in the scrupulous observance of the Sabbath; in abstaining from certain kinds of food; in eating only what clean hands had cooked; in being their own priests and offering their own sacrifices. If He had avoided the Essenes, He could have found many types of the theocratic ideal, Maccabaean, Apocalyptic, Pharisaic, popular and Messianic. Such an ideal had crossed His mind in the vision which showed Him "all the kingdoms of the world." Later it was to become the ideal of Mohammed; and he was so to organize his Church that while it was built on the Word it yet should like a State wield the sword; and by the use of these two it converted Arabia, subdued kingdoms, and founded Empires. But Jesus, more original and daring than either of these, conscious of a function for man which resembles nothing so much as the function of God in creation, disdained all positive laws, whether regulative, ceremonial, administrative or coercive, and founded His society simply by discipleship.

3. But the significance of His social ideal and method becomes apparent only when they and the idea of His person are looked at together. The person may be described as His social ideal embodied and organized for the creation of His society. The ideas He impersonates become the ideals it articulates; in other words, He is the Symbol of all it ought to be. His people were to be like Him, sons of God; and as He was "Son of Man" His society was to know no distinction of blood or birth or estate, but to be the home where men were to be born and nursed as children of humanity. As He impersonated the race before God, He also so personalized man to His Church that to live unto Him was to live for all mankind. As He saves by bearing the sin which was not His own, so His people must sorrow and suffer and die if they would save men. The apostle who conceives Christ as the Second Adam, the Head of the New Mankind, conceives the Church as His body, all its members being related to each other as well as to Him. Their life is His, their actions are inspired by Him, and it is only through their relation to Him that they can perfectly realize all other relations and faithfully fulfil all duties. In other words, His society was meant as His articulated person to be as ethical as Himself. In Hebrews His people are the people of the New Covenant, with the law of God written in their hearts, made by their faith independent of time, and lifted into fellowship with the Church of the firstborn whose names are written in heaven. In the Apocalypse His society appears under a most winsome figure: it is "the bride of the Lamb," arrayed in bridal garments; or, yet again, it appears as a multitude of saints redeemed "out of every tribe and people, nation and tongue." Possibly the last thing John and Paul thought of as they laboured to interpret the person, was that they were creating

an ethical ideal for a universal society; but it is not the self-conscious workman that accomplishes the grandest work. And no man ever did greater things for humanity than those who interpreted Christ into its ideal, personal and social.

§ IV. *The Christian not a Positive Religion*

1. The argument here touches one of the supreme and differentiating distinctions of Christianity: it is a personal but not a positive religion. The term "positive" is juristic rather than theological, and was introduced into theology by a distinguished lawyer who desired to construe the relations of God and man in the categories of his own science. It denotes an enacted, as distinct from a natural, law; the legislation which an established authority, whether personal like king or emperor, or representative like a Senate or Parliament, has promulgated and enforced, in distinction from the order, which nature is supposed to have constituted, the equity which issues from conscience and speaks in its name. Positive is public law, proclaimed and upheld by some public authority. Now founded religions are, by the very necessities of their origin, positive, i.e. they express some will; their beliefs are, as it were, public laws; their whole order is a legislation authoritatively enacted. Hence the religion of Israel, conceived as the creation of a lawgiver, is positive; but the older Semitic cults, which no statesman instituted or reformed, are natural. Buddha, in forming his *Sangha* or Church, and framing the laws as to dress, diet and social relations according to which his people were to live, founded a positive religion. So did Mohammed when he made the Koran the law for Islam; for his authority is ultimate, his words express God's will, and all we can know of God is what he has made known. But Christ is not related to Christianity as are these creators to the religions that bear their names. The pre-eminence belongs to His

person, not to His words; His people live by faith, not in what He said, but in what He is; they are governed not by statutes He framed, but by the ideal He embodied. In other words, His religion is an evolution of belief, not a product of authoritative legislation. Hence the extraordinary significance of His person, which, till it was interpreted, was but the immanent possibility of a religion. Hence, too, the value of the speculative idea to the ethical ideal; it was the universal Man of the one that created the potent humanity of the other. And so while positive legislation, like Buddha's or Mohammed's, emphasized the differences between those within and those without their societies, the Christian idea emphasized their common humanity. Through the Man who was all mankind, all men became kin. The idea that He who saves is not so much an individual as the collective race, compels His people to feel that in His presence all differences of blood and colour and caste vanish; that to be a man is to be His, redeemed by His death and passion; and that where He has loved we dare not cast out or despise. The people were not constituted like a state by positive law, but by those affinities of the Spirit which faith begot and developed.

2. But this method of constituting the people involved a correlative method of government. The ultimate sanction of positive law is the physical penalty. The magistrate is able to enforce obedience because he bears the sword. The idea of a free State is freedom to make its own laws, but not that its citizens are free to break the laws which have been made. Once the collective will has legislated, all single wills must obey; and if any one refuses obedience he will soon find the legislative become not a friendly and protective, but a hostile and retributive power. Though the bases of authority may be moral, yet the sanctions or penalties it uses to enforce its authority must be physical. The sovereignty of Christ, on the other hand, is in basis

and form, in precept and sanction, rational and moral. He governs man as an idea and an ideal, i.e. through his reason and by his conscience. Hence belief is a material, but polity is a formal question; imitation of Christ is essential, but church is more or less an accident of time and place. A man need not be either a monk or a Churchman to be a Christian; but if he be a Christian he may be both, or either, or neither. He may be a master or servant, a soldier or statesman, a merchant or mechanic; but he must be a man who obeys the Sovereign of his soul. The society that is not free to form its own polity lives in bondage to tradition and custom; but the rule of God is made possible only by the exercised and disciplined freedom of man. And so the immediate result of the spiritual sovereignty was the creation of conscience in religion, and with it the rise of a higher social and civil order. For the ancient mind so identified religion and State that no citizen was conceived to be at liberty to refuse to do honour to his country's gods; it was a grave act of treason not to worship the image or the symbol the emperor set up. Where this notion prevailed no change in religion was possible, save by means of a civil revolution; and out of it came tyrannies, hypocrisies and vices too many to enumerate. Christ's method left the man in his old world, but changed the man; and the man He changed He made so loyal in all civil duties, while so hostile to civil control over his conscience, that the State, to maintain itself, was forced so to change its functions and readjust its claims as to be able to include the man. These things are a parable, but they illustrate the wisdom of the action which, instead of constituting a people by positive, separative regulations, created one by the method of discipleship and faith in a transcendental idea.

3. The social ideal thus created and realized by the idea of Christ's person had four characteristics: (i.) His people were gathered out of all nations without any respect to blood or

rank or caste; they were called simply as men, and constituted into a new mankind. (ii.) They were so organized according to the idea of His person, that they may be described as, symbolically, its articulation. (iii.) As such they represented Him and continued His work. What this work is ought to be construed, not through the offices of organized religion, but through the character, the words and the history of Jesus Himself. (iv.) The most distinctive qualities of this society, its attributes and activities, were, like Christ's own, ethical, and consisted in a worship and service of God which ameliorated the state of man. Where the civil and military ambitions, the ceremonial and sacerdotal functions of the old States stood, the humane beneficences of the new people were now to stand. If His Church had conformed to His ideal, had followed His method in His Spirit, who can tell what man would have been to-day? All we can say is, the vision of the seer of Patmos,[1] who saw the kingdom of the world become the kingdom of our God and of His Christ, would have been infinitely nearer fulfilment than it is.

[1] Rev. xi. 15.

CHAPTER II

IDEAL RELIGION AND THE IDEA OF GOD

§ I. *The Idea of God in Religion*

1. HOW or under what conditions may the belief in one God be incorporated in a universal religion? To discuss this question we must resume certain positions already argued : (*a*) that a single universal religion is possible, but only through the belief in one God ; (β) that the belief may exist without the religion, though not the religion without the belief; and (γ) that the incorporation can happen only under certain terms or conditions, such as (1) that God is held to be equally accessible in all places, to all peoples and persons ; (2) that the terms on which access is granted are capable of fulfilment by all men ; and (3) that He has a character all can trust and qualities all can reverence. These principles imply others still more fundamental, such as (*a*) the correlativity of our knowledge of God, of nature, and of ourselves ; (β) the indissoluble connexion between the conception of God as a moral Being and the facts of our moral nature ; (γ) the co-ordination of His responsibility for us with our responsibility to Him, His responsibility being increased rather than lessened by the existence of evil ; and (δ) the witness borne (1) by man's universal search for God to His search for universal man; (2) by the universality of the religions to the possibility of a universal religion ; and (3) by the action of the higher religious ideas on man to his need of the highest of all ideas in its highest form in order that he may attain his most perfect state.

2. How, then, is this highest of all ideas to be worthily realized, i.e. incorporated in a religion which does justice to its intrinsic qualities and capabilities? There is nothing so easy as to change an idea in philosophy, nothing so near to the impossible as to change an idea in religion. What reason created reason can uncreate; what human nature has made can be unmade only by the dissolution or reconstruction of the nature. And religious beliefs have not only a more indestructible life, but a vaster potency than philosophical ideas. They have lived longer and gathered strength from their years; they speak to man and to more of him, with a more audible and more familiar and intelligible voice. If we try to represent a deity as he appears to those who worship him, how innumerable are the figures of speech we must employ! He is the highest known power, yet he is in the hands of those who address him. His interests are so theirs and his inclination such that if they but do the thing he approves, he will do what they desire. What he is to them he has been to their fathers; their history is the story of his action; their good fortune tells of his favour, their calamities tell of his displeasure. The events which sum up the meaning of life are associated with his name; the birth which promises continuance to the family, the marriage which brings it enlargement, the death which makes the living desolate, yet gives them dignity by binding their moment of being to the eternal. If they contend in battle, they ask him for victory; if they are confronted by famine, they beseech him for food; if their enemies perish, they sing his praises; if pestilence and death walk abroad, they appease his wrath. If they have imagination, their delight is the poetry that exalts his majesty and his power; if they are emotional, they either cultivate the mysticism that seeks absorption in him, or they offer the gifts that administer comfort by assuaging fear; if they are moral they put themselves under discipline and train themselves into asceticism and self-denial. There is no mood that the god who lives in the reli-

gion does not speak to, no conviction or affection, no passion or prejudice to which he does not appeal. It is no wonder, then, that the change of an ancestral and national deity is one of the rarest things in history ; and it is the rarer because in this region, where the ideas are all ideas of the reason, reason so seldom reigns, or reigns with shut or blinded or veiled eyes. Hence what may be to the thinker an obvious truism will be to the zealot or the devout person a " damnable heresy."[1]

Two things are to us so self-evident as to deserve the name of inevitable ideas, viz., the unity of God and His moral character; yet how does the case stand as regards the religions? Take the Unity. Monotheism is a very late and an infrequent faith. With that curious subordination of history to theory which distinguished him, Comte made Monotheism the last step in the first of the three stages through which man passes in the progress of his knowledge. But, as a matter of fact, Monotheism is a belief relatively recent; it has not been uniformly reached, was reached not by any general consensus, but by a small and exceptional fraction of the race, a single desert tribe, from whom all civilized men have received it. To-day Polytheism extends far further than Monotheism, for it is easier and more natural to man to embody in everything the Divine which he finds everywhere, to localize it, to split it up as it were into a multitude of definite and tractable individuals, than to refine it into an infinite personality, too abstract to be felt. But unless God be One He cannot be moral; in a multitude of deities morality is dissolved, for each of the multitude being divine has his own laws and does what is right in his own eyes. It is a matter of history that Polytheisms are by nature either unmoral or immoral. It is hard for us to conceive any sort of vice as godliness, or a pious man as other than virtuous. But our difficulty, which is due to centuries of Christian discipline, is one no ancient Greek would have felt, and no modern Hindu, or any modern savage who

[1] 2 Peter ii. 1.

worships as nature bids him, would feel. We must have one God before we can have the idea of a moral deity whose will is absolute law. But the moment this point is gained we are faced by difficulties of another order. On the one side the philosopher lays hold of the Monotheistic idea, elaborates it logically, reduces it to an abstraction, translates it into the terms of the schools, names it Substance or Entity, Nature or Humanity, the Infinite or even the Unknown; but the idea so transformed has ceased to be the living God which religion needs in order to live. On the other side there operate the sensuous temper and tendencies of the people. They cannot have a God afar off, they must have Him near at hand, manifest, palpable, living to spirit by being real to sense. Hence even within Christianity we find the energies of the Deity and His means of intercourse with man placed in stones, in temples, in images, in rites, nay, in the very garments men may wear as they worship. Men, indeed, will make anything into a god, if so be they can get command of the god they fear.

§ II. *Christ's Interpretation of God*

The abstract question, then, with which our discussion began, now assumes a much more concrete form: How far may it be justly claimed that God, as interpreted through Jesus Christ, has become, or is capable of becoming, the God of a universal religion? The positions assumed from our previous argument are: (*a*) The creative pre-eminence in religious history of Jesus Christ; (β) the special type of religion embodied in His character and life; (γ) the interpretation of His person by Himself, His disciples and apostles as containing (1) distinctive ideas of God and man; (2) the terms on which God comes to man, and man can find access to God; and (3) the modes in which man may worship Him.

One or two points suggested by the phrasing of the

question must be considered. (*a*) God is said to be interpreted "through Christ," not "by" Him. Interpretation "by Christ" would be limited to His teaching, what He said as expressing what He thought concerning God; but interpretation "through Christ," while it does not exclude the teaching, includes the person and character as well; what others thought concerning God because they thought as they did of Christ. (β) To interpret God is not to create man's knowledge of Him, though it may be to correct or perfect that knowledge. Men had known God and believed in Him before Christ came, as they still do where they have never heard of Him. Without the knowledge that existed before and apart from Him, the interpretation could not be understood. This means that He stands in an order governed by law, that He completes a process which has been going on ever since the birth of man, and still goes on wherever man is. Christ is more of a response to a nature dissatisfied with its own discoveries and knowledge, than an absolute miracle which violates all that nature's laws. (γ) The God He interprets is not an object of speculative thought, the causal or the synthetic idea of the nature we study; but He is an object of veneration, a Being man seeks to know that he may love and worship. What we have to do with, then, is not the metaphysical reality or philosophical warrant of the belief, but its religious value and efficiency, whether it has power to displace the ideas which the local cults have throned so firmly in the soul, and whether it has the qualities capable of organizing a fitting form for man's highest and most potent idea. (δ) The interpreter brings to more perfect knowledge the God in whose name He speaks, but does not supersede Him. While He Himself was construed as the God within God, the hands as it were by which Deity held and guided and saved humanity, yet He was not, in spite of strong tendencies to the personification and apotheosis here of an abstract nature, there of an ethical quality, set as an independent and isolated Divine Being over against the Godhead. And this is the more remarkable as supersession is a process so common in the religions as to be entitled to be termed uniform and constant. It finds barbarous expression in Greek mythology, especially as it is found in Hesiod. Zeus, though the father of gods and men, is himself a son who supplanted a father, who had attempted to keep his supremacy by devouring his own offspring. In the *Rigveda* we can trace the process by which Indra displaces Varuna, just as he had earlier stepped into the seat of Dyaus, and as all the gods vanished later into the bosom of Brahma, the youngest of the Vedic deities, who yet with his name slightly changed, so as to denote the highest philosophical idea, swallowed up all the older gods. In the Mahabharata we see Krishna rise, attain fame, climb from manhood into godhood, though the qualities and feats held to prove him divine are very manlike indeed; and he attracts to himself, as he sits amid the high gods in the Hindu pantheon, peculiar honours and a special cult. But Christ reveals or interprets without superseding Deity, enhances His grace without lessening His dignity. He does not break up the unity of God, for divided or individuated being is never claimed for Him. His own achievements do not form into a glory round His head, eclipsing the eternal Father. On the contrary He at once infinitely enriches and unifies the object of worship. He interprets without either superseding God, or reducing His majesty, or dividing His honour.

§ III. *The God Christ Interprets a Universal Ideal*

How far, then, may we say that God so interpreted through Christ is a Deity who could not be known and worshipped without forming a universal religion?

1. Let us note the action of the Interpreter on the idea. God was dissociated from a special State and associated with

a person; and this person was conceived as the symbol of humanity, an epitome of mankind. It is the characteristic of all ancient and unreformed religions to be tribal or national —for the nation is but the larger tribe; and the tribe loves its religion and reveres its god because they are its own, and are so bound up with its order and customs that their dissolution could only signify its destruction. If a stranger wishes to be admitted to the favour of the god, or the practice of the religion, he must become a member of the tribe, rebirth or naturalization being the only way to participation in its most solemn rites. The sanctuary was ever the spot most jealously guarded against the curious and prying alien. But Christ, as the interpretative personality, detached God from the customs of the tribe, and attached Him to the idea of man. There is nothing so universal as the individual who is the whole in little, as there is nothing so exclusive as the family which must, to maintain its being and its claims, keep its blood pure. But Christ, construed as the ideal of humanity, shows what God intended to be to every man, and what every man ought to be to God. He is an illimitable yet concrete and historical person; and as such He is at once the type of the man who alone can please God, and the symbol of the idea that one has only to be a man to be God's, and that the more fully He inhabits us the more completely human we become. The family from which Christ sprang disowned Him, and the act which cut Him off was like the truth told in parable: it meant that God had ceased to be the property of a people, and become the possession of mankind.

2. The change in the medium through which God was known involved a correspondent change in the way He was conceived, i.e. since Christ stood for man without any distinction of race, God, as interpreted through Him, was loosed from the qualities that bound Him to a peculiar people. The attribute of will which had been emphasized to justify His

choice of Israel, fell into the background, and grace, which is will spontaneously seeking the common good, came to the front. Christ was Son of God in no figurative or incidental sense, but essentially; and as the moment never had been when there was no Son, so there had never been, and could never be, a moment when there was or should be no Father. Thus love and fellowship, affinity and affection were bound up with the very being of God. He could not be conceived as loveless thought, or as abstract substance, or as almighty energy, so long as the terms Father and Son could be used to denote eternal facts and relations essential to His Deity. But even more significant was the correlative change in the conception of His manward activities and relations. To conceive the typical Man as essentially Son was to be driven to think of humanity in the terms of sonship. If by the very constitution of His being God was a Father, man by the very fact of his creation in Christ was constituted a son. And if collective man was God's son, it followed that God was man's Father, and so there stepped into the place of the tribal deity the universal Fatherhood. Before we can guess what this signified, we must have studied the spirit, traced the history, watched the action and the effects of the religions. To see how they have created caste, sanctioned and magnified the pride of blood, emphasized the distinctions of colour and race, justified the inhumanity of man to man, and then to discover how a religion has been based on a Fatherhood too universal either to know or to show "respect of persons," is as if one were suddenly taken from the study of crippling disease to the contemplation of sunny and buoyant health. The provincialism which justifies the jealousy and injustice of deity, his partiality for his own race, his insincerities and even ferocities to other races, directly hinders the birth and the growth of the idea of humanity, and encourages the terror which regards blood as the proper food of the gods. But when man thought of God in the terms of ideal humanity, as impersonated in Jesus Christ, his religion was at once universalized; the more thoroughly he believed, and the more piously he worshipped, the more humane he became in faith. The religion which did honour to the God who loved all men required the service of all mankind.

3. But the conception of man was changed as well as that of God. We may without extravagance say that man had never come by his rights in religion; for either, where God was great and of infinite majesty, he had been humbled into the dust; or, where God was very terrible, he had been degraded into an instrument that could be broken and cast away, or depraved into a coward who would offer the fruit of his body for the sin of his soul; or, where God was complaisant, he had taken him into his own hands and done with him as he pleased. To find a fit relation or a seemly equilibrium between God and man is a thing hard enough to be esteemed impossible, yet this was what Christ achieved. He made man stand upright before God, conscious of his dignity. It does not become a being of infinite promise to lie prone in the dust, even before the Infinite Majesty. To feel what it is to be the eternal Father's son, is to learn to behave as a son, possessed of his privileges as well as bound by his duties; and it is also to feel that all sons are equal in their potential, though not perhaps in their realized worth. Hence the Christian idea created two novel notions as to man: the value of the unit and the unity of the race. The ancient nations that most valued their collective existence attached least value to the individual man. If he was a slave, he was but a chattel; if he was an alien, his own gods might care for him, the native gods had other and better things to do. If his colour or his stature was not theirs, he would be described in terms more appropriate to a brute than to a man; and if his worship was noticed, his gods were said to be devils rather than deities. Refinement, intercourse, the decay of the martial spirit and the rise of the great empires may have created in the West

THE SANCTITY OF MAN AND LIFE

a milder temper and more restrained speech, but they did not add to the dignity of the individual. We admire the pyramids and temples of Egypt, but forget the misery of the men whose forced labour built them, or the pride of the king who wanted a splendid mausoleum, and thought, if he thought at all on the matter, that to sacrifice some thousands of men in building it made it all the fitter a tomb for a king. And so it seems to China, with its hundreds of millions of men, as if the waste of man by disease or the fierce forces of nature mattered little; there is the more to divide among the living if there are fewer mouths to be fed. We never cease to wonder at the art and literature of Athens, both so perfect in form, but we seldom imagine what is meant by the simple fact that when her life was bravest and her struggle hardest she had barely five thousand citizens, while of her slaves twenty thousand could desert to the enemy. Roman law was remarkable for its love of justice and its care for human rights; but to the Roman law the slave was a thing and no man, while Roman men were never so pitiless to others as when they were most concerned about their own privileges. And to-day the Hindu judges life by other standards and reads it with other eyes than ours. To him indeed life, simply as animal life, is sacred, a thing which he must not destroy; yet the feeling of its sanctity does not extend to the human personality, at least as the West understands it. If he argues as the divine charioteer in the *Bhagavadgita* does, he will hold that since man's being is indestructible, a mere moment in the circle of everlasting change, killing is no murder; but he may add for himself that to lose one's life in trying to rescue others from the jaws of famine and pestilence, is a most needless extravagance of mercy. The Englishman is—because of his passion to save the lives of men, combined with his pleasure in killing wild animals, a pleasure great in proportion to the wildness of the animal—a standing puzzle to the Hindu; but if he only could read the Englishman through his religion, he would see that the enthusiasm for the saving of men was the point where Christ had touched him, and made him so different in religion from what he is by nature. By nature he kills the tiger for sport, delights in perils and adventures, and finds amusement in facing or causing death in the jungle; but by religion he has become one who would die to save a man from death, whether he be a man of high caste, or of low caste, or of no caste. And how is it that man has become to the higher Christian peoples a being of such infinite possibilities and incalculable value that he must cease to be a slave, and be protected in his life and in his rights, however mean his nature and low his culture? How has it come about that the most truculent of races has come to act as if it were a fitter and more heroic thing for a man to sacrifice himself in saving life than to assert himself in destroying it? There is but one answer possible: it is due to the idea in his religion which holds him most strongly, and which never, whatever may happen to his faith, quite loses its grasp upon his conduct, that he ought to do for others what Christ did for him. He may die for man, but he cannot despise him. If he believes that Christ took his human nature, he must also believe that He dignified the nature He bore. Man seen through His humanity becomes a being of transcendent value; the nature which has been put of God to the most gracious of all uses is a nature that can be no more despised or mishandled. To the strong it was an imperious duty to help the weak, and a thing sternly forbidden to destroy the brother for whom Christ died. And so the religion began as a recreative humanity, which made it impossible to the parent to expose his child, or to the crowd to make holiday in the amphitheatre where the trembling man was thrown to the wild beast, or to the freeman to hold a brother man as his slave.

But this value of the individual needed for its full significance another and correlative idea, the unity of the race.[1] The most abstract of ideas was here destined to prove the most potent of practical beliefs. One person conceived as the symbol or epitome of man, in whose life all lived, in whose death all died, achieved the unification of mankind. The unity as it was held in ancient philosophy, especially by the Stoics, was a noble doctrine, but it remained a doctrine, an ideal which is an abstract; it did not walk about in the marketplace and deal with actual men. But the unity which Christ embodied was not ideal only, it was ethical and actual. The churches came into being as attempts to realize it, and these attempts grew into a fuller consciousness of what it signified. Ideals may take centuries to grow into realities, but they do grow, and the nearer the realities come the more infinite do the ideals appear. And this is pre-eminently true of this belief. We are but beginning to understand the responsibilities and obligations which lie upon the whole family of man for each member, and which lie upon each member for the family as a whole as well as for its several parts. Humanity as a whole was responsible for the sufferings of Christ, but though He suffered at its hands He was not free to inflict upon it suffering. On the contrary, His grace bound Him to submit that He might conquer, to die that He and His might live. He saw that sin as collective, inherent and inherited, rooted in nature and by nature propagated, was more a misfortune than a crime, and that sin as personal, active and expressed in acts, was a crime, though it might begin in misfortune. And He further saw that while it was the nature of the evil to harm the good, it was the duty and function of the good to save the evil. And so as the blameless Brother of a guilty family He bore the family's guilt, so bore it that all might learn of Him how to escape the sin that was sorrow and caused death.

Ante, pp. 444 ff.

§ IV. *The Condition of Realization*

1. But quite as significant as the ideas is the condition of their appropriation, the act and attitude of mind—for it is both—termed faith. It is an intellectual act, for it is a form of knowledge ; it is an emotional attitude and activity, for it trusts persons and works by love ; it is a moral intuition, for it sees obligation in truth and right in duty. It is not a single or occasional act, though it may be compared to a vision which for a moment looks into eternity and never forgets what it has seen; but it is continuous communion with the things the vision saw. Faith as knowledge studies the historical person, but as belief it sees in the ideal the symbol of God and the universe. The historical person is studied as if He were the realized religion, and He must be known that He may be imitated and obeyed. The ideal is contemplated that the soul may stand face to face with God, and endure as seeing Him who is invisible. In both aspects, as knowledge and as vision, faith is a receptivity ; it is man standing open to the touch and action of the eternal, yet as also sensitive and active, holding fast to what has been received. Its antithesis is the work which creates merit, the action which establishes a claim to reward ; but its correlative is grace, the spontaneous energy of the God who made man for Himself, effecting His conscious appropriation by the man He made.

2. Now faith, so understood, is an idea most characteristic of the Christian religion ; in no other does it hold the same place or fulfil the same functions. This is, no doubt, partly due to the kind and quality of the associated ideas ; it belongs to their household, has the face and features distinctive of the family. But this only emphasizes the distinction of the religion as a religion. Those before and around it were constituted by acts and customs rather than by beliefs ; and were more methods of approaching God than ways by which

He could approach us. They threw the burden of reconciliation on man and bade him do the things or use the means that would give him acceptance with God. The Christian was the first religion, as a religion, to say that custom has no worth, that work has no merit, that the only thing that can avail before God is the righteousness He gives and faith receives. In Greece, religion was a matter of oracles and shrines, of festivals national and civil, of conformity to law and custom, as both Protagoras and Sokrates found to their cost. Men might believe in the value of certain acts or the efficacy of certain institutions; but religion was too nearly identical with these to lay much stress on the faith that trusted the truth and acquired no merit. Its absence in the religion is reflected in the schools, where it has no recognition in a religious sense till we come to Proclus, who, in what is more a borrowed than a native tongue, speaks of faith as higher than knowledge and better than love, for love leads us only to the beautiful, but faith to God. The Roman worship consisted pre-eminently in expressions of joy, in lays and songs, in games and dances, and, above all, in banquets, "being grounded essentially on man's enjoyment of earthly pleasures, and only in a subordinate degree on his fear of the wild forces of nature."[1] In India the customs and laws of religion surround a man from his birth, govern his life as a whole, as well as its individual parts, his childhood, youth, manhood, and old age, his years, his months, his very days, but faith is no part of it. Certain philosophical sects have indeed made of *Bhakti*, which under one aspect is devotion, and under another faith, a cardinal doctrine; but while they may have known it, the multitude of religions we call Hinduism has not. The notion was native to prophetic Hebraism, and was fitly associated with the promise and its ethical Monotheism; but institutional Judaism was too much concerned with the acts and articles of worship to care for faith. Hence Christianity,

[1] Mommsen's *History of Rome*, i. 221.

in making faith the subjective pivot of religion, separated itself from uniform and invariable custom, boldly made itself independent of usage and institution, and brought the individual man and the absolute God face to face. It was the only mode in which a religion of universal ideas could have been realized by universal man.

This discussion leaves us with a question we must ask, though we shall not attempt to give it the answer it deserves and requires : What precisely did Christ, by these ideas and the condition of their realization, accomplish for religion? It is a small thing to say, He made a universal religion possible ; it is a greater thing to add, The religion He made possible is one that ought to be universal, for its ideal is the humanest and the most beneficent that has ever come to man. He completely moralized Deity, and therefore religion; and so made it possible—nay, obligatory and imperative—to moralize the whole life of man, individual and collective. His moral ideal expressed the beneficence of an infinite will, yet as impersonated in what we may term an actual yet universal Man. It was transcendental as God, it was immanent as mind ; and as incarnated in a religion, it concentrated the energies of the eternal for realization in the modes of time. If this can be said of Christ, what higher work could be ascribed to God ?

CHAPTER III

THE IDEAL RELIGION AND WORSHIP

WORSHIP as we have seen[1] is as essential as belief to religion. The man who thinks of God, if he thinks truly, must worship Him, for without this even nature would not be content. But is worship possible without some institution? and is an institution, which must bear the marks of time and place, possible in a universal religion? and what is a religion without worship save a philosophy or a system of more or less reasoned ideas?

Worship and belief differ in the nature and tendency of their action in religion; belief is the freer and the more expansive, worship is the more traditional and local. Thought is more open and accessible to new influences than custom, changes its forms more easily, and gains more by the change. And hence the frequency of such phenomena as the religion of Israel exhibited—the conflicts of the universal, the Monotheistic idea, with the local and consuetudinary, the spirit and institutions of the tribe.[2] Now these latter represent two forces or tendencies, a localizing, embodied in a place, and an externalizing, embodied in institutions.

§ I. *Place as it Affects Worship*

1. The holy place is perhaps the last and most inveterate of the forms which tribal particularism assumes. It may be described as the spot or the structure where the people of a

[1] Ante, pp. 480-481. [2] Ante pp. 244-257.

religion feel that they can offer the most acceptable worship to their God. Its sacred character is seldom due to a single cause, though complex causes may from some simple occasion become active. If we take the word "reason" as subsuming both cause and occasion, we should say that the reasons why a place becomes holy may be described as either physical, mythological, traditional, or historical. The physical reasons, though they never act without the impulse of a belief which is seeking to become articulate, may be a cave, as at Delphi; or a well whose waters have some peculiar virtue, as in the case of the innumerable holy wells of ancient religion and mediaeval legend, or whose springs make an oasis in the desert, as at the shrine of Jupiter Ammon, which Alexander visited; or it may be a tree through whose murmuring branches the god is heard to speak, as at Dodona. The mythological reasons, which never act without the physical, are the beliefs which place the gods either on special mountains, as the Greek seated his on Olympus or the Hindu his on Kailasa, the Himalayas, "formed by Visvakarman, in colour like a brilliant cloud and decorated with gold," whence they could hurl the thunderbolt or blow from their nostrils the devouring blast; or in some forest glade, where life does its silent but creative work, like the Germans of Tacitus, who "lucos ac nemora consecrant, deorumque nominibus appellant secretum illud, quod solâ reverentiâ vident,"[1] or like the Arician "templum nemorale Dianæ."[2] The traditional reasons may be the association of a district with some person or event, like the birth of a god, the burial of a saint, the wisdom of a teacher, or a miraculous appearance of deity; and to this class of places belong those regions of the Nile, where the weeping Isis wandered in search of the dismembered Osiris; Mathura, where the Yadavas thought Krishna achieved divine fame; Benares, where the dread Siva rolled the mighty river which

---

[1] *Germania*, ix.
[2] Ovid, *Ars Amat.* i. 259; cf. *Fasti*, vi. 59

THEIR ACTION ON THE RELIGION 553

had descended out of heaven upon his head; Ayodha, holy land of the Buddhists, where the Master was born and made the great renunciation; and the multitudinous Catholic shrines where, as at Lourdes, the Virgin has appeared to some devout and ecstatic maid. The historical reasons belong either to the life of a people, like those that made Jerusalem, because the city of their great king and the capital of their race, seem to the Jews the fit home of their God; or to the recorded experiences of some person, like those that made Mecca, the city where his youth had been passed, where his ancestors had dwelt, and whither the tribes of Arabia had for centuries gone to high festivals and such worship as they knew, so dear and so delightful to Mohammed.

Now, under these varied forms, different as they may seem, the action of place is in two respects the same, it localizes and it externalizes, working the more disastrously the purer and the broader the religion is. Thus sanctity comes to have a physical cause, bodily contact with the sacred object to have a specific religious value. The water that flows past the place becomes sacred, and to bathe in the Jordan or the Ganges, to drink of the well Zem Zem, or of the spring where the saint quenched his thirst, or above which the Virgin appeared, is either to be cleansed from sin or to acquire peculiar merit. If the pilgrim cannot go to the water, it can be brought to him; and for a price he buys his reward. The spot which the god touched, the cell where the saint lived, the cave where the prophet hid can be seen and handled; and the pilgrim feels as if he had done honour to the god and become worthier of heaven. The multitudes who go on pilgrimage are composed of persons intent on performing a religious duty, but they soon grow mixed, and the more mixed they grow the less devout they get, till what began in fervour may end in licence and riot. The people who keep the holy places grow as holy as they; priests increase, live on the alms and offerings of the faithful; and the industry of the place centres in the religion, and it becomes a commodity made and marketable, represented by articles that can be bought and sold. And so relics and memorials which can make his worship efficacious are manufactured, legends are invented to enhance the reputation of the god and the religious value of the place. The inevitable outcome is a materialized and localized deity and a coarsened worship. And this is a saying every holy place in the world illustrates if it does not justify.

2. But here it is necessary to distinguish : a local cult may suit the genius and type of a religion just as a side chapel falls in with the design of a cathedral ; but it is an altogether different matter where the religion is universal in idea and intention, while the place where men must worship, if they would worship acceptably, is but one. There are two examples of this inconsistency between idea and place, Judaism and Islam, but with most significant differences. Jerusalem was symbolical of the Jew, and though it perished he survived, and his God so survived with him that ever since they have dwelt together, God inseparable from the people and the people from God. To Mohammed, his people and land were alike holy ; the Arab was to conquer the world, but not to forsake Arabia ; thither, however far he wandered, he was ever to return, and the races he subdued to the faith were to come as pilgrims to the city of God and His prophet. But the success of the Arab arms destroyed the sanctity and separateness of the Arab people, though it only enhanced the sacredness of Mecca. The city towards which the Moslim pray is a city their feet must stand within if they would see God. But this localization of the highest act of worship keeps the religion racial, oriental, semi-barbaric, governed by Arab standards, ever confounded by the offer to physical endurance and achievement of those rewards which should be reserved for spiritual excellence. Emancipation from place is thus a necessity in the case of a religion that would be co-

extensive with man, and sufficient for his nature and its needs.

3. Now this emancipation Christ achieved, and His is the only religion which has achieved it. The association of worship with His person completely dissociated it from place, and it became possible to approach God anywhere, provided He was approached through Him. For union with Him needs but faith; the man who believes in the Son of God is identified with Christ, and when he worships it is as if Jesus worshipped. Since the act that relates the soul to the person through whom it finds acceptance is inner and spiritual, place and time are alike irrelevant, the spirit and the truth are all in all. Hence, too, the one medium is more ample than an infinity of local media, for their variety affects many things,—God, the sort of worship He approves, the acts that constitute it, the persons by whom and through whom it may be offered. A multitude of shrines means a multitude of deities, and not simply of men and the homes where they live. The man who worships the Virgin or prays to St. Joseph for a boon to himself or an evil to his enemy, who goes on pilgrimage to the tomb of St. Antony at Padua, or seeks from St. Francis at the Portiuncula healing for body or soul, finds in each place a different god, a being complexioned by the medium through which he is approached. But the one Mediator does not lower God to the sensuous needs of variable man, rather lifts man into the spiritual mood in which he feels his kinship with God. And the union of apparent incompatibilities in His person made it all the fitter a medium for this high purpose. He inhabits no place, yet He fills all time, which means that there is no spot where He cannot be found and no moment without His presence. He is as invisible and impalpable as God, yet as audible and tangible as man; and, we may add, to form an image of the image of the God no man can see is impossible. And it is unnecessary, for the Soul of Him, whom the art of no graver and the chisel

of no sculptor can represent, lives incarnate in speech which all men can hear or read.

And this has a high significance; the pictures which men delight to paint, or the statues they carve of Jesus on the cross or in the tomb, and which women love tearfully to kneel before, are not images of the Christ, nor in any sense representations of Him. There is nothing that fills me with darker horror or deeper aversion than the apotheosis of wounds and death which the Roman Church offers as its image of the Christ. Some months ago I stood in an Italian cathedral; it had been built by the wickedest, the fiercest, the most pagan, and probably the most learned of the Malatesti. Within it was the sarcophagus which held his remains, with his mocking inscription graven upon it, and the chapel where reposed those of his mistress Isotta, whose initials interwoven with his own were carved on every pillar and boss; while without in another sarcophagus are deposited the bones of Gemisthus Pletho, which he had proudly brought from Greece in days when men had been taught to seek miraculous virtue in the most gruesome relics of mortality. In this church, with a hideous moral heathenism looking out from every figure and line, what was conceived to be an act of Christian worship was going on. A crowd of priests was marching round, one at their head carrying a cross on which was fastened a contorted figure, together with nails, a hammer, a saw, and a pair of pincers, while from one of the beams hung a ladder of ropes. As the crowd paused to chant their monotonous strain before each altar, bending themselves and their symbol towards it together, I could not help saying, in what was not pride but utter humiliation of soul, " Your worship is not mine, nor is your God; and as for this cross you carry, it speaks rather of the wickedness of the men who slew the Saviour than of the grace of Him who saves man by His love." For how is it possible to make an image of Him without carnalizing a form that must be spiritual to be true? He is a type, an ideal, a symbol, which expresses at once the grace of the infinite God, and the promise, the potency and the inexhaustible possibilities of man. In His face divine pity shows, the tenderness of the everlasting Father as He looks out from an eternity that knows neither the haste nor the passion of time; and yet while the pity is divine the face is human, and speaks of man made by God for God, touched with the shame for sin which the pure alone can know, the sorrow for misery which none but the blessed can feel, the horror for death which only the dweller in immortal light can experience. And this is the person, "all glorious within," who has emancipated religion from the tyranny of place by teaching us that "he who hath seen Me hath seen the Father."

§ II. *The Institution as it Affects Worship*

1. The institution is the second and most potent of the forms under which the tribal spirit may affect religion. The term denotes all the customs and usages which constitute the local worship, or which determine the times and regulate the conduct of its several parts. Now the institution, so understood, is more potent in its action than the place; for it speaks more directly and authoritatively of God and to Him, describes His character and attitude to man, as well as what man's character, and what his attitude towards God ought to be; what he must do and what agents and agencies employ if he would please Him. In the worship therefore, as a consuetudinary or regulated system, the idea of God is presented in its most definite, concentrated and constant form; the worshipper learns, by doing the things which authority has declared and usage sanctioned as the most agreeable to Deity, what the Deity is and what kind and order of man He most approves.

While the ideas that underlie religion and organize its institutions differ, qualitatively and formally, almost to infinity, yet in one respect all worships agree, they are methods of approaching and pleasing God, means by which man seeks access to Him, tries to win His favour and gain His peace. Of course in the very way taken to reach Him, and the acts done, and the things offered in His honour, there is a most subtle yet concrete indication of character; but difference here does not affect the point of agreement: all worship aims at establishing harmony between two wills, God's and man's; whether it be by influencing man to surrender his will to God's, or by inducing God to do the will of man. These two may indeed imperceptibly shade into one another, but the rule is this—the lower the idea of God, the more He is conceived to be in the hands of man, but the higher the idea of Him the stronger becomes man's desire to leave himself in the hands of God.

2. If now the function of worship and its relation to the ideas of God and religion have been correctly described, it follows that this is the point where religion affects man and man religion most potently and most constantly. What its effect on character is to be does not depend so much on the idea of the relation between the persons as on the idea of the persons related. In the abstract worship ought to be the moment of most penetrative and illuminative exaltation in man's life, and it will be this if God is the highest and the holiest Being he can conceive or desire; but this it will not be if he simply seeks from God some advantage to himself which he can obtain from no other person or will. The advantage need not be material, may indeed be forgiveness of sins or acceptance of the person; but the mischief will be radical if the attempt be made to purchase it by offering to God something that will please Him in order that He may do something that will benefit us. For a God from whom anything can be purchased has fallen from the high estate of deity, who must give out of free grace if He is to

be honoured. If worship be conceived not as adoration of the only and absolutely adorable, but as giving a *quid pro quo*, then it becomes an effectual means of deteriorating religion and depraving man, and assimilating God to what in him is most depraved. And the more the externals of worship—the acts it consists of, the offerings it brings, the persons who present them—are emphasized, the more it bears this character and does this work. As a matter of fact the ancient religion whose worship was most domestic and least official, was the most lucid, imperative and impressive in its ethical teaching; while those religions that made most of priesthood and sacrifice were also those that most neglected the humaner and higher virtues. The highest ethics of the *Rigveda* are associated with the name of Varuna, and in his days the *rishi* or poet potently sang his praise, and the priest was only a shadow and a name; but in the later Sanskrit literature, as, say, in the epic which celebrates the deeds of Rama and the Law Book which bears the name of Manu, the tendency that began with magnifying sacrifice has ended in the decay of ethics, the death of all ideas of duty towards man as man, and the apotheosis of caste. Greek philosophy was a noble teacher of morals, but what ideals of good or justice do we owe to Greek religion? The Roman State jealously guarded the dignity and sacred character of the priesthood, and proudly supplied the college of pontiffs with "robes of purple and chariots of state," but had it not been for the Stoic teaching, especially as it affected Roman law, and the deification of the Empire, what would have become of Roman virtue? In Israel the conflict of prophet and priest reached its acutest issue in the idea of worship. What the one cultivated and delighted in, "the multitude of sacrifices," "the burnt offerings of rams and the fat of fed beasts," "the blood of bullocks or of lambs or of he-goats,"[1] the other despised and abhorred. The sacrifices the prophet

[1] Isaiah i. 11.

praised were those of joy and righteousness, of a broken and a contrite spirit. The notion that God was the Being whose mind needed to be changed, and that the change could be effected by things that could be purchased, a proper animal properly selected and properly killed, burned and offered by proper hands in the proper place, was a notion fatal to the ethical nature of religion and its power to create moral men. The more religion is bound to a special class of persons who officiate at special times and seasons, the more these persons become distinguished not by character but by descent, not by spiritual purity but by ceremonial cleanness, not by moral eminence but by distinctions of office and habit. And these things do not make for a high or a universal ideal in religion; on the contrary, without their abolition one could not be realized. The only institution possible in a universal religion must be an ideal; and Christ is at once an historical and a symbolical person. As the one He shows what the worshipper ought to be, as the other He is the cause of acceptable worship.

§ III. *Christ the only Institution for Christian Worship*

1. Now it is here where the discussions as to Christ's death and as to the emphasis laid upon it by Himself and His apostles will be understood. It was said that His person was conceived as an institution; and this signified that all the conditions and means needed by man for the perfect worship of God were realized in Him. He fulfilled the law; the ideas which the Levitical system showed in shadow He made substantive and final, realized "once and for ever." He was "the great High Priest," and in His priesthood He was alone. No one stood or could stand by His side. He was the sole Sacrifice needed by man or required by God, and offered through the Eternal Spirit. He lived for ever and His sacrifice for ever availed, for the temple where His priesthood was

exercised was eternal in the heavens. And He fulfilled the prophetic as well as the Levitical ideal. He was "the Lord our righteousness," the cause and means of man's acceptance with God, achieving the forgiveness of sins and the life everlasting. He was thus a whole institution of worship; in Him God was reconciled, in Him man was accepted, and He with the right arm of His Divinity round man, and the left arm of His humanity round God held the two together, knowing and known.

2. From this position several consequences follow.

i. Christ is the sole institution for worship which has divine authority in the Christian religion. He is the only Mediator, and no intermediation is provided for, though means to introduce man to the knowledge of His functions may be lawful and expedient. Hence His office does not exclude such minor or ancillary help as the weakness of man, his peculiar temper or stage of culture, may demand. These may be necessary to him while not essential to the religion, but they are permissible only as aids to the apprehension of the truth. The cardinal fact is the sole sufficiency of Christ; the man that comes unto God must come through Him, and through no other.

ii. The Eucharist is not in the strict sense an institution for worship, but a condition of higher fellowship, a means of communion. Through it the man speaks in symbol to his "great High Priest" and the Priest speaks to him; but this is not to worship God, though it may be to be better qualified for His worship. The reference is to the sacrifice, to our participation in it, to our dying in Christ in order that He and we may live together; but what this signifies is that the more we become in the sight of God and in our own experience one with Him, the fitter we are to worship God. The man who can most perfectly praise and serve God is he who can most truly say: "It is no longer I that live, but Christ that liveth in me."

iii. What is true of the Eucharist is also true of preaching, though it has a larger function and a more clearly recognized place in the chain of secondary causes. It has more of the essence or soul of worship in it; for it creates the enlightened intellect and the quick conscience, without which there can be no worship of a moral Deity. Jesus Himself was a preacher, formed preachers, and commanded them to do as He had done. The apostles were preachers, and while there is in all the apostolical writings but one explicit reference to the Eucharist, the Word is everywhere; to preach it was what they lived for, and the means by which the Churches lived. And this signifies that Christ appealed to faith; and the Christian lived by faith, and faith is knowledge, and knowledge is the exercised reason. He had nothing to fear, nay, He had everything to gain from the awakened intelligence. The slothful and the sensuous mind is His last enemy, which the preaching of the cross was meant to destroy. In the apostolic age this preaching was a "stumbling-block" to the Jew and "foolishness" to the Greek; but unto the called, whether Jews or Greeks, it was "Christ the power of God and the wisdom of God." What antiquity could have easily understood was a religion made up of offices, customs, and usages; what it could not understand was a religion whose only institution was a person realized by faith.

iv. In forming and founding this institution for worship the initiative was God's and not man's. It contradicted the belief that had governed man's action towards Deity and determined the acts and forms of his worship, viz. that God's mind needed to be changed and could be changed by gifts and sacrifices. The belief is venerable,—if age could authenticate any opinion this were the truest man has ever held; and it is common,—if to be believed everywhere, always, and by all make a belief true, this one could not possibly be false. And it is of all the beliefs known to religion the most pernicious; out of it has come the notion that God was harsher than man, that He loved blood and could be appeased by it; that man by satisfying His lust of death could buy from Him pardon and good will. The notion has been incorporated in multitudes of cults, has been coarsened and refined as it has dominated man or been subdued by him; but it has held its ground in the religions, most of all in those whose elaborate institutions, sacrificial and ceremonial, have been the proudest work of its hands. But the Christian idea reversed and undid all this. God it conceived as by nature merciful, immutably gracious in will, while man was the being who needed to be changed. Hence its very essence was stated to be "a ministry of reconciliation," and this was explained as "God in Christ reconciling the world unto Himself,"[1] or as "God commending His love toward us, in that, while we were yet sinners, Christ died for us."[2] The new institution for worship thus made God a real God for mankind. It may be that the old belief is not dead yet, that it still survives even in Christian societies, but it lives as the old Adam lives in the new man, the survivor from a more ancient world, out of harmony with its living environment.

v. The institution defines the kind and quality of the worshipper. He is to have the mind of Christ, to be an imitator of Him. While the worship is made possible by His death, His life shows what makes the worshipper acceptable. Here the value of His sinlessness appears: He is the ideal Man, and the Christian is to be in his own age what Jesus was in His. The New Covenant was created by a moral Person for the creation of moral persons. If the sacrifice shows how much God did for man, the life shows how much He expects from man. He saves the sinner that He may form him into a saint.

vi. The function of the worship is to qualify man to

[1] 2 Cor. v. 18–19.   [2] Rom. v. 8.

fulfil the divine purpose. It has an ultimate and a proximate end; the ultimate end is the glory of God, the proximate is to form the good man, but this is conceived as the way to that. In worship the man adores God, and he can adore only as he knows and admires; and God penetrates the man, becomes the energy of his will, or the soul of his soul, the heart of his heart, until it can be said : "Lo! God is in the man, and is using him to achieve the salvation of the world."

§ IV. *Conclusion*

1. Here then our long and not untoilsome journey ends, though I feel as if these later discussions raised problems too imperious to be dismissed unresolved. Yet our conclusion must be of the most practical kind :—if we do well to speak of the history of Jesus and the interpretation of Christ as the programme of a religion, are we not bound to compare the performance with the programme? The result may be humiliation, for so much of the programme remains unfulfilled; but also some instruction and enlightenment. The aggregation of the institutions and usages which we co-ordinate under the term "Church" round the central idea of the Christian faith, may have been inevitable; but it does not follow that the inevitable was the good, not to say the best. The Church which survived the Roman Empire was an assemblage of new ideas and of ancient customs that had proved their suitability to human nature by living in many religions and surviving many changes of culture and belief; and though it may have helped to preserve the Christian religion, yet it was at the expense of its higher ethical and finer spiritual qualities. The religion was saved by being assimilated to the world in which it had come to live; but the assimilation has cost it centuries of impotence, of bitter controversies, and of struggles, more or less fruitless, to escape from the toils in which it had been caught. Even if Nicaea affirmed the truth as to the deity of

the Son, it so did it as to help to form the Church into a civil state within the Empire and under the Emperor. Granted that Chalcedon rightly defined the two natures and joined them, properly distinguished and delimited, in the unity of the person, yet it conspicuously forgot alike in theory and in practice their ethical significance as to God and man. Would it not have been to the infinite advantage of the religion if these Councils had concerned themselves as much with the ethics as with the metaphysics of the person of Christ; and demanded that the Church should realize the fraternity, the unity of classes and peoples, the faith, hope and charity, the obedience towards God and duty towards man it symbolized? Even if we concede—though the concession, to be just, would need to be largely qualified—that Augustine was right and the Pelagians were wrong, must we not also maintain that his jealousy for the pre-eminence of Adam and for the organic being of man in sin, made him miss the most splendid opportunity that ever came to any Father or thinker for so applying the sovereignty of Christ to the higher moral, social, and spiritual life of the race as to show how the Christian idea could fulfil the ideal of humanity? Luther preached justification by faith alone, but he failed to see that equality before God was incomplete so long as the Church showed respect of persons, bowing low before kings, but trampling as with iron feet upon the peasants they oppressed. There is indeed in all history nothing more tragic than the fact that our heresies have been more speculative than ethical, more concerned with opinion than with conduct; that the Church whose claims are highest and most indefeasible in doctrine, has been the most prone to compromise in morals, consumed with jealousy for the honour and inalienability of the priestly office, while cynically indulgent towards the priestly character. But if Christ be rightly interpreted, the worst sins against God are those most injurious to man. His person is indeed a symbol of humanity in its double sense, as, subjectively, an emotion which becomes enthusiasm for the common good, and as, objectively, a race made one by the possession of a common and equal nature. Defined and explicated on its Godward side, the person yields a doctrine of God and redemption; but on its Manward side, it becomes a theory of the race which it is the primary duty and main function of the Church to realize. The ancient usages—the priesthoods, the sacrifices, the consecrations and transubstantiations, beliefs regulated by canon and discipline, enforced by law, as if it were an affair of state—which out of the old religions had stolen back into the Church, signified that the institutions the person had replaced were seeking to displace the person. They had on their side the innate and inveterate prejudices of human nature; it had on its side the ideal which was the supreme dream of the religion, and it has proved its power by compelling its very enemies to do its will, even when seeking their own ends.

2. The person, then, as institution made the religion universal in its aims and ideas, in its modes and action, and it has acted, in spite of the defective means and recalcitrant agencies it has had to employ, as became its high function. And what inference as to its constituents and character may be drawn from these discussions? Our purpose was not simply to co-ordinate historical phenomena, but to discover the causes that produce them, the ends they serve, the laws that govern their order and their movements. And certainly no discovery has in it more promise of scientific satisfaction than the relation between the conception of Christ which makes His person the source and epitome of a religion, and the function He has actually fulfilled in history. For what is the principle fundamental to all science? This: we do not live in a world where things come uncaused. We conceive nature as the realm where order and causation reign. Chance is a word science does not know. Accident is a

term which only denotes ignorance. It is used because vision has not found the secret it searched for. The growth of science is the decay of chance; when the one has finally prevailed there will be no place for the other. But order cannot reign in the nature now around man, and yet chance govern man himself; and if order reigns in history as in nature, then the great persons, who are in history what forces are in nature, must belong to this order, for they are the very factors by which it is constituted. But if we hold this most scientific principle, we must mark the inevitable question:—Can Christ stand where He does uncaused, unordered? If He had not been what He was, and stood where He did, could anything in history be as it has been or as it is? Is there any person necessary in the same sense as He is to the higher history of Man? May we not speak of Him as the keystone of the arch which spans the gulf of time? But can we conceive that the keystone came there by accident? or otherwise than by the hand which built the bridge, which opened the chasm and determined the course of the river that flows beneath? And can the nature or character of this Cause be known? Causes are known in their effects, for cause and effect ever correspond in quality and character. This Christ, then, as He stands in universal history, accomplishing those marvels of the Spirit which we have seen indissolubly associated with His person and His name, is an effect; and as He is the Cause of Him must be. Nay, more, is not the effect only as it were the cause embodied, the old force, unspent, persisting in a new form? And how shall we express the idea in this case better than in the evangelical formula, "the Word became flesh, and dwelt among us"? and how better describe His continuous action through all the centuries of our Christian experience than by the verse, "We beheld His glory, a glory as of the only Begotten from the Father, full of grace and truth"? The grandeur which thus comes to His person transfigures through it all nature and the whole history of man, and may well bid us adopt as our own the words which sum up the faith of an apostle, " God has been in Christ reconciling the world unto Himself."

True Religion is *no piece of artifice*; it is no boiling up of our *Imaginative* powers nor the glowing heats of *Passion*; though these are too often mistaken for it, when in our jugglings in Religion we cast a mist before our own eyes: But it is *a new Nature* informing the Souls of men; it is *a God-like frame of Spirit*, discovering it self most of all *in Serene and Clear minds, in deep Humility, Meekness, Self-denial, Universal Love of God and all true Goodness, without Partiality and without Hypocrisie*; whereby we are taught to *know* God, and knowing him to *love* him, and *conform* our selves as much as may be to all that Perfection which shines forth in him.

The *Glory of the Deity* and *Salvation of men* are not *allaied* by their union one with another, but both exalted together in the most transcendent way, for Divine love and bounty are the supreme rulers in Heaven and Earth. Φθόνος ἔξω θείου χοροῦ ἵσταται. There is no such thing as *sowre Despight and Envy* lodged in the bosome of that ever blessed Being above, whose name is LOVE, and all whose Dispensations to the Sons of men are but the dispreadings and distended radiations of his Love, as freely flowing forth from it through the whole orbe and sphear of its creation as the bright light from the Sun in the firmament, of whose benign influences we are then only deprived when we hide and withdraw our selves from them.—JOHN SMITH THE PLATONIST.

INDEX

A

Abraham, 248, 279 ; vision of (in the Koran), 280
Abu Bekr, 286
Acquired characters, transmission of, 72
Acts, Book of, 297, 442
Adam, 47 ; and Christ, 101, 301, 445 ; and Eden, 204
Aeschylus, 198
Agnosticism, religious instinct in, 197
Alexander the Great, 407, 552
Alexandria, school of, 254, 447
Ambrose, 428
Anarchy, a form of pessimism, 116
Anaxagoras, 246
Anthropology, 187, 192, 195, 204, 212
Antony of Padua, St., 555
Ape, The, history of, 42 ; and man, difference of, 45
Apocalypse, date of, 297 ; idea of Christ in, 450, 475 ; His death in, 501 ; idea of the Church in, 531
Apostles, and the Temple, 489
Apotheosis in Apostolic thought, 474
Aquinas, analytic power of, 13
Aristotle, 246, 387, 460
Art and religion, 198
Aryans, religion of, 217, 223, 230
Asceticism, mediæval, 114 ; of Schopenhauer, 125 ; of Buddha, 179, 274, 529 ; of the Essenes, 530
Asoka, 281
Assyria, religion of, 191, 193, 220 ; empire of, 231
Athanasius, on the Incarnation, 19 ; on Antony, 337
Athens, slavery in, 545
Atonement (*see* Christ, Death of)
Augustine, 13, 19 ; on evil, 100 ; on sin and grace, 101 ; theology of, 179 ; *De Civitate Dei*, 299 ; on miracles, 337
Ayodha, holy land of Buddhism, 553

B

Babylonia, religion of, 220 ; empire of, 231
Bain, Professor, on matter and mind, 52
Baur, 403, 427, 442
Benares, 552
Benedict, 263
Bentham, his theory of morals, 65
Beyschlag, on $\lambda \acute{v} \tau \rho o v$, 404
Bhak Li, 549
Bhagavadgita, 382, 545
Boehme, 241

Bolingbroke, Deism of, 106
Book of the Dead, 239
Brahma, 118, 219, 240, 541
Brahmanism, 232, 242; compared with Buddhism, 273; and Mohammedanism, 277 (*see also* India, religion of)
Browning, quoted, 430
Bruno, Giordano, 103
Buddha, his environment, 118, 271; his agreement with Fichte, 123; and Schopenhauer, 125; personal qualities of, 126; story of, 272; and Brahmanism, 273; his Church, 273; his individuality, 275; humanity of, 276; myths concerning, 335, 472; his social ideal compared with the Greek, 369; and Christ's, 483, 529 f.
Buddhism, 7, 193, 262, 270 ff.; its philosophy, 118, 230; idea of merit and demerit in, 120; a positive religion, 532; a missionary religion, 233; not an atheism, 242; its moral order theistic, 243; compared with Brahmanism and Mohammedanism, 277
Bunsen quoted, 229
Buridan's Ass, 77
Butler, on morals, 84 sqq.; his Sermons and Analogy, 85; on the difficulties of faith, 109; on moral evil, 150; compared with Kant, 84
Byron's pessimism, 115

C

Caesar, 407
Caiaphas, characterized, 314; his statesmanship, 316; his view of Jesus, 314 sqq.

Caligula, 344
Calvin, theology of, 179; on the Agony, 428
Caste in India, 232
Categorical imperative of Kant, 87, 123
Categories of experience supplied by personality, 35
Causation, Hume on, 25; in a pure naturalism, 28; in nature and in personality, 30; in nature a deduction from will in man, 34
Celsus, 427
Chalcedon, Creed of, 3
Character, natural factors of, 311
China, religion of, 192, 193, 266
Chinese idea of man, 546
Christ, the person of, a problem for the reason, 5; not a made mystery, 7; dialectic examination of, 8; literary and historical examination of, 10; defects of these methods, 13; idea of, 16, 18 absolute need of, 17; incompatibility of, with pure naturalism, 23; the historical and the ideal in, 477; epitomizes the mystery of Being, 478; contrasted with Buddha and Mohammed, 530; the universal man, 550; the keystone of the arch of history, 565; His names, 324–26, 438, 446, 449, 450, 456, 457; Logos, the, 326, 452, 455; Son of God, 446, 449, 543; Son of man, 11, 397, 406, 475; Messiah, 398, 400, 412; "the suffering servant of God," 398, 400, 501; Lamb of God, 457, 469, 501; idea of as generative of the apostolic

literature, 459; in Paul, 445; in Hebrews, 447; in the Apocalypse, 450; in John, 451, 502; mythical theory as to the person stated and criticized, 467; the idea not invented by Paul, 460; affinities in Greek religion, 473; its historic source, the mind of Christ, 474; His teaching concerning His death, 395; the teaching offends the disciples, 400; as a ransom, 404; as voluntary, 408; as a vicarious sacrifice, 499; its ends, 410; idea of, in Paul, 492, 504 ff.; in the Hebrews, 494, 500; in 1 Peter, 501; in the Apocalypse, 501; how Christ creates the Christian religion, 295, 305, 476; makes its ideas, 443–453, 460 ff., 541 ff.; becomes its only institution, 481, 514, 557; emancipates religion from the tribal Spirit, 555 (*see also* Epistles, Gospels)

Christianity, seems occidental to the Orient, 234; and Hebraism, 261; problem of, 295, 305; not a syncretism, 518; creates a people, 521; not a positive religion, 533

Cicero, 360

Civil Law (*see* Law)

Civilization, 177, 188

Clifford, The late Professor, 52

Coleridge on motives, 76

Colour not in nature, 31

Comte, empiricism of, 50; his great Being, 197; on monotheism, 538

Confucian classics, 382

Confucius, 266, 369, 482

Conscience, Bentham on, 67; Butler on, 85; origin of, 81; and the judgment of society, 82

Consciousness (*see* Self)

Consensus gentium, 381

Conservation of energy, 52

Constantine, 281

Corinth, church of, 529

Councils, ecclesiastical, 19 (*see also* Chalcedon, Nicæa)

Covenants, 422

Creation continuous, 59, 106, 171, 183, 293

Creeds, 19

Criticism, and Christianity, 10, 296

Cross, the (*see* Jesus Christ, Death of)

Cynicism, Greek, characterized, 113

Cyrus, 348

D

Daniel, Book of, its influence on Jesus, 11

Dante, 198, 510

Darwin, his doctrine of evolution, 39; his *petitio principii*, 47; on orchids, 54; his ethical theory, 70

David, 367, 488

Death, the human tragedy, 142; what life gains through, 144

Deism, and the problem of evil, 103; of Bolingbroke, 106; its shallowness, 108; its idea of a state of probation, 166

Delphi, 552

Democritus, 53

Dhammapada, 382

Disciples, their early view of Jesus, 313

Dodona, 552

Dominic, 263, 335

Domitian, 344
Dumas, the elder, 428
Duty, 81
Dyaus, 541

E

Education, as a factor of character, 312; influence of nature in, 137, 148
Edwards, Jonathan, on the will, 76
Egressive method, the, in the theistic argument, 48
Ego, universal, 90; of Fichte, 123
Egypt, religion of, 189, 193, 208, 219, 220, 239; empire of, 231; pyramids of, 545
Elijah, 367
Energy, how known, 34
Englishman and Hindu, 545
Enoch, Book of, its influence on Jesus, 11
Epicurus, 319
Epistles, relation of, to Gospels, 298 (*see also* Hebrews, Paul, Peter)
Essay on Man, Pope's, 106
Essenes, the, 491, 530
Ethical supersedes cosmical process, 183
Ethnography, 204, 208, 212
Eucharist, the, 561 (*see also* Supper, Last)
Euhemerism, 207
Euripides, 254
Evangelists as authors, 353, 358
Evil, problem of, 94 ff.; and faith, 97; and optimism, 99; and pessimism, 111; and immortality, 149; and the Incarnation, 168; not mere negation, 100; Leibnitz's idea of, 104; criticized, 155; kinds of, 134; physical, classes of, 136; arising from the interrelation of man and nature, 136; educative function of, 137; evils peculiar to man, 141; inflicted by man on man, 146; evil, moral, its problem, 96; defined, 150; not disciplinary, 150; and freedom, 161; Divine interference no remedy for, 162; connexion of with suffering, 166
Evolution, a theory of the creational mode, 38; if taken as a Causal theory, problem of, 38; must explain mind, 40; and speculation, 52; intelligence in, 54; means continuous creation, 59; and ethics, 68; differentiation in, 73
Experience, problem of, 6, 28; and pain, 135
Ezekiel, Book of, its influence on Jesus, 11; the Temple in, 488; priestly character of, 252

F

Faith, and reason, 18; and knowledge, 201; and religion, 286; described, 548; characteristic of the Christian religion, 549; and the Christian society, 528
Family as a factor of character, 312
Fichte, ego of, 123, 397; influence of, on Schopenhauer, 122
Forms of perception supplied by personality, 35
Founder, of a religion, and reformer, 263; and the religion, 286; operates in a congenial society, 264; significance of, for the religion, 264

Francis of Assisi, 263, 535
Frazer on sacrifice, 482 *n.*
Freedom, moral, problem of, 6; and personality, 30; and idea of energy, 34; and freedom of action, 75; implied in all moral judgements, 77; deduced by Kant from the categorical imperative, 88; and God, 157; the correlative of law, 160

G

Gamaliel, 447, 466, 490 *n.*, 527
Ganges, 553
Gibbon on Mohammed, 279
Gloatz, 476
God, the creative mind, 55, 57; idea of, immanent and transcendent, 58; omnipotent and omniscient, 58; Kant's deduction of, from categorical imperative, 88; not an abstraction, 153; omnipotence not a synonym for God, 134; impersonation of the absolute good, 154; no mere mechanic, 157; immutable, not immobile, 159; juridically described, 163; Hebrew conception of, 245; God in religion, 537; in the Christian religion, 539; moral sovereignty of, 86, 89, 103, 108, 151, 164, 292; law and sanction to Him a unity, 164; Fatherhood of, 350, 389, 543; God and man, disparity of, 8; real to each other, 57; ever in active interrelation, 58; the end of creation His glory or man's good, 156; as reflected in His creature, 156; mankind a unity to Him, 165; His immanence in nature and man, 171; religion a mutual relation between Him and man, 202; His action in history, 225; and on man, 18; God and evil: why does He permit evil? 96, 152, 159; His interference no remedy for evil, 162; how interpreted by Christ and through Him, 349, 339–41, 542–44
Goethe, 52, 115
Golden Rule, the, 382
Gospels, strata in the, 10; secondary element in, 13; criticism of, 297; significance of, 306; the natural view of Jesus in, 310; the supernatural view of Jesus in, 324; Jesus a unity in, 327; a study from life, 329; sanity of, 336; idea of God in, 349; reality of their world, 386; as creations in literature, 353; as books of religion, 358; unconscious art of, 359; not the work of literary men, 360; synoptics, date of, 297; relation to Epistles, 298, 436; sources of, 298; compared with each other, 300; with Pauline Epistles, 443; the fourth, 19, 457, 477 (*see also* Matthew, Mark, Luke, John)
Grace, doctrine of, 101, 165
Greece, religion of, 192, 207, 219, 236, 239, 473, 541, 549
Greek, the characterized, 522
Greek social ideal, 523
Gregory of Nyssa, 337; the Great, 332

H

Haeckel, 42
Hagar, 248

Happiness, as basis of morals, 78; indefinite term, 79; and highest good in Kant's ethics, 80

Hebraism and Christianity, 261; and Judaism, 549

Hebrew literature, its influence on Jesus, 11; narratives of the creation in, 246

Hebrew religion, 249, 488, 532; limitation of, by tribal instinct, 251; monotheism of, 244; influence of Moses on, 267, 269; and sin, 372; conflict of prophet and priest in, 559

Hebrews, Epistle to the, date of, 299; its affinities with Matthew, 300; Alexandrian, 447, 499; idea of Christ in, 448, 475; idea of the law in, 485, 492; of the Temple, 487; interpretation of Christ's Death in, 494; the idea of the Church in, 531

Hegel, on the Incarnation, 19; optimism of, 110; Schopenhauer's dislike of, 122; on Greek religion, 236

Hellenic spirit in the Gospels, 360

Hellenism, 254, 454, 463, 491; of Luke, 301; of Paul, 463

Heracleitus, 454

Heredity, problem of, 147; educative value of, 148

Hesiod, 239, 541

Hilarion, life of, 332

ἱλαστήριον, 493

Himalayas, 552

Hindu philosophy, 117, 241

Hinduism, 7, 219, 221, 240, 549; compared with Vedism, 260

Hiuen Tsung, 276

History, significance of, 176; order in, necessity of, 175; a late idea, 178; contrasted with the order of nature, 180; its cause mind, 181; how does it arise, 183; history a continued creative process, 183; and psychology, 380; and speculation, 470

Hobbes, on morals, 64

Holman Hunt's Shadow of the Cross, 395

Holy places, 550

Homer, 198, 222, 239, 255, 308, 510

Hosea, Book of, its influence on Jesus, 11

Hume, on miracles, 24; his philosophical principles, 24; speculation paralyzed in the school of, 50; his theory of morals, 66

Huxley, on Man, 41; his ethical theory, 70

I

Ideas and impressions, Hume's doctrine of, 24

Illusions in history, 15

Imagination, and mystery, 7; mythical action of, 12

Immanence (see God)

Immortality, Kant's doctrine of, 88; in relation to the problem of evil, 149

Incarnation (of Christ), what kind of mystery, 7; and problem of evil, 168; the idea in Hinduism, 275

India, social system of, 193 (see Caste), religion of (see Brahmanism, Hinduism, Vedism)

Intellect, the, and the intelgible correspond, 35; intelligence in evolution, 34

Isaiah, Book of, 250, 254, 367,

488; its influence on Jesus, 11

Islam, 7, 117, 217, 224, 230, 277, 532; and the sword, 281; as a state, 283; its ultimate ideas, 284

Isis, 552

Isotta, 556

Israel, religion of (see Hebrew religion, Judaism, Law)

J

James and John, the disciples, 401, 402–405

Jeremiah, Book of, 488; its influence on Jesus, 11; monotheism of, 250

Jerome, 332

Jerusalem, fall of, 299; Christ's entry into, 412; attitude of, to Christ, 416; the holy place of the Jews, 553, 554

Jesus of the Gospels and Christ of the Creeds, 3, 305–308; the natural view of Him in the Gospels, 310; supernatural view, 324; they constitute a unity, 327; a study from life, 329; Schmiedel on, 302, 392; difficulty in the case of an imaginary history of, 350; simplicity yet complexity of the Gospel view, 352; an unconscious sitter, 359; light and shadow in His life, 360; birth of, 326, 349, 374; the temptation, 337; its continuance, 341; Jesus and Nicodemus, 352; and the woman of Samaria, 352; and the young ruler, 363; the charge against Him, 320; His entry into Jerusalem, 412; cleansing of the Temple, 413; lamentation over Jerusalem, 416; His anointing for the burial, 417; before Pilate, 319; and His disciples, 400 ff. (see also James and John, Judas, Peter)

Jesus as teacher characterized, 381; nature and man reflected in, 383; universality of, 388; scope of, 389; influence of, 392; reticence of the earlier teaching, 391; claims advanced in, 393; on His passion, 395; His kingdom, 406; the Apocalyptic discourses, 417; interpretation of the Last Supper, 421; He changes the conception of God and man, 542; His parables, 384; parable of the barren fig-tree, 412; parable of the husbandmen, 416 metaphor of the corner stone, 416; parable of the marriage supper, 416; parables peculiar to Luke, 302; His miracles, 330, 347, 443; their ethical character, 337, 342, 347; unquestioned even by His enemies, 347; His social idea, 523; its religious nature, 526; His social method, 527; His character, its originality, 367; catholicity, 368; potency, 370; not depraved by power, 346; nor alienated by it from man, 347; His ethical transcendence, 357; sinlessness, 362; without consciousness of sin, 361; forgives sin, yet is guest of sinners, 364; His lowliness, 370; His passion in Gethsemane, 425; what it means, 427 ff. (see Christ)

Jew, the, characterized, 522

Job, 248
John, his conception of Christ, 326, 451, 475, 502
John the Baptist, 452; on Jesus, 362
Jordan, 553
Josephus, 299, 387, 491
Jubal, legend of, 143
Judaism, 253, 549
Judas and Christ, 362, 430
Julian, 427
Juridical idea of moral evil, 150

K

Kali, 240
Kant, compared with Mill, 51; on the moral law, 84, 87; the categorical imperative, 88; compared with Butler, 89; his influence on Schopenhauer, 122; dictum of, 228
Karma, 123 (see Merit)
Keble, 333
Keim, 414 n., 427
Kepler quoted, 37
Kingdom of God, 389, 524
Knowledge, ancient problem of, 28
Koran, 7, 388, 532; quoted, 278, 280, 282'; autobiographical character of, 278; vision of Abraham in, 280; miraculous character of, 285
Krishna, 7, 240, 541, 552
Kung Fu Tze, 224 (see Confucius)

L

Lang, Andrew, on religion,
Language, implies reason, 35
Lao Tze, 224
Law, and religion, 192; civil, 62, 164, 532; Jewish, 248, 465; curse of the, 504; distinction of Rabbinical and Levitical, 484, 503; moral and physical distinguished, 163; natural, 91; Roman (see Rome)
Leibnitz, optimism of, 104; and Schopenhauer, 125; criticized, 155; philosophy of, 179
Lewes, G. H., his History of Philosophy, 50; influenced by science, 52
Life, its gain through death, 144
Liddon's life of Pusey, 332
Literature and religion, 198
Lobeck, 236
Locke, 24, 31
Logia, 298, 380, 390, 435
Logos, origin of the idea, 454, Philonian, 255, 454; of John, 326, 452, 455
Lourdes, 553
Love, native to man, 508; of Penelope and Odysseus, 510; of Dante and Beatrice, 510; in the teaching of Jesus, 389; the law of the kingdom of God, 524; of Christ, 509; its power, 512; the new law, 514
Lucretius, 239
Luke's gospel, 296; Pauline, 300; characterized, 301; distinctive parables of, 301; style of, 325; idea of Jesus in, 325
λύτρον, 404, 410

M

Macedon, empire of, 231
Mahabharata, 541
Man interprets nature, 33; the key to all mysteries, 60; nature a problem to him, 172; acted on by nature, men, and

INDEX

God, 182; a doer as well as thinker, 61; his responsibility, 133; his moral freedom, 157; his capability of amelioration, 157; a problem to himself, 173; man and evil, 94, 133; man and physical evil, 134; his fallen state, 167; unity of the race, 173; the race a unity to God, 165; the idea of his unity distasteful, 174; signification of the idea, 175; the unity as an immanent teleology, 176; his unity realized through Christ, 547; his history continues the record of creation, 171; order in his history, 178, 181; material and spiritual outfit of savage and civilized man, 188; is before history, 204; primitive, 204; man and God: his capacity for God, 156; his relation to God in religion, 200; holy as God is holy, 250 (*see also* God and man); Man and Christ': idea of man in the teaching of Jesus, 359; conception of man altered by Christ, 544; man dignified by Christ, 546

Manu, laws of, 207, 559

Marcus Antoninus, 344

Mark, Gospel of, characterized, 300; idea of Jesus in, 324

Martha and Mary, 304

Mary (the Virgin), 301, 535; and Jesus, 313; immaculate conception of, 374; appearance of, at Lourdes, 553

Matter, problem of, 6; various definitions of, 52; mind has no reality for, 57; " matter, motion and force," 34

Matthew, Gospel of, characterized, 300; idea of Jesus in, 325

Mecca, the holy place of Mohammedanism, 283, 284, 553, 554

Medina, 281, 282

Melchizedek, 248, 496

Messiah (*see* Christ, names of)

Messianic hope, the, 314, 599; influence of upon the doctrine of the Person of Christ, 12

Metaphysics of the Creed, 3; in the school of Hume, 50; of knowledge and ethics akin, 64

Mill, James, *Analysis of the Human Mind*, 50; on morals, 67

Mill, J. S., his metaphysics, 51; his qualitative distinction of pleasures, 67; his definition of the right, 78; his indictment of nature, 95; his religious instinct, 197

Milton, 198; his Satan, 513

Mind, problem of, 6; interprets nature, 33; is open to God, 57; the cause of order in history, 181 (*see also* Personality, Self)

Miracles, Hume on their credibility, 24; ecclesiastical, 335 (*see* Jesus)

Mohammed, 224, 553; his influence on Arabia, 193; his story, 279; monotheism of, 280; myths concerning, 343, 472; sensuality of, 369; and Christ, 530; and his religion, 532

Mohammedanism, compared with Brahmanism and Buddhism, 277 (*see* Islam)

Monotheism, Semitic, 217, 219; Hebraic, 244, 269, 473; of Mohammed, 280; a late development in religion, 538

Moral ideal, the, immanent, in man, 90

Moral ideas, sources of, 64 ; judgements depend on the idea of freewill, 61, 63 ; law immanent in man and the universe, 84 ; preceptive and vindicative, 166 ; freedom its correlative, 160

Morality is social, 62

Morals, theory of : individualistic theory of Hobbes, 65 ; Hume's theory of social feeling, 65 ; Bentham's utilitarianism, 66 ; evolutionary ethics, 68 ; Darwin's social instinct, 70 ; Spencer's "ideal congruity," 71 ; determinism of Jonathan Edwards, 76 ; J. S. Mill's criterion of happiness, 78 ; Butler's doctrine of conscience, 85 ; Kant's categorical imperative, 87 ; deductions, 89

Morley, John, on Deism, 108 (note)

Moses, 254, 367, 482 ; his influence on Israel, 267 ; and Christ, 528

Motives, relation of, to will, 76

Music, not in nature, 33

Mystery, in religion, 4 ; of creation, 354 ; mysteries of nature, 5 ; of art, 6 ; man the key to all, 60 ; the Greek, 419

Mysticism, 366 ; Oriental, 522

Mythical imagination, morbidness of the, 332

Mythology, 7, 189 ; Vedic and Homeric, 222 ; Chaldaean, 246 ; Greek, 472 ; transitory character of, 356 ; continues history, 472

Myths of the Middle Ages, 335 ; of Buddha, 335, 472 ; of Mohammed, 343, 472

N

Napoleon, 407

Naturalism, 23

Nature, mysteries of, 5 ; Spinoza's view of, 24 ; idea of criticized on Hume's principles, 24 ; cannot interpret man, 28 ; relations of, with personality, 30 ; colour and sound are not in, 31 ; interpreted by mind, 33, 55, 291 ; evolves the involved, 40 ; stands in the supernatural, 56 ; Mill's indictment of, 95 ; as cause of suffering, 136 ; as educative of man, 137, 148 ; universal motherhood of, 140 ; inexorable for beneficent purpose, 140 ; cannot speak the last word on evil, 168 ; a problem to man, 172 ; order in contrasted with order in history, 180 ; action of, on man, 181 ; does not create religion, 210

Naturalism incompatible with the apostolic Christology, 23

Neoplatonism of Augustine, 100

Nero, 344

Nicæa, Council of, 3, 321

Nicholas of Cusa, 102

Nicodemus, 352

Nihilism, a form of pessimism, 116

Nirvana, 121, 274

O

Obligation, Bentham on, 67 ; origin of, 81 ; Kant on, 87

Odysseus, 510

INDEX 579

Old Testament, 367, 393, 463, 473
Olympus, 552
Omnipotence and omniscience (*see* God)
Opportunity as factor of character, 312
Optimism, and the problem of evil, 99; of Plato and the Stoics, 99; of Augustine, 100; of Nicholas of Cusa, 102; of Leibnitz, 104; of Pope, 106; criticized by Voltaire, 108; of Spinoza and Hegel, 110; of Socialism, 116; Buddhism, as an, 121
Order in nature and history distinguished, 180; the child of religion, 192 (*see also* History, Nature)
Osiris, 24, 552
Othman, 286
Ovid, quoted, 552

P

Pantheism, of Giordano Bruno, 103; of Spinoza and Hegel, 110; of India and Greece, 219; of Hindu philosophy, 241; not a religion, 241
Parables (*see* Jesus Christ)
Pascal, 97, 382
Passions, primary, their regulation, 184
Passover, the, illustrates the death of Christ, 493
Paul, an epitome of his day, 440; his epistles, 19, 207; their early date, 297; criticism of, 442; contrasted with the Synoptic Gospels, 443; idea of Christ in, 445; idea of the Church in 531; the psychological origin of his theology, 401;

its sources, 463; his relation to the Jewish Law, 465, 504
Paulus, 427
Penelope, 510
Persia, religion of, 193, 265; empire of, 231
Person, a social unit, 181; a supernatural and the modern view of nature, 56, 60
Personality, not to be eliminated from nature, 30; relations of, with nature, 30; interprets nature, 33; the vehicle of moral good, 91; natural factors of, 312 (*see also* Mind, Self)
Persons, in the Godhead, 9
Pessimism, causes of, 112; uncongenial to the Greek mind, 113; compared with mediæval asceticism, 114; of Goethe and Byron, 115; political, 116; of philosophic Buddhism, 119; of Schopenhauer, 120; of Von Hartmann, 127; appreciation and criticism of, 129
Peter, the informant of Mark, 300; rebukes Christ, 313; confesses sinfulness, 362; confesses Christ, 397; rebuked by Christ, 398, 462; spokesman of the disciples, 401; Epistle of, on the death of Christ, 501; his preaching at Pentecost, 527
Pharisees, their view of Jesus, 313, 490; their relation to the Apostles, 490
Pheidias, 91, 198
Philip, and Christ, 313
Philo, 447, 463, 491
Philosophy, problems of, 6; of religion (*see* Religion)
Phœnicia, religion of, 191, 220

Physical forces, the, and moral freedom, 34, 78
Pilate, an impersonation of Rome, 318 ; convinced of the innocence of Jesus, 320, 361 ; his famous question, 320 ; vision of, 321
Place, as a factor of character, 312 ; in religion, 551
Plato, quoted, 37 ; optimism of, 99 ; Schopenhauer on, 122 ; and religion, 198, 239 ; on Socrates, 361 ; his ideal of manhood, 368 ; and the Christian idea, 460 ; referred to, 241, 254, 360
Pleasure and pain as basis of morals, 65, 78
Pletho, Gemisthus, 556
Pliny, 321
Plotinus, 100, 241
Polytheism, vindicated by pantheism, 241 ; of the Semites, 268 ; cannot be moral, 538
Pope, and the problem of evil, 104, 106 ; compared with the speculative physicism of to-day, 109
Portiuncula, the, 555
Positivism (see Comte)
Preaching, Christian, 562
Priesthood, Aaronic, 494
Priests, the Jewish, their relation to Christ and the Apostles, 490
Probation, state of, a Deistic idea, 166
Proclus, 549
Protagoras, 549
Psalms, the, influence of, on Jesus, 11 ; sacred book of Monotheism, 250
Psychology of secondary qualities, 31
Ptolemies, the, 254.

Pujari, the, 240
Pusey, Dr., morbidness of his sense of sin, 333

Q

Qualities, secondary, 31 ; are not things of external nature, 33

R

Race, as a factor of character, 311
Raphael, 91, 198
Reason, antinomies of the pure, 5 ; mysteries of, 6 ; and faith, 19 ; can only live in a rational world, 35
Redemption, 166 (*see also* Christ)
Reformer and founder of religion, 263
Regressive method, the, in theism, 41
Religion, aesthetic, 4 ; mystery in, 5 ; creative of order, 185, 192 ; philosophy of, 186, 226 ; phenomena of, 187 ; scientific view of, 195, 205 ; is necessary to man, 196 ; as architectonic idea, 198 ; problems of, 199 ; idea of, 200 ; Herbert Spencer on, 205 ; ethnographic and historical method in, compared, 208, 213 ; rooted in reason, 210 ; conditioned by nature, 211 ; conflict of ideal and formal in, 216 ; influence of race on, 216 ; of place on, 218 ; of ethnical relations on, 220 ; of history on, 221 ; of social idea on, 222 ; of great personalities on, 223 ; of idea and institution in, 235 ; opposed action of custom

and thought in, 239; never a pantheism, 241; Hebrew idea of, 247; and founder, 286; and people, 520

Religions, vision of, in history, 191; of India and Greece compared, 221; as national and missionary, 230; spontaneous and founded, 259; positive, 532

Renaissance, and the problem of sin, 102

Renan, on Semitic languages, 217; on Luke, 325; on the Agony, 427

Responsibility, of the individual and the race, 165 (*see also* God and man)

Rig Veda, 207, 388, 541, 559

Rishi, the, 559

Ritschl, on λύτρον, 404; on the Death of Christ, 492 *n.*

Roman, the characterized, 522

Roman Catholic worship, 536; 553, 555

Romanoff, house of, 344

Rome, law of, 91, 231, 523, 545; religion of, 192, 193, 207, 518, 523, 549, 559; empire of, 231, 299; fall of, 299, 321; impersonated in Pilate, 318; influence of, on Jesus, 11; on Paul, 464

S

Sacrifice, Frazer on, 482 *n.*

Sadducees, their view of Jesus, 314

Samaria, woman of, 352

Savage man, mystery of thought in, 195; and religion, 215

Science, immensity of its field, 194; inadequacy of, 194; and religion, 195

Schleicher, on matter and spirit, 52

Schleiermacher, 428

Schmiedel, on the Gospels, 302, 392

Scholasticism, mediæval, follows Augustine, 102

Schopenhauer, pessimism of, 121; influenced by Kant, Fichte, and Buddha, 122; compared with Buddua, 125; representative of tendency of the age, 128; his idea of God, 154

Secondary qualities, 31

Seeberg on Ritschl, 492 *n.*

Seleucidæ, 253

Self, the, Hume on, 25; conception of, in a "system of nature" (*see also* Mind, Personality)

Self-realization, the law of human progress, 90

Semites, monotheism of the, 217, 219; social system of, 223; religion of, 230, 532

Seneca, on sin, 372

Septuagint, 254

Servant of God, the suffering, 398, 469, 501

Shelley, idealism of, 115; quoted, 131

Sigismondo Pandolfo Malatesta, 556

Simon Magus, 347

Sin, as the occasion of grace, 101; Christian idea of, 103; nature of, 150; original, 165; sense of, awakened by the cross, 373, 433

Sinlessness, idea of, 373, 376 (*see also* Jesus, character of)

Siva, 240
Slavery, ancient, 544
Social problem, the, 147 ; ideal of Greece and of Christ, 523
Socialism, a form of optimism, 116
Socrates, 361, 549
Solomon, 248, 488
Son of man, origin of the conception, 11
Sound, not in nature, 31
Sovereignty, moral, of God (*see* God)
Space, problem of, 6 ; Hume on, 25
Species, origin of, 38
Spencer, Herbert, on morals, 71 ; his anthropological theory of religion, 206
Speculative age, the, preceded by the historical, 470
Spinoza, his pantheistic optimism, 110 ; and Schopenhauer, 124 ; his idea of God, 154, 179 ; pantheism of, 241
Spirit, is thought made concrete, 55 ; the real creation of God, 57
Spontaneous generation, 49
State, judgement of the, 62 ; Islam as a, 281, 283 ; physical penalties of the, 533 ; and religion, 534
Steinmeyer, 428
Stephen, 491, 520
Stoic, ideal of perfect man, 90, 357 ; optimism, 99 ; opposition to pessimism, 113 ; definition of moral evil, 150 ; view of religion, 239 ; Logos, 454 ; influence on Paul, 464 ; idea of unity of the race, 547 ; ethics, 559
Strauss, 128, 427
Struggle for existence, 38 ; moral problem of, 109 ; pathos of, 128
Suffering, 166 (*see also* Evil)
Sulpicius, 337
Supernatural, modern antipathy to the, 23 ; true and false ideas of the, 56
Superstition, nature of, 206, 553
Supper, the Last, 419 ; narratives of, 419 ; interpreted by Christ, 421
Survival of the fittest, moral problem of, 109
Synagogue and Temple contrasted, 484, 487
Syncretism, 517 ; Christianity is not a, 518
Synoptists (*see* Gospels)

T

Tabernacle, the, 487
Tabula rasa, 29
Tacitus, quoted, 552
Tao-teh King, 382
Temple, the, 415 ; Christ the true, 457 ; and synagogue, 484, 487 ; and the Apostles, 489 ; in the Apocalypse, 502
Tennyson, quoted, 95
Tertullian, 337, 382
Théodicée, of Leibnitz, 104
Thucydides, 360, 387
Tiberius, 344
Time, problem of, 6 ; Hume on, 25 ; as a factor of character, 312
Trajan, rescript of, 321
Transcendence of will and thought, 78
Transcendental elements in knowledge, 51
Transcendental and supernatural, the, 55
Tyndall quoted, 55

INDEX

U

Unity of man (*see* Man)
Upadana of Buddha, 124
Upanishads, 388
Ur-Marcus, 435
Utilitarianism, 65, 78 ; cannot explain the categorical imperative, 83

V

Vanini, 427
Varuna, 541, 559
Vatican, Council, Decrees of the, 207
Vedantâ, 241
Vedic mythology, 222 ; religion, 260, 541 ; India, 271
Virtue as an element of the highest good, 88
Vishnu, 240
Voltaire, the *Candide* of, 108 ; unconscious theodicy of, 108 ; on Mohammed, 278
Von Hartmann, pessimism of, 127 ; Strauss on, 128

W

Wallace, Alfred, praises Darwin, 54
Weismann, 39
Wendt, 405, 476
Wheel of existence, 119
Will, problem of, 6 ; explains energy, 34 ; freedom of the, 76 (*see* Freedom) ; a creative force, 89 ; idea of, in Fichte and Schopenhauer, 123
Wisdom literature, influence of, on Jesus, 11
Witchcraft, 346
Worship and theology, 480 ; and religion, 551 ; and the institution, 557 ; potent influence of, on religion, 558 ; Christian, the creation of God, 562 ; defines the worshipper, 563 ; end of, 564

X

Xenophanes, 239
Xenophon on Socrates, 361

Z

Zem-Zem, the well, 553
Zeno, 254
Zeus, 349, 541
Zoroaster, 224, 265
Zoroastrianism, 7

www.ingramcontent.com/pod-product-compliance
Lightning Source LLC
Chambersburg PA
CBHW052041290426
44111CB00011B/1582